INNOVATION MANAGEMENT

INNOVATION MANAGEMENT

Context, strategies, systems and processes

Pervaiz K. Ahmed
Charles D. Shepherd

**Financial Times
Prentice Hall
is an imprint of**

Harlow, England • London • New York • Boston • San Francisco • Toronto
Sydney • Tokyo • Singapore • Hong Kong • Seoul • Taipei • New Delhi
Cape Town • Madrid • Mexico City • Amsterdam • Munich • Paris • Milan

Pearson Education Limited
Edinburgh Gate
Harlow
Essex CM20 2JE
England

and Associated Companies throughout the world

Visit us on the World Wide Web at:
www.pearsoned.co.uk

First published 2010

ISBN: 978-0-273-68376-6

British Library Cataloguing-in-Publication Data
A catalogue record for this book is available from the British Library

Library of Congress Cataloging-in-Publication Data
Ahmed, Pervaiz K.
    Innovation management : context, strategies, systems, and processes / Pervaiz Ahmed, Charles Shepherd. – 1st ed.
        p. cm.
    Includes bibliographical references and index.
    ISBN 978-0-273-68376-6 (pbk.)
    1. Technological innovations–Management.   2. Industrial management.
3. Knowledge management.   I. Shepherd, Charles.   II. Title.
    HD45.A477 2010
    658.4'063—dc22

                                                            2010009677

ARP impression 98

Typeset in 9.5/12pt Minion by 35
Printed and bound in Great Britain by Ashford Colour Press Ltd, Gosport, Hants

BRIEF CONTENTS

CONTENTS

Supporting resources

Visit **www.pearsoned.co.uk/ahmed** to find valuable online resources:

For instructors

- PowerPoint slides that can be downloaded and used for presentations.

For more information please contact your local Pearson Education sales representative or visit **www.pearsoned.co.uk/ahmed**

PREFACE

In a world of increasingly sophisticated customer needs, innovation is becoming central to corporate growth and prosperity, and is being recognised as a source of vitality and competitive advantage. But what do we mean by 'innovation', and what must companies do to leverage it in order to support their short, and long, term profitable growth objectives?

This book attempts to answer these questions by first building a common understanding of innovation and creativity and then examining how innovation can be used strategically. This is followed by examining structures, processes, frameworks and best-in-class practices for innovation. The book is structured in sequence, as illustrated below.

Firstly, we provide a definition and context for innovation, describing how it is seen to positively impact business performance. Many types of innovation are explored, and the different benefits they deliver are discussed. The economic argument for innovation is presented, and the relationship between innovation and creativity is offered,

With a basic appreciation of innovation and creativity in place, we turn our attention to the strategic questions that organisations may face. Firstly, we attempt to understand how organisations successfully position themselves for success in their target markets. With this

Part 1. Understanding innovation and creativity
1. Innovation in context
2. Creativity and innovation

Part 2. Strategic focus – setting a direction	
3. Strategy and innovation	4. Technology strategy

Part 3. Structure for new product development – frameworks	
5. Innovation process management	
6. Optimising innovation decision making and portfolio management	7. Innovation performance measurement

Part 4. Aligning people – culture and structure		
8. People, leadership and structure for innovation	9. Culture and climate for innovation	10. Innovation in a global world

Part 5. Execution within a structured development process		
11. Market learning	12. Design and manufacture for innovation	13. Supply chain management and innovation
14. Knowledge management and learning for innovation		

external view in place, we turn our attention to how they strategically focus so as to offer solutions of value into these markets by developing a clear technology strategy.

Once the strategic direction has been clarified, we go on to discuss structures that allow the strategy to be executed. Here we look at the implementation and use of innovation frameworks. These frameworks have evolved over time, and tend to comprise the four major elements of a senior management review board, cross-functional integrated teams, a structured development process, and a formal decision-making process. It is this decision-making process, enabled by emerging portfolio management practices, that is focused upon first, followed by a review of how the performance of the innovation framework can be measured.

Knowing the strategic direction we need to move in, and the broad framework we need to leverage to execute this strategy, we now need to ensure that the most critical resource is effectively engaged – namely the people in the organisation. In this next section, we review the various firm types that exist, which can dictate the need for specific innovation structures and teams. This requires a clear understanding of how people need to be aligned and what roles need to be fulfilled to support the business. To enable the teams and people requires organisation to build an innovation-friendly culture and climate. We go on to examine forms, roles and structures necessary for a firm to succeed in a world of global expansion and competition.

Finally, underlying any effective innovation framework is a set of effective and integrated processes, collectively known as the Structured Development Process. This can be as diverse as the nature of the business, but there are specific areas that are known to positively impact innovation performance. These are covered in detail. We cover issues of marketing, design, manufacturing and supply chain management. In addition, we review the emerging horizontal practice of knowledge management, which is increasingly driving efficiencies within innovative companies.

Throughout the book examples and case studies are introduced to aid understanding and provide insights across many industries and business scenarios.

ACKNOWLEDGEMENTS

I would like to acknowledge the love of my parents and family, who have been a constant source of encouragement and support in everything I have done.

Pervaiz K. Ahmed

To Diane, Jonathan and Michael, whose love, support and sacrifices have made this book possible. The weekends are ours again!

Charlie Shepherd

Publisher's acknowledgements

We are grateful to the following for permission to reproduce copyright material:

Figures

Figure 1.8 from *Knowledge, Technology and Economic Growth: Recent Evidence from OECD Countries*, OECD (Bassanini, A., Scappetta, S. and Visco, I. 2000) p. 26, OECD Economics Department working paper 259; Figure 1.9 from Cordis, 'The community innovation survey', March 2000, Innovation and SMEs Programme, http://cordis.europa.eu/itt/itt-en/00-2/dossier1.htm, adapted from OECD (1999), OECD Science, Technology and Industry Scoreboard 1999: Benchmarking Knowledge-based Economies, p. 93, www.oecd.org/sti/scoreboard; Figures 1.10, 1.11 and 1.12 from *2003 European Innovation Scoreboard: Technical Paper No.2, Analysis of National Performances*, European Commission (2003), © European Communities, 2003. Copyright of the document belongs to the European Communities. Neither the European Commission, nor any person acting on its behalf, may be held responsible for the use to which information contained in this document may be put, or for any errors which, despite careful preparation and checking, may appear; Figure 1.13 from *The Competitive Advantage of Nations*, Free Press (Porter, M.E. 1990), reprinted with the permission of The Free Press, a Division of Simon & Schuster, Inc., from *The Competitive Advantage of Nations* by Michael E. Porter. Copyright © 1990, 1998 by Michael E. Porter. All rights reserved; Figures 2.2 and 2.3 from Building the creative organisation, *Organizational Dynamics*, 22(4), pp. 22–37 (Gundry, L.K., Kickul, J.R. and Prather, C.W.), with permission from Elsevier; Figure 2.4 from Motivating creativity in organisations: on doing what you love and loving what you do, *California Management Review*, 40(1), pp. 39–58 (Amabile T.M. 1997), copyright © 1997, by The Regents of the University of California. Reprinted from the *California Management Review*, Vol. 40, No. 1. By permission of The Regents; Figure 2.7 from *Psychological Types* Volume 6: The Collected Works of C.G. Jung, Princeton University Press (Jung, C.G. 1971), © 1971 Princeton University Press, 1999 renewed PUP. Reprinted by permission of Princeton University Press; Figure 2.8 from Toward a theory of organizational creativity, *Academy of Management Review*, 18, pp. 293–321 (Woodman, R.W., Sawyer, J.E. and Griffin, R.W. 1993), copyright 1993 by ACADEMY OF MANAGEMENT (NY). Reproduced with permission of ACADEMY OF MANAGEMENT (NY) in the format Textbook via Copyright Clearance Center; Figure 2.9 from *The Creativity Tools Memory Jogger*, GOAL/QPC (Ritter, D. and Brassard, M. 1998), with permission of GOAL/QPC, www.MemoryJogger.org; Figure 2.11 from Illumine Training, 2008, Attacking Problems Mind Map; Figure 4.7 from A model of technology strategy, *Technology Analysis & Strategic Management*, 5(4), pp. 397–412 (Rieck, R.M. and

Dickson, K.E. 1993), reprinted by permission of the publisher (Taylor & Francis Group, http://www.informaworld.com); Figure 4.12 from Technology investment advisor: an options-based approach to technology strategy, *Information Knowledge Systems Management*, 2, pp. 63–81 (Rouse, W.B., Howard, C.W., Carns, W.E. and Prendergast, J. 2000), copyright 2000, with permission from IOS Press; Figure 5.11 from Doing it right: winning with new products, *Ivey Business Journal*, July/August, pp. 54–60 (Cooper, R.G. 2000) Stage-Gate (www.stage-gate.com); Figure 6.7 from How information technology will transform pipeline and portfolio management, *PDMA Conference on Portfolio Planning and Management* (McGrath, M.E. 1998); Figure 7.7 from The measurement of innovation performance in the firm; an overview, *Research Policy*, 19, pp. 185–92 (Cordero, R. 1990), copyright 1990, with permission from Elsevier; Figure 7.9 from Development of a technical innovation audit, *Journal of Product Innovation Management* 13(2), pp. 105–36 (Chiesa, V., Coughlan, P. and Voss, C.A. 1996), Wiley-Blackwell; Figure 7.11 from A proposed model for new service development, *Journal of Services Marketing*, 3(2), pp. 25–34 (Scheuing, E.E. and Johnson, E.M. 1989), © Emerald Group Publishing Limited, all rights reserved; Figure 7.12 from An interim report on measuring product development success and failure, *Journal of Product Innovation Management*, 10, pp. 291–308 (Griffin, A. and Page, A.L. 1993), Wiley-Blackwell; Figure 8.7 from A causal model of the impact of skills, synergy and design sensitivity of new product performance, *Journal of Product Innovation Management*, 14, pp. 88–101 (Song, M.X., Souder, W.E. and Dyer, B. 1997), Wiley-Blackwell; Figure 9.1 from Creating the climate and culture of success, *Organisational Dynamics*, 23(1), pp. 17–29 (Schneider, B., Gunnarson, S.K. and Niles-Jolly, K. 1996), with permission from Elsevier; Figure 9.2 from Corporate culture, customer orientation and innovativeness in Japanese firms: a quadrad analysis, *Journal of Marketing*, 57, pp. 23–7 (Deshpande, R., Farley, J.U. and Webster, F.E.), reprinted with permission, published by the American Marketing Association; Figure 9.3 from Toward a theory of organisational culture and effectiveness, *Organization Science*, 6(2), pp. 204–23 (Denison, D.R. and Mishra, A.K. 1995), copyright 1995, the Institute for Operations Research and the Management Sciences (INFORMS), 7240 Parkway Drive, Suite 300, Hanover, MD 21076 USA; Figure 10.3 from *Managing the Multinational Enterprise: Organisation of the Firm and Ownership of Subsidiaries*, Basic Books (Stopford, J.M. and Wells, Jr. L.T. 1972), copyright © 1972 John Stopford. Reprinted by permission of Basic Books, a member of the Perseus Books Group; Figure 10.10 from Designing global strategies: comparative and competitive value-added chains, *Sloan Management Review*, 26(4), pp. 15–28 (Kogut, B. 1985), from MIT Sloan Management Review © 1985 by Massachusetts Institute of Technology. All rights reserved. Distributed by Tribune Media Services; Figure 11.3 from Managing the market learning process, *Journal of Business & Industrial Marketing*, 17(4), pp. 240–52 (Day, G.S. 2002), © Emerald Group Publishing Limited, all rights reserved; Figure 11.8 from Online marketing research, *IBM Journal of Research and Development*, 48(5/6), pp. 671–7 (Agrawal, A., Basak, J., Jain, V., Kothari, R., Kumar, M., Mittal, P.A., Modani, P.A., Ravikumar, K., Sabharwal, Y. and Sureka, R. 2004), reprint courtesy of International Business Machines Corporation, © 2004 International Business Machines Corporation; Figure 11.9 from *Product development: managing a dispersed process, in Handbook of Marketing*, Sage Publications (Dahan, E. and Hauser, J.R. (B. Weitz and R. Wensley eds) 2001) figure 17, copyright 2002 by SAGE PUBLICATIONS INC BOOKS. Reproduced with permission of SAGE PUBLICATIONS INC BOOKS in the format Textbook via Copyright Clearance Center; Figure 12.6 from Architectural innovation: the reconfiguration of existing product technologies and the failure of established firms, *Administrative Science Quarterly*, 35, pp. 9–30 (Henderson, R.M. and Clark, K.B. 1990), The Johnson School at Cornell University.

Tables

Table 1.2 from Innovation and competitiveness: a review, *Technology Analysis and Strategic Management*, 10(3), pp. 363–95 (Clark, J. and Guy, K. 1998), reprinted by permission of the publisher (Taylor & Francis Group, http://www.informaworld.com); Table 5.2 adapted from

Winning at New Products, Gage Educational Publishing. (Cooper, R.G. 1988), copyright © 2001 Robert G. Cooper. Reprinted by permission of Basic Books, a member of the Perseus Books Group; Tables 6.2 and 6.3 from *Portfolio Management for New Products*, Addison-Wesley (Cooper, R.G., Edgett, S.J. and Kleinschmidt, E.J. 1998), copyright © 2002 Robert G. Cooper, Scott J. Edgett, Elko J. Kleinschmidt. Reprinted by permission of Basic Books, a member of the Perseus Books Group; Table 7.3 from An interim report on measuring product development success and failure, *Journal of Product Innovation Management*, 10, pp. 291–308 (Griffin, A. and Page, A.L. 1993), Wiley-Blackwell; Table 8.1 from *Managing Intellectual Capital: Organisational, Strategic and Policy Dimensions*, Oxford University Press (Teece, D.J. 2000), by permission of Oxford University Press; Table 11.2 from Real-time market research, *Marketing Intelligence & Planning*, 11(7), pp. 29–38 (Sanchez, R. and Sudharshan, D. 1993), © Emerald Group Publishing Limited, all rights reserved; Table 11.3 from Ethnographies in the front end: designing for enhanced customer experiences, *Journal of Product Innovation Management*, 23(3), pp. 215–37 (Rosenthal, S. and Capper, M. 2006), Wiley-Blackwell.

Text

Case Study on page 75 from http://www.innocentdrinks.co.uk/us/our_story/2009-investment/, Innocent Drinks Ltd; Box on page 97 from Message at Sony is tough times on the way, *Evening News*, 25 January 2005 (Hamada, R.), The Scotsman Publications Ltd; Box on page 126 from Pipeline=Lifeline, *Industry Week*, 254(5), pp. 45–50 (Teresko, J. 2005), Penton Media; Box on page 138 from Innovation for hire, *Global Cosmetic Industry*, 173(6), pp. 5–60 (Frazzolo, R. 2005), Allured Business Media; Box on page 176 from Nanotech innovations hinge on measurement technology and close alliances, *R&D*, 45(11), p. 16 (Keithley, J.P. 2003), based on Innovation Insider column originally published in R&D magazine, November 2003, pp. 16–17, Advantage Business Media; Box on page 209 from Rhodia adopts innovative alliances to foster product development, *Chemical Market Reporter*, 262(15), pp. 6–8 (Milmo, S. 2002) ICIS; Box on page 295 from IBM, http://www-03.ibm.com/ibm/history/history/decade_1990.html, reprint courtesy of International Business Machines Corporation, © 2010 International Business Machines Corporation; Box on page 311 from *Modern Tiger Teams: Team Problem Solving for the 21st Century*, Thales Research, Inc. (Pavlak, A. 2004) p. 27, http://mywebpages.comcast.net/apavlak/MTT_12-21-04.pdf; Box on page 319 from Product Design Speak 101: Product Champions *Carolina Newswire* (Roland, M. 2008), http://carolinanewswire.com/news/News.cgi?database=pipeline.db&command=viewone&id=6.

The Financial Times

Case Study on page 13 from Wind-up radio company to Aim listing, *Financial Times*, 16 February 2005 (Blackwell, D.); Box on page 37 from Space to breathe amid the crisis, *Financial Times*, 1 March 2009 (Schaffer, D.); Box on page 108 from Joint venture's new chip set to rival Intel, *Financial Times*, 8 February 2005 (Nuttall, C.); Case Study on page 159 from Going mobile: Velti builds global footprint for clients' campaigns, *Financial Times*, 4 June 2009 (Hope, K.); Case Study on page 212 from Outside the beauty box, *Financial Times*, 27 September 2008 (Aldin, B.); Case Study on page 259 from Brand is a big issue, *Financial Times*, 22 December 2003, 17 (Budden, R. and Burt, T.); Case Study on page 320 from Remedy for a malady, *Financial Times*, 14 August 2009 (Jack, A.); Case Study on page 351 from Chinese manufacturers bullish on exports, *Financial Times*, 11 August 2009 (Mitchell, T.); Boxes on page 363 and 372 from The invention house in the east, *Financial Times*, 17 June 2005 (Cookson, C.); Box on page 377 from Search for the right ingredients, *Financial Times*, October 2004, p. 15 (Buckley, N.); Case Study on page 425 from HP hits the right note with celebrities and piano-black case, *Financial Times*, 11 January 2008 (Allison, K.); Box on page 462 from Paying the bill after the price war, *Financial Times*, 30 September 2004 (Mackintosh, J.); Case Study on page 469 from Car manufacturing: vehicle makers appreciate the virtues of virtual design, *Financial Times*, 28 May 2008 (Cane, A.); Box on page 487 from Drive to offload risks on to the suppliers, *Financial Times*, 1 October 2003

(Mackintosh, J.); Case Study on page 500 from Control of the supply chain turns critical, *Financial Times*, 19 September 2007 (Pritchard, S.); Case Study on page 534 from Keeping the know-how of a retiring generation, *Financial Times*, 24 January 2006 (Baxter, A.).

In some instances we have been unable to trace the owners of copyright material, and we would appreciate any information that would enable us to do so.

PART 1

Understanding innovation and creativity

1

Innovation in context

Learning outcomes

When you have completed this chapter you should be able to:

- Critically evaluate the different meanings and formats of innovation, including the dynamic and static models of innovation.

- Recognise the importance of innovation and appreciate the role of innovation in economic development and prosperity (in the 'knowledge society') and how this has been illustrated through history.

- Understand the cyclical patterns of innovation creation and innovation destruction.

- Explain and evaluate the emergence of national and regional innovation clusters.

- Articulate and analyse the importance of developing a knowledge economy.

- Examine the role of the nation state, including government policy types, in promoting innovation.

The importance of innovation

Innovation is a defining feature of human society. It is especially important in the emergence of the 'knowledge society', in which the creation and commercialisation of new knowledge underpins both national and firm-level success. New ideas, new methods, new structures and new products are potent drivers of organisational vibrancy and economic growth. The modern world is engaged in unprecedented levels of innovative effort. Modern firms produce and deliver high quality goods and services across the globe. In the process new markets are created, existing ones extended and others closed. Technological progress is constantly remoulding markets by continuously playing out the drama of market creation and market destruction.

Innovation has always been a fundamental basis of competitiveness for firms, regions and nations. An Economist Intelligence Unit survey revealed that the creation of innovative products and services ranked among chief executives' top three concerns for the next five years (Pure-Insight, 2005). Heightened levels of competition arising from globalisation has sensitised companies to the importance of possessing an ability to develop and leverage knowledge and learning. Whilst the market system has always rested on its capacity to create new products and new ways of producing them, contemporary society's search for higher standards of living and thirst for new ways of fulfilling increasingly sophisticated needs requires more rapid innovation. Competition in this environment necessitates building innovative capacity through an enhanced knowledge and learning capability. There is little doubt that innovation is a critical factor in the success and prosperity of organisations and societies, but the precise nature of its role and its impact remains highly complex.

ILLUSTRATION

Ignore innovation at your peril

Lego, the Danish toy maker, once captivated the dreams of children across the world. It was the envy of all in the games sector. Yet at the height of its success it stood still whilst others around it were busy innovating. During the late 1980s and early 1990s electronic games started to appear in the market. At this time, Sega and Nintendo introduced electronic games at the top end of the market. Lego's executives saw them as an irrelevance: they were selling expensive games to teenagers and not to their market segment. As prices came down, the target market became younger. It took Lego quite some time to awaken to the reality of the threat it was facing, and by the mid-1990s, it remained far behind its competitors, despite significant reinvestment. Lego now licenses its products and brand to more established electronic games providers.

Defining innovation

Innovation is a source of advancement and development. Firms and nations that continuously innovate manage to sustain economic vibrancy. Thus, it is no coincidence that countries (US, Japan and parts of Europe) in which the highest patent activity or R&D investment intensity is observed are leaders on the ladder of economic development.

What do we actually mean by innovation? The answer is not as easy as one may think on first facing the question. Scholars observing the phenomenon from different perspectives arrive at many different meanings; some of which appear to conflict or provide no easy resolution with one another. The management guru Peter Drucker observes that 'innovation is the specific tool of entrepreneurs, the means by which they exploit changes as an opportunity' (Drucker, 1985). Tushman and Nadler (1996) focus on the firm in noting that 'innovation is the creation of any product, service or process which is new to the business unit'. Innovation comprises of two parts, the generation of an idea or invention and the fruitful commercialisation of that invention/idea (i.e. innovation = invention + exploitation). Another management guru, Michael Porter, shifts the focus of attention by highlighting that innovation cannot be treated solely from an individual or firm level since the process of innovation is embedded within the national or regional context (Porter, 1990). These viewpoints illustrate that beyond simple definitions innovation is an extraordinarily complex and even chaotic process. Indeed it is a subject that taxes the prowess of some of the most capable scholars and practitioners alike (Quinn, 1992).

In looking at the multiplicity of meanings given to innovation it is possible to discern a number of characteristics:

- *Innovation as creation (invention)*: The focus is on use of resources (people, time and money) to invent or develop a new product, service, new way of doing things, new way of thinking about things.

- *Innovation as diffusion and learning*: The focus is on acquiring, supporting or using a product, service or ideas.

- *Innovation as an event*: The focus of attention here is on a discrete event, such as the development of a single product, service, idea or decision.

- *Innovation as a (stream of innovations) trajectory*: This is recognition that a single act of innovation (as that in a discrete event) can facilitate a family of innovations to be derived from the original source.

- *Innovation as change (incremental or radical)*: Innovation enacts change. Some innovations are minor adjustments whilst other innovations are radical or discontinuous in nature.

- *Innovation as a (firm-level) process*: In this view innovation is not a single act, but a series of activities that are carried out by a firm to lead to the production of an outcome (namely, the innovation).

- *Innovation as a context (region, nation, etc.) level process*: This view sees innovation as an act beyond the confines of an individual or firm. The view captures institutional frameworks, socio-political networks, and proximal factor endowments as important factors in the act of innovation. The focus is switched from the firm to the peculiar endowments and characteristics of a specific context (region, nation, etc.).

It is clear from the above that innovation is a broad term. The term is often used loosely and is ascribed a variety of meanings. Scrutiny of the multiplicity of meanings allows two observations worthy of note to be made.

Firstly, innovation may be seen as a value-adding process as well as an outcome. Innovation as a value-adding activity is an enabling process. As an enabler, innovation is the process capacity to add value to any specified activity or outcome. Innovation as an outcome embodies the 'value-added' in products, services, thoughts and behaviours. Thus, innovation management is the management of the value-adding and embodiment process along the entire business chain and across macro and micro-infrastructures within which the agent (firm, entrepreneur, or individual) is enmeshed to produce a specified new or novel outcome(s).

Secondly, we can see that innovation as a term is used to describe a range of factors only some of which are under the control of the firm, some that can be influenced and some that are outside the firm's influence. The extent to which the firm can combine and turn these factors to its advantage defines how competitive the firm is vis-à-vis competition. In this sense, the ability to control and correctly utilise the variety of factors through a process of combination and alignment defines a firm's innovation orientation.

We often encounter the terms 'novel' and 'new' to refer to innovation. However, what does 'new' itself mean? By focussing on product innovation we can illustrate that there are many shades of newness.

- *New to world*: Products that are entirely new and novel to the world. For example, the first mobile phone, the first microwave, the Sony Walkman etc.

- *New to firm*: Products that take a firm into a new category, but are not new to the world, such as Asda's move into clothing retailing through the development of the George brand.

- *Product line extension*: These are additions to the current product lines, for instance, flanker brands in the firm's current markets. Examples are Persil Bio, Bud Lite, caffeine-free Nescafé, etc.

- *Product improvements*: Current products that are manufactured to improved standards of performance. Almost all modern-day products are improved, and often throughout their life.

- *Product repositioning*: These are products that are targeted to a new segment or put to a new use. Arm and Hammer's repositioning of baking soda from a fridge deodorant to toothpaste is a classic example of this.

ILLUSTRATION

Invention isn't everything

Only a few companies invent wholly new products. Most adapt and extend ideas that others have already tried. Apple's iPod was not the first MP3 player, but added enough to make its version innovative.

By developing the iPod personal music player and the iTunes online music store, Apple has dramatically altered the portable digital music industry. However, Apple did not invent digital music or portable digital players. It merely created a new and better value package by developing an easy-to-use music player with conveniently priced online music. The magic in its success is not of radical technology but the creation of higher added value for customers. This it achieved by clever use of design and combination of components to configure the best customer value-adding music proposition.

The lesson here is clear. Success in innovation is not driven by a development being radical or incremental, or whether it is invented in-house or out-of-house. Success is determined by the new value that it delivers to the customer.

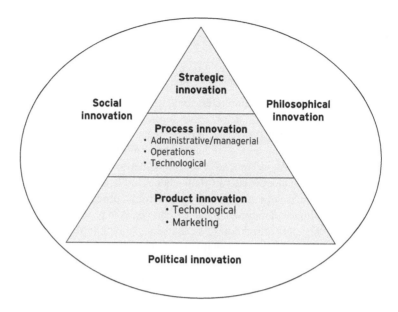

FIGURE 1.1 Innovation formats

Formats of innovation

Just as innovation has different meanings, it similarly manifests itself through different formats/types. These formats are derived from the variety of ascribed meanings, though one-to-one neat symmetrical allocation is not entirely possible. The formats fall broadly into two categories: those that are within a firm's control and those that reciprocally influence or are outside the firm's field of influence (see Figure 1.1).

Product innovation

More often than not, when we talk of innovation we are likely to be referring to product innovation (commonly referring to both products and services). This is so because product innovation is the most visible manifestation of the innovation process. Product artefacts consumed by the market represent the visible traces of the process or act of innovation. New products are the outcomes of the innovation process.

Product innovations are either technology driven or marketing driven. Technological or marketing advance is embodied in the features of the product. Technological embodiment of an innovation is often observed in the visible functional characteristics of a product. For example, the shift from mechanical typewriters to electrical typewriters to a word processor on a personal computer is a shift of technological embodiment. Marketing innovation involves an embodiment that may be tangible or intangible. For example, Unilever's Dimension 2 in 1 shampoo failed despite possessing a technological advancement not captured in any other competitive offerings at the time. Procter & Gamble entered second into the market with Wash & Go (a product with similar features to Dimension 2 in 1) and went on to become hugely successful. Wash & Go possessed the same technical features but was accompanied by a strong brand building and positioning effort as well as a highly persuasive marketing name to make it into a market-dominant product. In other words, technical innovation alone was insufficient to make Wash & Go successful; it additionally required marketing innovation to make the product a success.

Process innovation

Process innovation refers to the change in the conduct of a firm's organisational activities. The change in the way a firm organises and executes its functions may be a consequence of technological advance, or may emanate from the adoption of new structural or operational configuration ushered in through innovations in administration and management methods. Technological process innovations often improve the efficiency of manufacturing operations or enhance product attributes. For example, advances in semi-conductor technology allowed the development of a range of electronic products with attributes and features not possible with vacuum tube and diode technologies in products such as radios and televisions. Further advances in technology facilitated digitalisation of this family of products. As development of new product capabilities and features these represent product innovation. However, semi-conductor technology also altered the operational configuration of a firm and thus represents process innovation. Innovations occurring within the semi-conductor manufacturing process allowed the lowering of end-product prices. It was the underlying effects of these process innovations that actually fuelled the boom in the electronics sector.

Administrative or managerial innovations involve new methods of organising, structuring and operating the organisation. When Henry Ford revolutionised the production system by developing a mass production assembly line, he was involved in a managerial innovation. Operations were organised and managed in an entirely different manner to the then conventional batch and craft-based systems. Ford's system was subsequently challenged by another managerial and administrative innovation: Toyota's now acclaimed Toyota production system (TPS). The TPS is perhaps more correctly defined as a strategic innovation, but its sub-elements such as just-in-time (JIT), Kanban and Poka-Yoke are process innovations of the manufacturing system that transformed the mass-production environment. The implementation of the TPS or lean production system impacted upon and led to the re-shaping of the supply chain. In other words, the effective working of this administrative (process) innovation led to significant change in the way business was conducted and the strategic business model operated, i.e. it led to an attendant strategic innovation.

The shift from inspections to quality management, the adoption of Shigeo Shingo's Poka-Yoke for rapid flexible manufacturing set-up, Volvo's Udevella system of empowered teams are all examples of process innovation.

Strategic innovation

Strategic innovation often involves either a significant adaptive shift in the organisation's current business model or an adoption of a new business model. At times the strategic shift may be driven by innovations occurring within the organisation itself, such as product and process innovations, or it may be driven by external innovations and challenges. One recent external challenge that has required organisations to strategically shift from the old ways of doing things is the IT revolution. The arrival of the internet has led to development of e-business models. For many companies, adoption of e-business models has required development of new capabilities. E-business models have necessitated that conventional business models be complemented or supplemented by e-business building blocks or capabilities. The basic building blocks of e-business are: online information exchange, electronic execution and delivery of services, customised (or personalised) services, resource pooling, business intelligence, online collaboration, and offering aggregation (Baghci and Talsie, 2000).

Strategic innovation is not just driven by technological innovation. The merger in 2005 of Procter & Gamble with Gillette in the fast moving goods sector was partly to build brand portfolio strength but primarily to combat the strategic transformation of the supply chain by the retail giants. As retailers such as Wal-Mart, Tesco and others, grew in size they were able to exert control over the supply chain. To counter the change in the balance of power, manufacturing firms such as P&G have had to strategically consolidate their position in the supply chain by building brand portfolio strength.

External strategic shifts such as mergers, diversifications and consolidations are the most commonly observed outward expressions of strategic innovations. No less important, however, are the internally focussed strategic transformations. Internally focussed strategic innovations often involve structural reconfigurations. In fact, for the most part external expressions of strategy are reflections of internal reconfiguration and innovation. For example, many companies in recent times have moved to customer-centric configurations by switching from vertical hierarchies and functional organisation to horizontal process-based structures. The change in structure was a response to better meet customer needs but also to be able to make strategic supply-chain partnerships work seamlessly, end to end.

ILLUSTRATION

Strategic and process innovators

Companies that possess a strategic innovation capability exhibit a high facility to adapt to circumstances that in some cases may even threaten their very existence.

HP: re-invention is the secret

HP excels at strategic innovation. It transformed itself from an instrumentation company to a computer company in the 1980s and then into a leading manufacturer of printers. Slowly it re-emerged as a personal computer (PC) company and in the process shed its historical operations in electronics instruments and test equipment. In recent times it extended from a microprocessor chip and PC manufacturer to chip and equipment maker and then to computer networking. It is now moving into consumer electronics markets.

The Dell way: process innovation paves the way to redefine rules of competition

Dell is one of the world's largest makers of personal computers. Dell's success is not built around its PC products. Instead, Dell's success is derived from the way it configures and interweaves its processes with client IT departments. By interlinking its processes as a service module into the client systems Dell reduces the client's total cost and risk of PC ownership. It does this through a variety of mechanisms. For instance, it sets up a web-based order process that is company-specific, eliminates set-up and delivery expenses by preloading customised software configurations, tests and tags inventory at the factory and provides support and maintenance through remote monitoring and extensive e-service. Consequently, many of Dell's customers have reorganised their IT systems (e.g. purchasing, accounting) to allow a process interlock. Once customers make such relationship-specific investments they become less likely to switch to the competition. By structuring its organisational design around the delivery process and e-service capability Dell is able to engage in a highly interactive and close customer relationship. This allows Dell to create a system that becomes stronger as its customer network grows. In developing this 'new' mode of delivery Dell has transformed itself from a conventional transaction-based business model to a service delivery relationship business model. This transformation is an example of process-led strategic innovation.

The above innovations are primarily organisational. Organisations do not live in a vacuum but are part of the external environment. They are connected to the external environment through a complex web of intricate relationships and influences. Organisational innovation influences, and is in turn influenced by, external relationships. Indeed many organisational innovations are a consequence of innovations and shifts occurring in the external environment.

Social innovation

Society is in a constant state of change. More and more people are on the move across the globe leading to shifts in needs, tastes and aspirations. For instance, partly as a result of astute marketing, modern society has become more consumption- and self-orientated. This has provided companies greater scope to create and sustain premium brands. However, social innovation is not just market-driven manipulation by large corporations. It occurs far too slowly for it to be simply driven by companies. Social innovation is often an outcome of multiple factors coming together to push society in a new direction. For instance, the flower-power hippie revolution of the 1960s started off as a rejection of the corporate and institutional world but created opportunities for companies. Textiles and fashion houses flourished, as new fashions in colourful psychedelic clothing became part of the mainstream vogue and opportunities in niche markets such as vegetarianism emerged from nowhere. Thus, the movement that started off as a rejection was interwoven into a cycle of change that fuelled consumer culture. A simpler example of social innovation is Band Aid. The coming together of pop musicians to raise money for charity was a novel way of bringing attention to the plight of the needy. Band Aid led to the creation of numerous other events based on a similar format, such as Red Nose Day in the UK.

Heightened awareness of atmospheric pollution has made society environment-conscious, and this in turn led to social innovation. Before going further we need to disentangle change that is simply change from change that is innovation. When markets or society change this is not necessarily market or social innovation. As we noted earlier, social (or any other form of) innovation occurs when value is added to produce a hitherto novel outcome. Thus, environmental sensitivity or consciousness is not social innovation unless it acts as a value-adding process to produce a novel outcome with embodied added value. When environmental lobbying and pressures led to stricter controls on pollution, say as in the Kyoto Accord, then we have social innovation. Strictly speaking, the environmental pressures led to political innovation (definition of the amount of emissions allowed, and codes and procedures for carbon bonds that can be traded by countries). The political innovation led to a social outcome. The social outcome is considered as a social innovation outcome if value has been added by the activities of the process. In this instance this is in the form of greater protection of the environment. This example also shows the interconnection between the formats. In this instance, social innovation as an outcome arises from a political innovation as the enabling process. Indeed, most political innovations tend to have non-political innovation outcomes, such as growth of the economy, building capabilities and vibrancy in firms and people.

Political innovation

Shifts in the political arena often hold important consequences for the direction and development of society as well as organisations. Political innovations can take any number of shapes but most often are seen in the form of legislation, institutional reform, social direction and governance. For example, corporate scandals such as Enron in the US and Parmalat in Europe led to legislative and institutional innovations like the Sarbanes Oxley Act, and the formation of advisory institutes such as the Cadbury Commission.

Japan is a classical example of the impact of political innovation on the corporate arena. The post-Second World War Japanese government enacted a complex milieu characterised by an intimacy of government institutional advocacy arrangements. Japanese corporations rose from decimation through the active deployment of industrial policy by the Japanese Ministry of Trade and Industry (MITI) and Ministry of Finance. The peculiar institutional arrangements of the Japanese *ziabatsu* (business network) and government institutions supported the transfer of western technology and management methods to chosen Japanese corporate players. This set of arrangements was key in laying the foundations for Japan's remarkable economic growth and prosperity.

Philosophical innovation

Innovation in the philosophical arena appears to be very distant from the hustle and bustle of business action. However, new philosophical thinking impacts profoundly on society and the way it manages and conducts itself. Philosophical thought guides society by advancing knowledge and also by defining what is right and what is wrong. For example, Michael Faraday's discovery of electromagnetism or Isaac Newton's laws of science are philosophical advances that transformed society. Newton's laws of mechanics underpin a whole multitude of innovations, from bridges to spacecraft. In its guidance role, philosophical thought paves the ground for societal action and behaviour. Issues such as those surrounding the debate over the acceptance of the contraceptive pill, human cloning, genetically modified food typically start in the domain of philosophy before acceptance by powerful societal institutes and influencing agents/bodies. Subsequently, they spread out into the social sphere as socially accepted philosophical truths and often become embedded as rules of law through political enactment. The current era of what could be viewed as egocentric consumption is a part of a wider shift in society from a worldview of virtue rooted in religious faiths to the relativism of post-modernist society. The consumerism of modern society is a consequence of the philosophical acceptance of certain types of ideas in the arts, sciences and society. The impacts of philosophical innovation can be huge. Take for instance the philosophical revolution in China and Russia. The move from communism and socialism towards an acceptance of market capitalism has opened a market of more than 1.7 billion consumers.

Defining the innovation space: strategic mapping

The three organisational innovation formats defined above can be transposed into an innovation space map by scrutinising each of the dimensions (product, process and strategy) against level of change. Figure 1.2 shows an innovation space map. By compiling a plot of a company's portfolio of change the innovation space map allows scrutiny of an organisation's innovation approaches. The map can also facilitate examination of the company's position vis-à-vis its competitor firms, as well as allow longer term scrutiny by a process of compiling plots over time. The strategic space map can be used to study the direction that the company is taking, as well as the strategic interlinkages occurring between different levels of organisational innovation. The map can be used to develop an organisational prognosis as well as aid decision making. Examination of the product dimension against level of change produces the dimensions of: market penetration (or volume growth), product evolution and product revolution.

	Product/service	Process	Strategic	
Radical change	Product revolution	Process re-engineering	Strategic transformation	*(New to world/ new to firm)*
Incremental change	Product evolution	Process change/ improvement	Strategic development	*Product line extension/product improvement*
Current (no change)	Market penetration (volume)	Process efficiency	Strategic focus	*Repositioning*
	Product/service	**Process**	**Strategic**	

FIGURE 1.2 Mapping the innovation space

Market penetration (volume growth)

This dimension involves little or no product innovation. The main strategy here is to increase market share of the brand or product. This is often driven by marketing innovation. For instance, the development of a marketing programme that is able to communicate and capture the targeted market segment more effectively than competitors. This strategy is primarily based on developing a marketing proposition that outmanoeuvres competitor offerings in the marketplace.

Another way of developing market volume is to take the product into new markets or segments (this is termed *market development*). This a company may do by finding either new uses of the product or by identifying previously untapped market segments with the same or similar needs. The most common and traditional route to market development is one involving geographic market expansion. However, this is not the only mode for market development. Detailed study of market structures can often reveal market segments whose needs are very close but are currently unfulfilled or whose needs can be carefully developed to align with the current product offering.

Product evolution (product development)

This represents the classic domain of most corporate attempts to innovate, namely development of an improved product to more closely fulfil current market needs. Often when we talk of product evolution/development we are talking about improvements of the current offering, e.g. slightly improved formulation of a shampoo, or an improved dispenser.

This form of development utilises what is sometimes called *technology mining*. This strategy involves trying to find new uses of the same technology. Instead of just drilling downwards for efficiencies (from volume production) the technology is used to drive product extensions. For example, the microchip can be used in many different products.

Another way of evolving products is through *technology-led improvement*. Many products look the same yet they are often improved. This is typically found in complex products such as white goods. One fridge looks very much like another yet the product may be technologically enhanced. The auto sector is another example where advances in car engine technology and safety technology is unseen but plays a very important role in the product's performance.

Product evolution can also occur through market development. When a company evolves a new product from its current product but the evolved product is such that it fulfils needs of a market very different from its current one it is involved in an act of innovation that produces firm diversification. How 'distant' the market is from the firm's current operations determines the degree of diversification. Distant product-market offerings are referred to as unrelated diversification, and closer ones as related diversification. Related and unrelated innovation have an important bearing in terms of developing and extending knowledge, skills and competences, i.e. they stretch the competence base and by doing so open up further potential opportunities.

Product revolution

This represents a major shift in the product or technology. For instance, the shift from propeller aircraft technology to jet engine transformed the airline industry. Similarly, the changes from manual typewriters to electronic typewriters to computer software packages are radical revisions of the product offering. Some revisions can take the product into entirely new markets, but this need not necessarily be the case. Essentially, most of the radical shifts captured in this dimension are a consequence of technology-led transformation of products and markets.

ILLUSTRATION

Evolving your innovation – leveraging competences

Rory Stear founded Freeplay Energy after watching a television programme on a clockwork-powered radio. Trevor Baylis invented the radio in 1994 and Freeplay bought the rights to the invention. The world fell in love with the concept. In 2000, sales reached $37 million but the company still failed to make a profit. However, the company is now very different from the one that started making the famous radios in South Africa.

Running the company on a narrow invention manufacturing-driven business model was a mistake, admits Rory Stear. The company has spent the last four years reinventing itself as a research and product development company. The number of employees was cut from 600 to 30, and all manufacturing subcontracted. In 2004, on sales of just £3 million the company was making a break-even return. Now the business is led by consumer demand and based on a portfolio of products, of which radios are a small part.

The company has in the process developed a range of other products: torches, medical devices for monitoring unborn babies, and a charger for mobile phones. All of these are based on leveraging the original invention.

(*Source*: Based on D. Blackwell, 'Wind-up radio company to aim listing', *Financial Times*, 16 February 2005, p. 25)

Process efficiency

The game-plan here is to get the best out of the existing process. This means implementing and working the process more effectively. For example, when a new process is introduced into an organisation it is difficult to operate it to maximum efficiency. However, with repeated use experience accumulates and the process can be executed much more efficiently. This is the basis upon which the theory of learning and experience curve is founded, i.e. as more volume is produced the unit costs of operation fall as a result of learning effects. Process efficiencies play an important role in enabling price reductions, which are necessary to penetrate mass markets.

A narrow version of process efficiency is *technology process drilling*. This is an internal strategy based on process efficiency but by focussing on a particular technology to drive learning and cost efficiencies. The goal is to try and maximise the return of a particular technology in the current product market domain. As familiarity with the technology grows, it is applied with greater efficiency to reduce costs or improve the margin return to the organisation.

Another way to build process efficiency is to use the same process to manufacture a closely allied product. Quite often it is possible that variant products can be developed using the same basic processes. For example, ice creams that are packed into tubs can use a common production process, albeit with some additional packing and coating requirements, and be converted into a chocolate coated bar such as a Magnum ice cream bar. Thus, the core process remains the same but the product is evolved or extended. This is another enabling route to market innovation.

Process improvement

Process-led improvement occurs when the processes being utilised in the organisation are improved for greater efficiency of operation. Deployment of techniques such as quality-led improvement methodologies and Lean Six Sigma can yield internal efficiencies by reducing the level of waste as well as improving a product's conformance to the required customer expectations. Process improvement works at two levels: firstly, by improving manufacturing and other operations; and secondly by improving the product to ensure consistent and reliable performance to customer expectation. Almost all market launches of a product are improved over their lifetime. Without continuous refinement and improvement competitors can easily out-compete and out-position the firm by offering a higher quality product at a lower price.

Process re-engineering

Some shifts in process are such that they transform not only the production process but also open up the possibility of developing new products, or products with different attributes. For example, developments in the field of electronic technology transformed internal operations of firms that previously utilised electrical technology and the new process simultaneously opened up a new frontier of product possibilities. Process transformations need not just arise from technology but may do so through a radical restructuring of current operations and processes. When an attempt is made to radically change processes, the exercise is called business process re-engineering (BPR). Re-engineering is attempted when it becomes clear that no amount of small incremental change in the processes will produce the desired level of improvement benefits. Often this is the case when the efficiency of the company's processes lags very far behind competition, and the only solution is to start with a clean slate, and redesign and implement new highly improved processes.

Strategic focus

When current markets are emphasised the focus of attention is on stability and strategy implementation. The emphasis is to focus on core competences and develop strengths and capabilities in selected areas of market competition. Innovation rarely comes out of thin air. To produce innovation firms must first build, through sustained effort, the necessary expertise and competence in technical and market operations. In other words, innovation requires a depth of knowledge, and this requires strategic focus.

Strategic development

It is often the case that the market changes. If the change is small the old strategy may be sufficient to cope with the new market order. Sometimes, however, old strategies may not be appropriate to the changed market circumstances. New competitors may be entering the market or old ones stretching their products and evolving their markets in such a way as to make strategies that worked well in the past become inappropriate and jaded. The key role of innovation here is to find new and novel ways of leveraging and extending current competencies.

It is possible to deliver greater value to the market through strategic development. For example, some airlines have chosen to operate a booking system that ties retail and tour operators into their business chain. Thus, a greater amount of the business value chain is controlled and managed. Similarly, food retailers have engaged in strategic extension in using the internet to develop door-to-door delivery. In the services sector, insurance companies such as Direct Line Insurance are examples in which the traditional business model was challenged. Subsequently, with the advent of the internet further improvement was made to the service, i.e. strategic innovation was followed by technology-led process improvements. Essentially, innovation plays the role of stretching the current competencies in a new direction and therefore continuously reinvigorates the firm's strengths.

Strategic transformation

When companies change their products and markets they are almost invariably involved in a change of strategic direction. Development of entirely new competences and capabilities or transformations of conditions, such that they demand vastly altered strategies, are termed strategic transformations. Strategic transformations are often a result of major change in markets or technologies. For example, the watch industry went through a period of strategic transformation with the advent of electronic and quartz watch technology. Strategic transformation demands building new competences to compete in new or altered markets. Some firms ally or merge with other companies that possess the skills needed to operate in the altered environments. Others however, especially if response time to change is not a critical part of the equation for success, internally develop the skills and capabilities.

Figure 1.3 shows a hypothetical innovation space map for a company with a portfolio of three products at two time periods t1 and t2. The cross (x) product is one for which little innovation is taking place, and the major effort is to increase profits by developing market share and improve margins through cost reduction. It is product developed using the core skills of the company. The circle (o) product is similar but has been improved from its original form. In other words, some incremental product innovation is taking place. The star (*) product has undergone the most dramatic change. The strategic model for competing in this sector has altered, as has the product. The map also shows that the firm does not pay much

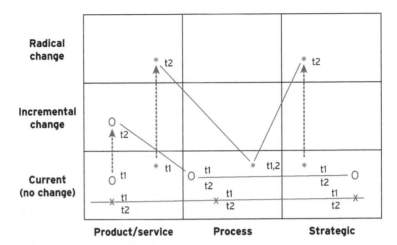

FIGURE 1.3 Hypothetical example of innovation space map

attention to its internal manufacturing and business processes. None of its processes have been improved over time. This is likely to place it at a disadvantage with companies who are improving their operational efficiency and product reliability and function through quality and other such process improvement efforts.

The above mapping matrix, whilst useful, misses out an important consideration in making an innovation a success: the behavioural dimension. Most instances of innovation require people to adapt to it to a lesser or greater degree. From a firm perspective there is an internal and external behavioural impact of innovation: consumers externally and employees internally are often required to behaviourally adjust to the development of an innovation (product, market or technology). It is important for the firm to fully comprehend the nature and implications of this change. The possibilities of impact depend on whether the change demanded is complex or requires simple behavioural adjustment.

The innovation may be incremental or radical but only require simple behavioural adjustment from employees internally and customers externally. In this case the behavioural impact of the innovation is not huge. The firm is able to get away with a small degree of retraining of its employees and education of the market. However, some innovations may require significant adjustment from both the firm's employees and/or the marketplace. Internally, the firm may need to develop new skills through retraining of employees, or devise new ways of conducting operations to cope with the change. Externally, the firm may have to spend time on educating the marketplace on the use of the new product, especially if misuse is likely to expose them to a health or other risk.

For instance, why was the initial uptake of mobile phones with camera technology surprisingly slow? Quite apart from technology factors there seems to have been at play a number of market resistances:

1. Not enough customers had mobiles with facilities such as cameras, making possessing one less attractive. There did not seem to be much point in having a camera phone if you could not send the picture or communicate visually with others.

2. There were issues of picture resolution and transfer speed, making downloads difficult.

3. Some of the internet connectivity features required a level of understanding and know-how that many users simply did not possess or wish to acquire by poring over technical manuals.

Many mobile phone owners either did not want the features or were unable to cope with the complex functions that it offered. To break into the market it was necessary for the tele-communications sector to (i) educate the consumers; and (ii) provide incentives to adopt the new technology. This was done by a strong marketing campaign as well as heavy discounting from the initial price of the phones.

Another example is from the food sector. For a long time now, companies have had the ability to produce synthetic food nutrients in tablet form. These could, theoretically at least, do away with the many problems of food products such as harvest, maintaining freshness in distribution and so on. But what is the likelihood of this happening in the near future? Eating food around a table with friends and family is a deeply rooted social custom that is not amenable to change. It requires extreme situations, such as space travel or being stranded, for people to convert to tablet-based food. To make such an innovation a commercial reality would require a firm to manage a tremendous change in consumer behaviour. In contrast, getting a consumer to switch from a washing powder to washing powder tablets or liquid packets for the washing machine requires little consumer education and little behavioural change.

From the discussion, it is clear that the success of innovation is not just dependent on being able to innovate technically. It is just as important that the firm is able to innovate the market itself, i.e. educate it and change it. Equally, the firm must innovate internally through a process of training and educating its employees. This is a key part of the process of creating an innovation capability. Innovation, therefore, is not just about producing product development outcomes. It is just as much, if not more, about managing people, processes, institutions and markets to enable it.

Models of innovation

Management scholars have been interested in understanding what type of firm is most likely to innovate. Schumpeter first suggested that small entrepreneurial forms were the sources of most innovations, but later found that large firms with some degree of monopoly power were more likely to be the sources of technological innovation. He argued that large firms have better access to capital than smaller firms, and possess the production and other complementary assets to commercialise an innovation. Since they hold a monopoly, they have no competitors who will imitate their innovations and are therefore more likely to invest in them (Schumpeter, 1950).

Empirical studies have not found a clear relationship between a firm's size and market power, and innovative activity (Kamien and Schwartz, 1995). Research has therefore attempted to explain a firm's success in terms of whether the innovation can be considered incremental or radical, and presented in terms of 'static' or 'dynamic' models.

Static models of innovation show a cross-sectional view of a firm's capabilities and the incentive to invest at a point in time, and therefore only view the difference between the old and the new. Examples of these models include:

- *Abernathy and Clark* (1985) looked at why some radical innovations fail. They suggested that technological and market knowledge underpins a firm's innovations. While new incumbents may introduce radical innovations that destroy the technological capabilities of a competitor firm, they can still fail if they are unable to destroy its market capabilities – especially if they are more important and difficult to acquire.

- *Henderson and Clark* (1990) investigated why some incumbents failed at incremental innovations. They recognised that innovations were comprised of components which were connected together and proposed an unbundling of technological knowledge into 'component' and 'architectural'. They suggested an innovation was 'incremental' if both the architectural and component knowledge are enhanced, while an innovation was 'architectural' if the component knowledge was enhanced and the architectural knowledge was destroyed. Using this typology, it was found that incumbents who were thought to fail in 'incremental' innovation were actually failing in 'architectural' innovation.

- *Teece* (1986) argued that the two factors of 'appropriability regime' and 'complementary assets' are instrumental in enabling a firm to profit from an innovation. 'Appropriability regime' is the extent to which a technology can be protected from imitation, thus allowing the inventor to collect rents from it. 'Complementary assets' are all the other capabilities (apart from those which underpin the technology) that the firm needs to exploit the technology, and includes manufacturing, distribution channels and the like.

- *Roberts and Berry* (1985) suggested that the firm has a choice in adopting an innovation (internal development, acquisitions, licensing, internal ventures or alliances, venture capital and nurturing, and educational acquisition), and this choice can determine success or failure.

- The *strategic leadership* view argues that the strategic incentive to invest in an innovation or the failure to exploit it as a result of destroyed competence come only after a firm's top management has recognised the potential of the innovation (Afuah and Bahram, 1995).

Dynamic models of innovation take a longitudinal view of innovation and explore its evolution following introduction. A technology here may then have its own unique radical and incremental phases, which may require a different type of firm for success. Some dynamic models include:

- *Abernathy and Utterback* (1978) suggested three phases in an innovations life cycle – fluid, transitional and specific. A lot of market and technological uncertainty surrounds the fluid phase, which is driven out during the transitional phase involving significant firm–customer interaction. Finally, the specific phase is entered when the innovation is driven based on a stable and dominant design. A firm will need different capabilities during different phases of this model (e.g. innovation competencies during the fluid phase, or low-cost competencies during the specific phase).

- *Tushman and Rosenkopf* (1992) explained that the extent to which a firm might influence the evolution of an innovation (e.g. guiding a design towards an industry standard) is governed by its complexity. The more complex an innovation, the greater the role of non-technological factors such as complementary assets and organisations. They outline a life cycle beginning with 'technological discontinuity' that advances a technological frontier by an order of magnitude, and drives a significant competitive advantage. This is followed by the 'era of ferment' when marketing and technological uncertainty is high, and competition for acceptance between different designs prevails. Eventually, a 'dominant design' emerges which reduces the technological uncertainty and ushers the beginning of an 'era of incremental change'. Again, it was recognised that different firms need different competencies at different phases of this life cycle in order to be successful.

- *Foster* (1986) attempted to predict when a 'technological discontinuity' might arise, suggesting that the rate of advance of a technology is a function of the amount of effort put into the technology and follows an S-curve. Technological progress increases rapidly (after an initial slow start) and finally diminishes as the physical limits of the technology are approached.

In each case, these dynamic models recognise phases of great uncertainty which are addressed through analysis and refinement, and lead to a dominant design. This design is then developed, released to market and incrementally improved to drive profitability. This is a broad structure which is mirrored in stage-gate innovation models today, and will be discussed in later chapters.

Innovation, trade and globalisation

Innovation, trade and globalisation are often treated as separate elements. Yet they are highly interlinked in the evolution of the modern world. Innovation is an activity that began with the ascent of humankind. The earliest known innovations were probably the discovery of fire and patterned tools. The history of humankind is the history of innovation. Around 6500 BC the Sumerian settlers of the Tigris and the Euphrates valley invented the wheel. The Mesopotamian (Greek for 'between rivers', i.e. between the Tigris and Euphrates) civilisation invented the cuneiform alphabet. The earliest known bricks, dated circa 6000 BC, were discovered in the Iranian plateau. The Sumerian practice of boiling alkalis together to create soap eventually culminated in the first cosmetics products in Egypt. This illustrates that the early civilisations were characterised by innovation and invention. The regional centres of innovation activity then moved from Sumeria to the Indus Valley, and thereafter a further shift eastwards occurred with the emergence of the Chinese civilisation. The Greek civilisation followed by the Roman Empire started the move away from the East toward Europe. Much activity in Europe was initiated within the Renaissance period (1498–1686) and further accelerated and capitalised upon during the Enlightenment period (1686–1849), and the Victorian period (1859–1900). In the twentieth century innovative dominance moved to the Americas. By the end of the twentieth century new hubs of innovation started to re-emerge in the South East Asia, particularly Japan, and also parts of Europe.

Innovation creation and innovation diffusion

Innovation is not a simple act. It does not happen in a vacuum and is a complex phenomenon underpinned by a number of elements. Two key elements of this phenomenon are: innovation creation and innovation diffusion. Innovation creation is primarily linked with the individual and the firm, whereas innovation diffusion additionally involves movement and adoption of the innovation (see Figure 1.4). Innovation diffusion in its rudimentary form occurred through trade, and is in many senses the precursor of the modern phenomenon of global convergence. Almost 3000 years ago, the Phoenician civilisation was

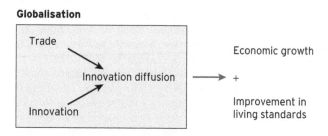

FIGURE 1.4 Innovation creation, trade and innovation diffusion

already engaged in long distance trade. The Phoenicians spread innovations through the movement of products to small clusters of settlements around the Mediterranean. The diffusion of technology subsequently followed, though in some cases this was seen to follow many centuries later. By the mid part of the twentieth century, the speed of diffusion had increased to a point where it had been compacted into under a decade. However, it was still limited almost entirely to trade in manufactured goods because of the dissimilarities in the ways of living and the relative unimportance of trade in services. In the 50 or so years that followed, the effects of trade and globalisation became ever more pervasive. Society in the latter half of the twentieth century came to be dominated by the economic triad of the US, Europe and Japan. During this period innovations occurring anywhere in the triad and in any sector (now including services) could be transferred and adopted elsewhere seemingly instantaneously (in around two years). This position has been further expanded with the emergence of new markets such as China, and the assimilation of former Eastern European nations into the European bloc. The process of diffusion has speeded up further and become more encompassing. It now incorporates services exchange in addition to manufacturing but also increasingly includes behaviour, aesthetics and other socially embedded artefacts.

Trade and more broadly globalisation is an ongoing consequence of technology transfer and economic convergence driven by the actions of firms to fulfil the desires and expectations of consumers and stakeholders. In this sense, globalisation is a complex phenomenon involved in the transfer of 'economic' innovations across the globe. It carries with it political and cultural adjustments and ramifications, which work via a process of economic convergence and diffusion of innovations to raise standards of living over time.

From the beginning of time, economics, politics and culture (the aesthetic, symbolic, ideological and value aspects of life) have regularly collided. The outcome pattern has

ILLUSTRATION

They forgot to invest

From almost nowhere the Prius, Toyota's hybrid-engine car has become an iconic product owned by Hollywood stars, Silicon Valley barons and increasingly the mass market beyond.

This is bad news for some auto manufacturers, especially the US companies Ford and General Motors. US auto companies refused to accept that American consumers would switch away from 'gas – guzzling' Sports Utility Vehicles (SUV) built on light truck chassis frames. However, as oil prices continued to rise, consumers changed. For a decade or so the SUV boom allowed Ford and GM to enjoy high margins and resist any inroads from Asian manufacturers, led by Toyota and Nissan. The formula no longer works. Both Ford and GM are suffering, particularly since the economic crisis of 2008.

GM and Ford's scepticism over the appeal of fuel-saving engines has made them technology laggards. Even worse, they are finding responding difficult because both are beleaguered by heavy pension and medical costs of an ageing workforce. A heavy capital structure makes it hard for them to change with the shift in consumer preference in their domestic market.

Asian companies have taken a strong lead in hybrids. Nissan and Ford have licensed the technology from Toyota, while Honda has developed its own system. Japanese manufacturers have always been adept at improving manufacturing efficiency and using product range as the platform to compete. They also continue to stress the long term rather than change direction to maximise short-term return. Ford and GM have constantly struggled to keep pace with Japanese technology, efficiency and quality.

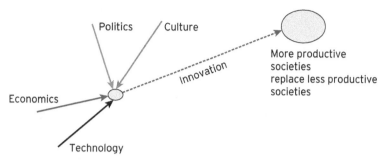

FIGURE 1.5 Innovation as the engine of economic growth

invariably been one in which culture and politics have adjusted to the opportunities presented by changes in technology, demography, ecology and economics (Lewis and Harris, 1992). Throughout history, the evolutionary principle that has repeated itself is one in which more productive societies have replaced less productive ones (see Figure 1.5). In modern thinking, it is generally postulated that innovation is one of the main factors underlying a country's international competitiveness, productivity, output and employment (Corley et al., 2002). However, the exact process through which this occurs remains unclear.

Cycles of economic growth

Economists have long struggled to explain the phenomenon of productivity growth. It was, however, not until the mid-1950s that the beginnings of an explanatory theory emerged from Massachusetts Institute of Technology (MIT) economist Robert Solow's work on the production function. According to this theory, output of the economy depends on the inputs, namely capital and labour (Solow, 1957). In essence, the basic theory postulates a doubling of outputs when the inputs are doubled (although this was latterly revised for anomalies arising from the law of diminishing returns. According to the law of diminishing returns, additions of labour to a fixed amount of capital, or vice versa, will after a point result in successively smaller output returns. This appears, on the surface, a perfectly reasonable explanation. However, evidence from real-world growth rates raises questions about the veracity of this explanation. For example, if this theory holds with its diminishing returns rider, how is it that the returns from the first half of the twentieth century were lower than the second half? What is the explanation for the widening of the gap between the developing and developed nations? According to the theory, when we are experiencing an increase of the stock of capital (as was the case for industrial nations) we would expect a fall in the return from each additional unit of capital. Yet the reverse was occurring. It would appear then that a substantial part of economic growth cannot be explained by increased utilisation of capital and labour, and is more aptly explained by 'multi-factor productivity' (MFP). MFP represents improvements in the efficiency of production as a consequence of technological progress plus other forms of new knowledge – in short, innovation. It is usually seen as a consequence of innovative activity from the world's leading firms, technological catch-up by others and re-allocation of resources across firms and industries. Stated simply, innovation accounts for the growth that cannot be explained by increases in capital or labour (illustrated in Figure 1.6).

Thus, even though lower returns are accrued from increasing labour or capital investment these can be more than offset by the leveraging effect of innovation. This explains why

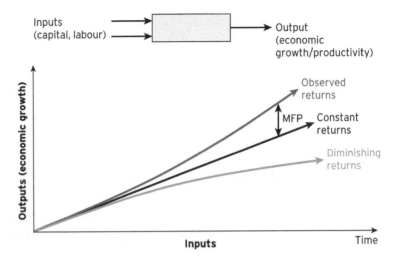

FIGURE 1.6 MFP in the economic growth equation

growth rates and returns have remained high in rich countries and the poorer countries have not, generally speaking, been able to catch up.

Technological change is central to the process of economic growth and development and appears to occur in a series of cycles. Among the first to notice this pattern was the Russian economist Nikolai Kondratieff. In 1925, using data on prices, wages, interest rates, and production and consumption drawn from France, Britain and the US, Kondratieff identified a series of long economic waves, of around 50-year cycles. The Austrian economist Joseph Schumpeter subsequently studied these in detail and found that each wave tended to be driven by entirely different clusters of industries, and could be divided into four phases: prosperity, recession, depression and recovery. Each wave was associated with a significant technological shift, around which other innovations (in production, distribution and organisation) clustered and the impacts of these rippled outwards into the economy. Typically, a new cycle was initiated with the advent and use of new technologies. Each upswing stimulates investment and expansion of the economy. The long boom eventually peters out as the technology matures and the returns to investors fall as potential opportunities reduce. Following maturity and decline, development of a new technology would bring fresh innovations and destroy the old way of doing things. Schumpeter labelled the process in which entrepreneurs actively fermented the displacement of old forms with new forms as 'creative destruction' (Schumpeter, 1943). This 'creative destruction' facilitates the environment for upswing. To date, four complete cycles have been discerned, and it would appear that we are in the middle of the fifth (see Figure 1.7). The fifth cycle, based on nanotechnologies, biotechnologies and networking software, offers a possible explanation of how the US managed to shake off the lethargy of the 1990s to leap ahead of those preoccupied in the preservation of the fourth-wave industries (Hepworth, 1989; Forster 1987). Indeed, the fifth wave may even be entering decline. Technology-led stimulation is important but is not sufficient itself to cause economic growth. Other factors, such as demographics, industrial, financial, social and demand conditions also need to be appropriately in place (Freeman 1982; Freeman and Perez, 1988). Thus, each wave is characterised by new forms of organisation, co-operation, competition and even location. In other words, technological leadership of one wave does not automatically guarantee leadership of the next wave (Rosenberg, 1982).

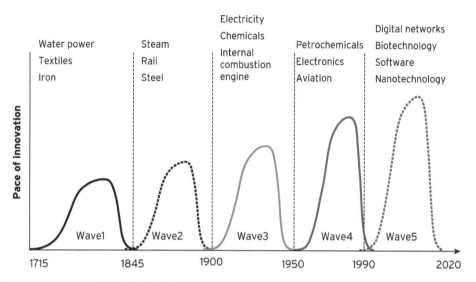

FIGURE 1.7 Schumpeter's business cycles.

The wave cycles appear to be shortening, from the early 50–60-year cycles to shorter durations of 30–40 years. The fifth wave is likely to peter out by year 2020. The shortening of the cycle can be explained by the fact that a much more directed effort at managing the waves was initiated in the early twentieth century. Such was the importance attached to the dominance of waves that governments and firms began actively searching for the next wave technology. One of the oldest symbols of an active approach to innovation was the foundation of Bell Laboratories in New Jersey, USA. Today all industrialised nations employ huge numbers of R&D staff, devices and processes to discern, induce and develop the next world-beating technology. Those who catch the upswing of the wave set standards that kill off weaker rivals, and enjoy the fruits of their dominance in the form of high premiums and profits. Latecomers to the wave have only the leftovers and even these may be quickly wiped out by the emergence of a new wave.

Two important points can be drawn from the discussion above. Firstly, the central role of entrepreneurial action in the innovation process. This indicates the centrality of firm-level factors in innovation. Secondly, the importance of institutional milieu within which a firm operates. This is often bounded either in a regional environment, but more often in terms of national boundaries. Both of these aspects are examined further in later sections.

Innovation and economic progress: some empirical evidence from Europe

Improvements in multi-factor productivity (MFP) play a crucial role in economic progress. Over the last two decades, the Organisation for Economic Co-operation and Development (OECD) estimates suggest that for most countries MFP growth accounted for 30–50 per cent of the business sector's GDP growth (Bassanini et al., 2000). Measurement of innovation is a difficult and tricky task, partly because of data limitations. Notwithstanding the major challenges in measurement it is still necessary to track innovation. A common measure of innovation is expenditure on R&D.

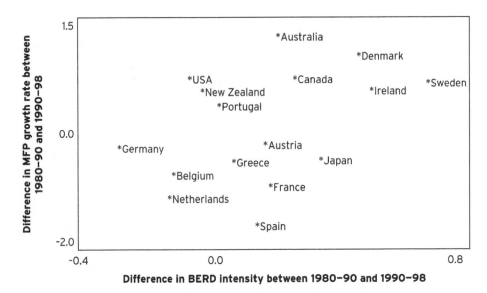

FIGURE 1.8 The relationship between changes in business enterprise expenditure in R&D (BERD) intensity and acceleration in MFP growth
Source: Bassanini et al., 2000. With permission from OECD

Figure 1.8 shows a positive relationship between investment in R&D and acceleration in MFP growth. Over the 1990s the differences across nation states appear to have been patterned by differences in MFP growth rates. Australia, Canada, Ireland, New Zealand, the Nordic countries and the US experienced accelerated growth in MFP. This indicated recovery from the slowdown experienced during the 1980s. However, over the 1990s for some countries MFP performance worsened, especially in Japan, France and Spain. Given that MFP growth is linked with developments and improvements in innovation and innovative practices and/or catch-up, the recovery of the US from the mid-1990s has been attributed to innovations in ICT (Integrated Computer Technologies) industries, the effects of which rippled over into other sectors. Similar ICT-led effect also occurred in other countries.

Patterns of innovation and MFP across countries depend on several factors and research by the OECD suggests that the policy environment has an important role in shaping these. For example, regulatory policies that limit product-market competition (e.g. imposition of entry or operational restrictions) or labour market adaptability (e.g. hiring and firing rules) can have important side effects on innovation, technology diffusion and MFP performance. There are essentially three main ways to improve MFP: (i) eliminate slack in the use of resources; (ii) adopt more efficient technologies; and (iii) increase innovative effort. OECD evidence suggests that MFP growth, over the short to medium term at least, is dominated by within-firm productivity, and therefore institutional environmental conditions are essential for robust MFP performance (OECD, 2001).

Another widely used indicator of innovative activity is cross-national variability of patents per capita (Figure 1.9). This measure is very similar to R&D intensity. The figures show that some European nations (Finland, Belgium and Sweden) are doing comparatively well but many others are showing signs of stagnation, especially Germany, France, and Switzerland.

In 2000, the Lisbon European Council set the European Union the goal of becoming the most competitive and dynamic knowledge-based economy in the world within the next

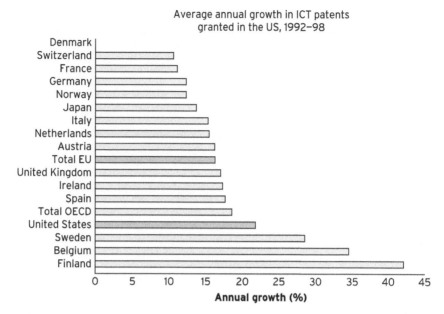

FIGURE 1.9 Annual growth rate of ICT patents
Source: Cordis, 2000. With permission from OECD

decade. The European Innovation Scorecard (EIS) was developed at the request of the Lisbon Council to aid tracking of progress. The EIS 2003 contains 19 main indicators, which capture the main drivers and outputs of innovation (see Table 1.1). The indicators are divided into four categories: human resources for innovation (five indicators), the creation of new knowledge (four indicators), the transmission and application of knowledge (three indicators), and innovation finance, output and markets (seven indicators). These indicators are used to operationalise data collection via a Community Innovation Survey (CIS). The third CIS survey was completed in 2003, and covers 32 countries – 15 member state countries, 13 acceding and candidate countries, three associate countries (Switzerland, Iceland and Norway), and the US and Japan.

The data from the 19 indicators of CIS-3 can be compiled into a Summary Innovation Index (SII-1). However, because of the non-availability of data for many indicators for acceding and candidate countries (ACC), the US and Japan, a second summary composite was also compiled (SII-2). The first composite (SII-1) covers all indicators for all member state countries, plus Switzerland, Iceland and Norway. The second composite (SII-2) is calculated for all countries, using only 12 widely available indicators (all five human resources indicators, all six knowledge creation indicators and ICT expenditures).

Finland and Sweden have the highest SII-2 from the European group of countries and are the European innovation leaders, matching the US and Japan (see Figure 1.10). Spain, Portugal and Greece are examples of countries catching up from low positions. Even though their performance is above the average of the EU15 (member states), the Netherlands, France and Germany appear to be in danger of losing momentum. Portugal and Austria (compared to 2001 SII) shifted to a catch-up position from a previous falling behind situation. Of concern Italy, in the company of Bulgaria, continues to fall further behind. Interestingly, several ACC countries rank higher than several EU15 member states. Only Cyprus, Romania and Turkey lag behind all the EU15 states.

TABLE 1.1 List of 2003 EIS indicators

Human Resources for Innovation	1. New graduates (% of 20–29 years age class) 2. Population with tertiary education (% of 25–64 years age class) 3. Participation in lifelong learning (% of 25–64 years age class) 4. Employment in med-high and hi-tech manufacturing (% of total workforce) 5. Employment in hi-tech services (% of total workforce)
Creation of New Knowledge	1. Public R&S expenditures 2. Business expenditure on R&S (BERD) (% of GDP) 3. EPO hi-tech patent applications (per million population) (USPTO hi-tech patent applications (per million population) 4. EPO patent applications (per million population) USPTO patent applications (per million population)
Transmission and Application of Knowledge	1. SMEs innovation in-house (% of manufacturing SMEs) SMEs innovation in-house (% of services SMEs) 2. SMEs involved in innovation co-operation (% of manufacturing SMEs) SMEs involved in innovation co-operation (% of services SMEs) 3. Innovation expenditures (% of turnover in manufacturing) Innovation expenditures (% of turnover in services)
Innovation Finance, Outputs and Markets	1. Share of hi-tech venture capital investment (% of total venture capital) 2. Early stage venture capital investment (% of GDP) 3. Sales of 'new to market' products (% of turnover in manufacturing) Sales of 'new to market' products (% of turnover in services) Sales of 'new to firm but not new to the market' products (% of turnover in manufacturing) Sales of 'new to firm but not new to the market' products (% of turnover in services) 4. Internet access/use 5. ICT expenditures (% GDP) 6. Share of manufacturing value-added in hi-tech sectors (% of manufacturing value-added) 7. Volatility rates of SMEs (% of manufacturing SMEs) Volatility rates of SMEs (% of services SMEs)

The link between innovation and economic welfare can be observed from Figure 1.11, which correlates the innovation index against GDP. It would seem clear from this that GDP growth is positively influenced by innovation. However, it is also interesting to note that the figure shows that innovation is not the sole way to achieve high per capita income levels. Luxembourg accrues its advantages from economic specialisation in finance and administrative services, and Norway benefits from its huge natural resources. Likewise, a high innovation (Index SII) does not always translate into high per capita income, as evidenced by Finland, Sweden and Japan.

Another interesting pattern is the difference in R&D-led innovation and diffusion-led innovation. Figure 1.12 shows the SII split into a R&D-based innovation creation component and an innovation diffusion component. It can be seen that larger and more developed nations perform better on R&D, and the less developed and smaller countries better on diffusion. The figure shows that with few notable exceptions countries that rank high in overall SII do well in R&D innovation. Most of the ACC states do better in diffusion than on R&D creation innovation.

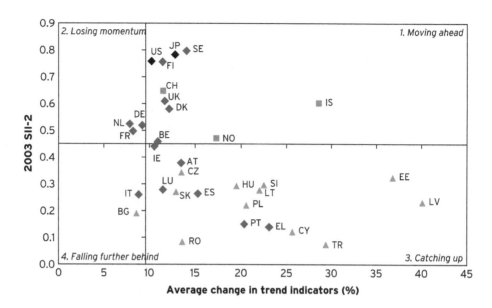

Member states	Acceding and candidate countries	Associate countries	Non-European
Austria (AT)	Bulgaria (BG)	Iceland (IS)	United States (US)
Belgium (BE)	Cyprus (CY)	Norway (NO)	Japan (JP)
Denmark (DK)	Czech Republic (CZ)	Switzerland (SW)	
Finland (FI)	Estonia (EE)		
France (FR)	Hungary (HU)		
Greece (EL)	Latvia (LV)		
Ireland (IE)	Lithuania (LT)		
Italy (IT)	Malta (MT)		
Luxemburg (LU)	Poland (PL)		
Netherlands (NL)	Romania (RO)		
Portugal (PT)	Slovakia (SK)		
Spain (ES)	Slovenia (SI)		
Sweden (SE)	Turkey (TR)		
United Kingdom (UK)			

FIGURE 1.10 European country SII index trends
Source: European Commission, 2003. With permission

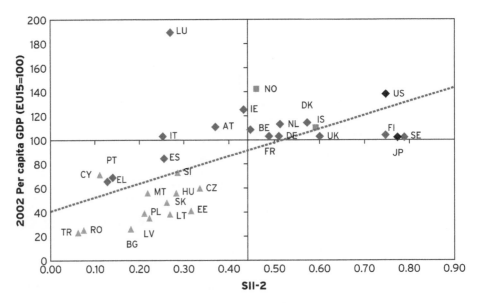

FIGURE 1.11 Correlation between innovation and GDP
Source: European Commission, 2003. With permission

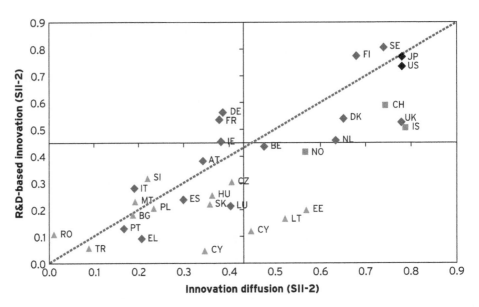

FIGURE 1.12 R&S innovation and innovation diffusion
Source: European Commission, 2003. With permission

Competitiveness, innovation, the nation state and the innovation milieux

So far, we have studied the meaning of innovation and its economic development aspects, where the primary focus was on the firm, its actions and strategies. In this section we return to address the tie between the micro-level and the macro-level view. In particular we examine how the competitive fabric of the nation state in the global environment (national competitiveness) is interlinked with a firm's actions for competitive advantage.

First it is necessary to clarify terminology, since there is a degree of confusion between the terms competitiveness and competitive advantage. At the firm level (micro-level), the term competitiveness is quite often used to refer to the ability of a firm to increase its profitability, market share and size. In traditional economic theory, typical measures of competitiveness are based on comparative cost of production, i.e. the way to become competitive is to produce a given output at lower cost. This may be achieved either by reducing the production factor costs or improving factor productivity. In other words, when used at the micro-level the term effectively becomes synonymous with the term competitive advantage. However, at the macro-level (national level) common indicators of competitiveness are framed in international trade terms. Under this perspective, competitiveness is the degree to which a nation can, under free and fair market conditions, produce goods and services that meet the test of international markets while simultaneously maintaining and expanding the real income of its citizens. Competitiveness thus is an evolving concept. Over time it has been defined in terms of trade, trade policy, industrial policy, technology policy and more recently simply as a way of raising living standards (OECD, 1996).

Regional innovation clusters: why do they form and where? Theoretical explanations for innovation sunspots

In the sketch of the evolution of humankind we discerned hives of innovation appearing in certain regions. The development of a hive of innovative activity concentrated in a certain region is sometimes called an innovation sunspot. A modern example of an innovation sunspot is Silicon Valley in California, USA. Given the impact of innovation activity on economic progress and firm vitality it is important to understand why and how such innovation sunspots emerge. A number of theories, arising from research in geography, economics and management try to explain why innovation is relatively concentrated in some places rather than others. These include the explanations listed below, which we will briefly elaborate upon:

- The swarm explanation;
- The transaction costs explanation;
- The knowledge economy explanation;
- The competitive explanation;
- The trade explanation.

The swarm explanation

One traditional explanation of the emergence of regional clusters of innovation is based on Schumpeter's (1943) argument that exogenous inventions (inventions created by others) sought by entrepreneurs create a swarming effect. In other words, companies and individuals wishing to take advantage of an opportunity or innovation are attracted to the locality. The attraction to the opportunity has a ripple effect, in that it highlights the region as one offering opportunity, and thus leads to further attraction. This creates a swarm effect. The main argument is that innovations are concentrated in regions because these environments are more conducive for the formation of new firms and incubation. This is partly because of the availability of inputs (ideas, people, supplies, etc.) into the innovation process and partly to do with the birth rate of new firms. The swarm effect formed the main wisdom of the relationship between innovation and geographic space up until around the 1970s.

The transaction costs explanation

The second explanation (or alternative to the traditional evolutionary economics explanation) of why innovations tend to concentrate in particular spaces is based on institutional analysis. This explanation is inspired by the work of Coase (1937), and Williamson (1975). The explanation argues that the traditional neo-classical cost minimisation calculus about the internalisation of firm functions can also be extended to consider the external market relations between firms. It suggests that local networks emerge in order to minimise transaction costs. By concentrating together into local supply chains, firms can reduce transaction costs, as well as take advantage of externalities, such as available skilled labour for which they do not have to pay directly. In addition, there are other non-market benefits that arise in the form of information exchange and shared business knowledge through clubs and meetings.

The transaction costs ideas inspired the concept of industrial districts and the concept of the innovative mileux (developed by Group des Researches Européen sur les Milieux Innovateurs (GREMI)). Both suggest that smaller innovative firms tend to cluster around local production systems. The smaller firms create networks that help them to minimise costs whilst at the same time gaining access to specialist knowledge and tied markets.

The knowledge economy explanation

Modern evolutionary theories and trade theories have also been used to explain spatial distribution of innovation. The evolutionary theories started by Schumpeter have been updated as modern explanations by a number of researchers (e.g. Dosi et al., 1988). Collectively, these theories explain innovation in terms of historical trajectories. The occurrence of innovation sets off a path of knowledge creation and accumulation. The more knowledge and learning accumulates the greater are the chances of further innovation. Innovation and knowledge accumulation are intertwined under this perspective. In other words, a chain or trajectory is initiated by an innovation. This form of explanation is referred to as *path dependency* or *evolutionary* theory. Thus, concentration of knowledge workers in certain regions allows higher levels of learning to take place and initiates an upward spiral of innovation and learning. This is why specific regions become innovation hotspots. From this we can see the importance of the state in nurturing conditions such as creating a skilled labour force and supporting certain types of incentives for innovation to take root. The state can help turn the mutually reinforcing wheel of innovation and knowledge creation. Because of government policies different nation states posses different national systems of innovation, which reflect how good local innovation systems are at acquiring and using new economic knowledge (Lundvall, 1992). Highly skilled or 'knowledge' workers feature prominently in this explanation because they are sources of innovation. Thus, developing a 'knowledge economy' becomes crucial to the nurture of innovation. It is upon such logic that an increasing number of advanced nations, as well as emerging economies, lay great store in developing themselves as knowledge hubs. The logic is simple: from knowledge comes innovation from which in turn comes further knowledge and economic prosperity.

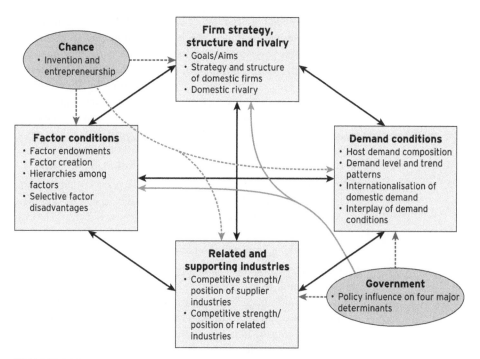

FIGURE 1.13 Porter's national competitive advantage diamond
Source: Porter, 1990. Reprinted with permission of The Free Press, a division of Simon & Schuster, Inc.

The competitive explanation

The three explanations developed so far focus on local production systems. However, there is an argument that for commercial success, innovations need to be internationally competitive. Trade and market competitiveness are important indicators of demand-pull and global economic activity. Porter (1990) built on earlier versions of the product life cycle theory to argue that local competition stimulates and strengthens world class performance.

Porter is generally regarded as the inspiration of *the competitive explanation* of regional clusters. The main objective of Porter's research in *The Competitive Advantage of Nations* was to uncover reasons why 'some social groups, economic institutions and nations advance and prosper' (Porter, 1990, p.xi). Porter noted that the particular combination of conditions within nation states has an enormous impact on the competitive strengths of the firms located there. According to Porter firm success is based on four characteristics, commonly termed as the Diamond framework (see Figure 1.13). The diamond is an interconnected system, in which each of the four determinants are mutually self-reinforcing.

Porter's diamond framework

1. *Factor conditions*: An industry needs an appropriate supply of factors (availability of skilled labour, infrastructure, etc.) in its home base if it is to be successful. Factors are divided into *basic* (e.g. unskilled labour, climate), *advanced* (e.g. highly skilled scientists, technical infrastructure, etc.) or *general* (those that can be deployed across several industries, or sectors). For instance, if the national environment has people with technical backgrounds, such as found in Germany, the competitive strength will be concentrated in engineering and high-tech sectors.

2. *Demand conditions*: The nature and type of domestic demand affects a sector's ability to compete internationally. Highly demanding and sophisticated consumers at home bring to bear pressures on the domestic firms to become more innovative and produce high quality goods. Additionally, a nation's firms gain if the buyers at home are able to anticipate the needs of buyers in other countries. By this mechanism home nation firms can gain a learning advantage in meeting such demands globally. Thus, a large market of demanding home consumers can have a positive impact on the firm's ability to compete internationally. For example, Japanese consumers value space saving. This forces Japanese companies to be innovative and lead in compact products. The US's desire for convenience foods gave it an advantage in fast food products.

3. *Related and supporting industries*: A nation's firms are able to compete more effectively, if they are surrounded in the home base by clusters of suppliers, buyers, distribution channels or technologies, who are themselves world class. For example, Denmark has a cluster in health and home products, Sweden in paper making, Germany in chemicals, metal-working, transportation and printing.

4. *Firm strategy, structure and rivalry*: Porter lays great emphasis on the fourth element of the diamond, which argues that intense rivalry in the domestic market strongly impels firms to innovate. Strong rivalry in the home market sifts out the poor quality and less innovative companies and leaves only ones with the strongest skills and competences to reap high returns. Thus the environment and the nature of competition in the environment play a key role in defining success on the platform of world markets.

In addition to the four factors, which constitute the primary elements of the diamond, two additional factors, chance and government, also influence competitiveness. Chance includes occasional random events and technological discontinuities that may create innovations or allow shifts in competitive positions. These do not feature as part of the diamond, but may alter the conditions within it. Similarly, the government has a role to play but only by affecting the corners of the diamond. Porter (in his original work) explicitly refused to regard government as a same order determinant as the other four factors of the diamond and demoted the role of active industrial policy as a secondary issue.

In later work, however, Porter and Stern (2001) extended the diamond framework by explicitly defining a common innovation infrastructure. This is a set of three cross-cutting factors that support innovation in the entire economy. The common infrastructure includes firstly the overall human and financial resources that a country expends for basic research and technological advance; secondly the long-term policy commitments that a country enacts (for instance, protection of intellectual property rights, tax incentives for innovation, openness of the economy to trade and investment); and thirdly the overall technological sophistication of the economy.

Porter's analysis, while becoming widespread, has come under strong criticism. It has been thought to be highly reductionist and simplistic in reducing the complexity into a four-edged diamond. It underplays the role of states, especially given the evidence from newly industrialising countries (NICs) (Stopford and Strange, 1991; Henderson and Appelbaum, 1992) and it does not adequately account for transnational activity of businesses on national diamonds (Dunning, 1992). Krugman (1994) provides one of the strongest criticisms in pointing out that the obsession with national competitiveness is a dangerous one. He asserts states are not like firms; international trade is not a zero-sum game (as it is in firm-level competition), and there is little empirical evidence to indicate that growth of one country diminishes the living standards of another. The only loss is perhaps in terms of diminishing 'status' that dents the nation's pride.

The trade explanation

Krugman (1991) put forward the hypothesis that comparative advantage of most advanced world economies has been lost to lower wage economies, and that advanced nations now must build absolute advantages on the basis of their innovative capabilities.

Krugman, in contrast to Porter, emphasises the significance of international trade in determining the success or failure of particular regions. Whilst Krugman does not explicitly address the issue of innovation, his examination of international trade provides insights into demand-led innovation. Krugman's basic argument is that the comparative advantage of advanced economies is being lost to developing low labour cost economies in routine production sectors. The way out of this dilemma is to develop absolute competitive advantages based on products and services that are geared specifically to the needs of international customers. Generally, this will require the use of 'knowledge' and 'quality' not available in less developed economies. Specialisation and greater division of labour is one route for gaining absolute competitive advantage. Innovation is the second route. Innovation is a key basis for securing absolute trading advantage. The capability of building absolute trading advantage is only available to a few regions possessing high levels of knowledge work. These regions are the hubs of international knowledge flows. Under the competition and trade explanations, innovation concentrations in a few areas arise from a complex interaction of international trading capabilities in combination with domestic environment factors.

ILLUSTRATION

The nano-boomerang

The Australian government is strongly backing nanotechnology. In 2004 it invested Aus$3bn as part of its 'Backing Australia's Ability' innovation strategy. Nanotechnology is the science of objects and materials less than 100 nanometres across, where one nanometre is a billionth of a metre.

According to Invest Australia, the government promotion agency, some Aus$100m a year is being spent on nanotechnology-based R&D at 70 research groups and about 40 companies in Australia. While this is a relatively small amount compared with other developed countries, Australia is reaping high returns in terms of a high market success rate in developing and introducing to market new everyday products.

Examples

One example is Cap-XX, a Sydney-based manufacturer. Cap-XX has developed miniature electrical power storage devices. Cap-XX has entered into partnerships with a number of computer giants such as Intel and Acer. The company has just finished setting up manufacturing operations in Penang. However, its CEO, Anthony Kongats, states that Cap-XX will maintain its core of manufacturing, research and product development in Australia.

Another example is Starpharma. Based on developments in nanotechnology, Starpharma developed VivaGel, a sunscreen cosmetic. Starpharma is now listed on the Australian stock exchange. The company intends to stay in its Melbourne base to take advantage of relatively low costs for R&D and its proximity to Asian countries, which are viewed as early market opportunities for VivaGel. However, its investment in Dendritic Nanotechnologies, a joint venture with Donald Tomalia, the US-based inventor of dendrimers, gives it access to US research and funds.

(*Source*: Based on L. Moldofsky, 'Smarter products with nanotechnology', *FT*, 20 November 2004, p. 3)

Government policies for innovation

As discussed earlier, path dependency theories (evolutionary theories) of innovation point to the importance of history and the idiosyncratic features of national economies. This implies that while competitiveness of firms is determined by management actions (of the firm), competitiveness also stems from the strength of a national economy's productive structure, its technical infrastructure and other externalities, all of which can be leveraged by firms to their advantage (OECD, 1996).

Economic benefits of new technologies chiefly originate from rapid and extensive diffusion. This process can be highly influenced (and leveraged) by putting in place policies that focus on developing strengths, combating blind spots and investing for the future. Policies can encourage firms by stimulating technology foresight. The Japanese were highly successful in this through instigation of collaborative long-term research programmes under the guidance of government institutes such as the Ministry of International Trade and Industry (MITI). These policy programmes were designed to compensate for the short-sightedness and blind spots of companies (Fransman, 1990). Japan is not alone in terms of policy guidance; others such as South Korea have also successfully conducted similar exercises (Jones and Sakong, 1980).

Over time the complexity of new technologies has increased. Development of new technologies can no longer be created through the efforts of a lone entrepreneur, but relies on complex mechanisms built on networks that often transcend national boundaries. This creates the case for government intervention. Governments are concerned about the competitiveness of their national economies, and the firms operating in them. Historically, national innovation systems have played a key role in securing competitive advantage and can be a driving force of economic dominance.

In global environments, it can be argued that national policies based on the simple premise of providing firms a competitive edge is obsolete because there is little value in government policies promoting innovation if the benefits can be transferred to other countries. Whilst there is debate over the nature and extent of impact of globalisation, especially with respect to R&D activities of large firms (Patel and Pavitt, 1991), nations cannot ignore the shift away from national oligopolies to global oligopolies. In a world of global competition it is all the more necessary to provide support for science, build a technology infrastructure, and select strategic technologies and expose them to appropriate levels of competition (Sharp, 1997).

Governments must play their role in nurturing the conditions that promote innovation. They have a number of instruments at their disposal. Clark and Guy (1998) indicate three policy formats for doing so (see Table 1.2).

Macro-economic policies have a broad impact on the terms of trade factors and thus are key in determining international competitiveness. Education policies shape the infrastructural condition of the labour market. Industrial policies are indications of the long-term direction of corporate support, and thus have a key bearing on the type of sector likely to receive support. These broader policies can be supplemented by more specific policies in the form of science, technology and entrepreneurship policies. Science policy is concerned with the development of basic science and training of scientists, while technology policy is concerned with the use of scientific knowledge in producing technological progress. Technology policy influences the decisions by firms to develop and commercialise or adopt new technologies. Entrepreneurship policies nurture start-up and incubation of new businesses. Innovation policy can be added to these as an additional strand. The various policies are summarised in Figure 1.14. The aim of innovation policy is to promote the development, diffusion and efficient use of new products, services and processes in markets or inside

TABLE 1.2 Three governmental policy formats to promote innovation

Supply side policies	Demand side policies	Developing networking and research infrastructure
Encouraging public R&D that complements private R&D	Financial subsidies for adoption	Improving industry–university relationships
Encouraging inter-firm collaboration	Provision for information	Developing other infrastructure elements
Targeting specific technologies	Facilitating technology transfer from abroad	
Providing tax breaks and subsidies for R&D	Developing technical standards	
Strengthening intellectual property rights	Government procurement	
	Providing SME support	

Source: Clark and Guy, 1998. Reprinted with permission of Taylor & Francis Group

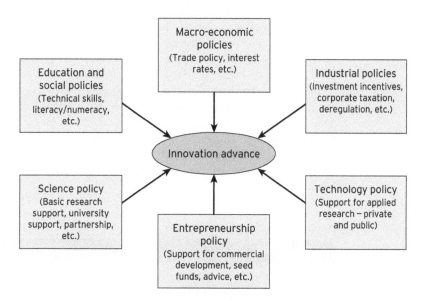

FIGURE 1.14 Policy instruments to promote innovation

private and public organisations (Lundvall and Borras, 1997). Innovation policies have a wider policy remit than science and technology policy. They take into account the complexities of the innovation process, focussing on policies to encourage innovation and diffusion. The aim is to facilitate interactions between different types of knowledge, firms and develop an infrastructure, including universities and R&D institutes. The main objective is to foster and speed up learning and innovation diffusion.

If the policy instruments can be correctly aligned they can act as powerful stimulants. The results of the Japanese miracle and also of the Tiger economies bear witness to the successful use of policy instruments. However, policy instruments in practice are rather unwieldy and take considerable time to produce the desired effect. Furthermore, governments change, and even when they do not themselves change they often fail to persist sufficiently with their advocated policies to produce the integrated impact intended of them as visions.

Conclusion

The chapter illustrated the different meanings of innovation to show that it is a complex phenomenon; one involving an intricate interplay of factors to successfully engender it. In particular it consists of two elements, innovation creation and innovation diffusion. Both must be managed systematically since they hold important consequences for individuals, firms and societies. Innovation is an act that involves adding value to a product, process or activity to produce a novel outcome. Organisationally, innovation can take the form of product, process or strategic innovation. However, non-organisational forms of innovation must also be borne in mind, since they can reciprocally affect the activities of the firm. To be successful at innovation requires a mastery over a number of complex activities. Not all such activities can be controlled by firms. Some of these influences are national and embedded in the national infrastructures and other determinants arise from supra-national forces such as trade and globalisation.

The very important role that innovation plays in societal evolution was highlighted. Innovation has been pivotal in human development. It is central to economic development and long-term prosperity. Historical evidence shows that innovation occurs in cycles, and each cycle is associated with a particular type of industry or initiative and conditions. Often these cycles of innovative activity are concentrated in specific geographic locations.

In addition, the chapter explored theories and frameworks that attempt to explain the underlying reasons and consequences of the emergence of regional clusters of innovation. In doing so it examined the role national governments can play in nurturing innovation clusters, and policies and instruments they have at hand to do so.

Innovation is too important for companies to leave to chance. Companies, hand in hand with governments and entrepreneurs, must work hard at the firm, national and international levels to foster innovation.

QUESTIONS

1. Why is innovation so important to society?

2. What is multi-factor productivity, and what does it tell us about innovation?

3. What general indicators can we use to assess national-level innovation? What are the advantages and problems with use of such indicators?

4. Name the different types of innovation that a firm may need to consider. Give an example of each from your own experience.

5. Explain Porter's diamond framework using real-life examples, and explain the pros and cons of his model. In doing so, evaluate how good it is at explaining formation of regional clusters of innovation?

6. Select an example of innovation cluster. Examine how it came to be formed and define the challenges for it into the future.

CASE STUDY

Space to breathe amid the crisis

Robert Bosch once came across a stray paperclip while wandering round one of his factories. He asked a nearby worker if he knew what it was. 'A paperclip,' the worker nervously suggested. 'No – this is my money!' the entrepreneur said.

The oft-told tale, possibly apocryphal, says a lot about Germany's largest privately owned engineering group. Frugality and financial discipline have underpinned Bosch's growth as an independent company since it was founded in 1886. Combined with a distinctive company culture and a reputation for innovation, they have since helped it expand to become the world's largest car supplier.

Franz Fehrenbach, chief executive and only the fifth company head since Robert Bosch, has this year put the company on a mission to single out every superfluous paperclip. 'We have to cut costs in all areas,' he says, sitting in the executive dining room at Bosch's headquarters in the hilly outskirts of Stuttgart. But he makes one exception: 'We will reduce spending in the ongoing business, but we will not cut back on research and development for important future projects.'

A sharp drop in revenues has prompted Mr Fehrenbach to slash output in recent months, making 17,000 German employees temporarily redundant and cutting jobs permanently at plants around the world. The news elsewhere in the sector is bleak: a succession of medium-sized suppliers has filed for bankruptcy in recent months.

In spite of appearances to the contrary, though, Bosch is in a markedly better position than many German manufacturers. Mr Fehrenbach has held fast to the company's long-term strategy amid the crisis: 'Our triple-pronged strategy comprises further diversification, investment in research and development and a targeted internationalisation.'

While other companies are taking drastic action in response to the crisis, Bosch's culture and solid financing position give it vital breathing space. The company thinks long term and has conservative, sometimes even reclusive, instincts. Employees take pride in its cutting-edge technology and the company's habit of reinvesting almost all of its profits in the business instead of funnelling them to anonymous investors.

'The company culture, especially our high credibility, is one of our greatest assets,' Mr Fehrenbach says. 'Our competitors cannot match us on that because it takes decades to build up.'

Bosch has almost €8bn in cash, while its financial liabilities have changed little from the €2bn last reported at the end of 2007. 'Bosch has a strong business risk profile and very conservative financial policies,' says Werner Staeblein, credit analyst at Standard & Poor's, the rating agency.

This has eased Mr Fehrenbach's job of steering the company through the crisis. He expects global car production to fall by 10–15 per cent this year, forcing companies to scale back capacity, close plants and consolidate further. 'The car industry is at the beginning of a radical structural transition,' he says.

For Bosch, there is a positive side effect to this industrial plight: last year, sales in the car parts business fell to below 60 per cent of total revenues for the first time, bringing Bosch closer to one of Mr Fehrenbach's strategic goals, a reduced dependency on the car industry. However, he had intended to achieve this not by a quirk of recession but by growth in the industrial and consumer goods sectors.

(*Source*: based on D. Schaefer, 'Space to breathe amid the crisis', *Financial Times*, 1 March 2009)
© The Financial Times Limited 2009

QUESTIONS

1. Why is Bosch in a relatively good position compared with similar German companies?
2. How did they deal with the economic crisis of 2008/9?
3. Carry out your own research and investigate how Bosch has performed since the crisis.

References

Abernathy, W. and Clark, K.B. (1985), 'Mapping the winds of creative destruction', *Research Policy* 14: 3–22.

Abernathy, W.J. and Utterback, J.M. (1978), 'Patterns of innovation in technology', *Technology Review* 80(7): 40–47.

Afuah, A.N. and Bahram, N. (1995), 'The hypercube of innovation', *Research Policy* 24: 51–76.

Bagchi, S. and Tulskie, B. (2000), 'e-Business models: Integrating learning from a strategy development experiences and empirical research', Working draft, 2000 IBM Corporation. **www.research.ibm.com/strategy/pub/ebbb.pdf.**

Bassanini, A., Scappetta, S. and Visco, I. (2000), 'Knowledge, technology and economic growth: Recent evidence from OECD countries', OECD.

Blackwell, D. (2005), 'Wind-up radio company to aim listing', *Financial Times*, 16 February, 25.

Clark, J. and Guy, K. (1998), 'Innovation and competitiveness: A review', *Technology Analysis and Strategic Management*, 10(3): 363–395.

Coase, R.H. (1937), 'The nature of the firm', *Economica NS*, 4: 386–405.

Cohen, W. (1995), 'Empirical studies of innovative activity', in P. Stoneman (ed.), *Handbook of economics of innovation and technological change*, Oxford: Blackwell.

Cordis (2000), 'The community innovation survey', March, Innovation and SMEs programme, **www.cordis.lu/itt/itt-en/00-2/dossier1.htm.**

Corley, M., Michie, J. and Oughton, C. (2002), 'Technology, growth and employment', *International Review of Applied Economics*, 16(3): 265–276.

Dosi, G., Freeman, C., Nelson, R., Silverberg, G. and Soete, L. (1988), *Technical change and economic theory*, London: Francis Pinter.

Drucker, P. (1985), *Innovation and entrepreneurship*, New York: Harper Row Publishing.

Dunning, J.H. (1992), 'The competitive advantage of countries and the activities of transnational corporations', *Transnational Corporations*, 1: 135–168.

European Commission (2003), '2003 European innovation scoreboard: Technical paper No.2 analysis of national performances', European Commission, 20 November.

Forster, T. (1987), *High-tech society: The story of the information technology revolution*, Oxford: Blackwell.

Foster, R. (1986), *Innovation: The attackers' advantage*, New York: Summit Books.

Fransman, M. (1990), *The market and beyond*, Cambridge: Cambridge University Press.

Freeman, C. (1982), *The economics of industrial innovation*, London: Pinter.

Freeman, C. and Perez, C. (1988), *Structural crisis of adjustment, business cycles and investment behaviour*, in G. Dosi, C. Freeman, R. Nelson, G. Silverberg and L. Soete (eds), *Technical change and economic theory*, London: Pinter, Ch.3.

Henderson, J. and Appelbaum, R.P. (1992), *Situating the state in the East Asian development process*, in R.P. Appelbaum and J. Henderson (eds), *States and development in the Asian Pacific rim*, London: Sage, Ch.1.

Henderson, R. and Clark, K.B. (1990), 'Architectural innovation: The reconfiguration of existing product technologies and the failure of established firms', *Administrative Science Quarterly* 35: 9–30.

Hepworth, M. (1989), *Geography of the information economy*, London: Belhaven.

Jones, L.P. and Sakong, I. (1980), *Government, business and entrepreneurship in economic development: The Korean case, studies in the modernisation of the Republic of Korea*, Cambridge, MA: Harvard University Press, 194–195.

Kamien, M.I. and Schwartz, N.L. (1975), 'Market structure and innovation: A survey', *Journal of Economic Literature* 13: 1–37.

Krugman, P. (1991), *Geography and trade*, Cambridge, MA: MIT Press.

Krugman, P. (1994), 'Competitiveness – A dangerous obsession', *Foreign Affairs*, March/April: 28–44.

Lewis, W.W. and Harris, M. (1992), 'Why globalisation must prevail: A report from McKinsey global institute', *McKinsey Quarterly* 2: 114–131.

Lundvall, B.A. (1992), 'Introduction', in B.A. Lundvall (ed.), *National systems of innovation: Towards a theory of innovation and interactive learning*, London: Pinter.

Lundvall, B.A. and Borras, S. (1997), *The globalising learning economy: Implications for innovation policy*, report from DG XII, Commission of the European Union.

Moldofsky, L. (2004), 'Smarter products with nanotechnology', *Financial Times*, 20 November, 3.

OECD (1996), *Industrial competitiveness*, Paris: OECD.

OECD (2001), 'Productivity and firm dynamics: Evidence from microdata', *OECD Economic Outlook*, No.69, Paris.

Patel, P. and Pavitt, K. (1991), 'Large firms in the production of the world's technology: An important case of "non-globalisation"', *Journal of International Business Studies* 22(1): 1–21.

Porter, M.E. (1990), *The competitive advantage of nations*, New York: Free Press.

Porter, M.E. and Stern, S. (2001), 'Innovation: Location matters', *Sloan Management Review*, Summer: 28–36.

Pure Insight (2005), 'Economist Intelligence Unit: Ideation and innovation trends and success indicators', 1 August, **http://member.pure-insight.com/library/item/552**.

Quinn, J. (1992), *Intelligent enterprise*, New York: Free Press.

Roberts, E.B. and Berry, C.A. (1985), 'Entering new businesses: Selecting strategies for success', *Sloan Management Review* 26(3): 3–17.

Rosenberg, N. (1982) *Inside the black box: Technology and economics*, New York: Cambridge University Press.

Schaefer, D. (2009), 'Space to breathe amid the crisis', *Financial Times*, 2 March.

Schumpeter, J. (1943), *Capitalism, socialism and democracy*, London: Allen-Unwin.

Schumpeter, J.A. (1950), *Capitalism, socialism and democracy*, 3rd edn, New York: Harper.

Sharp, M. (1997), 'Technology, globalisation and industrial policy', in M. Talalay, C. Farrands and R. Tooze (eds), *Technology, culture and competitiveness: Change and the world political economy*, London: Routledge.

Solow, R.M. (1957), 'Technical progress and the aggregate production function', *Review of Economics and Statistics* 39: 312–320.

Stopford, J.M. and Strange, S. (1991), *Rival states, rival firms: Competition for world market shares*, Cambridge: Cambridge University Press.

Teece, D.J. (1986), 'Profiling from technological innovation: Implications for integration, collaboration, licensing and public policy', *Research Policy* 15: 285–306.

Tushman, M. and Nadler, D. (1996), 'Organising for innovation', *California Management Review* 28(3): 74–92.

Tushman, M.L. and Rosenkopf, L. (1992), 'Organisational determinants of technological change: Towards a sociology of technological evolution', *Research in Organisational Behaviour* 14: 311–147.

Williamson, O.E. (1975), *Markets and hierarchies*, New York: Free Press.

2

Creativity and innovation

Learning outcomes

When you have completed this chapter you should be able to:

- Understand what creativity is and how it can contribute to innovation problem solving.

- Appreciate creativity as a complex process and not just a single act.

- Recognise that managing for creativity requires paying attention to the individual, teams as well as a variety of organisational factors.

- Understand that certain types of organisational systems, structure and practices hamper creativity, whilst others enhance it.

- Appreciate that creativity can be nurtured and developed in the organisation through a process of education, training and use of tools and techniques for creativity.

- Understand how to apply a select number of creativity tools.

Introduction

As organisational environments become more dynamic, the complexity and number of problems companies need to address rises seemingly exponentially. Competitors are getting stronger and better. Across all sectors, competitors quickly catch up with any new product release, any strategic move or new practice introduced by leading edge firms. To stay ahead companies are increasingly resorting to creativity in an effort to produce new products, improve organisational functioning and enhance decision making. Without a creative approach to the challenges facing them, there is a tendency to descend to the average of corporate practice. Many companies just mimic and implement the solutions and approaches that others improvise. This is not the basis upon which a company can become a leader in its class or the basis for it to survive dynamic change and cut-throat competition. Survival demands companies open themselves to new ideas and new ways of doing things. To do so companies must tap into the creative talents and energy of their people. Those that fail to leverage creativity regularly lose 50–60 per cent of employee power (Levesque, 2001). This figure is a lower end estimate; in quite a number of cases the loss is even greater. No company in the world can ignore this amount of potential and still hope to succeed in the modern world.

Notwithstanding all the attention and the rhetoric in corporate corridors and board-rooms all over the world, lack of innovation remains a key problem in business today. One reason for this is the continued failure to systematically manage for creativity. The first step in addressing this problem involves recognising that the creativity challenge is organisational, group and individual. It is the creativity in people and their ideas that produce innovation, but it is the organisation that must structure and encourage it for organisational benefit. In other words, attention must be paid both to the organisation (its systems, structures and culture) and the individuals within it.

Whilst the focus of creativity in the workplace is to produce organisational benefits, creativity also gives individuals significant personal benefits. Organisationally, developing creativity in employees strengthens their capacity to be more open, flexible and resilient and to see different opportunities and possibilities. These are important skills to deal with unstructured, ill-defined challenges, uncertainties and complexities of a changing world. For the individual, being creative builds self-esteem. When individuals are creative they feel good about themselves because creativity has an energising effect. People derive a great deal of personal satisfaction from being creative, which in turns leads them not just to be more productive but also to produce highly novel breakthrough ideas.

Approaches to creativity

The old-style hierarchical company often discouraged innovation. Even when such companies managed creativity, they did so under the assumption that 'thinking' was a managerial prerogative. Managers or their designated experts did the 'creative' stuff and employees lower down the hierarchy did the 'implementation'. In other words, the mass of the employees followed orders. They carried out tasks and worked to very precise prescriptions. They had little or no power to change, adapt or improve. Thus, their 'thinking' was redundant in such organisations. Reinforcing this position was the highly compartmentalised view of running organisations. Functions operated as specialists and work was executed in relative isolation. For instance, in R&D-orientated companies technology innovation was conducted in separate, designated parts of the organisation. In these organisations, the coupling between technology innovation and business process innovation is often overlooked. Fortunately, many companies have seen through the weaknesses of this approach. Highly innovative and creative companies have found that innovation and creativity cannot just be left to the aegis of a select few. Creativity and innovation must be fostered and harnessed throughout the whole organisation. Companies must become innovative across the entire spectrum of their activities, and this requires the involvement of all employees; from the top to the very bottom. Ritter and Brassard (1998) draw a contrast between the old approach and the new approach to creativity:

Old approach to creativity
- Only a few people in any organisation were considered the 'creative ones'.
- Breakthrough ideas are needed only in the 'strategic' areas of the business.
- Engineers were routinely brought in to fix major production or customer problems.
- Consultants were hired to help achieve a breakthrough in products and markets.

New approach to creativity
- Breakthroughs are required in every corner of a competitive organisation.
- Specialists in breakthroughs are still critical, but more people must become involved in creativity to tackle the increasing number of challenges that are emerging.
- The creativity that exists naturally within everyone in the organisation must be harnessed.
- A common process for dramatic improvement must be created.

Creativity and the creative process

Before proceeding much further, it is perhaps useful to gain a common understanding of creativity and the creative process, dispelling some myths as we go.

What is creativity?

Creativity can be defined in various ways, depending on the standpoint from which it is being examined. It can be defined from a psychological, a social, an individual or an organisational perspective. We tackle it from an organisational viewpoint. From an organisational standpoint creativity is the ability to consistently produce *different* and *valuable* results. A vital component in the production of valuable outcomes is a disciplined process that helps to channel creativity and keep it focussed to achieve results.

Creativity is a process of developing novel and useful ideas, whether an incremental improvement or a world-changing breakthrough. At a simple level, being creative involves:

- Consistently producing a lot of ideas.
- Putting existing, or new, ideas together in different combinations.
- Breaking an idea down to take a fresh look at its parts.
- Making connections between the topic at hand and seemingly unrelated facts, events or observations.

Creative outcomes are a consequence of making original and unique mental connections. This involves 'thinking in a divergent' mode. Divergent thinking arrives at numerous novel or unique meanings or new and original thought by a process of synthesising and representing images in an unusual or unconventional manner. According to Joseph V. Anderson (1992) there are three broad forms of creativity:

- *Creation* is the activity of making something out of nothing *(Creativity that makes things)*.
- *Modification* is the act of altering something that already exists, so that it can (a) perform its function better; (b) perform a new function; (c) perform in a different setting; or (d) be used by someone new *(Creativity that changes things)*.
- *Synthesis* is the act of relating two or more previously unrelated phenomena. Creation is nice, but synthesis is the real engine of survival and prosperity *(Creativity that combines things)*.

ILLUSTRATION

Cooking it up

The creative urge is alive and well in the professional kitchen. Chefs are drawing energy and inspiration from an unprecedented number of sources, including technology and the sciences. The ability to mix and match diverse ingredients and techniques from around the globe continues to spark new ideas and the development of previously unimagined dishes. At the same time, advances in technology and food science provide chefs with an array of new tools and precepts, enabling them to map out a new and largely unfamiliar culinary wonderland. For instance, Heston Blumenthal, chef-owner of the three-Michelin-star restaurant The Fat Duck in Bray, England, talks about applying the theories of 'molecular gastronomy' to menu development while exploring uses for such equipment as vacuum ovens and homogenisers. When asked to identify his chief source of inspiration, he unhesitatingly points to Harold McGee. McGee, a former instructor of literature at Yale, who in his groundbreaking book *On Food and Cooking: The Science and Lore of the Kitchen* turned to chemistry to debunk some long-held beliefs about cooking.

Other chefs, approaching the subject from a different perspective, maintain that creation arises out of experience. Rosario Del Nero, Chief Executive chef for Naked Fish Restaurants in Boston, calls creativity 'the sum of your experience as a human being – your growing up, your travels, your observations. When you create, you dig into a chest of experiences, of memories, of passion, of cravings.'

(*Source*: Based on Frumkim, 2005)

Myths of creativity

It is generally believed that creativity is a solitary practice. This belief remains prevalent despite the fact that most of the greatest inventions of the past century have emanated from inspired groups. Many believe that creativity cannot be managed. Yet in reality, managers can strongly shape the creative process. Most prevalent (and least productive) is the belief that groups must depend on a few, often eccentric, individuals for creative input, whereas any group can become more creative if its leaders understand and support the dynamics of creative collaboration.

Creativity often gets wrapped in mystery and talked about as if it were some genie from a magic bottle. Sebell and Yokum (2001) expose a number of common myths surrounding creativity and its organisational management. These are briefly highlighted below.

Myth 1. You can purchase an innovation

New products and services have always been the two most visible ways for companies to innovate, but other areas include manufacturing cost reductions, warehousing and distribution efficiencies, customer service improvements, creative marketing practices and promotions, and new forms of packaging. Many of these 'practices' cannot be bought on the market, because they tend to be organisation-specific. For instance, process innovation can take years to implement and master properly. Even when it is possible to buy or license a product or technological innovation the big challenge is still to make it work in the organisation. Absorbing an innovation is no easy task. The ability to absorb external innovation and knowledge is called *absorptive capacity*. New products and new services constitute only a small part of the spectrum by which companies can differentiate themselves and compete effectively. Companies must master innovation in all aspects of their operations: product, process and strategic innovation. Only those who are able to do so are likely to be the leaders in the new world.

Myth 2. All we need are some good new ideas

Too often, creativity is seen as the beginning and end of innovation. Such a conception impedes innovation from the very outset. Studies of innovative market leaders show that many of them are no more creative than their competitors. What they grasp, that poor innovators do not, is that coming up with good new ideas still leaves you miles away from achieving innovation. In addition to having the ideas, leading companies have mastered the second critical part of the creativity and innovation equation: the skills needed to steer fragile ideas over the barriers that block their implementation.

Myth 3. Once we shout 'Eureka' we'll be done

The forces that drive creativity and those that drive implementation of ideas are often different. The passion for creative people is the desire for the 'Eureka' moment. Innovation requires both innovation creatives and innovation implementers. It is rare for individuals to possess both capacities. Innovation implementers gain fulfilment from nurturing novel, fresh ideas through to reality. These people are not driven by pride of authorship and are not intimidated by the need to motivate a cross-functional team to overcome any problems that impede the development of the innovation. Organisationally, the ideal innovation team is a blend of idea creators and implementers.

Myth 4. The right idea will come out of nowhere

People and teams skilled at making creative ideas a reality know not to expect the instant answers implied by the 'Eureka' myth (the notion that out of nowhere will come the right answer). Rather, they appreciate that if they keep working on a problem, a solution will eventually come to them. Sometimes it will be piece by piece. At other times it may, in fact, appear quite suddenly. But whether the solution appears quickly or in piecemeal fashion, it will only come because they have been doing the hard work that, miraculously, seems to get turned into unexpected insight.

Myth 5. I'll recognise the breakthrough idea when I first see it

It is extremely rare that a breakthrough idea is recognised for its brilliance when first uttered. This is because most people evaluate ideas at a fixed point in time, usually when we first hear them. It is only with the benefit of hindsight that we come to realise that an idea labelled stupid at first blush was in fact brilliant. This mistaken belief that you will instantly recognise a brilliant idea on hearing it is extremely damaging to an innovation effort because new ideas are almost always flawed in some way when they first appear.

Given the risk-averse mind-set that thrives throughout the average corporate culture, most people work in an atmosphere where volumes of seedling ideas, with brilliant potential, are ignored because their inherent value is not immediately evident. The commitment to Thomas Edison's 1 per cent inspiration and 99 per cent perspiration that is needed to make ideas a reality simply does not exist in most organisations.

Myth 6. To be innovative, we need a clearly defined, repeatable process

There is no single roadmap for innovation, especially the creativity part. The search for an ordered, logical set of steps and procedures that will lead anyone and everyone to innovation overlooks the inherent messiness of creativity and innovation. Innovation and creativity efforts do, however, benefit from a flexible process approach.

Myth 7. Innovation has to be a home run

Businesses often resist change and newness of any kind until they realise they are lagging way behind on the innovation curve. They then decide they need to hit a home run to catch up. In this state of panic, if ideas that are put forth are not gigantic, breakthrough concepts, they get rejected. Since many big new ideas tend to appear blasphemous and/or are seriously flawed, the panic can build up to hysteria, usually with lots of finger-pointing and 'blame-storming'.

Myth 8. Innovation can be accomplished in one meeting

This is an impossible objective that is steeped in the confusion over creativity versus innovation. Creativity might be achieved in one meeting, but innovation requires an unpredictable number of interactions that bring together groups whose composition changes, based on where you are in the flow of the innovation.

Myth 9. We just implemented a great new idea, we can rest now

Innovation is continuous. Today's marketplace is dynamic and constantly changing. To respond, indeed, to stay in business, you must foster a culture that understands the need for continual change. Although, many know this intuitively, too few organisations respond in an effective or timely manner. Organisations that master the art of continuous innovation are the ones that win the competitive war.

Role of creativity in innovation: or creativity and problem solving

Creativity can take the form of single acts of creation. However, when it is directed to innovation 'problem solving' it becomes part of a process that may consist of several phases. 'Problem solving' processes may be divided into simple, compound and complex, according to the type of problem. In companies today, we see a move away from simple problems towards increasingly complex ones. Simple as well as compound problems can be solved by standard approaches. Complex problems, however, differ in that they are dynamic in nature. They are characterised by the rapid appearance of new patterns and the presence of interactions that are difficult to comprehend. This means that a complex problem can rarely be solved without developing new knowledge or new skills. In these circumstances, the ability of individuals to solve problems by creating new knowledge becomes a key qualification for success.

Creativity works by using *explicit knowledge* (such as expertise, rational and analytic knowledge) in conjunction with subconscious and deeper knowledge (called *tacit knowledge*) to produce creative outcomes (Leonard and Sensiper, 1998). It can be exercised in three ways. These three ways include problem solving, problem finding and prediction and anticipation, and are discussed next.

Problem solving

The most common use of creativity is indirect problem solving. Companies using creativity for problem solving tend to rely on experts with specialist knowledge in the problem area. The logic is that experts possess, in addition to their deep explicit knowledge, intuitive patterns born out of experience which they can tap into to find solutions to problems. Expertise combined with intuition helps them to more readily produce valuable outcomes than comparative novices without the skills or experience.

Problem finding

The second role of creativity is one of problem finding and framing. Creativity complements and adds to the analytical knowledge base of market intelligence. By bringing into play intuition, tacit knowledge and through questioning of basic assumptions, creativity can play an important role in the framing and finding of problems. This is often achieved by rejecting the most obvious answer in order to force an examination of alternative frames through a process of asking, which can look like totally different questions of the problem. Discoveries have often been the result of framing different questions about the same problem. Alternative framing often helps to reveal the real nature of the problem.

Prediction and anticipation

The third role of creativity is to predict or anticipate a new concept or future eventuality. New ideas, inventions and discoveries have often been observed to have been inspired from non-rational non-technical sources of inspiration. In other words, they arise only partly from the conscious and partly from the subconscious. Histories of discoveries suggest that the subconscious plays an important, albeit inexplicable, role in their enunciation. There are countless examples of breakthroughs that occurred by flashes of inspiration and hunches. Sometimes these have taken the forms of dreams, as in the case of Kekule's discovery of Benzene. Apparently, Kekule kept having a recurring dream of a snake that curled its body into a circle. This eventually inspired Kekule to conceptualise the ring structure of benzene. Most of the time these hunches and insights are supplements to expert knowledge, or what is often called 'being in a state of mind preparedness', and occur in the creative stages following extensive preparation and incubation.

Creative ideas do not emerge from thin air but are born from effort that combines the conscious, semi-conscious, and unconscious processes to modify, combine and/or extend existing pieces of knowledge to create new useful knowledge. Moreover, creativity in inno-vation is not just about a single meeting to come up with that one 'big idea' or develop a product; it is itself a process and it requires management.

ILLUSTRATION

In search of problems

Many people think that innovations come about by sitting down and thinking up something new.

Rather it is the case that most innovations result from thinking about problems. Innovators and inventors see a world full of problems, and it seems the creative answers come in due time, and with the right preparation.

Environmental problem

Toshiba of Japan has come out with a highly innovative solution to re-using paper. The company's e-blue disappearing ink allows paper to be returned to pristine condition and re-used repeatedly. The ink is erased by a heating process.

Security problem

Max Levchin, a Ukrainian, as a child of the Soviet Union was obsessed with cryptography, particularly with ways to keep information secret. In the 1990s Levchin noticed the internet problem, namely the lack of secure online transactions between individuals. His Soviet upbringing and his obsession set the ground for his solution. Mr Levchin went on to establish PayPal, the leading processor of person-to-person payments over the internet.

The creative process

Although innovation is often seen as a simple logical process, in reality it occurs through cycles of divergent creative thinking, which throws up many potential alternatives, followed by convergence to a selected solution.

The process of creativity can be broken into five steps (Hesselbein and Johnston, 2002):

1. *Preparation*: Creativity springs from deep wells of expertise. Research shows that most creative people have a towering command of a given discipline. Often such expertise comes about after serious study and experience. To develop such depth often requires 10 years plus of experience. However, creative groups also need beginners, mid-levels, and newcomers to the field who bring a fresh perspective and ask good questions.

2. *Innovation opportunity*: To be creative, in any field, requires as a starting point a *focus of attention*. Without a 'problem' no direction is given to the creative effort and so it remains idle, i.e. expertise must be applied to real-world problems and opportunities. Interestingly, this throws up perhaps what is the most critical challenge: defining the problem or area of opportunity on which to focus creative energies. Ultimately, the value of the solution to a problem is only as good as the problem/opportunity that was defined in the first place. In other words, the value of creativity is constrained by the question that it sets out to tackle. The 'right' question (problem/opportunity) must be posed to

open up the possibility of getting the 'right' answer. This is relatively straightforward if the problem or opportunity arises from a crisis or an external market-led demand. In its absence, asking the right questions becomes much more tricky, and indeed it becomes part of creativity itself, i.e. defining the problem may require an exercise in creativity.

3. *Divergence*: This part of the process is concerned with coming up with new ideas and solutions. This is the most dynamic and social phase of the creative process. Arriving at a 'good' solution requires first having a wide range of alternatives. Such choice can only spring from a breadth and diversity within the group itself: a diversity of working, thinking styles, professional and personal experiences, education and culture.

4. *Incubation*: Time and space is needed to reflect on solutions or considerations that may not be immediately apparent. It is no good just accepting the first solution that comes by.

5. *Convergence*: Once a rich and diverse group of 'ideas or solutions' has been assembled, the next step is to select one or the few from amongst them. The process of selection involves convergence to the single or few ideas that are to be taken further. Unless this is well managed, the most vibrant and innovative ideas may be lost.

From the above we can see that creativity hinges on a repeated cycle of divergence and convergence: to first create a rich diversity of options and then to narrow down and agree upon the best ideas to implement (see Figure 2.1).

Divergence expands the number of potential solutions through enactment of the processes of creativity. Convergence screens and weeds out non-feasible options. Most typically, the sequence is one in which divergence is followed by convergence. The activity of divergence underpins the creative process. It is the part of the creative process in which the most creative 'synthesis' takes place. Increasingly, the big challenge in the innovation process is not really that of screening (an aspect that most companies have become very adept at through the deployment of structured methodologies and frameworks) but one of ensuring that sufficient divergence activity occurs within the straitlace of the highly disciplined, structured innovation processes that have become commonplace in modern organisations.

A common mistake is to think of creativity just as a front-end activity, confined to the idea generation stage. It rather spans the entire innovation process. Creative input is just as critical to downstream activities such as marketing and launch of a new product, manufacturing and

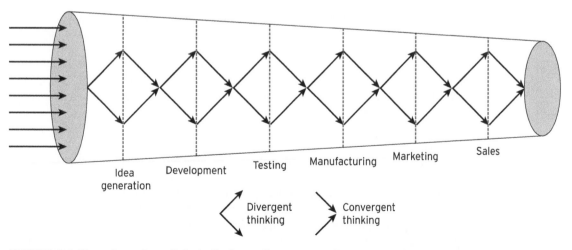

FIGURE 2.1 The nature of creativity in the innovation process: divergence and convergence

quality operations as it is to conceptualising the idea in the first instance. It is just as relevant in the first stages of the product development process as it is in the final stage. Moreover, its focus must not simply be limited to product development. It must be used to examine the entire business chain and processes. As we have noted before, innovation management is more than just product innovation, it is also process and strategy innovation.

Creativity must permeate the whole organisation. It is just as relevant to the shop floor as it is to top management. Indeed, if one considers frequency of use one may conclude that it is more important for shop floor workers since they need to exercise it on a daily process. Shop floor employees need to be regularly creative if they are to improve the processes that they work with. Indeed, the concept of quality circles is predicated on employee creativity to solve and improve process problems. The impact of senior management creativity tends to be longer lasting because of the nature of their function. However, senior management in terms of frequency typically do not exercise this muscle as much. Usually they leave this exercise for their annual strategy planning or other ad hoc sessions.

Theories of organisational creativity

Approaches to creativity theory are numerous. Broadly speaking, the various theories can be grouped into four general categories: attribute theories of creativity, conceptual skills, behavioural theories and process theories. The first two primarily place the individual as their centre of attention, while the latter two focus attention on the influence of organisational mechanisms and processes in the production of creative outcomes.

The attribute theories of creativity are based on the premise that specific characteristics and traits of individual beings predispose them toward being creative (e.g. Velthouse, 1990). Proponents of this perspective believe that creative individuals possess certain traits, such as openness, curiosity, intuitiveness, that bias them towards creative behaviour.

Proponents of the conceptual skills theory perspective centre their argument on the individual's cognitive abilities (e.g. Boone and Hollingsworth, 1990). The focus is on cognitive development, enhancement and use in producing creative outcomes.

The behavioural theories are predicated on the belief that creativity is an outcome of certain types of actions and activities (Amabile, 1997). The behavioural view tries to elicit certain types of behavioural outcome through the construction and deployment of mechanisms of creative behaviour reinforcements, such as rewards, setting expectations, and communications. This is probably the most familiar approach for managers.

Process theories of creativity posit creativity as a highly complex multi-level multi-faceted phenomenon, which relies on individuals' capabilities and capacities as well as organisational conditions and opportunities (Kao, 1989). Creativity occurs through the interplay of the individual, the task and the organisation.

Gundry et al. (1994) combine the various approaches to develop a model for innovation through creative behaviour (see Figure 2.2).

In building a creative organisation three areas need attention, as shown in Figure 2.3 (Gundry et al., 1994). The first is education and development of creativity skills. People must be trained and educated to be creative. They must be equipped with an understanding of creativity and problem-solving tools, in addition to the basic training for their jobs. The second is application of creativity competence to solve real business problems. There is little point in equipping individuals with tools if they are not going to be used. People must be set (empowered) to solve real problems. Third, the company must diagnose itself and its

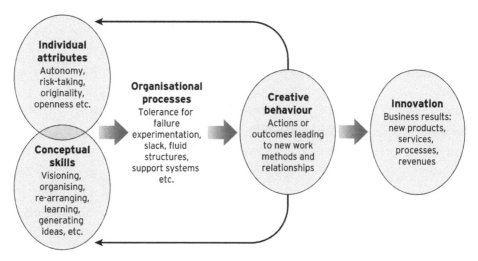

FIGURE 2.2 Creativity for innovation
Source: Gundry et al., 1994

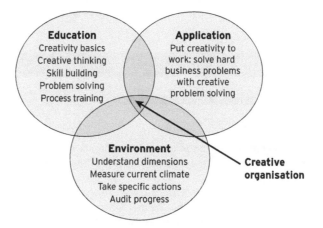

FIGURE 2.3 The three domains for creative action
Source: Gundry et al., 1994

organisational environment to define opportunities for creative performance. This means it must collect and process information about trends in the internal and external environment.

Amabile (1997) proposes a componential theory of organisational creativity and innovation, as shown in Figure 2.4. The upper three circles capture organisational work environment components, and the bottom three circles capture components at play in individual creativity. The theory indicates that the elements of work environment affect individual creativity, and the creativity outcomes from individuals or groups act as a primary source for organisational innovation. The main assertion in this theory is that the social environment (work environment) has a major impact on individual creative behaviour. Also, whilst the environment can have an impact on all the individual level components, its main direct effects are on a person's motivation to do the job (task motivation).

From the discussion above we can discern two important dimensions to creativity: an individual dimension and organisational dimension. We now turn to discuss these.

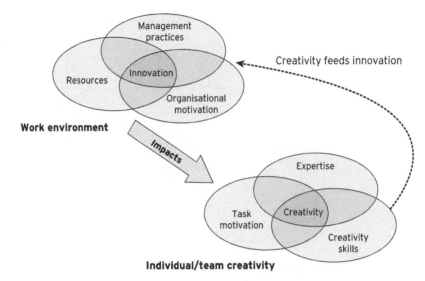

FIGURE 2.4 Componential theory of creativity and innovation

Source: Amabile, 1997, copyright © 1997, by The Regents of the University of California. Reprinted from the *California Management Review*, Vol. 40, No. 1. By permission of The Regents

ILLUSTRATION

Practice makes perfect

DuPont trains all its employees in the use of five techniques: lateral thinking, metaphoric thinking, positive thinking, association trigger, and capturing and interpreting dreams. Use of these techniques has been very profitable.

For example, DuPont researchers were trying to work out a way to dye Nomex fibres, which had proved to be impervious to dyes. Using the metaphor of a mineshaft, one researcher realised that timbers (metaphorically speaking) were needed to hold the fibre apart so that the dye could take effect. He then found a chemical agent that acted much like a timber in a mineshaft, holding the hole open until dyes could take effect.

The individual in creativity

Without doubt the centrepiece in the puzzle of creativity is people. Organisational systems and context factors are parts of the jigsaw that serve to induce and enhance the creativity of people within it, either as individuals or as groups. So, what makes people creative? Are some people more creative than others? These are questions that have occupied the minds of researchers for quite some time. These are complex questions with a variety of contentious and complex answers. Fortunately, explanations of creativity at the people level fall into two broad categories: cognitive (intelligence and physiological) and psychological explanations.

Cognitive explanations of creativity

Cognitive explanations fall into two interlinked yet distinct camps: one dealing with an individual's intelligence and the second examining the issue from a physiological perspective.

Human intelligence and creativity

A large body of research suggests that general intelligence defines an individual's ability to formulate and use abstract concepts (Sen, 1991). In simple words, it defines their ability to solve problems and develop new insights and ideas. This observation finds substantial support in the many studies reporting moderate positive relations between indexes of intelligence and creative production among artists, scientists and professionals, but weak, insignificant relations in lower level occupations.

Intelligence as a concept has a close relationship with knowledge. *Intelligence* is the 'capacity to acquire and apply knowledge' and *knowledge* is the familiarity, awareness or understanding gained through experience or study (Gardner, 1991, pp. 14–15). This is why we often see intelligence defined in terms of a person's accumulated knowledge. Yet it is not enough to have a mind full of knowledge. The main thing is to be able to use it well. Simple accumulation of knowledge has little to do with creative performance. Accumulation of knowledge makes for preparedness for creative performance but it is not a simple one-to-one substitute.

Howard Gardner (1991) defines intelligence as a 'relatively autonomous human intellectual competence' and claims that there are seven distinct types of intelligence: (1) linguistic, (2) logical-mathematical, (3) spatial, (4) musical, (5) bodily-kinaesthetic, (6) interpersonal, and (7) intrapersonal. Other researchers suggest intelligence is composed of various sensory processes: perception, memory, reasoning, intention, generation of action, and attention (e.g. Covey, 1990). And these aspects can be sorted into two distinct styles of thinking (Sinatra, 1989):

1. The deliberate ordering of thoughts with full awareness – the style of intelligence reflected in *conscious thinking*.

2. The thoughts that well up into consciousness without disclosing when they came or how they were formed – the style reflected in *subconscious thinking*.

These two thinking modes (conscious and the subconscious) lead to three external manifestations/abilities:

1. *Analytical thinking* (the ability to comprehend specific knowledge).

2. *Creative thinking* (the ability to combine areas of knowledge and come up with new ideas or approaches).

3. *Contextual thinking* (the ability to make practical use of this knowledge).

These three manifestations (or abilities) constitute intelligence in practice (Sternberg, 1987) and the most important aspect of these is not just in possessing them but also in knowing which is which and when to use it.

Even from this brief discussion we can see that individual intelligence is a complex and often highly contentious subject. It can be conceptualised in a variety of ways: a competence, a mode of thinking or an execution process. Thus, it is common to see intelligence in various ways, ranging from a competence such as verbal ability to 'street savvy-ness'. No matter how it is conceptualised, one thing is clear: all the different forms of intelligence play a role in contemporary problem solving. Thus, all the various types of intelligence need to be developed. And all can in fact be augmented by processes that build on and enhance the levels of intelligence, whether innate or developed. The interactions between human intelligence and creativity are summarised in Figure 2.5.

Perhaps, as the novelist and story-writer F. Scott Fitzgerald observed in *The Crack-Up*, 'the test of a first rate intelligence is the ability to hold two opposed ideas in the mind at the same time, and still retain the ability to function' (quoted in Rich, 1999).

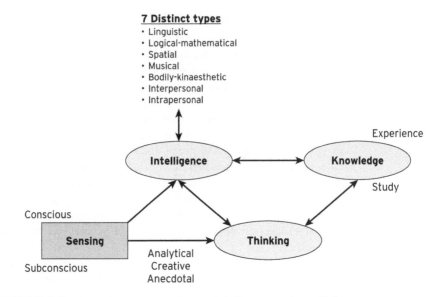

FIGURE 2.5 Interactions between human intelligence and creativity

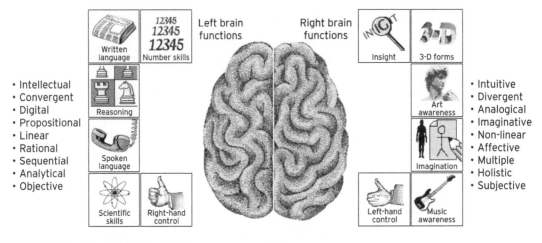

FIGURE 2.6 Left brain/right brain influences on creativity
Source: Adapted from MS-Encarta, Microsoft Corporation

Physiological explanations of individual creativity

The second explanation is closely allied to the first, but rather than focussing upon intelligence, its main attention is the functioning of the brain. The essence of this approach is around the different functioning of the cerebra of the brain (see Figure 2.6). Each of these is associated with different (information processing models) thinking modes. The left hemisphere appears to operate in a logical, analytical, computer-like fashion. The right side of the brain, in contrast, processes and makes senses of information through intuitive and non-linear complex patterns. It appears to be able to handle a vast quantity of complex and interlinked information. It is generally contended that the left brain's operation is inadequate for the complex synthesis readily achieved by the right. The forebrain combines the capacities of both left and right brain in the process of decision making.

The right brain's intuition and emotion is not the straight opposite of the left brain's rational and analytic capability. The right brain is neither the opposite of quantitative analysis, nor an attempt to eliminate quantitative analysis. Rather, the two are complementary cognitive strengths and powerful tandem tools in decision making. It becomes necessary to understand and rely on intuition because very few important decisions can ever be made on the basis of complete, accurate and timely information. One of the best ways to tap the power of the subconscious is to incorporate the idea of mental incubation. This is a process of giving the subconscious time to run free. In common parlance, we often refer to it as 'letting one sleep on it'. Whatever we call it, intuitive executives have found it a highly valuable way of tapping into their subconscious.

To solve problems effectively, it is necessary to use different thinking patterns at different times for different types of problems. Many highly effective business leaders practise what is called bi-modal thinking: combining macro- and micro-forms of attention (Garfield, 1986). Micro-macro-attention combines a worm's-eye and bird's-eye views. A micro-mode of thinking involves logical, analytical computation, seeing cause and effect in methodical steps. It is valued by those who prize attention to detail, precision and orderly progression. The macro-mode, the bird's-eye view, is particularly useful for shaking out themes and patterns from assortments of information. Whether you call the macro-mode intuitive or holistic or conceptual, it is good for bridging gaps. It enables us to perceive a pattern, even when some of the pieces are missing. In contrast, the logical sequences of the micro-mode cannot skip over gaps.

From our perspective, much of the research into the various cortices of the brain hemisphere or intelligence, while no doubt valuable, insightful and exciting, tells very little of how to use it to actually solve problems or become more creative in solving them. Clearly, a simple exhortation to use one side of the brain is insufficient. What is needed are specific principles and a process to develop and enhance the 'brain capabilities' as well as specific guidance on how and when to use which side during the 'problem-solving/solution-finding' process.

Let us accept for the moment that intelligence is not innate or genetic; that we can develop upon what we were born with. This means that we can develop and hone these neural capabilities via appropriate exercise or teaching. The challenge then, in one sense, becomes one of developing a whole brain pedagogy. And if this is the challenge, it is one that is poorly tackled. Most teaching emphasises the development of a rational and analytic capability. Even if teachers were capable of specifically targeting and developing the different cerebral competencies (of the left, right and frontal lobe) this by no means guarantees that people will be able to use the knowledge they acquire to solve the problems they confront. Why? Real problems are often poorly structured and hard to define, not neat academic exercises. Thus, people still need to be guided as to how to judge a problem, decide on the steps needed to solve it and follow it along to make sure these stems lead to a solution. Firstly, they need to be shown how best to apply their knowledge and experience to the solution (Sternberg, 1987) and secondly they need to be given the opportunity to do so.

Psychological explanations of individual creativity

This explanation moves the focus upon the individual and his or her predisposition towards certain behavioural patterns and forms of understanding. In other words, rather than one's intelligence or one's neurology, the state and predispositions of the individual become central to the explanation. These theories, because of their focus of attention, are often called personality or attribute theories of creativity.

ILLUSTRATION

Tapping into your different minds

The renowned creativity expert and thinker Edward de Bono has developed a system for tapping into the different aspects of one's brain. This system he calls the six-hat system. The six-hat system is sometimes confused with a creativity technique, which strictly speaking it is not. It is a system that deliberately taps into the different thinking and reasoning patterns of the mind, and does so in a way that makes time and space for creativity.

The six-hat thinking system

The six hats are metaphorical hats, which a thinker can put on or take off. Each of these hats indicates the type of thinking that is being used. This putting on and taking off is an essential part of the system. de Bono strongly cautions against the hats being used to categorise individuals, even if someone's behaviour invites this.

White hat: This hat is about facts, figures and information, asking questions, defining information needs and gaps. When someone calls out 'I think we need some white hat thinking at this point . . .', this indicates that it is time to move on to examine the facts and figures, market intelligence to check out the current thinking.

Red hat: This hat covers intuition, feelings and emotions. The red hat allows the introduction of feelings and intuition into the debate. It invites comments such as 'Putting on my red hat, I think that is a terrible proposal'. The red hat provides full permission to a thinker to put forward his or her feelings in the subject at that moment without fear that these will be laughed out of court by the heavy voice of 'facts or rationality'.

Black hat: This is the hat of judgement and caution. It is the hat of logic. It is used to assess why a suggestion does not fit the facts or the problem at hand. It is the hat that is most frequently employed but in no sense is it an inferior hat. The black hat is called the logical negative.

Yellow hat: The yellow hat is the logical positive. It asks why something will work and what the benefits are. It is used to forecast the likely outcomes of implementing a proposed solution.

Green hat: This hat is for creativity. It is used for finding new options and alternatives. It is about bringing forth new and novel insights from a process of provocation, challenge and change. de Bono has devised the term 'PO' (Provocation Operation) to deliberately introduce challenge of current assumptions or just simply a challenge. PO introduces 'movement' to a new position. The challenge may be introduced by several formal ways, the key of these include: Escape, Reversal, Exaggeration, Distortion and Wishful Thinking. In using these step-by-step methods, the lateral thinker is able to deliberately provoke his or her own thinking.

Blue hat: This is the overview or process control hat. This hat does not examine the subject/problem under scrutiny but the way it is being tackled. For example, one may say with this hat 'Putting on my blue hat, I feel we should do some more green hat thinking at this point'. In technical jargon, this hat is concerned with meta-cognition.

The system sets up a process in which a number of thinking patterns can be allowed to come into play. An individual can express his or her thoughts under the protection of one or another of the hats, or one person can ask another to put on or take off a particular colour of hat. For instance, if one person is being overly negative about an idea another person might say: 'Well that is brilliant black hat thinking, but now let us try some yellow hat thinking on that'. In this way a switch can be made immediately and without offence.

(*Source*: Based on de Bono, 1970)

Unsurprisingly, there is a huge amount of varied and complex research in the field of psychology dealing with human behaviour. From amongst these, one of the most insightful from our perspective is the work of Swiss psychologist Carl G. Jung (1875–1961). In 1923 Jung, whilst noting individual differences, found stable patterns in behaviour across individuals. He traced these patterns to preferences for recognising, paying attention to, and remembering people, ideas, and things and then making decisions or judgements about them. Jung defined eight different patterns for perceiving information and making decisions. He believed each of the eight patterns of difference to be equally valuable and equally creative. According to Jung, the creative instinct exists in everyone. You just need to identify, understand and refine your pattern preferences, or creative talents, to be more effective, productive and creative.

Jung proposed a wholly different perspective on thinking, based on his theory of personality types. He suggested that four psychological functions (*sensing, intuition, thinking and feeling*) comprise the basic attitudes that affect conscious behaviour. According to Jung (1971), people develop dominant preferences for certain types of data in their thinking: preference for either sensation or intuition.

1. *Sensation-dominant* people prefer precise, specific data. They see themselves as realists concerned with immediate problems.

2. *Intuition-dominant* people seek holistic information that describes possibilities, and their decisions use more general data.

Jung also found two dominant ways that people reach decisions: by thinking or by feeling.

1. *Thinking-dominant* people emphasise logic and formal modes of reasoning. They generalise and make abstractions.

2. *Feeling-dominant* people form personal value judgements. They explain things in human terms and emphasise affective and personal processes in making decisions.

On the basis of the two ways that people obtain data and the two ways they evaluate data, Jung defined four personality types: (1) sensing-thinking; (2) intuition-thinking; (3) sensing-feeling, and (4) intuition-feeling (see Figure 2.7).

1. *Sensing-thinking* types stress systematic decision making and hard data. They try to establish order, control and certainty. They focus on tasks and structured information. They take fewer risks than other types.

2. *Intuition-thinking* types tend to ignore specific, detailed information. They prefer to study patterns in data. Their thought takes bolder leaps into the unknown. They emphasise longer-range plans and new possibilities.

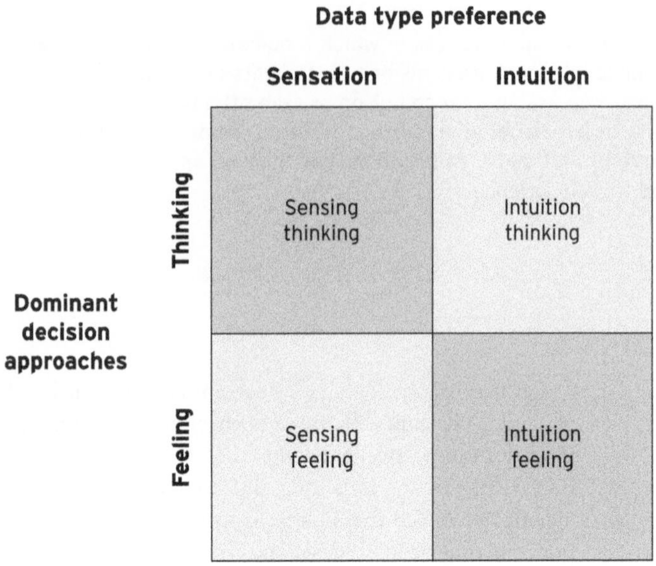

Data type preference

	Sensation	**Intuition**

FIGURE 2.7 Jung's four personality types
Source: Jung, 1971

3. *Sensing-feeling* types stress harmony, personal communication, and other people's opinions. Facts about people are more important than facts about things. They focus on short-term problems, with human implications.

4. *Intuition-feeling* types rely on their own judgement and experience, often portraying personal views as facts. They prefer holistic, intuitive perceptions to rules in decision making. They focus on broad themes and long-term goals.

Accordingly, each person displays a preferred method of understanding reality and people have different operating styles. In making decisions, people vary in how much data they want, whether they rely on intuition, gut feeling or logic, whether they play the 'doubting' game or the 'believing' game, and the way they arrive at a conclusion. In perceiving and judging, many people exhibit all four personality types at different times. Most people, however, have a dominant, preferred style. This is the style that they use more often than the others, across a variety of situations, particularly in situations that are fluid and not firmly structured.

From this, we see that one method of discovering people's creative potential and approach is to determine how they recognise information and define problems and challenges, as well as the way they go about producing creative responses and solutions (Levesque, 2001). To make Jung's model more accessible and help define these preferences, Katharine Briggs and Isabel Myers developed the Myers–Briggs Type Indicator personality indicator. Other instruments can also be used to address personal creativity styles, such as Kirton Adaption Inventory (KAI) and the Hermann Brain Dominance Instrument (HBDI).

Organisational factors in creativity

To get creative performance we must understand how organisational practices, processes and policies either enhance or inhibit creativity. A number of organisational factors

ILLUSTRATION

Motorola right brains it

Not only is Motorola one of the world's largest manufacturers of semi-conductors, it has many firsts to its credit. These include the car radio (the origin of the name 'Motorola'), the 'walkie-talkie', the 32-bit microprocessor, full-text two-way pagers, and a single-chip global positioning system (GPS) receiver solution.

Every year, the Motorola Labs team gathers together for a workshop to practise creativity and stimulate innovation in areas such as consumer systems, communications, advanced technology, networks, software and internet research, physical sciences and solid-state research. These activities from across the company were in fact combined in 1998 to form Motorola Labs, a single research organisation with a global team of scientists, engineers and technicians. Their focus is on discovering and developing new materials, technologies, architectures, algorithms and processes for smarter devices and systems.

The workshops aim to promote 'whole-brain thinking', combining right-brain creativity based on aesthetics and holistic feelings with left-brain linearity, logic, analysis and accuracy. The result helps better equip Motorola researchers to transform the promise of technology into something tangible that can be applied to solve real problems for customers and open new opportunities for the company's business.

Typically, the business-case workshops start with group brainstorming to generate creative ideas. The idea selection process follows, whereby individuals synthesise their ideas in order to aggregate similar business cases that may one day result in new and innovative products.

While the atmosphere of working through implementations as a team was always stimulating for the researchers, the teams and the implementers started to feel that the sessions seemed to lack real inspiration. They didn't always explore all the possible applications, and ideas were not always focused or organised. In the past, a variety of table toys such as Playdough and Tinker Toys were used to stimulate workshop brainstorming sessions. In 2004, in an effort to drive creative thinking to a more productive level, Motorola tried DesignAid.

Art Paton, Motorola's senior programme manager for advanced technical education, purchased the five issues of DesignAid published by Inventables. DesignAid stimulates right-brain thinking by allowing users to touch and feel. The hope was that the items in the DesignAid kits would assist the researchers. Paton's goal was to expose researchers to a variety of provocative materials and technologies from a broad range of industries to stimulate creative thinking and provide taking-off points. The various materials were used to spark creative ideas.

According to Paton the results were 'incredible'. Paton, who has run the Motorola Labs business-case workshop for the past three years, said the contents of DesignAid introduced the Motorola Labs team to innovations they would not otherwise have been familiar with, and helped them apply creative concepts in a variety of application spaces. Motivated by the hands-on engagement with the DesignAid samples, the research teams brainstormed and the exercise resulted in five new business proposals.

(*Source*: Based on Anon, 2004)

influence creative behaviours. These are briefly elaborated next. But before going on to these, it is important to note that just as there is individual intelligence, there is also organisational intelligence.

Our discussion in the previous section focused on human intelligence. A number of researchers have also conceptualised intelligence at a collective level (Williams and Sternberg, 1988; Walsh and Ungson, 1991; Glynn, 1996). Glynn (1996) highlights the key features that define the concept of organisational intelligence as:

- Organisations functionally resemble information-processing systems that process information from the environment (i.e. organisations have intelligence that is similar in function to that of individuals).
- Modelling organisations as information processing systems suggests that they are also able to act as interpretive systems, i.e. they are able to scan, interpret and diagnose their environments.
- The organisation is a network of shared meanings that are sustained and used through development and use of a common language and social interactions.

Although organisational intelligence is noted to bear resemblance to individual intelligence, it nevertheless is not the same. It is a social outcome resulting from the activities of the collective. It is based on accumulated wisdom of the individuals that form the collective, as well as the nature of their individual interactions amongst each other. Organisational intelligence is also a function of time and context. Over time and through different histories organisational intelligence may accumulate, ebb and even be lost through leakage. In other words, when we think of organisational systems, structures and culture we must remember that it is *not* just the individual that they influence and manage. They simultaneously influence and manage the collective: the group or the team(s), and they manage and influence the systems, values and processes (which in themselves are constituent parts of organisational intelligence) over time and over different environments and settings.

From the many organisational factors that influence creativity and innovation four have major consequences. These are: leadership behaviour, organisational structures, organisational culture and measurement systems. These are dealt with in later chapters, so we only briefly elaborate upon them here.

Creativity and leadership behaviour

Leaders can cultivate creativity by facilitating the five conditions of the creative process: (1) preparation (collecting both expertise and new perspectives); (2) innovative opportunity; (3) divergence (a range of options though professional and personal diversity); (4) incubation (time out for reflection); and (5) convergence (selection of options). Leaders establish the psychological and physical environments that support creativity. By virtue of their position they are best placed to identify long-term opportunities and define the direction in which to focus creative efforts. Leaders influence the creative process in the following ways: (Hesselbein and Johnston, 2002):

1. Forming heterogeneous groups (teams) comprising of a mix of individuals, some with specific types of expertise and others who are novices or outsiders.
2. Being sensitive and aware enough to recognise opportunities for innovation as they first arise.
3. Balancing the need to set an agenda, press ahead and push people towards an agreed upon outcome, with the need to have sufficient divergence of thought and alternative solutions.
4. Ensuring enough time is allocated to teams to support incubation.
5. Guiding idea selection by acting as a referee, coach, lobbyist, diplomat and conductor.

Leaders guide the change process by ensuring the presence of visioning, experimenting, pattern breaking, and bonding, and by keeping these four elements in balance. The individual who takes full charge of a large-scale change is necessarily strong, determined, and masterful at mobilising people around a vision. Successful leaders in uncertain environments need to maintain an on-going vision and commitment that gives an inherent strength in their organisations.

Creativity and organisational structure

Although command and control hierarchical structures can foster a sense of accountability and logic to the decision-making process, they are often too rigid. A key organisational form used for creative action is through the development and deployment of artificial structures or temporary structures such as teams or skunkworks. Teams such as specialist skunkworks have many characteristics – they are lean, agile and filled with cross-functional knowledge. Companies traditionally set up special teams for very important projects that require significant new ideas, new technologies and new processes. These teams are often successful because common corporate barriers have been specifically removed to facilitate quick and effective results.

Teams that manage to produce extraordinary results tend to be those in which team members worked well together in a climate of mutual trust and respect, effective communication, and commitment to growth and learning. These teams are usually made of individuals with complementary skills and talents.

Processes designed to facilitate constructive conflict resolution and successfully implement solutions can heighten the effectiveness, productivity and creativity of teams. When

ILLUSTRATION

Cola-innovation, it's the real thing

Several events conspired to drive down growth at Coca-Cola from 1998 to 2002 from 4 per cent to less than 1 per cent per annum: key of these was a shifting marketplace and management distractions. But in the process Coke has seen the need to establish innovation as a key strategic priority. To drive innovation Coca-Cola has developed three platforms.

Innovation centres: Three innovation centres located in the US, Europe and Japan are staffed with creative thinkers. These individuals report to marketers with new brand ideas, route to market approaches and new packaging ideas. They will oversee ideas from concept to commercialisation.

Marketing workbenches: This includes thinkers inside and outside the company responsible for developing creative ideas for driving the business. Participants in these look to develop innovative approaches around customer partnering, packaging, new product development, digital marketing beyond the internet and experiential marketing ideas.

Idea works: A database of abstract creative ideas that can be accessed around the world by Coke personnel. This includes consumer concepts, community events, promotions, new designs and new communications.

Coca-Cola uses as its yardstick three criteria:

1. *New consumers* from new beverage solutions and flavour extensions.
2. *Growth of categories* by transferring ideas from its operations around globe (quick wins).
3. Creation of *new profit streams* through radical innovations.

processes are designed with flexibility, customer service, optimal time to market and product excellence as the goals, they do not add bureaucracy but instead provide procedural guidance to save time in the long run (Kessler and Chakrabarti, 1996). Such processes are designed to ensure that the team balances planning with execution, and idea generation with delivery (Roberts, 2000). In fact, most of what happens in successful innovations is not the happy occurrence of a blind flash of insight, but rather the careful implementation of an unspectacular but systematic management discipline (Drucker, 1985).

Creativity and organisational culture

Innovation depends critically on people. People are creative and innovative when they are expected to be innovative, when they are given the resources to be innovative, and when they are rewarded for their innovations. Many company cultures have a negative impact on innovation. A rigid organisation that puts too much emphasis on 'the way things are done here' inhibits employee attempts to try new ways.

Continuing to use conventional thinking and even increasing the intensity of its application (i.e. get more facts, obtain more accurate measurements, do more studies, be more objective) as the means of improving the quality and quantity of solutions is perhaps the biggest inhibition to effective thinking. People struggling to do a job well will focus on what works for them. They adopt practices, refine them, gain confidence in them and make them their own. This embeds a 'Not Invented Here' syndrome. Overcoming this cannot be taken lightly. The solution is to promote a culture in which using ideas from any source is made part of the company's problem-solving discipline. The aim is for people to 'own' the ideas even if they were first generated by outside sources.

Innovation is about change. Most people react negatively to change, especially to that for which they are ill prepared. Also, the more comfortable they become with their work, the more unwilling they are to accept change. Sternberg (1987) notes the importance of helping people to become aware of and remove the emotional and motivational blocks that prevent them from applying their intelligence to everyday living: lack of motivation, lack of perseverance and fear of failure. Indeed, a great inhibition to effective thinking and full-spectrum creativity is simply the fear that arises naturally when one is called upon to do anything for the first time.

Companies can help nurture creativity by adopting innovation processes that provides the 'mental space' for new ideas to take root. For this to occur requires an open culture: one that shares extensively its knowledge and resources with the whole enterprise. As companies grow in size they find structure is required for the innovation and creativity process. Certainly, structure becomes a necessity as they grow beyond the size of an 'everybody knows everybody' team. However, these companies must guard against structures and systems that deaden new ways of thinking and doing. They need to implement structured processes that ensure that there is appropriate time, space and resource to seed, grow and develop ideas to fruition.

Creativity and measurement systems

Organisationally, companies need to measure their progress. Measurement is an important part of the continuous improvement cycle. However, they must take great care how they measure since measurement has both positive and negative aspects to it. Narrow measurement systems and metrics can easily suffocate creative behaviour. People respond to the metrics by which they are measured. For metrics to serve the intended purpose, they must be easily understandable, clearly defined to the people to whom they apply, understood by them and accepted as appropriate means to measure a given function. They must be such that they provide scope for creativity to take place, and rather than depress innovation, they should act as drivers of change and betterment. To achieve this aim it is often necessary to marry measurement with rewards.

Creative behaviour can be defined and also measured in many different ways but nonetheless in nearly all studies of creativity measures are drawn from only one of three basic categories (Garfield, 1986):

1. *Overt production criteria*, such as publication counts or patent awards. These measures assess creativity in terms of the frequency with which individuals generate innovative products having acknowledged social worth or the quality of these products.

2. *Professional recognition criteria* assess creativity in terms of the awards given to individuals for the production of new ideas or products held to be of some value in an occupational field.

3. *Social recognition criteria*: The judgements of knowledgeable others, such as peers or supervisors, afford a basis for assessing the value of an individual's novel contribution in some area. Although these criteria differ in many ways, they seem bound together by their common concern with the production of novel, socially valued products

It is important to ensure that a correct mix of the three is used. Over-reliance on production metrics tends to dampen innovation effort. The fuel for creative impulse must be provided through complementary emphasis on social and professional recognition.

Integrated multi-level models of creativity

Thus far, we have discussed a number of organisational models of creativity. From these we drew out the importance of two key elements, the individual and organisational dimensions, as key factors in determining and influencing creativity. We draw this section to a close by examining a number of multi-level models of creativity that attempt to integrate the factors that have been proposed. Three models are notable from amongst the many. Woodman et al. (1993) present an *interactionist view*, in which important influences on creativity at different levels are identified. Ford (1996) builds on Woodman et al. (1993) by proposing a co-evolutionary process model which describes how individual interpretations of multiple task domains within and between different levels impacts on their preference for routine or novel actions. Ford also examines how the introduction of novel actions influences the evolution of task domains. Drazin et al. (1999) extend the multi-level models by showing how a crisis shifts individuals' and communities' attention between two specific task domains (technical versus managerial) during a long-term creative project. They also show how the crisis re-frames the negotiated order of belief structures about creativity.

Here we elaborate on Woodman et al.'s interactionist model since it is the foundation upon which many other multi-level models have been built (see Figure 2.8). Woodman et al.'s (1993) model is based on the premise that behaviour is a complex interaction of a person and situation, and this is repeated at each level of social organisation. In other words, group creativity is a function of individual components as an input (i.e. group composition), as well as group-level factors such as group characteristics (i.e. norms, size, degree of cohesiveness, diversity, etc.), group processes (e.g. problem-solving approaches) and contextual influences (arising from the organisation at large and the nature of the task given). Likewise, organisational creativity, in turn, is a function of the creative outputs from the groups and contextual influences (e.g. organisational culture, resource constraints, etc.). The overall outcome in terms of new products, services, improved processes and new structures is a

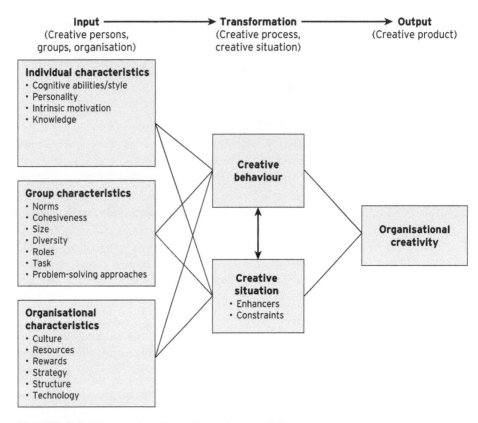

FIGURE 2.8 Integrated multi-level model of creativity
Source: Woodman et al., 1993

consequence of a complex interaction between the individual, group and organisational characteristics, which influence and define the salient creative context at each level of the organisation.

Woodman et al. (1993) show that the antecedents of individual creativity are defined by cognitive ability, personality factors, cognitive factors, intrinsic motivation and knowledge. These factors influence and are influenced by social and contextual factors. Group-level creativity is not a simple summation of individual creativities but is, in addition, determined by group composition (e.g. diversity), group characteristics (cohesiveness, group size, etc.) and group processes (problem-solving approaches, social network information, etc.), and contextual influences originating from the organisation. At the organisational level creativity is determined by contextual factors that define the organisations, such as organisational culture, reward systems, and training in creativity, external environment influences and group-level creativity.

 ## Creativity techniques

Although creative activity is recognised as being important, the potential of creativity is rarely fully exploited or managed. The best way to enhance creativity is by getting people to practise it. If we sit back and content ourselves with identifying creativity, rather than practising it, that makes us useless: all talk and no action (Sternberg, 1987). For creative outcomes to be produced, individuals must be trained in the tools and techniques of problem solving and creativity.

Innovative organisations have come to realise that every person needs to contribute their experience and creativity. However, some people have more fully developed their ability to piece together new ideas and to communicate them clearly. Creativity tools provide a structured way for an individual, group or team to combine intuition, imagination and personal experience to create interesting and eventually innovative concepts and solutions. These innovative solutions can be aimed at virtually any target:

- Reducing cost and waste.
- Developing new products and services.
- Resolving long-standing customer complaints.
- Dramatically cutting down cycle time.
- Developing new processes or dramatic process improvements.

For instance, the field of quality from which a large number of process innovations have arisen has realised the importance of creativity. Creative tools have been added to the basic quality planning tools. The aim of this addition was to improve the continuous improvement processes but also to ensure that opportunities for radical innovation are not lost.

There are numerous techniques for exploiting human creativity, far too many to fully enumerate here. Many of them are similar, and can be classed into a few categories (see Figure 2.9). One common method of classification is based on whether the technique pertains to the individual or group, and another common method is categorisation by the form of activity. Perhaps a more useful way of categorising the techniques is on the relative amounts of structure and the role in focusing (convergence) or expanding (divergence) options. Figure 2.10 illustrates the range of available techniques for such purposes. Techniques of divergence and convergence need to be employed in a cycle. Initially, one wishes to develop as many alternative solutions. This needs to be followed by a screening process to select one that is the most useful or appropriate for the problem at hand.

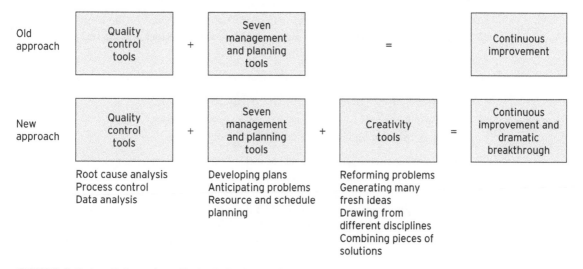

FIGURE 2.9 Creativity and quality tools for innovation
Source: Ritter and Brassard, 1998, with permission of GOAL/QPC

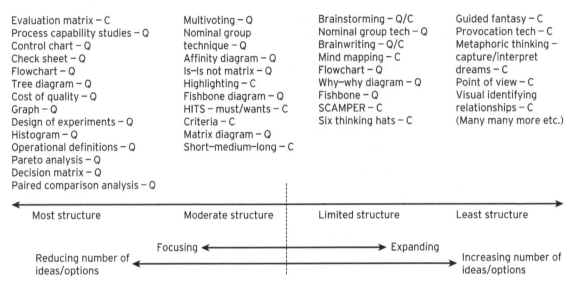

Evaluation matrix – C
Process capability studies – Q
Control chart – Q
Check sheet – Q
Flowchart – Q
Tree diagram – Q
Cost of quality – Q
Graph – Q
Design of experiments – Q
Histogram – Q
Operational definitions – Q
Pareto analysis – Q
Decision matrix – Q
Paired comparison analysis – Q

Multivoting – Q
Nominal group
technique – Q
Affinity diagram – Q
Is–Is not matrix – Q
Highlighting – C
Fishbone diagram – Q
HITS – must/wants – C
Criteria – C
Matrix diagram – Q
Short–medium–long – C

Brainstorming – Q/C
Nominal group tech – Q
Brainwriting – Q/C
Mind mapping – C
Flowchart – Q
Why–why diagram – Q
Fishbone – Q
SCAMPER – C
Six thinking hats – C

Guided fantasy – C
Provocation tech – C
Metaphoric thinking –
capture/interpret
dreams – C
Point of view – C
Visual identifying
relationships – C
(Many many more etc.)

Most structure   Moderate structure   Limited structure   Least structure

Focusing ⟵⟶ Expanding

Reducing number of
ideas/options   Increasing number of
ideas/options

FIGURE 2.10 Quality (**Q**) and creativity (**C**) tools for convergent and divergent thinking

Detailed description for the full range of creativity techniques is not possible. However, a select number of key techniques and the associated processes to execute them are elaborated in the section below. We confine our attention to association techniques (minimal structure), brainstorming (moderate structure), incubation methods (moderate structure) mapping techniques (higher structure) and the TRIZ system (highest level of structure).

Brainstorming

Alex Osborn developed the traditional brainstorming technique in the 1960s. It is a technique that introduces an element of structure to free association. The technique is traditionally used to help groups of 6–12 people free associate ideas suggested by a problem statement. A facilitator or recorder commonly stands at a board or flip chart and records ideas as group members verbalise ideas in their raw form, as quickly as they occur. Activities here include:

1. Identify the appropriate team to conduct the brainstorming session.
2. Convene the team and clarify the topic and ground rules.
3. Generate ideas.
4. Clarify the ideas and conclude the brainstorming session.

Brainstorming discourages the 'same old way' of thinking by creating more and more ideas which the team can subsequently build upon. Used effectively, it engages all the team, and enthuses them by putting an equal value on every idea. These ideas can be as creative as the individual team members wish, yet enables them to remain focused on the team's common purpose. Not only does this approach allow the known and obvious ideas to be identified, it also allows new ideas to emerge as the team members build on some of the ideas already posted.

Osborn drew up a set of four rules to increase people's willingness to share their ideas with the group. Usually, the facilitator states or posts these rules at the start of a brainstorming session – and, if necessary, politely corrects anyone who violates them. These rules are:

1. No criticism of any ideas. Save criticism for the evaluation stage.
2. Wild ideas are encouraged. Say whatever comes to mind.
3. Quantity, not quality. Generate as long a list as possible.
4. No proprietary ideas. Combining ideas or building on someone else's idea is encouraged.

The facilitator usually writes the problem statement for the group, making this a fairly directive method.

Once a list has been compiled, the groups critically examine the list of ideas, and work together to try to formulate several polished problem statements/solutions, which are then argued over and voted upon. In this manner, the group has a stronger hand in defining the problem, and brainstorming is used to bring creative insight to the initial stage of the creative process, often producing an 'out-of-box' problem definition that sets us off in a new and more productive direction.

Exploratory brainstorming/benchmarking

This is usefully applied during the early stages of any project or process.

Unlike traditional benchmarking, exploratory benchmarking is attuned to seeking novel approaches to a subject. You gather a hodgepodge of real-world examples, not all of which necessarily relate to your subject matter, and then find out just enough information about them to get the gist of what they are about or how they work. It is a quick sweeping process.

The product of exploratory benchmarking is an eccentric collection of designs or other ideas that may or may not be directly relevant to your subject but are certainly inspirational as you seek new approaches to the subject.

Breakdown brainstorming

This method is used to help groups explore complex problems or projects. It uses the free-association rules of brainstorming to generate as many sub-problems as possible.

Start by displaying and reading a formal statement of the problem to the group. Then point out that the problem statements tend to be fairly abstract and can often be broken down into sub-problems, or component parts.

The product of breakdown brainstorming is a lengthy list of sub-problems. Some of these will be very helpful in formulating creative solutions to the main problem, because they will surface aspects of the problem or suggest components of the solution that were not visible to the group when it tackled the problem on a higher level. Individuals can also use the method.

Electronic Brainstorming

In addition to the above, many creativity techniques have been enhanced by electronic and Internet media. This has increased the range of connectivity and sources of inspiration. Two techniques that are particularly amenable to this are the billboard and the chain letter.

Chain letter
This is used to get a large quantity of possible solutions outside of a formal meeting. In the chain letter, team members generate and pass ideas around via memo or e-mail. The steps in this approach are as follows:

1. Define your brainstorm objective.
2. Establish a medium and distribution method (paper or electronic, fax, internal mail, e-mail, etc., what's the order of routing and set a time frame for response).
3. First round, each person writes one or two ideas (then passes the letter on).
4. Next person builds on and/or adds to the ideas.

Billboard

This technique is used to gather ideas from a broader range of people, in a non-meeting format. The billboard is a public brainstorming tool – manual or electronic (Pande et al., 2002), and includes the following steps:

1. Define your brainstorming objective.
2. Post a message in a public place asking for ideas (and include the objective) – using flipchart, or intranet, etc.
3. Gather ideas at end of a specified time frame, and narrow and select from them.
4. Remember to thank the people for contributing.

Free association and creative association

Idea association is one of the most basic building blocks of individual and group creativity. Yet, oddly enough, there is no specific discussion of it in the traditional creativity literature. Perhaps the best-known technique for idea association is free association, a rudiment of the Freudian psychoanalytical method. Most people are familiar with the exercise in which a person is given a word and responds with the first thought that pops into their mind; this is free association in its most basic form.

Free association is a valuable aid for creative thinking since it helps people make connections they otherwise might not see. However, creativity in the business sphere requires quite a focused and goal-orientated approach. Companies want ideas that are related to the topic in hand, including many that are related to it in non-obvious ways. They also want a lot of these ideas: a small, random sample does not help much on the problem-solving front. Because of these requirements the art of free associating was developed into an approach called creative association.

In creative association, you free associate so as to surface the many patterns and relationships that surround your topic and lead on from it, bringing to light related ideas along the way. This approach is facilitated by the mind's tendency to produce ideas and retrieve memories in groups, based on patterns that link them. The patterns can be formal and conscious, as when we recall that red, blue and yellow all belong to a group called colours. They can also be less conscious, even accidental – as when we think of 'shell' and 'bell' in response to the work 'sell', just because these words rhyme. An accidental or secondary association such as this one cuts a path across the more obvious (and generally more useful) categories, connecting seemingly unrelated ideas and grouping them in new categories.

Two simple variants of the association techniques are described below.

Word associations and analogies

Word association and analogy are often used to move a team that is trapped in traditional thinking by using random, unrelated words as a way to stimulate fresh perspectives and new solutions.

By describing a random word, object or situation in detail, unusual connections can be made to a problem. This provides a virtually unlimited supply of inspiration for breakthrough thinking and enables all team members to create a new focus point for their thinking. It also helps re-energise the brainstorming process that has reached a lull.

1. Determine the source of stimulating words to use.
2. Define the problem clearly and brainstorm initial ideas.
3. Brainstorm associations or analogies that are stimulated by the selected picture or living thing:
   a. an *association*: a mental connection that is triggered by an idea, a memory, a picture, or an event.
   b. an *analogy*: a comparison of a primary characteristic, action or behaviour between two things.
4. Take the ideas identified in the previous step and re-state them as they apply to the problem.
5. Repeat the process as often as is helpful, using a new word each time.
6. Pool the best ideas.

Anti-solution

This technique is used to open mindsets to see things differently and from different perspectives. Here, individuals are asked to brainstorm the opposite of what needs to be accomplished.

1. Define your brainstorming objective.
2. Create a new objective, opposite to the 'real' one.
3. Brainstorm based on the 'anti' objective (have fun and be wild).
4. Examine each 'anti' idea and see what positive idea it suggests.
5. Record the positive ideas and add to them as possible.

For example, how about an anti-ageing cream that puts wrinkles on you, makes your skin sag, leaves your skin greasy and smelly.

Incubation methods

Incubation is the idea development that occurs when you sit on a problem for a while. The extraordinary value of this building block is well expressed by Bertrand Russell (1930, pp. 49–50):

> *If I have to write upon some rather difficult topic, the best plan is think about it with very great intensity – the greatest intensity with which I am capable – for a few hours or days, and at the end of that time give orders, so to speak, that the work is to proceed underground. After some months, I return consciously to the topic and find the work has been done.*

Of course, workplace pressures conspire against such intensity. No sooner do we get started on a tough problem than a new message, report, or order distracts us. Thus anyone who wants to incubate an important problem effectively must take special care to 'think about it for days with very great intensity' ignoring the pressures to multi-task. Instead, they must focus only on the problem.

Cyclical creativity

Cyclical creativity is a tool which helps teams incubate ideas. It involves fewer but longer work sessions, usually offsite or under 'lock down' orders to prevent interruptions. These intensive sessions are punctuated by several-day breaks, during which team members incubate ideas associated with a given problem. In the first intensive session, it is recommended that the team or group be 'overloaded' with as much information about the problem as possible. In subsequent sessions, it is recommended that a variety of creativity tools and processes are introduced and used.

The essential feature of cyclical creativity is the use of focus/un-focus/focus cycles. Although retreat-type work sessions offer many advantages for facilitating these cycles, it is possible to effectively integrate them into a single meeting or work session.

Basic method
1. Alternate intensive blocks of work and meditative break periods.
2. Take the group through at least one full focus/un-focus/focus cycle.

Focus periods
1. Use focused brainstorming techniques.
2. Diagram or flow-chart the problem.
3. Gather data on the problem or analyse data on the problem.
4. Write a full description or report of the work to date on the problem.

Break periods
1. Structure break periods so that the problem and related ideas can 'percolate'. Don't get distracted by other problems – disconnection is the key.

ILLUSTRATION

How General Electric hatches its eggs

General Electric is constantly striving for innovation. Driving this are three simple management tools: the management workout, best practices and process mapping.

The workout: A manager and his subordinates gather for a three-day retreat. The subordinates are given a set of problems to work on with the help of an outside facilitator. The manager is not allowed to participate in these sessions. On the third day, the manager is presented the solutions proposed by the subordinates. He has to respond with a yes, no or deferral for further study. The managers are encouraged to limit their deferral response.

Best practices: GE compares itself against other firms that are considered to be best in class in a particular function. GE then begins a process of study to improve its own performance by attempting to emulate the practices of these leading class companies.

Process mapping: The employees make a flow chart of a particular process. The flow chart breaks down the process and the product into its component and related parts. The employees are then set the challenge of how much time they can cut out of the process, and how they can improve the product. GE halved the time it took to manufacture aircraft engines through process mapping.

Mapping methods

Mapping methods are used to graphically break down a broad goal or problem into increasing levels of detail to better understand the existing knowledge about it.

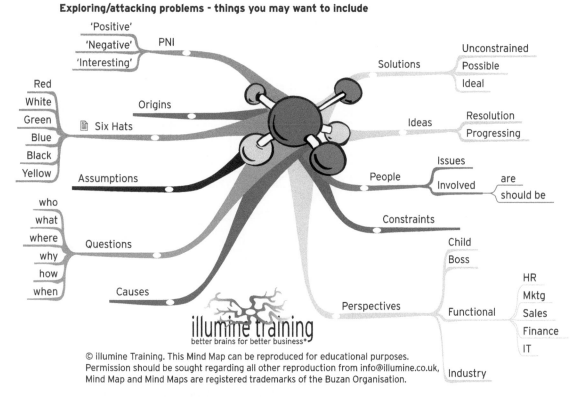

Exploring/attacking problems - things you may want to include

© illumine Training. This Mind Map can be reproduced for educational purposes. Permission should be sought regarding all other reproduction from info@illumine.co.uk, Mind Map and Mind Maps are registered trademarks of the Buzan Organisation.

FIGURE 2.11 Mind map example (exploring/attacking problems)
Source: Mind mapping examples from Illumine Training Ltd, 2008. Reprinted with permission

Mind mapping

This allows a team or individual to generate an enormous number of ideas by branching each idea into many more detailed ideas. The ideas in each branch can either be loosely or tightly connected with the 'limb' from which it grew. To create a mind map like that shown in Figure 2.11, follow these steps:

1. Write the topic (or draw a picture that represents it) in the centre or extreme side of a sizeable piece of paper.

2. Brainstorm ideas around the topic. For each major idea, draw a line directly from the main topic.

3. For each new idea, decide whether it is a new theme or a variation on an existing idea. Record ideas on the lines as they are generated.

4. Continue thinking, drawing and recording until the ideas (of the people involved) are exhausted.

Morphological box

This is used to map out all the combinations of potential solutions that address the essential parts of a problem.

Sample problem:
How can I determine which car is best for me?

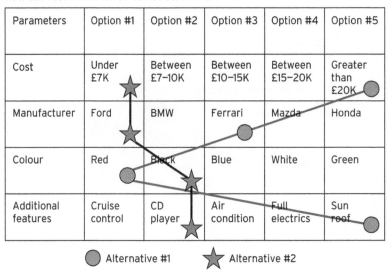

Parameters	Option #1	Option #2	Option #3	Option #4	Option #5
Cost	Under £7K	Between £7–10K	Between £10–15K	Between £15–20K	Greater than £20K
Manufacturer	Ford	BMW	Ferrari	Mazda	Honda
Colour	Red	Black	Blue	White	Green
Additional features	Cruise control	CD player	Air condition	Full electrics	Sun roof

⬤ Alternative #1   ★ Alternative #2

FIGURE 2.12 Example of a morphological box

It helps identify all parts of the problem that must be addressed to reach a successful solution. It builds a table that helps to display options for solving each essential part of the problem and allows the team to evaluate several solutions at one time (see Figure 2.12).

To do this:

1. Assemble a knowledgeable team.
2. Define the parameters that are necessary for any solution to the problem (a parameter being a characteristic that a solution must possess in order for it to be effective). Good parameters must be independent from other parameters, and create a complete solution when combined with other parameters.
3. Generate options for each parameter.
4. Build alternative solutions by linking different options.
5. Analyse the alternative solutions and select the best ones.

TRIZ: a structured methodology for creative problem solving

Whilst the above creativity tools work well as separate components, a number of structured systems for creative problem solving have been developed. From amongst these the most useful and increasingly prominent system is the TRIZ system. TRIZ is based on the work of Russian engineer Genrich S. Altshuller. Altshuller developed a system that he called ARIZ (a Russian acronym for Algorithm for Inventive Problem Solving). This was refined further by his students into TRIZ (Theory of Inventive Problem Solving). At the centre of the TRIZ process are five innovation patterns that emerged from Altshuller's historical scrutiny of innovations.

Pattern 1. Subtraction: In developing new products there is a tendency always to add features. The principle of subtraction works in reverse. Instead it takes away features from the product to look for developmental insight. For instance, caffeine from coffee leads to caffeine-free. Similarly, the principle can be used for other foods. For instance, in modern health-conscious society, subtract the fat for fat-free versions of the product. This can be used for other product categories to simplify and improve. Subtract a vacuum tube from a TV, what do you get? A slim-line plasma screen TV?

Pattern 2. Multiplication: This pattern requires adding a copy of an already existing component, but doing so in a way that alters the copy in some fundamental way. Perhaps the easiest example of this is adding an extra blade to a shaving razor. However, strictly speaking the extra addition must be altered in some way. For example, if the addition of the second blade is at a slightly different angle to allow for a closer cut following the skim of the first blade.

Pattern 3. Division: This principle operates by breaking the product down into its component parts, and then re-configuring it in some anticipated way. Let us use the old TV example again, for illustration. Imagine it is an old TV, say from 20 years ago. It has a screen, a base, on–off buttons, electronic circuits, etc. This is not how it came about, but the principle of division could potentially have led to the separation of the on–off buttons from the TV, i.e. led to the development of the remote control.

Pattern 4. Task unification: This principle sets the task of embedding a task or function into an existing element or component of the product. The most common example of this is embedding a car radio antennae function into the defrosting filament on the windscreen. By doing so, the car is more streamlined and you do not have to worry about remembering to ensure that it is drawn in when taking it to a car wash.

Pattern 5. Attribute dependency: This focusses on the relationship of the products and its attributes to its immediate environment. For example, in a car the pedals could be designed specifically in relation to its user (male or female). Let us say the attribute relationship is to be made with a female: the pedals are set in a way that allows higher heels and accounts for smaller foot-span. Or the relationship could be in terms of seat and height of individuals, thus leading to a seat that raises or lowers and expands or reduces leg-space.

The strength of this technique is its systematic decomposition and anchorage in a current product to drive development and improvement. Creativity techniques that start with a blank make it quite difficult to come up with something meaningful. Sometimes it is very difficult to come up with anything. As an experiment, just test yourself. Try and come up with something new, anything. Give yourself one minute to do so. Did you? Now, just pick up something and try and apply the above principles. Which one of the two methods led you to the most productive and innovative result? Most people find the second, since as a framework it directs your mind to use particular heuristics to reach the end goal. This makes it easier.

We've been creative: now what?

Going 'live' with a concept or product is often harder than striking the right spark in the first place. Many obstacles populate the enormous divide between vision and reality – between knowing what you want and actually doing something to make it happen.

Having the idea is just the beginning of the innovation process. To create a successful innovation the idea must undergo the often long and arduous task of implementation. Only if an idea can successfully negotiate the many obstacles in its way can it press the light of innovation. The structured methodologies of new product development are designed to help negotiate this path of uncertainty and 'fears'. Unfortunately, such structured methods exist only for the development and implementation of product ideas. Process and other innovation ideas have to chart a highly unstructured and sometimes ad hoc process. Implementation of process ideas is dependent on a complex web of organisational factors: management acceptance, resource availability, organisational commitment and so on. To get adoption of a new idea is no easy task. This is particularly so if the organisational culture, systems and management thinking are not accommodating towards new ideas. It is an unfortunate fact but many good ideas, especially process and organisational innovations, fall by the wayside simply because the organisation, particularly its management, either fails to appreciate the value of the idea or is simply resistant to change. In these companies, managers are busy protecting their status quo and operating in their comfort zone. It is no coincidence that these companies also have systems and practices that stifle and suffocate the emergence of new ideas. In later chapters we return to examine these organisational issues.

Conclusion

Creativity is the production of novel and valuable outcomes. Creativity plays a key role in innovation since it helps to define problems, solve them and even sometimes anticipate them. Creativity must be tapped at all stages of the innovation problem-solving and solution-finding process. It should not be confined simply to trying to generate new ideas. It is required for problem identification, problem selection and problem preparation. It is therefore important in developing innovative ideas and solutions, as well as installing and implementing the chosen solution. In other words, creativity spans the whole spectrum of innovation activity.

In this chapter we found that some approaches to organisation enhance creative performance whilst others dampen and stifle it. Hierarchical and bureaucratic organisational designs appear to be antithetical to innovation and creativity.

Innovation and creativity are phenomena that depend upon both the individual and the collective expertise of employees. Whether observed as an outcome embedded in new products, services, improved organisational structures or processes, creativity is rarely an individual undertaking. It requires managing the individual as well as the collective of employees' skills, knowledge and experience. Management of the individual and teams necessitates paying attention to a range of factors. Skills, competences and capabilities (intelligences) of employees need to be developed and enhanced. This can be done through a wide range of processes, such as training in creativity tools and problem solving as well as ensuring that jobs are designed to provide sufficient scope for creative performance. Each employee's specific predispositions and preferences towards problem solving need to be identified and managed in order to maximise their potential to contribute to organisational improvement and success. Whilst attending to these concerns, companies must take great care in constructing systems that reinforce creative behaviour and innovation. They need to examine their measurement and rewards systems, their structures and processes, their culture and the signal and behaviours of their leadership. All of these work together to weave a complex and intricate web of influence over acts of creativity and innovation.

QUESTIONS

1. Why is creativity important over the entire spectrum of innovation activity? What problems are experienced by companies that use only the idea-generation phase of the product development process?

2. What are the key steps in the creative process?

3. What factors stop creativity happening in the workplace?

4. Is creativity simply personal and individual? Explain why or why not.

5. You can't make people creative. They either have it or they don't. Do you agree?

6. Why do organisations frequently fail to tap into the right-brain thinking of their workforce?

CASE STUDY

As Innocent as a drink

Dan Germain, Head of Creativity at Innocent Drinks argues that creativity must be maintained in the fast growing company.

Innocent Drinks started in 1999. Dan Germain commented 'Try as we might to keep things as they are, we'll just have to face facts – our company is hopefully going to get a bit bigger. And we all know that once you get a bit bigger, you get a bit lazy; you stop caring; you cease to love the business that you took such care to nurture. And things get rubbish. That is what always happens'.

How could the company keep hold of its original spirit and keep on doing all of the creative things that made it special. There was unease that as the company becomes bigger, the less creative and fun it would get. According to Germain, this idea is un-revolutionary but it is surprising how many companies always just come up with product re-launches and new brand philosophies in order to try to keep their spirit intact.

Innocent is highly selective in hiring people. It uses interviews to ascertain skills and aptitude, but also screens for people who are 'innocent' – individuals who will fit in and enjoy themselves and take the initiative.

The people manifesto

Clarity is making sure that everyone knows what Innocent wants to do as a company. It means making sure that each individual knows his or her part. People love knowing how they can make a difference, so you should tell them, and make sure that they know how their work will make Innocent a mighty place.

Responsibility is about letting people get on with their job. Let them be the experts in their area, let them make mistakes and let them change things that could be better.

Fraternity means celebrating all of the good stuff: rewarding people for teamwork, and fostering an open, informal culture where people can say what they want without fear of recrimination.

→

When Coca-Cola made a minority investment in 2009, the founders commented: 'The three of us who set up the business will continue to run and manage Innocent. We will be the same people making the same products in the same way. Everything that Innocent stands for, remains in place – to only produce natural, healthy stuff; to push hard for better quality, more socially and environmentally conscious ingredients; to find more efficient and environmentally friendly ways of producing and packaging our drinks; to support charities in the countries where our fruit comes from; to have a point of view on the world, and to not take ourselves too seriously in the process. In fact, this deal will simply allow us to do more of these things.

'As we said, Coca-Cola is a minority investor. They have a small stake of between 10–20 per cent, which they paid £30M for. We chose Coca-Cola as our minority investor because as well as providing the funds, they can help us get our products out to more people in more places. Plus, they have been in business for over 120 years, so there will be things we can learn from them. And in some small ways we may be able to influence their thinking too.

'Innocent is ten years old this year. We sold 24 smoothies on our first day, back on 28th April 1999. This week, we will sell approximately 2 million.'

QUESTIONS

As the company develops following the investment by Coca-Cola:

1. How is it likely to change?
2. What impact is this likely to have on innovation and creativity?
3. What should Innocent be doing to adjust to these changes?

(*Source*: Based on Germain, 2005 and **www.innocentdrinks.co.uk**, 2009. With permission from Innocent Ltd).

References

Anon (2004), 'Remedy for the designer's block found in a clever blue box', *Design Engineering* 50(7): 66.

Amabile, T.M. (1997), 'Motivating creativity in organisations: On doing what you love and loving what you do', *California Management Review* 40(1): 39–58.

Anderson, J.V. (1992), 'Weirder than fiction: The reality and myths of creativity', *Academy of Management Executive* 6(4): 40–47.

Boone, L.W. and Hollingsworth, A.T. (1990), 'Creative thinking in business organisations', *Review of Business*, Fall: 3–12.

Covey, S.R. (1990), *Principle centered leadership*, New York: Summit Books.

de Bono, E. (1970), *Lateral thinking*, New York: Harper Row.

Drazin, R., Glynn, M.A., Kazanjian, R.K. (1999), 'Multi-level theorizing about creativity in organizations: A sensemaking perspective', *Academy of Management Review* 24: 286–307.

Drucker, P.F. (1985), 'The discipline of innovation', *Harvard Business Review*, May–June: 67–74.

Ford, C.M. (1996), 'A theory of individual creative action in multiple social domains', *Academy of Management Review* 21: 1112–1142.

Frumkim, P. (2005), 'Chefs seek new inspiration for culinary magic', *Nation's Restaurant News* 39(12): 75–79.

Gardner, H. (1991), *The unschooled mind*, New York: Basic Books.

Garfield, C.A. (1986), *Peak performers: The new heroes of American business*, New York: Harper Collins.

Germain, D. (2005), 'Nurturing creativity', *Brand Strategy*, February: 15.

Glynn, M.A. (1996), 'Innovative genius: A framework for relating individual and organizational intelligences to innovation', *Academy of Management Review* 21(4): 1081–1111.

Gundry, L.K., Kickul, J.R. and Prather, C.W. (1994), 'Building the creative organisation', *Organisational Dynamics* 22(4): 22–37.

Hesselbein, F. and Johnston, R. (2002), *On creativity, innovation, and renewal: A leader to leader guide*, Hoboken, NJ: Jossey-Bass Publishing.

Innocent (2009), *All about us*, **www.innocentdrinks.co.uk**.

Jung, C. (1971), *Psychological types*, Princeton, NJ: Princeton University Press.

Kao, J.J. (1989), *Entrepreneurship, creativity and organisation*, Upper Saddle River, NJ: Prentice Hall.

Kessler, E.H. and Chakrabarti, A.K. (1996), 'Innovation speed: A conceptual model of context, antecedents, and outcomes', *Academy of Management Review* 21(4): 1143–1155.

Leonard, D. and Sensiper, S. (1998), 'The role of tacit knowledge in group innovation', *California Management Review* 40(3): 112–121.

Levesque, L.C. (2001), *Breakthrough creativity: Achieving top performance using eight creative talents*, Mountain View, CA: Davies-Black Publishing.

Pande, P.S., Neuman, R.P. and Cavanagh, R.R. (2002), *The six sigma way team fieldbook – An implementation guide for process improvement teams*, New York: McGraw-Hill.

Rich, F. (1999), *New York Times*, 13 February, 19.

Ritter, D. and Brassard, M. (1998), *The creativity tools memory jogger*, 1st edn, GOAL/QPC.

Roberts, P. (2000), 'The art of getting things done', *Fast Company*, June: 162–164.

Russell, B. (1930), *The conquest of happiness*, London: Allen and Unwin.

Sebell, M.H. and Yocum, J. (2001), *Ban the humorous bazooka [and avoid the roadblocks and speed bumps along the innovation highway]*, Mansfield: Dearborn Financial Publishing.

Sen, A. (1991), 'Alternative to psychological testing', *Psychology and Developing Societies* 3(2): 56–64.

Sinatra, R. (1989), 'Brain functioning and creative behaviour', *Roeper Review*, September: 23–24.

Sternberg, R.J. (1987), 'Thinking better', *Bottom-Line/Personal*, 30 July, 12.

Velthouse, B. (1990), 'Creativity and empowerment', *Review of Business* 12(2): 13–18.

Walsh, J. and Ungson, R. (1991), 'Organisational memory', *The Academy of Management Review* 16(1): 57–91.

Williams, W.M. and Sternberg, R.J. (1988), 'Group intelligence: Why some groups are better than others', *Intelligence* 12: 351–377.

Woodman, R.W. and Sawyer, J.E. and Griffin, R.W. (1993), 'Toward a theory of organizational creativity', *Academy of Management Review* 18: 293–321.

PART 2

Strategic focus – setting a direction

3 Strategy and innovation

Learning outcomes

When you have completed this chapter you should be able to:

- Appreciate the importance of nurturing capabilities for innovation.
- Recognise the key strategic questions in developing innovation.
- Understand the basic strategic orientations for innovation.
- Understand the interlinkage between different innovation strategies.
- Appreciate that innovation strategies vary over the industry life cycle.
- Appreciate the advantages and limitations of following different innovation strategies.
- Appreciate the importance of being able to establish the dominant design in innovation.
- Recognise timing of entry as an important determinant of innovation strategy.
- Understand the different types of attack and defence strategies for innovation.

Introduction

Many companies are facing fundamental challenges in their organisational strategies and management practices. The changes are driven by the rapid pace of technological change, global competition and emergence of the knowledge-based economy. Market and product demands are changing faster than ever: customers are demanding more choice and more customised 'need' fulfilment; product life cycles are getting shorter and shorter; market boundaries are blurring and coalescing; global demand and competition is becoming the norm rather than the exception; and technological innovation is having transverse industry impacts. Due to the heightened effects of such forces of change, modern organisations must now capitalise on narrow windows of opportunity, introduce new products in rapid succession, and respond in real time to market dynamics. These shifts are uncertain, rapid and volatile, and often catch many firms unaware.

Collectively, the changes in the competitive environment hold important consequences for the development and management of products, markets and organisational capabilities. They precipitate a move away from monolithic and rigid organisational strategies and practices. Early success is no longer a guarantee of long-term survival. A pioneering firm can find its efforts eclipsed by an unexpected spin-off, a sudden shift in market conditions or a newer technological breakthrough. Managing the kaleidoscope of change is the challenge to strategy. Successful businesses are those that are able to innovate and strategically evolve.

Strategy, strategic capability and competitive advantage

The conventional view of strategy is one of matching internal resources with environmental opportunities and threats. Corporate strategy is the pattern of decisions in a company that determines and reveals its objectives and the plans to achieve these aims. Strategy is broken down into two fundamental activities: formulation and implementation. Formulation involves taking decisions over what to do, and implementation involves devising programmes and plans to achieve this. In this view of strategy the range of alternative possibilities is narrowed by matching opportunity to competence, once each has been identified and its future significance accurately estimated. This 'matching' encapsulates the company's goals and its position in the environment. The process is designed to minimise organisational weaknesses and maximise leverage upon strengths. In this traditional approach, strategy emerges from senior management's consideration of external and internal factors. Strategy is thus formulated in response to four basic questions (Leidtka and Rosenblum, 1996), which are framed below.

1. What might the business do?
2. What can the business do?
3. What do the people in the business want to do?
4. What ought the business do, from a societal point of view?

This approach of closing the gaps between external demands and internal capabilities works in relatively stable environments, in which strategy can get away with being relatively static. In a world characterised by stable customer demand, well defined markets and industry boundaries and visible competitors, the war of competitive survival is essentially a war of position. The key to competitive advantage from this perspective lies in *where* a company chooses to compete. The question of *how* it competes, while important, is demoted as being simply an issue of execution. However, dynamic environments, involving the type of change alluded to earlier, require disrupting current alignment and opening up new gaps in order to develop a basis for competitive advantage. Strategy, thus, becomes a war of movement rather than position. Success depends on acute anticipation and response to market trends. Successful companies rapidly enter as well as create products, markets and capabilities, and just as rapidly move out from them, sometimes even exiting entire businesses. In such environments the essence of strategy is not simply the positioning of a company's products to markets but the dynamics of its behaviour. Creating alignment, through the process of matching the external environment to internal strengths enables improved organisational performance. However, it does so only for the short run. Long-term survival requires the capacity to be able to deal with environmental disequilibrium through innovation and learning. To do this, the goal needs to become one of identifying and developing hard to imitate fundamental capabilities. These fundamental capabilities define the survival and long-term prosperity of the organisation. Stalk et al. (1992) note four basic principles for capabilities-based competition:

1. The building blocks of corporate strategy are not products and markets but business processes.
2. Competitive success depends on transforming a company's key processes into strategic capabilities that consistently provide superior value to the customer.
3. Companies create these capabilities by making strategic investments in a support infrastructure that links together and transcends traditional Strategic Business Units (SBUs) and functions.
4. Because capabilities necessarily cross functions, the champion of a capabilities-based strategy is the CEO.

David Aaker (1989) suggests that strategy involves discerning the way you compete (what you do), where you compete (the selection of the competitive area) and the basis of competition (see Figure 3.1). Competing in the right arena in the right way can be extremely profitable, but it is only so for a limited period of time. It is the assets and skills that define the basis of competition and provide enduring or sustainable competitive advantage. An asset is something that your firm possesses (such as a brand name, exclusive access to distribution channels, etc.). A skill is something that your company is able to do better than its competitors (e.g. efficient manufacturing). Without underpinning skills and assets it is highly unlikely that competitive advantage will be enduring, since where a company competes and the way it competes are both easily imitated. It is vastly more difficult, however, to imitate or neutralise specialised skills or assets. For example, any company may be able to distribute detergents and shampoo, but few are able to leverage it as effectively as Unilever or Procter & Gamble. The right assets and skills erect substantial barriers to erosive actions from competitors. Thus, the essence of strategic management is in the nurture and maintenance of critical skills and assets, and selection of strategies and competitive arenas such that these skills and assets are able to form sustainable competitive advantage.

Changing conditions can, however, undercut strategies and the assets and skills upon which they are based. In an attempt to come to terms with this dialectic of change, strategists have put forward new thinking. Mintzberg (1987) notes that strategy is not planned or intended but emergent. Planned strategies are static and inhibit learning, innovation and adaptability. Emergent strategy allows learning and adaptation via the incremental nature of its strategic steps. Hamel and Prahalad (1989, 1993) add to this the concept of strategic intent. Strategic intent not only incorporates strategy as designed and strategy as incrementally taking

FIGURE 3.1 Sustaining competitive advantage
Source: Adapted from Aaker, 1999

advantage of opportunity, but takes one step further in providing a stretch dimension to the potential opportunity. Strategic intent argues for a vision of strategy as a stretch of current capabilities rather than a constraint upon them. Burgelman (1991) refines this understanding by noting that successful firms survive through a process of renewal based upon internal experimentation and learning rather than strategic shifts to orientations that undermine cumulative learning.

The cumulated wisdom of these views highlights a number of dichotomies, which organisations must learn to balance. The strategy process must straddle between over-planning and too little guidance; between stability and change; between control and autonomy; efficiency and effectiveness. The above contrast of strategic approaches throws up an 'adaptation' paradox. Alignment through a process of matching strengths and weaknesses to opportunities and threats bestows efficiency and performance through enactment of stability. This it does by closing out variation. However, this very act of adaptation simultaneously detracts from the capability to change to newer circumstances. In other words, adaptation precludes adaptability (Burgelman, 1991). Liedtka and Rosenblum (1996) attempt to reflect these realities by adding to the earlier set of questions concerning fit and implementation, a new set of questions that emphasise shaping and participating:

Q1. How can we shape tomorrow's value system to create new possibilities, in partnership with our stakeholders?
This question shifts the focus of attention from a purely self-centred individual firm's strategic intent to how that intent aligns with other stakeholder and powerful players, and what the intent delivers to all other stakeholder parties.

Q2. What new capabilities are we committed to developing and learning to care about?
This question ties together mindsets with skill-sets, on the belief that the two are inseparable. Innovation and learning of new skills only becomes possible when the 'something new' becomes personally important. We engage in and learn about what we care about (Senge, 1990). Senge's observation highlights the central problem in the strategy formulation and implementation dichotomy. Organisational renewal starts by opening a gap between today and tomorrow's strategic intent. However, corporate change and individual change are intricately interlinked. Without behavioural change at the individual level corporate intent becomes empty. To get innovation and learning, the individual must move away from the comfort of the current and become receptive to the opportunities that the future offers. Learning occurs more effectively if it is self-initiated rather than

FIGURE 3.2 Questions driving innovation strategy
Source: Adapted from Liedtka and Rosenblum, 1996

driven by directives from the top. Individuals need to feel they can discover and shape new possibilities into which they can invest personal energy and commitment. This view of strategy widens the perspective from a top-down approach to wider participation in strategy enactment.

The two questions link industry environment to corporate social responsibility, and organisational capabilities with the primary values held to be important by organisational agents (see Figure 3.2). Both of these questions are drivers of innovation. The first question focuses on the innovation outcomes that the firm wishes to deliver to the marketplace, and the second on the enabling capabilities to deliver these outcomes.

ILLUSTRATION

The dynamics of strategy

Strategies for innovation are not straightforward. There have been times when companies such as IBM, Apple and Xerox have invested in R&D without reaping significant benefits and were outperformed by competitors with more meagre R&D budgets.

During environmental turbulence and strategic uncertainty, many previously successful companies decline; some even fail outright. These trends are particularly clear in technology-related industries. For instance, IBM pretty much owned the mainframe business but was slow to see the development of the minicomputer business, which was controlled for years by Digital Equipment. Digital failed to see the transition to smaller and cheaper PCs and rapidly declined, along with Data General, Prime and other players in the minicomputer industry. Wang took the word processing market away from IBM, which had long dominated it with its Selectric Typewriters. Wang's stand-alone word processors, however, were soon overtaken by word-processing software systems such as WordPerfect and Word.

Similar patterns, only slightly less extreme, can be found in other industries. Experience suggests that core competences of the past can become codified and inflexible. In times of rapid change they become core rigidities and, ultimately, core incompetences. Indeed, past success can often be a precursor of market failure. It is, however, important not to judge strategies at a single time frame.

Apple

Apple developed the PC menu system but it was Microsoft who came to dominate the sector. Thus, Apple was deemed to have a poor R&D record, until it developed the ipod and iTunes Music store. The iTunes Music Store reportedly sold 1 million music tracks within the first week of product launch, sold 85 million tracks within the first year and currently sells nearly 2.5 million tracks per week. Apple's iTunes is supported by iPod, already a pop culture icon that is boosting Apple's revenues and brand.

IBM

IBM managed to avert impending crisis during the 1990s by altering its strategic focus and programmes of innovation. In doing so, IBM exhibited a high level of market adaptability. Sparked by the leadership of Lou Gerstner, the company underwent a paradigm-shifting change that resulted in a far stronger focus on the needs of customers. IBM realised it needed to shift its innovation focus to upstream parts of customer value chains, i.e. devote more time to systems integration technologies than fundamental device technologies. In addition to maintaining strong internal R&D, IBM began to out-license and in-license activities, a sign of open innovation. IBM organised for a more open and market-based innovation by creation of Emerging Business Units (EBOs) that provide start-up opportunities to creative employees. By following such strategies, IBM made a successful transition away from its historical focus on computer hardware such that, today, it spends over 65 per cent of its resources on software and systems.

(*Source*: Based on Homes and Glass, 2004)

 ## Generic strategies for innovation

A number of attempts have been made to codify innovation strategies (e.g. Porter, 1980; Kerin et al., 1992). Each of these typologies presents what are commonly called generic (or archetype) strategies. Each typology is based on a theory of competitive advantage, and theoretically each proffers an insight over how to reap high returns. Typically, in each typology there is some conceptual overlap within the proposed strategy archetypes. Nevertheless, these archetypes tend to be recognisable as discrete approaches. The potential of these strategies can be achieved if a firm is able to implement one (or a combination of these), and competitor firms have difficulty emulating the firm's chosen strategy.

The generic archetypes can be classified/grouped according to the basic orientation of each approach. Three basic types of orientations can be discerned: (1) product-market-focussed strategies, (2) opportunity–risk-focussed strategies and (3) time- (or industry-) focussed strategies.

Product-market-focussed strategies

The primary focus of these strategies is to develop products and markets in a manner designed to capture a superior competitive position. Porter's (1980) generic strategies (cost leadership, differentiation and focus/niche) and the strategy of diversification fall into this group. For instance, a differentiation strategy focuses on the development of distinctive products delivering superior value to the end customer. This allows the company either to penetrate the market, develop the market or diversify into a new market. Similarly, a low-cost strategy, whilst it is based on efficient organisational processes, focusses on the competitive dynamic within the product-market arena, i.e. the emphasis is to deliver a product that provides superior value to the customer. The focus (or niche) strategy targets a segment or sub-segments of the market for whom specific value can be customised. It is obvious that these strategies are closely allied to the exploitation of the strategic trajectories captured in the Ansoff matrix (product development, market development, market penetration and product-market development (or diversification) strategies).

Cost reduction

A company that focusses upon cost leadership chooses to compete by being able to lower its costs relative to competition. The theory of cost reduction is that a firm with lowest costs is able to accrue higher returns, or greater market share, or both. This strategy does not mean, however, a single-minded focus on just reducing costs since there is no point in reducing costs of products that no one wants.

The most common method of reducing costs is through volume production to gain access to economies of scale and learning effects. This requires heavy up-front investment in large-scale equipment and machinery, as well as complementary management of a large throughput within the supply chain. The higher margins breed a cycle of re-investment and thus allow the strategy of low cost volume production to be sustained. Driving this to an even higher level is the phenomenon of globalisation, in which market size is expanded, so allowing access to further economies of scale. The cost leadership strategy, however, should not be confused with lower prices. Lower costs allow the company to increase its margin. The price charged in the marketplace is determined by factors such as the relative prices of competitors and the relative superiority of the product offering against those of competitors. It is often, naively, assumed that cost reduction occurs simply through production volume increases. The fact is that cost reductions must be systematically managed through learning and process innovation. Cost reduction can be achieved through three possible paths:

1. Downsizing (including divestment and workforce de-layering).
2. Experience effects in volume production (learning).
3. Organisational improvement (process innovation).

Differentiation

Differentiation is an organisational strategy in which attempt is made to offer products/ services that are unique or superior to competitors. The strategy is based on perceived value of products relative to competitor offerings or substitutes. Through a process of *adding value*, differentiation is able to enlist customer loyalty and lower sensitivity to price. This insulates against the effects of competition. Differentiation is a particularly favoured strategy during the emergent stage of the product life cycle, when the novelty of the innovation is able to attract customers who value the benefit of having the product at a higher price more than the cost of having to wait for a lower price product to emerge.

Differentiation is also appropriate in the mature stage of the life cycle, where it can be highly effective in rejuvenating the market through clever niching or marketing. Strategies based on differentiation require highly creative and innovative approaches to marketing. Another aspect of differentiation is that it requires speed and agility of action to create brand uniqueness and strength to constantly stay one step ahead of imitative brands.

Even from this brief discussion it is clear that one of the fundamental drivers of the differentiation strategy is product-market innovation.

Niching

The theory of niching suggests that a firm is able to attain superior returns by identifying and positioning itself in sub-sectors of the market where competition is less intense. There are essentially three types of niches:

- Those abandoned or overlooked by others.
- Those not subject to the general decline affecting the business as a whole.
- An emerging market, not yet identified by competitors.

Niche strategies are most frequently employed by small firms because of their limited resources. Many small entrepreneurial firms develop their strategies through a process of identifying the very specific needs of small niche markets and innovating to fulfil these. By locking onto a niche, companies are able to avoid direct confrontation with other players. The niche strategy can use either a differentiation premise or a cost premise to serve the specific needs.

Diversification

The theory of diversification is based on the logic that a move away from the firm's core business can lower risk or yield higher returns than remaining in the core area. The justification for pursuit of this strategy is based primarily on enhancing shareholder value by engaging in an activity that is outside the firm's core operations. Diversification can be seen as innovation in the sense that a movement outside of the firm's core activity constitutes a new or novel act for the firm, even if it is not new or novel to others, i.e. it is innovation local to the firm.

Innovation and the effect on product success

While a number of different strategies exist for companies to exploit their innovative capabilities, it is important to understand some limitations. 'Product innovativeness' is concerned with the technical and marketing discontinuities whereas 'product advantage' refers to a product's superiority relative to other products in the marketplace on dimensions such as quantity, benefit and function. Although product innovativeness enhances product advantage, a high level of innovativeness reduces customer familiarity, indicating that product innovativeness can be detrimental to new product success if customers are not sufficiently familiar with the nature of the new product and the innovativeness fails to improve product advantage. When controlling for both product advantage and customer familiarity, product innovativeness has no direct effect on new product profitability. This finding has strong implications for companies that mistakenly pursue innovation for its own sake:

- Companies should emphasise product innovativeness when it relates to the market relevant concepts of product advantage and familiarity.

- Existing technical and distribution abilities can be used to enhance product quality and customer understanding. Distribution channels in particular should be exploited to counter customer uncertainty toward newly introduced products.

Opportunity–risk-focussed strategies

This group of strategies are based on the risk and future orientation of companies. Miles and Snow's (1978) strategic typology of Prospectors, Analysers, Defenders and Reactors best illustrates this type of orientation. This strategic typology is built upon scenarios of the future coupled with strategic intent. The typology encapsulates an approach that emphasises out-thinking or out-strategising other players. The Prospector and Analyser strategies are risk-taking orientations, while Defenders and Reactors are risk-averse. Paradoxically, Defenders and Reactors are risk-averse yet often as the future enfolds they find themselves at risk of extinction. In other words, they become burdened with risk, and therefore could be labelled as *risk-carriers*, in contrast to prospectors who are *risk-takers*.

Defenders

Defenders are organisations that have a narrow product-market domain, and do not tend to search outside of their domains for new opportunities. They attempt to locate and maintain a secure niche in a relatively stable product/service area by offering a limited range of products/services than competitors, but with higher quality, superior service and lower prices. As a result of this narrow focus, these organisations seldom make major adjustments in their technology, structure or methods of operation. Often, they are not at the forefront of developments in the industry. They tend to ignore industry changes that have no direct influence on their current areas of operation and concentrate instead on doing the best job possible in a limited area. They devote primary attention to improving the efficiency of their existing operations.

Defenders seek out stable environments in which to locate. Defenders' organisations are optimally designed to serve their current domains but possess little capacity for locating and exploiting new areas of opportunity.

Prospectors

Prospectors are organisations that almost continuously search for market opportunities. These firms regularly experiment with potential responses to emerging environmental trends. They are the creators of change and uncertainty through product and market innovation. Marketing is used heavily to search out new opportunities. These firms are acutely sensitive to potential opportunities. Prospectors value being 'first in' to new product and market areas, even if not all of these efforts prove to be highly profitable. They typically operate within a broad product-market domain that undergoes periodic redefinition. The prospecting strategy is risky, and many projects simply will not be successful. Prospectors in one sense 'misutilise' resources because they operate across a broad product-market domain making it difficult to be technologically efficient across all areas. Prospectors find it difficult to maximise short-run profitability because they invest heavily to prepare themselves to respond to tomorrow's demands. In contrast to Defenders, Prospectors suit a more dynamic environment. Prospectors are, by definition, highly innovative and forward-looking companies. They continually modify their product-market domain to take advantage of perceived opportunities. This they achieve through flexibility in technology and organisational systems, which facilitate rapid adjustment to emerging environments.

Analysers

Analysers are organisations that operate in two types of product-market domains: one relatively stable and the other changing. In the stable domain, they operate routinely and efficiently through the use of formalised structures and processes. In the more turbulent domain, top managers watch competitors closely for new ideas and rapidly adopt those showing the greatest promise. Analysers tend to maintain a stable, limited line of products or services, while at the same time moving quickly to follow promising new developments in the industry. They seldom are 'first in' with new products or services. However, by carefully monitoring the actions of major competitors in areas compatible with their core product-market base they can frequently be 'second in' with a more cost-efficient product or service.

Marketing plays a dual role: first, locate new product or market opportunities; and second, promote the sale of the organisation's traditional products or services. Analysers avoid the expense of R&D, choosing instead to imitate the successful actions of Prospectors. Analysers compete by creating a dual technological core. The stable component of the technology is to develop a near efficient production system that creates products or services on a standard basis. The flexible component exists in the form of a large applied research group whose function is to adapt new product designs to fit existing technological capabilities. The dual nature of the Analyser's technology allows the organisation to produce familiar products or services efficiently while keeping pace with the breakthrough developments of Prospectors.

Analysers possess a combination of Prospector and Defender characteristics. The Analyser defines its entrepreneurial 'problem' as how to locate and exploit new product and market opportunities, while simultaneously maintaining a firm base of traditional products and customers. The organisation solves this problem with a mix of stable and emerging products.

Reactors

Reactors are organisations that encounter change and uncertainty occurring in their environment, but are unable to respond effectively. Reactors lack a consistent product-market orientation or a consistent strategy–structure relationship. They are neither aggressive in maintaining established products and markets nor take as many risks as competitors. They seldom make adjustments of any sort until forced to do so by environmental pressures. Reactors are unstable organisations because they do not respond consistently to their environments, over time. Often, they fall into an unpleasant cycle of responding inappropriately to environmental change and uncertainty, which is worsened by their reluctance to act aggressively in the future.

Time-based (industry- and competitor-focussed) strategies

These strategies consider dynamics of competition to establish favourable entry and industry positions. In one sense, they may be referred to as competitor-focussed strategies because they have the aim of out-manoeuvring competitors within an industry. These strategies are dependent on timing of entry into market. Market entry is made at a point in the evolution

TABLE 3.1 Inter-relationship between the strategy types

Competitive orientation	Time	Opportunity–risk	Product market
Pioneer	First entrant	Prospector	Differentiator, offensive stratetgist (pre-emptive)
Fast follower	Early entrant, out pacer	Prospectors, Analysers, Imitators	Differentiator, low cost, hybrid
Late follower	Late entrants, put pacer, leap frog	Defenders, Reactors, Imitators	Differentiator, low cost, hybrid

of the industry when structural conditions are stacked in their favour. Kerin et al.'s (1992) first-mover strategy falls into this group. Success is dependent on a keen understanding of the structural conditions of an industry at a given moment in time as well as its future evolution.

This set of strategies draws a primary distinction in terms of innovation, notably whether the firm intends to be a first or early entrant into the market, or a follower and late entrant. These generic formats are discussed in further detail in the sections that follow.

There is an inter-relationship between the strategic formats in each of the group orientations, especially between time and risk–opportunity dimensions. This can be evidenced by the conceptual overlap between the generic strategy archetypes in these groups. Table 3.1 provides an indicative synthesis of the various strategic forms used in the extant literature and their approximate association to each other. The combinative interlinkages between these are made clear in the discussion that follows.

Proactive strategic orientation and innovation

Companies' strategic orientations are crucial in understanding product innovation and performance (Atuahene-Gima and Ko, 2001). A proactive strategic orientation is characterised by aggressive firm strategies and bold action, and decision making to enhance competitiveness. Those exhibiting a proactive strategic orientation encompass an aggressive focus on innovations, meeting both the articulated and latent expectations of customers, and promote the pre-emptive identification of new market opportunities and acting on them (Kohli and Jaworski, 1990). The goal here is to lead or alter the competition, and requires an increased level of market intelligence generation and responsiveness.

In addition to responding to explicit customer needs, proactive companies also explore opportunities for developing new products that customers cannot describe. A market orientation enables a business to anticipate changing market conditions and respond to market requirements, but may also include incremental changes.

Alternatively, if a company incorporates a strong market orientation into a proactive strategic posture, the result is an aggressive initiation of product innovation with high levels of risk (e.g. Hult and Ketchen, 2001). Proactiveness and a market focus should provoke the development or improvement of products (i.e. exploitation) and new methods of doing so (i.e. exploration). In short, a proactive strategic orientation should enhance innovativeness.

Innovation strategies over time

Competitive conditions change and co-evolve with the emergence, development and maturity of any specific industry. Whilst each specific product or industry goes through a unique change, a general pattern can be discerned which is often labelled as the product life cycle (if the focus is on a specific product), or if aggregated as the category or industry life cycle. Typically, a life cycle is represented as a graph of sales over time. The general, or ideal pattern of the life cycle is divided into four phases: introduction, growth, maturity and decline. Initially, sales are slow as a new product is introduced. Depending on the 'newness' of the product, potential users must be informed and persuaded to purchase the product through effective marketing of its features, attributes and advantages. In the next stage, rapid growth occurs as market acceptance takes place. In the maturity stage, sales stabilise, and in the decline phase unit sales start to fall. The observed pattern of sales in the life cycle is a cumulative depiction of the effect of the rate of innovation diffusion and innovation adoption. Rogers (1983) clarifies the rate of innovation diffusion by identifying five categories of adopters depending on how soon individuals adopt an innovation. Rogers postulates a bell-shaped normal curve (see Figure 3.3), in which the first 2.5 per cent of people who adopt an innovation are labelled innovators, and the next 13.5 per cent the early adopters. The rate of adoption of these individuals typically constitutes the introduction stage of the life cycle. The following 34 per cent segment of adopters, called the early majority, define the growth phase. The maturity stage is defined by the adoption of the innovation by the next 34 per cent slice, labelled the late majority. The final 16 per cent of the adopters define the decline phase.

The life cycle pattern is closely associated with innovation patterns and strategies. As a product class evolves, the type and amount of innovation changes (see Figure 3.4). This is

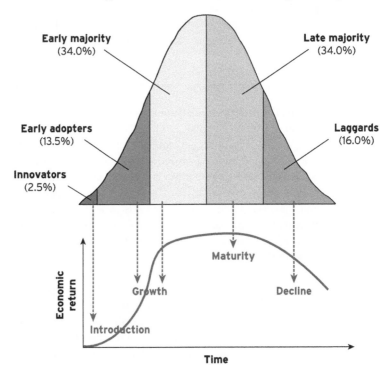

FIGURE 3.3 Alignment of strategic types to life cycles

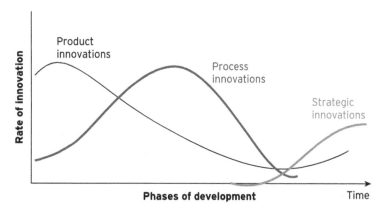

FIGURE 3.4 Patterns of innovation over time

most apparent in the life cycle pattern of a product arising from a technological innovation or discontinuity. The industry life cycle (or more precisely, the product class life cycle), begins with an introduction of a radical new innovation. This initiates other incumbents to release their versions of the product, resulting in a large quantity of product variants arriving onto the market. The variant product forms vie with each other for dominance. Competitive intensity increases until a dominant design emerges. Once a dominant design takes hold within the marketplace, the emphasis shifts from introduction of technical innovation(s) to process innovation. Process innovation strives to build efficiency in the customer value delivery process. This can be achieved by adopting a variety of approaches. Strategies for cost leadership work at improving the process of manufacturing and delivery, whilst differentiation works to create value by creating distinctiveness in the product offering. The impact of process innovation is often to reduce price significantly and/or improve the offer significantly. From after this point onwards, technological innovations are incremental, and the main focus becomes one of improving quality and performance. Maturation of the life cycle is typified by a high level of copy-cat introduction in almost all realms of the product class, leading to the erosion of most, if not all, product differentiation. To cope with these conditions many companies begin to adopt consolidation strategies. The process of upheaval can then be re-started by a fresh round of strategic innovation, which lends impetus to further development of the life cycle or makes the current trajectory redundant through introduction of a radically transforming innovation.

Pioneering (or first-mover) strategy

Success of a firm can depend to a large degree on its ability to produce new, innovative products or services. If the product is so new as to start a whole new market and industry, the firm that introduced it is usually referred to as the Pioneer. A pioneer is not necessarily the inventor of a technology or product innovation. It is the firm that first introduces the innovation to the market, i.e. not just the developer but the first one to commercialise the innovation.

Being a pioneer is an expensive and risky business. However, the rewards often translate into a larger market share and profits. These rewards are labelled *first-mover advantages*. Research on timing of entry into new markets has shown that pioneers tend to enjoy an enduring competitive advantage over later entrants (Lambkin, 1992). The order of entry not only affects market shares but gives the pioneer an advantage such as cost production, cost

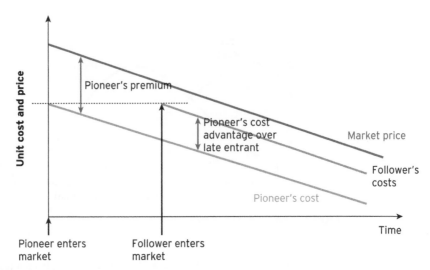

FIGURE 3.5 Pioneers advantage: impact of speed to market on costs and prices

of advertising, brand loyalty, quality, and the like. These advantages subsequently translate into a market share differential (see Figure 3.5).

Speed to market endows the pioneering firm with advantages. Entry at the early stage allows the firm to capture a lion's share of the market and profits. As competitors introduce products, the pioneer's profits may decline. By then, however, the pioneering firm will have moved down the learning curve, and be able to enjoy significant cost advantage over later entrants. This generally tends to last over the life of the venture, unless actions taken by late entrants are able to overturn this advantage in their favour (see Figure 3.5). In sum, pioneering (or first-mover advantage) refers to lower unit costs and greater market control than later entrants. It provides an opportunity to set product standards and greater opportunity to differentiate the organisation from followers.

At the beginning of the life cycle, pioneers dominate the market and often continue to hold onto a significant proportion of market even after entry of competitors. According to Robinson and Fornell (1985) this arises from three sources of market advantage:

1. *Relative consumer advantage*: By coming into contact with and using a company's products before competing offerings are available, customers receive differential information. Product and brand familiarity translates into higher market shares, i.e. a differentiation advantage is gained by the pioneer firm from the demand-side of the market.

2. *Relative marketing mix advantage*: With relative direct costs held constant, market pioneering can provide marketing mix advantages from the supply-side. Product differentiation advantages arise because customers have become familiar with and understand the pioneer's marketing mix. This relative advantage in marketing mix also allows capture of market share.

3. *Relative direct costs advantage*: The third source of pioneering advantage is derived from the pioneer's lower relative costs. Being first into the market can allow it to lead on cost saving with respect to purchasing, manufacturing and distribution. These cost savings can be used to invest more on the marketing mix, and thus increase further the market share.

Using more recently developed terminology first-mover advantages arise from three primary sources, 'technological leadership', 'pre-emption of assets' and 'buyer switching costs'.

Technological leadership provides an advantage derived from the learning or experience curve, where increased knowledge results in falling costs with cumulative output. Additionally, success in patent and R&D races can occur here, but needs to be tied into advances in product or process technology.

The first-mover may also be able to gain an advantage over rivals by *pre-emptive acquisition* of scarce resources. Pre-emptive strikes can take numerous forms, including the pre-emption of input factors and pre-emptive investment in plant and equipment. Another approach is the pre-emption of key geographical locations. In many markets there is only 'room' for a limited number of profitable firms, and the first entrants can select the most attractive niches.

The third source, *buyer switching costs*, recognises that late entrants have to incur switching costs, which requires them to invest extra resources to attract customers away from the first-mover firm.

In presenting these advantages, it is important to balance the argument by classifying some disadvantages that might accrue from a first mover strategy:

- Higher costs due to the hidden costs of accelerating development, such as risk of trivial innovation driving out more profitable breakthrough innovations.
- Higher costs as a result of the required investments in technology.
- Elevated costs due to more thorough concept and prototype testing.
- Consumer-based disadvantages related to the inability to exploit opportunities arising from shifts in consumers' preferences and purchase criteria as the market develops.
- Disadvantages related to being locked in on first-generation technology, which prevents firms from taking advantage of the latest technology.
- Disadvantages related to possible positioning and pricing mistakes inherent with accelerated development.

It is now generally accepted that market share is closely related to order of entry. Market pioneers usually achieve a larger sustainable market share than late entrants. As a rule of thumb, the ratio of market share advantage is about 1.0 for the pioneer, 0.6 for early followers, and 0.4 for late followers. In other words, late followers can expect to get 60 per cent less, and early followers 40 per cent less market share than the pioneer (Robertson and Gatignon, 1991).

Pioneering can be risky in terms of identification of market demand and choice of appropriate technology to meet that demand. Seemingly promising markets can easily vanish, with loss of huge investments and corporate effort. For example, Exxon invested hundreds of millions into shale oil technology but the market failed to transpire according to plan. The major problem is that the one technology that will eventually become the industry standard, and hence dominate the sector, is unclear at the embryonic stages of market development.

As we shall elaborate in later sections (see section on dominant design, p. 103), pioneering risks mainly stem from the fact that several technologies are competing for product supremacy during the early stage of the life cycle. Typically, one of these technologies will win the battle and oust the others from the marketplace. The classic example is in the VCR market, in which beta technology, despite offering higher quality, lost out to VHS technology. Early movers may not always succeed because of three main effects: market uncertainty, technological uncertainty and the free-rider effect (Boulding and Christen, 2001).

ILLUSTRATION

Differentiator versus cost leader (HP – Dell)

Not every firm chooses to compete using innovation as a prime lever of value. Consider HP and Dell in the consumer printer market. HP clearly competes as an innovator while Dell competes on price (and through differentiation in its PC business).

'The days of engineering-led technology companies are coming to an end' Michael Dell declared, while HP's Carly Fiorina says 'We're the biggest, we're the best, and we're getting better in a growing market.'

Clearly, firms compete using various angles of competitive positioning. HP will continue to innovate products as the basis of its success. And Dell will continue to succeed so long as it can find innovative hosts from which it can leverage technology and then compete on price.

(*Source*: Based on Homes and Glass, 2004)

Follower (late entry) strategy

Follower companies are those that are not first to market. These companies allow others to innovate, and then wait for the time that is the most opportune for them to enter the market. The follower strategy can take a number of forms, depending on the timing and order of entry, as well as the mode of competition they adopt.

A follower firm can be:

1. An early follower (or *fast follower*).

2. In step with majority of competitors (simply a *follower*).

3. A late follower (also known as *late entrant*).

Almost all industry sectors have fast followers. Fast followers introduce their products as soon as the Pioneer has shown that demand exists by educating consumers about the benefits of the new offering. Successful fast follower products tend to be significantly different from the first entrant's offer because they are able to closely incorporate consumer preferences to the pioneer's product. Whilst potential disadvantages exist, there are definite advantages to being second to market (Buzzell and Weisema, 1981). Understanding the relative advantages and disadvantages is key to the success of the strategy, irrespective of whether the company is small or large.

Fast followers can enjoy some of the benefits of the pioneers while avoiding the initial risks and costs of the first entrant. Fast followers are also able to learn lessons from the market's response to the first entrant's offering. Late followers can also avoid high R&D and 'market building' costs but due to the lateness of their entry they encounter severe competitive pressures on price as well as difficulties in building strong positions of differentiation. Strategies of competitive parity and late followership often do not result in high performance in a rapidly changing environment (Stalk, 1993).

Advantages of fast follower strategy are essentially derived from lower costs and lower risks. The major benefits of this approach are:

1. Allowing market uncertainty to disappear.

2. Learning from the pioneer's experience (mistakes and successes).

ILLUSTRATION

Followers reduce the window of opportunity for premium profit skimming

Companies in the consumer electronics sector are facing difficult times. Panasonic (its owner Matsushita), Samsung, LG Electronics, Sony and Philips are all experiencing a rocky ride. The market-place is crowded and the struggle to stay one step ahead of competitors is relentless.

Philips was in 2004 rumoured to be considering cutting down or even abandoning its consumer elec-tronics offerings. The Philips consumer electronics unit is Europe's biggest and generates more than a quarter of group revenue, but has consistently low profit margins. In the same year, Samsung blamed a 42 per cent profit drop on falling mobile phone margins and tumbling prices for flat-screen televisions.

So, how have these electronics manufacturers found themselves in such a precarious situation? The fact is, while consumer demand for new products is high, once a product has been out for a few years prices have to be slashed to shift units. Major supermarket chains are selling equipment from smaller, niche suppliers at low prices resulting in major manufacturers being forced to cut prices to compete.

The period between the launch of a new consumer electronics product and its reaching rock bottom price seems to be ever-decreasing. When the VHS video recorder was launched in the late 1970s, prices remained high for many years. DVD players, however, took a comparatively short time to drop from their entry price. Plasma televisions have also been steadily dropping in price since their release.

Multi-billionaire Microsoft founder Bill Gates said this year the digital evolution of technology is progressing faster than expected. This may be good news for consumers, but what does it mean for manufacturers? It means they have to stay on their toes and always be ready to produce and market the 'next big thing', almost before it has been invented.

It also means they have to keep watching their costs. A cheap workforce becomes a necessity rather than an option when profit margins become so narrow. For instance, Matsushita, which makes Panasonic and Technics products, closed its television factories in Wales in 2004 and relocated the jobs to the Czech Republic. Sony cut hundreds of jobs at its plants in Wales in 2005.

(*Source*: Based on Hamada, 2005)

3. Introducing superior manufacturing techniques.

4. Introducing products with superior technology or design features.

5. Fine-tuning the marketing mix.

Allowing market uncertainty to disappear

One key reason many companies enter second, or late, is because it carries less risk. They prefer to conserve their resources while the pioneer tests the viability of the market. The pioneer in effect does the expensive upfront market-testing, from which followers are able to use to gauge market attractiveness and profit potentiality. For example, Coca-Cola initially refrained from the caffeine-free, juice-added, and cherry flavours but now commands all three markets. IBM entered mainframe computers after Sperry, and in the PC market followed on after Apple. In the clothing sector this strategy is deployed regularly. Fashion houses bring out new styles, and the retail giants select the designs that show the greatest potential for the mass market. By the time the retailers get 'into' the new product a lot of the risk has been taken out.

Learning from the pioneer's market experience

The first-mover charts its innovation through unknown territory. The pioneer's trials and tribulations are an invaluable source of experience for others to learn from. Learning from the pioneer's mistakes is very useful. Typically, market research for new product introductions can be in the range of £7–10 million, and followers can capitalise on this by simply keeping track and carefully analysing the pioneer's market strategy and actions. For example, California Cooler introduced wine coolers, which were very successful and appealed to females who did not want to drink beer. Gallo noted how female orientated the drink was, and how important the different flavours were to the market, and used this insight in developing Bartles & Jaymes. The introduction of Bartles & Jymes, accompanied by a highly focussed advertising campaign, had a devastating impact on sales of California Cooler.

Introducing superior manufacturing techniques

Pioneers with strong manufacturing competences and resources can leverage their innovation maximally by adopting an aggressive policy of low-cost volume production and using price to under-cut competition. Likewise, if the follower possesses such strength it can use it to overtake the pioneer. A follower strategy that is designed to overtake the pioneer, or other competitors, is referred to as an *out-pace* strategy. Out-pacing strategies, as used here, refers to deliberate plans and strategic actions designed to overtake existing competitors in an industry.

For example, Texas Instruments was able to take out Bowmar, the pioneer of hand-held calculators by leveraging its superior manufacturing capability. In only a matter of three years the pioneer had to exit the market. Matsushita is another company that regularly employs this strategy to devastating effect. 3Com's Palm pilot has out-paced Sharp's Wizard in the personal electronic organiser category, and Amazon.com sped past Barnes & Noble in the book retailing industry.

Introducing products with superior design attributes

Followers have the advantage of time to perfect their product offering, whereas the innovator tends not to enjoy such luxury. Often the product that is brought out first will in fact not be the right product because nobody could have predicted precisely what the right product should have been. Followers have the benefit of using the pioneer's hindsight. They follow on the heels of the pioneer with a second product that is an improvement on the original entrants. Pioneers can pre-empt this from happening if they correctly predict market needs. Doing so enables them to occupy the best spaces in terms of market positioning. In such scenarios, followers are forced into inferior market positioning spaces. If the pioneer's product does not fit perfectly, it leaves room for the fast followers to gain immediate advantage by filling in the gaps. For example, Toyota was able to overtake VW in the small car market by commissioning specific research to probe what aspect of the car VW owners liked, disliked and what they desired the car to have. Toyota used this to design a small car with all the desired attributes and none of the turn-offs.

Fine-tuning the marketing efforts

Followers can fine-tune their marketing efforts specifically to lure customers away from the pioneer. This strategy was used by Gallo against California Cooler. In 1982, California

Cooler had 75 per cent market share. One year following the introduction of Bartles & Jaymes, the share had fallen by 20 per cent. By 1986, Gallo's B&J was the market leader. Gallo achieved this by identifying a slight mismatch in the fit between the California Cooler's product and the market. Instead of beer type of packaging, B&J designed a more sophisticated wine type of package. Fruit sediment was removed from the product to give it a wine-like taste. Also, by eschewing higher price they cut out the possibility of their product being perceived as a higher-end niche product. These creative modifications gave the follower a more sophisticated look and positioning, which appealed to a larger market. In other words, a follower with creative imagination can modify a pioneer's idea to build a more desirable product and with it a more profitable business.

Followers are often labelled as imitators. Unfortunately, this label is used in a derogatory manner. The huge success of imitators should indicate that imitating is a positive and pro-active strategy and it requires considerable skill. Imitation strategy used by companies such as Matsushita is not a secondary or inferior strategy. It is a primary strategy that requires honed competences, which enable its proponents to overhaul even the strongest of pioneers.

There is a a distinction between *pure imitation*, a simple one-way transfer of knowledge, and the *reflective imitation* practised by Japanese firms. Pure imitation provides little competitive advantage to the borrower. However, reflective imitation, as practised by the Japanese firms, is an elevated strategy that goes far beyond simple copying and transfer of knowledge. It requires active adaptation to a new setting and reflects specific requirements of new user(s) or segment(s). Accordingly, when followers employ this form of elevated imitation they are able to successfully challenge pioneering firms.

ILLUSTRATION

Inventors, pioneers and followers

Have you heard of Gablinger or Chux? Most likely not, but perhaps you should have since each has an important place in the history of product innovation. Gablinger developed low-alcohol lager and Chux sold the first disposable nappies.

For most people, these are forgotten companies because none of them were able to make a commercial success of their innovations. More likely than not the low-alcohol beer you drink is Miller Lite, and the nappies your children are wearing are made by Procter & Gamble. In each of these markets the innovator was swept aside.

The business world is not always kind to pioneers. Take EMI as an example. The company's history is one of a remarkable record of innovation. EMI was a pioneer in television and computing and its CAT scanner transformed radiography. Yet it has not made any of these products for many years. Our televisions come from Sony and our computers from Dell.

Contrast EMI's experience with that of Glaxo Wellcome. Each had, in the 1970s, a product that would ultimately take the US healthcare market by storm. Both the CAT scanner and anti-ulcerants were to win Nobel prizes for the British scientists who invented them.

But there the similarities end. EMI was proud to employ Geoffrey Houndsfield, who invented the scanner. It established a US distribution network and manufacturing facility to exploit his innovation – and was quickly crushed by the superior political, marketing and technical skills of GE.

James Black, who developed anti-ulcerants, did not work for Glaxo, but for SmithKline. Glaxo's Zantac was an imitative product, second to market. US distribution was initially contracted out to Hoffman la Roche. The superior marketing skills of Glaxo and its partners enabled Zantac to overtake

→

SmithKline's Tagamet and become the world's best-selling drug. Glaxo's achievement was based not on the speed or quality of its innovation but on its commercial skills in exploiting it.

It seems that what we take as a first-mover advantage is often only that because we tend to mistake the successful innovator as the first mover.

There are two closely related lessons. One is that being first is not often very important. The other is that innovation is rarely a source of competitive advantage on its own. Individuals and small companies can make a great deal of money out of good new ideas. The success of large established corporations is generally based on other things: their distribution capability, their depth of technical expertise, their marketing skills. Time and again these characteristics enable them to develop the innovative concept far more effectively than the innovators themselves.

(*Source:* An updated version of J. Kay, 'Why the last shall be the first and the first shall fade away', *FT*, 13 May 1998, p. 19)

Choosing between strategies: pioneering versus following

In some industries it seems there are distinct disadvantages in pioneering. One such industry is electronics, in which it pays to wait for the market to materialise and then leapfrog past the pioneer. A *leapfrog strategy* is one in which firms bypass the current innovation in order to adopt a future innovation.

In general both pioneering and follower strategies are capable of producing success and long-term competitive advantage. The choice of strategy requires weighing the relative advantages and disadvantages of each approach for the specific entry question at hand. Consideration of two specific factors is helpful in arriving at this decision.

1. Sustainability of product market leadership position

Pioneering should be selected if competitors can not easily imitate the firm's innovation or the firm is able to innovate at a faster pace than competitors. The *out-strip* (or *out-innovate*) strategy is predicated on creative destruction, which renders duplication efforts redundant. For example, Gillette has been able to maintain its position in the low-tech sector of shaving products by continuous product introductions and effective marketing to avoid product cannibalisation. The ability to sustain such a strategy depends on the rate of innovation diffusion, and the ability of the firm to control it. Firms can slow the rate, or at least partially control it, by means of:

- Patents.
- Trade secrets.
- In-house development of product prototypes.
- Vertical integration into competitor-sensitive areas.
- Enlightened personnel policies and innovative reward systems.

Pioneering is also favoured when it is possible to clearly identify characteristics and needs of the early adopter segment(s), and predict shifts in socio-economic trends, and their nature and impact on emergent markets. Pioneering also benefits when few alternatives or substitute technologies exist on the horizon.

2. Ability to dictate rules of the game

Pioneering is likely to be successful if the firm is able to dictate the rules of the game, and by so doing create specific competitive advantages. These advantages may be derived from:

- Reputation for quality and service, which translates into long-term brand loyalty.
- Pre-emptive positioning in the most attractive market segment(s).
- Higher share of 'voice', which is reciprocally related to market share.
- Freedom of choice in market channel(s), allowing the first-mover to choose the best distributors, retailers and agents as partners. This is especially the case if the pioneer can form exclusive links that deny the follower market access.
- Skill and experience in manufacturing, allowing for a permanent cost advantage.
- De facto definition of category/standards against which late entrants are judged.

Many companies, such as Coca-Cola, McDonald's, Wrigley and Del-Monte have vigorously built and protected their positions by constantly changing the rules of the game in their favour.

The conditions under which an imitation or follower strategy may provide equivalent, if not superior, returns to innovation are, in general, converse to conditions favouring the pioneer. Five such conditions include (Bolton, 1993):

1. Industries with weak intellectual property.
2. Technologically interdependent industries.
3. Industries with high market and technical uncertainty.
4. Industries with rapid technological change.
5. Industries with rapid information flow.

Defensive strategies by the pioneer

Whilst pioneers are generally market dominators, reversal of their fortunes can, and do, occur. In the consumer goods industries companies such as Bird's Eye Walls, Campbell, Goodyear, Hallmark, Kleenex and Wrigley have been market leaders for years. In the industrial market sector, companies such as DuPont, Alcoa, Xerox, Pitney Bowes and John Deere have been leading their markets for decades. However, in both consumer and industrials markets, some pioneers have fallen by the wayside. Unsuccessful pioneers include Reynolds International Pen (ball-point pens), Bowmar Instruments (hand-held electronic calculators), Royal Crown Cola (diet and caffeine-free colas) and Advent (large-screen television). The British firm EMI was the first to enter the CT scanner market but GE rapidly overtook it by quickly coming out with a second-generation technology. SmithKline's Tagamet was the first to market as a treatment for heartburn but Glaxo's Zantac surpassed it. The question is how can the pioneer defend against being overtaken?

Defensive steps against potential incumbents need to be planned by pioneers before the actual competitive threat takes place. The nature of defence must be appropriate to the nature of the new entrant threat. Failing to recognise significant threats can ultimately be disastrous but at the same time over-reacting to minor threats is a waste. IBM ignored Cray as a competitor by thinking of it as a limited niche operator in the supercomputer market. As the niche grew, IBM was forced to take note and respond. However, protecting all niches can be expensive and tricky because it can extend a company thinly across too many fronts. On the other hand, niches offer footholds which allow followers opportunity to launch battles for market dominance, or grow the niche market to a dominant market. Robertson and Gatignon (1991) propose three types of defence reactions:

- Attack or retaliation strategy.
- Co-operation or accommodation of a new entrant.
- Abandoning the market.

Attack or retaliation strategy

This is the most aggressive of actions, and is often the pioneer's first inclination, but it may not be the optimal. The pioneer should take pre-emptive strikes if:

- It holds a significant competitive advantage in critical areas of operation. For example, Philip Morris found it very difficult to get a foothold in the beer market because Anheuser-Bush enjoyed distribution and image advantages. The strength of the Budweiser brand, an intangible asset built over a long period, made it extremely difficult for Philip Morris to overcome Anheuser-Bush's advantage.

- The new entrant is not able to build economies of scale enjoyed by the pioneer (i.e. the pioneer can price the new entrant out of the market). For example, Coco-Cola had to withdraw from its entry into the market because Gallo enjoyed large distribution and cost advantages. A second example is Nutrasweet, which utilised pricing to foil competitive market entry by leveraging its superior cost structure and scale of operation.

- The new entrant's access to resources is low to medium.

If a retaliation strategy is adopted it is necessary for the firm to decide how and in which domain this attack is to be conducted. The firm has a number of options:

- Direct attack in pioneer's 'home' market domain.
- Indirect attack, in which the counter-offensive takes place in markets where the new entrant is already operating.
- Direct and indirect attack.

Co-operation or accommodation of new entrant

This strategy is based on the realisation that either there is no point in a full-frontal attack because the action would be detrimental in the long run for both parties, and/or because there is room in the marketplace to accommodate more than one player. Moreover, it may be the case that the pioneer welcomes the newcomer because the new entrant's investment is necessary to fuel market development, i.e. not all new entrants are necessarily threats, instead they can be co-operative partners in developing the market. Pioneers also need to take into account that reacting aggressively against strong entrants can lead to reverse retaliation. In the chemical sector, investment in even setting up a single plant can easily run into hundreds of millions. Here, given the level of investment, any reaction by the pioneer is likely to be met with equal counter-force. Conditions leading to adoption of this strategy are:

- Lack of minimal advantage vis-à-vis competitors.
- Equivalent scale of new entrant.
- New entrant has equivalent accessibility to resources.

Abandoning the market

It is quite possible that the pioneer is overwhelmed by the superiority of a new entrant. The new entrant may have a better product as well as depth of resources and competencies. When outclassed across a number of critical dimensions the pioneer is left with little choice but to manage a graceful exit rather than incur losses in an unwinnable battle. The exit may be speedy or a slow planned retrenchment.

Pioneers' response to competition

Pioneers naturally expect competition, and thus take steps to try and circumvent entry as far as possible, especially from strong rivals and have counter-plans at hand when it does happen. A number of marketing-based counter-measures that can be used are briefly elaborated below.

Price response

Price should be reduced if:

- The market is price-sensitive.
- There is high cross-elasticity of demand.
- Experience curve and economies of scale are strong.

Product response

Late entrants may pursue differentiation instead of cost to penetrate the market. This requires the pioneer to enhance its offering as soon as competitor products are able to achieve product parity. The pioneer can combat entrant attack by incorporating innovations into the core product, thereby constantly enhancing it.

The pioneer may reposition or extend positioning if market needs are heterogeneous, and differentiation and segmentation are possible. The pioneer needs to ensure that it subsumes any salient product dimensions that the new entrants offer. For example, Toyota's entry with the Lexus into the luxury car market led to BMW, Mercedes and others in the luxury end of the market to 'up' their game in terms of quality and price performance.

The pioneer may consider introducing a second brand, or more brands, if market demand is growing and substantial. This is a good strategy to follow if the likelihood of cannibalisation is low, and the segment is sufficiently price-insensitive as to allow for a second differentiated offering.

Communications response

Communications strategies can build significant barriers to entry. By establishing a strong brand identity new entrants can be kept at bay. For instance, it has been very difficult for new entrants to get a foothold in the breakfast cereals market because the existing corporate and brand identities are so strong in the minds of the consumer. New entrants in such markets do so by buying brand equity via acquisitions. For example, Philip Morris acquired Kraft Foods and General Foods to purchase brand names.

Distribution response

The pioneer may choose to broaden its distribution channels as it progresses through the stages of the life cycle to reach the mass market. If the market is evolving, new distribution channels can be developed, or channels can be tied up to slow the sales from new entrants.

Emergence of dominant design over the life cycle

To develop strategies, an organisation must possess intimate understanding of the evolution of a product, particularly the process through which a dominant design emerges. The emergence of a dominant design is a defining event that drastically affects the pattern of competition and drastically reduces the probabilities for success for subsequent entrants (Utterback and Suarez, 1993). Firms that incorporate key attributes of what will in the future become the dominant product design into their product line have twice the likelihood of survival than those that ignore the emergence of the dominant design (Christensen et al., 1998).

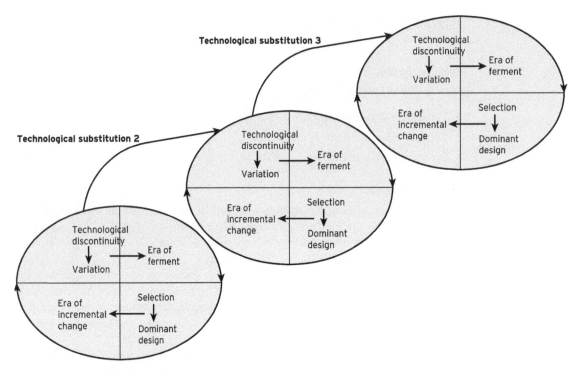

FIGURE 3.6 Technology cycles over time
Source: Adapted from Tushman et al., 1997

A widely used model to describe organisational adaptation to technologial change is the punctuated equilibrium model (Romanelli and Tushman, 1997). A central feature of this model is the concept of dominant design. Industry leaders can lose out to late entrants because they have difficulty in managing technological discontinuities. As noted earlier, industry evolves through a succession of technology cycles, which can be patterned as S-curves.

Each technological cycle comprises of alternating periods of technological variation, competitive selection and retention (convergence) (see Figure 3.6). Each cycle begins with a technological discontinuity, which represents a radical technological shift. The radical innovation initiates a technology cycle. A new radical innovation has the effect of rupturing the existing pattern of incremental innovation and initiates an era of ferment, in which competing technological regimes vie for market acceptance and dominance.

The era of ferment can be divided into two sub-stages: the era of substitution and the era of design competition (see Figure 3.7). In the era of substitution the new technology displaces the old. However, older technology rarely exits without a fierce fight. The new technology is frequently attacked, especially in its embryonic introduction because in its formative development it may not work well and is based on unproven assumptions and untested competences. To ward off threats from newcomers, the existing community attempt to improve their offer by innovating incrementally upon the existing technology. For example, mechanical typewriters, mechanical watches, and piston jets all exhibited performance improvements once they were challenged by new technologies. The second sub-stage involves design competition. This is an overlapping stage with the first, in which the original radical innovation is refined from its crude introduction. Typically, several competing design variants emerge, each embodying the fundamental breakthrough technology in a

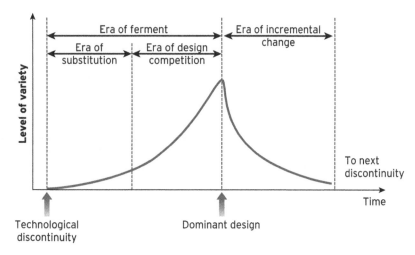

FIGURE 3.7 Nature of competition over the technology life cycle

different way. For example, once the first personal computer was introduced, it was quickly followed by numerous versions, each with its own (and often different and incompatible) microprocessor architecture, disk and operating system format.

The period of design variation eventually comes to a head with the emergence of a single dominant design, a single basic product architecture that becomes the market standard. The dominant design is a specific path along an industry's design trajectory that establishes dominance among competing design paths.

CASE STUDY

Compatibility partnerships

Matsushita and Sony agreed to jointly develop Linux operating system software for digital consumer electronic products in a highly unusual co-operative deal between two of the fiercest rivals in the industry. The deal was a boost to Linux, an open operating system that is written in non-proprietary code and is widely used in personal computers and servers. The agreement between two of the world's largest consumer electronics makers was a blow to Microsoft, which also wanted to expand its presence in the home user market.

Matsushita and Sony aimed to establish a forum of electronics producers supporting the project, including Hitachi, IBM, NEC, Philips, Samsung and Sharp.

The agreement highlighted the growing complexity of consumer electronics products. Devices from TVs to air conditioners use operating systems to perform sophisticated tasks such as processing digital signals or maintaining room temperature. So far, manufacturers such as Sony and Matsushita have used a variety of operating systems including their own proprietary systems. By jointly developing Linux for consumer electronic use and encouraging the wide adoption of Linux within the industry, Matsushita and Sony hope to significantly improve the efficiency of product development.

They chose Linux mainly because it is widely used, open to the public and has many supporters. This means it is easier for manufacturers to seek the support of their suppliers and subcontractors, Sony said.

→

'We are not forming an alliance to compete against Microsoft', said a Matsushita representative. Nevertheless, the intent was relatively clear. Sony and Matsushita continued to use existing operating systems for specific products – such as Windows for Vaio – but expected the newly developed version of Linux to be increasingly used in consumer electronic devices, such as portable and home audio–video products.

By 2008 the Linux development had led to a 'Web appliance' that could browse the Web and perform simple e-mail tasks. Unfortunately, although there was the software and engineering talent available to produce these devices, customers did not want to be limited to only these tasks, particularly since mobile phones were gaining many of the same technologies. However, the companies had also developed 'embedded systems' that used very limited amounts of memory and could thus be used in many domestic appliances such as mobile phones, digital TVs, set-top boxes and automotive telematics.

QUESTIONS

1. Why do you think Matsushita and Sony decided to use Linux? What advantage(s) may this confer and what potential future problems may this also cause?

(*Source*: Updated version of M. Nakamoto, 'Matsushita, Sony to develop Linux for home devices', *Financial Times*, 19 December 2002, p. 27)

The emergence of a dominant design marks the transition from a period of ferment to a period of incremental change. The dominant design reduces the level of uncertainty and risk associated with the technological discontinuity by locking in to a specific product design format. This process is facilitated by the support of a network of suppliers, customers and other firms. From this point onwards, the rate of design experimentation drops, and the focus of organisational attention switches to market positioning and customer targeting, as well as lowering of operational costs through design simplification and process innovation.

Dominant design and the notion of a 'standard' are used often interchangeably. An industry standard, when narrowly defined, is largely the outcome from technical rivalry. In contrast, when broadly defined, a standard is the format that is accepted for current use through authority, custom or general consent. The broad notion of dominant design indicates the role of factors other than technology alone as a key influence over the adoption of a specific design format and its emergence to a position of dominance. Dominant designs emerge from an interplay of firm-level factors, strategic manoeuvres, environment factors and chance events.

- *Firm-level factors*: Firm endowments such as size, strength, reputation and image play a role in pushing forward a specific design path in the race to establish dominant design.
- *Strategic manoeuvres*: Strategic manoeuvring such as building alliances with other competing firms and supply chain participants can help in the adoption process. Sony's betamax was defeated by JVC's VHS technology primarily because VHS licensed its technology and built numerous alliances with worldwide manufacturers, as well as initiating schemes with retailers to draw customer patronage.
- *Environment*: A host of general environmental factors (suppliers, customers, competitors) can play a role in the emergence of the standard. From amongst these, one of the most prominent is government regulation, which can have the effect of enforcing upon an industry a specific standard. For example, the Federal Communications Commission's (FCC) approval of the Radio Company of America's (RCA) television broadcast standard effectively drove out other competing claims, making RCA design dominant in the TV industry.

- *Chance*: Besides systematic strategies to establish the firm's variant as the standard, good fortune, timing and coincidence can all play a role in the emergence of the standard.

A dominant design enforces standardisation, and thereby allows accumulation of gains from economies of scale and learning. Contrary to popular belief and expectation, a dominant design need not necessarily be the best from the competing designs. It is simply the design format that emerges from a complex combination of fortuitous circumstances, encompassing technology, economic and organisational factors.

The emergence of a dominant design leads to a period of incremental change, in which process innovation replaces product innovation as the engine of change and improvement. During this period the dominant design is incrementally changed, yet over time it undergoes profound improvements. Additionally, the emergence of dominant design allows the development of product platforms. Product platforms allow development of product families, which share common architecture, components and interfaces.

Which design format will win out is an uncertain process. The consequences of betting on the wrong technology can have disastrous consequences. Since the dominant design represents the 'winning technology', the pay-off from developing, choosing or adopting the dominant format is higher. Once the dominant design establishes itself as the winning format it usually becomes the single accepted industry architecture, and over time other designs fade out. Even if more than one technology persists, because of technology lock-in, higher returns are likely for dominant design adopters. Optimal design strategies are contingent upon whether the firm enters before or after a dominant design emerges (see Figure 3.8). Firms will either:

- Enter early and if necessary change to the dominant design. Firms that enter early find that the dominant design is an evolution of the original innovation, and not the innovation itself. In most cases the initial choices made by early entrants are not likely to be the finally chosen format. Thus, for early entrants the key to success and the maintenance

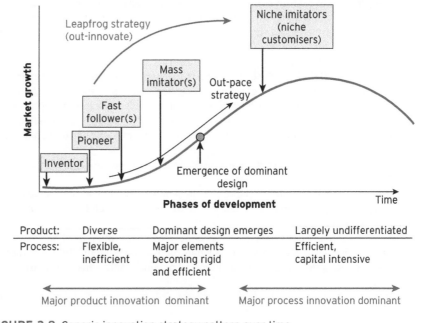

FIGURE 3.8 Generic innovation strategy pattern over time

of first-mover advantages is their ability to change their product designs in line with the emerging dominant format.

● Or delay entry so as to increase the likelihood that they choose the dominant design the first time. This strategy leads to obvious benefits but incurs switching costs as well as strong competition from established companies.

The emergent dominant design fulfils the requirements of many users but at its early inception often does not meet exactly the requirements of any particular market segment. The company responsible for the creation of this design accrues significant returns during this period because the battle for customers swings in their favour. Companies that follow have to emulate the design format. Follower companies emulate the dominant design by incorporating features into their version of the dominant design to attract customers to their offering. For instance, if price is a key factor for customers the follower firms should adopt low cost strategies. If specific features or additional services are required then differentiation strategies ought to be implemented.

ILLUSTRATION

Challenging Wintel

Semiconductor architects from IBM, Sony and Toshiba unveiled details of a 'supercomputer on a chip' [in February 2005]. This chip was a serious challenge to industry leader Intel, particularly for its ambitions to move into the digital home.

Just at the same time that Intel announced it had completed initial production runs of its latest processor featuring just two cores, IBM, Sony and Toshiba revealed that their four-year-old joint venture had produced a chip containing nine separate processors, or 'cores'. Intel, however, maintained that its dual-core products would be available in the second quarter of 2005, compared with a 2006 launch date for products containing the joint ventures Cell processor. The Cell processor made its debut in Sony's next-generation PlayStation 3 games console, high-definition TVs from Sony and Toshiba and a Sony home server for broadband content.

Cell features a new version of IBM's PowerPC processor controlling eight other 'Synergistic Processor Elements' (SPEs), which can also act autonomously carrying out separate tasks. Its designers said this would mean complex graphics processes could be shared out to achieve photo-realistic effects, while users would not suffer the waiting time currently experienced when data-intensive applications were being run. In a hint that they planned to challenge the dominance of the 'Wintel' alliance of Microsoft's software and Intel's hardware, the designers said that Cell could run multiple operating systems simultaneously.

'I would be really concerned if I were Intel', said Dan Sokol, analyst with Envisioneering, a research firm. 'This looks one hell of a processor.'

An Intel spokesman countered that Cell's developers would need time to build a software ecosystem supporting the chip and that Intel had learnt to incorporate chip innovations into its own industry-compatible architecture.

With computing and consumer electronics devices converging, Intel has set up a Digital Home division that is showcasing a prototype of a living-room entertainment PC. But, there is no denying that Cell poses a serious threat to Intel's ambition to dominate this emergent market.

(*Source*: C. Nuttall, 'Joint ventures new chip set to rival Intel', *Financial Times*, 8 February 2005, p. 23)

Innovation protection strategies

Once a firm introduces a product onto the market it needs to protect its position and profit stream from encroachments from competitors. To ensure a flow of profits the innovating firm must take action not just in the marketplace but across the entire business chain. During the battle for dominant design and in the period after its establishment the focus of the competitive challenge switches to one involving customer lock-in, competitor lock-out and establishing a proprietary standard for network participants to adopt.

Locking in customers

A firm can increase switching costs if it is able to enhance the appeal of its product by matching more closely the needs of customers. This requires it to build a superior product offer through effective leverage of the marketing mix. Providing technical support, service support and ease of customer access to the product through good management of distribution channels facilitates customer lock-in. Customised product offerings take the 'lock-in' strategy a step further by incrementally raising the customer's switching costs.

Locking out competitors

Companies can lock out potential competition by taking steps that restrict access to key activities in the value chain. Companies that own strong brands can leverage bargaining power to ensure that their products are stocked instead of competitors, or are located in premium positions within the retail store. Competitors can be locked out by a constant stream of innovations (out-innovate strategy), making competitor offerings redundant. Patents offer a highly effective method for locking out competition. For some industries, such as the pharmaceutical industry, patents are the main way of circumventing competitive encroachment.

Sustaining proprietary standards

Companies that are able to establish a network of suppliers, manufacturers and users are able to erect significant barriers to entry. These protective strategies involve to varying degree three sub-elements: block, run and team-up.

Blocking as a defensive strategy

The basis of this defensive strategy is to take action to stop competitors entering the industry and/or limit the effectiveness of their entry. Blocking may be achieved by:

- Maintaining, enhancing and sustaining unique capabilities. Capabilities of the firm are unique, and difficult to copy.
- Protecting knowledge sources. Proprietary knowledge can be protected by legal means, patents, etc.
- Signalling intent to stay and compete fiercely in the market. Signals may be of managerial commitment, as well as marketplace threats such as dropping price.
- Increasing commitment by scaling up operations to reap economies as well as signalling intent to remain in the industry for the long run.

Running as a defensive strategy

Firms following the run strategy try to keep ahead of the competition through continuous innovation. In doing so, they often cannibalise existing products and make obsolete parts of the existing capabilities. This strategy is followed if it is believed that competitors are able to navigate around patents, copyrights and other protective measures. In other words, the strategy concedes that all its blockades will eventually be overcome. Here, the profit stream is maintained by adopting an active defence, namely one of becoming a constant innovator and first mover.

Teaming up as a defensive strategy

The team-up strategy looks like the opposite of a block strategy. Instead of preventing entry it invites entry. However, it does so only by inviting those participants that will help the company build a stronger position and protect it from direct competition. The logic of this strategy is based on the relative gains from such action. The gain can be in the form of the following:

- *Allow it to win the battle for dominant design*: As more firms use the design variant of the firm the higher is the likelihood of it becoming the industry standard. The process works through a virtuous cycle: the more other manufacturers use the design, the more likely that complementary innovators will commit to it in developing their products. The more innovators that commit to the design the higher is the likelihood of customers choosing it. The more the customers choose it, the likelier that other manufacturers will adopt it.

- *Stimulate market demand*: By giving away technology to others, the company can stimulate market demand without having to bear by itself all the burden of capital and marketing investments.

- *Build capabilities*: Some innovators do not possess the full range of resources, and have to rely on partnerships to realise innovation. For example, licensing is common practice in small pharmaceutical firms. These firms need the resources of larger firms to conduct clinical trials that are required to get through the arduous process of drug approval.

- *Second source effect*: In some industries, particularly those involving large-scale customer investment and long-term commitment such as the defence sector, and semiconductors, etc., buyers insist on the existence of alternative (or second) sources of supply. This is to ensure that future generations of products and components are available to them when they need them.

- *Access to markets*: Teaming up is a rapid way of gaining access to markets, especially international ones.

CASE STUDY

Strategies for pace of innovation in fast-moving consumer sector

In the world of fast-moving consumer goods, innovation has long been recognised as one way of staying ahead of competitors. Another is marketing. Gillette, the US company that dominated the global shaving products market, combines both.

Since it introduced the first twin-blade razor (the Trac II) in 1971, Gillette had launched a razor about every nine years. In 1977 the Atra added a pivoting head. Released in 1990, the Sensors spring-mounted blades promised an even closer shave. Sensor helped Gillette establish dominance over the wet-shave market in North America and Western Europe, with 70 per cent of sales.

In 1998 Mach3 was launched as Gillette's latest wet-shave razor, with the Boston-based company investing more than $1bn (£600m) in the new product, with a $300m advertising budget for the first year alone.

'Each of these [innovations] is protected by patents, making it next to impossible for competitors to copy', said Bob King, head of the company's North Atlantic group.

Manufacturing strategy

Gillette installed a production line to reduce unit costs on Mach3. It made the cartridges in a continuous process. This allowed Mach3 to be launched in more than 100 markets by year end – a roll-out that had taken more than four years with Sensor.

Schick's four-blade surprise

In September 2003 Gillette then found itself on the defensive after Schick launched its four-blade Quattro razor. Immediately, Gillette reacted by filing a suit against Schick.

Gillette wanted Quattro banned from the market. 'An injunction is not the norm', said David Schlitz, a patent lawyer. 'It is an extraordinary remedy.' Despite this Gillette could not block Quattro's introduction to market; the legal process was long and arduous. Schick was stressing the differences from Mach3, whilst Gillette was trying to focus on the shaving systems' similarities.

As shoppers began buying the four-blade razor, the stakes for both Schick and Gillette started to rise dramatically. Accumulating profits for Quattro would be good news for Schick but only if the company was able to keep them. A judge might have ruled that Quattro earnings belong to Gillette.

The case was risky for Gillette as well. If the injunction filing was found to have no basis, a judge could have awarded Schick substantial damages.

The patent suit against Schick centred on the position of Quattro's blades. In developing the Mach3 in the 1990s, Gillette hit upon a way to achieve a closer shave without irritating the skin: the razor aligned blades progressively closer to the skin so that each one cut closer than the last. The patents covering Mach3 – and there were more than 50 of them at that time – described the positioning of those blades in excruciating detail, specifying the ideal millimetres of distance between the blades. 'The technology applies, whether you're using three blades, four or five', says Eric Kraus, a spokesman for Gillette.

One obvious question was why Gillette failed to invent the four-blade razor itself. The company had long held that simply adding more blades did not ensure a better product. But Schick said four blades achieved a closer shave, and that its product accomplished this without skin irritation.

The case was settled out of court in 2006. In 2005, Gillette released the Fusion Model with five blades.

QUESTIONS

1. What type of innovation strategy was Gillette following?
2. What type of protection strategy did it use, and how effective was it?
3. Why do you think Schick stole the lead on Gillette? How did Gillette allow this to happen?

(*Source*: An updated version of V. Griffith, 'Schick and Gillette take fight to edge', *FT*, 16 September 2003, p. 31)

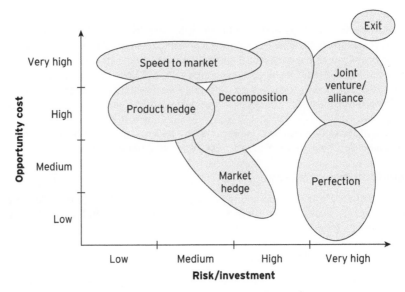

FIGURE 3.9 Options map for innovation strategies

Strategic alternatives: mapping for innovation options

Being fast to market is of little advantage if the wrong choice of innovation is made (technology, design, etc.), i.e. if it is not what the customers want. Being a late entrant is equally unfeasible if the market is going to be totally captured by early entrants. The opportunity of missing a fast-moving window of opportunity and the risk of entering have pulls in opposite directions. In the world of practice, managers rarely have the time to consider the range of issues and competing demands. Often they yield to the momentum of historical circumstance. Strategies used in the past are often repeated without due diligence to emerging contexts. But one size does not fit all. Situations in which market needs are clear and competitors predictable warrant markedly different approaches than those appropriate for high degrees of uncertainty. Each situation has a different context, and these differences imply different management actions and strategies. A simple way to capture the strategic options facing the firm at a given moment is to map its context along two dimensions: risk of entry and opportunity cost (see Figure 3.9).

This strategic map is useful in highlighting the strategy most appropriate to the specific cost–opportunity dilemma facing an organisation. The main elements of the map will be discussed briefly here.

Speed to market

When entry risk is low but opportunity cost is high, it is important to manage the innovation process to get to market as soon as possible. Under these circumstances an innovation strategy, and thus implicitly the management of the innovation process, stressing speed rather than risk reduction is the best option.

Perfection strategy

At the other end of the continuum to the speed-to-market strategy is the perfection strategy. In this strategy, the opportunity cost is low but the risks of not getting it right are so high that it is necessary for the firm to ensure that it takes minimal or, even better, no risk. A typical industry facing this type of scenario is the aircraft manufacture industry. In the development of an aircraft, a company like Boeing or Airbus can take no risks. Product shortfall, even in a minor way, has the potential of bringing the entire company to its knees.

De-composition strategy

This is used when the development risk and opportunity cost are equally important. This approach involves breaking down a complex development task into a series of smaller discrete steps. By breaking a complex innovation into a sequence of limited challenges it becomes possible to contain development risks and keep development costs under control.

Northern Telecom used this strategy in developing the DMS 100 switch. The DMS 100 was a digital system that challenged the then leader of analogue systems AT&T/Western Electric. The challenge of development included overcoming numerous technical hurdles: development of a family of local transit and international switches, development of advanced semiconductor technology, filter-code chips, high-density packaging and a new high-level software language. The technical challenges were estimated to require $200 million in development investment. This amounted to nearly half the entire company's equity. Also, moving to a radically different technology and system meant that there was high uncertainty (technological and market) at the outset over which features the DMS would include. Under this scenario, the only safe route was to break the task into smaller 'bite sizes'.

Market hedge strategy

This strategy is most appropriate when opportunity costs matter, but not as much as entry risk. To reduce market risk it is necessary to test the product but the test has to be conducted outside the company's normal activities and markets, i.e. in an outside niche. The market hedge (or outside niche) strategy reduces the development risks without exposing the company's innovation to its current product's customers. This strategy allows the innovating company to hold onto its mature products as long as possible without cannibalisation or competitor disruption. Sony used this in its audio studio business when moving its products from analogue to digital.

Product hedge strategy (mixed product: old and new)

This strategy is relevant when entry risk matters but not as much as the opportunity cost. Under such circumstances there is pressure to enter the market quickly and it may be that the product and the market are not entirely prepared for a newer version. Under these circumstances, companies may put out a product hybrid variant that contains elements of the new mixed in with the old. Sweden's Ericsson used this approach in putting to market the AXE 10, a partially digitised local switch. Ericsson did so because it was faced with a situation in which, if it did not make it to market first, a competitor would do so, and this would result in it being effectively locked out of its markets for 20-plus years. This threat made it

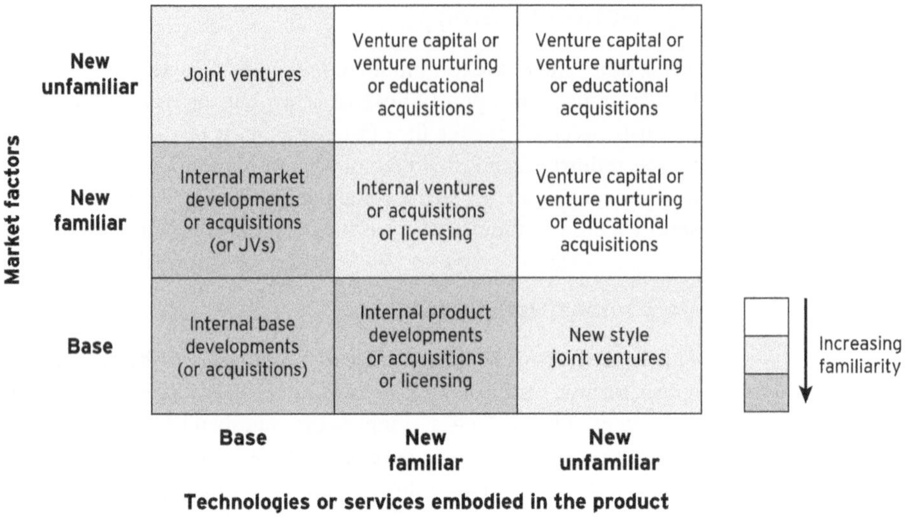

FIGURE 3.10 Optimum entry strategies

imperative that Ericsson got its AXE 10 system into market as early as possible, even though it lacked experience in digital switch technology. To overcome this dilemma, Ericsson offered a new full local switch, but one which was also partially digital. This move allowed Ericsson to slow the move to a fully digital environment, but also allowed it to reduce development and market test costs. Importantly, it allowed AXE to be first to market and establish itself as the front-runner, i.e. opportunity costs were substantially reduced.

Outsource and alliance strategies

In situations where both opportunity cost and entry risk are extremely high, it makes little sense to carry the full burden of development risks and costs in-house. Here, outsource (external collaborations) arrangements, such as joint ventures make sense. If rapid entry is required and the joint venture route is too slow, a financially strong company may opt for the acquisition route. This allows the company to buy into the market. Once a decision to enter a new product market has been made, the mode of entry becomes critical. Figure 3.10 summarises seven alternative entry modes with their advantages and disadvantages.

Internal development and external development (acquisition) represent two opposites of the continuum in terms of approach. Other approaches have a mixture of the characteristics of these two. Developing a new business internally avoids the limitations, liabilities and costs of an acquisition. An internal venture is a variant in which a separate entity within the existing firm is established, so that the business will not be constrained by existing culture, systems and structures.

The selection of the right entry strategy depends on the firm's familiarity with the product market to be entered (Roberts and Berry, 1985). Familiarity is defined along two dimensions:

1. *Market dimension*

    With respect to market factors, three levels of familiarity are defined (familiarity decreases going down the list):

1. *Base*: Existing products are sold within this market.
2. *New/familiar*: The company is familiar with the market because of extensive research, the presence of experienced staff, or by having links with the market as customer.
3. *New/unfamiliar*: Experience and knowledge of the market is lacking.

2. *Technology dimension*

   Three levels of familiarity are associated with the technologies or services embodied in the product dimension (familiarity decreases going down the list):

   1. *Base*: The technology or service is embodied within the existing products.
   2. *New/familiar*: The company is familiar with the technology because of work in related technologies, an established R&D effort in the technology, or extensive focussed research in the technology.
   3. *New/unfamiliar*: Experience and knowledge of the technology is lacking.

As the level of familiarity on these two dimensions declines, the commitment level should be reduced. The figure above shows the optimum strategies recommended from a familiarity assessment. There are, of course, times when a high commitment approach in a new/unfamiliar cell makes sense. However, Roberts and Berry (1985) caution against this approach, since it undertakes high risk, and suggest that gaining familiarity should be seriously considered.

ILLUSTRATION

The logic of alliance strategies

Alliance networks are increasingly becoming a norm in the business model of large companies, especially those in the high-tech sector. For instance, IBM, Fujitsu, NEC, Intel, Microsoft, Merck, Netscape and Monsanto all operate through well-established networks of strategic alliances. Why?

There are a number of reasons:

1. Alliances can be an extremely important strategic tool, especially in industries in which standards (i.e. a set of co-ordinated product designs enabling the components of a system to work together) play, and are influential in, determining the success of one innovation against a competing standard. This is the case in computers, software, telecommunications and video games. These industries often end up being dominated by a single standard. For example, the Microsoft/Intel platform known as Wintel controls the major share of the PC market.

2. Alliances are a very useful tool to introduce major changes in the core business activities of large, conservative and slow-moving companies. Industry leaders tend to be relatively large, highly complex bureaucracies that experience difficulty in making fundamental changes in product market and technology strategy. Alliance networks can be structured to link the hub company to the developers of an array of emerging technologies, allowing the hub of the network to experiment with different technical, operational, and strategic approaches through external linkages.

3. Linked to the above point, alliance networks are vital in areas experiencing technological convergence. The convergence phenomenon is characterised by an increasing interdependence since no single company has mastery over the full range of the technical capabilities to compete in the emerging domain. Such trends are being observed in sectors such as multimedia, telecommunications, and drug discovery.

Monsanto

Monsanto, the life sciences powerhouse, is an excellent example of an organisation that has used an alliance network over decades to spearhead the transformation from an old-line chemicals concern to the cutting edge of biotechnology, and then to cope with the recent, rapid technological convergence in the life sciences.

Under the leadership of John Hanley, CEO in the mid 1970s, Monsanto became very interested in the promise of biotechnology – at the time, a radical new scientific breakthrough – in revolutionising the agriculture business. Since that time, the company has entered over 50 biotech-related alliances (in addition to a number of acquisitions, most notably of the drug company G.D. Searle). Although public concern about the introduction of genetically modified organisms into the food supply has dented some of the potential economic returns from Monsanto's bold strategy, the result nonetheless has been one of the most radical corporate transformations in recent business history.

Monsanto has re-made itself, converting from a plastics and chemical outfit to one of the world's premier life sciences companies, with deep capabilities in biotechnology and major businesses in herbicides, genetically engineered plants, and human drugs. Monsanto's collaborative history includes alliances with a diverse array of organisations: universities, start-up biotech companies, leading drug companies, seed companies and diversified food producers. These partnerships have spanned an equally diverse set of business opportunities.

Four alliances illustratively portray a cross-section of Monsanto's alliance network.

- *Millennium Pharmaceuticals*: Monsanto committed $200m to form a joint venture company, Cereon Genomics, with gene hunter Millennium to develop genomics-based plant and agriculture products. Millennium transferred to Monsanto a range of genomics technologies for use in the development of life sciences products, including pharmaceuticals. This deal followed earlier ones in the genomics area with Incyte Pharmaceuticals, Calgene, Synteni and Ecogen.

- *Cargill*: Partnership to develop genetically enhanced food and animal feed. It combines Monsanto's genetics technology with the resource base of the leading grain and food processing company, which has the capabilities to produce and deliver custom-made foodstuffs worldwide.

- *Pfizer*: Co-development and co-marketing agreement for Celebrex, Monsanto's novel anti-inflammatory compound (the first FDA-approved Cox-2 inhibitor). Among potential drug company partners, Pfizer had the largest US sales force.

- *ArQule*: Monsanto acquired the right to use data produced by Arqule Inc. and its capabilities in structure-guided drug design, modular building block chemistry, combinatorial chemistry and informatics. These data will be used to accelerate the identification of promising molecular candidates for the development of novel crop protection products, herbicides, insecticides and fungicides.

In 2009 Monsanto continued to demonstrate its ability to change its strategy to match changes in the marketplace. 'Over the last six years, Monsanto's business has undergone a dramatic transition from a company historically built on chemical innovations to one focused on delivering enhanced seed offerings', said Chief Executive Hugh Grant. 'Our 2009 fiscal year represents a milestone for our business as our seeds and traits business alone will deliver more gross profit than all of Monsanto did in 2007.'

(*Source*: T.E. Stuart, 'Alliance networks: View from the hub', *FT*, 15 November 1999, p. 4; H. Weitzmann, 'Monsanto earnings beat expectations', *FT*, 24 June 2009)

Disruptive innovation strategy

One type of innovation emerging as strategically important is disruptive innovation – a powerful means for broadening and developing new markets and providing new functionality, which in turn disrupt existing market linkages (Christensen and Raynor, 2003; Gilbert,

2003). This work explored how new technologies came to surpass seemingly superior technologies in a market.

Disruptive innovations are considered to have the five following characteristics:

1. The innovation under-performs on the mainstream customer value.

2. The new features offered by the innovation are not valued by the mainstream customers' value.

3. The innovation typically is simpler and cheaper and is offered at a lower price than existing products.

4. At the time of its introduction, the innovation appeals to a low-end, price-sensitive customer segment, thus limiting the profit potential for incumbents.

5. Over time, further developments improve the innovations performance on the attributes mainstream customers value to a level where the innovation begins to attract more of these customers.

A valuable observation here is that the disruptive technology initially under-performs the dominant one on dimensions the mainstream market demands, but with steady improvements, it meets or exceeds those demands. A second valuable insight is that dominant incumbents are displaced, even though they did what generations of strategists and the basic philosophy in marketing say they should: listen to their mainstream customers (Tellis, 2006).

By way of illustration, a series of disruptive innovations exist and are easily recognised by many; digital cameras relative to analogue cameras, iPod relative to Walkman, gasoline engine relative to the steam engine. In each case, new capabilities were brought to bear on an established market which forced a 'change in the rules'. Consequently, such a strategy depends on the extent an incumbent wishes to either disrupt the market, or the extent that the substitute offering is considered radical from the incumbent product or service.

Innovation ecosystems: a network strategy perspective

We have thus far examined innovation strategy mainly by considering it from an individual firm's perspective. However, as we have noted in earlier chapters, and also indirectly alluded to in this chapter, firms in the modern day rarely act in isolation. Firms, and therefore their strategies, are intermeshed into complex networks of competition. We draw out some of these issues by developing an ecological perspective of firm innovation.

The dynamics of competition over time has been modelled by proponents of the population ecology school of thought (e.g. Moore, 1993). This school of thought models competitive dynamics by adopting a biological analogy. Taking as a reference point the way organisms adapt to their environments, the perspective shows that successful organisations are also those that are able to evolve rapidly with changes in their environment. According to population ecology, the initial entrants into an environment enjoy low levels of direct competition. These initial entrants are called R-strategists. Population density is low and firms are able to freely select segments they wish to serve. If the firm wishes to serve a few segments they are known as R-specialists, and if they choose a large number they are R-generalists. Once a firm makes this decision it becomes difficult for it to change because its historical investment creates barriers to an alternative strategic path (this is known as path dependence). As the environment continues to change fresh opportunities emerge that allow new firms to enter. These late entrants are referred to as K-strategists.

The early stage of the evolution is characterised by significant opportunity but also by great uncertainty. Typically, this phase contains mainly R-specialists and/or perhaps one or two generalists. R-specialists often are small entrepreneurial firms, lacking in resources, and therefore typically focus on small high-return segments. Because of their focus, R-specialists are able to survive better than R-generalists which attempt to serve large segment block(s) at a time of high uncertainty.

Arrival of large numbers of late entrants occurs as market uncertainty is reduced. Typically, the new entrants tend to be of the type labelled K-generalists. These firms focus on areas of inefficiency of early entrants and capitalise upon them. A number of entrants at this stage are K-specialists who customise to reach highly specialist segments that are often too narrow to be served by others. The number of entrants at this stage rises exponentially, until a point of time when the environment's carrying capacity (market capacity) is saturated. This begins an industry shake-out, in which weaker firms, either those that do not fulfil their target segment needs well or those that are not able to withstand competitive under-cutting, are weaned out. Empirical support for the population ecology model was provided in Romanelli's (1987) study of minicomputers. Interestingly, Romanelli's study highlighted, contrary to theoretical expectation, that the majority of entrants were specialists, especially at the emergence stage. The most successful firms adopted a fast-moving and aggressive approach. These firms rapidly adapted and moved from one segment to the next by vigorously introducing new products.

Moore (1993) built on the logic of population ecology model by arguing that businesses do not evolve in a vacuum. The strategic challenges of business success and survival, especially those involving innovation, cannot be viewed purely in terms of an organisation as the unit. Businesses are part of an ecosystem that cuts across a variety of industries (those engaged along the entire business value chain). In a business ecosystem, a network of businesses co-evolve capabilities around a new innovation. Often for an innovation to succeed a number of companies will have to work together, in competition as well as cooperation. For example, Apple computers is a leader of an ecosystem, which involves personal computers, consumer electronics, information and communications. The Apple ecosystem consists of a web of suppliers and distributors, including companies such as Motorola, Sony and large customers. Moreover, in most environments a number of business ecosystems compete for dominance. IBM and Apple are an instance in point. Thus, companies need to be aware of the competition from other ecosystems as well as birth of new ecosystems. Quite often, in business ecosystems organisations face each other as partners as well as competitors.

The challenges of the business ecosystem evolve over time (see Figure 3.11). In the pioneering stage (stage 1) of the business ecosystem, providing customer value is key. It is vitally important for the business ecosystem leader to focus on identifying what customers want and how the product is able to deliver to the identified customer proposition. Survival goes to the network partnership in the ecology that is best able to identify and meet customers' needs. At this stage, it is vitally necessary to ensure that the customer value proposition is fully catered. The network leader must create partnerships with capable firms to ensure that a total solution is delivered. An additional benefit of attracting and making important partnerships for the ecosystem leader is that it partially ensures that these companies do not help out another emerging ecosystem or precipitate their own competitive ecosystem. The Apple ecosystem had to woo and tie in hardware manufacturer, software designers, and distributor and customer support service companies to build its total package.

Established companies, with large amounts of resource, can bide their time watchfully and allow market uncertainty to die down. It is usually difficult for larger organisational behemoths, with unwieldy corporate cultures, to try and conduct iterative probe and learn

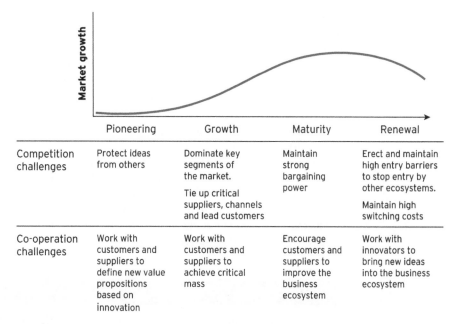

	Pioneering	Growth	Maturity	Renewal
Competition challenges	Protect ideas from others	Dominate key segments of the market. Tie up critical suppliers, channels and lead customers	Maintain strong bargaining power	Erect and maintain high entry barriers to stop entry by other ecosystems. Maintain high switching costs
Co-operation challenges	Work with customers and suppliers to define new value propositions based on innovation	Work with customers and suppliers to achieve critical mass	Encourage customers and suppliers to improve the business ecosystem	Work with innovators to bring new ideas into the business ecosystem

FIGURE 3.11 Innovation network strategies over the life cycle: competition and collaboration

processes to discover which solutions are being sought by the market. Such experiments are conducted much more ably by nimble entrepreneurial firms. The task of the large resource-rich onlooker firms is to select from the gene pool the DNA template that fits most closely the requirements of the given environment. Thus, established firms can enter at stage 2 because they are able to appropriate capabilities and development work of those in stage 1 by virtue of their resource (particularly financial leverage) strengths.

The growth stage (stage 2) often sees fierce battles between competitor business ecosystems. The ecosystem leaders not only engage in direct battle but also try to lock suppliers, customers and partners of the competitor into their system. At this stage either a single ecosystem establishes itself as the dominant player, or competitive deadlock is reached between a few (most often two) ecosystem leadership rivals. Success at stage 2 (expansion stage) often requires meeting two preconditions: first, a large number of customers who value the proposed business/product concept; and second, the company possesses the potential to ramp up its operations to meet the demand of the mass market segment. Another task at this stage is to stimulate demand, but to do so at a rate such that it does not exceed the company's capability to meet it. Over-stimulation of demand either makes the market attractive to new ecosystems or the excess demand is satiated by competitor ecosystems. IBM's late entry into the PC market is typical of second-stage entry. Stage 2 is based on rapid expansion that erodes the margins of other ecosystems, such that it forces them into extinction or near to extinction. Preparation must also be made for the stability of the maturity stage (stage 3).

Stage 3 of the business system necessitates establishing a leadership position by control of critical and core value-adding activities of the innovation. To attain ecosystem leadership position, companies have to cultivate bargaining power. This requires the firm to posses control over a critical activity which others in the ecosystem are not able to easily duplicate or provide. This status may be gained through contractual means or a patent, but more often than not it relies on the ability to constantly innovate and create value for the whole ecosystem.

IBM was unable to do so, and lost its leadership footing to the chip and software producers Intel and Microsoft. Currently, Microsoft and Intel control the critical component of the microcomputer ecosystem, and by virtue of their constant innovation are able to maintain their role as ecological contributor and thus leader. This position has major benefits because they are able to take away the lion's share of the total value produced by the ecosystem. Intel's and Microsoft's margins are more than double the average of other participants in the ecosystem. Stage 3 leaders have a pressure to continue to shape future directions and industry horizons, as well as maintain profitable stability in their ecosystem. The major fuel for this is from innovation activity.

The renewal stage (stage 4) occurs when the ecosystem matures and becomes open to attack from new innovations and emergent ecosystems. How ecosystems face the threat of obsolescence is an enormous challenge. A number of renewal options are available. First, they may attempt to stunt the development of new innovations and ecosystems. Second, they may incorporate these innovations into their own ecosystem; or third, they restructure and perhaps even exit from their current business arena.

Conclusion

In this chapter, we highlighted the need for corporate strategies to look to future environments and from this to nurture organisational capabilities to allow delivery of high-value innovations to the marketplace. In constructing strategies it is necessary to understand what innovations will be valued in the future and to take action to ensure that the firm possesses the capabilities to deliver on these.

Innovation strategies comprise three basic orientations: product market, opportunity risk and time (or industry development). Often these are dealt in isolation, whilst in reality the three basic orientations are interconnected. In developing innovation strategies companies need to bear in mind the connections since they hold important consequences for each other. The chapter elaborates on these by examining changes occurring over an industry's life cycle to illustrate key consideration in development and deployment of generic strategies for innovation. The advantages and limitations of the different strategies are considered.

There is no one best strategy for innovation. Innovation strategies depend on the particular circumstances of the specific organisation. For companies that are risk takers and future-orientated the strategy of pioneering innovation is the most appropriate. For risk-averse but resource-rich firms, a follower strategy may be more appropriate. Moreover, innovation strategies cannot be static. The nature of competition in innovation is highly dynamic and evolves over time. Fortunately, there is a general pattern that can be discerned over the industry life cycle. The chapter elucidates this pattern and discusses the changes in the nature of competition and innovation and the consequences these hold for firms. One key challenge in the industry is the battle by innovating firms to establish their innovation as the dominant industry standard.

The chapter shows that developing the innovation is not a simple strategic challenge. Once the innovation has been developed it must be carefully guided through a range of competitive onslaughts and market changes. This requires the company to possess an armoury of aggressive and protective innovation strategies.

The chapter concludes by highlighting that the challenge of innovation is rarely that of a single firm going it alone. Most often innovators need to build a network of partnerships to succeed in delivering the 'package of value' demanded by the marketplace. The network aspect of strategies is drawn out by discussing innovation from an ecosystem perspective.

QUESTIONS

1. What key strategic questions need to be asked for innovation? What do these tell you about the nature of an innovative organisation?

2. Discuss the three basic orientations of innovation strategies. Highlight the relationship between the generic strategy archetypes in each of these categories.

3. Over the industry life cycle highlight when product innovation, process innovation and strategic innovation start to predominate. Explain why.

4. What are the advantages and disadvantages of a pioneering strategy over a follower strategy?

5. Identify the factors that you need to consider in deciding between which strategy to follow.

6. Discuss strategies that a pioneer can take to defend its innovation from attack.

7. What is dominant design? Why is it so important for a firm to win the battle in establishing a dominant design? Identify what actions/strategies could be used to swing the balance in favour of the firm.

CASE STUDY

Building and controlling an ecosystem: mobile makers versus Microsoft

This case study describes two stages in the battle for supremacy in the use of software for the mobile phone market.

The situation in 2002

If attack is the best form of defence, then the mobile phone companies are striking out to repel the advances of Microsoft in their market. The reason is simple: if Microsoft's Smart Phone operating system becomes the de facto standard for the next generation of mobile phones, mobile phone manufacturers could become little more than assembly companies. Bob Schukai, Motorola's 3G product manager for Europe, says: 'We're determined not just to be box providers. That puts you in the PC game and you can get commoditised very quickly.'

Mobile phone companies are using three major defence strategies: alliances, licensing and application development. The latter has seen manufacturers offer consumers content as well as hardware products. Motorola, for example, has linked up with AOL Time Warner to provide handset owners with downloadable ring tones, screen savers and games featuring TV and film characters. Motorola has also formed the MAGNET (Motorola Applications Global Network) programme which helps third-party application developers with training, technical assistance and marketing support.

In 1998, the major handset manufacturers joined forces with Psion to form Symbian, a software licensing company that has developed an operating system (also called Symbian) for data-enabled mobile phones. Today, Symbian's members are Matsushita, Nokia, Motorola, Psion, Siemens and Sony

→

Ericsson, representing almost half of the handset market. Symbian's operating system has been licensed to manufacturers representing more than 70 per cent of the handset market, although so far only a handful of Symbian-enabled mobile phones have been announced or launched. Symbian has also worked with Intel to optimise the latest version of its operating system to work with processors that use Intel's Xscale technology, designed for wireless computing.

Nokia is also licensing its Series 60 platform to handset manufacturers wanting to develop smart phones. Series 60 includes Nokia's software source code, Texas Instruments' Open Multimedia Applications Platform (OMAP) chipset and the Symbian operating system. But not every handset manufacturer has opted to join OMAP or license Series 60 technology. Sendo, a mobile phone manufacturer with headquarters in the UK, is one of the new players in the market (it was founded in 1999) and has opted to support Microsoft's smart phone operating system. Ron Schaeffer, Sendo's head of product strategy and planning, explains why: 'Microsoft has done a good job in getting Windows CE [the technology behind Smart Phone 2002 operating system] down to a size and processing requirement that was reasonable to put in smart phones. They also did lots of work on the user-interface and didn't just dump Windows on to the size of a telephone screen.'

Another attraction, adds Mr Schaeffer, was the number of Windows developers: 'There are 6m Windows developers out there with Microsoft development tools that can readily support Smart Phone 2002. The interest we've had from developers has been tremendous'. Mr Schaeffer admits that Sendo's decision to support Microsoft wasn't solely about the technology: 'With Smart Phone 2002 we have a higher seat at the table than we would with OMAP.'

'Whoever comes out top in the smart phone battle still has to win over consumers and that may not be easy', says, Phillip Riese, chief operating officer of AirClic, a mobile solutions company: 'The companies have a WAP-antagonistic attitude to overcome a reference to inflated expectations created by the marketing of Wireless application protocol for use as an internet standard with 2G phones.'

The situation in 2008

A new deal with Sony Ericsson sees the Swedish–Japanese mobile handset maker use Microsoft's Windows Mobile operating system in a new flagship handset. The deal is a coup for Microsoft, which is now working with four of the world's top five handset manufacturers. It already has deals with *Samsung*, *LG*, and *Motorola*. Only *Nokia* has resisted working with Microsoft, and this is unlikely to change, given the company is backing rival mobile phone operating software from Symbian.

Microsoft has been trying to push into the mobile market for the last five years. With around 3.5bn mobile subscribers worldwide compared with some 1bn computer users, mobiles will eventually be by far the larger market for software.

However, Microsoft has been slow to progress in this space. It expects to have an installed base of around 35m handsets running Windows Mobile by the end of the year, but this is just a tiny fraction – around 13 per cent – of the global market for smart phones.

QUESTIONS

1. Why are there battles going on between mobile manufacturers and Microsoft? What is the logic behind this?

2. Critically assess the logic behind the strategies of the main contenders.

(*Source*: G. Cole, 'How mobile giants are defending their patch', *FT*, 31 May 2002, p. 1; M. Palmer, 'Microsoft unveils software deal with Sony Ericsson', *FT*, 11 February 2008)

References

Aaker, D.A. (1989), 'Managing assets and skills: The key to a sustainable competitive advantage', *California Management Review*, Winter: 91–106.

Atuahene-Gima, K., and Ko, A. (2001), 'An empirical investigation into the effect of market orientation on new product performance: A contingency approach', *Journal of Product Innovation Management* 12(4): 275–293.

Bolton, M.K. (1993), 'Imitation versus innovation, lessons to be learned from the Japanese', *Organizational Dynamics* 21(3): 30–45.

Boulding, W. and Christen, M. (2001), 'First mover disadvantage', *Harvard Business Review*, October: 20–31.

Burgelman, R. (1991), 'Interorganisational ecology of strategy making and organisational adaptation: Theory and field research', *Organisational Science* 2(3): 239–262.

Christensen, C.M. and Raynor, M.E. (2003), *Innovators Solution*, Boston: Harvard Business School Press.

Christensen, C.M., Suarez, F.F. and Utterback, J.M. (1998), 'Strategies for survival in fast changing industries', *Management Science* 44(12): S207–S220.

Cole, G. (2002), 'How mobile giants are defending their patch', *Financial Times*, 31 May, 1.

Griffith, V. (2003), 'Schick and Gillette take fight to edge', *Financial Times*, 16 September, 3.

Gilbert, C. (2003), 'The disruption opportunity', *Sloan Management Review* 44(4): 27–32.

Hamada, R. (2005), 'Message at Sony is tough times on the way', *Evening News*, 25 January, 4.

Hamel, G. and Prahalad, C.K. (1989), 'Strategic Intent', *Harvard Business Review*, May/June: 63–76.

Hamel, G. and Prahalad, C.K. (1993), 'Strategy as stretch and leverage', *Harvard Business Review*, March/April: 75–84.

Homes, J.S. and Glass, J.T. (2004), 'Internal R&D vital but only one piece of the innovation puzzle', *Research Technology Management* 47(5): 7–11.

Hult, G.T.M. and Ketchen, D.J. Jnr. (2001), 'Does market orientation matter? A test of the relationship between positional advantage and performance', *Journal of Product Innovation Management* 14(4): 243–257.

Kay, J. (1998), 'Why the last shall be the first and the first shall fade away', *Financial Times*, 13 May, 19.

Kerin, R.A., Varadarajan, P.R. and Peterson, R.A. (1992), 'First mover advantage: A synthesis, conceptual framework and research propositions', *Journal of Marketing* 56(4): 33–52.

Kohli, A., and Jaworski, B. (1990), 'Market orientation: The construct, research propositions and management implications', *Journal of Marketing* 54: 1–18.

Lambkin, M. (1992), 'Pioneering new markets: A comparison of market share winners and losers', *International Journal of Research in Marketing* 9: 5–22.

Leidtka, J.M. and Rosenblum, J.W. (1996), 'Shaping conversations: Making strategy, managing change', *California Management Review* 39(1): 141–157.

Miles, R.E. and Snow, C.C. (1978), *Organisational strategy, structure and process*, New York: McGraw-Hill.

Mintzberg, H. (1987), 'Crafting strategy', *Harvard Business Review*, July/August: 66–75.

Moore, J.F. (1993), 'Predators and prey: A new ecology of competition', *Harvard Business Review*, May–June: 75–86.

Porter, M. (1980), *Competitive strategy*, Cambridge, MA: Harvard University Press.

Nakamoto, M. (2002), 'Matsushita, Sony to develop Linux for home devices', *Financial Times*, 19 December, 27.

Nuttall, C. (2005), 'Joint ventures new chip set to rival Intel, *Financial Times*, 8 February, 23.

Palmer, M. (2008), 'Microsoft unveils software deal with Sony Ericsson', *Financial Times*, 11 February.

Roberts, E.B. and Berry, C.A. (1985), 'Entering new businesses: Selecting strategies for success', *Sloan Management Review*, Spring: 3–17.

Robertson, T.S. and Gatignon, H. (1991), 'How innovators thwart new entrants into their market', *Planning Review* 19: 4–11, 48.

Robinson, W.T. and Fornell, C. (1985), 'Sources of market pioneer advantages in consumer goods industries', *Journal of Marketing Research* 22: 305–317.

Rogers, E.M. (1983), *Diffusion of innovations*, New York: The Free Press.

Romanelli, E. (1987), 'New venture strategies in the minicomputer industry', *California Management Review*, Fall: 160–175.

Romanelli, E. and Tushman, M.L. (1994), 'Organisatioal transformation as punctuated equilibrium, An empirical test', *Academy of Management Journal* 37: 1141–2266.

Senge, P. (1990), *The fifth discipline: The art and practice of the learning organisation*, New York: Doubleday Press.

Stalk, G., Evans, P. and Shulman, L.E. (1992), 'Competing on capabilities: The new rules of corporate strategy', *Harvard Business Review*, March–April: 57–69.

Stalk, G. Jr. (1993), 'Time and innovation', *Canadian Business Review*, Autumn: 15–18.

Stuart, T.E. (1999), 'Alliance networks: View from the hub', *Financial Times*, 15 November, 4.

Tegarden, L.F., Hatfield, D.E. and Echols, A.E. (1999), 'Doomed from the start: What is the value of selecting a future dominant strategy', *Strategic Management Journal* 20: 495–518.

Tellis, G.J. (2006), 'Disruptive technology or visionary leadership', *Journal of Product Innovation Management* 23(1): 34–38.

Tushman, M., Anderson, P.C. and O'Reilly, C. (1997), 'Technology cycles, innovation streams and ambidextrous organisations: Organisational renewal through innovation streams and strategic change', in M.L. Tushman and P. Anderson (eds), *Managing strategic innovation and change: A collection of readings*, Oxford: Oxford University Press.

Utterback, J.M. and Suarez, F.F. (1993), 'Innovation, competition and industry structure', *Research Policy* 22: 11–21.

Weitzmann, H. (2009), 'Monsanto earnings beat expectations', *Financial Times*, 24 June.

4 Technology strategy

Learning outcomes

When you have completed this chapter, you should be able to:

- Recognise the stages in the technology life cycle and the associated strategies.

- Appreciate the difference between specific and generic technologies and technology bundles.

- Understand the process of strategic management of technology.

- Appreciate the issues, tools and techniques involved in developing and implementing technology strategies.

- Recognise the factors involved in the technology investment decision.

- Understand a range of technology protection strategies.

Introduction

Even a cursory look at modern society shows technological innovation has transformed our lives in profound ways. We take for granted many technologies as if they have always been present. The comforts of modern life are heavily driven by technological innovations. For instance, today we hardly notice the novelty of instant connectivity provided by mobile telephony and e-mail. We have treatments for illnesses that not too long ago were incurable. Technology not only affects the world of the consumer, but it also fundamentally shapes business organisations themselves by effecting change in the way they conduct business. Radical innovations play a major role in challenging competitive balances and redefining the rules of competition. It is difficult to underplay the importance of technology. It has been a constant force underlying human (and economic) progress.

The term technology is part of the common lexicon. Sometimes it is used narrowly to refer to a specific product, science or process, and other times it is used more broadly to refer to knowledge and its use. At other times it is simply used as a catch-all term to define a whole multitude of things. We can consider technology as the ability to create a reproducible way for generating new and improved products, processes and services. Technology allows the development of new products, goods or services (product technology), new processes (process technology) or to better adapt one or the other to the needs of consumers or users (design technology). Technology is thus a core capability of an enterprise to provide its customers with its goods and services both now and into the future.

Basically, technology is the 'study of techniques', just as sociology is the 'study of society'. A common theme in the numerous definitions of technology is the view of technology as a capability to achieve certain objectives. The end objectives can be the fulfilment of a customer's product needs, an organisation's managerial needs, its process or performance needs. Technologies affect firms in three key areas: product, process and administration. Product technologies are the set of ideas and knowledge embodied within the product, and are often the basis of product differentiation. Process technologies are the set of ideas and knowledge involved in the manufacturing and delivery processes. Administration technologies are the set of ideas and knowledge that are used in the planning, control and marketing of the product.

ILLUSTRATION

Trends shaping R&D

Innovation is driven by the mega-trends in science, technology and society.

Jules Duga, a Battelle senior research scientist, is co-author of the annual funding forecast with *R&D Magazine*. For example in 2005, Duga noted that overall R&D spending by industry was essentially flat. In the 2009 report he comments: 'I think we are seeing a funding future that is a reflection of the world's current economy. We all are intertwined and everyone, whether they know it or not, is linked in some way to the fundamental importance of research and development.'

'As we look toward the anticipated levels of R&D support and performance, it is important to consider some of the major factors that are either active at the present or which will surely be the precursor of megatrends in the near future', says Duga. He sees major R&D opportunities in the following categories:

- *Materials technologies*: The development of new classes of materials suitable for medical implants and other high-performance applications.
- *Medical diagnostic imaging*: The expansion of techniques for rapid and less expensive, non-invasive medical diagnostics methods, with emphasis on obtaining and interpreting images.
- *Information mining and assessment*: The development and expansion of techniques for the gathering and mining of information in a wide range of topics and the capacity to rapidly analyse content.
- *Environment*: The management of the environment including, but not limited to, the reduction of factors that contribute to global warming.
- *Energy production and distribution*: Renewable and/or low-waste production, including nuclear options, bio-energy, hydrogen and fuel cells.
- *Medical technology*: Emphasis on the development and deployment of methods for diagnostics and therapeutics – including feedback systems, early-warning systems and emergency response equipment.
- *Anti-terrorism technologies*: Identification, isolation and deactivation of materials, systems and devices that can produce physical, economic and psychological disruptions.

Duga also noted that there were signs of fundamental shift in R&D – toward outsourcing what was traditionally considered a manufacturer's core competence. 'Specifically what started as a movement toward utilizing captive facilities located primarily in Japan and Western Europe has blossomed into a significant increase in the support of R&D in non-captive, independent-performing institutions in developing or re-developing countries.'

The most visible examples of this is the amount of R&D outsourced to China and India and the growing efforts in other parts of the world. Companies that have developed globally distributed R&D capabilities can leverage significant operating benefits. What is different today from past outsourcing is that some of the variations of R&D outsourcing seem to reflect fundamental changes in the current corporate business model. Much of it is fall-out from management's new global strategies for revenue growth. An example is General Electric Co.

(*Source*: Based on Teresko, 2005 and Anon, 2009)

Technology life cycle

Technologies appear to grow and evolve in a pattern that generally follows a S-curve (Foster, 1986). This pattern is often used to describe what is commonly called the technology life cycle.

The technology life cycle can be described as a sequential process consisting of four phases: generic research, applied R&D, production scale-up and technological maturity. At the introduction stage of a new technology the firm has to make significant up-front investments in generic research (see Figure 4.1). Generic research is the pool from which fundamental revisions of the current technological paradigm arise. Many companies under-invest or steer clear of generic research because of the high uncertainties and risks involved. Consequently, public funding from governments is necessary to ensure fundamental research and technological development is not under-nurtured.

The second stage is that of applied R&D. Attempts are made in this stage to exploit generic research to fulfil market needs. The phase involves trial and error improvement of the technology to fit with market needs. In this stage, new knowledge from generic research begins to be conceptualised as new products, services or technology. Investment into the technology speeds up as the economic benefits of the new knowledge become clearer and uncertainty decreases.

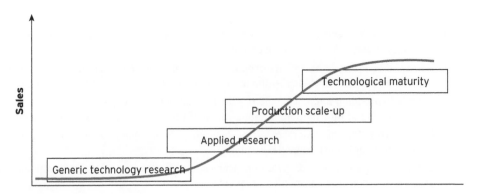

FIGURE 4.1 Stages of a technology life cycle

The third stage is characterised by increased commitment to the technology and deciphering of strategies for exploitation. This is the starting point of the commercialisation of technology with development of initial versions of marketable products. In the fourth stage the technology becomes more widely understood, and numerous competitors begin to utilise it to develop offerings of their own. This marks the transition to technological maturity. During this stage the technology is exploited to its limits through the competitive activity of the many who have entered the sector. Gradually returns and improvements from further investments become smaller. By now, the technology begins to reach its physical limits in terms of exploitation and so the gains to be made from the technology begin to peter out. Around this stage companies begin to actively search for new research and technologies so as to build the next level of competitive advantage. This often starts the process of a shift to a new technological paradigm.

Technology curves and the stages are not as straightforward in practice as they appear in theory. They suffer from problems associated with general cycles of this form. First, not all technology follows this ideal pattern. Even when it does it is not always possible in practice to gauge the stage one is at. After passage of time the stages become clear but not during the event, thus making it problematic as a decision-making tool. Additionally, industry sector technology cycles are typically a complex aggregate of sibling S-curves and are rarely stand-alone trajectories (see Figure 4.2).

Technology entry strategies

Discussion of life cycles often leads one to think of technology development as a single linear sequence. However, not all companies develop technologies from the beginning to the end of the technology cycle. Indeed, it is only a rare few that compete in the entire technology cycle. Most come in at a point when they are relatively sure of being able to gain benefits, and exit when competition begins to significantly erode their margin return. Most companies have to make decisions over when to enter, how to enter and when to exit.

As discussed earlier, the technology evolution cycle can be broken down into a number of basic stages. However, the nature of technology changes over the life cycle (Roussel et al., 1991). Four basic technology forms can be identified, and they tend to predominate at different stages of the life cycle. Figure 4.3 shows the investment decisions linked to stage of technology development. Investment strategies for the different phases characterise different forms of technologies.

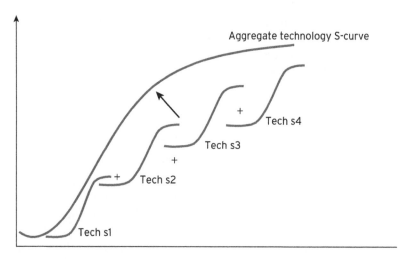

FIGURE 4.2 Sibling technology S-curves

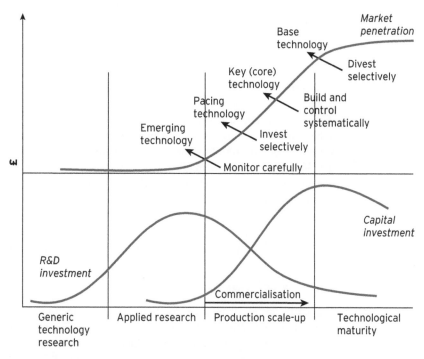

FIGURE 4.3 Investment strategies across the technology life cycle

To clarify Figure 4.3, we can state that emerging technologies potentially hold profound implications in overturning current paradigms, but their relevance for competitive use is, at this early stage, unclear. Pacing technologies, on the other hand, have the potential to change the basis of technological competition. Key technologies (also known as core technologies) are embodied in products and processes, and usually are the basis from which to build positions of differentiation. Finally, the base technologies are essential, but are widely accessible and known by all of the competition.

A company may choose to develop a technology by entering at any one of these junctures. In the initial stage, there is little known market demand for an emerging technology. By mid-stage, however, the economic value of the technology starts to become clearer, and there is much applied research and development activity. As the technology matures, its commercial potential is high because the market has already shown an acceptance of it. At this stage firms begin to change their focus from finding uses for the technology to additionally refining and improving the technology to deliver better-quality products.

Development entry strategy

This entry strategy is based on doing basic R&D. The end outcome of this strategy is highly indeterminate at the moment of investment since it is not known whether the basic research will culminate in a commercial outcome or not. The advantages of this strategy are that it nurtures a pool of knowledge that opens up the possibility to pioneer an industry sector through radical innovation. By being the pioneer, a firm can gain proprietary rights to the technology. This strategy generally requires the firm to have sufficient slack (spare) financial resources as well as a strong scientific and technological capability. It is most appropriate for companies with strong and significant R&D departments, and is largely the domain of firms operating in advanced nations with easy access to an abundance of scientific resource.

Early–mid entry strategy

This entry strategy is primarily focussed towards commercialisation. The main objective is to exploit generic research and emerging technologies developed by others. Entry is usually through technology licensing. Large firms using this entry strategy, especially those wishing to be early movers to capitalise upon an emergent technology, will often acquire or merge with the proprietary firm(s). Buy-outs and acquisitions are especially common if the inventing firm is small and the entering firm large. This entry mode avoids the uncertainty and costs of conducting basic research, and yet, if executed well, allows the company to build dominance in the industry sector. Prerequisites for using this model, however, are that the company has a research capability and resources to take the emerging technology and turn it into a marketplace success. In other words, it must possess a strong applied research capability, a strong marketing capability and an abundance of finances to develop and capture the market.

Mid–late entry strategy

This entry strategy is built on the basis of out-competing existing firms in the sector by virtue of more effective production. It is often a strategy used by firms that are attempting to accrue cost advantage from volume production, or by firms in less developed countries without an indigenous research and technological capability. It is especially relevant to firms that can move to low-cost offshore locations. Technology, because it is generally more widely available at this stage, can be bought or licensed cheaply (relative to the initial stages). The focus of the strategy is to quickly master the target technology and develop strategies for use of the technology to drive price–value competition, i.e. the technology is used to develop quality products, which are at the same time highly price-competitive. An alternative to this is to simply develop low-price basic products for currently unserved markets, such as those in developing and under-developed nations.

Besides the points made above it is important to note that the development technology strategy is complicated because of the nature and type of uncertainty. In using this strategy it always advisable to keep in mind that most technology products do not function in isolation. Research, especially in the high-technology sector, appears to indicate that partnerships and links with complementary products is crucial for success of new products that embody very novel or radical technologies (Nambisan, 2002). By partnering and integrating the new technology with other already existing and reputed complementary products, the level of uncertainty surrounding the new introduction can be reduced.

ILLUSTRATION

The long cycle of technology gestation before application

The typical focus of technological innovation is creating breakthrough technologies that make completely new things possible. Having developed a successful business with core product lines, many R&D executives think about allocating resources to the creation of new, breakthrough technologies that will serve as the basis of entirely new product lines and even new businesses within the corporation.

However, creating and commercialising a breakthrough technology can often take more than a decade to commercialise. The concept of Global Positioning Systems, for example, was brainstormed in a 1973 Department of Defence meeting as a foolproof method for satellite navigation. But this would not have happened had Aerospace Corporation not started early GPS development in 1961, work which in turn would not have occurred had people not started working on portable atomic clocks during the mid-1950s. While the first operational GPS satellite was launched in 1978, the full 24-satellite capability was not in place until 1993. Since then, GPS has been rapidly applied to trucking, commercial fishing, surveying, personal navigation on foot, on the water, in the car, and in many other applications.

As exciting as breakthrough science can be, potential paradigm shifts need a very long time to take hold in target markets. As noted above, GPS took 20 years to achieve widespread commercialisation. It took PCs more than 20 years to achieve 20 per cent market penetration, and cell phones about 15 years. The discovery of a new drug is still largely approached as an R&D effort that integrates both basic science and product development. The average time and cost for new products introduced in the last several years is now about 13 years and $800 million per product.

(*Source*: Based on Meyer et al., 2005)

Technology forms: specific, generic and bundles of technologies

So far we have seen that the nature of a technology changes as it moves through the technology life cycle. We now turn to another issue defining technology. We often look upon technologies as being stand-alone and specific, i.e. a technology is used for a specific purpose, such as in the development of one type of product. However, this is often not the case. Technologies can be generic. Generic technologies are those that can be put to a wide range of uses, and are not confined in their application or use to one specific industry or sector. For example, Canon's competence in generic imaging and optics technology has allowed it to develop a diverse range of products from copiers and laser printers to cameras. Generic technologies typically arise from fundamental scientific and technical research, such as that conducted in universities and specialist research labs.

There is another dimension that adds further complexity to the management of technology. For the most part, technologies are not developed or used in isolation from other

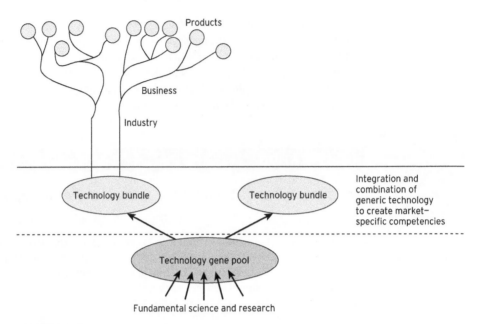

FIGURE 4.4 The technology bonsai

technologies. Most technologies are developed and used in parallel or even in combination with one another. This pattern of co-development is sometimes called technology clusters (Daussuage et al., 1987), but in order not to confuse the term with regional technology clusters we will refer to this form as *technology bundles*. Technology bundles represent the number of applications that originate from a core technology or from the fusion of a number of generic technologies developed in parallel or combination. Technology bundle strategies are common in Japanese companies such as Canon, NEC and Honda.

Generic technologies provide a wide spectrum of exploitation opportunities across many sectors. However, to take advantage of these opportunities firms in specific sectors must take the generic technology and adapt it to develop industry- and market-specific products. This means that companies need to fuse the generic technology with other technologies, either specific to the sector or generic, in order to develop market-specific products. This fusion creates the technology bundle that can be subsequently used to develop a range of products. Thus, the selection of an appropriate technology bundle is an important feature and defines the long-term technical and product development trajectory of a firm. Technology bundles are often captured as technology tree depictions (sometimes called the technology bonsai) (see Figure 4.4). In the technology bonsai, the general rule of depiction is that the roots define the key technologies, the trunk the industry, the branches the business sectors, and the leaves the products.

Technology bundles clearly depend on the decision regarding which generic technologies are selected to constitute the bundle (the mix of generic technologies), and how they are subsequently developed. Technology bundles have important consequences in terms of strategy. When strategies are predicated on this logic, the traditional concept of industry-bounded competition makes little sense because a technology bundle opens up a wider radius of market opportunity and competition. The potential applications of a technology bundle allow the firm to diversify into a number of market sectors. However, this also means that the basis of assessing competition has to be expanded accordingly. The basis of competition changes from a firm's industry to the radius of the firm's technological bundle and the overall market

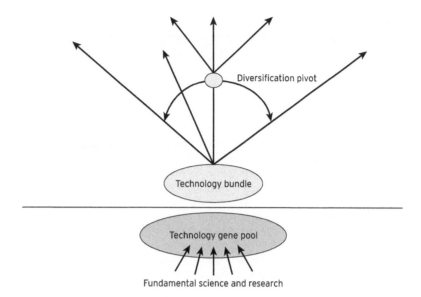

FIGURE 4.5 The technology diversification pivot

viability of applications derived from the bundle. The potential market applications define the diversification pivot, and each trajectory develops a capability that can, in turn, be the basis for further technology development and fusion, and create from it further diversification (see Figure 4.5). This suggests a much more dynamic path to the firm's growth, in which the potentiality to shift direction is greater. It also gives more meaning to the fundamental question of business: what business are we in? Answers to this question often end up being rather trite, but when the radius of opportunity is large, the question starts to take on more meaning and the answer becomes not only much more difficult to derive, but also more telling in defining the strategic trajectory that the firm has chosen to follow. Technology bundles also challenge current portfolio logic as well as business structures and organisation.

Technology dominance: optimal versus sub-optimal technology

How do new industries form and evolve? This is a question that we touched upon and developed in terms of the life cycle pattern depicted in classic S-form curve. In the development of these trajectories, though we have not stated it, it is almost always assumed that the best technology (or products) gets selected and over time are improved and developed. However, research during the 1980s and 1990s observed an interesting phenomenon: inefficient or sub-optimal technologies were establishing themselves as industry standards and coming to dominate the marketplace. David (1985) looked at how the QWERTY board became supremely dominant. Cowan (1990) examining the nuclear reactor sector noted that the light-water nuclear reactors became dominant over other nuclear energy formats not because they were the best technology, economically or technically, but because they were able to make the largest and quickest advances along the learning curve. In situations where there are competing technologies and strong and increasing returns, it is not possible to ex ante predict which of these technologies will come to dominate. To take for granted that the best (optimal) technology will always win out is a poor, if not invalid, assumption.

ILLUSTRATION

P&G cross-fertilises technology to stop you sneezing

At last, a cure for the common cold? Well, not quite. But with Vicks First Defence, Procter & Gamble hopes it might have the next best thing. First Defence isn't a drug. It doesn't actually attack the cold virus. Instead, it neutralises it by a clever combination of physical mechanisms. A nasal spray creates a gloop that wraps itself around virus particles while creating a protective barrier on the skin inside the nasal passage. This prevents viruses from replicating. Meanwhile, because the gloop has a low pH, it also deactivates them.

Vicks First Defence is a 'technological breakthrough with a revolutionary formula that will step-change the way consumers, doctors and pharmacists pre-empt a cold', it boasts. It took five years of research and development to get the gloop working properly, but the fundamental elements of the product – nasal sprays, lower pH levels – are not new. P&G just put them together in a new way to tackle an old problem from an unexpected direction. This is cross-fertilisation.

P&G's development is indicative of a new, more pragmatic approach to innovation sweeping through many companies. The biggest thing in innovation right now is that companies are being innovative with innovation. Cross-fertilisation is the basic ingredient underlying this change.

Cross-fertilisation is not just for technology. It can take a variety of forms: across technologies, across market and category boundaries, and across departmental and organisational boundaries. For example, Diageo Head of Global Innovation Strategy, Syl Saller, noted that the key to Smirnoff Ice's success was a determination to cross-fertilise the previously separate markets and marketing strategies of spirits and beer.

(*Source*: Based on Anon, 2005a)

One explanation for this type of sub-optimal occurrence is the presence of network effects, or network externalities (Besanko et al., 2004). There are two types of networks, actual and virtual. Actual networks involve some form of physical connection between members (via e-mail or telephone, etc.) and the 'product', whilst virtual networks arise through the use of complementary goods. Classic examples of this type of network externality effect can be observed in computer operating systems, video games, and mobile phone technology in which the utility of the technology increases as the number of users increase. Where such network externalities exist they can lead to technological lock-in. Technological lock-in can also give rise to another effect: technological lock-out. Microsoft's software, such as MS Office, is a good example of technological lock-out. In order to secure the full advantage of the software it is necessary for users to also purchase Microsoft's operating systems and computer architecture. This locks out competitors such as Sun, Oracle and Apple.

Theories of path dependency show that history plays an important role in determining the selection and reinforcement of a particular trajectory of technology over others. Once a pathway has been established it co-evolves with a network that reinforces itself and the technology, despite the existence of other better technologies. Path dependence, however, does not mean technological determinism since one historical event does not rigidly prescribe all subsequent technological development, but it does make development in that direction easier. This is referred to as *soft technological determinism*. Rycroft and Kash (2002) show that path dependence is evident at the micro- and macro-levels of technology evolution. They identify three sets of factors that play an important role in technology and network evolution: culture and institutions, organisational learning and technology design. They find that technological paths are closely linked with cultural processes that arise from national, local and trans-national influences. From these national patterns, culture and social networks hold the most important consequences for technological development. For instance, distinct national innovations systems promote certain directions in innovation and technology development. These are reinforced by the cultural predispositions towards certain types of innovation, especially through institutional rules and restrictions. For example, Germany's skills in the electrical and non-electrical machine sectors and France in Aerospace, etc.

Second, the act of acquiring tacit and explicit knowledge leads to self-sustaining routines. As more learning takes place in a specific technology (and hence path), the less likely is the firm, or participants of the network, to explore different technology paths. Moreover, the focus of future learning is narrowed to the search of a domain close, or complementary, to previous learning. Thus, the range of likely future paths becomes constrained by a local search for learning. Third, technology paths are interlinked with the co-evolutionary contexts of other technologies with which they are connected or integrated. In many cases, systems interdependence is a major influence for technology path development since a set of technical relationships, once embedded, can have a powerful lock-in effect and thus prevent embarking on a new technology path. System interdependence and common standards emerge from co-evolutionary processes. Moreover, the setting of a common standard is more often than not an active and aggressive process in which firms try to create co-operative networks amongst competitors because they believe that, by so doing, they will promote the technology pathway that will serve to protect and promote the interests of their network. The battle is, thus, between competing networks to set into motion technology paths that ultimately move markets and industry in directions that favour them.

Normally when network externality effects are discussed, the focus is on technological lock-in. However, another explanation is found in a different type of lock-in: behavioural lock-in (Barnes et al., 2004). Behavioural lock-in occurs when a product has become an industry standard and users have invested time and effort in learning to use it. In this situation they become less willing to change to a new product, process or technology even though it is superior. Behavioural lock-in occurs when agents (both users or producers) become stuck into an inefficient format due to habit, learning or culture. Barne et al. note a number of factors that can lead to this. First, institutional influence can habituate behaviour because institutions often provide incentives to encourage societies and people to act in certain ways. Once these commitments have been made they can be difficult to reverse. Second, employees, such as professionals, tend to create inertia against 'new ways of doing things' that may displace their positions of power and control. Workers become accustomed to work practices and organisational structures. Third, even customers can easily develop attachments to specific products despite the existence of better or cheaper alternatives. Whatever the cause of lock-in, it seems market forces alone may not be sufficient to overcome them.

Path dependency theories are useful in explaining the potential for less than efficient or optimal technologies to survive and prosper. The focus of path dependency case histories is on the evolution of the production processes, and the mechanisms through which lock-in occurs. However, path dependency stories are derived from a passive historical explanation, and fail to account for an active interpretation of firm agency (Stack and Gartland, 2003). In other words, the firm's role in shaping and creating its environments is minimised, whilst events in the firm's history are given precedence. Building upon path dependency insights, another group of researchers stress the firm as an active agent (Garud and Karnoe, 2001). This group of researchers belongs to the *path creation* school of thought, in which the role of entrepreneurs is emphasised. In path creation, entrepreneurs in real time attempt to shape the processes, social practices and actions that are at work in their environments. Accordingly, new technologies, production processes and products that win out in the marketplace are the result of an interplay between producers, consumers, regulators, and the public, and not a simple outcome of a battle between efficiency versus inefficiency. Contrasting the two approaches, Stack and Gartland (2003, p. 490) note that path dependency places the entrepreneur passively on the outside looking in, while path creation has the entrepreneur active on the inside looking out.

Strategic management of technology

Strategic management of technology emerged as a phenomenon because of the failure of traditional R&D to exploit technology. Traditional R&D approaches were particularly poor at absorbing external technologies as well as implementing new (internal or external) technologies. In particular, traditional R&D approaches were unable to handle the social consequences arising from new technologies. Whereas traditional R&D management was primarily focussed on the internal production of new technological knowledge, technology management considers a portfolio of approaches for this purpose. New technological knowledge can be acquired externally, not just developed internally. The acquired technological knowledge must then be managed (stored in easily retrievable and useable forms) and used both inside (in the processes of the company) and outside of the organisation (products for customers). Thus, technology strategy is about the acquisition, management and exploitation of technology (Clarke et al., 1995). These three elements of technology strategy are depicted in Figure 4.6.

By developing the notion that management of technology is a strategic activity, a distinction between technology and the management of technology can be made. Technology

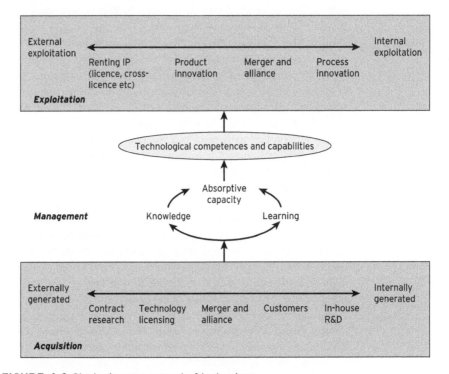

FIGURE 4.6 Strategic management of technology

management is 'the integration of technology throughout the organisation as a source of competitive advantage'. In this viewpoint, rather than perceiving technology as an organisational black box, managers must monitor, evaluate and make decisions over the role technology is to play in their future positions. Strategic management of technology requires facing two key challenges: first, developing the link between technology planning and business planning; and second, reconciling the tension between the short-term perspective of evaluating the value of investing in efforts that lead to gains in the current marketplace (marketing-based strategy) against evaluating technology in terms of its future potential (Madsen and Ulhoi, 1992).

Acquisition of technology

Internally generated R&D is often considered as the primary method for acquiring technology. However, technology can be acquired from a variety of sources, and internal development is but one source from amongst them. Technology licensing is a commonly used external sourcing method. Some companies go one step further by developing either a joint venture or a merger with firms in possession of the needed technology or knowledge (Hagedoorn, 1993). The case for bringing in-house what was previously out-of-house is based on the need for the firm to exert greater control over the technological process. When no strong case exists for control, external sources are best left to independent development. Partnerships and arm's-length relationships can be built with independent research agencies, such as universities and other specialists through research contracts and sponsorships. An important external source of technology and knowledge are network alliance of a company. Thus, competitive advantage is secured not just through the company's own knowledge and technology, but also its relationships with partner companies in the network.

Management of technology

It is not sufficient for a company just to acquire technology and knowledge. Whatever the source of knowledge the firm must be able to use it to develop useful competencies and capabilities. This requires an explicit effort from the company to assimilate and develop new knowledge into core competencies, i.e. the firm must actively engage in a process of knowledge transfer and use. Effectiveness of knowledge transfer depends on the organisation-specific variables (such as prior experience, cultural distance and organisational distance), and knowledge-specific variables (tacitness and complexity) (Simonin, 2004). However, not all knowledge and technology can be imbibed into the organisation and turned into a competence. Knowledge transfer spans across a spectrum: knowledge that has low potential for becoming an organisational competence to knowledge that has high potential for conversion into a competence. The ability to transfer and use knowledge is defined by the organisation's absorptive capacity (Cohen and Levinthal, 1990). Absorptive capacity is the ability of a company to use prior knowledge to recognise the value of new, external information, and assimilate it, and exploit it for commercial ends.

Technology exploitation

Technology can be exploited in numerous ways. The most obvious of these is the incorporation of technology into the firm's processes and products. However, technology can be

Who puts the shine in your lip-gloss?

Over the past few years the cosmetic industry has been shaped by two somewhat conflicting trends: on the one hand, the concentration of dozens of brands in single companies; and on the other hand, the shortening of product life cycles. As a result, large cosmetic marketers face the challenging task of providing fast-paced innovation for hundreds of different product lines, ranging from fragrances to skin care treatments and make-up. In many cases, this would be impossible without the help of specialised contract manufacturers.

For instance, in the make-up products category, cosmetic companies are having to increasingly turn to contract manufacturing for powders. 'Powders are difficult to produce. They require special technologies. Even marketers that do have their own manufacturing plants for make-up tend to use contract manufacturers for powders', said Renato Ancorotti, CEO of Gamma Croma, based in Italy, a contract manufacturer providing colour cosmetics to many world-leading brands.

In turn, contract manufacturers today are heavily involved in their customers' strategies. To succeed, cosmetic contract manufacturers need to think and act much like an internal department of major cosmetic clients. They get to know the client's product ranges and are able to detect weaknesses that even the client often overlooks.

'We tend to focus on our strategic customers: analyze their product ranges, their promotional cycles, their marketing plans for the next three to five years. We try to really understand their needs', said Arabella Ferrari, vice president for global strategic marketing, Intercos. Intercos, headquartered in Italy, is one of the largest contract manufacturers. It provides colour cosmetics to many of the world's leading brands. 'For each key customer, we have one marketing person, who internalises a passion for that specific brand. This way we can really customise our products in all of their phases, from conceptualisation to development to production.' Ferrari also pointed out that this level of involvement must be achieved even for competing clients. 'We would never provide the same product to more than one customer. They will get two different options. Even though they may be based on the same core technology, they will be customised', she added.

Richard Nicolo, president and CEO of D'Arcy Laboratories, expressed a similar view. 'Contract manufacturers are constantly looking for the right fit for the marketers, in terms of emerging products and trends. We analyse the customers' needs, we look for holes or gaps in their product mix and try to determine which new products can suit their market. A perfect example is what we did with a major worldwide beauty company', explained Nicolo. 'Four years ago, we developed a very innovative depilatory cream and we submitted this technology to that company because we saw they were not in this product category at all. We brought it into their R&D department, they found it interesting, and when they investigated the category further their interest grew. They didn't understand how big the category was until they bought products from us and entered that market. Their initial contract with us increased by more than 400 per cent when the product went to market.'

To a large extent, new product ideas originate from contract manufacturers, as these companies are directly responsible for developing products. Cosmetic marketer companies express new needs, chemical companies offer new possibilities, and contract manufacturers create new products. And they do it by using all the tools available for innovation (new marketing concepts, new manufacturing or packaging techniques and new raw materials). This is why large cosmetic contract manufacturers experiment with new raw materials on a daily basis.

Part of what the contract manufacturers do is blue-sky research, and part is applied research.

(*Source*: Frazzolo, 2005)

exploited through selling of proprietary knowledge on the market by methods such as licensing out, or using it to negotiate beneficial alliances. This is discussed further in the section on patent strategies.

Formulating a technology strategy

Decisions concerning technology (acquisition, management and exploitation) cannot just be left to technical specialists. Technology strategy is about making decisions over alternative technologies and deciding how they are to be used and implemented within new products and processes. Technology strategy plays a crucial role in determining what knowledge and capabilities a firm pursues, refines and retains over time, and how it goes about this task. In turn, technological capabilities have a major impact on the survival and success of a firm because they determine how well a firm can innovate or respond to competitor innovations. In linking technology to strategy, Coombs and Richards (1991) highlight four strategic areas that impinge upon the planning process.

1. The setting of an R&D budget.
2. The internal allocation of that budget between long-term and short-term R&D.
3. The allocations between particular business-related areas of R&D.
4. The allocation of specific performance improvement goals to individual or technological fields.

The process of technology strategy formulation can be structured along six tasks (Rieck and Dickson, 1993). These are depicted in Figure 4.7 and discussed below.

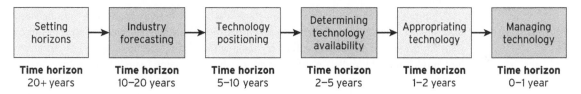

FIGURE 4.7 Process of technology strategy formulation
Source: Rieck and Dickson, 1993. Reprinted with permission of Taylor & Francis Group

Setting horizons

In this initial step, we ask the questions 'Where are we?' and 'What are the boundaries of our universe?'. The main task here is to assess whether or not the industry in which the firm currently operates is able to provide the profit potential necessary for the firm to meet its corporate objectives. This can be assessed from industry and technology forecasts.

Industry forecasting

The aim of the forecast (at this stage) is not to predict new products, but to define and understand the forces that are likely to shape the long-term direction of the industry. Tools that are useful in conducting this analysis are technology trajectory projections, based on current and future forces. At this juncture it is worth reiterating that consideration of technology trajectories alone creates blind-spots because it fails to account for the role that social actors play in influencing the path, i.e. paths can be shaped by the specific actions of firms. For instance, Benetton developed its own technology trajectory by importing existing technologies from outside its sector into its own sector. Techniques, such as value chain analysis, can be usefully employed at this stage. By examining technologies at each stage of the value chain, it is possible to check the nature and impact of interaction between technologies in the different parts of the chain. This provides insight as to how to develop the best configuration to optimise the entire value chain. The focus on the value chain is also a helpful reminder that technology bundles rather than just single technologies ought to be considered.

Technology positioning

The company needs to establish the strategic posture that will allow the firm, with its given capability and history, to build success in the future. The firm must decide the strategic space it wishes to occupy in the industry, i.e. technology position. For example, Sony's goal of being a leading product innovator necessitates it being at the forefront of a range of technologies. The key task is for the firm to decide how it is going to use technology to secure competitive advantage.

Determining technology availability

By this stage the company has already gained an appreciation of the potential directions of its sector and technologies, and how it wishes to use them. The next step is to assess the best way of acquiring the technologies that it needs for success into the future. As noted earlier, it can do this either by developing them through in-house R&D or gaining them from an external source (license, acquire, or hire staff with the required knowledge, etc.), or use a mix of both.

An important issue to explore at this stage is whether there exist any synergies between technologies. This is because very often competitive advantage is derived from a fusion or joint application of technologies. Rather than focus on a single technology it is important to look at technology bundles. A different approach on the same issue is to examine whether the technologies are base or core. Base technologies are those that are essential to an operation but are known widely by competitors. Core technologies are those that the firm will use to build a differentiated competitive position. These are the ones that should be the focus of investment. Unfortunately, many firms tend to over-invest in base technologies and under-invest in those that are important for future competitive advantage.

Appropriating technology

Once a preliminary decision as to which technology and source has been defined it is necessary to see how the technology can be most effectively incorporated into operations. This is usually called assessing/defining *appropriability*. Appropriability is the ability to derive 'economic rent' from the innovation (Klien, 1991). The challenge of appropriability is essentially twofold: first, how to implement or transfer knowledge into the organisation, and second, how to protect the 'knowledge' from leakage out to competition, i.e. sustain and protect its competitive advantage.

Managing technology

Once technology has been acquired and implemented it is important to ensure that its role in competitive advantage is sustained through a process of continuous improvement and protection. By constantly improving the technology, especially by aligning it to shifts in the marketplace, an internal dynamic is built into the process of building competitive advantage.

Dynamic technology strategy formulation model

Many of the classic models treat technology as an input to strategy formulation process. They treat technology strategy simply as another functional strategy involving decisions at the Strategic Business Unit (SBU) level. Technology is linked to strategy through a series of decisions such as technology screening, selection, acquisition, R&D project selection, resource evaluation, and so on. The focus of such technology strategy formulation processes is to examine how technology can be embodied in the strategies of the firm, and how the changes in technology are likely to affect strategy, i.e. how to gain competitive advantage by changing the solution for a need through a technology-driven product. Here, winning against competition is through correct positioning of the firm. Under this perspective, technology (and technology strategy) plays a support role in achieving the desired strategic posture. This approach to technology strategy is rather narrow, and not particularly amenable to dynamic conditions (Chisea and Manzini, 1998).

The focus in these conventional technology strategy approaches is on the product and its constituent technologies. In other words, only technologies embodied in the product and the production process are emphasised. This makes the approach only relevant to a restrictive set of industries and contexts, i.e. only relevant to industries where competitive success is primarily defined by a product's functional performance or cost. In environments where there is a high degree of dynamism, and product and production process paradigms are not stable, this type of approach is severely limited and inappropriate. In highly dynamic environments the current product or process is not a sound reference point. In such environments the search for continuity on which to base and leverage technology strategy must be founded upon the skills and knowledge used in the product and processes, i.e. innovation capability is derived from the competencies and resources developed over time. Thus, competitive advantage is derived from the capability to develop and accumulate competencies on a long-term trajectory and not upon the current product or the process per se. Chisea and Manzini (1998) combine features of the conventional approach into a resource-based model to develop a technology formulation model for dynamic environments. This dynamic technology strategy formulation model takes the traditional steps of external and internal environment analysis but changes the focus and content (see Figure 4.8).

Stage 1. External analysis

In conducting external analysis the emphasis is first to determine what makes value for the customers, and how this will evolve into the future. The product thus becomes a transient feature of fulfilling customer needs and not the ultimate focus of the technological solution,

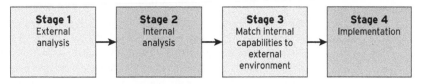

FIGURE 4.8 Technology formulation for dynamic environments

i.e. fulfilling *evolving* customer needs is the technological focus. This makes consumer behaviour and consumption a key input into the process. The second part of the process is to identify those skills and competencies that will be critical enablers of fulfilling customers' future needs (both known and latent needs).

Stage 2. Internal analysis

Internal analysis is the second step in the process. The focus in this step is not on outputs (such as products or technologies used), but on the underlying skills and knowledge. The reason for this shift in focus is that in dynamic environments, outputs are less stable than the enabling skills and competences, though these too can become obsolete. The main activities in this stage are threefold:

1. Identify the skill base, i.e. compile a map of the skills in the firm.
2. Benchmark skills against other companies (not just competitors). Assess the breadth and depth of these skills. Breadth is the range of their applicability, and the depth is the level of skill appropriability.
3. Identify skills that are critical, namely those that can deliver high value to customers, possess a wide range of application, and are difficult to imitate (high degree of appropriability).

Stage 3. Match the internal capabilities to the external environment

The third step involves matching the internal to the external environment in order to identify areas in which to build a technological base for the future, i.e. defining the content of technology strategy. To help decision making at this point a matrix map of existing and future critical skills to existing and potential application can be highly insightful. This is developed further in the section on technology roadmaps, later in this chapter.

Stage 4. Implementation

In this stage, actions necessary for implementation of the chosen technology strategy alternatives are taken. These actions lead to five different categories of effort: competence deepening, competence fertilising, competence complementing, competence destroying and competence refreshing.

Competence deepening: These are technology investment actions that strengthen existing skills and applications. Following this option is appropriate when existing technological skills are useful and effective in developing products desired by the marketplace, and the skills are likely to remain appropriable.

Competence fertilising: These are investments into technologies that show high promise for creating new applications. This involves investing in current capabilities but with an explicit view of stretching them into new areas, thus enriching and extending the capability pool. When a firm has little experience in a new application area it may wish to enter into a joint venture or alliance with others with more experience of the market. This option also explains why firms do not divest from certain areas that are not profitable or are even loss making. For example, Sony continues investing in VCR technology although it is no longer profitable because it is critical for the company to continue to build capabilities for future applications in the consumer electronics sector.

Competence complementing: This strategy involves making a bridge to shift from the current skill base to a new one. Investment is made in technological areas that can be integrated into current skills, such that it becomes possible to develop new applications and new processes (ways of doing things). Sometimes competence-complementing actions are taken not to advance into the future but simply to leverage upon the applicability range of current skills and technology.

Competence destroying: In certain circumstances shifts occur that make the firm's current skills base redundant. The development of a new technology may make an old one obsolete. For instance, advent of electronic technology rendered obsolete skills in diode valve technology (used to make products such as TVs and radios, etc.). The need for TVs and radios remained but the competencies needed to succeed in the marketplace changed dramatically. Thus it is important for the firm to detect competence-destroying change, and take action either to refresh competences, or exit from the sector.

Competence refreshing: These are investments to develop new skills that show high potential for the future. This strategy involves taking high risks, especially if the environment is highly dynamic as well as uncertain. To hedge against high risk exposure, firms following this strategy often do so by building partnerships or off-lay some of the risk by sourcing external venture capital investment. Internal development is usually left for later stages when uncertainty is lowered.

A firm should build a technology strategy path that it wishes to execute over time. For instance, the technology strategy path could begin by competence deepening and fertilising, followed by complementary integration and refreshment.

Analytical tools and techniques for developing and implementing technology strategy

As discussed earlier, the general technology strategy process involves assessing the current position of the company's technology base. Technology dynamics in the external environment are then used to consider the variety of technology options. This is followed by development of plans for how the company will realise its chosen technological path, and construction of an investment and implementation strategy to support this. In this section we examine the issues that need to be considered, and main tools and techniques that can be used to assess technologies and link them to strategy development. These tools and the related questions that they help to answer are summarised below:

- *Technology portfolio*: Where are we now? What do we need to be developing for the future?
- *Technology forecasting*: Where is technology going, and what does the future hold?
- *Roadmapping*: How can we link the present to the future?
- *Technology valuation*: What and where should we be investing for future gain?
- *Technology protection*: How do we protect and sustain our technology positions?

Technology portfolio

A technology portfolio is a useful way of assessing the firm's overall position. The portfolio can be created in numerous ways. One method is to map product, process and administrative technology on a matrix with the level of maturity as one dimension and the level of

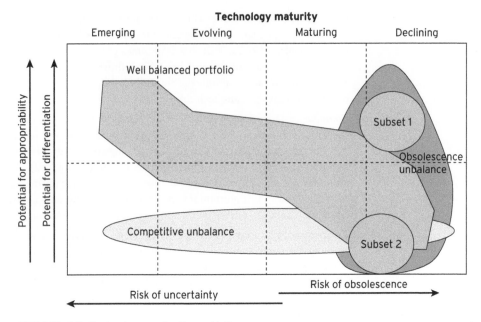

FIGURE 4.9 Technology maturity portfolio

technology appropriability on the other (see Figure 4.9). The map visually shows whether the company has a balanced portfolio of technologies. The mapping can be conducted for product, process and administrative components separately or on a single matrix. The exercise is most useful, and hence most common, for examining product technology portfolios. The portfolio is useful in defining technology strategies for the future, and also illuminates the possibilities for product market strategies.

A number of different balance positions can be discerned on the basis of competitive impact and risk exposure. Risk exposure changes over the maturity life cycle: uncertainty is high during the emerging stage but reduces over time. However, as uncertainty declines the risk of obsolescence starts to grow. The risk of obsolescence becomes high in the late stages of the life cycle.

Figure 4.9 shows three basic portfolio balance positions. The *balanced portfolio* represents a good mix of technology in terms of risk exposure, competitive impact and return to the firm. It contains a balance of new and maturing technologies. As old technologies become obsolete, new replacements with high potential for profits are already in place. Thus gaps appearing over time are being continuously filled.

In the *unbalanced portfolio 1 – competitive unbalance* scenario, whilst the company has a spread of technologies at various levels of maturity its investments are in technologies that are commonplace and unlikely to secure it a position of strength or differentiation in products.

In the *unbalanced portfolio 2 – obsolescence unbalance* position, the company has an overabundance of highly mature technologies. If the mix is dominated by technologies that remain inappropriable then the balance is in fact acceptable, since it allows the firm to continue to operate successful endgame strategies through these technologies (sub-set 1). If, on the other hand, the mix is dominated by base technologies then the strategic position is weak. In this case, exit and divestment strategies need to be considered, and they also need to be coupled with refreshment strategies (acquisition or development of new technologies).

ILLUSTRATION

Shell's technology portfolio

Shell successfully implemented 4-D technology in the early 2000s with an estimated saving of hundreds of millions of dollars and improved oil production of hundreds of thousands of barrels.

4-D technology portfolios

Shell breaks down 4-D seismic technology into three portfolios. They include the traditional, or today's proven technology; a higher risk portfolio; and a third portfolio of tomorrow's technologies.

The traditional portfolio takes the present low-risk technology and applies it to areas where Shell knows it will succeed. This includes monitoring fluid movement in offshore reservoirs from information gained by comparing reservoir models with actual survey information. Areas where proven 4-D technology has been applied include the Gulf of Mexico, North Sea and offshore West Africa.

The higher risk portfolio includes technologies on the edge, such as monitoring gas reservoirs. This also includes applying the technology to land data, carbonate fields and pressure monitoring. Areas where this higher risk portfolio of technology has been applied include repeat land surveys in the Middle East, gas depletion monitoring in offshore Northern Europe, and time-lapse swath surveys in the Far East and New Zealand.

The third portfolio of future technologies, or the portfolio with the highest risk, includes downhole seismic monitoring, permanent seismic arrays for future 4-D surveys and passive monitoring of areas surrounding wells. Applications in progress include steamflood monitoring in the Middle East and North America utilising permanent downhole arrays, and passive listening projects in the Middle East and Northern Europe.

Future technology in the third portfolio includes integrating seismic technology with smart wells and smart fields where permanent surface and downhole sensors constantly monitor the wells. The information would be used to optimise the field development by continuously updating the reservoir model.

(*Source*: Based on Anon, 2002)

Technology forecasting

In deciding which technology path to follow firms need to have a reliable assessment of the future development and potential of a technology. The decision of selecting a particular technology over another is a complex and risky task because of its long-term ramifications. Technology forecasting helps in this. Technological forecasting has its origins in the defence sector, and subsequently found favour in the space sector industries. There are a whole host of techniques that can potentially be used. In this section we briefly elaborate some of these.

The forecasting methods can be divided into five major classes of forecasting: expert opinion, trend extrapolation techniques, systems analysis, parameter analysis, and creativity methods.

Expert opinion

Expert opinion is a common basis of developing forecasts. A number of ways of inputting expert opinion into the forecast can be defined.

● *Visionary forecasting*: This procedure relies on the personal intuition of a chosen expert. It is a widely popular and commonly used method.

- *Panel consensus method*: Rather than rely on the intuition of a single individual, this method uses a group of experts. The logic is obvious: a group-based forecast is likely to be more reliable and less error prone.

- *Delphi panel*: Originally developed by the Rand Corporation, the Delphi panel method adopts a systematic consensus-building approach to develop forecasts. The Delphi panel is a useful way of tapping into experts' knowledge to define new factors and assess how they influence the future development of a technology. These factors may be technological or non-technological, and some may hinder while others encourage the development. The Delphi method is most useful for longer term forecasts or in the definition of the new technologies or influences which may introduce discontinuities or modifications to a time-series forecast.

The Delphi technique facilitates structured anonymous interaction between experts using a questionnaire approach and feedback designed to reduce shortcomings of a face-to-face meeting. The classical process involves devising a series of questions or 'event statements' about the future, which then follow an iterative cycle of rounds.

- *Round 1*: The questionnaire is circulated separately to individuals who are asked to make their individual forecasts about the event. The responses are returned to the administrator who analyses them.

- *Round 2*: The data from round 1 (median and inter-quartile) is re-submitted to the individuals. They are asked to provide reasons for their forecast and then asked to re-forecast.

- *Round 3*: The data is analysed again, and fed back to panel participants. This time the list of reasons from everyone is also provided. Once again they are asked for their forecasts and explanatory comment.

- *Round 4*: Repeat of round 3, as above.

This sequence is repeated until consensus occurs. A consensus typically emerges by the fourth or fifth iteration.

Trend extrapolation techniques

This set of techniques is based primarily on statistical modelling of time-series observations and mathematical simulations, with the common techniques outlined below.

- *Linear projection*: This assumes a simple linear relationship, in which the slope defines the rate of change. These techniques are most often based on simple correlation and regression analysis. Unfortunately, most phenomena do not follow such a simple trend.

- *Trend curves*: Extrapolations can be made on a hypothesised general pattern of development. For example, Forster's S-curve pattern is often used to extrapolate from the present moment, using past data, a pattern into the future. Another common approach to define the pattern of evolution is to use adoption-diffusion models. Trend curves have often been used to analyse substitution of one technology for another. For instance, plots of technical-economic performance data of competing technologies allow estimation of when one technology will be able to deliver superior value over the other. This allows pinpointing the point in time at which technological switchover is likely to occur.

- *Mathematical models*: There are a variety of complex models that use mathematical simulation models for forecasting. From amongst these one of the most popular is the biological growth analogy. In these, technology development is patterned in terms of a biological system.

Systems analysis

This range of techniques uses current weaknesses and problems as the staring point to develop suitable technical solutions for the future.

- *Present system analysis*: By identifying shortcomings of a current technology it becomes possible to develop courses of action for the future. The main benefit of this technique is that it defines the key areas that need further attention and focus. For example, if weight is identified as a problem for car fuel economy then attention is directed to using lighter material substitutes in body and engine fabrication.
- *Hypothetical future*: A hypothetical future problem or scenario is constructed. From this a range of solutions can be developed. It is a technique that is useful in preparing for contingencies that may potentially arise.
- *Impact studies*: This is similar to hypothetical studies but the technique's focus is to look at impact. For example, if we (or our competitor) had technology X how would it affect us, the industry, our customers, the economy?

Parameter analysis

These techniques focus on a single aspect of the technology rather than examine the entire system.

- **Theoretical limits test**: The technology (or object) under study is pushed to its theoretical performance limits to identify potential applications.
- **Analysing unique properties**: The technique focuses on a specific unique feature or property in order to identify potential market applications. For example, high weight-to-strength ratio and the cost of developing such performance.

Creativity methods

There are many creativity techniques, such as synectics, morphological analysis and TRIZ, that can be used for examining technology. We briefly discuss two techniques here.

Scenario analysis

The scenario method overcomes the limitation of deterministic forecasting. Scenario methods allow envisioning a number of alternative possible outcomes.

Analogies

This technique involves drawing an inference on the basis that if two things share at least one thing in common they may be similar in other respects. For example, man's attempt to fly and birds. Whilst the flapping of the wings fails to deliver useful information, the shape of aeroplane wings, tail and retractable ailerons have been derived from analogical observation. The value of the method relies on finding the correct analogy and translating it onto a specific problem of development.

Analogies are of two types and contain two elements (O'Connor, 1971). The first type of analogy is casual. Here there is some resemblance but it is the starting point for further examination, which leads to the second type of analogy: formal. Formal analogy emerges after close examination of the phenomenon is made. Each form of analogy is made from two elements: (i) physical manifestation (features in products, processes or systems) is first noted, and then (ii) principles of operation (laws, theories or ideas on which the physical manifestation depend) are defined. The definition of basic principles of operation is the critical part of analysis, and is key in developing the forecast. Analogies can be derived from a range of sources, such as biology, history, geography, and so on. Numerous technological developments have drawn on analogy for development. For example, solar panels to domestic heating (aerospace analogy); hovercraft to lawn mowers (engineering analogy); silver halide colour change of photography to optical lens that change shade depending on sunlight (chemical process analogy); aircraft groundspeed/altitude indicator based on the selective eye sighting of the beetle; liquid ejection principle for movement of marine animals for ski-jets (biological analogy).

ILLUSTRATION

The aeronautical vision roadmap

The aeronautical industry has three stages of development, known as Vision 5 for the five years between 2005 and 2010, Vision 10 and Vision 20. Vision 5 incorporated the sort of advances that were being incorporated in the Airbus A380 which was rolled out during this period. Vision 20, the longer view, encompassed conceptual developments, such as the blended wing plane.

Between these two extremes was the time-frame where engineers often find much of their most practical creative work. The big decisions on concept and direction have been made, the investment committed: it is now up to engineers to make it happen.

Providing sufficient electricity to drive the plane is illustrative of the mid-range technology challenges facing the sector. The giant Airbus A380 requires 1 megawatt of electricity to meet its in-flight power requirements for passenger entertainment and so on. This is about the same as an office block or a small shopping centre. Yet this is still a relatively conventional aircraft, carrying heavy, high-pressure hydraulic systems to power its brakes and undercarriage.

The next generation in the Boeing family of aircraft, the 787, first took to the skies in 2009. It is significantly smaller than the Airbus, powered by two engines and carrying 300 passengers, yet it also requires 1 megawatt of electricity. Why? The explanation for this surge in demand is that the 787 has a lot more electrically activated systems. 'The industry is moving towards the electrically activated craft', explains David Clarke, Rolls-Royce's head of technology strategy. All that heavy and costly hydraulic equipment will now be superseded.

'At the moment we're having to find ways of installing electricity generators inside the engine without increasing its weight', says Clarke.

A consortium of European companies including Rolls-Royce is working on the ANTLE – the Affordable Near Term Low Emissions engine – which has generators embedded inside the core of the engine and will be ready for testing within a year. This engine is designed for the next generation of ever more electricity-hungry aeroplanes.

Engineering advances do not happen in isolation; the Vision 10 trend in aircraft engines has a parallel in marine engine technology, which is also moving towards all-electric drives. The ships of the future will have the power unit suspended beneath the hull, changing angle to steer the ship instead of using a hydraulic rudder.

(*Source*: Based on Anon, 2005b)

Technology roadmapping

Technology roadmapping (TRM) is a method to ensure that investments in technology are geared to the development of capabilities aligned to marketplace opportunities. TRM is a process that enables integration of technology issues into the strategy process. It identifies those technologies that have the greatest potential for leverage by the firm and locates the transfers of technology into products. TRM is an important technology co-ordination and decision-making tool (Albright and Kappel, 2003).

Roadmaps can be compiled using different formats but in general they comprise a time-based chart linking technology development and investment to products and markets. TRM has been used by a number of leading-edge companies to aid their strategic planning and new product development process. For example, Lucent Technologies, ABB, Motorola and others have used such methods for a number of years. The roadmap is a visual depiction of critical items that are important in delivering to the market. It links internal enablers (resources, skills, and technology) to the external landscape (competitors, competitive products, alternative technologies, etc). It summarises how the organisation plans to use technology over time as a basis to build enduring competitive advantage.

The generic roadmap is typically organised into a number of layers: market, product, technology and resources. The top layer is used to capture key market and business trends. The second layer captures business factors: key products and processes. The third and fourth layers capture technology and resources that are required to deliver upon the chosen business objectives. One often comes across the roadmap as a high-level visual document. Nevertheless, it is an aggregation of in-depth assessments that are integrated into the final map. The component assessments are illustrated in Figure 4.10.

The process of deriving the roadmap is just as important as the map itself, because it forces cross-functional communication and sharing of long-term objectives to build shared understanding of where the company is heading in the future. It also surfaces underlying assumptions as well as highlights potential gaps in the current armoury of skills and competencies. Thus, it serves as an impetus for short- to medium-term actions. Phaal et al. (2003) recommend a four-stage process, built around workshops for each stage. Each stage focuses on compiling a different assessment in the layers for the roadmap. However, before commencing roadmapping it is important to clarify the remit of the exercise:

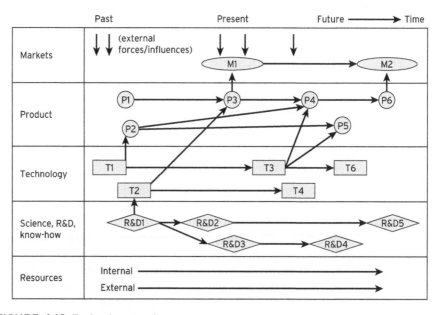

FIGURE 4.10 Technology roadmap
Source: Adapted from Albright and Kappel, 2003

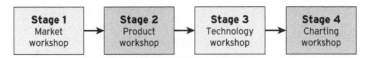

FIGURE 4.11 Technology road mapping stages

- What is the scope and focus of the exercise (unit of analysis, e.g. SBU, corporate portfolio, etc.)?
- What is the objective for the exercise?
- Who is to be involved? (Normally this should include a range of functional areas, i.e. R&D, manufacturing, marketing, HR, and should include people from all levels of the organisational hierarchy, and certainly not just senior managers!).
- What is the information that is likely to be required, how will it be sourced, when will it become available, etc.?
- What is the planning timescale and resources for the exercise?

The steps commonly covered during technology road mapping are outlined in Figure 4.11 and expanded upon briefly.

The first stage, the Market workshop, is intended to identify key drivers of the chosen business market(s). Once completed, the Product workshop can be entered into, where the product features that can deliver to market needs are defined. Product features can also be linked to market by compiling a simple 'product-features to market-segment' matrix grid, which allows product strategy options to be more easily considered.

The Technology workshop then considers the technology that can be used to build desired product features. Constructing a technology solution product features matrix grid can be useful in highlighting the possible options. For further insight, the different technology solutions should be ranked on their ability to deliver desired performance. Finally, the Charting workshop links the information and analysis of the previous workshops to structure a roadmap that links all the layers together. The map should depict key milestones, and show product evolution with technology programmes to achieve these aims, i.e. the map should indicate a migration trajectory, from the past to the future. Next, it is necessary to explicitly address specific implementation issues and detail plans and resource commitments to overcome current deficiencies and build future capabilities.

The final roadmap is a living document that evolves as market and technology changes over time.

Technology and R&D valuation

Two characteristics of technology investment make the application of simple investment analysis tricky: risk and time. First, technology investment involves a high degree of risk because at the time of investment it is not certain that the investment will lead to any positive outcome. Second, pay-off occurs in the long-term future, if it occurs at all.

Most companies have to make some level of investment in technology and R&D (*option creation investments*). Their purpose in making these investments is to realise future gains. They are a way of expanding future options through which the firm can build future competitive advantage, i.e. these investments do not lead to immediate and direct business results but play an important role in building value into the future. Not all investments are likely to lead to returns. Some will never lead to significant returns, and some may never be needed. Nevertheless, they are useful in that they create viable technology options, and thus investments in technology need to be considered from this potentiality.

Investing in technology is not the same as investing in machine capital. The purpose of technology, especially science- and research-led technology, is to create alternatives (options) that the investors may subsequently exploit. Whether they choose to exploit these options depends on the emerging trends and factors that define whether competitive advantage can be developed from these options. Moreover, the decision to exploit the option often requires substantial further investment in equipment, space, labour and so on. This is called *option realisation investment*. The option creation investments represent only part of the total investment. Indeed, the option realisation investment may be much greater than the technology option creation investment. However, the technology realisation option decision is made later, when the level of uncertainty is much reduced and knowledge about the technology option in securing market advantage much improved. This knowledge is inherently not available when making the original investment.

Traditional methods of investment analysis are rather poor when it comes to making assessments of investments that have an initial component and a later component based on contingent factors. This type of decision is most effectively dealt with by a group of models known as option pricing models (e.g. Luehrman, 1998; Wu, 2005). Essentially, options pricing models deal with investments that are made to create potential for a future investment with subsequent return. This is the case for R&D and technology investment. Investments in R&D and technology are often made simply to create intellectual capabilities that may be subsequently developed by further investment to eventually create new products or services. The interested reader is referred to Luehrman (1998) for an accessible treatment of the subject.

In dealing with this issue, Rouse et al. (2000) note that technology investments involve two fundamental and inter-related questions:

- For alternative investments under consideration *in the present*, what are the likely impacts of these investments *in the future*?
- Given likely *future impacts* of alternative investments, what *current value* should be attached to these future impacts?

The answer to these questions is difficult because the returns to technology are uncertain, and occur in the future. The uncertainty makes it difficult for long-term research and technology investments to compete against short-term investments with more certain returns. However, strategy requires investments in short-, mid- and long-term technology projects to ensure a balanced technology portfolio. There is a need to strike a balance between risk for today and risks for tomorrow. In terms of risks, returns today are worth more than the same returns tomorrow. Similarly, risk-free equivalent returns are worth more than those that carry risks. Discounted investment flow analysis is the traditional approach for investment decisions. However, this form of analysis tends to portray long-term technology investments in a poor light due to the heavy discounting of future flows. Proponents of this approach argue that this can be easily corrected by inflating projections of the returns. Unfortunately, this simply sinks the decision process into a hazy mire of subjectivity. Rouse et al. (2000) present a model that attempts to assess the true value of technology investment return by incorporating into the assessment a number of key models (see Figure 4.12):

- *Options pricing models*: These allow valuation of downstream cash flows with contingent assessment for further investments to bring the technology to market.
- *S-curve models*: based on Foster's market and technology maturity pattern to assess/ predict likely cash-flow patterns.

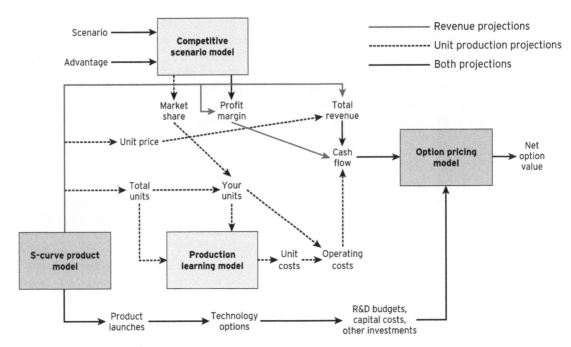

FIGURE 4.12 Integrated framework of models for technology investment value assessment
Source: Rouse et al., 2000

- *Production learning models*: These models take into account the lowering of unit costs as cumulative production volume increases.

- *Competitive scenario models*: These models examine the likely impact of competitors moving into the market. The effects of competition on market share are based on four scenarios: no competition; first in with others as follower; second in with one follower; and second in but with many followers.

The models can be integrated into a computer-based tool called the Technology Investment Adviser. In this tool, the S-curve is used to project revenues. The production learning model comes into play when the production technology is proprietary, and volume gains from experience curve effects can be realised. Projected competitive scenarios coupled with other inputs are fed into the options pricing model, which on the basis of a probabilistic assessment of technical and market success rates develops an assessment of the net value of each technology option. Since estimates of parameters are used in developing the projection it is good practice to conduct sensitivity analysis and Monte Carlo modelling to get a feeling for the level and form of imprecision in the projections.

On a broader scale, technology investment options can be built into standard NPD portfolio management practices to ensure adequate R&D funding exists for broad ventures, which can then be analysed in more detail using some of the technology and R&D valuation models discussed here.

Protecting intellectual assets: patent strategy

Once developed, a technology becomes part of the intellectual portfolio. In recent times, many companies have discovered the importance and value of intellectual property.

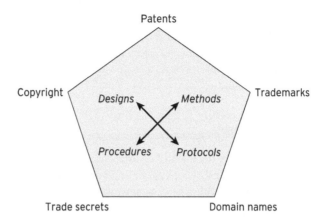

FIGURE 4.13 Forms of intellectual property

Intellectual assets (or intellectual property) are very different from tangible assets. IP consists of patents, trademarks, copyrights, domain names, trade secrets and other knowledge related to the processes of manufacture and delivery of goods and services (see Figure 4.13) It is estimated that around 75 per cent of the Fortune 100 companies' total market capitalisation is represented by intangible assets (Rivette and Kline, 1999). Despite this, very little attention is paid to the subject of how IP needs to be managed strategically, how it can sustain competitive advantage, and how it can help to shape industry structure and circumvent competition.

IP falls into two basic categories: first, assets that can be legally protected (such as patents, trademarks), and second, knowledge that resides in the heads and experience of people (see Figure 4.13). Whilst companies have come to recognise the importance of IP, how to manage IP remains rather opaque. In the past much of the IP activity was left to specialists. Typically, corporate lawyers and other IP specialists were called in for advice, and it was rare for IP to be treated strategically by senior management (Reitzig, 2004). However, innovation is not just about developing new technologies, products and services. This is only part of the challenge. Another part of the challenge is to ensure that the new innovations (products, services and technology) can earn a steady and good stream of revenues. Otherwise the burden of risk-taking is not worthwhile.

In the discussion we focus on patents, but the principles are similar for other categories of intellectual property (copyright, trademarks, etc.).

Patents

Patents are one of many methods used by governments to encourage innovators to engage in inventive, risk-taking behaviour. Patents are awarded by governments to protect an innovation for a stipulated period of time (which varies from country to country, and depends on the type of patent) from competitive copying. Basically, the patent is a form of contract between the inventor and the public (represented by the nation's government) which grants the inventor(s) an exclusive right to exploit the innovation in the national region for a limited period of time. In effect, the inventor is given monopoly rights for a specified time period to maximise returns on the innovation, and thus make their efforts worthwhile. Governments believe that without such protection from copying, inventors would not dedicate the necessary time, effort or investment. Patents fall into a number of different classes (utility, design, plant and business model, to name a few).

Utility patents

Utility patents are the most common form of patent, and most often spring to mind in common discourse. There are five classes of utility patent: (i) a process, (ii) a machine, (iii) an article of manufacture, (iv) a composition of matter, (v) an improvement of any of the other four classifications that results in a useful outcome. Typical patent protection period: 17–20 years.

Design patents

Design patents offer protection to design (lines, images, configuration, etc.) that gives uniqueness to the form of an article. The key factor of determination in a design patent is appearance. Design patents can be requested for different time frames: 3.5, 7 or 14 years. The fees for the patent depend on the time requested by the patentee.

Plant patents

Plant patents emerged primarily with the advent of biotechnology. These patents protect invention of distinct and new asexually propagated plant variants not found in nature.

Business method patents

Until 1998, patent protection was not available for methods of doing business because it was deemed that abstract ideas are not patentable. In 1998, the US Federal Court presiding over *State Street Bank & Trust vs Signature Financial Group Inc.* upheld a patent for a computer software program that was used to allocate assets in mutual funds. This paved the way for statutory recognition of business method patents. From that point onward business method patent, especially internet-based patent, activity rose frenetically. Business method patents include new and non-obvious methods of performing business functions, such as accounting, financial, inventory control, management, distribution and other such functions (Alderucci and Maskoff, 2000). Unfortunately, some of the rise in business method patents has been from frivolous applications. For example, Priceline.com has more than 60 business process patents and another 400 pending. Among the patented techniques are ways to automatically bill subscribers for magazine renewals they do not want, or relieve fast-food customers of their spare change (Preston, 2000). Another similar example is of Amazon.com. Amazon.com has secured a business method patent for a shopping process that allows returning customers to buy items without having to re-enter credit card or shipping information. This form of frivolous activity has led to some controversy over internet patents. The concern is that many people are receiving patents for ideas that are not new or original, but simply old ideas re-devised for the internet. Of course, the counter-argument is that should this be the case then these internet patents can be attacked in court based on 'prior art' (i.e. the invention is not original or is obvious). However, the problem with this line of argument is that it takes on average £0.5 million to mount a challenge against the validity of a patent. It is often cheaper to pay royalties than try and establish that the patent isn't deserved.

Patent process

The time period of a patent varies from nation to nation. Typically, the time period varies between 14 and 25 years, and also depends on the type of patent. For example, a general patent in the US and Japan is normally for 20 years, whereas in the UK it varies between 14 and 21 years.

To be eligible for a patent, the innovation must meet three criteria:

- *Novelty*: The invention must be different from *prior art* (past inventions).

- *Non-obviousness*: The invention must not be anticipated or a simple extension of prior art.
- *Utility*: The invention must be useful to society.

In arriving at a decision to grant a patent the government office takes the above criteria, especially the first two, into account. In particular, the invention must not be known or be disclosed within the nation in which the application is being made. Patents are nation-specific, and currently there is no such thing as a world patent. It is necessary to apply for a patent on a nation-by-nation basis. This has obvious cost implications. At the moment, there is a harmonised patent system in Europe, administered by the European Patent Office, and there is on-going debate over the development of a global patent. Whether this can be made a reality depends on whether significant progress in international law takes place.

The patent process starts off with a patent application. The application usually carries a processing fee (in the UK, this is currently around £200–300). In most countries the first to file applicant is given the patent rights. The exception is the US, where the inventor is given priority, i.e. even if the inventor is second to file for a patent they will receive the patent. Nevertheless, even in the US the inventor must make a timely application. In all cases, if the inventor makes public the invention they must file for a patent within a year, failure to do so loses their right to patent the invention. To file for a patent, documentation and drawings of the invention must be provided and must be certified by independent witnesses. The help of a legal advisor may be necessary to ensure the disclosure document is valid and secure. Being systematic at this stage is important in defending against any ownership claims later on from other parties.

Once lodged with the Patent Office, the claim is assigned to an appropriate category and examined by a group whose role is to search for prior art and literature to determine if the invention is original. If the decision is approved then the patent is granted, and the patent fee must be paid. This fee varies. In the UK, it is in the region of £1000–2000. If the patent application is rejected it is possible to revise and re-submit, or even take the matter to a Board of Appeal.

Patent strategies

Taking out a patent is just the starting point. Companies must protect and use their IP strategically. The first step in this process of managing IP is to check that the assets fit with long-term strategic plans. This can be done by vigorous scrutiny of the assets along the following lines (Tao et al., 2005):

- Which internal patents support your current business? Which ones are key?
- Which external patents could block you, now and in the future?
- Which internal patents can block your competitors, now or in the future?
- Which intellectual assets (internal or external) provide you with *freedom to practise* (the legal ability to practise its technology without infringing other IP rights)?
- Which assets drive or protect market share in your business now, and which in the future?
- What IP or know-how can be acquired externally?
- What is the total value contributed by your intellectual assets in your protected products, services, licensing revenues, joint ventures etc.?

Companies should aim to build IP asset portfolios that support the firm's technology roadmap. By so doing they will enhance their competitive position, maximise returns, block competition, and be aligned to market needs. A number of IP strategies can be adopted. These are elaborated next.

Defensive IP strategies

In this strategy the firm accumulates patents to prevent direct competition in related or even unrelated areas. The company builds a firewall of patents that it can use to establish a strong competitive position. This strategy requires the company to continuously patent, as well as improve upon its current patent to ensure that they are updated and sustained. For example, as part of its IP strategy, Intel has erected a thicket of patents to protect its large-scale investments in state-of-the-art wafer production plants (Hall and Zeidonis, 2001).

Prospective IP strategy (or development)

This is an outwardly focussed IP strategy in which the firm monitors innovations and developments occurring in the external environment. One activity under this format is 'bibliometrics'. In bibliometrics a statistical scan of patents and scientific papers is made to sift out the most important ones. A second activity commonly used in this approach is benchmarking of competition and non-competition. This is used to build appreciation of potential opportunity areas to focus research and development energies. The prospective strategy monitors the external environment to assess potential ways to develop as well as leverage the firm's patent portfolio.

Co-operative IP strategies: cross-licensing

Co-operative strategies involve a cross-licensing of patents. In this strategy patents are shared between companies. This is a particularly effective strategy to follow if the aim is to establish a design or article as a standard. Cross-licensing speeds the diffusion process as well as adding organisational muscle (investment and marketing) behind a particular technology.

Large-scale cross-licensing can lead to monopolistic positions over a technology or format. The Japanese companies Sony, Matsushita and JVC extensively cross-licensed dual-deck VCR technology, at nominal royalties between them, and so were able to exclude any newcomers for a considerable period of time.

Market-based IP strategies: licensing

A company can extend its invention by licensing out its invention to others for a royalty payment. The motive for this strategy may be purely pecuniary or strategic. When a patent is of little direct use to the firm it may capitalise on the patent by selling it in exchange for royalties. On the other hand, licensing, much like cross-licensing, can allow the company to build market presence and dominance of a particular technology. Dominant presence may be critical in establishing the product/technology as the standard format. Becoming an industry standard or the most visible technology in the market can lead to high returns into the future for all the firms in the licence network. In following this strategy the firm must take care to ensure that it devises a licensing contract that best allows the firm to maximise upon its objectives.

Pioneering companies such as Texas Instruments, IBM, Fairchild have used licensing and cross-licensing strategies very successfully. They allow other companies to use their technologies in return for access to their future technologies or licence fees. IBM's annual revenue from licensing patents alone in 2001 was over $1 billion: a growth of 2000 per cent from the position in 1988 (Sandburg, 2001).

Aggressive IP strategies

In the past many companies adopted a passive attitude toward patents. However, the cut and thrust of modern-day competition has changed all this. This strategy adopts an aggressive

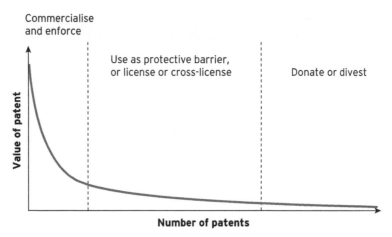

FIGURE 4.14 Generic strategic options for patents

litigation stance. This strategy is one in which the patented technology is not necessarily used by the company for production of its own products, but is 'hired out' to manufacturers of consumer products. These aggressive companies try and sign up as many companies as they can and make money from this. What is an interesting feature of this strategy is the combined use of licensing, or cross-licensing, with a strong litigious approach by a company to lever its products into other companies' final products. Predatory companies with large patent portfolios threaten competitors and non-competitors alike with costly litigation, with the hope of at least getting some royalties fees. Attacked companies find it difficult and very expensive to defend against continuous aggressive litigation. One way of avoiding fees and preventing continued aggression is to arrange some form of cross-licensing agreement. However, this means that the attacked companies must have patents in the quiver to offer in exchange. Faced with high levels of predatory action many companies have started to build defensive portfolios. For example, Autodesk (the fourth largest PC software developer), after experiencing attacks by large systems companies, decided to build a strong portfolio of patents to protect itself in case of any future attack. The defensive portfolio took years to build but gave Autodesk the potential to negotiate cross-licensing agreements with any aggressors (Roberts, 1998).

By clever use of these basic IP strategies it is possible to favourably shape and alter the industry structure and competitive positions (Reitzig, 2004).

In arriving at a decision as to what type of strategy to employ, firms should first assess the nature and value of patents. In most patent portfolios the Pareto principle is applicable, with the first 10–20 per cent of patents accounting for a vast proportion (80–90 per cent) of the total value. On the basis of value and fit with strategic priorities it is possible to devise generic options for patents (see Figure 4.14). The first 10–20 per cent of patents that comprise the major patent value should be exploited in the marketplace and patents strongly enforced and defended. The next tranche of patents have value but perhaps are of nominal value or non-direct value. The approach to these should be to license them out or use them as a defensive hedge. The final group of low-value patents can be divested or donated to bodies such as universities that are able to make use of them.

The importance of knowledge management, in the context of patents, cannot be over-stated, as the case study below exemplifies.

Conclusion

Technology is a fundamental force in human progress. For quite some time the management of technology was treated as a black box phenomenon, and left alone to manage itself. Increasingly, firms have found that they cannot leave technology unmanaged since the repercussions of doing so are manifold. Technology development has important consequences for firm innovation at all levels: product, process, administration and strategic.

Technology development follows a life-cycle pattern over which different strategies and approaches to management need to be adopted. The chapter delves into the implications of these. Technology is rarely developed or used by itself. More often than not it is developed and fused with other technology to develop new innovations.

It is normally assumed that the best technology or new product is the one that survives in the marketplace. This chapter has shown that this is not always case since a large number of factors, other than technological or product functionality, come into play in determining market dominance. This makes the systematic management of technology even more important. Strategic management of technology requires firms to acquire, manage and exploit technology cleverly and astutely so as to build sustainable positions of advantage. The chapter has elucidated the process of technology strategy formulation under stable and dynamic conditions. Assessment of the firm's position through construction of a technology portfolio coupled with assessment of future trends through forecasting was elaborated. The technique of roadmapping was amplified to show how the present can be linked to the future. The chapter examined the technology investment decision through discussion of options pricing techniques. Finally, technology protection strategies were elaborated by developing a discussion of patent strategies.

QUESTIONS

1. Describe the main stages of the technology life cycle. What are sibling S-curves? Think of an example of sibling curves.

2. What is the difference between specific technology, a generic technology and a technology bundle? Provide an example of each.

3. Explain why the best technology does not always succeed in the marketplace.

4. Describe the main tasks in the formulation of a technology strategy. What are the shortcomings of this model in dynamic environments? How can these shortcomings be overcome?

5. Why are technology investments difficult to assess? Discuss a method of developing such an assessment.

6. What forms of intellectual property exist in a firm? Discuss the types of protection strategies available to the firm, and consider the types of circumstances in which each should be deployed.

CASE STUDY

Going mobile: Velti builds global footprint for clients' campaigns

It takes determination to sustain a high-technology start-up in Greece, where the government has been slow to update labour and tax regulations and offers few incentives for entrepreneurs. Yet Alex Moukas, a software scientist with a master's degree from MIT, decided there was enough talent at home to justify the risk. 'There are a lot of smart people here plus other advantages – a reasonable cost of living and the availability of European Union funding', Mr Moukas says.

However, about 90 per cent of Velti's business comes from abroad. 'Many of our clients are multinationals so we've developed a global footprint', Mr Moukas says. Velti opened offices last year in New Delhi, Shanghai, San Francisco and Moscow to support local clients.

Velti handles mobile advertising campaigns in more than 30 countries. It works with leading operators, among them Vodafone, Wind, Orange and MTS, which controls Russia's biggest network.

In a fragmented marketplace, it has become a leading force thanks to a proprietary marketing platform that handles the planning, execution and monitoring of multiple-level campaigns across different mobile formats and channels.

The latest version of the platform offers 70 'templates' that businesses seeking to cut costs can use for mobile marketing campaigns. Customers also make savings under a software-as-a-service arrangement, or a revenue-sharing deal for a campaign run by Velti, rather than licensing and hosting the platform themselves.

'This is a new market that moves fast and there aren't so many businesses with resources to buy a software platform', Mr Moukas says.

Despite its potential, mobile advertising has been slow to take off, partly because usage is still low compared with the fixed internet. But increasing numbers of advertisers are including mobile in their media mix.

Simple campaigns using SMS messaging to run competitions or offer product discounts to subscribers have proved effective, Mr Moukas says.

According to industry forecasts, the global market is set to grow from around $4bn last year to almost $20bn by 2012. By then mobile subscriptions are expected to reach almost 4bn, covering just over half the world's population.

Velti claims a bigger reach than its competitors thanks to a joint venture with Interpublic, a leading holding group of international advertising agencies.

Recent projects included building a mobile community for Johnson & Johnson, the healthcare manufacturer; promoting content sponsored by Vodafone Live! for Disney, the entertainment group; running an SMS contest for cash prizes for MTS; and a campaign for Argos, the UK retailer, allowing consumers to check prices and reserve items using SMS texts.

'Innovation is key', Mr Moukas says. As well as spending heavily on research and development, Velti has started to consolidate its position by acquiring smaller competitors using cutting-edge technologies.

(*Source*: Based on K. Hope, 'Going mobile: Velti builds global footprint for clients' campaigns', *FT*, 4 June 2009)
© The Financial Times Limited 2009

QUESTIONS

1. What are major challenges of managing technology in a globally disperse organisation such as Velti?
2. What is the logic of Velti's approach?
3. How could Velti ensure that it stays at the forefront of global innovations in this market?

References

Albright, R.E. and Kappel, T.A. (2003), 'Roadmapping in the corporation', *Research Technology Management*, March–April: 31–40.

Alderucci, D. and Maskoff, K. (2000), 'Monetisation strategies for business method patents', *Licensing Journal*, November/December: 1–6.

Anon (2002), 'Shell's research and development philosophy', *Oil and Gas Investor*, May, 10–13.

Anon (2005a), 'After some innovation? Maybe you need to just ask around', *Marketing Week*, 16 June, 28.

Anon (2005b), 'The electric plane', *Sunday Times*, 19 June, 9.

Anon (2009) *Funding forecast reflects global economic turmoil*, **www.techconnect.org/news/press/item.html?id=150.**

Barnes, W., Gartland, M. and Stack, M. (2004), 'Old habits die hard: Path dependency and behavioural lock-in,' *Journal of Economic Issues* 2: 371–377.

Besanko, D., Dranove, D., Shanley, M. and Schaeffer, S. (2004), *Economics of strategy*, Hoboken, NJ: John Wiley.

Chiesa, V. and Manzini, R. (1998), 'Towards a framework for dynamic technology strategy', *Technology Analysis and Strategic Management* 10(1): 111–129.

Clarke, K., Ford, D., Saren, M. and Thomas, R. (1995), 'Technology strategy in UK firms', *Technology Analysis and Strategic Management* 7(5): 169–190.

Cohen, W.M. and Levinthal, D.A. (1990), 'Absorptive capacity: A new perspective on learning and innovation,' *Administrative Science Quarterly* 35(1): 128–152.

Cowan, R. (1990), 'Nuclear power reactors: A study in technological lock-in,' *Journal of Economic History* 50: 541–567.

Coombs, R. and Richards, A. (1991), 'Technologies, products and firm's strategies. Part 1a Framework for analysis,' *Technology Analysis and Strategic Management* 3: 77–86.

Daussauge, P., Hart, S. and Ramanantsoa, B. (1987), *Strategic technology management*, Chichester: John Wiley & Sons.

David, P. (1985), 'Clio and the economics of QWERTY', *American Economic Review, Papers and Proceedings* 75: 332–337.

Foster, R. (1986), *Innovation: The attacker's advantage*, New York: Summit Books.

Frazzolo, R. (2005), 'Innovation for hire', *Global Cosmetic Industry*, 173(6): 5–60.

Garud, R. and Karnoe, P. (2001), *Path dependence and creation*, in R. Garud and P. Karnoe (eds), *Path dependence and creation*, London: Lawerence Erlbaum Associates.

Hagedoorn, J. (1993), 'Understanding the rationale of strategic technology partnering: Inter-organisational modes of co-operation and sectoral differences', *Strategic Management Journal* 16, 241–250.

Hall, B.H. and Ziedonis, R.H. (2001), 'The patent paradox revisited: An empirical study of patenting in the US semi-conductor industry, 1979–1995'. *RAND Journal of Economics* 32(1): 101–128.

Hope, K. (2009), 'Going mobile: Velti builds global footprint for clients' campaigns', *Financial Times*, 4 June.

Klien, J. (1991), 'Why strategists shun technologists', *Technology Analysis and Strategic Management* 3(3): 251–256.

Luehrman, T.A. (1998), 'Investment opportunities as real options', *Harvard Business Review*, July–August: 51–67.

Madsen, H. and Ulhoi, J. (1992), 'Strategic considerations in technology management: Some theoretical and methodological perspectives', *Technology Analysis and Strategic Management* 4(3): 311–318.

Meyer, M.H., Anzari, M. and Walsh, G. (2005), 'Innovation and enterprise growth', *Research Technology Management*, 48(4): 34–44.

Nambisan, S. (2002), 'Complementary product integration by high-technology new ventures: The role of initial technology strategy', *Management Science* 48(2): 382–398.

O, Connor, W.J. (1971), 'A methodology for analogies', *Journal of Technological Forecasting and Social Change* 2(3): 279–293.

Phaal, R., Farrukh, C., Mitchel, R. and Probert, D.R. (2003), 'Starting-up roadmapping fast', *Research Technology Management*, March–April: 52–58.

Preston, R. (2000), 'E-businesses take eye off ball with patent tactics', *Internetweek*, 23 October, 834.

Reitzig, M. (2004), 'Strategic management of intellectual property', *Sloan Management Review*, Spring: 35–40.

Rieck, R.M. and Dickson, K.E. (1993), 'A model of technology strategy', *Technology Analysis and Strategic Management* 5(4): 397–412.

Rivette, K. and Kline, D. (1999), *Rembrandts in the attic: Unlocking the hidden value of patents*, Boston: Harvard University Press.

Roberts, B. (1998), 'Patent strategies: For profit or protection, companies are getting more aggressive about patents', *Intellectual Property*, October: 79–84.

Rouse, W.B., Howard, C.W., Carns, W.E. and Prendergast, J. (2000), 'Technology investment advisor: An options-based approach to technology strategy', *Information Knowledge, Systems Management* 2: 63–81.

Roussel, P.A., Saad, K.N. and Erikson, T.J. (1991), *Third generation R&D: Managing the link to corporate strategy*, Cambridge, MA: Harvard Business School Press.

Rycroft, R.W. and Kash, D.E. (2002), 'Path dependence in the innovation of complex technologies', *Technology Analysis and Strategic Management* 14(1): 21–35.

Sandberg, B. (2001), 'You may not have a choice: Trolling for dollars', *Tech Search*, 30 July, **www/techsearch-llc.com/trolling_7-31-01.html**.

Simonin, B. (2004), 'An empirical assessment of the determinants of the process knowledge transfer in international strategic alliances', *Journal of International Business Studies* 35(5): 407–438.

Stack, M. and Gartland, M. (2003), 'Path creation, path dependency and alternative theories of the firm', *Journal of Economic Issues* 2: 487–494.

Tao, J., Daniele, J., Hummel, E., Goldheim, D. and Slowinski, G. (2005), 'Developing an effective strategy for managing intellectual assets', *Research Technology Management*, January/February: 50–58.

Teresko, J. (2005), 'Pipeline=lifeline', *Industry Week* 254(5): 45–50.

Wu, M.-C. (2005), 'Evaluating investment opportunity in innovation: A real option approach', *The Journal of American Academy of Business* 2: 166–171.

PART 3

Structure for new product development - frameworks

5 Innovation process management

Learning outcomes

When you have completed this chapter, you should be able to:

- Describe the evolution of innovation management over the past 50 years.

- Explain the major components of New Product Development (NPD) models, and how these components interact in a cohesive framework.

- Understand the benefits and problems of adopting a structured methodology, such as the Stage-Gate® innovation system.

- Show how 'NPD' models are evolving to address today's increasingly complex customer and market needs.

- Appreciate through the specific example of the solutions approach the key challenges of network innovation.

- Explain how NPD frameworks might differ between a product- (or service-) focussed business, and one that is positioned as a network-based solutions provider.

Introduction

Innovation is central to corporate growth and prosperity and can be defined in many different ways. Broadly speaking, there are two theoretical approaches to studying business innovation: an enabling perspective and an outcomes perspective. The enabling perspective focusses upon factors that hinder or help innovation to occur. This perspective considers issues such as internal processes, systems, structures, culture, people and organisation. The outcomes perspective is much narrower in its outlook and is focussed on transformation activities and processes. Transformation of inputs into outputs primarily defines the activities involved in the development and commercialisation of a company's products or services – referred to as new product development (NPD). In theory, and unfortunately in practice, these two aspects have tended to be treated separately. However, they are closely intertwined and inseparable. The enabling part is directly responsible for the efficiency and effectiveness of the outcomes. A structured approach to product development process can help successful commercialisation of ideas, but how well it operates is constrained by organisational culture, general systems such as rewards, strategies and other resources.

Innovation is often measured from an outcomes perspective. One proxy measure of innovation effectiveness is new product development success. Because of this, there is a tendency to narrowly focus on managing the new product development process at the expense of managing the enablers of innovation. In this chapter, we examine innovation from the new product development process perspective. This is done at this stage to set the context for the enabling processes, systems, structures and strategies that are dealt with in later chapters.

Providing value and winning customers remains a constant business challenge. The main factor of change is the customer. Customers are becoming more and more demanding. They are on a constantly upward cycle of self-fulfilment. New products launched today seem to lose their appeal at an ever quickening pace. To survive in such environments companies have to keep pace with changing market needs. They must quickly and accurately identify changing customer wants and develop more sophisticated products to satisfy those needs. Customers increasingly demand greater functionality, greater performance and greater reliability from their products and services.

Innovation is fundamental in meeting this challenge, especially when you consider that 40 per cent of sales come from new products (Cooper and Kleinschmidt, 1991) and services (both 'pure' and product support) constitute around 70 per cent of the aggregate production and employment in the Organisation for Economic Co-operation and Development (OECD) nations (Berry et al., 2006). Unfortunately, a wide body of research has shown that companies endeavouring this route encounter numerous problems and a high level of failure (e.g. Calatone et al., 1995):

- One product concept out of seven becomes a commercial success; and only one project in four results in a winner.
- Roughly half of the resources that industry devotes to product innovation is spent on failures and killed projects.
- Around two-thirds of executives are 'somewhat' or 'very disappointed' with the results of their firm's NPD efforts.
- New products face an average 35 per cent failure rate at launch.

It seems 'making' innovation is no easy task. The capability to innovate is not a common one. It is a difficult and complex competence to nurture. However, those who can build this capability can reap huge rewards. A large body of research shows a strong correlation between innovation and company health. Indeed, long-term success and survival is heavily dependent on a firm's capability to innovate, and was illustrated in a survey that revealed that 78 per cent of FTSE 100 respondents planned to invest in innovation in 2005 in order to drive growth (Pure Insight, 2006). Additionally, it revealed that the creation of innovative products and services ranks among chief executives' top three concerns for the next five years.

Notwithstanding the risks and problems, the potential benefits from innovation are such that it is considered one of the most important processes within organisations. For many companies, success in innovation has been brought about by development of a superior NPD system or framework, and these frameworks are seen as an important source of competitive advantage. However, the development and implementation of a NPD framework is by no means simple, nor is it a guarantee for new product success; it should come as no surprise that the causes of innovation success and failure can often be traced back to the NPD framework.

Evolution of innovation process management systems

Diverse approaches to managing innovation have been attempted over the years, beginning with rudimentary efforts to grapple with technology to sophisticated and encapsulating complex systems of management. Fortunately, these approaches to new product development can be categorised into relatively distinct patterns and evolutionary phases of development.

Stages in the evolution of innovation management systems

Adapting and extending Rothwell's (1994) original phases of evolutionary development of innovation systems we identify the existence of six phases of development. These development phases are informative in that they help to define the likely trajectory for future progress in the management of innovation (Figure 5.1).

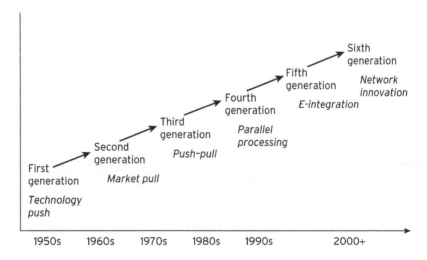

FIGURE 5.1 Evolution of innovation process management systems

FIGURE 5.2 Technology-push innovation process

The first generation: linear technology-push innovation process (1950s–)

This first generation, known as technology-push, depicts an early approach to innovation (Figure 5.2). In this approach companies believed that doing 'more R&D' would result in the development of more successful new products. Hardly any attention was given to the internal transformation process or the role of the marketplace in new product development.

This approach can still be found in companies that have an acknowledged technological leadership in the market, or who are considered subject matter experts and trusted advisors by their own customers.

ILLUSTRATION

Iridium – satellite telecoms that didn't take off

The idea for Iridium was conceived in 1987 when a Motorola engineer and his wife were planning a vacation on a remote island in the Caribbean. The wife, a real estate executive, was wary of travelling to a spot where she'd be out of telephone communication with her home office. Just what would happen if travelling businesspeople had the wherewithal to 'stay in touch' from anywhere in the world with a single, fit-in-your-briefcase telephone unit? The proverbial light bulb clicked on, the vacation was cancelled, and Motorola found itself on the threshold of wireless communications – an industry that a decade or so later would have a global value in the hundreds of billions.

Iridium's first-of-its-kind plan to utilise low-level satellite technology (called LEO, leap-frogged over the competition, which relied on more traditional high-altitude satellites requiring comparatively huge dishes. Iridium's satellites would orbit the earth at an altitude of about 420 miles.

In November 1998, Iridium unveiled its first handheld satellite phone, after spending $140 million on an international advertising blitz and setting a goal to sign up 500,000 customers within six months. By April, however, only 10,294 people had signed up – and they were to pay $3000 each for the clunky, oversized telephones and up to $5 per minute to talk on them.

'We're a classic MBA case study in how not to introduce a product', John Richardson (Iridium's CEO) said. 'First we created a marvellous technological achievement. Then we asked the question of how to make money with it.'

Plagued by problems with its suppliers, batteries that needed to be recharged 2–3 times a day, frequent cut-off calls and interference, and limited global coverage, Iridium also had to compete against cheaper cellular competitors whose technology was considered better.

In July 2000, Motorola made the decision to pull the plug on the entire Iridium operation. Iridium was told to issue orders to its 66 LEO satellites – now effectively 'space junk' – to, individually and over a period of several months, fire their thrusters, and alter orbit to a new course that would send each into the earth's atmosphere to burn up. For a moment it would blaze like a shooting star.

'A lot of engineering went into making Iridium possible', said Herschell Shosteck, a Washington DC based analyst, 'Iridium can serve as a reminder to the entire wireless industry in the future... a reminder not to let technological exuberance override business prudence.'

(*Source*: Based on White, 2002)

FIGURE 5.3 Market-pull innovation process

The second generation: linear market-pull innovation process (mid-1960s–)

As competitive pressures increased it became increasingly clear that technology push was failing to cope with the new market circumstances. This resulted in the emergence of the second-generation or 'market-pull' (also referred to as the 'need-pull') approaches to innovation shown in Figure 5.3. The market-pull approach incorporates a market focus into the innovation process to overcome the technology-push blindness to customers' needs. This is a simple sequential model in which the market is a primary source of ideas for directing R&D. R&D becomes a passive and in some regards even a reactive player in the process.

One of the primary dangers of following this model is that it produces a tendency to neglect long-term R&D programmes. Thus companies can easily become locked into a regime of technological incrementalism. For the most part, companies using this approach simply adapt existing products to meet changing user requirements along maturing performance trajectories. By doing so they run the risk of being outstripped by radical innovators.

ILLUSTRATION

How not to follow marketing

Campbell's soups

Campbell's, the U.S. food producer, discovered that although the British reacted favourably to the quality of its products and were accustomed to buying canned soup, they were not used to buying it in condensed form. According to one source, it appeared to them that Campbell was offering them half the amount of soup they were used to at the same price. The company simply added water to its existing product and repackaged it, thus putting it on par with the local competition.

The third generation: push-pull innovation process (early 1970s–)

In making the transition to the market-led model of innovation many companies began to suffer from a weakening of R&D. Companies using this approach produced few radical breakthroughs. To counter these weaknesses steps were taken to combine features of the market pull with the technology push model. This is sometimes referred to as the interactive, 'coupling' or push–pull model (see Figure 5.4).

This coupling model is deemed by many, certainly up to the mid-1980s and even presently, as presenting best practice. It essentially is a sequential process but with feedback loops.

Commenting on this approach Rothwell (1992) notes two sets of issues for success, namely, project execution and corporate level factors. These are summarised in Table 5.1.

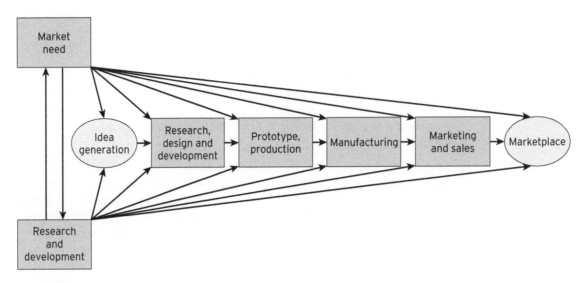

FIGURE 5.4 The 'coupling' model of innovation (third generation)

TABLE 5.1 Factors in innovation success

Project execution factors	Good internal and external communication. Treating innovation as a corporate wide task, i.e. effective inter-functional co-ordination. Careful planning and project control procedures. High efficiency and quality in production. Strong marketing orientation to satisfy user needs and create user value. Product champions and technological gatekeepers as owners of the process. High quality, open-minded management committed to the development of human capital.
Corporate level factors	Top management commitment and visible support for innovation. Long-term corporate strategy with associated technology strategy. Long-term commitment to major projects. Top management acceptance of risk. Innovation-accepting, entrepreneurship-accommodating culture.

Source: Rothwell, 1992

These factors show that success or failure can rarely be explained in terms of one or two factors only. Success is multi-faceted and rarely associated with performing one or two tasks brilliantly. It requires doing most tasks competently and in a balanced and well co-ordinated manner. At the very heart of a successful innovation process are 'key individuals': people with ability, flair and a strong commitment to innovation.

The fourth generation: interactive-parallel processing innovation process (mid-1980s–)

As markets became internationalised, competition intensified and product life cycles shortened, speed of development became an important competitive weapon. Japanese companies pioneered a process that conducted activities simultaneously rather than in sequence. This

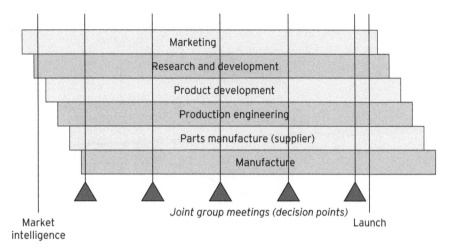

FIGURE 5.5 Parallel processing innovation process

approach is called the interactive parallel process. In deploying this model of innovation Japanese companies began exhibiting remarkable performance in world markets because they were innovating more rapidly and efficiently than their western counterparts. The Japanese innovation system possesses two striking features: *integration* and *parallel development*. Japanese companies not only integrate external partners (such as suppliers) into the new product development process at an early stage but simultaneously integrate the activities of the different functional parties (working on the innovation) in parallel rather than sequentially (see Figure 5.5).

Many companies, even today are trying to come terms with the essential features of this fourth-generation process. Companies in the West trying to follow this model have found it a very difficult model to emulate. One reason for the difficulty is that they have focussed on the tangible skeleton of the process. The secret to the Japanese success is not just in the hard-wiring of the process but in the soft underbelly, i.e. it is in the wiring of the enabling factors. The Japanese culture of consensus and team, of individuals working together to succeed rather than individual victory, provided the tight coupling and alignment necessary for parallel processing to take place. In contrast, many Western companies paid scant attention to management of the softer issues necessary to enable parallel processing. Even when issues such as culture were considered, they were managed to further promote individualism and competition. In other words, the focus was heavily on the 'outputs' part of the innovation equation.

The fifth generation: e-integrated innovation process

As noted above, many companies in the West had problems trying to emulate the Japanese concurrent model because it is not possible to transfer a culture or ways of behaving with ease or immediacy. This can only come about gradually and slowly over time. Fortunately, the advent of new technologies provided an alternative solution to achieve a similar or the same solution. Developments in information technology (IT) made it possible to induce integrated and concurrent product development.

The electronification of the innovation system is a major feature of the fifth generation system (Figure 5.6). Electronic product development tools allow efficient real-time handling of information across the whole system of innovation. In essence, 5G is a process of parallel information processing that enhances the traditional informal face-to-face interaction

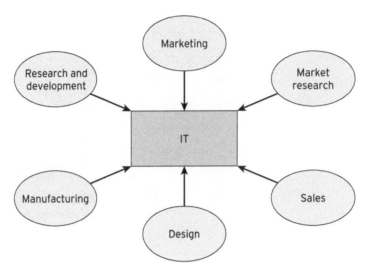

FIGURE 5.6 E-integrated innovation process

ILLUSTRATION

MatrixOne delivers e-integrated solutions in PLM

Manufacturing companies across myriad industries are investing in PLM (Product Lifecycle Management) application suites – to the tune of $2.3 billion in 2003, according to AMR Research (Stackpole, 2003). Why? Because they see PLM's potential to vastly improve their ability to innovate, get products to market and reduce errors.

PLM is an integrated, information-driven approach to all aspects of a product's life, from its design through to manufacture, deployment and maintenance – culminating in the product's removal from service and final disposal. PLM software suites enable accessing, updating, manipulating and reasoning about product information that is being produced in a fragmented and distributed environment. PLM allows the integration of business systems to manage a product's life cycle.

MatrixOne Inc. is a recognised leader in delivering collaborative PLM solutions, giving companies the ability to rapidly deploy a secure collaborative environment for their value chain that eliminates the barriers caused by geographically dispersed organisations and multiple disparate systems. This enables companies to dramatically accelerate time-to-market and significantly reduce product development costs. For example: JDS Uniphase.

JDS Uniphase is a global leader in the design and manufacture of products for fibre optic communications for the industrial, commercial and consumer markets. Challenged with complex products, a fragmented and corporate structure due to a series of mergers and a globally dispersed value-chain, JDS needed to consolidate work practices and share information more effectively across many discrete entities. As a result of a MatrixOne solution, the product transfer process has been greatly simplified, resulting in design-to-manufacturing gaps being eliminated. This was illustrated by engineering changes being turned around in 5 days rather than the previous 50 days.

(*Source*: Based on MatrixOne, 2005)

through electronic means. Additionally, the electronification process has a positive side effect: it greatly increases the potential for sharing knowledge and learning. Electronic technology can add significant value to the process when the innovation system is developed with the intention to manage knowledge flows.

The sixth generation: the open (network) innovation process

By the late 1990s, most companies were faced with the challenge of creating speed to market. The early part of the twenty-first century added another element to this challenge: customers desiring customised products to fulfil their unique needs. This added a further dimension of complexity to the management of innovation. Organisationally, faster development and greater efficiency required the creation of tighter internal linkages and access to additional resources and capabilities. However, it was unlikely that a single firm would (or could) possess all the necessary competencies and content to deliver the unique solutions demanded by customers. In addition to this challenge, companies still recognised the need for incremental development (line extensions, next generation products, etc.), but breakthrough innovation was where the game-changing opportunities were found to exist. To be successful, companies needed to look externally more, and challenge their own business models and approach to R&D.

This began the move towards what is now recognised as 'Open Innovation'. Open innovation is defined as the 'leverage of capabilities and expertise of others to deliver differentiated and meaningful innovation' (Perkins, 2008). The open innovation philosophy recognises that issues such as workforce mobility and venture capital have eroded the ability of corporate R&D labs to contain their knowledge and that significant innovation can often occur in smaller companies or global innovation clusters. In addition to this, a new breed of independent research labs has created a new source of R&D that has an increasingly active and distributed market for ideas.

In its initial incarnation, this model was based upon a partnership premise consisting of loose and tight relationships to form a network. Partnerships could include those from the entire value chain, from raw material suppliers to end customers, and even competitors. In this network, the partners became willing participants in the development process. As a result, it was no longer sufficient to just manage an internal process for successful development, but additionally a set of external interfaces and processes must simultaneously be looked at and managed. Consequently, greater focus was given towards the use of parallel and integrated (cross-functional) development processes which encouraged earlier participation by key stakeholders, including suppliers and leading-edge users in product development.

Open innovation is not about outsourcing innovation or surrendering an important competitive advantage. They key lies in achieving the right balance between internal R&D (where a core competency exists, or it is cost-prohibitive to go outside) and being capable of identifying and harvesting some of the great ideas that are being developed by start-ups, inventors, entrepreneurs and other companies. This requires organisations to be able to provide for the in-sourcing of technologies, products, or even businesses at various stages of the development life cycle. It also requires the ability to leverage or spin-out internally developed ideas and technologies that are under-utilised, and put them into the hands of external parties in order to capture value from them. This is depicted in DSM's Open Innovation Model (shown in Figure 5.7), where different activities may come into play at different stages of the product development process, and includes licensing capabilities to others, rendering R&D services to others, venturing by participating in start-ups, mergers and acquisitions and disposals/divestments.

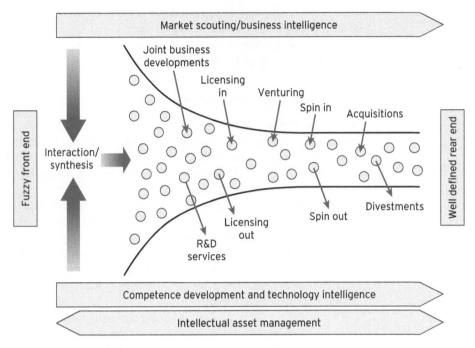

FIGURE 5.7 DSM's open innovation model

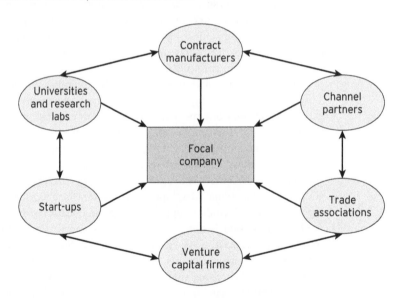

FIGURE 5.8 Open innovation model

To fully benefit from the open innovation model, companies have now realised that they need to evolve from a technology scouting approach to one of developing an innovation ecosystem (or network of opportunities) made up of a series of nodes (small start-ups, brokers, inventors, etc.), which are held together by mutual self-interest, trust and open communications (see Figure 5.8). Nodes can be populated by a number of roles, with the most common including inventors, transformers, financiers and brokers.

Inventors are those individuals or organisations who create new ideas, products, services or business models and can be driven from within an organisation via R&D departments, advanced product development teams or any employees (e.g. via idea/innovation systems). Other sources of inventors include start-ups, contract labs, academia, freelance experts, consultants and creative customers.

Transformers take their inputs from inventors and convert them into market-relevant and usable products or services, and can commonly be seen in the forms of internal supply chain and operations departments, while external sources are found in the form of contract manufacturers, channel partners, consultants and lead users.

Another important node is that of the financier, who funds activities of inventors and transformers. Corporate venture capital groups and a company's CFO may assume the role of finance internally, while externally, this may be satisfied by economic development agencies, risk-sharing business-to-business (B2B) clients and venture capital firms.

Since the businesses/nodes associated with an innovation ecosystem will already be focused on their own 12–18 month product pipeline, open innovation is best applied to game-changing opportunities. This means that companies need to know the sources of new ideas for the market (more obvious trends and sources will be open to heavier competition), so an ability to find information from non-traditional sources can be as important as the traditional sources. Brokers fulfil the role of finding and connecting inventors, transformers and financiers, which can be performed through internal groups (business development, IP licensing offices, etc.) or external forums (trade associations, solver network portals, loyal customers, etc.).

Moving from a closed innovation to an open innovation model is not easy. The organisation needs to be adapted in terms of breaking down any 'Not Invented Here' culture by adjusting compensation schemes to the market success of ideas, and by enabling the culture through the introduction of an idea submission and management system. Additionally, great care should be taken in how best to manage and govern partners, while also ensuring an effective sharing of intellectual property. And finally, serious consideration needs to be given to the ways in which customers are to be engaged in the innovation network, especially in moving away from a reactive towards a proactive approach to anticipate needs and satisfy customer needs.

These may seem considerable barriers to overcome, however the benefits can be equally considerable. Successful adopters of open innovation are able to leverage someone else's R&D, allowing them to extend reach and capability for new ideas and technology while also re-focussing internal resources. Consequently, they are seeing a far greater impact on their own internal R&D performance. Additionally, improved payback (up to 50 per cent) in internal R&D through sales/licences of otherwise unused IP is also generating otherwise untapped benefits. As an example, Nintendo has benefited from open innovation with the development of its Wii product. The company brought together a group of lead users, start-ups, academics and entrepreneurs to develop the brand new games console aimed at a new target customer group – specifically families,

Components of the generic NPD framework

Having sketched the evolutionary trajectories of developing new products, we present a detailed discussion of a basic generic framework that captures the common features across all NPD system models. A number of NPD frameworks have been developed to satisfy the needs of different organisations operating in different markets. Their goal is to bring products

ILLUSTRATION

Too complex to handle: nanotechnology commercialisation requires more than one pair of hands

Nanotechnology has opened up a wide frontier such as faster electronics, huge storage capacities for PCs, cheaper energy through efficient energy conversion, and so on. However, before these future possibilities become commercial realities, researchers must be able to fully characterise nanotech material and device properties.

Tools and techniques, such as scanning electron emission and ultra-violet microscopy, provide valuable information on nanostructures. However, electrical characterisation is essential to understand what is happening beneath the surface of nanomaterials. For example, gate dielectrics in advanced semiconductors can have thickness dimensions of less than one nanometer; the performance of these dielectrics can only be predicted by evaluating their equivalent electrical thickness. Similar considerations apply to carbon nanotubes (CNTs) and silicon wires, which are the basis for many nanotech innovations.

Government funding supports a large proportion of fundamental research in nanotechnologies. To move beyond basic research, it is crucial for companies to build partnerships with university labs and companies with complementary expertise. This is especially true in testing, where complex devices and materials have diverse properties that present unique measurement challenges. Historically, many scientific advances occur only after suitable investigative instruments become available, so nanotech researchers must either rely on instrumentation companies or take time away from R&D to develop their own measurement systems.

More often than not, research specialists know the material and device physics intimately, but are not experts in measurement technology. They are usually under pressure to commercialise research results as quickly as possible, and often do not have the time or resources to spare to develop in-depth measurement expertise.

On the other hand, instrument companies have the resources and expertise in measurement but do not have the insight that researchers possess to develop measurement innovations that will advance the state of the art more quickly. This is because nanotechnology cuts across multiple scientific disciplines, including electrical and electronic engineering, computer science, biotechnology, materials engineering, chemistry and physics. This translates into commercial pressures on instrumentation manufacturers that cannot afford the time needed to become experts in all these disciplines.

In this world, partnerships can allow them to leverage the expertise of individuals and organisations to create better solutions for researchers. Therefore, alliances between instrumentation designers and manufacturers of nanomanipulation and nanoprobing tools have become essential in constructing a complete measurement solution.

An example of this is Keithley's alliance with Zyvex Corp., a manufacturer of probers and nanomanipulation systems. This allows scientists and engineers to manipulate objects ranging in size down to the molecular level under a scanning electron microscope. By integrating Zyvex technology with Keithley's nano-level measurement expertise, researchers get powerful new solutions that neither company alone could provide.

By working together closely, nanotechnology researchers and instrumentation manufacturers can create innovative and comprehensive measurement solutions that are essential for developing the next generation of nanostructures, nanomaterials, and semiconductor devices. These partnerships are likely to be instrumental in speeding up the transfer of nanotechnology from the research lab to the production environment.

(*Source*: Based on Keithley, 2003)

to market on time, to optimise business results by reducing cycle times and costs and to manage the programmes according to agreed business plans over a product's life cycle. The majority of these NPD frameworks possess a number of common components, which when executed in a balanced and effective manner can significantly improve NPD performance. These components generally include:

- Use of a *Structured Development Process (SDP)*. This comprises a structured process containing activities and tasks, which serves to set the 'rules of the game' and describes entry and exit criteria between key programme milestones, primary tasks, schedules and resource assignments.
- A team of senior executives, called a *Review Board*, provide oversight of the programmes by resolving cross-project issues, setting project priorities, resolving issues and make Go/Kill decisions.
- Use of *Realisation Teams* (cross-functional execution teams), operating under a product 'champion' and reporting to the assigned Review Board. Many terms are used to describe these teams, including Integrated Programme Teams (IPTs) and Core Teams.
- *Phase (or Stage) Gate Reviews*. These represent decision points in the process, and define major development milestones. These are points in time when funding, resources and project schedules are approved or rejected by the Review Board.

A common way of looking at the NPD framework is to view it as a stage-gate system, in which a series of product development activities occur during each phase and are reviewed periodically by management at major checkpoints or gates. This is illustrated in the NPD Framework called 'PACE' (Product And Cycle-time Excellence) devised by the consultants PRTM (McGrath et al., 1992) (see Figure 5.9).

These key structural components through which the structured stage-gate model is executed and arranged will now be elaborated upon. (Stage-Gate® is a registered trademark of Product Development Institute Inc.).

Structured product development process (SDP)

In many companies, the way products are developed is completely unstructured. There is no consistent terminology; each project team uniquely defines its activities even though many are similar. The need for additional structure is demonstrated by the high penalties arising from an unsystematic approach to development. The following problems are symptomatic of poorly structured development processes (McGrath et al., 1992):

- *Inconsistent terminology and definitions*, leading to garbled or confused hand-offs between functions or stages (up to 39 per cent has been estimated) causing wasted effort and misdirected work. This leads to an increase in the number of clarification meetings.
- *Inability to estimate resource requirements and schedules*, resulting in sub-optimal planning and execution in support of programmes considered vital to the company.
- *Excessive task independence*, resulting in complex and inefficient communication channels and plans being made disjointedly between groups and a poor understanding of responsibilities. In some instances, 42 per cent of work is repeated because of upstream change that occurred due to late customer input, something being overlooked or errors in specifications.
- *Attention focussed on fire-fighting*. Estimates indicate that in some cases, at least 48 per cent of development work is spent fire-fighting caused by unplanned work, which appears unexpectedly but requires immediate attention.

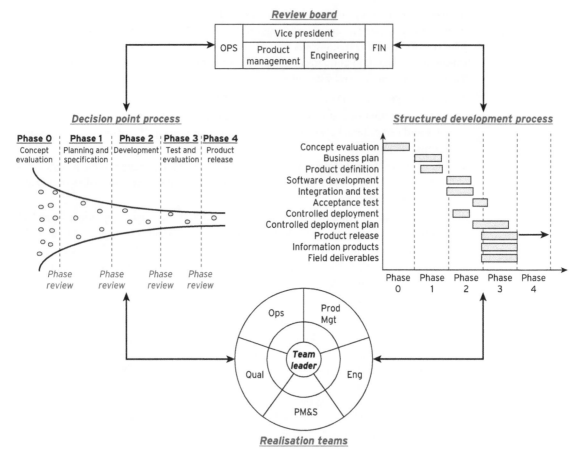

FIGURE 5.9 PRTM's PACE NPD framework
Source: Adapted from McGrath et al., 1992

Before going further, it is perhaps necessary to appreciate what we mean by a process. A process is a sequence of steps that transforms a set of inputs into a set of outputs. In this sense, a Structured Development Process (SDP) is simply a sequence of steps or activities to conceive, design and commercialise a product. Theoretically, numerous ways of conceptualising the process exist (e.g. Wheelwright and Clark, 1992). Most of the modern-day conceptualisations are based on these original descriptions. We re-conceptualise the process as a seven-stage description (see Figure 5.10). Note, in later discussion we compress the seven stages into fewer stages. We do this, firstly, for ease of presentation and discussion but also to demonstrate that the stage-gate can be (and often is) conceptualised in a variety of ways.

The Structured Development Process (SDP) offers a framework consisting of terms that describe what needs to be done in development and allows them to be consistently applied across all projects. For this the SDP must be used uniformly across the company and compliance must be mandatory. Through this process the SDP becomes part of the organisational culture. 'Best in Class' companies create guidelines around the SDP to ensure major tasks are performed across all projects and ensure mistakes, once identified, are not repeated. The clarity offered in these documents concerning key cross-functional linkages and responsibilities ensures an effective overlap of activities, improved hand-offs between functional groups, setting of realistic and more achievable schedules and improved planning and control.

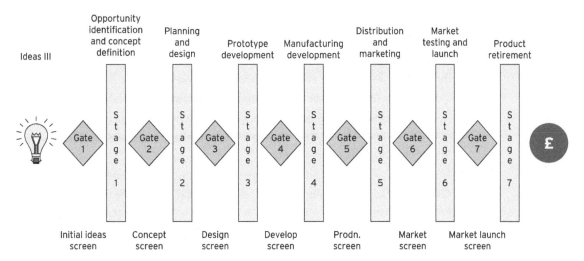

FIGURE 5.10 The Stage-Gate activities model
Source: Based on Cooper 2000

The framework presented here is organised as a linear sequence of activities. However, the same activities can be structured and organised in parallel to reflect a concurrent, rather than linear, model. It can also be arranged in a completely different manner to meet the specific needs of the organisation (e.g. Rapid Application Development (RAD) environments).

Each of the stages outlined here will be elaborated upon further.

Stage 1. Opportunity identification and concept definition and evaluation

This stage starts the NPD process by defining the opportunity to develop a product and then developing a number of possible solutions to meet the requirements such that they fulfil customer needs. From these the best concept is selected. This stage is sometimes referred to as opportunity screening and feasibility study, or simply the 'fuzzy front end' in reference to the ambiguity that exists at this early stage.

Activities and tasks associated with this stage are:

- Identification of customer needs and market opportunity.
- Definition of the problem (statement of opportunity with the company as a reference point, i.e. assessing the corporate challenge).
- Market intelligence gathering (for opportunity assessment).
- Concept generation (development of a number of possible solutions for the problem).
- Concept evaluation (identifying the best solution to meet the needs).

Stage 2. Planning and design

During this stage the structured development of the concept occurs. The concept is embodied with the functional attributes that are required by the customer. The best configuration to meet customer needs is defined and appropriate plans to meet these specifications are defined.

Activities and tasks associated with this phase are:

- Breakdown of the problem (using techniques such as quality function deployment (QFD) and product design specification (PDS), benchmarking, project planning).
- Information gathering (for engineering design purposes).
- Design review (to assure that design is physically producible and economically viable).
- Review and refinement of product design specification (to ensure that selected alternative is feasible in terms of critical design parameters and cost versus performance trade-offs).
- Market and competitiveness assessment.
- Identification of legislative and regulatory requirements that will need to be addressed.
- Creation of a supporting contracts/bids, or a business case clarifying the financial attractiveness of an opportunity and its relative positioning in the market, and a business (or programme) plan which pulls together the individual functional plans (engineering, quality, operations, marketing, etc.) into a co-ordinated and aligned plan.

Stage 3. Prototype development

This phase brings about a complete engineering description of a producible product through a process of preparing detailed engineering drawings and purchasing specifications. The process can be greatly aided by computer aided 3-D modelling and drawing.

Activities and tasks associated with this phase are:

- Detail drawings and specifications.
- Review to reconsider implications of the design for development activities that follow.
- Product architecture definition (divide the overall design system into sub-system or modules, which are then used to define the arrangement of physical elements to provide desired functionalities).
- Configuration of parts and components (preliminary modelling and sizing of parts and identification of suitable materials and manufacturing methods. Techniques such as simulation and prototyping aid this process).
- Sourcing of components and services from outside suppliers who might provide important content in the overall solution.
- Parametric design of parts and components (design configurations are tested for robustness through evaluations of exact dimensions and range tolerances).

Stage 4. Manufacture evaluation and development

This stage involves assessing manufacturing capability to produce and assemble each of the components. This is captured in a process map that specifies the sequence of operations, materials, tooling and arrangement of machines to be used.

Activities and tasks associated with this phase:

- Engineering test and product certification (e.g. Health and Safety, etc.)
- Early market testing and controlled deployment into 'lighthouse' accounts.
- Specification of production plant to be used, and any specialised tools or equipment.
- Planning production arrangement and layout.
- Planning work schedules and inventory control (production system).

- Planning quality assurance.
- Establishing costs of production.
- Planning information flow to facilitate production.

Stage 5. Distribution and marketing

For the product to reach the consumer in the 'way' and place they wish to acquire it requires business as well as technical decisions. For instance, the shipping package may be critical and shelf-life also may have to be considered early on in the development. There is also the need to develop technical briefings for the sales brochure and performance test data to consider. All of these must be married with marketing decisions to portray the desired brand image and market positioning.

Activities and tasks associated with this phase are:

- Supply chain configuration.
- Marketing planning.
- Packaging design.
- Shelf-life planning.
- Shipping or transport design.
- Support material (performance specifications, etc.).

Stage 6. Market testing and launch

The use of the product by the end consumer is a key consideration since the customer ultimately decides the success of the product. Customers assess the performance of product along a number of critical dimensions such as product quality, reliability and safety, ease of maintenance, aesthetics, serviceability and of course overall performance to desired expectation. The company needs to ensure that the product complies with the needs of the customer. Otherwise it risks market rejection, i.e. even though the idea is good and a market need exists, the actual product that is developed may not always match sufficiently with the customers' expectation of it. Thus, the company must trial products before full release into the market.

Activities and tasks associated with this phase are:

- Focus group testing.
- Marketing strategy simulation testing (adverts, communications, price etc.).
- Market testing.
- Launch planning (including localisation and channel validation).

Stage 7. Post-launch and product retirement

It is quite common to assume that the task of product development ends with market launch. On the contrary, it is necessary to ensure that the process remains alive for some time after the launch. After launch the company may find it needs to make minor modifications to the product, and if it is unfortunate major ones. Of course, if the company produces the right product with the right attributes and quality at the right time there would be no need for this. Unfortunately, nothing is completely certain in the real world.

An additional issue must also be considered in the post-launch planning phase, namely that of product retirement. This aspect is increasingly relevant with the growing concern for the environment and the enactment of laws constraining pollution and protection of the eco-system. Product developers must explicitly consider the disposal of a product when it is past its usefulness stage.

Activities and tasks associated with this phase are:

- Recycle and disposal plan.
- Market and competitive monitoring, resulting in incremental refinements to the product.
- Cost reduction activities to maintain margins.
- Product phase-in/phase-out plans.
- Discontinuation (including inventory management and depletion).

ILLUSTRATION

Stage-Gate® innovation model

A standard Stage-Gate® innovation model is provided in Figure 5.11 (Cooper, 2000) and consists of five stages and five gates. Each stage consists of a set of prescribed, cross-functional and parallel activities. The entrance to each stage is a gate: Idea Screening Gate, Business Case Gate, Development Gate, Testing and Validation Gate and a Launch Gate. Each of the gates has an associated set of mandatory deliverables which helps tough Go/Kill decisions to be made, and complies with previously approved screening criteria. Different implementations of this basic model exist across many companies and industries (e.g. more gate reviews).

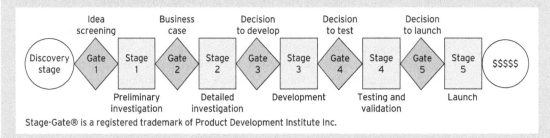

Stage-Gate® is a registered trademark of Product Development Institute Inc.

FIGURE 5.11 Simple map of a Stage-Gate® Process
Source: Cooper, 2000

Realisation teams

The realisation team is a team given responsibility for a specific development project. The secret to successful product development teams lies in organising them to achieve effective *communication, co-ordination* and *decision making*. Many different organisation structures can be used to implement the innovation process. A large number of companies continue to use hierarchical structures to implement innovation processes. Hierarchical structures with extensive rules and procedures often create functional boundaries and barriers. They thus work against cross-functional co-operation which is required in the product development process. With premium rewards being accrued to those with speedier and improved development processes, some companies, unfortunately a large number, have resorted to simply mimicking the concurrent approach by imposing their functional structures onto a parallel NPD framework. Not surprisingly, they have experienced low levels of success. To successfully move from a serial approach to innovation to a concurrent approach requires adjustment along numerous dimensions. Functional structures seem particularly inept at driving the transition to more advanced innovation processes.

A number of studies have been conducted to identify the most effective team structure to support NPD activities. They indicate many different approaches to teams can be employed. Work by Corey and Starr (reported in Cooper and Kleinschmidt, 1991) in their survey of 500 manufacturing firms, suggests that core teams or autonomous teams were the most successful amongst all alternatives. Use of traditional functional teams produces the lowest success in controlling cost, meeting schedules, achieving technical performance and overall results (Larson and Gobeli, 1989). The value of using empowered senior cross-functional teams to drive such programmes is one that is not lost to the majority of companies. Trygg (1993) found 96 per cent of all groups that had halved product development times employed cross-functional teams. A further contributing factor to the success of these teams was the extent to which leadership is provided by a 'product champion' (Frey, 1991). It would seem therefore that successful NPD teams are:

- Cross-functional.
- Empowered.
- Well supported by resources.
- Led by a strong product champion.
- Under visionary management and clear goals.

Self-managed cross-functional teams are a cornerstone to a leaner and more flexible organisation; one capable of managing the intensifying competitive pressures and the inexorable acceleration of technology. They also appear to be the logical means to generate more creative, less problem-riddled solutions, faster. These teams are key enablers of the NPD framework. They facilitate a change in focus within the company away from the functional and towards project-specific goals. Their empowered accountability and responsibility for project-related goals fosters a greater sense of ownership and commitment and creates a highly effective and dedicated team.

ILLUSTRATION

Lockheed's skunk works – probably the most famous team effort in the world

In 1943, a small group of aeronautical engineers working for the then Lockheed Aircraft Corporation (headed by Clarence 'Kelly' Johnson) were given the rush job of creating an entirely new plane from scratch, the P-80 'Shooting Star' jet fighter.

This secret project was housed in a temporary structure roofed over with an old circus tent, which had been thrown up next to a smelly plastics factory. Staffed with the right mix of expertise, and given complete autonomy, unhampered by bureaucracy or the strict application of regulations, this team met their objective in 143 days – 37 days ahead of schedule.

Source: Based on Quinion, 2005

Review boards

Senior management monitor and control the product development process through formally designated Review Boards. These bodies are also referred to as the Product Approval Committees (PAC), Resource Boards or New-Product Executive Group. This group is responsible for approving and prioritising new product development investments. Specifically, it has the authority and responsibility to:

- Initiate new product development projects.
- Cancel and re-prioritise projects.
- Ensure that products being developed fit the company's strategy.
- Allocate development resources.

Because this is a decision-making group it should remain small. It typically includes the Chief Executive Officer (CEO), Chief Operating Officer (COO) or General Manager, and the Heads of the Marketing, Engineering, Finance and Operations areas. In this capacity, each person is expected to dedicate around 10–15 per cent of their time on oversight-related activities. The specific roles expected of these members include:

- *Establish the vision*: Set strategy by establishing a vision for the company's products. A clear vision is important in helping the entire company to achieve its development activities.
- *Make decisions*: Senior management needs to review project progress at each of the decision-gates to make 'Go' or 'No-Go' and other product portfolio decisions.
- *Cultivate the product development process*: The senior management group must garner support for the new product development process and the portfolio of projects going through it. It is important to have a standard common NPD process operated by the entire company to ensure smooth and consistent execution of product development activities.
- *Motivate*: The senior team must provide leadership and motivation for all participants involved in product development.
- *Recruit the best development staff*: It is of crucial importance that senior management have access to individuals with specific technical skills and expertise to work on development projects. If the best (most appropriate for the task at hand) staff are recruited into other tasks, product development projects will suffer.

It is important to get a balance between the review team's authority and the empowerment exercised by the realisation teams. Top management need to balance their need for information and control against the development team's need to own the process of conceptualising, designing, testing, manufacturing, launching and screening new products (Anthony and McKay, 1992). Too much control makes the review team overbearing and too little leads to poor alignment. The issue of project and resource management in NPD is an important one and can lead to the control of a NPD framework being unbalanced. Unbalance can be either through insufficient control, over-control, or inappropriate control because of poor information.

Four syndromes of unbalance can be discerned (Figure 5.12):

- *Autocratic leadership syndrome*. In this form of unbalance one senior executive dominates product development decisions. It typifies the 'I know best' and 'Do as I command' syndrome. It leads to frustration in the senior team as well as the development team.

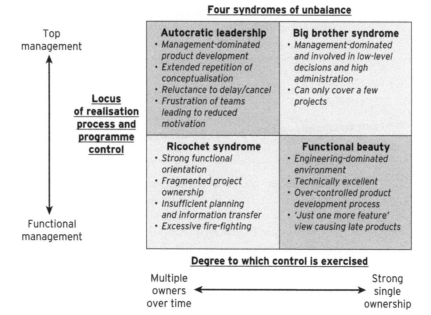

FIGURE 5.12 Four syndromes of unbalance
Source: Anthony and McKay, 1992

- *Big brother syndrome.* In this syndrome, the senior management team gets involved in low-level decision making. They oversee every little decision and create high loads of administration and bureaucracy for the development team. The development team feels powerless and unable to openly express their voice in the process.

- *Functional beauty syndrome.* This occurs when one function exerts excessive control over the project. In the past this type of syndrome was prevalent in engineering and technically orientated companies, such as Rolls-Royce where engineering considerations led to constant refinements. In the modern day, this syndrome can be found in the heavy dominance by marketing of the development process leading to constant minor refinements that are of marginal value to the end customer.

- *Ricochet syndrome.* Here control is passed from one function to the next as the project proceeds through the different stages of development. In principle this seems sensible enough, since the baton of control is being passed as a different role becomes primary. However, in practice it is easy to lose a sense of direction if the different individuals taking hold of the baton wish to stamp their own authority and direction on the project. The project thus ricochets from one direction to the next, and fails to make clear progress.

Improvements due to balancing the NPD framework can be dramatic: a 50 per cent reduction in cycle time is not uncommon. Other benefits include better products, lower development costs, improved predictability and the ability to handle more development projects concurrently (Anthony and McKay, 1992).

Phase review (decision point) process

All companies possess a decision-making process for new products, even though it may be an informal or non-explicitly defined process. Absence of a formal decision-making process can lead to inconsistent and unreliable decisions, which consequently introduces significant delays to product development programmes. This can be overcome by applying a well-defined phase review process.

The phase review process drives the product development processes. It is the process whereby the Review Board:

- Makes the difficult strategic-level product decisions.
- Allocates resources to product development efforts.
- Provides direction and leadership to the project teams.
- Empowers the realisation teams to develop the programme on a phase-by-phase basis.

These decisions are made through approval at the conclusion of specific phases in the development effort, and are generally guided by a list of deliverables and milestones that are expected to be completed in support of a Go/No-Go decision.

The phase review process is intended to cover all significant product development efforts, including all major new product development opportunities. Very small projects, such as minor enhancements, can however be managed by a simpler process or grouped and managed as a package. While the NPD process can be conceptualised in different ways, most conceptualisations incorporate project review decision points. Review Boards use these review decision points to examine projected technical, marketing and financial performance of programmes to determine whether to proceed with developing the new product or to terminate it prior to commercialisation. The model shown in Figure 5.13 has five stages, although more or less may be employed by different companies. The phase review process can be viewed as a funnel with many ideas entering at the concept phase and through a series of screenings over the course of development narrowed to a few appropriately resourced projects with high likelihood of market success. At the conclusion of each phase, a review is held to determine the direction of the project: proceed, cancel or re-direct.

For instance, in a parallel arrangement of the stage-gate development a number of activities are executed concurrently across a number of different functions. At specific points,

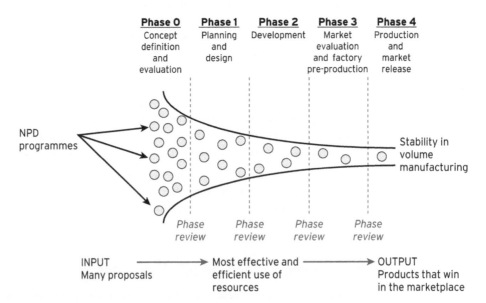

FIGURE 5.13 Funnel approach of new product development frameworks

	1	2	3	4	5	SCORE	WEIGHT	WEIGHTED SCORE
Market volatility	High/erratic				Very stable			
Probable market share	4th Best				Leader			
Probable product life	<1 year				<10 years			
Similarity to product life	No relationship				Very close			
Sales force requirements	Have no experience				Very familiar			
Promotion requirements	Have no experience				Very familiar			
Target customers	Perfect strangers				Close/current			
Distributors	No relationship				Strong			
Retailers/dealers	Trivial				Critical			
Importance to task user	No relationship				Current/strong			
Degree of unmet need	None/satisfied				Totally unmet			
Likelihood of fulfilling need	Very low				Very high			
Competition to be faced	Tough/aggressive				Weak			
Field service requirements	No current capability				Ready now			
Environmental effects	Only negative ones				Positive ones			
Global applications	Domestic only				Fits global need			
Market diffusions	No other uses				Many other uses			
Customer integration	Very unlikely				Customer seeks it			
Probable profit	Break even at best				ROI > 30%			

FIGURE 5.14 Screens for commercial assessment

these are brought together in the form of specific phase review deliverables that are presented to the Review Board. On the basis of the information provided, the product development project will be permitted to proceed to the next phase (with commitments in funding and resources given), given instructions to re-focus, or cancelled. This review activity ensures that funded programmes are consistent with the company's strategic and financial goals and are supported and resourced in a manner that increases the likelihood of success.

The decision to proceed with the project or drop the project is usually made on the project meeting certain criteria. These criteria act as screens to help senior management arrive at a decision, and are often supported by a business case and plan. The screens define pertinent objectives and considerations that need to be assessed in order to facilitate the decision. Figure 5.14 provides an example of a screen to assess technical and commercial factors.

In addition to such screens, it is common that phase review checklists are applied to ensure due diligence is applied to complete prescribed tasks in a logical and effective sequence. These checklists enforce the use of the SDP and therefore reduce the level of variability in the NPD framework. An example of such a checklist is shown in Figure 5.15.

The use of screens and phase review checklists help to kill off unattractive opportunities earlier. It also is a process of committing increasing levels of investment to attractive opportunities as their associated risk is reduced (see Figure 5.16).

 ## New service development models

Service innovation has, in the past, been seen to differ from product innovation in three important ways. Firstly, for labour-intensive, interactive services, the service providers (service delivery staff) were part of the customer experience and therefore part of the innovation.

ITEM	Yes/No	N/A	Owner/Date	COMMENTS/REFERENCES
Product management marketing				
Final Deployment Plan Completed				(Insert Document Reference)
Sales Forecast Available				
Business Impact Model Completed				
Collateral Materials Completed				
Sales Training Available				
Sales Readiness Review Completed				
Customer Engagement Model Available				
Area Release to Sell (ARS) Declared				
Area Release to Install (ARI)				
Development				
Development Plan Finalized				(Insert Document Reference)
Solution Definition Completed				
Program Aligned with Quality Plan				
Acceptance Test Specifications				(Insert Document Reference)
Interoperability Test Specifications				(Insert Document Reference)
Services				(Insert Document Reference)
Customer Services and Professional				
Customer Education/Training Available				
Development Risk Assessment Review				(Insert Document Reference)
Controlled Deployment Plan Completed				(Insert Document Reference)
Guidelines and Input Document for				(Insert Document Reference)
Support planning delivery				
Worldwide Services Plan Finalized				(Insert Document Reference)
Maintenance Pricing Complete				
Risk Assessment Finalized				(Insert Document Reference)
Area Release to Deliver Service (ARDS)				
Team				
Resources/Deliverables Committed				
Business Plan Updated				(Insert Document Reference)
Program Risk Assessments				Planned and Completed
Team Leader Approval: Solution: _____				
Offer Name: _____				

FIGURE 5.15 Example of a phase review checklist (joint development and deployment review)

Secondly, services requiring a physical presence of the customer necessitated 'local' decentralised production capacity. Finally, service innovators have not had a tangible product to carry a brand name.

However, ever-increasing economic and competitive pressures have forced product and service innovators to think in similar ways. Services can now be consumed at a considerable distance from where they are produced through the use of web-based technologies – while also allowing integrated service and product branding to be achieved. Similarly, the cost of product development from central manufacturing sites have given way to low-cost regional centres, resulting in an increase in globally distributed development and manufacturing models.

ILLUSTRATION

Example of NPD screening

High levels of waste are not uncommon in many 'funnel like' NPD processes. According to Cooper and Kleinschmidt (1991) only one new product concept out of seven becomes a commercial success. This translates into 46 per cent of corporate resources being expended in cancelled projects or failures.

Percentage of R&D spent on cancelled projects is a standard measure in NPD screening performance. Analysis of this metric suggests these figures have dropped to around 3–5 per cent as a result of more stringent screening, earlier in the NPD funnel.

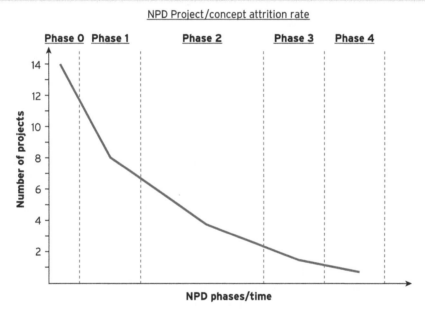

	Phase					
	Concept	Plan	Develop	Deploy	Lifecycle	Total
Number of projects	14	8	4	2	1	
Phase effort (X time units effort)	X	X	4X	2X	2X	10X
Total project commitment (phase effort X number of projects)	14X	8X	16X	4X	2X	44X
Lost R&D through cancelled projects	−6X	−4X	−8X	−2X		−20X
	20X/44X = 46% lost resource due to project attrition					

FIGURE 5.16 NPD project/concept attrition rates

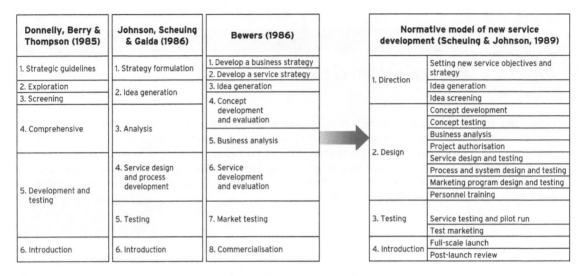

Donnelly, Berry & Thompson (1985)	Johnson, Scheuing & Gaida (1986)	Bewers (1986)	Normative model of new service development (Scheuing & Johnson, 1989)	
1. Strategic guidelines	1. Strategy formulation	1. Develop a business strategy	1. Direction	Setting new service objectives and strategy
		2. Develop a service strategy		
2. Exploration	2. Idea generation	3. Idea generation		Idea generation
3. Screening				Idea screening
4. Comprehensive	3. Analysis	4. Concept development and evaluation	2. Design	Concept development
				Concept testing
		5. Business analysis		Business analysis
				Project authorisation
5. Development and testing	4. Service design and process development	6. Service development and evaluation		Service design and testing
				Process and system design and testing
				Marketing program design and testing
				Personnel training
	5. Testing	7. Market testing	3. Testing	Service testing and pilot run
				Test marketing
6. Introduction	6. Introduction	8. Commercialisation	4. Introduction	Full-scale launch
				Post-launch review

FIGURE 5.17 Normative model for services innovation

With a convergence of thinking between product and service innovators, it makes sense that common innovation models are applied within many firms. However, this has not occurred through design, but rather as a result of many service-orientated firms lacking appropriate innovation structures and processes, and now leveraging the extensive research that has been conducted for products. Many service-orientated firms now rely on formal review (evaluation) committees, new-service project teams and pre-defined review points. Additionally, they are increasingly employing models which are very similar in nature to the product development structures proposed by Booz, Allen and Hamilton (1968).

This was illustrated by Scheuing and Johnson (1989), who proposed a 'Normative Model for Service Innovation' based on earlier service innovation models (see Figure 5.17).

Each model considers the need for strong strategic objectives to be set before ideas are generated and screened. The best ideas are then analysed in more detail, before being developed and tested through a series of pilots and being successfully deployed. This sequence of activities, and the key review points closely mirror generic 'product-related' stage-gate innovation models (see Figure 5.18).

It is only when we drive down to the detailed implementation level of these process models that we might uncover differences, in terms of intangibility, customer contact, non-homogeniety and perishability.

● Service products are normally *intangible* and do not have components that can be perceived by touch. Consequently, the design of the production and delivery mechanism must be carefully planned and creative approaches will be required to help conduct effective market research in this area.

● Deciding on the appropriate degree of *customer contact* is essential. Timing, intimacy and information exchange all need to be considered, and this may necessitate re-training of staff should the new service offering be sufficiently different. In addition, new service prototypes can only be tested with customers – no laboratory testing is possible, so ways in which this is to be performed can also be critical.

● In terms of *non-homogeniety*, service innovations need to take account of the dependency of the service offering on both the consumer and either consistency or customisation

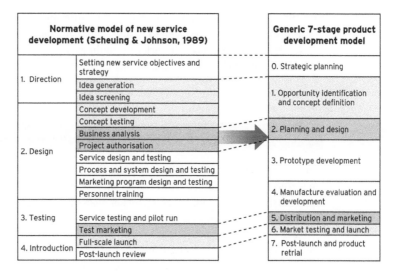

Normative model of new service development (Scheuing & Johnson, 1989)		Generic 7-stage product development model
1. Direction	Setting new service objectives and strategy	0. Strategic planning
	Idea generation	1. Opportunity identification and concept definition
	Idea screening	
2. Design	Concept development	2. Planning and design
	Concept testing	
	Business analysis	
	Project authorisation	
	Service design and testing	3. Prototype development
	Process and system design and testing	
	Marketing program design and testing	4. Manufacture evaluation and development
	Personnel training	
3. Testing	Service testing and pilot run	5. Distribution and marketing
	Test marketing	6. Market testing and launch
4. Introduction	Full-scale launch	7. Post-launch and product retrial
	Post-launch review	

FIGURE 5.18 Comparing service and product innovation models

can be a valid aim. Different customer segments can require changes to both the service and the service augmentation. It is important to identify the main market segments and drivers.

- Since services cannot be stored, the location and timing of the delivery are crucial. The production and consumption of a service are still essentially simultaneous, so it is important to identify the right capacity levels that are required, and where they are to be deployed.

While this does not change the shape of the NDP frameworks, it does introduce the need to be more cognisant of services needs from the customer. Additionally, the power of the internet and open-source communities have enabled customers to share their experiences more readily, allowing them to have a far greater impact on a company's reputation than ever before.

However, it seems clear that these differences will continue to reduce as service and product innovators increasingly attempt to gain a competitive edge by leveraging any number of best practices, for example:

- Service innovation is more effective when the services are consistently defined, deployed and executed against. This attempt at reducing variability is conceptually the same as product platforming approaches.

- Service innovations will be continually defined, refined and improved through successive pilots. Rapid Application Development (RAD) approaches for software have achieved this same goal for many years.

Despite these nuances, it is fair to assume that while significant literature refers specifically to 'product' innovation, the lessons and practices can equally apply to services, with one caveat – the notion of service augmentation.

Customers generally consider both the service offering (the core service received) and the service augmentation (the delivery of the service in terms of customer contact and intimacy). Much research has shown that a competitive advantage is often gained as much by the service augmentation as the service itself. Often, competitors can easily copy new service products, and the speed with which new services can be introduced can create an oversupply. As a result, great care should be taken to ensure service augmentation is explicitly included in the service development process in order to minimise the risk of the innovation being quickly copied. This also helps counter the problem that services are hard to protect through patents (Goffin and Mitchell, 2005)

NPD practices in non-profit organisations

Studies of practices in new product and service development have focussed predominantly on for-profit organisations. However, recent research in this area has yielded some interesting results and conclusions focussing on key areas of strategy, portfolio management, process, market research, people and metrics and performance measurement (Barczak et al., 2006).

Large non-profit organisations tend to be very good at articulating their mission, embedding it throughout, and using it to drive programmes and activities. These organisations tend to view product development as a tactical endeavour versus a strategic one, and do not engage in portfolio management practices. Instead, broad criteria such as fit with vision, funding availability, and presence of a champion are used for evaluation programmes. Additionally, the NPD process tends to be informal, with little structure, and individual departments tend to undertake their own NPD initiatives and have their own processes for doing so. Non-profit organisations also place a heavy emphasis on ideation and less emphasis on other activities such as concept development and testing, project evaluation, and business analysis. It appears that in many cases, the practices applied across for-profit and non-profit organisations are similar, although at different levels of maturity. It also appears that they share some of the same weaknesses, specifically around performance measurement.

Product development performance

Possessing a NPD process is not itself a guarantee for success. A number of factors determine whether a particular project is likely to be successful, and the types of benefits and problems arising from such frameworks can be wide-ranging. To understand the areas in which product development methodologies can be improved, it is beneficial to know the reasons why new products fail. We review the key success factors in NPD, and the benefits they can yield, before turning our attention to the challenges that these frameworks present.

Key success factors in new product development

According to Robert Cooper (1990), who is considered by many as the father of 'stage-gate' development models, there are eight key factors that distinguish winning projects from the losers. Briefly, these are (in descending order of importance):

1. A superior product that delivers unique benefits to the user, rather than 'me too' offerings with little differentiation. Superior products:
   a. Have a commercial success rate of 98.0 per cent, versus 18.4 per cent for undifferentiated ones.
   b. Experience market share of 53.5 per cent, versus 11.6 per cent for 'me too' products.
   c. Rate profitability of 8.4 out of 10 (versus 2.6 out of 10 for undifferentiated products).

2. Possess a well-defined product concept prior to the development phase, which is three times more likely to be successful and capture higher market share (by around 38 per cent on average).

3. Are supported by high-quality technical activities, such as strong technical assessments, trial or pilot production, and/or in-house product or prototyping testing.

4. Driven from a strong fit between the needs of the project and the firm's R&D or product development and engineering competencies and resources.

5. Possess highly effective practices at the (fuzzy) front-end of the development funnel; this includes initial screening, preliminary market and technical assessments, detailed market studies, and business/financial analysis.

6. Feature a strong fit between the needs of the project and its sales, distribution, marketing, advertising and customer services capabilities.

7. Involve effective execution of marketing activities, such as preliminary market assessments, detailed market studies, customer tests of prototypes and market launch. When well executed, success rate can be more than doubled.

8. Are more successful when targeted at more attractive markets (i.e. large markets with high growth rates, or high market need).

When implementing, or operating, a NPD framework, it is important to consider these key success factors and ensure they are being proactively and consistently driven. It is also important to consider the interplay between different success factors, and identifying and driving towards those which the company truly desires. A common example is the relationship between development speed (time-to-market) and product profitability. Companies that succeed in bringing new products to market faster than competitors can obtain first-mover advantages, however more innovative new products are associated with slower development speeds. Recent analysis has suggested that there is an inverted U-shaped relationship between development speed and new product profitability, and that the optimal point in this U-shape differs for product improvements and line extensions. This relationship is important for managers in determining to what extent they wish to accelerate development of new products, and how the associated spending should be spread across the product portfolio.

Benefits of a structured development process

The benefits to be gained from implementing a structured NPD process are many, and are generally divided into benefits that are experienced internally within the organisation (process and business benefits), and those benefits derived externally (market benefits), which are summarised next.

Organisation (process) benefits

Implementing a structured NPD process provides a discipline to what would otherwise be an ad hoc and chaotic process. The provision of a 'roadmap', defining the tasks and deliverables for the project leader, helps improve visibility and understanding of the process by the members of the company. The introduction of evaluation points focusses the attention on quality of execution and ensures no steps or activities are omitted. Its cross-functional coverage forces input and involvement from all parties at the right time, and can help accelerate the process by identifying and allowing opportunities for concurrent activity (Cooper and Kleinschmidt, 1991).

Organisation (business) benefits

A range of business benefits can be obtained by the effective implementation of a structured NPD framework. These can include:

- Improved new product success rates.
- Rapid generation of economies of learning curve with lower overhead and labour costs.
- More information sharing and problem solving across the organisation.
- Lower requirements of working capital.
- Less need for engineering and design changes due to environmental variations (Gehani, 1994).

External (market) benefits

In addition, structured NPD models have also been seen to deliver a range of key market benefits, including higher quality of goods and services, greater customer satisfaction, faster development and more effective and timely launch (Gehani, 1994; Cooper and Kleinschmidt, 1991).

Deficiencies of stage-gate NPD systems

Regardless of the potential gains from adopting a NPD framework, it is not a problem-free process and success is not guaranteed. Analysis of the adoption of NPD by companies raises a number of issues for concern. In some cases NPD programmes have even had a negative impact on the success of the organisation (e.g. Trygg, 1993). Some key causes for concern are:

- Around a quarter of companies who implemented a NPD framework reported worse 'time-to-market' performance.
- Almost two-thirds of company executives state they are 'somewhat' or 'very' disappointed in their firms' new product efforts.
- About half of resources invested in new product programmes are wasted on technical and commercial failures.

The less than startling rate of success is associated with a number of problems and inefficiencies. Most of the potential problems arise from the implementation of the new product development structured methodology. Many implementations of the NPD process have been accompanied by increases in bureaucracy. Additionally, if controls are made too tight they can thwart creativity and slow down decision making. Instead of promoting innovation the process can easily become a deadly plague. Fortunately, many of the problems appear to be caused by implementation-related issues rather than any fundamental failing of the NPD framework. Planning and care in implementation can remedy the problems.

Analysis of product development failures shows a lack of market orientation, weak product uniqueness, little added value, consumer use dissatisfaction, high price, and low quality as the main causes of failure (Lee and Na, 1994). In an extensive study by Cooper (1988), the most common reasons for new product failure were identified as shown in Figure 5.19.

This seems to indicate that major external problems lie in the market-related dimension, particularly the lack of market analysis, reaction of competition and the lack of an effective marketing effort. Internal factors such as technical or production problems also contribute to this by raising internal costs or contribute to poor timing of product introduction. A

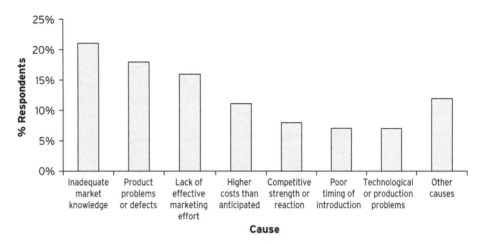

FIGURE 5.19 Common reasons for new product failure

TABLE 5.2 Deficiencies in new product development processes (%)

Deficiencies in the new product development process		Done inadequately	Mistakenly omitted	Total
Market *(average 42%; inadequate, 18% omitted)*	Detailed market study	50	25	75
	Test marketing	37	23	60
	Preliminary market assessment	38	21	59
	Product launch	50	5	55
	Prototype testing with customer	36	14	50
Technical *(average 26%; inadequate, 9% omitted)*	Prototype testing in-house	30	9	39
	Product development	32	6	38
	Pilot production	17	18	35
	Production start-up	22	10	32
	Preliminary technical assessment	28	3	31
Evaluative *(average 35%; inadequate, 10% omitted)*	Detailed financial analysis	40	11	51
	Limited screening	30	9	39

(Source: Cooper, 1988)

further breakdown of these figures offered by Cooper (1988) reveals deficiencies in the new product development process as highlighted in Table 5.2.

From the results shown in Table 5.2, it can be clearly seen that customer orientation is particularly important in successful innovation. It is surprising that many employees, not only scientists and engineers but even marketers, do not understand their customers. The problem is not just a lack of market research making the organisation unsure of customer needs but largely a result of the company's inability to effectively transmit the 'voice of the customer' internally (the classic problem of the ineffective Marketing–Engineering interface). This requires the company to devise ways of correctly exposing employees to customers' needs.

NPD frameworks are also plagued by many problems which are internal to the organisation, and which need not exist. Shortage of resources (time, money, people) occurs because too much attention is given to current activities, leading to insufficient efforts for long-term and radical activities. The present versus future conflict is a central and common source of contradiction, and the problem of inadequate resources can also be felt by taking on an excessive number of projects (e.g. through weak 'kill' criteria or the tendency to consider too broad a range of development directions). Consequently, people work on too many activities, which leads to a tendency to pull expert individuals off one project to fix another one. In some cases, problems here can result in damaging competitive behaviours internally, as individual teams battle fiercely for resources, resulting in one or two teams winning out, but the organisation, as a whole, losing.

Aligned to this can be a vagueness resulting from poor planning, which leads to frequent changes in priorities. Additionally, poorly developed and poorly understood organisational goals lead to a lack of synergistic actions and behaviours. This compounds the problems that may already exist from the chopping and changing of personnel from one project to the next. Consequently, scarce resources are wasted by running in many and often wrong directions.

A lack of commitment and support from top management can also strongly dampen innovation. Leadership that leans toward excessive retrospection and possesses attitudes that reinforce a 'we have always done it this way' view deadens radical innovation. Management, by signalling and reinforcing the norms of behaviour, either encourages or stifles innovation. Innovation begins and ends at the top. One way to try to combat negative tendencies and turn them into positive ones is to introduce initiatives for creativity. Encouraging open communication and providing creativity training are good techniques for doing just this. However, at times it may be necessary to mandate sharing of activities across functional disciplines. Similarly, biases of senior management, especially if toward a single dominant functional area such as marketing or engineering, can actually be very troublesome for well-rounded decisions to be reached. Decisions that take longer than two months often deflate the energy to get things done. The net result: frustration in the recipients.

It is clear that a great deal can be gained if companies are able to improve their customer orientation, and their integration between the technical and marketing functions. Another area for attention is the quality of internal project and resource management. If product development projects are not controlled or poorly resourced the new product development effort will almost invariably end up being a failure.

 ## Modern developments in managing the NPD process

The discussion thus far has presented a structured innovation process system that currently represents the majority of practice. It is a generic structure that is generally considered as a state of the art process. However, new developments are taking place that are taking the innovation and new product development process towards a more advanced stage. We will firstly discuss some significant incremental improvements that have been applied to the standard NPD framework. Next, we elaborate two models that are suggestive of the type of move towards a more advanced generation of innovation framework. The first model is essentially a refinement of the existing structured approach and the second is indicative of the transformation towards a network model (sixth generation) in response to environmental shifts and added complexity.

How companies are evolving their NPD frameworks

Research in the automotive industry has suggested that a third of companies have modified their NPD frameworks, and are likely to use (amongst other things) virtual teams and adopt collaborative and virtual NPD software support tools (Etlie and Eisenbach, 2007). These companies are not alone, as others have adopted capabilities, such as:

- Tailoring to suit different risk level projects.
- Adaptable process to support different development approaches (waterfall and spiral models).
- Efficient, lean, rapid systems.
- More creative approaches towards NPD governance, including self-managed and virtual, electronic decision gates.
- Accountable and continuous improvement.

We will discuss each of these briefly in turn, and show how the NPD frameworks are continuing to innovate.

Tailored NPD structures

Perhaps the most significant change in NPD frameworks over the past few years has been that they have become a scalable process, scaled to suit very different types of risk level projects – from very risky and complex platform developments through to lower level extensions and modifications, and even to rather simple sales force requests (Cooper, 2006; Cooper and Edgett, 2005).

Many companies have attempted to apply a simple stage-gate model for all projects, but found it cumbersome and overbearing. As the NPD frameworks evolved, and were incrementally improved based on previous lessons learned, it became the collective knowledge and experience of those that used it. However, this tended to add administration and bureaucracy as the demands to adhere to the process became more onerous.

To address this challenge, many have tailored their NPD frameworks to allow only the relevant elements to be included in different projects based on need and applicability. One such tailored model is offered by Cooper (2008), who suggests that the initial gate (decision point) acts as a clearing house to direct different projects down different execution routes. The full-blown product developments continue to be driven through the formal NPD structure and decision-making processes, while smaller, low-risk, projects pass through different types of increasingly compressed and lean frameworks (see Figure 5.20).

Adaptable development processes

Just as NPD frameworks have been adjusted to become tailorable, so too have the underlying processes in the 'Structured Development Process' (SDP) become more flexible. Consequently, the concept of spiral/iterative or agile development is now accommodated, allowing project teams to move more rapidly to a final product design through a series of 'build–test–feedback' iterations (Cooper and Edgett, 2005; Hauser et al., 2005). This concept is covered more fully in Chapter 12.

Efficient, lean, rapid systems

In a series of bi-annual benchmarking activities, the Performance Measurement Group (PMG) (2003) identified and refined different stages of maturity in NPD frameworks. Many companies appeared to have stalled at stage 2(b), which was reflective of a mature, functionally strong and standardised NPD process which was beginning to falter as increasing and incremental improvements added further administration and bureaucracy (see Figure 5.21).

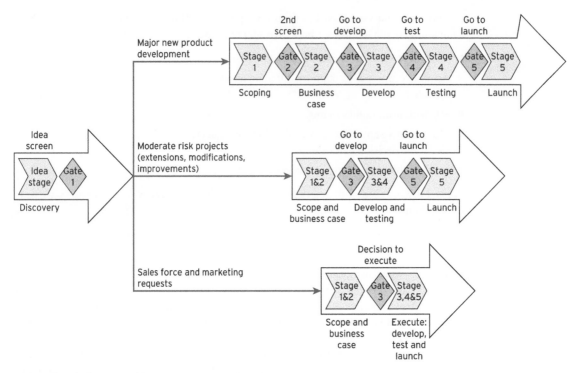

FIGURE 5.20 Tailoring NPD frameworks (the NexGen model)
Source: Cooper, 2008

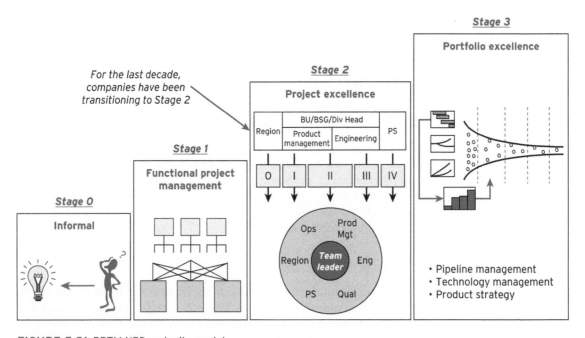

FIGURE 5.21 PRTM NPD maturity model

As a response to this, some companies have made their NPD frameworks lean by removing waste and inefficiency at every opportunity. Key areas of focus have included documents and templates, decision processes, functional deliverables, and the use and attendance of various supporting committees and review boards.

Creative approaches to governance

Deficiencies in NPD governance have already been identified and addressed by some companies (see Chapter 6). Ensuring decision points have teeth, clarifying the roles of the Review Board (gate keepers), and applying portfolio management principles are becoming increasingly common.

Additionally, some companies are making use of scorecards and make better go/kill decisions (e.g. Procter & Gamble, ITT Industries, Johnson & Johnson), while others employ pre-defined success criteria at gates. Other improvements in this area include:

- *Self managed gates*: Where teams conduct their own reviews (or local reviews) for low-cost/low-risk projects.
- *Electronic and virtual gates*: Where decision point review materials are distributed and reviewed remotely by Review Board members, who score and recommend go/kill decisions, which are then consolidated and discussed via teleconference or video-conference, and aided by the use of collaborative IT tools.

Accountable and continuous improvement

Applying disciplined improvement methodologies, such as 6-Sigma, has allowed many companies to drive continuous improvements in NPD, focusing on three major elements (Cooper and Edgett, 2005; Cooper, 2006):

- *Having performance metrics in place*: These metrics measure how well a specific new product project has performed.
- *Establishing team accountability for results*: All members of the project team are fully responsible for performance results when measured against these metrics.
- *Building on learning and improvement*: When the project team misses the target, or when deficiencies occur, or variances to forecasts are seen, they focus on fixing the root causes, not the symptoms (Ledford, 2006).

Iterative learning innovation model of new product development

One interesting refinement upon the basic generic structured model is captured in the iterative model proposed by Hughes and Chafin (1996). Hughes and Chafin propose a value creation model, called the Value Proposition Process (VPP). The focus of this model is on continuous (or iterative) learning to improve the certainty of knowledge used in NPD decision making. By utilising an iterative methodology the model breaks the seemingly linear sequence of the generic model. The model encapsulates the basic steps of the generic model but configures these into a cyclical process. Whilst this departure is essentially incremental it does show potential to refine and advance the current structured approach to new product development.

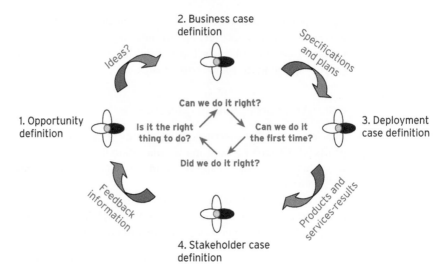

FIGURE 5.22 Continuous life cycle process
Source: Hughes and Chafin, 1996

The objective of the Value Proposition Process is to determine if an organisation can convert an idea or an opportunity into a proposition that adds value to a number of stakeholders: the end users, the company, and the value chain. The VPP consists of a framework of four continuous planning cycles. Each cycle is based on going through a series of sub-loops and passing through an integrated screening methodology. The screens are very much like the stage-gate review point screens in the structured development process.

The VPP is essentially an encompassing life-cycle process that focuses on answering the question: Can we do it right? This is captured in Value Proposition Cycle (VPC). However, often there is an even more basic question that should be answered first: Is it the right thing to do? This question is tackled in the Value Sensing Cycle (VSC). After the VPP, there is another question that usually needs to be asked: Can we do it right the first time? This is answered by going through the loops of the Value Introduction Cycle (VIC). Once the product or service begins to be commercialised, there is an ongoing evaluation question: Did we do it right? This question must be answered from the point of view of the four stakeholders: the customers, the employees, the suppliers and the stockholders, and is captured in the Value Management Cycle (VMC) (see Figure 5.22). In other words, four cycles are used to answer questions that frame the portfolio of a product development life cycle.

Value proposition cycle

The VPC methodology is presented in detail, since the basic sequence is repeated in the other cycles but with a different set of questions and screens. The VPC comprises four iterative loops (see Figure 5.23). Each loop raises a set of critical questions and addresses the following activities: defining the market value of the opposition (Does the customer care?); developing the business value (Do we care?); delivering a winning solution (Can we beat the competition?); and applying project and process planning (Can we do it?).

Each turn of the VPC loop requires going through a screen, very much like the screens shown for the generic process. The screens summarise the critical factors for success. The number of success factors varies according to product newness, complexity, and amount of

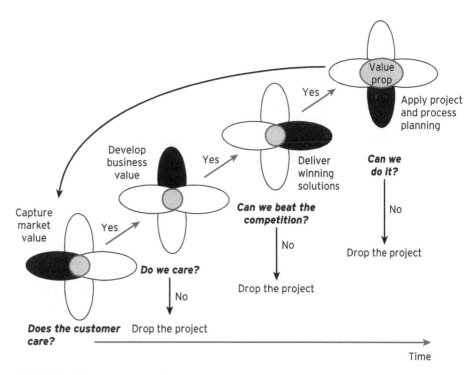

FIGURE 5.23 Value proposition cycle
Source: Hughes and Chafin, 1996

risk. New and risky products with a high cost of failure require more items in the screen. A simpler project such as a line extension can use a reduced set of evaluation criteria.

Value Sensing Cycle

The portfolio life cycle process can begin at any point in the life cycle if a product already exists. A really new product would begin at the idea generation stage, known as the Value Sensing Cycle (VSC). This cycle continuously scans the market, the business environment, competition and technology to identify new ideas or opportunities. These ideas are screened and reduced to a manageable few, which are then passed along to the VPC.

Value Introducing Cycle

Once the team and the organisation have used the VPC and agreed that they can do it right, the proposition is translated into the final specifications and plans, and fed into the Value Introduction Cycle (VIC). This cycle consists of a highly disciplined process to develop, produce, verify and deploy the solution initially to all target market segments, and over time any additional market segments. The output of this cycle is products and services and the required support infrastructure that provides the input for the Value Management Cycle (VMC).

Value Management Cycle

The VMC continuously screens market and business performance to answer the question: Did we do it right? The monitoring is from the point of view of customers, employees, suppliers and stockholders. Critical questions must be answered at each of the four loops in the VMC such as:

- Do our customers perceive that they are paying a fair price for the benefit received?
- Do the project team members feel motivated by what they accomplished?
- Do we have strong supplier partnerships that will assure favoured customer treatment from them?
- Are we profitable and adding shareholder value?

Metrics from each of these four loops are an important part of the CEO's dashboard. Critical feedback from the VMC is linked and fed into the VSC to complete the life cycle. The cycle is then continuously reiterated.

The iterative model is interesting because it reinforces the focus on the value delivery in innovation. But perhaps of even more interest is that it examines value from a number of stakeholder positions. Most models of innovation unfortunately just focus on one or two stakeholder interests: either the shareholder by looking after the bottom line of the organisation or the customer. Under such positions the role and importance of the other stakeholders is either completely ignored or given short shrift. Yet for a company to build an innovative culture and a positive image and standing in its environment it must provide value to its employees and society too. By examining development projects using a broader 'stakeholder value' approach, it is possible to identify the multiple dimensions a company must focus upon to drive sustainable success.

Network innovation: the solutions innovation model

As discussed earlier, there has been a shift toward network models for innovation over time. The questions arising are 'why is this move occurring' and 'what are the fundamental issues of this transition'. In order to illustrate these issues, we elaborate a specific variant of network innovation: the solutions innovation approach.

Companies that have relied on traditional structured NPD frameworks, such as those encapsulated by the generic development process described earlier, are coming under increasing pressure. Technologies are evolving ever more rapidly. This has reduced the span of an average product life cycle, making products less profitable than comparable offerings in previous generations. Products are also increasingly becoming commoditised and payback periods shorter. Furthermore, market segments have begun to fragment as customers' needs become ever more sophisticated. Customers are demanding unique customised products or solutions. They are no longer satisfied with a generic fulfilment of their specific 'individual' needs. Adding to this, shareholders are also demanding greater returns on their investments, and unlike in the past they now exhibit a greater and quicker tendency to switch their investments to other more profitable portfolios. On top of all this, there is no let-up in the intensity of global competition. Given these changes, it is small wonder that many senior executives are becoming overwhelmed by the challenges facing them. They are experiencing pressures that undermine the advantages they have established over many years.

Some companies have chosen to address these problems by attempting to strengthen their current business models (e.g. by intensifying efforts to reduce costs and maintain margins) or rationalising their current portfolios (e.g. discarding less profitable product lines). Unfortunately for these companies, if they continue simply to drive incremental improvements internally, the nature of the external forces will be kept at bay only for a short while. In order to tackle these trends it is necessary to fundamentally question the existing new product development framework. Shepherd and Ahmed (2000) propose solutions-based innovation as a method to cope with the new environment. They argue that under fast-changing complex environments, in which there is heightened demand for customised need fulfilment, companies must move to building solutions for end customers rather than just developing simple products. If they can do this they will be able to build long-term sustainable positions of competitive advantage and profitability.

Some features of this approach are already being observed in leading-edge companies. The solutions innovation phenomenon started in the corporate consultancy sector and the high-end computing and electronics sector. Faced with the new environmental challenges many leading-edge companies across all sectors have been quick to realise the importance of innovating 'solutions' as opposed to just products. So what exactly is solutions innovation? To answer this, we need first to examine the underlying features of the traditional product-led innovation paradigm.

Traditional NPD frameworks have been employed to effectively design, develop and manufacture products to meet the needs of established markets. In this paradigm, all decisions are made at the product level. This perspective is based on a simplistic and atomistic view of products and services. Each product is considered, developed and evaluated in isolation. The investment decision to develop a product is made on the product's projected revenue stream, and each product that is developed is evaluated separately and independently (Figure 5.24). Additionally, each product is developed to meet a specific yet generic mass-market need. While the needs of end customers remained relatively simple this approach to innovation was able to deliver competitive advantage. However, when the needs become more sophisticated and complex this paradigm beings to reach its limits.

When customers begin to demand complex and uniquely customised 'solutions', the product-centric development process begins to break down. A few illustrative examples are helpful in understanding these developments. For example, a number of select and increasingly sophisticated holidaymakers are now looking for a customised solution to their needs. They do not just want to book an airline to fly them to their destination. They want a taxi to

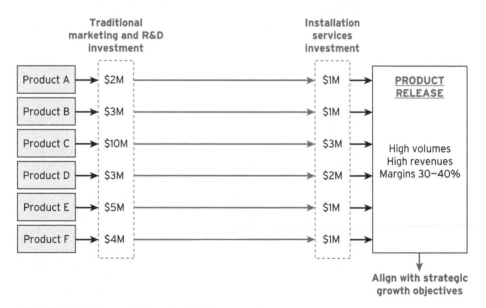

FIGURE 5.24 Product focus in NPD frameworks
Source: Shepherd and Ahmed, 2000

take them to the airport, they may have a gluten food allergy or they may be diabetic and so they want the airline to remember their particular dietary requirement, they want an onwards taxi to their hotel and they want the hotel to know of their dietary restrictions too. They may even want their pets to be looked after while they are away on holiday. Now a traditional company would focus on providing a product, such as say pet care or booking tickets, but a solutions-led company would perceive the need to develop a total solution to fit the customer's needs. They would compile the different narrow needs into a package that provides an entire solution. The solutions company would be able to offer a service for pets, taxi for transport, and have an interconnection with hotels to ensure dietary needs and other relevant information was communicated.

To deliver on such a promise the solutions company would need to possess an extended capability, one that is well beyond the realms of a simple product innovator. Let us look at a few more illustrations to demonstrate this point. In the banking sector, affluent customers are not just looking for safe deposit of their money but a financial solution to manage their income wisely. In addressing this need, leading-edge banks such as Lloyds TSB have for certain categories of customers (such as platinum card carriers) privilege managers, whose role is to provide an array of services, advice and support. These privilege managers assist in investment planning, insurance advice, pension planning to arranging a mortgage and so on. The emphasis is on providing a financial solution rather than just a product. In other words, they cater to the specific and complex needs of the end customer. An alternative example is from the telecommunications sector. This is a sector where solutions innovation is gaining increasing relevance. Telephones are no longer just devices for simple communication. Mobile phones provide a full connectivity solution. The range of features in a mobile phone are indicative of a complex packaged solution: voice communication, text-based communication, a camera facility, WAP-based internet connectivity, radio facility, time clock, diary organiser, calculator, and even applications that help to track and plan shares and stocks portfolios. In this sector, it is not possible to simply offer a narrow product. Mobile phone companies have to bundle a large range of components into a single package. This requires companies to either possess or have control over a vastly larger range of capabilities. For example, Samsung made great inroads into the mobile phone market because it was able to leverage a capability from its other operations, namely camera technology. The sharper picture resolution and design of Samsung mobile phones was in large part from the company's strength in electronics and cameras. Bundling the camera facility into the mobile phone helped Samsung rise to a prominent position in the mobile market.

Clearly, when customers demand customisation or complex products the challenge of innovation becomes greater. Rather than just developing new products the companies are faced with the challenge of configuring a solution. This is a much more demanding task. Shepherd and Ahmed (2000) define a solutions company as one that integrates component products (or sub-components of a product) and services to provide a solution to a complex customer problem.

To further illustrate solutions innovation let us look at Automatic Teller Machines (ATM) as an example. Consumers come across ATMs as cash machines. ATM manufacturers are part of the computing and electronics sector. One of the largest companies in the sector is NCR. The clients of NCR are primarily banks and building societies. The end customer is however the person on the street, wishing to withdraw cash. The traditional approach to innovation at NCR was simply to focus on the hardware, i.e. develop a high-quality cash point machine. NCR's market intelligence indicated that ATMs could be potentially turned into 'solution providers' rather than just cash dispensers for end customers. For instance, an ATM could function as a computer by allowing internet access, etc. If you examine newly installed ATMs you are likely to find a number of additional features linked into the cash dispensation function. One that has recently taken off is the incorporation of a mobile phone top-up facility. Other features allow payment of bills and engagement in other financial transactions. To be able to incorporate these features NCR had to develop new software and services in the ATM hardware. In other words, to move from a product innovator to a solution innovator the company had to not only innovate new hardware, but also innovate in terms of creating new software and services. The hardware, software and services are separate components of product development. However, when appropriately combined they create a solution. This requires the company to innovate not just hardware but also software and services. However, once the software, service or hardware components have been developed for the specific needs of the client they can be used as components to develop solutions for other customers through a careful process of bundling and integration. In other words, each of the components may be subsequently leveraged to compile bundles as customised solutions for other customers (see Figure 5.25).

The solutions innovator gains access to a double revenue stream: one from the product innovation alone (i.e. component parts of the solution, such as hardware, software or services in our example). The second stream is from creating the solution through effective bundling. In fact, the way this works is that the company first undertakes to provide a unique customised solution for which it can charge premium price. The customised solution is subsequently examined or broken down into components, and each component if possible is used to produce other unique solutions through recombination. In the process of innovating new solutions it is often necessary to innovate along one or more component parts. These component innovations can then be either used in future bundling of unique solutions or released/sold to the market as product developments of themselves. Thus, a dual stream of income is realised.

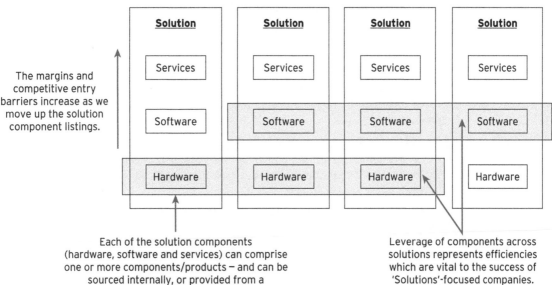

FIGURE 5.25 Solutions portfolio – a generic model
Source: Shepherd and Ahmed, 2000

ILLUSTRATION

BASF looks to develop customer solutions

In 2003, BASF AG signed an agreement with Omya, a Swiss-based producer of white minerals, to co-operate in the development of paper making and coatings products by using each other's R&D facilities. While Omya makes calcium carbonates and talcs for use as fillers and pigments, BASF produces binders and dispersions for paper makers.

'Paper companies are increasingly demanding solutions from their suppliers that have already been tested and shown to work', says a BASF official.

Under the agreement, Omya gets access to a pilot coating machine at BASF's paper technical centre in Ludwigshafen, Germany, after closing its own testing coating equipment at its headquarters in Oftringen, near Zurich, Switzerland. At the same time, BASF will be able to test its products at Omya's printing centre at Oftringen.

'The alliance with Omya makes it easier for us to offer holistic system solutions to our customers', says Hans Richard Schmidt, a spokeperson for BASF's European business unit for paper. 'It also enables us to make the process of rendering services less costly.'

(*Source*: Based on Milmo, 2003)

Any company embarking on this type of strategic repositioning must first establish exactly what kind of solutions it wants to provide as part of its solution portfolio, and also articulate a business model to drive growth through an effective move from 'products' to 'solutions'. The realignment from a 'product' to 'solutions' focussed innovation model represents a significant strategic repositioning, for which senior executives need to provide answers to some fundamental questions, such as:

- Is there more money to be made in fixing more complex problems than the ones we address now?
- Is there more money in being the first to understand and fix a problem?
- Are we close enough to our customers (particularly high-level management) to understand their industry trends as least as well as they do, and influence those who make the key decisions?
- Which core competencies do we possess that offers a significant competitive differentiation?
- Since leverage is essential to profitability, what products, services and competencies are available to us to provide the necessary solutions, and which do we need to acquire through alliances/partnerships?
- What strategies do we need to fill the gaps in our intended solutions, and what is the desired roadmap?

An important challenge for the solution innovator is the dramatically higher requirement in terms of a company's core capabilities. Creating a solution demands not only greater resources but more importantly much broader and wider capabilities. It is more than likely that no single firm alone possesses all the skills and expertise to produce a solution. To create the solution the company must link up with partner firms that possess specific skills and expertise in the components necessary to develop the solution. In other words, the innovation challenge is one that extends beyond the company's boundary of expertise and experience. The challenge of managing innovation in a solution-led organisation is one of managing external partnerships, and not just internal participants.

In moving to solutions innovation a company needs to extend its range of innovation competencies. A solution innovator requires to build four key competencies for success:

Market/business knowledge competence

The area that best articulates what it means to be a solutions-focussed company is defined at the customer interface. The success of solutions-based innovation rests on identifying customer needs for solutions in the first place. A key objective in defining solutions is to identify opportunities for increasing the mix of higher margin components. Ultimately, if no such complex need exists then there is little value to becoming a solution-centric organisation. The solutions provider must understand end customer needs in detail and more holistically since solutions require the bundling of what on the surface may seem to be separate product needs. To uncover, or better define, problems for which solutions are required the solutions innovator must find new ways of delving into customer need-bundles. As such, solutions innovators need a closer and deeper relationship with end customers than product-centric firms. They need to be involved in the customer's world in order to uncover their complex bundles, and they need to involve the customer in their world by finding ways of eliciting customer participation in the innovation development process. Rather than conducting transactions the solution innovator must develop strong symbiotic relationships.

For instance, in a business-to-business context, where the customer is another business, the solutions provider must build a strategic understanding of the client's business. The solutions innovator must understand the industry in which the client operates, its current position and future direction of development even better then the client does. Only by having such deep knowledge can the solutions provider begin to construct convincing solutions for the client themselves. This deep market knowledge capability is essential to develop long-term win–win solutions. Without such in-depth insight it is not possible to configure solutions. In a business-to-business context this would involve developing relationships not at mid-manager level, such as with the purchasing manager, as is the case in product-centric development but with senior executives. Links with the client company at the senior executive level are necessary to appreciate their strategic aspirations and long-term objectives. These become the basis from which to develop solutions.

Technical competence

Adopting a solutions-focussed business model requires a company to control and manage a wider set of competencies. The company needs to strengthen existing competencies and also develop new competencies either alone or in partnership with others. The technical challenge is to be leading edge in a number of key areas that are critical to the formulation and delivery of the solution. This can be achieved in a number of different ways other than just through internal development. Especially in making the transition from a product innovator to a solutions innovator, most companies will find they simply do not possess all the competencies to develop solutions. They can address this through a number of alternative routes such as mergers, acquisitions, sub-contracting or partnerships. This leads on to the next critical competence for solutions innovation, namely network or partnership competence.

Partnership competence

In highly complex environments it is unlikely that any single organisation will possess, or wish to possess, all the necessary skills and technological collateral to meet the broad enterprise-wide needs of its customers. To develop a solution usually demands sourcing and integrating both internally and externally supplied components into the solution. It is therefore necessary that effective and enduring relationships are established with partner firms, who possess a strong knowledge and capability base in the different components. In this network, the solutions innovator adopts the role of a trusted focal integrator who identifies and develops the 'solution' by integrating the components such that all the partners in the network benefit. A strong project management competence is needed here!

Integration competence

To develop solutions means that the company must be able to integrate the components seamlessly and efficiently so as to deliver high value. This demands an integration capability to put together the different components to compile a solution. However, the expertise required is not only in technical integration of components but also an ability to identify valuable business, process and organisational integration opportunities. This requires the solutions innovator to first have an appropriate network of partners and second, the ability to manage the relationships to facilitate integration. Underpinning this, of course, is trust and the management of a complex web of partner relationships.

It is clear that an organisation adopting a solutions focus needs to be able to articulate its solution offerings clearly and ensure the components that they comprise can be provided. Consequently, the competence profile of the solutions-focussed company sees a progressive move away from a strong technical competence to one which is more balanced with market/business knowledge, partnership and integration competencies. Figure 5.26 illustrates the move required to become a solutions innovator.

It is important to note that although we have discussed solutions innovation in seemingly discrete block components (product components, service, hardware, software, etc.), the solutions concept is actually quite generic. It extends to complex products, and even in some cases to what look on the surface like simple products. For instance, often it is the case that complex products, such as drugs, are viewed as simple product entities by customers. However, their development frequently involves the coming together of several different component technologies and capabilities, i.e. the product is actually made up of sub-components

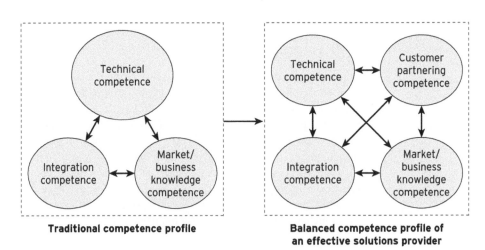

Traditional competence profile   **Balanced competence profile of an effective solutions provider**

FIGURE 5.26 Organisational competence of a solutions provider
Source: Shepherd and Ahmed, 2000

which a single firm alone may not possess. This is particularly the case in the new drug development sector, which is now experiencing a convergence between nanotechnology, bio-science with pharmaceutical development. Such 'complex products' are actually made up from sub-component elements that must come together to produce a seamless product solution. Additionally, products that one may think of as simple, are also being examined and innovated from a solutions perspective. Take, for example, toothpaste. It is no longer developed as a simple tooth-cleansing paste, but is formulated as a bacterial wash for the mouth and tongue. Nike is a great example of solutions positioning. Nike is not just designing shoes for performance but it is now beginning to consider bundling an athletics solution by providing sports coaches to its customer geared to develop the customer skills in the specific type of Nike shoe they purchase.

In this section we have presented an overview of the challenges facing traditional, 'product'-focussed companies in a world of rapidly changing technologies, increasing product commoditisation and more sophisticated customer needs. A number of world-class companies recognising that their traditional business is under threat are adopting a solutions-focussed business model to sustain their long-term profit and growth aspirations. The solutions model encourages companies to integrate component products (or component parts of a product) and services in a manner that allows them to meet the complex needs of their customers. Such a strategic change requires a significant overhaul in the company's NPD frameworks. An adjustment in the skills mix and organisation structure is often demanded to execute solutions innovation effectively. Solutions innovators must develop new practices and frameworks to exploit 'solutions' opportunities. Moreover, management in these environments need more and better quality information to guide their decision making as well as track performance. This is not a trivial, or simple, thing to achieve.

The challenges we have defined specifically for solutions innovators are the general challenges of network innovation. We have used the solutions approach to highlight the organisational demands that must be tackled by companies wishing to move to a network system of innovation. The network approach is based on collaborative links and relationships. Chesborough (2003) conceptualises this shift to links and relationships as 'open innovation'. In the developing the solutions model we have highlighted not just the challenges but also the reasons for the shift toward network systems of innovation. Becoming a solutions innovator specifically, and network innovator broadly, demands significant organisational shift. Companies that attempt this are engaging in an act of strategic and process innovation. Organisational innovation is required to develop the new competencies to become a solutions innovator. The evolution to a network (or solutions-focussed) business model is a high-risk and complex strategy, but in today's rapidly changing economic and technological climate there seems little alternative.

ILLUSTRATION

From technology to functionalities: Rhodia's partnership approach to innovate solutions

R&D partnership between speciality chemical companies and their customers are relatively common-place in the development of new products. Several European chemical companies are taking this further and extending product development to include not only suppliers and customers, but also other players in the chain, such as retailers and designers in the home and personal care markets.

With a current allocation of around 20 per cent of its R&D budget to such broad-based research partnerships, Rhodia considers itself to be pioneering a new way of conducting research and development in the chemicals sector.

'This is truly a revolution in the approach to new product development', says Jean-Julien Baronnet, Rhodia's group executive vice-president responsible for developing the new partnership business model.

'Companies in sectors such as detergents, automobiles and food are moving away from a culture of secrecy in research into one involving strategic alliances', he adds. 'The future of R&D now lies in these sort of alliances. Trying to develop products alone is wishful thinking. The discovery of new products has become more and more complex because it involves so many different competences in addition to chemicals.'

In October 2002, Mr Baronnet, speaking at the World Detergents Conference in Montreux, Switzerland, stated that when tackling new product development, companies like his own are beginning to think more in terms of functionalities than technologies.

'Our organization is market- and customer-oriented, so that we may have an intimate understanding of market trends and our customers' expectations', he explains. 'This enables us to identify unmet customer needs. These needs are translated in terms of functionalities, and we determine what technologies and expertise are necessary to satisfy them.'

Functionalities in detergents include surface modification for easy cleaning, surface adhesion for textile fabric care and controlled release for time-controlled discharge of perfumes.

'A major problem with perfumes in detergents is that 80 to 90 per cent of them are destroyed in the wash, yet they can account for around 30 per cent of the cost of the formulation', Mr Baronnet notes. 'The solution to the problem in terms of functionality is controlled release, which can help to reduce the destruction level down to 40 per cent and generate huge savings. But a control release system can involve three to four complementary technologies in areas like latex, polymers, [and] minerals such as silica and surfactants.'

Like technologies, similar functionalities can be applied across a range of markets. Rhodia is using surface modification in sectors such as fabric care, hygiene and automotives.

'Our polyamide fibers division is working on the surface modification of fibres so they can capture smells like dog odours in cars', says Mr Baronnet. 'We are using surface modification of fibres to eliminate stains, while we also see opportunities for applications in areas like babies' tissues.'

Around half of Rhodia's R&D expenditure is allocated to one-to-one co-operation projects with individual customers, which are based on the company's system of cross-fertilisation of technologies. Over the last two years, Rhodia has pursued a strategy of cross-linking its own technologies to help build close R&D partnerships with customers. In these, Rhodia businesses that have helped launch the new strategy, research partnerships have boosted average returns on capital employed to around 15 per cent, roughly a fourfold increase. The partnerships have been such a success that the company is rolling out the concept across the company and extending the scope of the alliances beyond direct customers.

'We are bringing together companies which are complementary to each other', explains Mr Baronnet. 'In the field of surface modification, for example, we would want to get around the table a textile manufacturer, our own polyamide and detergents businesses, a soaper, a retailer and a designer.'

The company is already helping to develop clothes using fibres with antibacterial and anti-odour properties for Benetton, the retail chain.

'If necessary, we will bring into these alliances competitors who are strong in a specific technology relevant to a functionality we are working on', Mr Baronnet says. 'The important thing will be that we will not be in competition with these chemical companies in the same markets with the same functionality.'

Rhodia is finding that in sectors such as detergents, these broader alliances tend to comprise three to four companies. In its automotives activity, the partners number five or more.

'What we are helping to develop are virtual companies whose members have the same objective of satisfying unmet consumer needs by working together on the same research programs', Mr Baronnet explains.

(*Source*: Based on Milmo, 2002)

Conclusion

In this chapter we examined how innovation management processes have evolved into their current state of being. This is instructive in that it highlights a trajectory of continuous improvement in the approaches and it emphasises the need to build upon the current legacy of innovation systems. The effectiveness of the approaches is very much contingent upon the specific context a company faces. Unquestioned adoption of frameworks and associated tools is likely to result in failure. Success requires careful understanding of the specific constraints and opportunities both internal and external to the organisation, and selection and adaptation of an innovation framework that capitalises on this context.

In elaborating the generic structured development model we defined the fundamental activities and structures required for a modern product development system. We went on to highlight the iterative learning and the solutions model as two formats that potentially define the trajectory of development for modern innovation practice. The iterative learning model focusses upon continuous learning more thoroughly than earlier innovation processes. It is also driven by a stronger focus on incorporating value for a wider set of stakeholders than previously, i.e. using more than just shareholders as a yardstick of success and decision making. The solutions model focusses on the challenges facing management of innovation as environments become more complex and end customer needs become more sophisticated. The solutions model is a specific illustration of the shift toward network-based innovation. It shows that the current structured product development methods are inadequate in the face of new environmental challenges. And to move from product-centric innovation to solution-centric will require companies to undertake strategic innovation in the process of innovation itself. Perhaps taken individually these models represent moderate improvements to current understanding of the innovation process. Taken together, however, the models are representative of the evolutionary trajectory towards a new generation of innovation management processes.

QUESTIONS

1. What are the six major stages through which innovation process management systems have evolved? Define the pros and cons for each approach.

2. What are the four basic components that constitute a generic NPD framework?

3. What are the advantages of implementing a structured product development (SDP) model? What are potential limitations or problems of this approach?

4. Explain the reasons behind the Japanese ability to parallel process new product development activities. Why do some western companies find it difficult to emulate this model? How have western companies been able to come to grips with the parallel processing model of development?

5. How do NPD frameworks differ between a product/service-focussed business, and one that is positioned as a network innovator or solutions provider?

6. Define the key organisational challenges in becoming a network innovator.

7. What dynamics are driving the shift towards network innovation generally, and toward solutions innovation specifically?

CASE STUDY

Outside the beauty box

When Molton Brown chief executive Sara Halton wanted to inject fresh life into the 34-year-old brand, she didn't just talk to the people in new product development. She set up an advisory board – calling in Hip Hotel founder Herbert J.M. Ypma, interior decorator Andrew Martin and horticulturist Guy Barter, and six other experts. 'I thought it would help us to think differently', Halton says. 'Ideas come out of the most surprising places sometimes.'

This is a new way of thinking about beauty product development. Traditionally, a company would see a gap in the market and talk to its laboratories or create a product in response to a competitor's launch. But lately, the approach has been quite different. Nivea, for example, has just set up a discussion group with Stephen Bayley, creator of the Design Museum, in the chair. Its aim is to answer this question: 'what is beauty?' 'Creating new products is not the reason for the group', says Ann-Louise Holland, PR manager for Nivea's parent company, Biersdorf UK. However, 'if light bulbs for new products come out of it, we'll pick up on them.'

Five years previously, Chris Sanderson at the Future Laboratory, a trend-forecasting strategic consultancy, received a call from Procter & Gamble. 'We were commissioned by them to look into the concept of light, without knowing why', Sanderson says. The outcome was *The Book of Light*, a report that offered insights into how the cosmetics market was set to change over the coming decade. And the result in product terms is rumoured to be the bestselling Olay Regenerist range.

Then there's the Mind Gym, a corporate consultancy famed for coming up with the concept of the stuffed crust pizza during one of their workshops, who were approached by GlaxoSmithKline to run a 'Generating Creative Sparks' workshop with its oral hygiene team.

'It's a cornucopia of stimuli to the senses', explains Octavius Black, global managing director of the Mind Gym and co-author of *The Mind Gym: Wake Your Mind Up*. One exercise, for example, involves objects such as teddy bears or rubber being proffered with the objective to create ideas in a specific field.

According to Sarah Leonard, vice president of leadership and organisation for GlaxoSmithKline, 'in just 90 minutes, the business generated over 60 innovative concepts for new product development, of which 30 were then taken and further progressed.' One new, top-secret toothpaste is being launched on the back of the workshop.

It's not just idea generation that is being revolutionised, though; these days the big beauty giants are creating products using more esoteric sources.

For example, the technology used to develop protective clothing in Japan has been modified for use in skincare. It takes the form of an ingredient called Diakalyte in an anti-ageing product by L'Oréal's Biotherm, called Source Thérapie Superactiv serum.

'L'Oréal has a worldwide open innovation process that looks for any new technologies and concepts mastered in other industries that could be of interest to the cosmetics industry', says Patricia Pineau, L'Oréal's director of scientific communications. 'We took the technology from the waterproof fabric and translated it to work for a skin cream. We wanted to preserve skin transparency as well as increase the diffusion of light. In other words, create the optical effect of a skin surface that is at once smooth, transparent and matt.'

The food industry, too, is proving fertile territory for the beauty industry. Clinique's Supermoisture make-up is made using a machine similar to that traditionally used in ice-cream vans. 'Our textural prototype to research and development was yoghurt', explains Scott Miselnicky, Clinique's executive director of worldwide make-up product development. Clinique was interested in the ice-cream technology 'for the reason that it changes the chemical properties of the emulsion and comes out as a mousse.'

In fact, changing the intellectual properties of the beauty industry itself is what this is really all about. 'During our first meeting [with the advisory board], the conversation ranged from elephant polo to organic food', recalls Molton Brown's Sara Halton. 'It was like being at a very interesting dinner party.'

(*Source*: B. Aldin, 'Outside the beauty box', *FT*, 27 September 2008)
© The Financial Times Limited

QUESTIONS

1. To what extent does this case study justify being innovative in an organisation's approach to innovation?
2. Analyse and categorise the different approaches that are described.
3. Consider another industry very different from skincare and suggest ways in which they could benefit from looking at that industry from outside the box.

References

Aldin, B. (2008), 'Outside the beauty box', *Financial Times*, 27 September.

Anthony, M.T. and McKay, J. (1992), 'From experience: Balancing the product development process: Achieving product and cycle-time excellence in high technology industries', *Journal of Product Innovation Management* 9: 140–147.

Berry, L.L., Shankar, V., Parish, J.T., Cadwallader, S. and Dotzel, T. (2006), 'Creating new markets through service innovation', *MIT Sloan Management Review* 47(2): 56–63.

Barczak, G., Kahn, K.B. and Moss, R. (2006), 'Exploratory investigation of NPD practices in non-profit organisations', *Journal of Product Innovation Management* 23(6): 512–527.

Booz, Allen and Hamilton (1968), *Management of new products*, Chicago: Booz, Allen & Hamilton.

Bowers, M.R. (1986), 'The new product development process: A Suggested model for banks', *Journal of Retail Banking* (8): 19–24.

Calantone, R.J., Vickery, S.K. and Droge, C. (1995), 'Business performance and strategic new product development activities: An empirical investigation', *Journal of Product Innovation Management* 12: 1–10.

Chesborough, H. (2003), *Open innovation: The new imperative for creating and profiting from technology*, Boston MA: Harvard Business School Press.

Cooper, R.G. (1988), *Winning at New Products*, Scarborough, ON: Gage Educational Publishing.

Cooper, R.G. (2000), 'Doing it right: Winning with new products', *Ivey Business Journal*, July–August, 54–60, **www.stage-gate.com**

Cooper, R.G. (2006), 'Formula for success', *Marketing Management Magazine* (American Marketing Association), March–April: 21–24.

Cooper, R.G. (2008), 'Perspective: The stage-gate idea-to-launch process – update: What's new and NexGen systems', *Journal of Product Innovation Management* 25(3): 213–232.

Cooper, R.G. & Edgett, S.J. (2005), *Lean, rapid, and profitable new product development*, Ancaster, ON: Product Development Institute.

Cooper, R.G. and Kleinschmidt, E.J. (1991), 'Formal processes for managing new products: The industry experience', Faculty of Business, McMaster University, Hamilton, Ontario, Canada.

Donnelly, J.H., Berry, L.L. and Thompson, T.W. (1985), *Marketing financial services*, Homewood, IL: Dow Jones-Irwin.

Etlie, J.E. and Eisenbach, J.M. (2007), 'Modified stage-gate regimes in new product development', *Journal of Product Innovation Management* 24(1): 20–33.

Frey, D. (1991), 'Learning the ropes: My life as a product champion', *Harvard Business Review*, September–October: 46–56.

Gehani, R.R. (1994), 'Concurrent product development for fast-track corporations', *Long Range Planning* 27(2): 40–47.

Goffin, K. and Mitchell, R. (2005), *Innovation management: Strategy and implementation using the pentathalon framework*, Houndmill: Palgrave MacMillan, Ch.3.

Hauser, J., Tellis, G.J. and Griffin, A. (2005), '*Research on innovation: A review and agenda for marketing science*, Cambridge, MA: Marketing Science Institute.

Hughes, G.D. and Chafin, D.C. (1996), 'Turning new product development into a continuous learning process', *Journal of Product Innovation Management* 13: 89–104.

Johnson, E.M., Scheuing, E.E. and Gaida, K.A. (1986), *Profitable service marketing*, Homewood, IL: Dow Jones-Irwin.

Keithley, J.P. (2003), 'Nanotech innovations hinge on measurement technology and close alliances', *R&D* 45(11): 16.

Larson, E. and Gobeli, D.H. (1989), 'Significance of project management structure on development success', *IEEE Transactions on Engineering Management* 36(2): 119–125.

Ledford, R.D. (2006), 'NPD 2.0: Raising Emerson's NPOD process to the next level', in *Innovations*, St. Louis: Emerson Electric.

Lee, M. and Na, D. (1994), 'Determinants of technical success in product development where innovative radicalness is considered', *Journal of Product Innovation Management* 11: 62–68.

MatrixOne (2005), *MatrixOne success stories*, MatrixOne Inc, Marketing Publications.

McGrath, M.E., Anthony, M.T. and Shapiro, A.R. (1992), *Product development: Success through product and cycle-time excellence (PACE)*, London: Butterworth-Heinemann.

Milmo, S. (2002), 'Rhodia adopts innovative alliances to foster product development', *Chemical Market Reporter*, 28 October 262(15): 6–8.

Milmo, S. (2003), 'BASF and Omya form paper chemicals alliance', *Chemical Market Reporter*, 12 May 263(19): 6.

Performance Measurement Group (2003), 'NPD benchmarking survey', PRTM (Pitigglio, Raban, Todd & McGrath).

Perkins, C. (2008), Innovation leader summit: Open innovation executive roundtable, Pure Insight.

Pure Insight (2006), Insight library paper entitled 'Ideation and Innovation Trends and Success Indicators, **http://member.pure-insight.com/library/item/552.**

Quinion, M. (2005), *World wide words*, **http://www.worldwidewords.org/qa/qa-skul.htm.**

Rothwell, R. (1994), 'Towards the fifth-generation innovation process', *International Marketing Review* 11(1): 7–31.

Rothwell, R. (1992), 'Successful industrial innovation: Critical factors for the 1990s', *R&D Management* 22(3): 221–238.

Shepherd, C. and Ahmed, P.K. (2000), 'From product innovation to solutions innovation: a new paradigm for competitive advantage', *European Journal of Innovation Management* 3(2): 100–106. Scheuing, E. & Johnson, E. (1989), 'A proposed model for new service development', *Journal of Service Marketing* 3(2): 25–34.

Stackpole, B. (2003), 'There's a new app in town', *CIO*, 15 May: 93–98.

Trygg, L. (1993), 'Concurrent engineering practices in selected Swedish companies: A movement or an activity of the few', *Journal of Product Innovation Management* 10: 403–415.

Wheelwright, S.C. and Clark, K.B. (1992), *Revolutionary product development*, New York: The Free Press.

White, M.D. (2002), *A short course in international marketing blunders: Mistakes made by companies that should have known better*, Novato, CA: World Trade Press.

6 Optimising innovation decision making and portfolio management

Learning outcomes

When you have completed this chapter, you should be able to:

- Understand the importance of decision making as a risk-abatement mechanism.

- Appreciate the different types of decisions that need to be taken to drive new product development specifically, and innovation generally.

- Recognise the shortcomings of current decision-making approaches in product development.

- Appreciate the importance of portfolio management decisions for short term, and long term, profitable growth objectives.

- Describe the different methods of development programme valuation.

- Appreciate methods and techniques for strategic alignment.

- Understand how portfolio management practices can be integrated into existing decision/review stages in the NPD framework.

Introduction

The development and implementation of innovation processes is no easy task, nor a guarantee for new product success. In fact, there is no single best way to organise for innovation, and many causes of success and failure are often traced back to the NPD framework.

Failures to innovate draw attention to the veracity of the decisions taken and the processes used to arrive at these decisions. Complex and dynamic environments accentuate these problems. Many companies experience difficulties in making correct decisions across a wide range of areas supporting their NPD frameworks. Firms are facing an increasing dichotomy between the external expectations of the market and internal competencies producing current product offerings. This can create *strategic inflection points* (SIP), where companies are forced to adjust their competitive positioning to reduce the associated 'strategic dissonance' between 'strategic intent' and strategic action (Burgleman and Grove, 1996). In such situations, it is critical that the right decisions are made by the right people at the right time. In this chapter, we examine the decisions and decision-making processes within NPD frameworks, which are being increasingly adopted by high-performing companies. Whilst

ILLUSTRATION

Accantia's simple balance

Accantia is known, among women at least, for its feminine hygiene brand Lil-lets. The company makes 500m tampons a year. That is enough, according to Accantia's marketing, to reach from England to Australia if laid end to end. Accantia is the end result of a series of disposals made by Smith & Nephew in 2000, as it quit consumer products to concentrate on medical devices. Geoff Percy, managing director of the division, and Peter Hatherly, the finance director, led a £175m management buy-out backed by ABN Amro, the Dutch bank. This bought them Lil-lets, Simple, Wright's Coal Tar Soap and Cidal, an anti-bacterial cleansing brand.

Accantia's other main business, Simple skincare, is another substantial consumer brand, with about 8 per cent of the market for skincare products used by British women. The company itself is not widely known: few private equity-backed businesses are. But there is encouragement for other private entrepreneurs in the success with which Mr Percy and finance director Peter Hatherly, a fellow shareholder, have defended and extended Accantia's market position in the face of competition from big multinationals.

Accantia punches above its weight

The company has the ability to make decisions and act on them faster than is possible in many large corporations. It combines two businesses with strikingly different characteristics:

- Skincare provides growth, while the highly stable Lil-lets feminine hygiene business generates the cash needed to pay back the debt raised in a secondary buy-out.

- It has strong brands. Simple, the skincare brand, has a wide appeal across different categories of customers, something that has supported the product innovation on which Simple's growth is based.

- It has a close relationship with shareholders: private equity ownership imposes tough discipline in terms of financial targets but gives the business a strong sense of direction.

(*Source*: Anon, 2004)

the focus of elaboration is on NPD processes, the points discussed are of relevance and applicable to a wider range of innovation problems that support and enable strategy implementation and alignment. It is also recognised that organisational decision making is very much a people-based, and at times even a highly politicised, activity. These specific issues are discussed within Chapters 8 and 9.

Decision making in NPD frameworks

All companies have a process for making decisions, even though it may not be recognised as an explicitly defined process. The NPD process has already been shown as a generic process consisting of stage-gates or phases. Traversing the process requires making decisions at each stage-gate (see Figure 6.1). Each stage-gate review is used by senior management to decide whether to proceed with developing the new product or to terminate it. Each phase transition point requires taking a fundamental decision to ensure that the company's strategic goals can be realised.

In each phase, a number of activities are executed concurrently across a number of different functions. At these transition points, information from different parts of the organisation is collected to allow the building of a jigsaw from the pieces. The collated information (generally presented in the form of a business plan, supported by an agreed checklist of mandatory elements needed to guide the specific phase review) is scrutinised at these critical junctures by the senior team of decision makers (called the Review Board). It is only when the decision makers are in timely possession of correct and accurate information that they stand a chance of making correct decisions for long-term success. Figure 6.2 illustrates the types of information input to construct an appropriate business plan for a project and thereby aid decision making at a gate-post review.

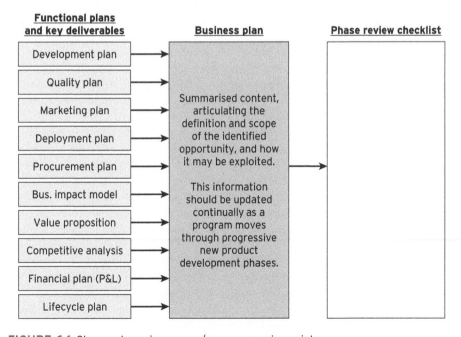

FIGURE 6.1 Stage-gate reviews as go/no-go screening points

	CONCEPT	PLAN	DEVELOPMENT	DEPLOYMENT	LIFECYCLE MANAGEMENT
FOCUS	High Level/ External	Balanced Internal/ External	Low Level/ Internal	Low Level Internal/ Increasing External	Balanced Internal/ External
LEVEL OF DETAIL	Rough Estimates	Detailed Estimates	Detailed Actuals	Detailed Actuals	Detailed Actuals
Marketing	High level definition, trends & historical performance (e.g. CAGR)	Detailed definition, with current market trends and performance	Ongoing monitoring/ Focus changes to outward messaging	Strong marketing of solution/Drive demand	Ongoing marketing efforts
Product/ Technology	High level architecture/ Capabilties identified	Clear requirements, with high level design/ architecture	Detailed decomposition/ Focus on development	Validation & verification/Pilot of products leading to customer acceptance	Cost reduction initiatives/ Productivity improvements
Business Case/ Gate Pack	Prelimiary business case covering high level details	Detailed business case & plan ready for Review Board review and approval	Refinement of plans for later gates	Refinement of plans for later gates	Strategies to prolong product life and revenue/ Profit streams
Financials	Rough estimates & assumptions	Detailed estimates, supported by clear basis of estimates	Actual vs plan tracking & refinement	Actual vs plan tracking & refinement	Actual vs plan tracking & refinement

FIGURE 6.2 Focus, detail and content alignment to reviews

The front end of the stage-gate funnel characteristically carries high levels of uncertainty. Typically, very little may be known about a concept or the target market to which it is to be applied. As a result, the information to support the opportunity can be rather rough and incomplete. Over time, as the programme (project) moves through the development funnel, the levels of completeness and accuracy of the supporting information improves. As the quality of information improves, the overseeing senior management team tends to approve increasing levels of resource to support an opportunity since uncertainty and risk is now much reduced (see Figure 6.3).

Given the uncertainty, it is not surprising that only 8 per cent of a product's development cost is committed during the design phase whereas the subsequent development phase accounts for 80 per cent of total costs (Pawar et al., 1994). The ability to review programmes and commit resources based on an increasing understanding of the opportunity is an important risk-abatement mechanism for companies. Thanks to the implementation of NPD decision-making frameworks, today's portfolios of NPD projects waste less money on unsuccessful products (Griffin, 1997). It allows them to identify undesirable and low-value programmes and cancel them prior to the development phase, during which most resources are expended. In fact, current practice indicates that the highest attrition of programmes in the funnel takes place at concept screening. The second largest number of cancellations takes place in the next phase, namely business planning. Programmes are eliminated much earlier in the NPD process than in the past, resulting in less time and money being spent on a particular idea (Page, 1993; Souder, 1988).

Clearly, the contribution of NPD frameworks to a firm's innovation efforts is governed by the effectiveness of decision making they allow. If the NPD frameworks can facilitate

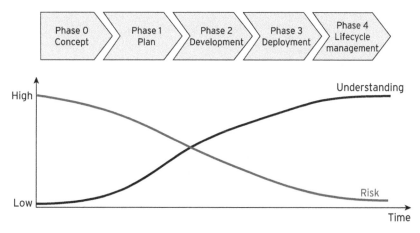

FIGURE 6.3 Risk abatement in NPD decision points

better, quicker, more accurate and timely decision making then they are playing the role for which they were designed. A NPD framework should allow accurate assessment of the value and costs of an opportunity, and thus help the firm in making the decision as to which opportunities it wishes to pursue. Since the stage-gates are decision-making points they become junctures that define decision-making effectiveness.

Decision-making weaknesses of NPD frameworks

The major milestone reviews are points for establishing programme risk and opportunity, which then determines whether funding is to be continued. They are the pivotal practice in any NPD framework, as they bring together the co-ordinated execution defined by the structured development process (SDP), the cross-functional teams that execute the underlying processes and the senior members of the company who make the critical go/no-go investment decisions.

However, this is an area which is rated as one of the weakest in product development, with only 33 per cent of firms having tough, rigorous gates throughout the idea-to-launch process (Cooper and Edgett, 2005). Further, only 44 per cent of projects meet their sales targets, which means that they are not doing their job. Too many bad projects, and too many projects, are sliding through (Cooper, 2008).

Research has identified a number of common problems that lead to sub-optimal management and flawed decision making within the NPD framework. Development funnels have been found to be loaded significantly beyond capacity. This occurs through two phenomena – 'Gates with no teeth' and 'Hollow decision gates'. Where the milestone reviews have 'no teeth', projects are rarely killed, resulting in NPD 'funnels' becoming 'tunnels', in which projects never stop until they reach their destination (Jenner, 2007). 'Hollow decision' points result in meaningless approvals being given without resources being formally committed (Cooper, 2008), and this often drives informal and reactive resource re-assignment later. Some of the impacts of these practices include:

- Development funnels have been found to be loaded significantly beyond capacity. Projects are often added to the pipeline without any visible link to resource capacity, resulting in resources frequently being over-committed by 2–3 times (Harris and McCormack, 1997), and sometimes even up to 10 times. (e.g. Lamy, 1998; Edgett, 1998).

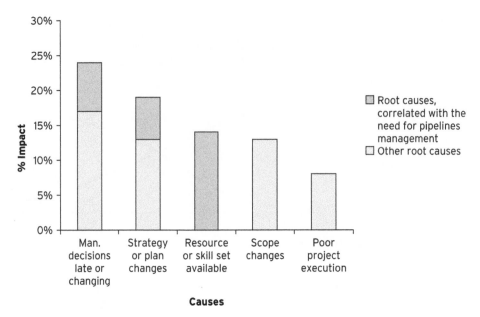

FIGURE 6.4 Root causes of development delays
Source: Harris and McCormick, 1997

- The primary involvement in decision making is through visibly dedicated groups, such as the Marketing and R&D functions, while other important support groups (Product management, Procurement, Manufacturing, etc.) are often overlooked.

- The above can be exacerbated by senior management adopting a 'zero-based budget' mentality. This is a mentality in which managers believe 'anything that is attractive has got to be done'. As a result, the senior management decision team manages the input (on the belief that 'more is more') rather than output where fewer projects into the development pipeline may produce more successful outcomes ('less is more').

Some of the root causes of these problems were researched by Harris & McCormick (1997) and are summarised in Figure 6.4 which illustrates the dual challenge in NDP decision making – to ensure the go/kill decisions are appropriate at a programme level, and at a portfolio level.

The general impact of these problems, and the flawed decisions that arise, is that critical functions, or key individuals, are overloaded and required to work on an increasing number of simultaneous tasks (see Figure 6.5). The result is task fragmentation. This has a critical impact on both individual and organisational productivity since most individuals find that they cannot optimally handle more than two tasks at any one time.

By having too many projects underway at any one time, it appears that projects tend to stall in the middle phases of the development process. The development phase is the point that generally places the greatest demands upon the project team and the organisation's resources. Typically, at this point project teams make requests for extra (financial and human) resources to overcome earlier constraints (imposed because of having too many projects and too few resources. Unfortunately, the organisation's resources are already at full stretch and there is little possibility of securing further support. A further problem with having a large number of programmes being executed concurrently is the increase in complexity and lack of focus it brings. Increasing amounts of time and effort are required to address

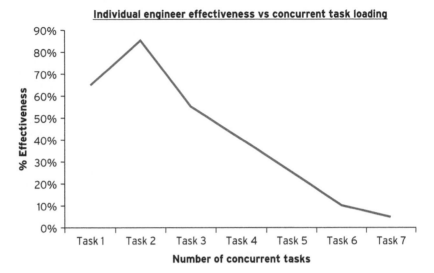

FIGURE 6.5 Time impact from task fragmentation

execution problems. The result is a fire-fighting mentality that undermines the smooth running of important projects. It also makes the company less able to address any unforeseen or unpredictable problems that may arise in the future. Unsurprisingly, productivity suffers. The reduction in productivity, in conjunction with a reluctance to kill programmes, can lead to an overall increase in product development costs, degradation in 'time-to-market' performance, and compromises in product quality. R&D investment is undermined through an increased programme failure rate, the bottom line suffers and shareholder value falls. In such situations, the very reason the NPD framework was originally implemented starts to be significantly undermined. Such companies experience a loss of potential revenue from late market releases, a tarnished reputation due to poor on-time delivery and/or delivery of inferior products.

A common reaction to these problems is to re-prioritise programmes and attempt to focus on only the newly prioritised 'key' programmes. This leads to mid-course corrections in projects. When this practice becomes pervasive it leads to chronic fire-fighting and resource realignment (PRTM, 1998). Consequently, teams are delayed as they come across unpredictable functional bottlenecks and this translates into further schedule slippage (Cooper et al., 1998). Constant changes in priorities have the effect of introducing a constant resource overload on key functions, whilst others may remain under-utilised. Moreover, not only does this reduce organisational performance but it also introduces confusion in teams over what are the true priorities and why they differ between project teams and functions. This and other issues are illustrated in Figure 6.6, and indicate a need for more effective management of projects in the development funnel.

In addition to the various mechanical problems associated with NPD decision points, a series of bad behaviours has also been witnessed which further undermines the effectiveness of NPD frameworks (Cooper, 2008), and includes:

● Executives' 'pet projects' receiving special attention and bypassing the gates.

● Gate meetings cancelled at the last minute due to availability of key personnel (gate-keeper/chairperson).

● Gate meetings held, but decisions not made or resources committed.

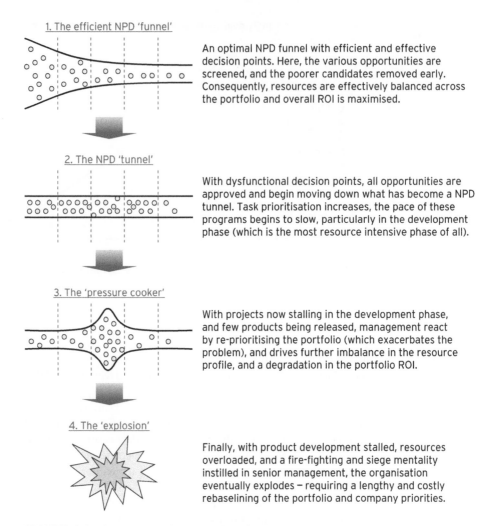

1. The efficient NPD 'funnel'

An optimal NPD funnel with efficient and effective decision points. Here, the various opportunities are screened, and the poorer candidates removed early. Consequently, resources are effectively balanced across the portfolio and overall ROI is maximised.

2. The NPD 'tunnel'

With dysfunctional decision points, all opportunities are approved and begin moving down what has become a NPD tunnel. Task prioritisation increases, the pace of these programs begins to slow, particularly in the development phase (which is the most resource intensive phase of all).

3. The 'pressure cooker'

With projects now stalling in the development phase, and few products being released, management react by re-prioritising the portfolio (which exacerbates the problem), and drives further imbalance in the resource profile, and a degradation in the portfolio ROI.

4. The 'explosion'

Finally, with product development stalled, resources overloaded, and a fire-fighting and siege mentality instilled in senior management, the organisation eventually explodes – requiring a lengthy and costly rebaselining of the portfolio and company priorities.

FIGURE 6.6 Stages of NPD funnel dysfunction

- Gatekeeper/chairperson and key resource owners missing the meeting, or not delegating authority to designee.
- Single-person gate meetings, or decisions by 'executive edict' (one person knows all).
- Go/kill decisions based on opinion or speculation rather than facts.
- Using personal and hidden go/kill and prioritisation criteria.

While some of these issues can be addressed by some simple mechanisms (e.g. go/kill criteria, success indicators, mandatory/core attendance at decision reviews, approval sign-off limits, etc.), it demonstrates the inconsistencies in the guidelines and behaviours surrounding NPD decision making which can have an adverse effect on NPD performance in terms of increased costs, reduced NPD ROI, and programme delays (Harris and McCormack, 1997). This indicates the need for more effective management of projects in the NPD funnel. The rise of such problems has led to the development, and increasing adoption, of portfolio management practices in NPD.

CASE STUDY

The portfolio paradox

An in-depth study of successful and unsuccessful innovation over the previous 40 years at Exxon Chemical (now Exxon-Mobil Chemical) provided evidence for executive concern: the company's substantial R&D activities produced only two major breakthroughs during that entire period. Rather than big new ideas and products, the company generated mostly smaller, lower-value process innovations. If it was of any comfort to it, Exxon was not alone. The same problem was dogging the entire chemical industry, and research-intensive sectors beyond.

What was driving the scarcity in major innovations?

For many companies the experience in managing innovation has been paradoxical. Faced with low success rates and increasing pressure to deliver consistent, predictable revenue growth they have reacted by adding more projects to the R&D pipeline. The consequence is that many relatively small, low-risk projects receive support in order to maintain a full portfolio of growth options leading ultimately to research fragmentation. Resources and talent quickly become thinly spread and there is general lack of focus in the pipeline. This leads to weaker commercialisation with little in the way of big wins. In turn this feeds the erroneous conclusion that still more projects are needed.

It would seem from this that the very approach of improving the innovation rate, namely the portfolio model with its structured stage-gates for the rigorous management of projects is at the heart of the dismal chain of events. Whilst the stage-gate system brings discipline to the often undisciplined world of research, the approach is failing to adequately address the problem of managing R&D, especially in generating radical innovation. There are several reasons for this failure:

1. Aggressive goals that are part and parcel of radical innovation invariably look 'impossible' at project outset. They rarely fit neatly into the typical stage-gate review process. It is usually not long before the organisational focus drifts from the quality of projects to the quantity.

2. The Exxon study highlighted that a high percentage of commercialised innovations were motivated by 'getting the ox out of the ditch' during hard times. Rarely were they part of a pro-active R&D programme, i.e. the motive driving innovation shifted, and it did so in most cases unintentionally. R&D was being driven by the aim of surviving the next budget review rather than on inventing 'the next big thing'.

3. Another problem is that the sheer number of projects intended to 'balance' a portfolio can actually crowd out innovation. The Exxon Chemical study found that fewer projects may actually lead to more radical innovations. According to the study, had the total number of projects been reduced by 30–50 per cent, complemented by a sharper focus on a handful of major innovation projects, the company would have realised shorter commercialisation cycle times as well as higher value product and process innovations.

QUESTION

Given this dilemma, how can senior managers motivate their R&D organisations to become more innovative? If conventional strategies to sustain and manage a diverse project portfolio lead to fewer, less exciting innovations – the very opposite of management intent – then what is a better approach?

(*Source*: Based on Canner and Mass, 2005)

Portfolio management in NPD frameworks

Many firms find it difficult to realise their business strategies. Some focus on the trivial, easy, quick and cheap programmes (the 'low hanging fruit') that meet their short-term objectives whilst the projects designed to create tomorrow's big winners are simply ignored. Others attempt to focus only on the big programmes. These firms have portfolios that assume too much risk for their associated return, i.e. their portfolios are all high risk/high reward. And there are some that make investments without consideration of risk at all. These behaviours, ultimately, have the effect of increasing the probability that a firm will fail to meet its strategic growth objectives since many of the high-risk projects will inevitably fail. In any case, the problem is caused by projects not being aligned with strategic goals in a balanced manner, or being aimed at a multitude of different markets with little strategic focus or leverage (Cooper et al., 1998). Another factor making business strategies unachievable is the disconnection between various budgets and plans. Functional budgets are often out of sync with project budgets and plans (PRTM, 1998), with the outcome that revenue and profit plans are not based on realistic or agreed project schedules.

As we have noted in the previous section, deficiencies in decision making contribute to sub-optimal business performance in NPD programmes. Poor criteria for decision making, or criteria based on politics, emotion and opinioneering are unfortunately commonplace (Cooper et al., 1998; Edgett, 1998). The result is too many mediocre programmes in the pipeline. This subsequently starves good programmes of resources, and results in too few winners being released to the market. This condition can also be caused by operating in markets that are opportunity constrained.

Clearly, from the above observations and research, the decision-making practices in NPD frameworks need careful attention and improvement. Companies who have become mature in the development and institutionalisation of NPD frameworks have started to recognise the value of introducing a higher level decision-making capability, in the form of portfolio management models (PMM) to support their NPD models.

Portfolio management for new product development is a dynamic decision-making process in which the full list of a company's active development (new and existing) projects are evaluated. It is a process that adds to the go/kill decisions on individual projects using the stage-gate process two additional, yet key, interlinked decision-making processes:

1. A periodic comparative assessment of the company's portfolio of projects (in which the entire set of projects are compared against each other).

2. Development of a strategically aligned new product strategy for the business, complete with strategic resource allocation decisions.

Portfolio management is vital to a business performing well because it is one route by which senior management can operationalise business strategies. Portfolio management allows articulation of the types of markets that management has chosen to attack, the technologies and products to leverage, and the relative importance of each. The choices that are made today determine what the business will look like in five years' time.

Portfolio management is concerned with the effective allocation of scarce and vital resources. It attempts to balance resources across a workable number of programmes in order to maximise productivity, reduce time to market and maintain the desired strategic positions in markets. These actions help execute an organisation's business strategy. Markets are moving too fast, are too unpredictable and too uncertain to rely on conventional management approaches. Previous management paradigms were formed during periods of

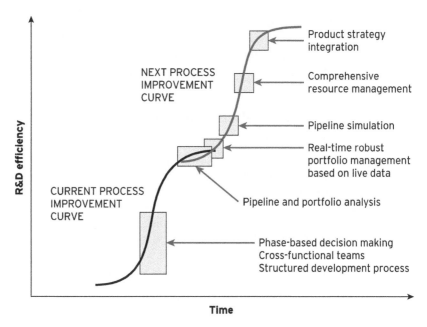

FIGURE 6.7 NPD frameworks – current and future improvement opportunities
Source: McGrath, 1998. Reprinted with permission

relative stability when demand outpaced capacity. These paradigms are outmoded and too sluggish to respond to the present-day competitive drivers/environment of speed, ceaseless innovation and uncertainty (Gould, 1996). A portfolio management model, operating within a NPD framework, can assist by offering an environment through which strategic objectives can be challenged and programmes aligned to strategic growth objectives. Portfolio management is thus an attempt to introduce a capability to ensure development programmes support strategies. McGrath (1998) highlights that portfolio management offers a major opportunity for improvement in NPD frameworks. This and other potential improvement possibilities of NPD frameworks are shown in Figure 6.7.

Once the basic stage-gate process has been implemented, portfolio management is the next critical task for success in product innovation. At least, this is the predominant view of senior management in technology (CTOs, VP of R&D, etc.). Findings from a survey revealed that the top 20 per cent of corporate performers place more importance on portfolio management than the bottom 20 per cent (Cooper et al., 1998). Portfolio management is perceived to be vital because it attempts to maximise financial return, properly allocate scarce resources, provide focus and balance, forge a link between project selection and business strategy and help communicate priorities. However, those who have implemented portfolio management processes, in the main, are not particularly satisfied with them. Portfolio management processes are perceived to be complex and not easy to use, and in turn are not well understood by senior management. Because of this they are used inconsistently and inefficiently.

Currently, two models are prevalent. First, the 'Pipeline Management Model' developed by the consultants Pitiglio, Raban, Todd and McGrath (PRTM) provides some focus on business drivers to identify which opportunities should be targeted. However, it concentrates more on the effective allocation and management of resources to be applied to programmes/projects. Second, Cooper, Edgett and Kleinschmidt (CEK) introduce a series of techniques and tools that provide greater business rigour around the programme selection and prioritisation activities than that offered by PRTM. However, the CEK model only briefly discusses effective resource management to support NPD. Both models are discussed next.

PRTM's 'Pipeline Management' model

According to the consultants PRTM, before a strong competency in the key portfolio excellence can be achieved, a capability in project excellence must first be established (PRTM, 1998). Project excellence is founded on the guiding principles upon which all stage-gate frameworks operate (namely, implementation of the structured development process with established decision-points, realisation teams, and a review board). Project excellence is about getting effective cross-functional integration through implementation of a common set of interlocked functional processes that are supported by a strong project management competence (encompassing project scheduling, resource/capacity management and risk management). Only after this has been established is it possible to begin to fine-tune the performance of the stage-gate processes via portfolio management (see Figure 6.8).

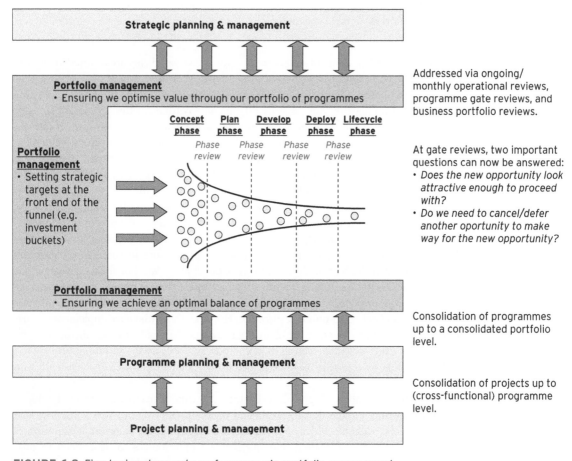

FIGURE 6.8 Fine tuning stage-gate performance via portfolio management

PRTM's pipeline management is proposed as a process that dynamically integrates product strategy, project management and functional management. It optimises the development pipeline (i.e. the cross-project management of all development-related activities, such as new product development, product support, technology development, process improvements, etc.). Pipeline management emphasises building long-term capabilities to handle projects coming down the pipeline. Functional managers have to shift from being reactive to anticipating requirements and addressing bottleneck issues before they occur. A well-functioning pipeline management process has the following elements (Harris and McCormack, 1997):

1. A strategic balancing process that sets priorities among the numerous opportunities, and adjusts the organisation's capabilities to deliver new products.

2. A pipeline loading process that actively manages the entry and exit of development projects into the pipeline and handles mid-course corrections.

3. A pipeline delivery process that ensures that functional managers maximise the flow of projects through the organisation in both the short and long term.

The pipeline management process is implemented with two categories of tools: decision assistance and data handling tools. With both types of tools, automation is an important facilitator. However, it is important to bear in mind that this does not necessarily require building a complex automated, or even a fully integrated, tool. These elements are illustrated in Figure 6.9.

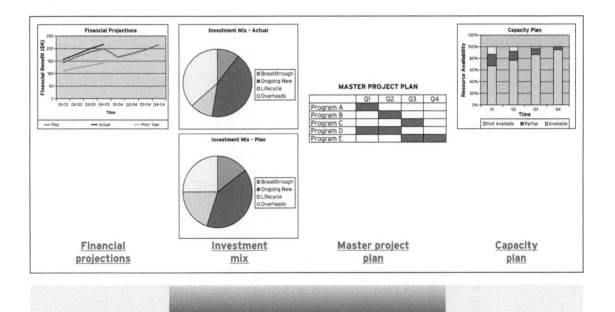

Strategic resourcing balancing
- Setting strategic investment levels
- Rationalising aggregate product line plans with resource capacity
- Long-range functional skill set planning

Pipeline loading
- Managing entry, exit and mid-course corrections of development projects.
- Upgrading project reviews with fact-based 'what if' resource analysis.

Pipeline delivery
- Efficient individual project assignment and loading
- Look-ahead capability for shared resource organisations.

FIGURE 6.9 Pipeline management process
Source: Harris and McCormick, 1997

The focus of the pipeline management model is to continually develop resources to meet the demands of current and future programmes, and to ensure that the resources are optimally deployed during programme execution. Unfortunately, the pipeline management model fails to provide adequate detail to assist in effective model definition, deployment and execution. It also fails to provide any formal mechanism for achieving strategic alignment of the NPD portfolio beyond matching core competencies to future programmes.

The CEK model

Cooper, Edgett and Kleinschmidt (CEK) propose a set of discrete methods to deal with the challenge of managing the portfolio of development projects. CEK's portfolio management model provides greater focus and definition than that offered in the PRTM model. However, no attempt is made to bring the discrete models together in a manner designed to provide an integrated view of the portfolio. The CEK model is based upon providing discrete views based on the three established objectives of portfolio management in new product development, specifically:

1. Maximisation of the value of the portfolio.
2. Achievement of an optimal balance in the portfolio.
3. Effective alignment to strategic objectives.

Each of the major areas of the CEK model, described as key objectives of the CEK portfolio management, is discussed next.

Objective 1: Maximising the value of the portfolio

A clear objective in the mind of any senior leadership team is to maximise the value of the firm's portfolio. In tackling this task, many managers resort to significant guesswork and assumptions because of poor information. It has already been observed that inadequate up-front work can lead to poor-quality data. Fortunately, many different techniques exist to assess the value of a programme and thus, through consolidation of all programmes, the portfolio. The most common of these techniques include net present value (NPV), internal rate of return (IRR) and payback.

The NPV of a project can be expressed as the value in today's terms of the cash generated from that project, over and above the opportunity cost of investing at its cost of capital rate, i.e. defines the present value of the project by reflecting the value of future cash flows. Using NPV as a decision rule, all projects with a positive NPV should be accepted, as they will increase shareholder wealth. The NPV method has proven to be a better method of investment appraisal than other techniques (such as IRR), as it has always indicated the optimal investment alternative. Indeed, the accounting rate of return method has lost its appeal over the past 20 years, especially in the evaluation of new technology. Additionally, in a survey of the 150 largest firms in the UK, 79 per cent used payback as a means of investment appraisal, although only 32 per cent used it as the primary evaluation technique (Ogg, 1999).

Present value methods allow estimates for certain criteria to be developed based on the choice of a criteria considered to be the most important aspect to the organisation in its decision-making process, e.g. use for revenue streams, gross margins, investment levels, etc. Unfortunately, naïve use of such methods has also been responsible for sales revenue estimates being wrong by an order of magnitude. For instance, when using NPVs, the values can drop dramatically as a project progresses through the NPD funnel. Now, consider the fact that many projects will be at different stages of completion in the funnel. The result can be a set of figures that may be so far divorced from reality that they provide little tangible value. It is often the case that the use of such techniques induces 'imaginary precision' (discussed later), in which great weight is placed on such estimated figures.

ILLUSTRATION

Portfolio and programme management tips from Ford

An important aspect of Ford's portfolio management approach involves understanding the value of each programme. Once that is known, the value of the portfolio can be better understood. The value of a programme is not simply the sum of the individual programme's timing, quality, cost and content but rather a non-linear combination of these factors. Time, quality, cost and content have different weights based on specific targets and strategic goals; for instance, in some cases quality might have more weight while in others 'timing' might be more significant in terms of the overall value of the programme.

As an illustration of a case where one priority is weighted more heavily than another, a hypothetical example is offered where Ford is beaten to market by a competitor with a derivative product. In such a case, the time factor becomes the predominant value component. Quality would not be as much of an issue, because known sub-systems from the current platform will be used. Costs will be allowed to temporarily exceed the norm and content is going to carry over from previous development projects – plus any extra content needed to stay competitive. In this case, timing carries the greatest weight. In general, the newer and bolder the product, the more important timing becomes. If timing is missed, then synchronisation with tooling manufacturing plans, advertising, promotions, etc. is lost. Under other conditions, content has a greater weight than other factors, where additional features are being made to luxury-end products.

(*Source*: Mueller, 2004)

To be useful, it is important that the technique applied not only provides realistic information based on current intelligence but also yields a sound base from which comparisons between programmes can be made. A number of techniques have evolved to meet this need, which can be applied to achieve ranked listing of projects. These techniques generally focus on determining a risk-adjusted net present value, after which estimated costs can be deducted. This gives an estimated value of the project and allows consolidation of all projects to obtain the overall value of the portfolio. The common methods are the economic commercial value (ECV), productivity index (PI) and dynamic rank ordered lists (DROL). In addition to these, non-financial models can also be used to construct rank-ordered lists. Interestingly and worryingly, surveys have repeatedly shown that a clear majority of firms do not formally analyse risk. Pike (1982) estimated this figure to be as high as 63 per cent.

A number of techniques have been developed that permit the consideration of the 'uncertainty dimension' as part of the process of (capital) budgeting. Two categories of techniques exist: *intuitive*, relying on simple rules of thumb ('heuristics'), and *analytical*, involving the quantification of the uncertainty surrounding a project. Analytical techniques are being increasingly applied, particularly in the area of developing risk-based financial valuations of programmes. However, such techniques suffer from a number of drawbacks. The most obvious is the dependency on specific financial and risk information that often is itself an estimate. Second, the treatment of the probabilities (being multiplied together) will always tend to unfairly punish more venturesome projects. Third, such techniques fail to look at the balance of the portfolio with respect to high- and low-risk projects. Therefore, analytical

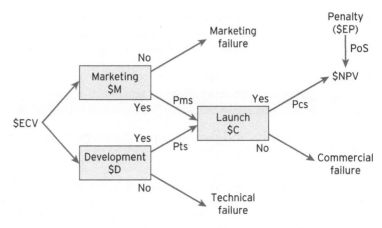

Where....

ECV = *Economic commercial value*
NPV = *Net present value*
EP = *Expected penalty*

M = *Marketing investment associated with the programme*
D = *R&D investment associated with the programme*
C = *Launch costs associated with the programme.*

Pms = *Probability of marketing success*
Pts = *Probability of technical success*
Pcs = *Probability of commercial success*
PoS = *Overall probability of success (Pms * Pts * Pcs)*

FIGURE 6.10 Portfolio maximisation – the Shepherd–Ahmed valuation model

techniques such as these are useful in establishing a preliminary ranked list and estimated value of the portfolio but should not be applied in isolation.

Economic commercial value (ECV)

Economic commercial value (ECV) seeks to maximise the commercial worth of the portfolio, subject to certain budgetary constraints. It looks at the continuum of activities from development through launch and commercialisation, applying appropriate risk factors at each major stage and deducting associated expenses to arrive at a risk-adjusted NPV (see Figure 6.10).

Based on the decision tree in Figure 6.10, the ECV can be calculated using the following formula:

$$ECV\$ = (NPV * PoS) - (\$C * (1\text{-}Pcs)) - ((\$M + \$D) * (1\text{-}PoS)) - (\$EP * (1\text{-}PoS))$$

In this technique, a simple model can be applied to quantify the marketing, development and launch risk (see Table 6.1).

Validated in over 60 NPD projects, this risk model identifies around 10 critical elements each for marketing, technical and commercial dimensions that affect the success of any given NPD programme. A simple yes/no subjective assessment of the extent to which the programme being audited meets the intent along the specified criteria leads to an assignment to the element a score of 0.1. The values for each of the three areas can be added to produce the overall risk score for the dimension. The individual dimension scores can then be employed to calculate the overall risk (or probability of success) of the programme. (Note: This calculation can also be used to determine the positioning of projects in the risk/opportunity profile, discussed later.)

TABLE 6.1 Simplistic risk model supporting (Shepherd–Ahmed) ECV calculation

Attribute (R&D/product fitness)	Score
Start at value 0.0	
Validated requirements definition available (yes = +0.1)	
Supports the company's solution approach by providing all, or some, of the components which comprise an offer (yes = +0.1)	
Commitment of suitable development resources to meet objectives (yes = +0.1)	
Experience already gained with complexity (scale or scope) of the offer (yes = +0.1)	
Solution leverages proven/existing technology (yes = +0.1)	
Combined plan/develop and deploy cycle times will be under 33–45 weeks (yes = +0.1)	
Experience in creating like offers (yes = +0.1)	
Dependent external groups (partners, ISVs, suppliers, OEM providers, etc.) are strategically and operationally aligned (yes = +0.1)	
Solution conforms to the company's architecture (yes = +0.1)	
Any tools and/or processes required to support offer development in place (yes = +0.1)	
Total	

Attribute (market readiness)	Score
Start at value 0.1	
Validated value proposition (yes = +0.1)	
Fit with the company's strategy (yes = +0.1)	
Commitment of suitable marketing resource available to support programme (yes = +0.1)	
Market/sales plan readiness (yes = +0.1)	
Market segmentation complete and reliable market research data used to validate opportunity (yes = +0.1)	
Market builds on existing strengths/market leadership of the company in other areas (yes = +0.1)	
Market has progressed beyond the 'early adopter' stage (yes = +0.1)	
Low market entry barrier exists for the company (yes = +0.1)	
High market entry barriers to competition/competitive strategy defined (yes = +0.1)	
Total	

Attribute (deployment readiness)	Score
Start at value 0.0	
Adequately defined targeted customer within market segment (yes = +0.1)	
Availability of an associated business impact model (yes = +0.1)	
Entrenched competition in market/key customer sites (no = +0.1)	
Channel readiness (and lack of conflict) (yes = +0.1)	
Deployment collateral availability (yes = +0.1)	
Support services committed and available (yes = +0.1)	
Experience in the delivery and support of like offers (yes = +0.1)	
Realisation teams and regional deployment teams operational plans interlocked (yes = +0.1)	
Suitable sales and professional/pre-sales and consultancy services committed and available to support programme (yes = +0.1)	
Any tools and/or processes required to support offer deployment in place (yes = +0.1)	
Total	

Source: Shepherd, 1999

The ECV method carries with it certain benefits. It is based on a decision tree. Thus, if a project is cancelled, some costs will not be incurred or factored into the project value. Additionally, since the investment is discounted, longer-term programmes will be appropriately penalised. A further advantage is that sunk costs are not considered, allowing programmes which are nearer completion to be considered more valuable (potentially). As a result, projects receive a higher priority when they are closer to launch, have little left to be spent on them, have a higher probable earning stream or lower risk, or the programme utilises less of a scarce/constraining resource.

Productivity index

Another technique for assessing the value of a firm's portfolio is the productivity index (PI). The PI also attempts to maximise the financial or economic value of the portfolio for a given resource constraint, and is akin to the constraining variable applied to the ECV to arrive at a rank-ordered list. This is calculated as follows:

P.I. = [ECV X Pts – $R&D] / $R&D
Where ECV is a probability weighted stream of cash flows for the project, discounted to the present and Pts = probability of technical success.

The focus of this technique is on the effective application of R&D resources, rather than cross-functional investment impact that includes marketing. It is subject to all the advantages and disadvantages of ECV, but has the advantage of being applied across many industries. As a result, it provides a means by which external benchmarking can be performed.

Pipeline index

The pipeline index was developed by PRTM and compares the product load in a company's product development pipeline to the flow of projects that the company has demonstrated it can handle. This therefore provides an assessment tool for determining the probable outcomes of development pipeline decisions. The pipeline index is calculated as follows:

Pipeline index = pipeline load/demonstrated pipeline flow

Where:
Pipeline load = Number of projects in development between concept approval and launch
Demonstrated pipeline flow = Average annual products released X average major product time to market
Pipeline load and annual products released are measured in major product equivalents
Time to market is the time in years between concept approval and launch.

Theoretically, a pipeline index of 1.0 means a company has committed to a portfolio of projects it has proven it can handle. Over 1.0 means overload, under 1.0 means under load. Given the approximations of the Pipeline Index equation, PRTM have suggested that values fall into four ranges:

Pipeline index range	Description
PI < 0.9	Underload, wasting capacity.
0.9 < PI < 1.3	Optimal load, maximising productivity
1.3 < PI < 1.6	Probable overload, somewhat degrading productivity
PI > 1.6	Definite overload, significantly hurting productivity.

TABLE 6.2 Example of dynamic rank ordered list

Project name	IRR (%)	NPV ($m)	Prob. tech. success (%)	IRR X Pts	NPV X Pts	Strategic importance	Ranking score
Alpha	20	10.0	80	16.0 (2)	8.0 (2)	5 (1)	1.67 *(1)*
Epsilon	15	2.0	70	10.8 (4)	18.0 (1)	4 (2)	2.33 *(2)*
Delta	10	5.0	90	11.1 (3)	7.8 (3)	2 (4)	3.33 *(3)*
Omega	17	12.0	65	18.7 (1)	5.1 (4)	1 (6)	3.67 *(4)*
Gamma	12	20.0	90	9.0 (6)	4.5 (5)	3 (3)	4.67 *(5)*
Beta	22	6.0	85	10.5 (5)	1.4 (6)	2 (4)	5.00 *(6)*

Source: Cooper et al., 1998

Dynamic rank ordered list

The dynamic rank ordered list attempts to apply several criteria concurrently, such as NPV, IRR or ROI. Probabilities of technical success are applied to each criterion in each active project and the individual results ranked in order. Additionally, a strategic importance value is determined for each active project and the associated ranking assessed. Table 6.2 illustrates a simple example of this.

The average ranking score is arrived at by adding all the ranking values for each criterion (in bold) and dividing by the number of criteria applied (the result in bold italic). The list can then be rank ordered according to the ranking score.

This technique benefits from its ability to handle several criteria concurrently and tends to be fairly simple to apply. However, it is largely based on uncertain and often unreliable financial information, which when exposed to a simplistic treatment of probabilities may result in unsound results. It also fails to consider the appropriate balance of projects required to meet both short-term and long-term strategic growth objectives.

Scoring models

A non-financial technique used in building ranked lists involves the use of scoring models. These models identify key success criteria within an organisation, and require project-specific scores (and risk or importance weightings to be applied). The success criteria may even be tied to the stage-gate hurdles that need to be passed in order to achieve a successful 'GO' decision. The resultant accumulation of weighted scores, covering many concurrent facets, produces an overall project score. This project score can then be used to compile a rank ordering of projects.

The attractiveness of scoring tools lies in their simplicity of use and the ability to handle multiple goals concurrently. As a result, assessments are performed in a complete and rigorous manner and can aid the decision-making process. It is worth bearing in mind that in practice, however, when scoring models have developed and applied during stage-gate reviews they have been burdensome, in the sense that discussions get bogged down in unnecessary detail. Additionally, the subjective application of scores and associated weightings can give rise to two interesting phenomena: *imaginary precision* and the *halo effect*.

- *Imaginary precision* arises when greater emphasis is placed on the precision of the scoring model rather than the right decision to be made (e.g. a project scoring 50.1 per cent is permitted to pass a previously agreed 50 per cent threshold, yet a programme scoring 49.7 per cent is cancelled).

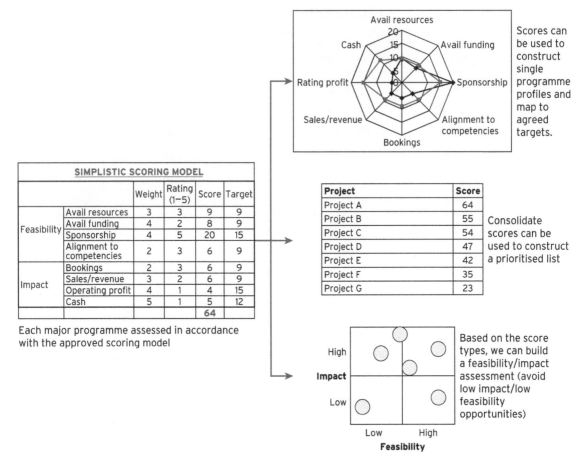

FIGURE 6.11 Using a scoring model (including feasibility/impact modelling)

- The *'halo effect'* occurs when projects score well due to extremely high values being achieved for a number of key variables, yet may have poor scores elsewhere. As a result, programmes may be permitted to pass because of the attractiveness of a minority of attributes rather than a more balanced whole.

As this technique is increasingly used, the sensitivity of scoring from different groups/ sources has come to the fore as an issue. To address this, various consensus-based methods of scoring can be used to achieve greater organisational consistency. However, these can further burden the stage-gate review process, complicate prioritisation, and add to the imaginary precision and halo effect behaviours.

In some cases, these scoring models may contain elements which not only focus on the economic benefits, but also on other more subjective elements, such as the 'feasibility' of progressing with an opportunity. As a result, a 'feasibility/impact' analysis can be conducted and used to focus on portfolio maximisation (see Figure 6.11).

Objective 2: Achieving a balanced portfolio

Before discussing the various tools to help achieve a balanced portfolio, it is perhaps useful to discuss what a balanced portfolio means. It is usual for strategic planners to set long-term objectives for an organisation. These are articulated in what is called the 'intended strategy'.

However, environmental changes usually mean that adjustments to a corporation's activities and course must be made. These adjustments are embodied in what is termed the 'emergent strategy'. Furthermore, companies use 'strategic intent' (Hamel and Prahalad, 1989) to drive the short-term objectives toward the longer-term intended strategy. In other words, business leaders need to balance short-term with long-term activities, which can often contain conflicting objectives.

The purpose of portfolio balancing is to articulate key desired organisational objectives (which often conflict), and then enunciate views to assess the extent to which an organisation is participating in a mix of projects that balances the corporation's objectives appropriately. Management can take either a short-run versus long-run view or a combination of both in developing their product portfolios. Having a balanced portfolio, that is putting emphasis on both short-run and long-run programmes, is more desirable than an unbalanced (or negative) portfolio that optimises only one or the other (Samli, 1996).

A common representation of portfolios is through construction of Risk-Opportunity profiles. CEK use such profiles to construct a classificatory matrix that indicates the relative positioning of programmes (see Figure 6.12). Such categorisation allows the identification and removal of undesirable activities (high risk/low return) from the portfolio.

The terms 'Pearls', 'Oysters', 'Bread and butter' and 'White elephants' were devised by CEK, and generally describe products in a life-cycle context. This is analogous to the strategic business units (SBUs) definition in the BCG/growth share matrix (Question mark, Star, Cash cow and Dog). These are defined as follows:

- *Pearls*: Potential star products. These are projects with a high likelihood of success, which are expected to yield very high rewards.

- *Oysters*: Long-shot projects with a high expected payoff, but a low likelihood of technical success. They are the projects where technical breakthroughs will pave the way for strong payoffs.

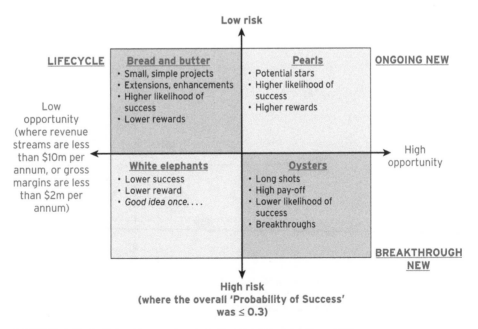

FIGURE 6.12 Defining the quadrants in the risk/opportunity exhibit
Source: Elaborated from Cooper et al., 1998

- *Bread and butter*: Small, simple projects with a high likelihood of success but low reward. They include simple extensions, modifications and updating of projects.
- *White elephants*: Low-success/low-reward projects that are difficult to kill but began life as good prospects. Unfortunately, over time these projects have become less attractive.

Clearly the quadrants are defined according to the different levels of risk and opportunity. However, one of the biggest problems with such a system lies in the definition of the various quadrants, i.e. how do we set the dividing boundary lines for the matrix? A general guideline for dividing boundary lines is as follows:

1. Boundary between a high and low reward of £10m, or £2m gross margin (but this is clearly industry dependent!)
2. The dividing line for overall risk limit (probability of success) of 0.3 or greater – which equates to approximately 7/10 score in each of the three risk categories in the risk model discussed earlier. The inherent shortcomings that apply to growth-share matrix are equally relevant to this system.

Once the definitions have been discussed with senior management and boundary limits agreed, the positioning of the programmes can be established and reviewed. The most common type of chart employed to illustrate balance amongst key variables is the 'bubble diagram' (although histograms and pie charts may also be applied) (see Figure 6.13). This allows the senior management team to look at the quadrants in which the programmes are positioned, and discuss conflicts or discrepancies.

Depending on the desired objectives of the company, several different types of bubble diagrams may be required to ensure an effectively balanced portfolio can be achieved. A number of the more commonly used criteria for establishing the bubble formats are shown in Table 6.3.

These bubble charts tend to be extremely easy to follow and show balance far better than any list. They are versatile in that they can provide information on many factors of interest. It is important to note though that these charts should be employed as information displays rather than pure decision tools.

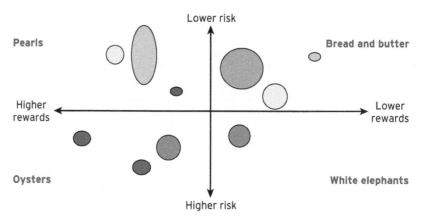

Size = resources (annual)
Colour = timing
Shading = product line

FIGURE 6.13 Sample bubble diagram (risk/reward)

TABLE 6.3 Popular bubble diagram plots

Rank	Type of chart	Axis (X)	Axis (Y)	%
1	Risk vs reward	Reward : NPV, IRR, benefits after years of launch, market value.	Probability of success (technical, commercial)	44.4
2	Newness	Technical newness	Market newness	11.1
3	Ease vs attractiveness	Technical feasibility	Market attractiveness (growth potential, consumer appeal, general attractiveness, life cycle)	11.1
4	Strengths vs attractiveness	Competitive position (strengths)	Attractiveness (market growth, technical maturity, years to implementation)	11.1
5	Cost vs timing	Cost to implement	Time to impact	9.7
6	Strategic vs benefit	Strategic focus or fit	Business intent, NPV, financial fit, attractiveness	8.9
7	Cost vs benefit	Cumulative reward	Cumulative development costs	5.6

Source: Cooper et al., 1998

One drawback of these charts is that they stimulate discussion rather than point to project choices, although some would argue that the accompanying discussions are a vital component to portfolio reviews. Overcoming this issue is a positioning technique proposed by Luehrman (1998). Luehrman applies an options pricing approach to classify strategic investment decisions. In brief, the options pricing approach can incorporate into the assessment of a development project's prospects an element of uncertainty in the trajectory of development of a project. The options pricing logic is relatively simple: when we invest in a project we do so by evaluating its future prospect. However, it is rare that we follow this path of investment in a direct line or that the future outcomes will be as we initially predicted. In the course of a project, new information will come to light, new opportunities may arise, competitor actions may make the project less likely to succeed or reduce its potential returns. All of these are uncertainties, which as they unfold the company must respond to and learn from. In other words, the development of a project is a chain of real options. In financial terms, the decision to invest in a project involves a series of options rather than a single large static decision. Strategies are executed as a series of decisions taken over time. Some decisions are taken immediately while other others are deferred until more information is available or circumstances evolve. By accounting for this, the options pricing approach defines the space within which future investments are to be made, i.e. leaves room for discretion and accommodation of ongoing and unfolding events. Traditional methods, such as discounted cash flow (DCF) valuation, fail to incorporate this dimension into their assessment of prospects. To capture and plot these considerations, Luehrman proposes two metrics:

1. *Value to cost metric*: This captures net present value (NPV) but adds to this the time value of being able to defer the decision. In other words, it assesses the value of the underlying asset that is being built (i.e. value of new product that will be released to market)

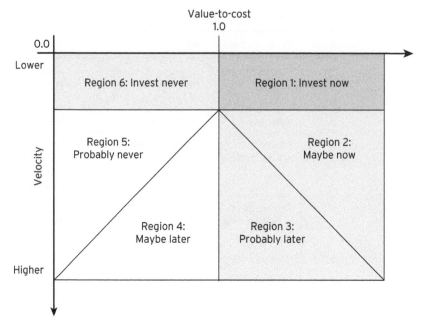

FIGURE 6.14 Volatility vs value-to-cost positioning

divided by the present value of the expenditure to build the asset (i.e. cost to develop the product). When the value of this metric is between 0 and 1, we have a project that is worth less than it costs. When the value is greater than 1, the project is worth more than the present value of its costs.

2. *Volatility metric*: This measures how much things can change before an investment decision must finally be made. This depends on (i) how risky/uncertain the future value of the assets is. This is captured by *variance per period of assets*; and (ii) how long we can defer a decision (captured by the option's *time to expiration*).

Using these two metrics allows mapping of opportunities as bubble charts (see Figure 6.14). The additional benefit, of course, is that in this chart the relative positioning of an opportunity guides the recommended investment decision.

Where . . .
Value to cost metric = $S/PV(X)$
Volatility metric   = $\sigma\sqrt{t}$
And . . .
S   Underlying asset value ($ millions)
X   Exercise price ($ millions)
T   Time to expiration (years)
σ   Standard deviation (per year)
rf   Risk free rate of return (% per year)
S-X   Conventional NPV ($m)

In the use of any of these techniques a key factor of success is to employ charts and reports that the decision makers can readily understand, and which support their own views and perceptions around the current state of the NPD portfolio. If the techniques are too complex or fail to accurately capture the realities of practice, it is more than likely that they will fall into disuse.

Objective 3: Need to build strategy into the portfolio

As markets evolve, it is important that the NPD portfolio remains aligned to the company's strategic objectives. In many NPD management frameworks, the alignment of strategic intent and strategic action fails to take place. This is surprising, given this ability is considered critical to NPD success (Bacon et al., 1994). Research has shown that innovation strategies often fail because the project mix is not aligned to strategic goals (Cooper et al., 1998; PRTM, 1998). Many companies recognise the importance of framing product development within their chosen strategic space but few manage to do so. Leading to this position is the fact that often information needed to create alignment is either not available or not made available. Consequently, decisions are made on politics, opinioneering and emotions (Cooper et al., 1998; Edgett, 1998).

Different strategies require different types of investment. Companies aiming for significant growth are likely to have adopted a *Prospector* strategy. The prospector requires higher levels of investment in innovative and ground-breaking programmes, which if they succeed will allow premium pricing (Thomas and Ramaswamy, 1996). Other companies, targeting less ambitious growth, may spend less in groundbreaking programmes but have a strong competence in analysing competitive products and quickly mimic them in a cost-effective manner. These companies are *Analysers*. They tend to enter markets at a time where revenues, gross margins and market share are still increasing, but not at quite the same rate as initial entrants. Finally, companies specialising in cost reduction enter late in what may still be a growing market but are able to pick up marginal market share because of their strategy to operate at low gross margins. These companies are *Defenders*. Clearly, companies must purposely allocate a specified proportion of their investment funds towards specific types of programmes on the basis of the strategies they wish to execute.

Whilst companies recognise the importance of framing product development within an integrated strategic vision (PRTM, 1998), no formal mechanism has yet been validated to achieve this integration. Traditionally, strategic planning activities are simply geared toward articulating expected growth objectives in key areas, such as revenue, market share and gross margin. How these growth objectives are to be realised is often left unclear at the point of defining the posture of the company in its chosen market, i.e. the way the strategy is to be operationalised by development programmes is typically left undefined and unclear. A key decision that determines to what extent actions are aligned to strategies is the funds-allocation decision.

One method of ensuring funds are allocated according to strategic priorities is proposed by CEK. CEK define a concept they call Strategic Investment Buckets (SIBs), where a company determines what proportions of investments will be spent in specific areas – very much like deciding where to place chips in a game of roulette. The first step in agreeing this investment profile is to define/agree the investment buckets to be applied. A common way of classifying strategic investment buckets is to position opportunities in the context of relative newness to the company and to the market. On the basis of this consideration different types of SIBs can be defined. These are shown in Figure 6.15.

Once the investment buckets have been defined, senior managers need to discuss and decide on a potential investment profile that they wish to follow over the next 2–3 years. This investment profile decision serves to define a baseline of objectives against which the firm can monitor its achievements over time.

A useful technique in conducting this exercise is to get senior managers to estimate what profiles their key competitors are investing in, what strategies they are following (first movers, fast followers, defenders, analysers, etc.). An illustrative example is provided in

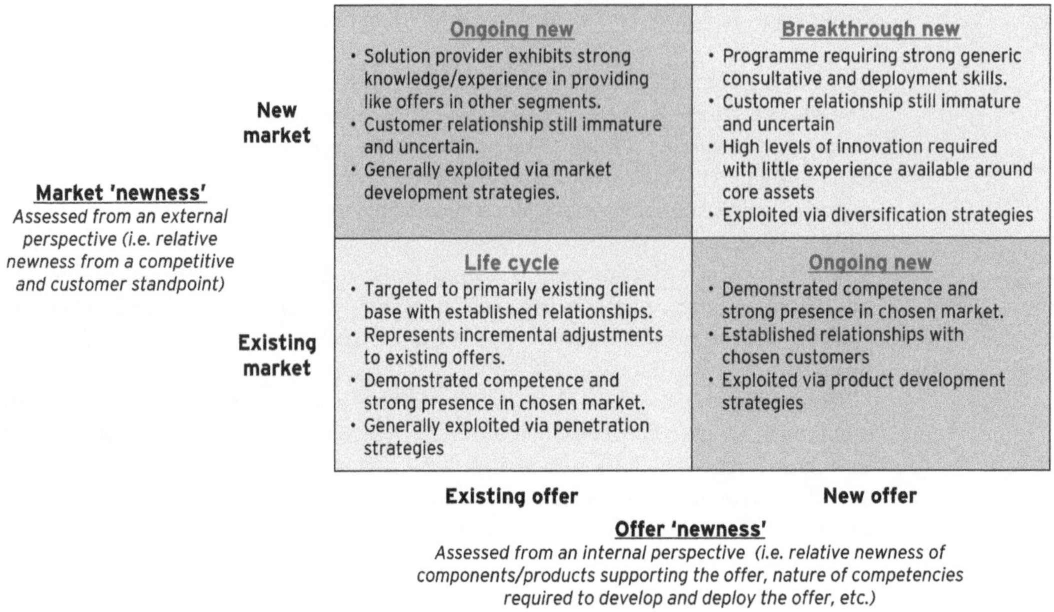

Market 'newness'
Assessed from an external perspective (i.e. relative newness from a competitive and customer standpoint)

	Existing offer	**New offer**
New market	**Ongoing new** • Solution provider exhibits strong knowledge/experience in providing like offers in other segments. • Customer relationship still immature and uncertain. • Generally exploited via market development strategies.	**Breakthrough new** • Programme requiring strong generic consultative and deployment skills. • Customer relationship still immature and uncertain • High levels of innovation required with little experience available around core assets • Exploited via diversification strategies
Existing market	**Life cycle** • Targeted to primarily existing client base with established relationships. • Represents incremental adjustments to existing offers. • Demonstrated competence and strong presence in chosen market. • Generally exploited via penetration strategies	**Ongoing new** • Demonstrated competence and strong presence in chosen market. • Established relationships with chosen customers • Exploited via product development strategies

Offer 'newness'
Assessed from an internal perspective (i.e. relative newness of components/products supporting the offer, nature of competencies required to develop and deploy the offer, etc.)

FIGURE 6.15 Defining strategic investment buckets

TABLE 6.4 Baselining the strategic investment buckets based on competitive profiles

Competitor	First mover	Fast follower	Defender	Breakthrough new (%)	Ongoing new (%)	Life cycle (%)
Competitor A	YES			30.0	60.0	10.0
Competitor B	YES			40.0	50.0	10.0
Competitor C		YES		15.0	70.0	15.0
Competitor D		YES		30.0	55.0	15.0
Competitor E		YES		10.0	70.0	20.0
Competitor F			YES	10.0	60.0	30.0
Competitor G	YES			40.0	50.0	10.0
Competitor H		YES		10.0	80.0	10.0
GENERIC PROFILE				10.0	50.0	10.0

70% assigned as a baseline. Now agree how the remaining 30% will be allocated (use 15%/60%/25%)

Table 6.4. This type of assessment yields a benchmark for the firm to assess its own investment strategies and check for any potential strategic openings.

From this competitive assessment it is possible for the firm to look at the lowest possible investment levels in each strategic bucket, and depending on the strategic posture they wish to adopt into the future use these as a guidepost to develop a baseline investment position for the company. In other words, having an understanding of how competitors are applying their funds and the strategic postures that they have adopted allows the company: (i) to

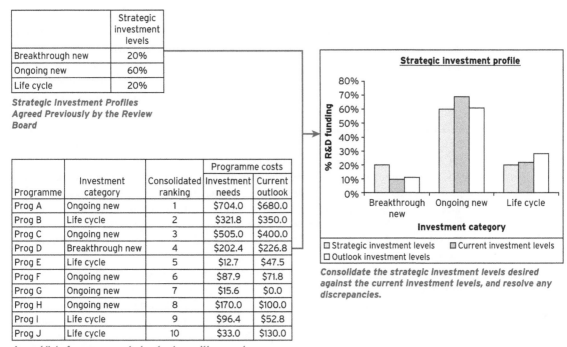

	Strategic investment levels
Breakthrough new	20%
Ongoing new	60%
Life cycle	20%

Strategic Investment Profiles Agreed Previously by the Review Board

			Programme costs		
Programme	Investment category	Consolidated ranking	Investment needs	Current outlook	
Prog A	Ongoing new	1	$704.0	$680.0	
Prog B	Life cycle	2	$321.8	$350.0	
Prog C	Ongoing new	3	$505.0	$400.0	
Prog D	Breakthrough new	4	$202.4	$226.8	
Prog E	Life cycle	5	$12.7	$47.5	
Prog F	Ongoing new	6	$87.9	$71.8	
Prog G	Ongoing new	7	$15.6	$0.0	
Prog H	Ongoing new	8	$170.0	$100.0	
Prog I	Life cycle	9	$96.4	$52.8	
Prog J	Life cycle	10	$33.0	$130.0	

Consolidate the strategic investment levels desired against the current investment levels, and resolve any discrepancies.

Agreed list of programmes to track, along with current investment profiles.

FIGURE 6.16 Aligning the investment strategy to funded programmes in the NPD funnel

define the baseline to stay in the race with competitors, and then (ii) decide where the outstanding funds should be applied to try and lever winning positions. It is generally easier to decide where to allocate the outstanding funds than start from a point where 100 per cent of the investments are to be allocated. Once the investment buckets have been defined, and a planned profile has been agreed, it is possible to classify current and future opportunities and assess the extent to which the intended investment profile is being executed. The process is illustrated in Figure 6.16.

Through a process of monitoring and tracking, it is possible to discuss why specific variances may exist. For example:

● Why current outlook levels are different from those originally approved by the NPD Review Board?

● Why current outlook levels differ from the agreed investment profile intended to support strategic objectives?

● How levels of funding already committed may limit funding for certain types of opportunities in future years.

The results of this discussion can yield insights into whether and to what extent the firm's actions and decisions will lead to the attainment of strategic growth objectives. Additionally, such discussions can serve to create stronger support for the intended investment strategy.

Crafting strategy into the firm's development portfolio is conducted to achieve *strategic fit* and *strategic prioritisation*. *Strategic fit* is intended to ensure projects are consistent with the business strategy, whereas *strategic prioritisation* focuses on the breakdown of spending to reflect associated programme priorities. Needless to say, the incorporation of strategy into the NPD framework and processes introduces an added layer of complexity. However, it has been established that NPD processes used by 'best practice' firms tend to start with a strategy step, and are somewhat more complex than practices adopted by the not-so-successful performers (Griffin, 1997). Indeed, research indicates that strategic alignment of product development efforts with the overall business strategy is critical to project success (Burgleman and Grove, 1996; Bacon et al., 1994).

Three different approaches are generally available to achieve strategic alignment of innovation programmes in the context of the business portfolio. These are 'top down', 'bottom up' and 'top down/bottom up' approaches.

The *top-down* approach demands the existence of a strategic plan, containing the mission, goals and strategy for each business. Different categories of projects are then defined, and specific amounts (or proportions) of R&D expenditure are assigned to each strategic investment type (or 'bucket'). This process can ensure that investments are allocated to support both short- and long-term goals, and ensure new product spending reflects the priorities of business strategy for sustainable advantage.

This model provides a clear link of strategy and strategic priorities to the choice and prioritisation of projects. It also prevents different types of projects being unfairly compared and ranked together, thus ensuring an effective means of enforcing portfolio balancing. The process supports the need for all resources to be considered together and to be allocated across many different project types. While this technique has already been found to be beneficial, it does suffer from a number of drawbacks. If too many 'buckets' are identified, there is a real danger of overly fragmenting resources across too many tasks. This has clear implications from a productivity perspective. A purely top-down view also prevents new product opportunities from driving the strategy, thus restricting any emergent strategies from evolving. Fortunately, many of these problems can be overcome by using a *targeted spending approach*, in which spending levels are assigned across a single dimension (or bucket classification), resulting in a high-level prioritisation list focussed on both long- and short-term objectives, i.e. X per cent of investment to be spent on breakthrough projects, Y per cent on ongoing, and Z per cent on life-cycle projects rather than focusing on specific programmes.

The '*bottom-up*' approach looks at the strategic fit of individual programmes, determines the extent to which each supports the intended investment strategies and prioritises them accordingly. A first cut of 'GO' decisions is then made and the expenditures for all are added up by each business. This alignment generally takes place at the stage-gate review point and can be augmented by scoring models. In this manner, strategic alignment is driven from the project level upwards. However, the process can lead to a spending spiral or spending pattern that exceeds budget constraints. This typically demands some tough decision making on the part of senior management, especially when strategic bucket thresholds are breached or lucrative projects are cancelled when no funding remains for specific types of projects.

A combination of the '*top-down*' and '*bottom-up*' models encourages the use of different components to drive portfolio decisions. Senge et al. (1990) suggest that good results most often are achieved by bringing to bear many perspectives. Bringing both the 'top-down' and 'bottom-up' models together, through a series of iterations and discussion should, theoretically at least, result in a more optimal strategic alignment of projects. Of course, the contradictions between the two approaches may make the process more complex and tricky.

In addition to alignment, adopting a systematic approach helps protect the company against the variability of an individual decision maker's predispositions. Research shows that when confronted with the same objective environment, different managers make different decisions based on their individual experiences and values (Prahalad and Bettis, 1986), and their personal characteristics and professional background (Miller and Toulouse, 1982). Thomas and Ramaswamy (1996) report that firms led by confident CEOs adopt risky and innovative strategies, while firms led by CEOs given to feelings of helplessness tend to pursue more conservative strategies. Additionally, firms pursuing internal diversification tended to have CEOs with backgrounds in marketing and production. On the other hand, firms that pursued acquisitive diversification were more likely to have CEOs with backgrounds in accounting (Song, 1982).

ILLUSTRATION

The innovation challenge in the pharmaceutical sector

Innovation is a key driver in the pharmaceuticals sector. Companies in the sector constantly search for new and better medicines for common conditions to replace the value of their most successful drugs before their patent expires. The economics of the sector revolve around research-led discovery and patent protection and post-patent expiry strategies. When patent protection expires, generic drug companies can supply identical formulations at unmatchable prices. Research-based firms find they are unable to compete on price because of their heavy investment in research and marketing of a proprietary product. So the survival of the research-based pharmaceutical companies depends on continual discovery of new drugs.

Increasingly, despite being old hands at drug development, pharmaceutical companies are struggling to respond to the innovation imperative. R&D investments in the sector have increased more than tenfold since 1980, reaching $49 billion in 2003. Yet the number of new drugs launched over the past five years by the top pharmaceutical companies has not moved much above historic levels of the 1980s and 1990s. Between 1996 and 2002, the number of new drugs brought to the market plunged from 53 to 17. GlaxoSmithKline, the Number 2 player in the industry, introduced just three new products in 2003, only one of which it discovered.

The dismal record of discovery over the last few decades led many of the major pharmaceutical companies to the realisation that the hands-off 'leave-it-to-the-scientists' policy was no longer working. They needed to identify priorities, understand and make trade-off decisions between projects, and actively manage project portfolio risks. During the 1980s and 1990s many started to introduce a more commercial approach to innovation management, in which the attention of scientists was redirected from the far horizon to customer-focussed innovation functions as a way of improving performance and accountability of business units.

This shift toward a more commercial approach to managing innovation was a step forward in some cases but in other instances it was a step back. The market focus works well where an intimate understanding of customer needs is the basis for innovation, but is less relevant in sectors such as drug discovery where scientific advance is the stronger driver of value.

The problem with applying the commercial approach to drug development is that it assumes that a more customer-centric focus for allocating innovation resources will be more effective. Yet just knowing customers needs is of little value until you have also found a way to meet it. A customer-centric focus does little to improve the discovery process and decisions based on this logic can actually work to hinder the process. Such criteria is likely to focus business unit managers on short-term performance and encourage them to fund research that provides modest but quicker paybacks at the expense of longer-term projects seeking breakthroughs.

So how should discovery processes be managed? The trick is to be more commercially disciplined when allocating resources without de-motivating the discoverers. McKinnon et al. (2005) propose three elements for this:

→

1. *Run discovery as a separate business*: This separation has a number of advantages: first, it allows senior managers to look at and allocate resources to their key value drivers directly instead of indirectly through intervening business units. Second, it directs the focus of innovation managers on outputs while leaving their destiny in their own hands. This ensures research horizons are not confined within the parochial interests of existing business units. Third, it gives the scientists the freedom they need to orchestrate internal and external discovery activity effectively.

2. *Focus on the economics of the process, not of the project*: Treating the discovery teams as businesses acknowledges a vital, inescapable truth about discovery-led innovation: that not all projects add value directly, and should not, therefore, be evaluated on a purely financial basis, particularly in their early stages. One dramatic example is Viagra's failure as a treatment for heart disease, but its remarkable success for a totally different condition. The principle of 'funding strategies, not projects' is as valid in the lab as it is in the boardroom. In effect, it raises the focus of measurement and judgement from projects to the project portfolio and encourages the movement of scientific talent between projects to its highest-value use.

   An important consequence of this shift of focus from projects to portfolios is that traditional net present value calculations are no longer the best tool for evaluating individual research programmes. More sophisticated innovation measurement tools, such as real options analysis, which take into account the uncertainty of research projects, are more effective.

3. *Focus on decision-making effectiveness, not functional efficiency*: Although managers should never tolerate inefficiencies, the fact is that in industries like pharmaceuticals, the savings from a very effective cost-efficiency drive can be wiped out by a decision to continue developing a product that should be abandoned, or to abandon a project that could, were it allowed to continue, produce a blockbuster. Companies that focus their cost control efforts on improving the quality of their project portfolios – by identifying their stars and dogs early – create much more value than those that focus on the less demanding but less important task of maximising operating efficiency.

Executives who fail to make the distinction between discovery project and incremental market development projects will find themselves in positions whereby they weaken their long-term market positions and destroy intrinsic value, either by spending too much on the wrong projects or by spending too little on the right one.

(*Source*: Based on McKinnon et al., 2005)

Integrating the parts

Discussion earlier in this chapter has highlighted the disconnection between key management levels (strategic, programme and project). Another key issue is the lack of data integrity used in decision point reviews (Edgett, 2007). It is clearly important for any portfolio model to provide an effective interlock between these levels. Interlink between the three levels helps drive the alignment to strategic goals. Figure 6.17 illustrates the way the portfolio is consolidated by different levels of management. In one sense portfolio management can be described as an attempt to take programme-specific information and consolidate it in a manner that interconnects and supports a holistic view and execution of the business.

Individual projects are executed to support broader programmes. The individual projects are tightly controlled using well-established project management practices and measured through metrics such as cost, quality and schedule adherence. The programmes that co-ordinate these projects are focussed on meeting specific business objectives (e.g. growth in revenue, margins or market share). Consequently, these programmes are assessed along two criteria: project-specific objectives (cost, quality and schedule needs) and business

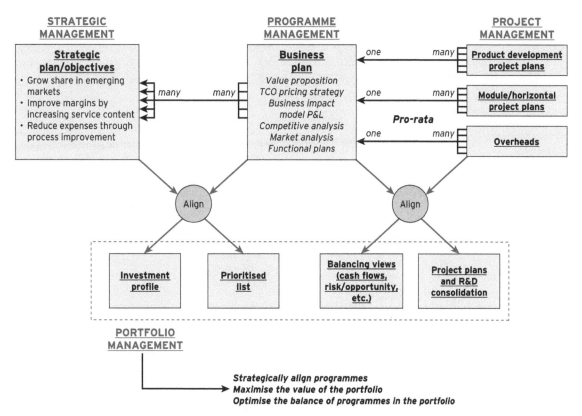

FIGURE 6.17 Aligning project, programme, portfolio and strategic management
Source: Shepherd, 1999

objectives. The activities within the programmes are defined by business plans (articulating the attractiveness of an opportunity, and the way in which a company will mobilise its resources to exploit it), which themselves are interlocked to deliver upon strategic objectives.

An integrated portfolio management model should ensure short-term operational targets are being actioned in accordance with long-term strategic objectives. This is what is meant by *strategic balancing*. By linking strategic and operational planning, an integrated model should allow clear tracking of the linkages between high-level decision making and subsequent operationalisation.

Whilst work in the field to date has provided insights into the variety of components that can constitute a portfolio management framework, little is elaborated on how the pieces come together into a workable and integrated model. To this end, the model in Figure 6.18 provides a top-down/bottom-up integrated view of a portfolio management framework. This framework indicates the interconnections and mechanisms to manage the key activities for portfolio management by offering the following elements:

● By aligning development projects to agreed programmes, a mechanism is introduced which helps reinforce availability dates (through agreed cross-functional milestones), and drives agreement on costs.

● By ensuring key information is made available at the programme level, which makes it possible for it to be used in compilation of different portfolio exhibits. Information that

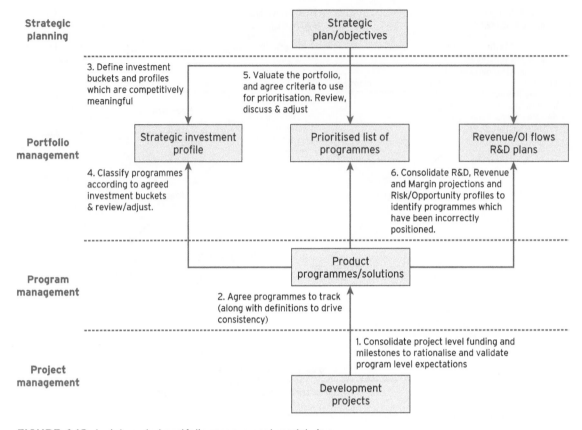

FIGURE 6.18 An integrated portfolio management model view

is typically required includes R&D costs, projected revenue, margin streams and associated risk profiles. As a result of the availability of such information, it is possible to construct risk/opportunity profiles, R&D profiles, and revenue/margin flows to drive portfolio balancing.

● By agreeing funding profiles which are comparatively aligned to competitive activities, the likelihood that specific investment profiles will meet the intended strategic objectives increases.

● By aligning product programmes to agreed strategic investment buckets, it is possible to assess the consolidated and actual funding profile against the intended profile.

● By agreeing factors that are important to the business (e.g. such as project value to the company), it is possible to arrive at a single, agreed prioritisation list that everyone can adhere to. This drives greater focus on key projects and thus supports execution against agreed objectives.

The sequencing of activities outlined in Figure 6.18 provides guidance on how portfolios can be progressively built up and base-lined.

As a result of these integrative steps/elements, it becomes possible to construct exhibits that clearly and accurately define the product portfolio in any company. Additionally, by using information that senior management should already be familiar with, the level of uncertainty and distrust of the new model can be greatly reduced.

ILLUSTRATION

Huber uses Sopheon Accolade to automate and integrate portfolio model

J.M. Huber is a diversified, multi-national supplier of engineered materials, natural resources and technology-based services to customers spanning industries from food products and pharmaceuticals, paper and energy to plastics and construction. As one of the largest family-owned companies in America, Huber is present in more than 20 countries. Its global research and development organisation is tasked with developing new products that will drive growth and profitability.

As part of a corporate commitment to become more market driven and develop new applications for J.M. Huber Corporation products and technologies, the company set a strategic goal of generating 25 per cent of revenue from new products by 2005.

Previous attempts at introducing a formal product development process had failed, primarily due to the process being paper based, which made it difficult to share information globally. This impeded project communication and slowed progress. Huber launched an initiative it called market-driven innovation (MDI) to drive its new product development strategy. MDI included the introduction of a structured development process that would enable the company to optimise its new product investments and resources. To automate this integrated process, Huber implemented the Accolade product from Sopheon. Accolade allows rapid and effective comparison of projects in the Huber portfolio, and allows priorities to be more effectively and consistently set. Since this portfolio information is accessible throughout the company, it has increased accessibility and collaboration.

As a result of this successful linking of an integrated process and supporting IT tool, Huber has realised some impressive benefits:

- Increase in the NPV of the Huber portfolio by four times within 12 months.
- Time spent preparing for portfolio reviews has been reduced by more than four man months per year.
- Approximately one man month per year, per team member, has been eliminated in completing deliverables and project documentation.

(Source: Anon, 2004)

Benefits from an effective portfolio management model

NPD frameworks have historically been introduced to address three specific objectives, time-to-market, development cost and first-mover advantages. However, the effectiveness of their implementation has affected their ability to deliver these benefits at a level that matches senior management expectations.

A major problem of the prevalent structured funnel NPD systems has been poor decision making, which has either been arbitrary, or highly complex and rather intractable. Portfolio management offers an opportunity to address some of the major concerns in this area by more clearly aligning operational process and resources to programmes intended to drive growth. Additionally, by being able to make investment decisions that support the vital few opportunities, the performance of the organisation can be increased.

A number of intangible benefits have also been identified to be associated with an effective portfolio model (Harris and McCormack, 1997).

- The company can quickly re-allocate resources to higher priority projects.
- Strategic and financial plans are based on realistic development skills and capabilities, and detailed plans are put in place to address deficient areas.
- Functional budgets are aligned with project needs and strategic plans.
- Bottlenecks are eliminated, enabling all projects to proceed rapidly through development.
- Functional managers free up time as fire-fighting is minimised and proactive, cross-project trade-offs are made continuously.
- Decisions on all projects and in every function are co-ordinated, based on aligned priorities and factual information.
- Ripple effects on projects due to external changes of development problems are smoothly resolved.
- Project team leaders can succeed, because projects are staffed for success.

The types of potential benefits offered are illustrated in Figure 6.19.

The use of 'portfolio management' within NPD frameworks developed during the late 1990s. However, the importance placed on this area can be deduced from the number of organisations that tried to implement such a framework. Between 1997 and 1999 there was an increase from 1 per cent of companies using portfolio-based decision making to 7 per cent (PRTM, 1998). By 2001, this had risen to 13 per cent. However, more recent findings suggest a slow-down in the speed at which companies are embracing portfolio-based

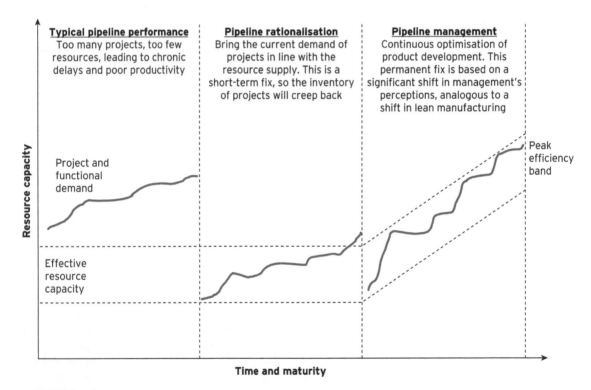

FIGURE 6.19 Creating peak efficiency in pipeline management
Source: Harris and McCormick, 1999

models because of their complexity and difficulty in use. This is so, despite the fact that many companies still rate this capability as one of their most important priorities.

Integrating portfolio management practices into NPD governance

NPD frameworks can be represented as a steady stream of products (or services) flowing through a pipeline. The classic funnel shape is representative of a process that evaluates many ideas and selects only the best for full-scale development and deployment. Unfortunately, the decision point reviews are usually inadequate for making trade-off decisions, since the focus is on one programme (rather than many), and conducted at a detailed programme (rather than overarching portfolio) level. So what is the best way to integrate both programme and portfolio reviews into the NPD governance structure?

Existing programme reviews, using the NPD decision process, tend to occur in an 'event-based' manner. They reach different review milestones at different times, and have cycle times that reflect the unique nature of the opportunity they attempt to exploit. Supported by a major deliverable, such as a 'gate review pack' or business plan, these reviews are intended to allow senior members of the company to assess the opportunity and risk associated with a programme and make the necessary go/kill decisions. To better integrate with the portfolio management model, these deliverables should be updated to provide the Review Board with information on how the current programme might change the profile and priorities of the portfolio. This tends to represent a bottom-up approach to portfolio management, where the focus is on exceptions and minor change, and could specifically address:

- Impact on current investment strategies to meet strategic long-term, and short-term, growth objectives (e.g. funding taken away from a 'breakthrough new' opportunity to fund an immediate 'life cycle' opportunity).

- Impact on the overall valuation of the portfolio (e.g. where the cancellation of one programme over another may increase the overall value in the long term, but possibly not in the short term, due to the associated risk).

- Overall portfolio priorities, which subsequently governs how resources are assigned within the company (e.g. where the major programmes are given the best players to ensure success).

Portfolio-based reviews should tend to occur in a time-based manner, perhaps occurring quarterly (or even monthly in a highly dynamic environment). Ideally, the timetable for portfolio-based reviews should align to the company's strategic and operational planning cycles. The intention of these reviews should be to assess the value of the portfolio, its mix (based on planned profiles), balance and strategic alignment. Decisions made here should be made at a portfolio level (i.e. across all products/services) and be intended to maximise portfolio performance. Trade-offs between programmes and strategic business units can take place here, and broader organisational targets and profiles may be fine-tuned as appropriate. This is very much a top-down view, where changes in the portfolio may have an impact on any number of programmes. The integration of these two approaches is illustrated in Figure 6.20.

In this manner, the urgency of progressing programmes through the NPD funnel will be achieved via event-based decision points (which ensure strategic/portfolio alignment), but also enables broader issues and fine-tuning to be addressed at a portfolio level. At all times, major planning and review points are synchronised to prevent confusion and duplication.

	01			02			03			04			01			02			03			04		
	Jan	Feb	Mar	Apr	May	Jun	Jul	Aug	Sep	Oct	Nov	Dec	Jan	Feb	Mar	Apr	May	Jun	Jul	Aug	Sep	Oct	Nov	Dec
Major planning events (strategic)				Strategic plan kick off			Strategic plan approval									Strategic plan kick off			Strategic plan approval					
Major planning events (operational)							Operational plan start			Operational plan approved									Operational plan start			Operational plan approved		
Quarterly portfolio reviews (time based)			Port review			Port review			Port review			Port review			Port review			Port review			Port review			Port review
Program decision points/gate reviews (event based)																								
Program Alpha			Gate 0	Gate 1			Gate 2							Gate 3		Gate 4								
Program Beta				Gate 0		Gate 1					Gate 2					Gate 3			Gate 4					
Program Gamma		Gate 0			Gate 1		Gate 2					Gate 3		Gate 4										
Program Delta	Gate 0		Gate 1	Gate 2							Gate 3							Gate 4						
Program Epsilon				Gate 0	Gate 1		Gate 2				Gate 3										Gate 4			
Program Omega							Gate 0			Gate 1				Gate 2							Gate 3			

Annotations: "Alignment of portfolio reviews to strategic and operational plans"; "Alignment of portfolio reviews to decision point reviews".

FIGURE 6.20 Integrating portfolio management into NPD decision points

Conclusion

A number of strategic planning methodologies have been developed over the past 20 years which are intended to aid companies in achieving long-term, sustainable, profitable growth objectives. While significant efforts have been directed towards improving these methodologies, little has been achieved in aligning these to operational activities. Consequently, great difficulties have been experienced in translating strategic plans into action.

NPD frameworks were introduced to improve operational performance in product development and were seen as a mechanism whereby a company's strategy could be articulated. During the past 10 years or so, a great deal of research has been conducted to improve the effectiveness of cross-functional teams, execution and optimisation of functional processes and the improvement of cross-functional linkages.

While demonstrable benefits have been realised in such frameworks, primarily in time-to-market and product development cost reductions, many senior executives remain disappointed in their NPD frameworks to realise specific growth objectives. Problems were identified in decision making and the strategic alignment of development projects. It is only in the past few years that work in NPD frameworks has been directed toward improving the associated decision making of programmes. Most of the progress has been in the area of portfolio management, but remains tentative and fragmented. Nevertheless, it is the first step towards better alignment of product development projects to strategic objectives and associated strategic positioning.

QUESTIONS

1. Select 5 important characteristics that would influence the prioritisation of a product portfolio. Show how you would use these to provide an initial prioritised list for the senior management team to review and discuss.

2. If you had five exhibits to present to the Review Board, providing an effective coverage of the company's current product portfolio, which ones would you select, and why?

3. Based on the following information, build a risk/opportunity bubble chart, then discuss what issues the company is facing.

Programme	Strategic investment bucket	R&D allocated ($m)	Total opportunity (revenue $m)	Marketing risk score	Development risk score	Launch risk score
A	Ongoing new	3.0	9.0	0.8	0.8	0.7
B	Life cycle	0.5	5.0	0.8	0.9	0.7
C	Life cycle	0.3	4.0	0.9	0.9	0.8
D	Breakthrough	15.0	45.0	0.3	0.3	0.3
E	Ongoing new	10.0	30.0	0.5	0.5	0.5
F	Ongoing new	5.0	15.0	0.7	1.0	0.6
G	Lifecycle	9.0	5.0	1.0	1.0	0.4
H	Breakthrough	5.0	10.0	0.9	0.8	1.0
I	Ongoing new	4.0	11.5	0.9	0.3	0.4
J	Lifecycle	1.0	3.3	0.9	0.9	0.9

4. Based on the following information, calculate the ECV for the proposed opportunity, and position it in the available list explaining what recommendations you would make to the senior management team (Review Board).

Measure	Value
Marketing investment	$1.0m
Development investment	$10.0m
Launch investment	$10.0m
Probability of marketing success	0.7
Probability of development success	0.8
Probability of commerical success	0.6
Estimated NPV over 5 years	$250m
Penalty for missing commitment	$50m

5. Select two companies within a specific market, and explain how you would differentiate their portfolios using the models described in this chapter, with particular emphasis on strategic alignment.

CASE STUDY

The bitter pill – can you help save the company?

Company A is an established player in the pharmaceutical market, specialising in analgesia (pain killers) possessing around 33 per cent of the available market share, which it shares equally with two other competitors (Companies B and C).

Company A currently sells products of different strengths to medical organisations, chemists (prescription only) and supermarkets (non-prescription). The products in this market have not changed radically in the last 5–10 years, although improved practices have allowed the cost-to-manufacture to drop significantly.

Recent market analysis has indicated some interesting activities which need to be considered by the senior management team of Company A. These include:

- Competitors are aggressively entering new geographical markets

- Competitors are looking to diversify into new product areas, and are supported by strong relationships with influential research groups.

This has been supported by some externally commissioned research which has indicated that both Companies B and C have adjusted their R&D funding profiles, with an intention to drive a 'first-to-market' positioning with estimated profiles as follows:

Investment profile/year	Current year	Current year +1	Current year +2
Breakthrough new	33%	38%	43%
Ongoing new	34%	34%	34%
Life cycle	33%	28%	23%

To remain competitive, Company A now recognises that it needs to adjust its strategies and portfolio. Consequently, recent strategic planning activities have uncovered a strong need for Company A to aggressively grow market share, revenue and margins.

Before it can do so, it needs to understand the issues that are faced by the current portfolio. Some specific detail around the current portfolio is offered below:

Product	Investment category	Current year's R&D ($m)	Probability of marketing success	Probability of technical success	Probability of commercial success	Associated NPV ($m)
A	Ongoing New	3.0	0.8	0.8	0.8	55.0
B	Lifecycle	2.5	0.9	1.0	0.8	25.0
C	Breakthrough New	6.0	0.5	0.4	0.3	90.0
D	Lifecycle	2.5	0.9	0.9	0.7	30.0
E	Ongoing New	4.0	0.8	0.8	0.6	65.0
F	Lifecycle	5.0	1.0	1.0	0.7	40.0

QUESTIONS

1. Which elements are missing that make it difficult for Company A to baseline its activities?
2. What challenges are being faced by Company A?
3. Based on these challenges, which five exhibits would you present to the Review Board to provide an effective review of the company's current product portfolio? Please state reasons why you selected these exhibits.

References

Anon (2004), *J.M. Huber increases value of portfolio by four times*, Bloomington, MN Sopheon Corporation.

Bacon, G., Beckman, S., Mowry, D. and Wilson, E. (1994), 'Managing product definition in high technology industries: A pilot study', *California Management Review*, Spring: 32–56.

Burgleman, R.A. and Grove, A.S. (1996), 'Strategic dissonance', *California Management Review*, 38(2): 8–28.

Canner, N. and Mass, N.J. (2005), 'Turn R&D upside down', *Research Technology Management* 48(2): 17–22.

Cooper, R.G. (2008), 'Perspective: The stage-gate idea-to-launch process – update: What's new and NextGen systems', *Journal of Product Innovation Management* 25(3): 213–232.

Cooper, R.G. and Edgett, S.J. (2005), *Lean, rapid, and profitable new product development*, Ancaster, ON: Product Development Institute.

Cooper, R.G., Edgett, S.J. and Kleinschmidt, E.J. (1998), *Portfolio management for new products*, Reading, MA: Addison-Wesley.

Edgett, S. (2007), *Portfolio management: Optimising for success*, Houston, TX: American Productivity and Quality Center.

Edgett, S.J. (1998), 'Portfolio management for new products', *PDMA Conference on Portfolio Management*, Fort Lauderdale, December.

Gould, M.R. (1996), 'Getting from strategy to action: Processes for continuous change', *Long Range Planning* 29(3): 278–289.

Griffin, A. (1997), 'PDMA research and new product development practices: Updating trends and benchmarking best practices', *Journal of Product Innovation Management*, 14 November: 429–458.

Hamel, G. and Prahalad, C.K. (1989), 'Strategic intent', *Harvard Business Review*, May/June: 63–76.

Harris, J. and McCormick, M. (1997), 'Benefits of establishing a pipeline management process for high technology companies', *Insight*, Summer: 9(2), PRTM.

Jenner, S. (2007), 'Gates with teeth: Implementing a centre of excellence for investment decisions', Paper presented at the First International Stage-Gate Conference, 20–21 February, St. Petersburg, FL.

Luehrman, T.A. (1998), 'Strategy as a portfolio of real options', *Harvard Business Review*, September–October: 87–99.

McGrath, M.E. (1998), 'How information technology will transform pipeline and portfolio management', PDMA Conference on Portfolio Planning and Management, 10 December.

McKinnon, R., Gowland, C. and Worzel, K. (2005), 'From breakthrough to value creation: Mastering profitable discovery', *Strategy and Leadership*, 33(3): 17–23.

Miller, D., Kets de Vries, M.F.R. and Toulouse, J.M. (1982), 'Top executive locus of control and its relationship to strategy making, structure and environment', *Academy of Management Journal* 25: 237–253.

Mueller, J. (2004), *Portfolio and program management tips from Ford* (Ford Motor Company), **www.scribd.com/doc/25221842/Fords-Case-Analysis.**

Ogg, A. (1999), 'Investment appraisal techniques', MBA Thesis, University of Abertay.

Page, A.L. (1993), 'Assessing new product development practices and performance: Establishing crucial norms', *Journal of Product Innovation Management* 10: 273–290.

Pawar, K.S., Menon, V. and Reidel, J.C.K.H. (1994), 'Time to market', *Integrated Manufacturing Systems* 5(1): 14–22.

Pike, R. (1982), *Capital Budgeting in the 1980s*, London: ICMA.

Pittiglio, Rabin, Todd and McGrath (PRTM) (1998), 'Managing the product development pipeline', 1 June, Internal Consultative Document to NCR Payment Solutions – Waterloo, Canada.

Prahalad, C.K. and Bettis, R.A. (1986), 'The dominant logic: A new linkage between diversity and performance', *Strategic Management Journal* 7: 485–501.

Samli, A.C. (1996), 'Developing futuristic product portfolios: A major panacea for the sluggish American industry', *Industrial Marketing Management* 25(6): 589–600.

Senge, P. (1990), *5th discipline field book*, New York: Currency-Doubleday Publishing.

Shepherd, C.D. (1999), 'Strategic alignment of new product development processes', Ph.D. Thesis, Bradford European Management Centre, University of Bradford.

Song, J.H. (1982), 'Diversification strategies and experiences of top executives in large firms', *Strategic Management Journal* 3: 377–380.

Souder, W.E. (1988), 'Managing relations between R&D and marketing in new product development projects', *Journal of Product Innovation Management* 5: 6–19.

Thomas, A.S. and Ramaswamy, K. (1996), 'Matching managers to strategy: Further tests of the Miles & Snow typology', *British Journal of Management* 7: 247–261.

7 Innovation performance measurement

Learning outcomes

When you have completed this chapter you should be able to:

- Understand the role of performance measurement in driving business performance.

- Describe the evolution of business performance measurement systems.

- Appreciate the main components of a business performance measurement system.

- Appreciate the integrated performance measurement frameworks and methodologies.

- Recognise the different levels of measurement.

- Understand the different types of measurements and metrics.

- Recognise and appreciate the different metrics of innovation measurement, and the relationship between them.

- Understand the characteristics of a successful measurement system.

Performance management in the modern business context

Measurement in innovation is somewhat of a necessity. We all have heard the rhetorical expression, 'innovate or die' which is designed to impel innovation activity on an on-going basis. However, to innovate requires not just an expression of commitment or even effort, but a systematic approach to the management of innovation. This must include an insistence from top management on continuous measurement, monitoring and improvement. Measurement is a key trigger for action. It keeps the minds and people's energies focussed on adding value and is one of the best means possible for preventing complacency. Innovation is generally deemed to drive competitiveness. This makes monitoring and measuring innovation all the more relevant. On the basis of its importance, it is often assumed that organisations, generally speaking, are good at measurement and use it effectively to drive innovation. Is this really the case?

Lingle and Schiemann (1996) report findings of a survey of 203 executives from a cross-section of industries in the US. The survey attempted to establish answers to the following questions:

- What are companies doing to increase performance?
- Does measuring strategic performance make a difference?
- Is measurement being used to manage change?

The survey found that measurement is not widely pervasive as an integrated practice and its implementation is not a straightforward process. Moreover, the value and impact of measurement is significant, and greatly distinguishes good companies from the rest. As Lingle and Schiemann (1996) argue, 'For those executives who have gone beyond the given eyeshades and stopwatches to assess the pivot points of their company's strategy – from how well customer expectations are met to the ability to manage relevant environmentally and regulatory forces, to how adaptable the organisation is – the measurement effort will yield ongoing results to the bottom line.'

Despite the importance of measurement, the survey highlighted that the quality of measures related to innovation and change is much worse than in areas such as finance, productivity, and customer satisfaction. More often than not, the survey findings suggest that measures on innovation are not included for management review and meetings, are not widely used for bringing about organisational change and are not linked to employee compensation.

The survey concluded that some of the chief reasons for the lack of commitment to making measurement work in the area of innovation are because many companies:

- Possess fuzzy objectives without any clear statements or a process for generating buy-in and commitments.
- Place unjustified trust in informal systems. Many companies tend to rely on feedback from informal, subjective sources, but as Lingle and Schiemann (1996) state, 'Non-measurement managed companies often learn too late that an apparent problem which has absorbed resources is the concern of only a few squeaky wheels, while a more critical problem has gone unattended.'
- Ignore the fact that measurement is closely associated with alleviating fear and inducing positive behaviour for making the system in question work. They simply continue with old entrenched measurement systems and get caught up in a measurement mania, where the focus is more on the measurements of activity rather than results. This is known as

the 'activity trap' in which it is pre-supposed that just because we are doing something we are producing some results.

Every organisation is involved in some form of measurement, whether naïve or sophisticated. Without measurement a company would not know if it had achieved its goals. Through measurement, companies are able to control, evaluate and improve processes. Measurement is itself a process, involving decisions over what to measure, how to measure, and what actions to take after measurement. Measurement is a way of enhancing understanding. Lord Kelvin put it well in noting, 'When you can measure what you are speaking about and express it in numbers, you know something about it. [Otherwise] your knowledge is a meagre and unsatisfactory kind' (Lord Kelvin 1824–1904, quoted in Heim and Compton, 1992, p. 1). Leading-edge companies have acted upon such wisdom and have carefully devised measurement metrics and systems to help them reach their performance goals.

Many businesses follow programmes of innovation, and yet after some time begin to wonder whether this investment of large sums of money and time has been worthwhile. Those that do not possess an innovation tracking system operate in the dark and are unable to answer the question. Many become disenchanted because they have little or no understanding of the value being derived from their investments and effort. Only businesses with a measurement system in place are able to track their progress, or lack of it, and take corrective actions to ensure that the company's strategic and short-term objectives are being met through the innovation strategies being followed. This underscores the importance of measurement. Measurement is important because:

- It draws attention to areas that need improvement.
- It highlights areas of high performance and strengths.
- It allows comparisons to be made to historical performance as well as relative to competition.
- It surfaces the costs of poor implementation of strategy.
- It highlights the gap between objectives and actual attainment.

Without measurement, management becomes a game played in the dark. No one really knows what they are doing, how well they are doing, and indeed if it matters at all.

ILLUSTRATION

Measurement – the other half of creativity?

A popular view of business is that it is split into two halves. One half is the creative right side of the brain: product developers, marketers, researchers and others who dream big dreams and think in the future tense. The second half is the rational left brain, made up of financial analysts, accountants and other number-crunchers who don't look farther ahead than the next quarter's spreadsheet.

It is a nice little image, but it is wrong. Business innovation is a lot more about synthesis than just the singular act of invention. The greatest breakthroughs are made by those with the broadest perspectives and the deepest knowledge: they can see the potential in a new idea while also understanding the economics of production and distribution, the motivations of competitors, and the needs and moods of consumers. And this analytical creativity is far more likely to be found among the suits than those who wear high-fashion trainers. The fact is that both types are needed.

One great example of this is Samuel Insull, a starched English bean-counter who took care of all the business details that Thomas Edison, the inventor, couldn't be bothered with. With a deft combination of discipline and insight into the market and the economics of electricity, he sowed the seeds of General Electric, now one of the world's largest companies.

Not every accountant is an Insull, of course, but there are plenty of individuals who pay attention to the detail required to turn inventions into commercial realities. If executives took a hard and open-minded look at the operating and financial sides of their business, they would probably find a good number of individuals with such skills. Unfortunately, few managers seem to make that effort. They buy into the popular but false distinction: innovation should be left to the creatives, and that is a shame. Think of how much more productive corporate innovation could become if those with a deep understanding of the numbers were brought more fully into the processes for generating and commercialising new ideas.

(*Source*: Based on Carr, 2005)

 ## The measurement conundrum

Measurement is not a simple phenomenon. It carries with it a range of problems and ramifications. The nature of measurement is complex and has resulted in the view that it is 'a mystery . . . frustrating, difficult, challenging, important, abused and misused' (Sink, 1991). Different organisational actors, such as strategists, accountants and human resource managers, have their own definition of measurement and use measurement in different ways. For instance, human resource managers deploy metrics and measurement for internal assessment, such as an individual's performance appraisal, whilst the focus of others is on external reporting, such as financial accounting ratios. One way to overcome the many definitional problems is to define measurement as the systematic assignment of numbers to entities. This definition can be universally applied to hold meaning for the requirements of various stakeholder groups. What is important is that the function of measurement and actual metrics are appropriate and useful. The function of measurement must be to develop a method for generating a class of information that will be useful in a wide variety of problems and situations (Zairi, 1994). Functionality is important because it is possible to devise many measurement systems and metrics; but unless they are useful they are meaningless.

Measurement is not easy. In attempting to measure, what often happens is that select attributes of performance that are used to characterise a specific construct are examined rather than the performance per se. The issue of measurement is further complicated by the fact that measures are aggregated either upwards from individual activity to organisational performance, or disaggregated downwards from strategic goals to individual targets. With so many different levels of measurement, ranging from the individual to organisation-wide, it is hardly surprising that so many contradictions and conflicts emerge in the world of practice. Measurement raises a number of difficulties and conundrums:

- Measurement, if not implemented well, can easily become counter-productive and induce rigidity. Organisations and people start to focus on the number rather than the raison d'être of the number, namely as a driver for continuous improvement.

- Measurement can too easily become an internally focussed and unwieldy bureaucratic nightmare. Measurement systems and metrics must be carefully constructed. It is easy, if too many metrics and measurements take place, for the organisation to be paralysed through information collection.

● Measurement through objective assessment can be highly revealing, but it must be conducted with great care because it can induce fear in the people being measured. Moreover, the claim to objectivity must not be taken too far, since what is being measured, by whom and for what purposes is essentially a selection dictated by the subjectivity of certain agents of the organisation.

● Processes with human elements are very complex to measure. It is often mistakenly believed that measures track behaviour. On the contrary, behaviour tracks measurements since, in most instances, behaviours are induced to maximise the performance indicator rather than effectiveness of the process. For example, we only have to observe the way measurement has induced undesirable ways of reducing waiting lists and patient handling in National Health Service (NHS) hospitals in the UK. Rather than tackling process inefficiency, the measurement metric became the focus of attention for manipulation in order to show improvement.

● When measurement is either very small or very large it introduces added layers of complexity and challenge.

From a systems perspective, performance measurement is a process of determining how successful an organisation (or individual or process) has been in attaining objectives. Under this approach, inputs and outputs of a specified organisational process or activity become the central focus of attention. Generally, at the organisational level, measurement provides an assessment of whether strategic aims are being met. At the individual level, performance measurement serves as a device through which to focus and enunciate accountability, and acts as an objective, impersonal basis for performance evaluation. Measurement metrics are usually constructed to reflect the desired organisational and behavioural outcomes, and in this way they become useful as ways of providing feedback on activities that motivate behaviours for continuous improvement in customer satisfaction, flexibility and productivity.

CASE STUDY

Vodafone's integration and alignment challenge

Arun Sarin succeeded Sir Christopher Charles Gent in the summer of 2003, to run Vodafone, the £2bn telecommunications giant, after it had gone through a period of intensive acquisitions. The acquisition phase, Sarin says, is largely over. The focus now is to complete the integration of Vodafone's disparate companies. 'We acquired a lot of companies to become what we are today. Now we have to make this series of companies work as one operating company.'

Mr Sarin says he is happy to be steering that course. 'No company runs on automatic pilot. You need to manage and steer and direct a company not as an individual but as a group of senior team members that bring different skills to the table. After the discussion we figure out where we want to go, at what speed we want to go, what sector we want to go in. All of those things are important.'

That approach reflects a management style built on consensus. The new chief executive spreads the Vodafone operating mission in person at so-called 'town-hall meetings' to some of the group's 68,000 employees in some 28 countries. Sir Christopher, who started the practice, addressed more than

30,000 workers in such meetings in 2002 alone. Mr Sarin also relies on the company's flagship wireless devices to communicate with the workforce by e-mail and webcam.

A graduate of the Indian Institute of Technology and the University of California at Berkeley, he relies heavily on performance targets, benchmarking and stiff financial measures to monitor results. Anything that threatens Vodafone's annual revenues of €50bn, underlying earnings of €20bn and free cash flow of €10bn is viewed dimly.

Referring to Vodafone's 'play-book', he says: 'One of the nicest things about Vodafone is that we benchmark everything. We benchmark churn, we benchmark revenue, we benchmark cost of acquisition ... and then we put all the charts up and we say, "OK, Italy does this really well and the UK does this really well and Germany does this really well. Can we learn something from their business model that we can apply in our other markets?"'

'We do this absolutely rigorously and with great enthusiasm every month. But, frankly, we don't talk a lot about it externally. I would say this is part of the internal management and process that helps us stay ahead of the competition.'

Vodafone's new chief executive does not see anything particularly smart about employing such measures. They are seen as logical tools for a global corporation in evolutionary mode.

Sarin pays tribute to his predecessors: the company 'is in very good shape'. As a long-serving Vodafone non-executive director, he could hardly do otherwise. But colleagues suggest he is also determined to strip out duplication and savings from far-flung areas. This is expected to involve more centralised product development at Vodafone's new headquarters campus, where 3000 staff work in seven large buildings, each named after a communications legend such as Baird, Bell and Edison. Marketing, branding and sales will be more carefully co-ordinated across different territories.

Summing up the Sarin challenge, one executive says: 'The verdict is that Vodafone has got through its acquisition phase with a range of decentralised operating businesses. The issue now is to run it like one business while giving local operations a measure of autonomy. It's not an easy trick to pull off.'

QUESTION

What role can performance measurement play in aligning and integrating Vodaphone's operations to become a market-facing innovator?

(*Source*: Based on R. Budden and T. Burt, 'Brand is a big issue', *Financial Times*, 22 December 2003, p. 17)

 ## Performance measurement

To be useful, metrics of measurement should allow comparisons to be made. However, in practice there tends to be a large degree of inconsistency in definition and measurement. For example, productivity can be defined as a quality measure, a financial performance measure, or even given some other classification. This type of apparent inconsistency makes measurement a tricky issue and one that needs to be approached systematically and with care in developing an appropriate measurement system.

Performance measurement must encapsulate all aspects of business decisions in order to align and move the organisation in the desired direction. This requires discipline and a systematic methodological approach to implement the right metrics and track them over time. A good measurement should possess the following characteristics to make it useful:

- *Clarity of purpose*: Provide the right information necessary to achieve aims.
- *Correct and precise*: 'Good' information.

- *Timeliness*: Provide the right information to the right people, at the right time.

- *Reflect process visibility*: Be able to capture how work is being done and provide feedback for continuous improvement of the process.

- *Reflect progress visibility*: Be able to capture how well work is being done. The metrics here should be those leading to customer-focussed outcomes.

- *Focussed on core value-adding activities*: Measures and measurement must be only on critical activities that lead to performance outcomes. It is important to ensure that only a few select and key measures are implemented.

- *Improvement focussed*: Measurement should be such that it leads to feedback that helps reach corporate targets.

Phases of performance measurement

Performance measurement has evolved through three relatively distinct stages (Ghalayini and Noble, 1996), summarised in Figure 7.1. The first of these systematic approaches to measurement began to emerge in the early 1980s. During this stage the emphasis of measurement was on financial measures such as profits, ROI and productivity. In this era, measurement systems were designed on the traditional logic of management accounting. Unfortunately, this perspective suffered from numerous limitations. Briefly, these are:

- *Traditional accounting measures are lagging metrics that lack relevance for day-to-day improvement decisions.* Metrics based on a system of conventional accounting were designed to attribute costs, not aid decision making. Traditional measures quantify performance only in financial terms, but are not readily amenable to driving improvement actions, such as customer satisfaction, delivery time adherence, etc. Moreover, financial information is collected after the event, and so provides only an historic account of what

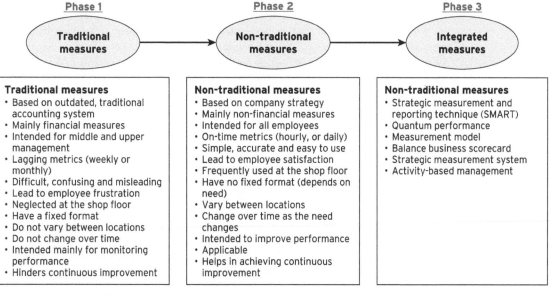

FIGURE 7.1 Evolution in measurement approaches
Source: Adapted from Ghalayani and Noble, 1996

has already happened. Thus, it is not highly relevant for controlling live events as they happen, i.e. it is not operationally relevant.

- *Corporate strategy.* Traditional measures are poor at driving alignment actions for corporate strategy implementation.

- *Relevance to practice. Conventional measures can breed narrowness of focus and inflexibility into the organisation through formulation and adherence of rigid standard(s).* Traditional measures are not only difficult to collect and expensive but, additionally, are narrow in focus and fixed in format. They are typically used to set narrow financial standards of performance, sometimes across all departments and parts of the business. Often what is relevant for one section is not relevant for others, making the information somewhat redundant in many cases. Setting standards for performance can easily act against the philosophy of continuous improvement since it can lead to the establishment of bounds (upper or lower) in the norms of output and behaviour. For instance, workers may hesitate to improve their performance if they begin to think that the standard for the forthcoming period is to be revised upwards on the basis of current results. Additionally, traditional financial reports used by middle managers do not reflect the organisational reality of fluid structures with shifting responsibility and new market conditions warranting rapid and flexible response to shifting customer requirements.

These problems fuelled a move to incorporate non-financial measures. This shift of emphasis is reflected in the second stage of development. In the second stage, the emphasis moved to the development of non-financial measures such that they facilitated decision making for managers and workers. New metrics were developed that were more closely related to operational processes, and therefore allowed 'online' actions to be taken to control and improve the process rather than just monitor past performance. These measures were flexible in that they could be changed to reflect emerging requirements arising from the dynamics of the marketplace.

The third stage built upon the second by developing integrated systems of financial and non-financial metrics to drive organisational performance. The basic aim of the integrated systems was to allow examination of performance from multiple angles and openly explore the trade-offs in arriving at the final decision. A variety of such integrated systems have been developed, and from amongst these the most well known is the Balanced Scorecard, the Strategic Measurement and Reporting Technique (SMART), the Quantum Performance Measurement Model (QPMM) and the Strategic Measurement System (SMS). These integrated measurement frameworks are sometimes called performance measurement systems but, as we highlight in the discussion later, these are actually a component of the full performance measurement system.

Performance measurement systems

A performance measurement system is a tool for balancing multiple measures (cost, quality and time) across multiple levels (organisation, processes and people) to systematically monitor, and control the organisational transformation process (Hronec, 1993). The logic of implementing a performance measurement system is based on the simple principle: what gets measured gets done. Essentially it is a system that relies on development of a set of rules and procedures to collect specific pieces of information for organisational assessment and improvement purposes.

An effective performance measurement system should provide timely and accurate feedback on the efficiency and effectiveness of operations. It is of utmost importance to ensure data provided by the performance measurement system is relevant, factual information that reflects accurately core business processes and key activities (Miller, 1992). Having precise and accurate information is the foundation for sound business decisions, and can be the critical difference between prosperity and death. Dixon et al. (1990) identifies five characteristics of a good measurement system. The performance measurement system should:

- Be mutually supportive and consistent with the business's operating goals, objectives, critical success factors and programmes.
- Convey information through as few and as simple a set of measures as possible.
- Reveal how effectively customers' needs and expectations are satisfied. Measures should focus on critical factors that customers' want and can see.
- Provide a set of measurements for each organisational component such that they demonstrate to all members of the organisation how their decisions and activities affect the entire business.
- Support organisational learning and continuous improvement.

Historically, performance measurement systems have looked to serve the needs of shareholders and senior management in providing a top-level overview of how the company operated in the previous financial year. Such measures, whilst providing consistency in measurement, were of limited use to drive the organisation since they were a retrospective collation, being often produced a long time after the year-end. To be organisationally more useful the measures must assist managers in making decisions and taking action.

Adoption of the wrong measures within the performance measurement system is not only wasteful but can be highly damaging to the morale and motivation of employees. Indeed, many performance measurement systems fail because they contain too many metrics (measurement paralysis) or metrics that are vague, confusing and contradictory to desired outcomes (diffusion-confusion paralysis). More often than not, such systems engage in measuring activities that are of a local or individual interest to a manager rather than a key activity for the business.

To drive the organisation forward the measurement system must enable a wide, yet deep, appreciation of what is happening to factors that govern business performance. It is no use just focussing attention on the financial bottom line. In addition to the bottom line, it is necessary to identify and track 'top line' performance measures. What are the critical processes that add value, how can people's behaviour be improved (productivity), how well is strategy implemented, and so on, are the type of questions the measurement system should be able to answer, in addition to highlighting financial returns to investment. These questions capture the enabling drivers that underpin financial performance, and require the definition and tracking of non-financial metrics capable of identifying in real time the progress that is being made, and where to take corrective actions. This linkage between strategy, actions and measures is essential and unless companies adapt their measures and measurement systems to facilitate this, the measurement system will fail to deliver the expected benefits (Dixon et al., 1990).

The performance measurement system is often considered simply as the framework of metrics. However, it is more than a system of measurement metrics. The measurement system is a process which involves translating the organisational vision and mission into specific goals and targets. It is the goals and targets that determine the nature of the metric that is to be implemented and monitored for business performance. The process does not end at the point of data collection. It is followed by critical evaluation and appraisal of the achieved performance to define appropriate actions for future success. These decisions must be

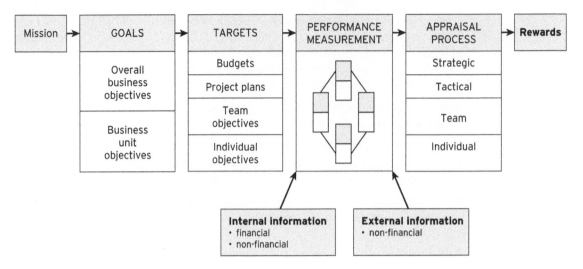

FIGURE 7.2 Performance measurement system

complemented by development of appropriate training, rewards and motivators to drive implementation actions. The process is illustrated in Figure 7.2.

No company would say that it is not committed to continuous improvement, yet few realise that the way they deploy performance measurement may be harmful and incompatible with improvement initiatives (Zairi, 1992). Performance measures need to promote and encourage the right behaviours, i.e. those behaviours that assist the organisation in achieving its goals. The measurement system and metrics must be non-threatening and motivational, promoting involvement and ownership in a cycle of continuous improvement.

In developing measurement systems, soft behavioural aspects tend to be underemphasised or neglected because they are difficult to measure. Yet, it is generally the case that the sound management of the soft aspects leads to high performance as a natural consequence. Therefore, the tendency to focus on the tangible hard metrics must be supplemented by inclusion of a good balance of soft measures.

Traditional performance measures have focussed on outputs, whereas there is a need to look towards the enablers that lead to the production of results. Enablers can be multifaceted and include elements such as leadership, people, systems, strategy, communication, etc. It is from these enablers that improvement benefits flow. This distinction defines two basic types of measures: *Process-based measures* and *Output- (or Results-) based measures* as illustrated in Figure 7.3. Process measures are attached to a process, so to speak. They relate to a particular process, and are used by people to control, manage and improve their work process. They are online measures since they provide quick feedback to guide actions in the

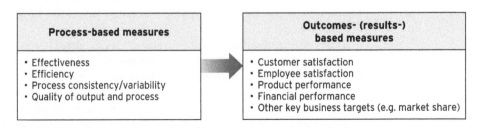

FIGURE 7.3 Process- and outcome-based metrics

workplace. In contrast, output measures relate to broad business targets and goals, and are used more by management as a broad yardstick of how the organisation has been running. Typically, output data is collected from the workplace but is analysed and presented to the higher echelons of the organisation. Consequently, the information is a retrospective assessment of performance, and usually is collected weekly, monthly or annually. Output measures capture aggregate pictures of the organisation and therefore, whilst useful for planning purposes, have lower value in guiding daily operations.

So, what are the characteristics of an effective measurement system? Firstly, the measurement needs to capture the reality of the organisation at various levels (strategic, tactical and operational). As a result of this, it seems obvious that the performance measurement needs to be a distributed activity reflecting various levels of ownership and control within the organisation. Consequently, the performance measurement needs to comprise a mix of measures ranging from specific metrics for individuals to improve their own performance through to broader measures assessing the alignment to, and fulfilment of, strategies. If defined and implemented effectively, these performance measurements should then be able to highlight opportunities for improvement in all areas of the business.

Many companies appreciate the concepts, and the need, for measurement, but still fail to develop measurement systems that enable superior performance. There are a number of reasons for this, with some of the more common causes being listed below:

- Fail to operationally define performance.
- Fail to relate performance to the process.
- Fail to define the boundaries of the process.
- Misunderstand or misuse measurement and measures.
- Fail to distinguish between control and improving measures.
- Measure the wrong things.
- Misunderstand/misuse information.
- Fear measurement will somehow distort performance priorities.
- Fear measurement may expose poor performance.
- Perceive measurement will reduce their autonomy.

Clearly, the purpose for measuring should be to help monitor the value of initiatives (in our case, innovation) and, by linking the key performance indicators to organisational activity, to drive performance. Unfortunately, this is not always the case, since purposes are quite complex and varied. If the results are to be used for policing reasons they work against the principles of capturing, sharing and learning within the organisation. In essence, we have to answer two basic questions:

1. What is the purpose of measuring?
2. Who are the results for?

In today's competitive environment businesses compete on such things as opportunity recognition, learning speed, innovation, cycle time, quality, flexibility, reliability and responsiveness. Financially orientated systems are obsolete in business environment where competitive success is secured through tapping into the knowledge capital of people, in which success comes from on how managers and workers think about their business and how they invest their time and resources. Such environments demand effective measurement systems. Effective measurement systems are ones that are balanced, integrated and designed to highlight the firm's critical inputs, outputs and process variables.

ILLUSTRATION

Technology-driven performance measurement

Business performance management and programmes for lean and improved product innovation are among a handful of prescriptive measures being applied by manufacturers to achieve competitiveness. In the case of Dallas-based Celanese Corp, an industrial chemical company, this is a global effort.

Brenda Hightower, manufacturing business systems manager for Celanese, sees value in delivering real-time key performance indicators (KPIs) to managers. Celanese (an industrial chemical company with about 9500 employees) had 2003 revenues of $4.6 billion.

'The translation of operational parameters into financial parameters makes work more meaningful', says Hightower. 'But we only deliver actionable information – in other words, those few KPIs whose results a given individual can influence through good decision-making. Our portal solution, Lighthammer's Illuminator, was rolled out to more than 20 sites worldwide – including nine sites in 2004, and the others in 2005 and 2006.'

Sudipta Bhattacharya, VP of manufacturing applications for enterprise vendor SAP, said, 'People need to understand that what we're talking about is access to events on the plant floor as they unfold, not control of the plant floor.' Bhattacharya spearheaded SAP's efforts aimed at increasing relevancy on plant floors, including its support of the S95 integration standard, which defined interfaces between applications at the industrial control level, and applications at the manufacturing execution system level.

Celanese is an SAP user, and SAP has a partnership with Lighthammer, so the integration accomplished was already 'internal' to Illuminator, says Russ Fadel, CEO, Lighthammer. He said Celanese's approach to the project includes going horizontal across sites, and then 'burrowing down' as the company becomes proficient at identifying applications that can be launched on the Illuminator platform – another dynamic being seen repeatedly in manufacturing environments, regardless of the platform.

At most of the Celanese sites, the project also included integration with OSIsoft's plant data historian, which was core to the vendor's RtPM (real-time performance management) platform. Hightower said Celanese developed templates for similar plants, and was replicating an identical process at each plant as the roll-out proceeds. This horizontal approach brought a quick accumulation of benefits, as well as eventual comparisons of similar plants' performance.

(*Source*: Based on Anon, 2005)

Integrated performance measurement frameworks and methodologies

At the heart of a performance measurement system is the integrated performance framework (IPF). This framework captures the blend of metrics that are to be used in the system. Another important aspect of the performance measurement system is the process by which the metrics of components of the performance measurement system are defined and implemented, i.e. a measurement system methodology. In this section, we illustrate through select examples the range of corporate practice in integrated measurement frameworks (SMART, Balanced Scorecard) and measurement system methodologies (QPMM, SMS).

Balanced business scorecard

Following a year-long research project, examining 12 leading-edge companies, Robert Kaplan and David Norton concluded that a balance between financial and non-financial measures is important to modern business (Kaplan and Norton, 1992). They developed from this research one of the most widely known and popular integrated performance

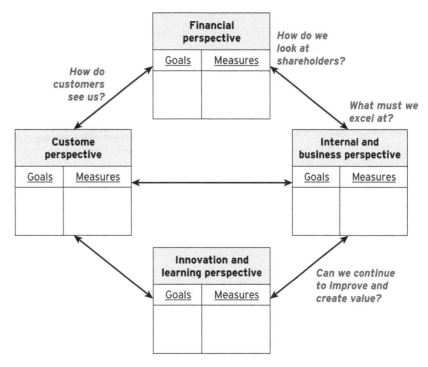

FIGURE 7.4 Balanced scorecard

measurement frameworks, called the Balanced Scorecard (see Figure 7.4). The balanced scorecard does not discard financial measures but integrates financial measures with complementary operational indicators along three additional dimensions of performance: customer satisfaction, internal processes, and innovation and improvement activities. The financial perspective metrics allow the company to answer how well it is performing with regard to shareholder returns. The internal perspective focusses on and tracks what the company must do well. Measures from the customer perspective inform the company how well it is performing for its customers, and the internal measures should show how well the company is faring in terms of innovation and improvement.

The four perspectives capture different dimensions of performance and thus allow a broader and more rounded understanding of performance than narrow financial measures. The historical practice of only looking at financial indicators failed to provide a balanced and clear view of the health and progress of the company. The additional three perspectives maximise the effectiveness and usefulness of measurement. The effectiveness of the balanced scorecard is highly dependent on the metrics populating the four 'balances'. Thus, the definition and selection of 'indicators' is a critical aspect in the development of an effective scorecard.

This balanced approach to performance measurement, when developed and cascaded into the organisation systematically, can provide greater strategic alignment and appropriate measures to drive actions. For instance, Apple executives (one of the 12 companies in the original study) viewed the scorecard approach as essential in expanding discussions beyond gross margin, return on equity and market share. To work, the balanced card should not be over-populated with a large number of measures. The number of metrics must be limited to those that clearly and concisely specify improvement and progress along critical activities.

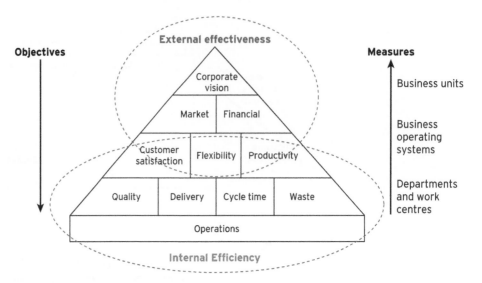

FIGURE 7.5 The SMART performance pyramid system
Source: Adapted from Lynch and Cross, 1991

The four perspectives should provide information that drives integrated action from all quarters of the organisation.

Strategic measurement and reporting technique (SMART)

The SMART approach to measurement was developed by Wang Laboratories in 1989 (Dixon et al., 1990). The SMART system incorporates financial and non-financial metrics to develop a system of measurement for engendering customer satisfaction. SMART seeks to translate strategic aims by linking high-level strategic metrics with lower level operational process metrics.

The SMART system (see Figure 7.5) starts at the apex of the pyramid by first defining, and then using the corporate vision to identify the markets in which the company will compete. The vision is then broken down into marketplace and financial goals, which in turn are translated into business goals for success in terms of customer satisfaction, flexibility and productivity. The business operation objectives are then further deciphered into specific process level goals in terms of quality, delivery, process time and waste. For each goal, objective or criterion at least one measure is used. Wang Laboratories reduced by over 40 per cent the number of metrics that they had been using through the implementation of the SMART system.

Quantum performance measurement model

The QPMM (see Figure 7.6) highlights a cascade system that illustrates how to break down corporate goals into lower level goals associated with process functioning, which is ultimately responsible for delivering superior performance. The key processes are monitored for performance by tracking process outputs, process inputs, and process activities. By doing so, the system can act as a method for integrated planning and control system (Bemowski, 1996). The metrics within the QPMM are classified either as process (the activity) or output (the output from the activity), and are divided to measure three key parameters: quality, cost and service (Hronec, 1993).

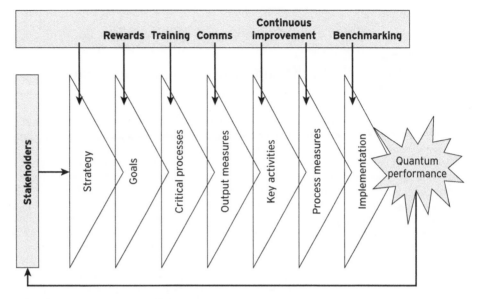

FIGURE 7.6 Quantum performance measurement model
Source: Adapted from Hronec, 1993

Strategic measurement systems (SMS)

Another methodology for developing an integrated measurement system is captured by the SMS framework. SMS, though it is now more widely applied, was originally developed to provide managers with data that they needed to support investment proposals or where R&D backing was required based on non-financial measures (Vitale and Mavrinac, 1994). SMS was developed to assist management in defining and gaining clarity on their strategies and priorities.

The steps in development of a SMS are:

1. *Specify the goal*: What do we wish to achieve?
2. *Match the measure to the strategy*: What are critical success factors that we need to focus on to reach our goals?
3. *Specify the measures*: What measure will be the most useful, how will it provide us feedback to take improvement actions, and who is the measure for (i.e. who is the target audience – customers, employees, managers, investment analysts and industry experts)?
4. *Predict the results*: What will change and what are the implications of the metric and change? All aspects of the measure, both positive and negative, need to be considered.
5. *Build commitment and inspire action*: Who is committed to the measurement process, why are some individuals/parties not on board and what needs to be done to get their commitment?
6. *Plan the next step*: Once the metrics and system is in place how to improve it, make it better, adapt it for future circumstances and strategies? These actions may take any number of forms, such as setting targets, developing a formal incentive scheme or communication system.

Thus far, we have reviewed pertinent theoretical aspects and frameworks of measurement. In the discussion that follows, we highlight more specifically innovation measurement and metrics used by companies.

CASE STUDY

Driving the company through measurement

When going on a car journey you need to know how far you have travelled and how much fuel you have; but you also need to know whether your road will take you towards your destination. Performance measurement in most businesses is good at showing how things are going now but poor at showing how they will be in future. The reason is that two sorts of performance must be measured.

One type, organisational performance, shows how the organisation is doing today and is analogous to speed, fuel consumption and the state of the car.

Strategic performance measurement, however, is about how well the organisation will perform (whether you are on the right road). It is like knowing you need a new map before discovering you are lost.

Research involving 27 UK-based companies such as BP, CGNU, Kingfisher and Vodafone, shows that many struggle to choose the right measures and targets and the right performance measurement and management systems (PMMSs). The study also shows failings in how organisations make use of what is measured. In the US study, 80 per cent of respondents believed PMMSs should help achieve results but did not, and 65 per cent rated their PMMSs as poor or merely 'adequate' for helping strategy deployment.

There is no shortage of PMMS techniques. Half of our interviewees claimed to use at least 10 different approaches. There is no 'silver bullet' but some better practices are emerging.

The Balanced Scorecard is an increasingly popular approach that goes beyond pure financial measurement to include such elements as customers, human resources and innovation. About half of our sample claimed to use it. Some forecasters believe more than 70 per cent of US-based companies will be using it within two years.

Key performance indicators (KPIs) are also widely used. These are measures chosen to reflect performance in high-impact areas, especially in operations such as error rates.

Balanced Scorecard gurus tend to be dismissive of KPIs, pointing out that using too many measures without any organising principle leads to 'measurement paralysis' – although this criticism can equally be applied to the way many use the Balanced Scorecard. Whatever the theory about balanced scorecards and KPIs, research shows that the practice often falls short of expectations. Also, most approaches fail to measure strategic performance.

Another gap is the measurement of 'strategy deployment', i.e. how effectively you are progressing towards your strategic objectives. Organisational performance is no substitute because it measures this only after the fact. For example, sales growth is a good organisational measure of the success of a strategy to launch a new product or service. But it is not forward-looking. It could not predict failure to meet the target launch date, say.

The remedies are not complex but they require sustained management effort. Aim to connect the way strategy is formulated with the way goals are set and communicated, with the choice and use of PMMS tools, with performance review and reward mechanisms. Emphasise getting things done. Lou Gerstner, when appointed chief executive of IBM, said: 'This organisation had plenty of great strategies – it didn't successfully implement any of them.'

A good strategy is insufficient – you need to manage its deployment and for that you need effective strategic performance measurement. Success comes not only from having a map but also making sure you follow the right roads.

QUESTIONS

1. What are the problems with traditional measurement metrics?
2. Why do companies struggle with performance measurement?
3. How should a business performance measurement system, such as the balanced card, be implemented?

(*Source*: Based on N. Britten, 'Bigger picture of performance', *FT*, 7 August 2001, p. 16)

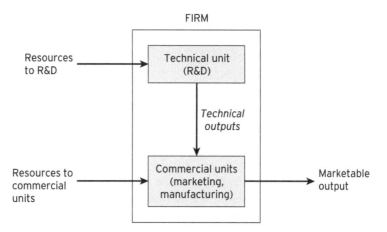

FIGURE 7.7 The innovation development process
Source: Cordero, 1990

Performance measurement and innovation

A fundamental element of sustaining competitive advantage is the ability to repeatedly and successfully commercialise new products. To do so requires that innovation processes are managed and controlled and the key in this challenge is to measure processes that govern an organisation's innovation performance (Cordero, 1990). However, measuring and defining metrics to drive innovation is complex. One of the major sources of complexity is the multi-dimensionality of innovation. This is further compounded by the fact that studies of innovation measurement are fragmented. Many organisations focus on measurement of innovation inputs and outputs and ignore the processes in between.

A systems picture outlining the relationships between inputs, outputs and the innovation development process is offered by Cordero (1990), who characterises technical output as a function of leveraging R&D resources (see Figure 7.7). However, business success depends not only on the output of R&D development outputs, but also on the efficiency and effectiveness of commercially focussed resources that convert the technical outputs into marketable products. Cordero refers to this variable as the 'quality of resource deployment', a term that basically fits his concept of productivity.

Developing further this type of systems logic, Loch et al. (1996) propose a model that reflects a process–output–success chain, in which the development performance concept is divided into two. The first is process performance, which captures performance in the operational management of processes involved in executing the projects. The second is development output performance. It captures the output of the development processes to create marketable outcomes (using Cordero's terms).

Development process performance is an important driver of output, however it is not directly so of business performance (Loch et al., 1996). For instance, development processes determine the cost, speed and quality of product development. However, new product success is not solely defined by these factors. Additional factors such as excellence in marketing and commercialisation strategies also play a key role in determining market share and business profits. Thus, a company may possess processes that are capable of excellent delivery in terms of new products to the marketplace, but if the market fails to perceive value, irrespective of whether they actually do possess value or not, profit performance is unlikely to

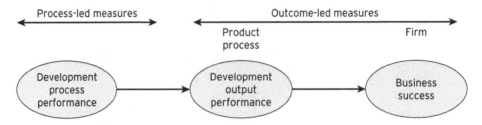

FIGURE 7.8 The input–output–success view of the development process

materialise. Accordingly, what is necessary is to monitor, align and drive innovation performance across the three levels (see Figure 7.8).

Bearing in mind the above, and turning our attention to measurement, it is often the case that the measures are defined at the micro-level (e.g. metrics for an individual project) or at the macro-level in terms of broad financial outcomes. This creates a gap between discrete/unique projects and firm performance at the industry level. This gap can be closed in delineating metrics at three performance measurement levels (Loch et al., 1996). These are:

1. *Development process performance*: Measure of the quality of the development function's efficiency and effectiveness in deploying and using competencies that drive the performance

2. *Development output performance*: Measure of the development function's contribution to the firm's business objectives

3. *Firm's business performance*: Measure of a firm's success in the market.

ILLUSTRATION

The tricky business of assessing innovation by measurement

The good news is that innovation can be measured; the bad news is that it can become a complex exercise fraught with difficulties and many differences between organisations.

A report by the National Academy of Sciences (Brown et al., 2004) notes that innovation measures must cover five activities:

1. The introduction to the market of new products;

2. The development of new processes to produce or deliver products to the market;

3. The funding of new sources of supply of raw materials;

4. The development of new markets; and

5. Changes in the organisation of firms.

However, measuring the number, value and actual economic success of newly introduced products by an organisation is a somewhat subjective measurement of the organisation's innovation capabilities. The degree of novelty within this environment can vary from product to product and from organisation to organisation. Measurements in this framework are best performed within the organisation's own framework – making a comparison to another organisation's new products is often not comparable and, at best, subject to debate.

Quality of patents

Measuring the number of patents obtained by an organisation is more of a quantitative measure of its innovation capabilities than a purely product-based evaluation. However, outside of the absolute number of patents obtained, the actual quality and innovative value of an organisation's patent portfolio can also be somewhat subjective.

For each of the 12 years up to 2005, IBM had been granted more US patents than any other company. It has an active portfolio of more than 25,000 patents in the US and 40,000 patents worldwide. Does that make it the most innovative organisation in the high-tech community? Not necessarily. It can be considered an innovative organisation, but what sets IBM apart from others is in having an infrastructure that is conducive to creating patents out of its intellectual property.

IBM has led the US for a long time in the ability to create patents and to earn large sums of money by licensing them. But even that policy may be changing slightly. Recently, IBM made more than 500 of its information technology software and hardware patents available to anyone developing open-source software in an effort to foster continued innovation.

According to research by Jean Lanjouw and Mark Schankerman published by the UK's Royal Economic Society and by the US's National Bureau of Economic Research (NBER), 'R&D productivity is not strongly related to the quality of patents held by an organisation. But there is a strong association between the stock market valuation of an organisation and the average value of the patents they hold.' This is particularly relevant in the pharmaceutical and instrumentation industries and likely in the IBM situation as well.

Other measurements

The number of publications produced by an organisation's technology staff, the licences they obtain, and technology awards they receive are among other measurements that can be used.

Traditional bibliometrics utilises quantitative analyses and statistics to describe patterns of publications within a given field. This highly technical endeavour can provide very quantitative measures of the innovation capabilities of an organisation by the number of citations and citation-coupling obtained within the organisation's published works.

A new growth in the area of bibliometrics has been in the area of webmetrics, or cybermetrics. Similar bibliometric statistical techniques can be used in webmetrics to scientifically map areas of the Web that are referenced to an organisation's IP, based on the number of times they are hyperlinked to other websites.

Licensing is another highly quantitative technique that can be used to gauge the value of an organisation's innovation capabilities. Often intrinsically linked to an organisation's patent portfolio, licensing continues to provide a substantial revenue stream for many technology-based organisations.

(*Source*: Based on Studt, 2005)

Development process performance

Classic studies on development performance have generally focussed on the project aspects of innovation. These studies identified a number of key project success drivers. For instance, the important and statistically significant drivers for innovation success are understanding user needs and internal and external communications (Marquis, 1969); attention to marketing 'efficiency of development' and authority of R&D managers (Rothwell et al., 1974); and product superiority, project definition and synergies with marketing (Cooper and Kleinschmidt, 1987). In a similar vein, Zirger and Maidique (1990) derived a framework of key R&D capabilities for project success. They identify three key functions for effective

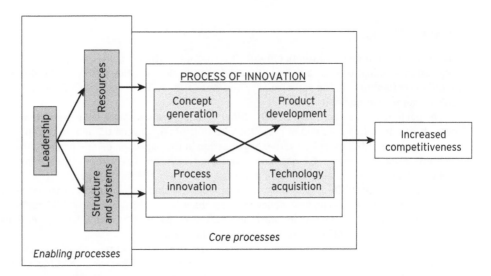

FIGURE 7.9 Core and enabling processes
Source: Chiesa et al., 1996

product commercialisation: marketing, R&D/engineering, and manufacturing. Associated with these, they note three key success factors:

1. Functional competence of the three functions.

2. Strong communication with the customer.

3. Strong management execution (or the ability to hold together the three functions, and steer them in a coherent direction).

These initial studies led to scrutiny of other key processes involved in innovation. The problem with innovation processes is that they are complex, in that they cut across functional, hierarchical and organisational boundaries. To identify the core and enabling processes of innovation requires examining human and capital resources involved in: (1) creating new knowledge; (2) generating ideas aimed at new and enhanced products, manufacturing processes and services; (3) developing those ideas into working prototypes; and (4) transferring them into manufacturing distribution and use. On the basis of such criteria, and adapting Chiesa et al. (1996), the following core processes and enabling processes for innovation can be discerned (see Figure 7.9).

Core innovation processes:
- Identification of new product concepts – concept generation.
- Taking the innovation from concept, through development and transfer to manufacturing and use – product development.
- The development of innovations in manufacturing processes – process innovation.
- The development and management of technology per se – technological acquisition.

Enabling processes:
- The deployment of human and financial resources – resources.
- The effective use of appropriate structures and systems – structure and systems.
- Providing the top management leadership and direction – leadership.

Each of these processes needs to be tracked through the implementation of appropriate metrics. Chisea et al. (1996) propose an audit tool for this purpose, such that its use increases the capability of the firm to meet strategic and tactical business objectives. By tracking, through the use of such an audit tool, it becomes possible to check for improvements in performance of processes that are key to yielding innovation outcomes. The metrics for each of these core processes are summarised in Table 7.1.

TABLE 7.1 Some of the metrics to support these enabling and core processes are summarised in Table 7.1.

Broad focus	Broad capability	Definition	Example of some useful metrics
Enabling processes	Leadership	Performance and conformance metrics that indicate that the innovation process is operating effectively.	• Gating process effectiveness & consistency (e.g. checklist compliance) • Adherence to predefined investment profiles for the company's portfolio mix
	Structure & systems	Effectiveness of the organisational structure and supporting infrastructure to meet business needs.	• Floor space utilisation • ROIC for IT projects • Organisational span-of-control metrics • Functional performance metrics
	Resources	The extent that available resources meet the demands of the product development programs.	• Resource availability vs plan • Funding actuals vs plan (including Earned value/estimate at complete performance)
Core processes	Concept definition	Efficiency of the innovation process that generates the ideas for commercial success.	• Number of invention disclosures • Number of new products released in the last 5 years • % sales from products released in the last 3 years
	Product development	The efficiencies associated with taking a concept to market.	• Product development cycle time • Product cost vs plan • Programme schedule vs plan
	Technology acquistion	Extent to which technology is bought vs developed in house.	• Product margins • Design to cost (DTC) measures (e.g. variance of cost to 'Price To Win') • Technology profile/mix vs company core competencies
	Process innovation	Effectiveness associated with continuous improvement within the business	• 6-Sigma financial benefits • Number of improvement projects completed • Number of employees formally trained/certified in 6-Sigma
	Production efficiency	Extent that products are manufactured/assembled as effectively as possible.	• Indirect vs Direct Labour costs per unit • Unit cost trends • Labour utilisation • Cost of quality • Production yields

TABLE 7.1 *Continued*

Broad focus	Broad capability	Definition	Example of some useful metrics
Performance indicators	Customer acceptance	Success enjoyed by customers recognising the value of a company's products and/or services	<ul><li>Customer retention rates</li><li>Customer satisfaction scores</li><li>Market share</li></ul>
	Financial performance	Resultant financial success derived from effective investment, and execution, in product/service development	<ul><li>Break even time (BET)</li><li>Plan vs actual (profit, revenue, cash)</li><li>Adherence to functional budgets</li><li>Return on investment capital (ROIC)</li></ul>
	Organisational compliance & maturity	Adherence to legal, regulatory and industry recognised certifications required to compete in a given industry or market.	<ul><li>Attainment/retention of quality standards (e.g. ISO9001, ISO14000)</li><li>Compliance to internal auditing requirements (legal, safety, etc.)</li><li>Maturity of industry standard models (e.g. CMMI)</li></ul>

Development output performance

The measures associated with the development process let you determine how (whether) each process affects outcomes. The outcome measures, on the other hand, tell the story of what happened, not only to development time but also in terms of product market success as well (Griffin and Page, 1993). The development processes' outputs can be mapped along the three dimensions of product performance, the product's market performance and the process output performance. The product performance dimension assesses whether the product matches expected standards of functional performance desired by the development team. The market performance dimension assesses how well the product performs relative to marketplace competitors, and the process performance dimension assesses how well the innovation process in its totality has performed. Metrics to capture progress along these dimensions are summarised in Table 7.2.

When using measurement, one must take care to note that not all firms pursue innovation for the same reason. The different goals of firms are typically captured by the different strategies that they follow. Different strategies produce different types of success, and this is also reflected in the way internal processes are managed. Thus, measurement metrics must not be unilaterally implemented but must take into account strategy-led differences.

One of the most widely used business strategy typologies, relevant for innovation, was developed by Miles and Snow (1978). The Miles and Snow typology divides firms into four categories, on the basis of the speed with which an organisation responds to changing environmental conditions by changing its products and markets. The four strategies are:

- *Prospectors*: These are firms that value being 'first' with new products, markets and technologies, even if not all efforts prove to be profitable. These firms move rapidly to seize opportunities.
- *Analysers*: These are firms that are seldom first to market with new products. However, by carefully monitoring the actions of major competitors, they capture significant shares through a strategy of fast following or imitation. They capture market share by delivering a lower cost or improved product than that offered by the pioneering firm(s).

TABLE 7.2 Development outcome performance metrics

Area	Description	Example metrics
Product output performance	The measurements should capture the product's functional, quality and technical performance.	• Technical product performance • Proportion of significant changes in product introduction • Product performance level • Quality guidelines met • Technical success • Unit cost reduction
Product's market performance	The measurement metrics should be indicative of the product's ability to create competitive advantages through customer satisfaction.	• Customer acceptance • Customer satisfaction • Margin goals met • Break-even time • Profitability goals met • Market share goals met
Process output performance	This measurement should assess the overall outcomes from the innovation process.	• Development cost • Proportion of products that arrive first to market • % sales from products in last 12 months • % sales from products introduced in last 3 years • New major products launched compared to industry

- *Defenders*: These firms attempt to position themselves in secure niches within relatively stable product or service areas. They protect their domain by offering higher quality, superior service or lower prices. Defenders tend to ignore industry changes that have no direct influence on current operations.

- *Reactors*: These firms are highly complacent to change and fail to aggressively maintain their established products and markets. They respond only when forced to do so by strong environmental pressures. These companies tend to be very passive.

Research in the strategy field (e.g. Slater and Narver, 1993) has found evidence linking these four strategy types to product development differences. The key differences are:

- Prospectors and analysers place greater emphasis on growth through new product development than defenders and reactors.

- Prospectors tend to be pioneers, whilst analysers tend towards imitation of new products. Analysers focus attention on business processes that allow them to rapidly add product lines to their existing portfolios.

- Defenders are likely to emphasise product line extension strategies rather than 'new' product market development.

- Reactors are likely to be very inconsistent in their approach to innovation and product development.

On the basis of these differences, Griffin and Page (1996) recommend that different metrics should be used for different strategies. The most useful overall success measures for different business strategy are captured in Table 7.3.

Strategic differences are also mirrored by differences in the aims of the portfolio of development projects. Product development projects are undertaken for a myriad of different reasons. For example, some projects are undertaken to retain customers, others to arrest margin erosion, grow market share, drive revenue growth, etc. These different project

TABLE 7.3 Measures across different strategies

Measure	Prospector	Analyser	Defender	Reactor
% Profits from products < 'n' years old	X	X		
% Sales from products < 'n' years old	X			
Degree today's products lead to future opportunities	X			
Degree products fit business strategy		X	X	X
Development programme ROI		X	X	X
Success/failure rate		X		X
Subjective overall programme success				X

Source: Griffin and Page, 1996

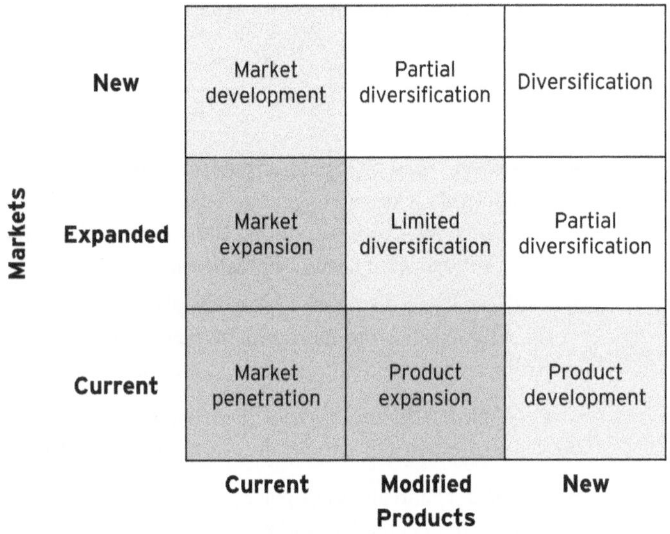

FIGURE 7.10 Ansoff nine-box version: product–market matrix of project development options

motivations can be captured by the Booz, Allen and Hamilton (1982) framework, which is an extension of Ansoff's original product/market matrix. This framework arrays projects based on newness to the market and newness to the company, and groups projects into six distinct categories (see Figure 7.10). The framework links business strategy, product strategy and technological newness (Ansoff, 1957).

- *New-to-the-world* products are those which create an entirely new market.
- *New-to-the-company* products allow the company, for the first time, to enter an established market.
- *Additions to existing lines* are new products that supplement a company's established product lines.
- *Improvements in/revisions to existing products* provide improved performance or greater perceived value and replace existing products.

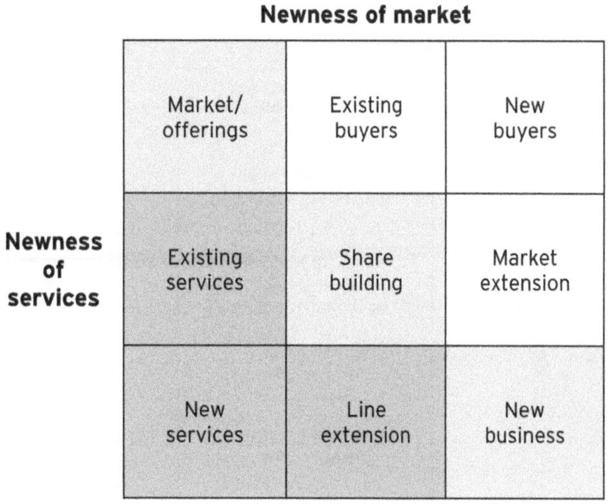

Newness of market

Market/ offerings	Existing buyers	New buyers
Existing services	Share building	Market extension
New services	Line extension	New business

Newness of services (row label on left)

FIGURE 7.11 New service strategy matrix
Source: Scheuing and Johnson, 1989

- *Repositionings* are existing products that are repositioned to new markets or market segments.
- *Cost reductions* are new products that provide similar performance at lower cost.

A comparable view has been proposed by Scheuing and Johnson (1989) to link business strategy to service newness and target markets (see Figure 7.11).

- 'Share building' aims to sell more existing services to current buyers, and often involves an aggressive implementation style, e.g. heavy discounting.
- 'Market extension' offers existing services to market segments not previously served by the firm.
- Under a 'line extension' strategy, a service firm will attempt to market new services to existing buyers. This is common in mature service industries which leverage their current customer base.
- 'New business strategy' is the riskiest alternative where a firm cannot capitalise on any existing strength.

To be useful, measurements must be in line with the differences in objective of each development project. This means implementing yardsticks that are appropriate to the aims being sought. Griffin and Page (1996) highlight useful success measures by project strategy (summarised in Figure 7.12), and note that:

- The 'Degree to which the project met profit goals' is the most useful measure of financial success for most project strategies.
- The 'Degree to which the project provides a competitive advantage' is generally the most useful indicator of project performance-based success – with the only exception being for 'Cost reductions' where the focus is upon retaining previous performance levels rather than providing a competitive advantage.
- Customer-based measures tend to vary depending on the specific product strategy.

Newness to market

	Low		High
High	**New to the company** Market share Revenue or satisfaction **Met profit goal** Competitive advantage		**New to the world** Customer acceptance Customer satisfaction **Met profit goal or IRR/ROI** Competitive advantage
	Product improvements Customer satisfaction Market share or revenue growth **Met profit goal** Competitive advantage	**Additions to existing lines** Market share Rev./Rev. growth/Satis./ Accept. **Met profit goal** Competitive advantage	
Low	**Cost reductions** Customer satisfaction Acceptance or revenue **Met margin goal** Performance or quality	**Product repositionings** Customer acceptance Satisfaction or share **Met profit goal** Competitive advantage	

(Left axis label: **Newness to firm**)

Legend: Customer measure #1 and #2
Financial measure
Performance measure

FIGURE 7.12 Metrics across different project development options
Source: Griffin and Page, 1993

CASE STUDY

Not always a number: goals and aspiration as metrics

Powerful ideas bring people together, often without managerial intervention, to solve apparently unsolvable problems in unexpected ways. Sending a man to the moon by the end of the 1960s, the Manhattan Project, and the race to create the silicon chip were all compelling causes that inspired and helped organise research in both government and the private sector that did not have a formal structure of gate-keeping and carefully calibrated resource allocation. What characterised them – and what's most useful for large corporate organisations – was the use of an ambitious goal to motivate and drive research. In each case, the people involved in the project saw it as a 'must-complete' task. The search for a solution was the prime motivation, and it played to the natural curiosity and persistence that distinguishes many scientists and engineers.

Some of the most successful corporate innovators have used precisely this type of cause to create a highly productive R&D organisation. Intel engineers, for example, are constantly motivated by the shadow of Moore's Law to create faster, higher capacity silicon wafers. Danaher Corporation's focus on the 'breakthrough goal' of creating low-cost infra-red detectors for a new, 'invisible' market in predictive and preventive maintenance netted the company the 2003 NASA Product of the Year award and a spike in sales to new customers. And Sun Microsystems was similarly inspired by an ambitious belief – that the future of computing was to be found on the internet, not just the hard drive of a PC – to create the now ubiquitous Java language.

In the 1980s and early 1990s, when Al Giacco was the CEO of Himont, then the world's largest producer of polypropylene, he instilled a sense of a great cause to transform this fast-growing but historically low-margin business into a high-tech producer of high-value engineered materials. Giacco quantified the cause and made it tangible by setting an 'impossible' goal for his organisation: each year, commercialise two wholly new applications of polypropylene in which Himont would have a significant, proprietary lead-time advantage. Giacco and his senior team did not prescribe what those new applications should be; instead, they simply provided the funding and autonomy to researchers who understood they had to create meaningful results, year after year.

Not all causes need to be articulated by corporate leadership, nor do they need to be on the scale of the Apollo mission. Often, innovation is driven from the bottom up, by engineers or scientists dedicated to the cause of discovering a breakthrough medicine, perhaps, or simply a more convenient product for consumers-like 3M's Post-It Notes. In each case, the sense of an important goal that has significance beyond the company's bottom line helps drive the research agenda and signals to researchers that their capacity for innovative thinking is valued.

QUESTION

What does this illustration tell you about narrow, numbers-based metric for innovation?

(*Source*: Based on Canner and Mass, 2005)

Firm business performance

Ultimately, for innovation performance to be beneficial to the firm it has to lead to improvements in firm competitiveness and the bottom line. Innovation outcomes such as new launches and brand position have to translate into durable business returns if the firm is to continue investing in its innovation strategy. As we discussed earlier, how an individual innovation (new or enhanced product or process) contributes to enhancing the firm's bottom line is not a simple process but depends on a multitude of factors (product, market and process factors) coming together as a bundle to create potential for competitive advantage.

Whatever the source of competitive advantage, from a measurement perspective the bottom-line impact of an innovation on the business is measured by traditional accounting measures such as sales and profits generated from that innovation and by the market share gained. Given the standard nature of accounting measures these metrics can be compared against direct competitors in the sector and indirectly across industries. A firm's performance can also be adjudged against its predicted or expected results. These business/firm-level measures are primarily financial, and present an aggregated picture of the performance of the organisation. Their use to direct innovation has to be carefully guarded because they can lead to focus upon short-term gains rather than accounting for the long run whilst managing in the short term. A basic set of financial indicators are highlighted in Table 7.4 for illustration.

From the discussion we can observe that in order to measure the impact that innovation can have on business competitiveness, the measurement activity has to travel through the spine of the entire innovation process by focussing not only on outputs of the products/services per se but also on the performance of the whole process of innovation itself. Three categories of measurement have been proposed, which are broad enough to capture the full complement of measures to fuel innovation. These are: process-level measures, product-market-level measures and business/firm-level measures.

TABLE 7.4 Basic financial measures

Area	Description	Example metrics
Profitability ratios	Measure returns generated on sales or investment, often in comparison with industry.	Profit margin on sales Return on capital employed (ROCE) Return on investment (ROI) Return on assets (ROA)
Activity ratios	Measure the use of resources and are best used in comparison with industry standards.	Fixed asset turnover Total asset turnover Average collection period Inventory turnover

All of these three types of measures are interlinked in the sense that changes in one almost invariably affect the others. Process-based measures are online measures because they allow taking immediate actions to deal with problems. They help to direct attention to activities that are happening in real time, and therefore drive actions that need to be taken so as to optimise aspects of critical concern within the innovation process, such that bottlenecks do not occur. Outcome measures (product-based measures, and especially financial measures) are very often *retrospective* in nature. They can only be compiled once the information is made available, i.e. once the project has been completed and the product is performing in the marketplace.

Being overly concerned with outcome-based measures, too early in the innovation process, often serves to distract development teams from doing the right things (i.e. progressing the project forward). Imposing these types of measures early on in development encourages

ILLUSTRATION

Understand your business beyond the aggregate metric

When Charles Miller Smith, a former Unilever veteran of 31 years, was appointed as Chief Executive of ICI in 1995, he was faced with the challenge of radically transforming the company.

After battling through the recession and the Seneca de-merger, ICI found itself facing tough targets for a group-wide average return on net assets (RONA) over the business cycle of 20 per cent.

'Those were clear targets and people were anxious to deliver', says Miller Smith. '1995 was good for the business; it made genuine progress and RONA sharply increased. Clearly, as that happened, people became more confident and there was a growing sense of comfort and confidence about the future. You could feel that leeching into the bloodstream of the business.' But that, so far as Miller Smith is concerned, only brought the new ICI to first base. Take RONA: 'The 20 per cent RONA target was straightforward, clear-cut, simple, well understood across the business, sometimes too well understood, because everybody assumes that 20 per cent is the reality for everyone, when you have to differentiate.' Paints, for instance, should make 30 per cent. Overall, he says: 'We are still short of the best in the industry, which is about 6 per cent above where we were last year.' ICI's RONA average in 1995 was 18 per cent.

By the best, Miller Smith meant America's Du Pont.

(*Source*: Based on Lorenz, 1996)

a mentality of 'let's work on less risky options/projects', 'let's play safe'. This results in development teams focussing on minor projects and a failure of the firm to make any significant leaps or real impact in the marketplace. Measures, therefore, must be carefully balanced and constructed to allow:

- Continuous flow of projects.
- Facilitate speed in the development process.
- Lower costs of development through process improvements.
- Optimise the capability of the process, by structuring its functioning to be in line with adopted strategies.
- Create a balance between large and small projects to reflect a healthy portfolio that incorporates short-, medium- and long-term business needs.

All this also needs to support the longer term goals of improving profit, growth, customer satisfaction, market share, retaining a competitive supremacy in the business categories concerned.

Making the measurement system work is always a difficult task. In tackling this challenge it is important to pay attention to key factors that facilitate or hinder its implementation. Benchmarking experience (Zairi, 1994) suggests that success in implementing an effective measurement system lies in:

1. Having top management play a strategic role in directing and allocating adequate resources to facilitate the measurement system.
2. Making measurement activity an integral part of the innovation strategy.
3. Getting top management commitment to create a positive climate for innovation and an atmosphere of trust to allow measurement to positively drive actions of individuals.
4. Creating effective communication processes from the corporate level downwards, with clear objectives and a thorough understanding of the organisational goals. Communication includes sharing information on results as well as action plans.
5. Formulating clear processes and systems, which are vital to effective management of innovation activity and are important for setting up goals and managing performance at the individual, project and business levels.

Applying maturity assessments to NPD frameworks

In many disciplines, maturity models are being defined to help management understand the extent of their capabilities, and how these capabilities compare with the competition – e.g. CMMI modelling is available to assess development maturity, SCOR models for supply chain maturity, MEM (manufacturing excellence models) for manufacturing, etc. These models all tend to be constructed from a series of 'key practice areas' which need to grow and mature together for an organisation to realise business performance improvements. Moving up a maturity curve is a matter of bringing the whole organisation along at an equal pace and capability, not to have an unbalanced capability which results in bottlenecks and constraints through the company's value stream.

Having a maturity model to work from often provides an initial point from which a company can begin to look for weaknesses and opportunities within its operations, which can then be investigated through more formal 'deep dives' of performance and conformance (lagging and leading) indicators. While no standard maturity model exists for NPD frameworks, a number of organisations have defined their own models and applied them as part of their strategic objectives to improve NPD performance.

This should ideally be applied at a business unit level, with involvement from a statistically significant number of people in key roles within the NPD framework. The assessment can be conducted individually, and average ratings determined, or by consensus amongst a representative group. The important outcome here is that a base line is set from which specific areas can be targeted to improve NPD performance, and also provide a benchmark against which improvements in maturity can be measured and compared.

Conclusion

Performance measures are vital for companies to ensure that they are achieving their goals. Measurement provides an important mechanism to evaluate, control and improve upon existing performance. Measurement creates the basis for comparing performance between different organisations, different processes, different teams and individuals.

Performance measurements have traditionally focussed on financial measures designed for the benefit of the shareholder rather than the line manager. Innovation managers require data and information that assists them in making business decisions. For example, if the innovation process is beginning to become inefficient, the sooner the development manager becomes aware of this the quicker corrective action can be taken. Performance measures are an important means of providing managers with the information they require in order to innovate effectively and efficiently. Financial information is received much too late for line manager and development teams, and so does not assist in identification and rectification of the cause of the problem. Thus, innovation success requires developing and implementing a balance of online process measures and outcome measures. This balance can be created through the adoption of integrated performance measurement frameworks such as the Balanced Scorecard. In addition to using the appropriate balance of metrics, innovation success requires possessing the right approach to measurement. In other words, the task is not just one of the defining appropriate metrics, but critically one of implementing these through a systematic process across the entire spectrum of innovation activity.

QUESTIONS

1. In what sense is measurement an important driver of business performance?

2. Identify the three stages of performance measurement, and state what are the perceived advantages and limitations of each.

3. What is the difference between Process measures and Outcome measures?

4. Briefly describe an example of one integrated performance framework and one measurement systems methodology.

5. Identify the three levels of innovation performance measurement. Provide an example of metrics to capture each of these.

6. What are the characteristics of a good measurement system? What features would make it a useful system.

Making performance measurement work

In a typical organisation, business units act independently of each other and make decisions based on information that is relevant to them. For example, the sales and marketing department might collect data on the effectiveness of the various special promotions that the company employs. It would then repeat promotions that substantially increased sales, and abandon those that had little impact. Meanwhile, the operations director might independently implement an IT solution enabling warehouse managers to reduce stockpiles and respond more efficiently to fluctuations in demand. This approach might work at a departmental level, but how does an organisation obtain a high-level view of the business as a single, organic entity?

Performance management (sometimes also called corporate or business performance management) aims to bring these individual business units together and ensure that they are working towards a single corporate strategy. This means that decisions taken at board level can be used to inform performance measures, which can then be adopted by individual business units. It is a combination of two disciplines: business intelligence, which looks at historical data (such as how many units of a particular product were sold last week) and enterprise planning, which aims to steer the organisation's future. Recently its capabilities have been boosted by technological developments that make it possible to extract and analyse data from different sources and report on them on a daily, rather than a weekly or monthly, basis. Traditionally, senior managers who wanted to see detailed reports about performance would have had to request the information from the IT department; now, they can have a dashboard on their desktop displaying up-to-date reports tailored to their specifications. Central to performance management is performance measurement, and the question of how an organisation can determine, and then measure, the indicators that are key to its success. Many organisations choose to use a formalised methodology, such as the balanced scorecard or Six Sigma, while others prefer to use a system customised to their specific requirements. A recent report from Cranfield School of Management, entitled 'Business Performance Management: Current State of the Art', which surveyed 780 US corporates, found that 46 per cent of those that took part were using formalised performance measurement systems; of those, 75 per cent were using the balanced scorecard technique.

First expounded by Harvard professor Robert Kaplan and consultant David Norton in the early 1990s, the balanced scorecard proposed the measurement of performance from four different perspectives: financial performance; information about customers; internal business processes; and learning and growth. They believed that this combination would enable companies not just to evaluate current performance, but also to understand how well they were likely to perform in the future. As a formalised technique, it has proved enormously popular for businesses needing to make sense of the mass of data gathered from internal and external sources. For example, knowing from the learning and growth perspective that a high rate of employee churn has a negative impact on profitability makes it possible to put in place strategies to retain staff. It would be a mistake, however, to focus too closely on whether the balanced scorecard, say, is better than Six Sigma or any other system. 'It doesn't matter which methodology you pick', says Frank Buytendijk, research vice-president of corporate performance measurement at Gartner. 'What explains success is the fact that the managers have a shared view of looking at the business.'

Bernard Marr, author of the Cranfield report, agrees, arguing that an essential part of a performance management project is to think through corporate strategy and devise appropriate metrics, even if data on those measures will be harder to collect initially. Yet, he says, many organisations fail to do this, making the elementary mistake of measuring what is easy to measure rather than what is useful to measure: 'Companies measure how many hours people spend on training courses each month and other useless metrics.' He suggests that the balanced scorecard, although useful, is limited by considering the perspectives of only two stakeholders – the shareholder and the customer. Instead, he suggests, organisations should consider a technique known as the 'performance prism', which takes in the perspectives of other stakeholders, such as employees, suppliers and pressure groups. 'Another aspect of the prism', explains Mr Marr, 'is to ask what I as a company can get from my key stakeholders. There is a difference between what I want from my customers and what they want from me. You can satisfy all your customers 100 per cent but this might not be the most profitable option.' Equally, says Chris Knighton, chief executive of Aspiren, a consultancy firm, many organisations become bogged down in the detail of the performance management framework. This leads to a 'scattergun approach', in which too much time and money is spent on attempting to create a perfect system. 'Ultimately', he explains, 'they're adopting the same approach in every area of the business without necessarily thinking about which areas are going to contribute most significantly to the delivery of the strategy.' Successful performance management also depends on getting the cultural change right and ensuring that new sets of indicators are accepted throughout the organisation. There is no easy way of doing this, particularly in an organisation where different business units have been using their own spreadsheets or business intelligence systems for years.

A performance measurement framework can only work if the indicators are cascaded down through the organisation. 'If you have a strategic scorecard for how you deliver projects across the organisation, it is fundamental to drive that scorecard down, so that every project manager and every person within every project is absolutely clear about the actions they must undertake to impact the strategic success of the organisation', says Mr Knighton. If necessary, the indicators can be tied to rewards and remuneration, so that there is a clear incentive to adopt the new indicators. In the US, Brigham & Women's Hospital of Boston claims that the success of a balanced scorecard methodology has been dependent on cascading the indicators to employees. The hospital uses technology from SAS, a business analytics vendor, to draw data from 29 sources relating to 50,000 patient encounters a year. The information is analysed and then filtered down to 650 employees in the form of a scorecard containing 30 metrics linked to reports on finance, productivity and workload. The scorecards are used to improve performance and cut costs – doctors, for example, can spot anomalies in patients' length of stay or assess the cost of introducing certain tests. The biggest technical challenge for implementing performance management lies in drawing data from many different sources; a report from Butler Group, published in June 2004, entitled 'Corporate Performance Management: A New Approach to Business Control and Planning', suggests that 'a significant percentage of organisations are infested with inconsistent or erroneous data'. Estimates of how much existing corporate data is inaccurate vary; Gartner puts it as high as 25 per cent in Fortune 1000 companies. Cleaning up data and putting processes in place to eliminate mistakes in initial data entry is, therefore, essential. 'Performance management is a way to steer the organisation, and to control fundamentally strategy and execution. If you're going to do that, you'd better be pretty sure that the data you're relying on to build metrics is 100 per cent accurate', says Ian Charlesworth, a senior research analyst at Butler Group, and co-author of the report.

Having put a performance management framework in place, a surprising number of organisations then fail to act on its findings. This is a phenomenon described by the Cranfield report as 'drowning in data' or 'paralysis without analysis'. To remedy this, believes Mr Charlesworth, it is necessary to decide how particular parameters will be used within the organisation: 'If customer activity drops down to a particular level, then we have to create an alert and have an agreed and documented process in place to decide what action we take. So, you're proactively considering what the reaction to that information should be, rather than waiting for the alarm bells to go off and saying, "Gosh, customer activity has dropped to nearly zero, what on earth are we going to do about it?"' Perhaps the greatest threat to the success of performance management is what the Butler Group report refers to as the 'strategy gap' – the fact that, over time, indicators slip out of phase with corporate strategy. Performance management has to be dynamic: key individuals need to take responsibility for their own portfolio of KPIs, amending them in line with the wider issues.

QUESTIONS

1. Discuss ways that IT can help performance management.
2. What are the difficulties and challenges in developing and implementing a successful performance management system?
3. Taking into consideration your understanding of the balanced scorecard, the Cranfield prism, and other such systems, develop your own version of a performance management system for innovation. Evaluate its relative strengths and weaknesses relative to previous approaches.

(*Source*: K. Thomas, 'The pursuit of performance', *FT*, 6 October 2004, p. 12)

References

Anon (2005), 'Celanese's improvement goals in tune with times', *Manufacturing Business Technology* 23(4): 12.

Ansoff, I. (1957), 'Strategies for diversification', *Harvard Business Review* 35: 113–124.

Bemowski, K. (1996), '1994 Baldrige award recipients share their experience', *Quality Progress* 28(2): 35–40.

Booz, Allen and Hamilton Inc. (1982), *New product development for the 1980s*, New York: Booz, Allen and Hamilton Inc.

Britten, N. (2001), 'Bigger picture of performance', *Financial Times*, 7 August, 16.

Brown, L.D., Plewes, T.J. and Gerstein, M.A. (2004), 'Measuring R&D expenditures in the U.S. economy', Ed. Panel on Research & Development Statistics at the National Science Foundation, National Research Council, 91–101.

Budden, R. and Burt, T. (2003), 'Brand is a big issue', *Financial Times*, 22 December, 17.

Canner, N. and Mass, N.J. (2005), 'Turn R&D upside down', *Research Technology Management* 48(2): 17–22.

Carr, N.G. (2005), 'Suits to the rescue', *Strategy+Business*, Spring, **www.strategy-business.com**.

Chiesa, V., Coughlan, P. and Voss, C.A. (1996), 'Development of a technical innovation audit', *Journal of Product Innovation Management* 13(2): 105–136.

Cooper, R.G. and Kleinschimdt, E.J. (1987), 'New products: What separates winners from losers', *Journal of Product Innovation Management* 4: 169–187.

Cordero, R. (1990), 'The measurement of innovation performance in the firm: An overview', *Research Policy* 19: 185–192.

Dixon, J.R., Nanni, A.J. and Vollmann, T.E. (1990), *The new performance challenge: Measuring operations for world class competition*, Homewood, Illinois: Business One Irwin.

Griffin, A. and Page, A.L. (1993), 'An interim report on measuring product development success and failure', *Journal of Product Innovation Management* 10: 291–308.

Ghalayini, A.M. and Noble, J.S. (1996), 'The changing basis of performance measurement', *International Journal of Operations and Production Management* 16(8): 63–80.

Griffin, A. and Page, A.L. (1996), 'PDMA success measurement project: Recommended measures for product development success and failure', *Journal of Product Innovation Management* 13: 479–496.

Heim, J.A. and Compton, W.D. (eds) (1992), *Manufacturing systems: Foundations of world-class practice*, Washington DC: National Academy of Engineering.

Hronec, S.M. (1993), *Vital signs: Using quality, time and cost performance measurements to chart your company's future*, New York: Amacom.

Kaplan, R.S. and Norton, D.P. (1992), 'The balanced scorecard – Measures that drive perform-ance', *Harvard Business Review*, January–February: 71–79.

Lingle, J.H. and Scheimann, W.A. (1996), 'From balanced scorecard to strategic gauges: Is measurement worth it?', *Management Review*, March: 56–61.

Loch, C., Stein, L. and Terweisch J. (1996), 'Measuring development performance in the elec-tronics industry', *Journal of Product Innovation Management* 13: 3–20.

Lorenz, A. (1996), 'ICI's long march', *Sunday Times*, 12 May, 1.

Lynch, R.L. and Cross, K.F. (1991), *Measure up! Yardsticks for continuous improvements*, Cambridge, MA: Blackwell Publishers.

Marquis, D.G. (1969), 'The anatomy of successful innovations', *Innovation* 11: 28–37.

Miles, R.E. and Snow, C.C. (1978), *Organisational strategy, structure and process*, New York: McGraw-Hill.

Miller, J. (1992), 'Designing and implementing a new cost management system', *Journal of Cost Management*, Winter: 41–53.

Rothwell, R., Freeman, C., Horley, A., Jervis, N.I.P., Robertson, A.B. and Townsend, J. (1974), 'SHAPPO updated – project SHAPPO, phase II', *Research Policy* 3: 258–291.

Sink, D.S. (1991), 'The role of measurement in achieving world class quality and productivity management', *Industrial Engineering*, 23–28 June: 70.

Slater, S.F. and Narver, J.C. (1993), 'Product-market strategy and performance: An analysis of the Miles and Snow typology types', *European Journal of Marketing* 27(1): 33–51.

Scheuing, E.E. and Johnson, E.M. (1989), 'A proposed model for new service development', *The Journal of Services Marketing* 3(2): ABI/INFORM Global.

Studt, T. (2005), 'Measuring innovation . . . Gauging your organisation's success', *R&D* 47(2): 42–45.

Thomas, K. (2004), 'The pursuit of performance', *Financial Times*, 6 October, 12.

Vitale, M. and Mavrinac, S.C. (1994), 'New process/financial scorecard: A strategic performance measurement system', *Planning Review* 22(4): 12–17.

Zairi, M. (1992), *TQM based performance measurement: Practical guidelines*, Letchworth, Hertfordshire: Technical Communications (Publishing) Ltd.

Zairi, M. (1994), *Measuring performance for business results*, London: Chapman & Hall.

Zirger, B.J. and Maidique, M.A. (1990), 'A model of new product development: An empirical test', *Management Science* 36: 867–883.

PART 4

Aligning people – culture and structure

People, leadership and structure for innovation

Learning outcomes

When you have completed this chapter, you should be able to:

- Describe the characteristics that distinguish organisations as being more or less innovative.

- List the different firm types for innovation.

- Illustrate how organisation structure can affect innovation.

- Articulate the importance, advantages and drawbacks of cross-functional integration.

- Discuss general aspects of teams, appreciate the enablers and constraints of effective teaming and the various stages teams will pass through before they become truly effective.

- Show how teams support NPD and how global/virtual teams are being increasingly used by organisations.

- Appreciate other organisational forms that exist outside standard innovation frameworks which play an important support role.

- Describe the key roles that individuals play in innovation and appreciate the two types of leaders commonly found driving innovation – executives and champions.

Introduction

Innovation without people simply is not possible. The types of people involved in innovation and how they are organised can have a significant impact on a company's innovation performance and its ability to meet specific business objectives. In this chapter we initially discuss characteristics of innovative firms before examining the different firm types, such as 'Individual inventors', 'Hierarchical firms' and 'Silicon Valley' firms that can be used for meeting very different business challenges. After the high-level view of how firms might competitively position themselves to meet their innovation goals, we go on to examine how internal structures can be used to drive innovation. This includes a review of groups that might initially work outside the NPD funnel and includes discussion of research laboratories, incubator departments and skunk-works.

Teams are a fundamental element of most NPD frameworks and are used with an expectation that the results of any team will be greater than the sum of the results of each individual within the group. After reviewing some basic aspects of teams, we discuss how teams can be structured to support innovation. This has attracted a significant amount of research, particularly in the interface between R&D-marketing and R&D-manufacturing.

With new challenges being faced in the market, companies are relying less on co-located teams, and more on virtual or global teams. Aspects of these types of teams are developed and discussed. Finally, we discuss individual roles and leadership in innovation by elaborating where and how they fit into a company's product development framework. The role and importance of team leaders in directing teams and making key decisions and product champions in guiding innovation project through hurdles and challenges of innovation are also presented.

What makes a firm creative?

Companies of all types need to innovate to a degree if they are to thrive and survive. The way companies are structured to meet the specific challenges they face in the market can determine how successful they will be. How companies approach certain tasks, activities and process is a general indicator of their attitude towards innovation. A number of simple general characteristics that can be used to distinguish between highly creative and less creative organisations include:

- How a company sets its *goals* and drives their achievement throughout the organisation.
- The extent to which critical *information* is identified, collected, communicated and used.
- The importance placed on *generating* and *evaluating new ideas*.
- The way in which individualism and *involvement* is nurtured as part of the company's human relations ethos and how that drives *motivation* within the company.

Highly innovative companies place great emphasis on creativity and the alignment to long-term goals. These companies allow considerable freedom in how people in the organisation go about attaining clearly defined strategic goals. Less innovative organisations tend to focus on a much shorter time horizon and are generally driven by short-term profits. They tend to be fearful of risk. As a consequence of trying to control risk they exert tight control throughout the business. Tighter control often has a tendency to turn the organisational focus inwards; and people in companies focus on creating efficient operations to meet narrow functional objectives. This focus can lead to departments working in isolation and rarely communicating with each other. Highly creative organisations, by way of contrast, place great store on being responsive to their external environment by being not just efficient but also effective in their responses. To achieve this they rely on a wide variety of sources of information, knowledge and impetuses to drive the organisation. Not surprisingly, highly creative organisations welcome and encourage new ideas and generally challenge their personnel to achieve the impossible. They often have systems to collect new ideas. These ideas are then evaluated in a manner that balances the need for inquisitive exploration and speed. In stark contrast, less creative organisations tend to be more dismissive of new ideas or show greater resistance to them. In these companies greater emphasis is placed on operational matters and so-called 'realism'.

A significant characteristic that distinguishes highly creative organisations from those that are less creative lies in the way they view their employees. Highly creative organisations show a respect for individualism and value diverse opinions. They also value consensus but not at the expense of deadening diversity in their employees' thinking, behaviour or actions. They control their employees but diligently take care that this does not to stifle initiative. Hence, they provide the individual considerable scope to define and execute their job tasks. This helps satisfy the individual's need to have influence over how they go about achieving their task and provides scope for the individual to derive self-satisfaction through achievement and recognition inside the company. Internal recognition and achievement often go hand in glove with external recognition. Indeed, for the most part such companies actively support their employees to get external recognition. For example, by giving freedom to write papers, speak as experts at conference venues, etc. These companies promote the taking of the initiative and reinforce this by selecting and promoting individuals on merit. They are also acutely aware, nonetheless, that not every single initiative can produce a positive outcome, so they strive to create environments in which there is freedom to fail. Less creative organisations tend to have little respect for individualism and attempt to drive (rather than seek) consensus. In this environment, supervisors tend to be responsible for assigning work to meet short-term performance objectives. In such highly directive environments there is little in the way of individual task autonomy, empowerment or individual freedom. Promotions are driven by administrative capability with an emphasis on length of service.

Innovation firm types

Besides the characteristics that make companies more creative, firms differ in how they organise to implement their chosen innovation strategies. Teece (2000) proposed a number of organisational types that are structured to support innovation in different ways. These include Individual inventors, Multi-product integrated hierarchical firms, High-flex 'Silicon Valley' firms, Virtual corporations, Conglomerates and alliances.

Individual inventors

The simplest form of innovative firm is the *Individual inventor* (although not strictly an organisational form) and is characterised by a single person acting as an inventor or entrepreneur. Acting from a base of specialist knowledge, the inventor often experiences significant funding issues that constrain successful commercialisation. This places limits on the 'value' the inventor can capture as a result. In order to establish an organisation that can exploit the innovation more effectively, the inventor may use intellectual property as collateral. Other types of contractual transactions may also be employed to secure funding and allow the innovation to be developed. These include the exchange of patent(s) for equity in a new venture funded firm, or for cash or equity in an established firm. In the case where the inventor has strong grounds to assume the innovation can be extremely successful, or its value faces time constraints, he/she may attempt to license the innovation to incumbent firms who already have the necessary complementary assets in place. In all these cases, there is a fundamental paradox for the inventor in that the intellectual property will not be bought until the nature of the innovation has been shared with the purchaser, at which time they have acquired it without cost.

ILLUSTRATION

Marconi – the wireless pioneer

The young Guglielmo Marconi indulged his passion for science in two attic rooms of the family home in Bologna, Italy. After reading about the work of Heinrich Hertz (who had developed equipment to send and detect electromagnetic waves), Marconi wondered whether these waves could be used to send messages as signals through the air, just as messages could be sent along wires in the telegraph and telephone.

One night in 1895, Marconi completed an experiment where a transmitter was set up at one side of the room to send out radio signals, which were then picked up by a receiver connected to a bell 9m away. Soon, Marconi had developed his prototype to send and receive such signals over a distance of 2km.

Marconi was quick to seize on the commercial applications of wireless telegraphy and obtained his first patent in 1897. He used this to form the Wireless Telegraph and Signal Company Limited, which then became Marconi's Wireless Telegraphy Company Ltd in 1900 – the forerunner of Marconi plc.

Encouraged by the construction of a number of radio stations on the west coast of England and Ireland, Marconi was able to improve his equipment and grow his business. By 1901, he had successfully transmitted a signal from Cornwall, England to Newfoundland, Canada, and the Atlantic Ocean had been bridged by radio for the first time.

In 1909, Marconi was awarded the Nobel Prize for Physics, and in 1931 (on the 30th anniversary of his first transatlantic signal), his own voice circled the globe in a radio broadcast.

(*Source*: Based on Briggs, 2001)

The organisational equivalent to the individual inventor is the *Standalone research laboratory*. Standalone research laboratories face many of the challenges of the individual inventor. The major distinction lies in the laboratory being able to bring more skills together, leverage some economies of scale and perhaps have access to a larger financial resource base.

Multi-powered, integrated, hierarchical firms

This organisation type is characterised by the presence of a highly stratified structure and bureaucratic decision making. Mostly, though not always, these tend to be large firms with a poor aptitude for change. In dynamic environments they find themselves entrenched in competencies and practices that served them well for many years but which now limit their competitiveness. Because of their size they are generally protected from attack from smaller competitors, i.e. they are protected by significant entry barriers. In possession of a large resource base they are often found initiating large projects, especially those in which they can establish standards by incrementally evolving technologies or products pioneered by others.

A number of options are available to such organisations to drive greater innovation and break out of their current apathy. Firstly, new venture divisions can be spawned to address new opportunities. New venture divisions are an attempt to create environments that are free from the ponderous and risk-averse nature of the parent organisation. Alternatively, large integrated firms may enter into symbiotic relationships with other firms that already have entrepreneurial structures in place to promote creativity and innovation.

ILLUSTRATION

IBM in the 1990s

During the 1980s and early 1990s, IBM was thrown into turmoil by back-to-back revolutions. The PC revolution placed computers directly in the hands of millions of people. And then, the client/server revolution sought to link all of those PCs (the clients) with larger computers that laboured in the background (the servers that served data and applications to client machines).

Both revolutions transformed the way customers viewed, used and bought technology. And both fundamentally rocked IBM. Businesses' purchasing decisions were put in the hands of individuals and departments – not the places where IBM had long-standing customer relationships. Piece-part technologies took precedence over integrated solutions. The focus was on the desktop and personal productivity, not on business applications across the enterprise. By 1993, the company's annual net losses reached a record $8 billion. Cost management and streamlining became a chief concern, and IBM considered splitting its divisions into separate business independent businesses.

Louis V. Gerstner Jr. arrived as IBM's chairman and CEO on 1 April 1993. For the first time in the company's history, IBM had found a leader from outside its ranks. Gerstner had been chairman and CEO of RJR Nabisco for four years, and had previously spent 11 years as a top executive at American Express.

Gerstner brought with him a customer-orientated sensibility and expertise in strategic thinking that he had honed through years as a management consultant at McKinsey and Co. Soon after he arrived, he took dramatic action to stabilise the company. These steps included re-building IBM's product line, continuing to shrink the workforce and making significant cost reductions. Despite mounting pressure to split IBM into separate, independent companies, Gerstner decided to keep the company together. He recognised that one of IBM's enduring strengths was its ability to provide integrated solutions for customers – someone to represent more than piece parts or components. Splitting the company would have destroyed a unique IBM advantage.

(*Source*: Based on IBM, 2005. Reprint courtesy of International Business Machines Corporation, © 2010 International Business Machines Corporation)

High-flex 'Silicon Valley' firms

Silicon Valley-type firms are highly innovative and are characterised by shallow hierarchies, which provide significant local autonomy. Change culture within such companies tends to be very strong, allowing innovation to occur at many levels within the company (product and process, and strategic). Any attempt to drive hierarchical restrictions into the company through imposition of seniority and rank or move towards overly functional specialisation is strongly resisted if it is seen to destroy the flow of ideas.

Typically, in their early stages, Silicon Valley companies are led by founders. Decision making is often simple and informal, and is supported by very quick and open communication and co-ordination. This characteristic seems to endure even as these companies grow. During the embryonic stages, these companies have a limited stream of internally generated cash with which to fund new opportunities. This often results in Silicon Valley firms building connections with the venture capital community, the public equity market or other firms with available cash to fund their venture.

Virtual corporations

Virtual corporations are businesses that sub-contract as much of their operations as possible. As a result of this, they tend to have very shallow hierarchies and are smaller than they might otherwise be. With very light organisation structures, virtual corporations can be extremely creative. They operate best by overcoming internal skills deficiencies by establishing strong alliances with competent (often best in class) organisations. As a result of this, they are proficient in early-stage innovation activities and often have the capacity to be first to market.

This organisational form, however, is not considered to be viable in the long term because it finds it difficult to capture value from an innovation over its entire life cycle. Generally, these companies find it difficult to retain control and exclusive rights of the innovation as the industry evolves and big players with large resources enter the market. Quite often it is the case that research from the virtual corporation is acquired and leveraged by a larger company.

ILLUSTRATION

Managing the virtual product development organisation – lessons from Navitrak

Navitrak International Corporation is a Canadian developer of products that provide navigation information for commercial and consumer applications, and has cultivated a distinct approach to managing the virtual organisation. A small and aggressively entrepreneurial company, Navitrak was conceived from the beginning as a virtual organisation, and has created a strong market presence through developing a robust, inter-networked approach with high levels of flexibility.

By leveraging its core skills, taking advantage of a growing pool of displaced technical and business talent, and skilfully optimising available technologies, Navitrak was able to generate a virtual organisation that responds quickly to new opportunities. This required an understanding in the core skills needed to support technical and market changes, then securing these skills through strategic partnerships, acquisitions, value-added re-sellers, industry associations and universities.

Navitrak's approach is to bring only the most necessary and most highly skilled players to the core team. Then these players bring with them their own networks. Over time this generates an exponentially larger and more complex network.

(*Source*: Based on Knowledge Roundtable, 2000, 2004)

Alliances are a variant form of the virtual corporation. Alliances exhibit a stronger commitment to other enterprises that may lie upstream, downstream, horizontally and laterally from the core business than the level of commitment in the sub-contracted relationship of the virtual corporation.

ILLUSTRATION

The Airbus consortium

Airbus Industrie (Airbus) began as a consortium of European aviation firms to compete with American companies such as Boeing and McDonnell Douglas. In the 1960s, European aircraft manufacturers competed with each other as much as the American giants. In the mid-1960s, tentative negotiations regarding a European collaborative approach began.

Airbus Industrie was formally set up in 1970 following an agreement between Aerospatiale (France) and Deutsche Aerospace (Germany) (joined by CASA of Spain in 1971). Each company was expected to deliver different sections as fully equipped – such as engines, fuselage, wings, etc.

Conglomerates

Conglomerates are a set of disparate business units that are loosely integrated through some kind of holding company structure. These business units are expected to remain viable in their own right and will therefore attempt to gain venture capital from many sources. The more diverse these business units and the more financially independent they are, the more they begin to resemble a portfolio of stand-alone firms. The conglomerate structure suggests high levels of decentralisation, which generally favours the innovation process but can also restrict the ability to build a strong internal change and alignment across all business units.

Aligning innovation to firm types

From the description of the different firm types, it is clear that they are suited to different competitive environments (that demand very different specific capabilities) and innovation strategies. The desired capabilities for a specific environment in which the company operates may exist internally within the company, may exist outside the company or may be sufficiently unique that they need to be created. It is important for any company to recognise which capabilities it needs and how these may be secured. It is also important that the nature of innovations being implemented to drive the business is understood. *Autonomous* innovations are generally used to create improved products and processes that fit comfortably into existing systems, and either fit or reinforce existing standards. Conversely, *systemic* innovations change technological requirements in a way that entirely new opportunities are identified. These may demand significant overhaul of the organisation and its processes.

Understanding where the desired capabilities reside and what type of innovation a company needs to engage in provides a high-level view of the most appropriate organisational format for the firm to adopt (see Table 8.1).

In autonomous innovations, where capabilities can be sourced externally and are considered reasonably stable, the use of decentralised and virtual structures works most effectively. Under these circumstances using bureaucratic, centralised structures lowers the performance of the company.

Systemic innovations favour integrated structures. These are required to achieve the tight integration necessary to drive successful development and commercialisation. In these

TABLE 8.1 Firm types for innovation

	Type of innovation	
	Autonomous	Systemic
Capabilities exist in-house	Silicon Valley-type	Multiproduct integrated
Capabilities exist outside	Virtual	Alliances
Capabilities must be created	Alliances Silicon Valley-type	Silicon Valley-type

Source: Teece, 2000. By permission of Oxford University Press

organisational formats sharing of information, knowledge and co-ordinated effort is a must. This is precisely what multi-product integrated firms attempt to achieve. If these organisations, however, operate as autonomous units (departments or firms in the case of alliance formats) without alignment to a strategic outcome it becomes quite difficult to successfully develop and commercialise the systemic innovation.

 ## Organisation structures for innovation

Organisational structure can be defined in terms of 'centralisation' and 'formalisation'. Centralisation is concerned with the consolidation of specific practices and/or functional boundaries within an organisation, while formalisation describes the extent that roles, responsibilities and organisational integration are achieved by formal roles and operating procedures. In these terms, the literature regarding innovation is somewhat inconsistent. It has been suggested that centralisation may actually facilitate innovativeness by reducing conflict and ambiguity, thus leading to a more uniform response to changes. In contrast, it has been argued that firms should be less centralised under conditions of high uncertainty and change. Individuals may have a greater level of autonomy in how to decide and act in a decentralised organisation. This may be helped by allowing a greater exchange of disperse ideas which familiarise employees with changes in the status quo, and decreases associated uncertainty (Ayers et al. 1997).

With respect to formalisation, it has been asserted that formal procedures can regulate tasks and assign role responsibilities, thus facilitating input and involvement from other departments. However, the contradictory (and dominant) view suggests formalisation engenders and enforces the status quo and inhibits the diffusion and communication of ideas. With such contradictions in the research, one thing can be stated with confidence, that an appropriate choice of organisation structure can have a significant impact on innovation performance. It has been shown that the success in new product introduction is related to the flexibility of organisational structure (e.g. Karagozoglu and Brown, 1993). Innovative firms tend to be loosely structured. This gives them a flexibility that permits speedy response to external changes.

In this section we briefly explore some common organisational structures and how they affect innovation and also address the pressing challenge of integrating key functions to drive effective innovation. Thereafter, we turn our attention to the use of teams and virtual global teams as a common feature in innovation. We also go on to explore additional structures and forms that support and extend corporate efforts to innovate.

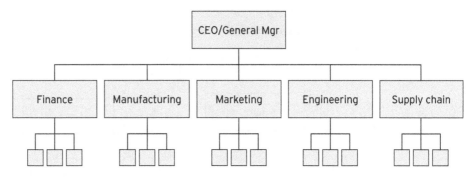

FIGURE 8.1 Functional organisations

Common internal structures

Internal structures of organisation have evolved over time. There are numerous variant structures that have been used for internal structuring of operations. Of these the two most common underlying structures from which a large proportion of variants have been constructed are the functional and matrix forms.

Functional organisations employ a hierarchical division of work between workers and their supervisors according to the principles of 'scientific management' proposed by Fredrick Taylor (1911). In this environment, the relationship between different functional departments is generally governed by Max Weber's principles for ideal bureaucracy. With extensive rules and procedures in place, different departments operate almost independently of each other.

Functional organisations (see Figure 8.1) tend not to encourage or value co-operation across functions. In some cases, performance standards and objectives are not consistent across the groups and can result in time-consuming conflict resolution. Since formalisation may be disjointed, the responsibility for designating cross-functional tasks and applying reward systems may be unclear resulting in further dysfunction in cross-functional teams.

Matrix organisations (see Figure 8.2) are an attempt to maintain functional specialisation while improving cross-functional integration. Functional specialists reside in functional groups and report to a functional manager. In innovation projects, they also report to project leaders, who may require their expertise during a particular phase of the development.

The matrix structure allows organisations to adapt to the needs of a project by flexibly manipulating the company's resources and expertise. On the downside, many companies find it difficult to balance the time spent in a functional group with time spent on projects. Nevertheless, firms using matrix organisations exhibit product development market success rates about twice those found in functional organisations (Larson and Gobeli, 1986).

In addition to the two major forms of structuring, some organisations use complementary structural formats to enhance innovation outcomes (see section on 'Other Structures for Innovation', p. 310). For example, some companies use permanent *co-ordinating groups* to manage the cross-functional flow of new product development (Souder, 1987). These groups are composed of personnel who possess a balanced perspective enabling them to work effectively with several specialist groups over a long period of time to both facilitate and monitor progress. Lorsch and Lawrence (1965) found that these groups produced high firm-level performance in terms of market and technological success where the level of uncertainty in one of these elements was extremely high. They found that these groups

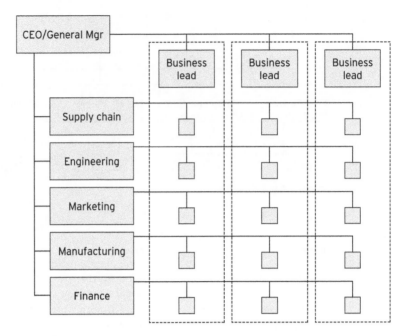

FIGURE 8.2 Matrix organisations

provide a means by which conflicts are resolved and decisions are made, thereby mediating the differences in organisational responsibilities.

The adoption of a specific organisational structure is dependent on the nature of the business in which a company is engaged. For instance, established companies operating in stable markets benefit from functional structures since these structures are geared for high efficiency within an unchanging environment. Under these circumstance, these structures can help innovation projects to meet time, cost and quality constraints more effectively than other structures. Alternatively, matrix organisations seem to handle uncertainty and change in dynamic markets more effectively than their functional counterparts. One important element determining how well innovation is supported by organisational structure lies in its ability to integrate and align skills and disciplines from different functions in a given environment.

Integrating key functions in innovation

Cross-functional co-operation facilitates completion of projects on schedule, within budget and with fewer design changes (Griffin, 1992). Frequent and effective communication between various functions allows different perspectives to be shared and explained. This stimulates greater levels of creativity than that experienced by functional departments working in isolation and increases the likelihood of product development success (Ford and Randolph, 1992).

While many different functions may be involved within an innovation project, the core functions are of R&D/engineering (to create), manufacturing (to make) and marketing (to market). The effective integration between these functions has attracted a significant amount of research attention, most of which suggests a positive correlation to innovation performance (Griffin and Hauser, 1996). However, the propensity for conflict between these functions is great. To some extent, R&D and marketing have similar goals. Marketing and R&D share responsibilities for setting new product goals, identifying new opportunities for the next generation of products, understanding customer needs, and resolving engineering design and customer-need trade-offs. Both are interested in creating change through new products and new technology. R&D is rewarded for creating new products, while marketing is rewarded for creating and maintaining markets and satisfied customers. In contrast, manufacturing is more concerned with achieving maximum efficiency in production and minimising associated costs. Consequently, the manufacturing function prefers narrower product lines to gain economies of scale and minimise change-over problems, while marketing prefers broad product lines to satisfy every customer.

As far back as 1983, Cooper found that projects that balance marketing and R&D inputs have a higher rate of success. The greater the harmony between marketing and R&D, the greater is the likelihood of success (Cooper and Kleinschmidt, 1987). Further enablers to success include:

- Joint effort in new product design significantly improves chances for new product success, for both industrial and consumer goods.
- Functional integration positively correlates to innovation success.
- Innovation success is significantly determined by interfunctional climate, information received by R&D, interaction and information exchange, and richer and broader communication (i.e. across all relevant topics).
- Underpinning this success is organisational synergy – the fit between the firm's R&D capability, management skills and market research resources.

Thus it appears that management strategies need to be developed that balance marketing and R&D.

Barriers to cross-functional integration

Simply increasing the level of functional integration is not sufficient to improve innovation success (Henard and Symanski, 1999). In fact, a blind promotion involving all functional areas in all stages of innovation can actually decrease NPD performance. From a theoretical standpoint, cross-functional integration violates two classic management principles. Firstly, assuming that authority should equal responsibility and every subordinate should be assigned to a single manager, cross-functional integration complicates the relationship between functional areas and innovation teams. This can increase organisational conflict (Katz and Allen, 1985). Secondly, conflict is introduced at an individual level as personnel from different functional areas often have different orientations, goals and values (Song and Parry, 1993). Thus, diversity in a team or organisation can lead to conflicting expectations, resulting in stress that can disrupt work patterns and performance.

Several potential barriers to cross-functional integration for innovation have been uncovered (Song and Parry, 1996).

Functional jargon as a barrier

Firstly, companies often suffer from the use of language (jargon) specific to each function. Each function uses its own set of technical terms and these differ from each other due to the context in which each function uses them. For example, marketing professionals tend to speak in terms of product benefits and perceptual positions, while R&D professionals speak in the more quantitative language of specifications and performance. The subtle differences in language often imply vastly different solutions and can make the difference between a successful and unsuccessful development.

Different reward systems

Another major barrier lies in the different organisational responsibilities and reward systems that exist in different functions. Behaviour within specific functional groups, whilst optimising their own outcomes, can undermine the overall performance.

Barriers caused by physical location

It is not uncommon for R&D and marketing functions to be physically located in different areas. R&D facilities tend to be located close to a rich source of skills (e.g. vendors and universities), whereas marketing offices tend to be located close to specific customers or physical markets. Increasingly, with aggressive cost-reduction objectives, manufacturing facilities are also being located in areas where cheap labour and components are available. Subsequent isolation of key functions across distant geographies increases personality, cultural, language and organisational barriers (Allen, 1979). The management skills needed to co-ordinate the complexity of such environments are an added expense (e.g. by hiring skilled individuals, or purchasing necessary training from external suppliers). For instance, getting physically dispersed personnel to share common values and reference points through socialisation is both costly and time-consuming.

Personality and cultural differences

In addition to the physical separation between functional groups, these are also personality and cultural differences between functions – particularly between technical and marketing personnel. Different functional areas possess very different paradigms and approaches to work. Empirical research shows that disharmony between marketing and R&D is the rule, rather than the exception (Moenaert and Souder, 1990), and is driven by personnel from each function differing in their respective training and backgrounds. Fortunately, there is evidence that this gap is not so huge or unbridgeable. For instance, Gupta et al. (1986) in a study of marketing and R&D managers of 167 high-technology companies found little substance to support the assertion that R&D and marketing managers are simply 'different' and thus cannot co-operate with each other. Rather, it was found that the functions had very similar traits and tended only to differ in their time perspective against specific dimensions (See Table 8.2).

R&D managers tend to have a longer time orientation and a stronger preference for high-risk, high-return investments. This supports a basic characteristic of innovative people: they prefer to solve complex problems and exhibit higher levels of patience when refining a

TABLE 8.2 Differences in orientation across functions

Dimension	Marketing	R&D
Time orientation	Short	Long
Projects preferred	Incremental	Advanced
Ambiguity tolerance	High	Low
Professional orientation	Market	Science

solution. Marketing managers exhibit a shorter time orientation and focus on lower risk incremental projects that have a greater certainty for success. Interestingly, marketing personnel show a higher tolerance for ambiguity in development projects than their R&D counterparts who are longer term orientated.

Additionally, there are differences within functions depending on firm context. For instance, comparing firms that can be described as 'low integration' (relatively simple products) versus 'high integration' (complex integrated solutions), the characteristics between the marketing and R&D functions change somewhat. For example, marketing managers in high-integration firms show a higher tolerance for ambiguity and a longer time horizon than those in low-integration firms, perhaps in recognition of the more complex products they are responsible for, and the comparative lifespan of their products.

How organisations value and reward different functions

Perhaps even more worrying than the different perspectives of functional area is the difference in perception of how the organisation values and rewards its different functions. Many R&D managers feel that they are accorded a lower status than their marketing counterparts (in terms of salaries, power and career prospects). This creates feelings of inequality and adversely impacts on R&D performance.

One thing is clear from the studies of R&D–marketing integration – the level of joint involvement between these two departments critically affects new product success rates (Parry and Song, 1991). In these studies, the one group of firms that is consistently successful (in terms of both 'percentage of sales from new products' and 'sales from new products') is the one that balanced these two areas through better communication and co-operation.

Teams in innovation

Teams are key in executing innovation projects. In their use a company must appreciate the variety of formats that can be implemented to meet the business goal of innovation. Teams can be formed at any level within an organisation – at corporate, product division, individual project or research level. Teams are generally formed under the basic premise that they are more productive than using individuals and generally provide a better solution to the problem at hand. The logic behind teams is simple: teams tend to combine and offer a range of skills and perspectives that go beyond that of any individual whilst also providing the structure for constant exchange and interaction amongst its members.

Teams can be created on either a part-time or full-time basis, and have a tenure which can be as short or as long as the company needs to resolve a specific challenge. Full-time project teams are generally created to deal with large, important projects where the company recognises that dedicated effort will result in the best solution and performance. Consequently, full-time teams can be quite powerful and influential in the company.

Teams are a basic building block in frameworks designed for structured management of innovation. For example, at the senior management level is the Review Board. This typically comprises senior managers, representing the key functions, who make go/no-go decisions. Lower down at the operational level of the organisation are cross-functional programme teams, who are responsible for executing projects within specific time, cost and quality constraints. Cross-functional teams are now used in around 67 per cent of all NPD projects and their use increases to 85 per cent for projects aimed at developing highly innovative products or services (Griffin, 1997).

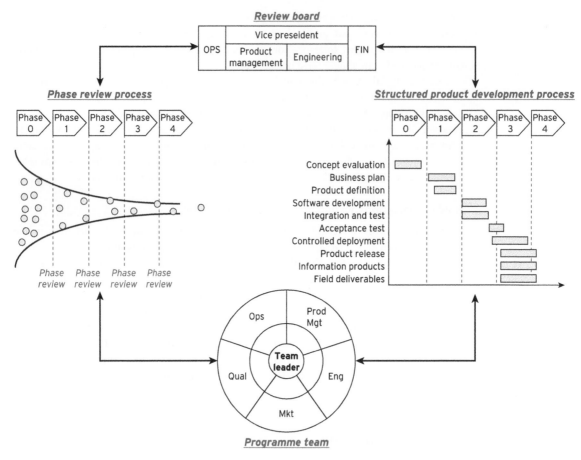

FIGURE 8.3 The basic architecture in which teams are deployed
Source: Adapted from McGrath et al., 1992

The most common approach for executing innovation projects is the cross-functional programme team. Such teams face a number of challenges for success (Kono and Clegg, 2001). First, it is necessary to gain the support of top and middle management in order to facilitate and drive co-operation with other departments. Management must move beyond simply espousing teams. They must model and actively practise teamwork to create environments where people prefer and are comfortable with teamwork. Second, team goals, responsibilities and schedules need to be clearly defined and understood by all. Team environments are where mistakes are not followed by punishment; where people are willing to give and receive constructive feedback and are motivated by work and collaboration. Teams need outstanding project leadership skills and high-calibre members, possessing complementary knowledge, skills, attitudes and capabilities. Access to supporting tools and information is also critical in the effective functioning of teams.

Another important enabler of teams is 'co-location' – the extent to which personnel from different departments are brought together in the same physical location. The purpose of co-location is to enable easier and more frequent interaction between team members of different departments, with the assumption that barriers will be broken down and more effective NPD will be achieved. Physical proximity of team members can reinforce social similarity and create shared values and expectations. When team members work in close proximity there is an improvement in the levels of co-operation, and in commitment, trust and communication. Thus, co-location of teams improves cross-functional integration and NPD performance (e.g. Ross-Flanagan, 1998, Chappell, 1995; Connelly, 1995)

As teams become established it is important that their value is not undermined by other forces. For instance, team members over-burdened with too much work and pressurised into making decisions quickly can work to destroy teams. A similar outcome results if teamwork is expected but rewards are given for individual 'heroic work' instead. A further element that negatively affects teams is an environment where facilitation is neither used nor available to help build trust and mutuality between members. Mismatch between team design, team membership characteristics and team objectives lowers team performance. Moreover, teams have a tendency to plateau in their effectiveness over time, especially as the lustre and excitement of working as a team wears off. Under this scenario, teams can be revitalised by increasing or modifying performance targets or bringing in new constituent members.

Team dynamics

Team members are typically drawn from different backgrounds, represent different functions and levels within the organisation and may have different reasons for being involved in the team. There may also be cultural, linguistic, religious and/or social diversity amongst the members. As a result, it can take a significant amount of time and energy to successfully transform a group of individuals into an effective team. This journey can be mapped against specific stages of maturity – forming, storming, norming and performing (Tuckman and Jensen, 1977), as illustrated in Figure 8.4. Generally, teams progress sequentially from one stage of maturity to the next, but there may be occasions when members regress to one of the previous stages, particularly when dealing with a complex problem.

The initial stage is when the team is formed and the members feel anticipation, optimism, excitement and perhaps fear or anxiety. At this time, team members generally look to the team leader to provide structure to the team, and identify specific roles and responsibilities. As goals and objectives are clarified, the team moves from the 'forming' to the 'storming' stage. Here, team members begin to see gaps between their initial expectations and reality. This can lead to dissatisfaction and re-examination of goals, team structures and team roles. As team members become more competitive or defensive, it becomes critical that the team leader keeps the team focussed on the task at hand and provides frequent encouragement.

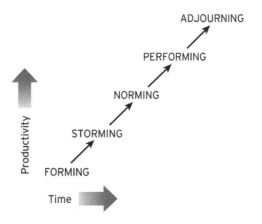

FIGURE 8.4 'Norming' model of team maturity

Over time, team members become more familiar with each other's working styles and knowledge and they begin to resolve conflicts with increasing co-operation and trust. This 'norming' stage sees the team working towards common ground-rules and common objectives. Plans and procedures are established on how these objectives will be met. Eventually, the team will enter the final stage – 'performing', where all the members work productively together to produce high-quality results. At this stage, they will have taken responsibility for decision making, problem solving, conflict management and goal achievement.

These stages of maturity are not confined to innovation only, but apply equally to any team setting. From an innovation perspective, it is important that the team can quickly move through the forming, storming and norming stages as quickly as possible, and therefore reduce the effects of team dysfunction on the goals they may have been set.

Team structure for innovation

The secret to successful product development teams lies in organising to achieve effective communication, co-ordination and decision making. Many different team formats have been used in organisations. A number of studies have been conducted to identify the most effective team structure to support NPD activities, resulting in the identification of many different approaches to team composition (see Figure 8.5).

Autonomous cross-functional teams operating in a matrix organisation have been found to be generally the most successful format from amongst all other team alternatives (Corey and Starr reported in Cooper and Kleinschmidt, 1991). The use of traditional functional organisations produces the lowest success in controlling cost, meeting schedules, achieving technical performance and overall results (Larson and Gobeli, 1989). The value of empowered cross-functional teams to drive such programmes has not been lost to the majority of companies. Indeed, research shows 96 per cent of all companies that had halved product development times employed cross-functional teams (Trygg, 1993).

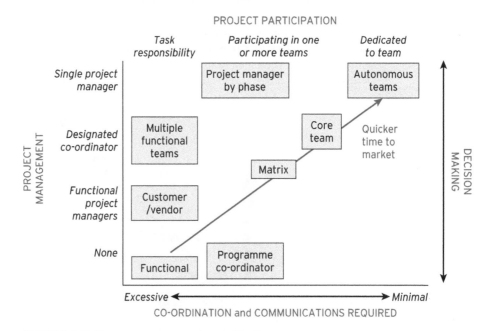

FIGURE 8.5 Teams, empowerment and effectiveness

Cross-functional autonomous teams are key enablers of innovation. They facilitate a change in focus within the company: away from functional and towards project-specific goals – this is supported by the high level of budget control they are assigned. Team accountability and responsibility for project-related goals foster a greater sense of ownership and commitment, ultimately facilitating the development of a highly effective and dedicated team. Such teams solve a number of integration problems within the company – they encourage information exchange, provide a degree of formalisation and encourage co-operation by providing a forum in which conflicts are resolved directly without intervention from management.

Using cross-functional project structures leads to higher R&D performance, especially for short duration projects, but also in projects where technology is not changing rapidly (Allen, 1979). Short duration project teams are an organisational mechanism most often used in situations where there is moderate uncertainty in both the marketing and technology dimensions, but extreme uncertainty in neither (Lorsch and Lawrence, 1965). Under these circumstances, use of cross-functional teams for product development has been found to shorten product development cycle time (Griffin, 1997) and improve commercial (market) success rates (Souder, 1987).

To gain benefits, however, such teams must be successfully embedded within the organisation. To do this requires careful and systematic development, management and alignment of teams. This often means using extrinsic and intrinsic levers for individual engagement and team performance. For some individuals, being part of a successful team is rewarding enough. Yet team-initiated evaluations and intrinsic consideration should also play an important role. For the most part it is necessary to go beyond a chance approach to motivation. In NPD projects, rewards are often allocated to team members based on the team's behaviour and performance relative to some pre-defined formal performance standard. However, performance-based financial incentives play a minor role in overall compensation, but assume increasing importance as one moves up the ranks (e.g. share options). Additionally, compensation typically rewards team members, not teams. In practice, one observes that team efforts tend to be recognised by non-financial rewards (e.g. plaques) and financial rewards, if given, are small-scale in nature.

Rewards for team-based innovation

How compensation and benefits are provided is an important issue in how teams are managed. Asking people to work in cross-functional teams and then rewarding them individually and on a functional basis strongly undermines team-work. Under traditional hierarchical reporting structures, compensation is determined primarily on individual contributions. In an environment where teams become more important, however, the implementation of team benefits becomes more pressing. Studies have shown that marketing and R&D personnel tend to be evaluated most frequently on individual functional performance (Coombs and Gomez-Meija, 1991). For instance, only 7.4 per cent of companies tie compensation to successful performance of new products (Page, 1993). Marketing personnel frequently receive bonuses based on increases in market share. R&D personnel, on the other hand, are given bonuses based on technological innovations (e.g. patents) regardless of whether the technology has been successfully productised (Zettelmeyer and Hauser, 1995). Since individual performance objectives do not reflect the interdependence required in an innovation team, they can actually discourage the very efforts necessary to develop successful new products (Donnellon, 1993).

Overall, team approaches produce lower production and labour costs and more committed employees. Indeed, self-managed cross-functional teams are believed by many to be a keystone to leaner and more flexible organisations capable of managing competitive pressures and the inexorable acceleration of technology. Teams are increasingly being seen as the logical means to generate more creative, less problem-riddled solutions, faster (Donnellon, 1993).

Global/virtual teams

In the past companies relied on co-located teams. These teams comprised of individuals who worked together in the same physical location and were culturally similar. However, in order to support a global customer base, companies have become more disperse in their operations. As a result, it has become more expensive to bring critical resources into a central location for the purposes of innovation. In order to bring the expertise needed many companies are relying on global or virtual teams (Boutellier et al., 1998), and this reliance is growing.

Past research has consistently revealed the quality of teamwork as an important driver of innovation performance (Easley et al., 2003), and that new product development teams regularly have team members who are not co-located (Hoegl and Proserpio, 2004), increasingly relying on *virtual* teams to drive product development programmes.

A *virtual* team can be defined as one comprising of individuals who reside at a moderate level of physical proximity and are culturally similar (e.g. a team where members are dispersed within the same country). *Global* NPD teams tend to comprise individuals who work and live in different countries and also have the added complication of cultural diversity. Despite the greater physical distance and cultural differences, many of the challenges faced by these two team formats are essentially similar in nature, differing only in severity. Therefore, we will consider them as synonymous and hereafter use the term 'global team'.

Global teams are an important means of developing products for global markets. They allow the company to draw on the local experience of individuals who reside in the countries

ILLUSTRATION

Boeing employs radical virtual team concept to create a breakthrough innovation

Rocket propulsion and power is an industry with very long cycle times. To develop a new rocket engine usually takes a team of about 400 to 600 people, and usually occurs in a periodicity measured in years.

Rocketdyne Propulsion and Power and the Boeing Company developed an innovative rocket engine using a groundbreaking model for managing product development projects. Faced with stringent cost, time and performance requirements, Rocketdyne reached beyond the company's walls to assemble a virtual team composed of world class professionals focussed on a key set of core competences.

The team transcended the boundaries between disciplines and companies, to create one of the first two, new, liquid-fuelled rocket engines in the United States in over 25 years. The virtual team achieved the following results:

- The first unit cost was reduced from $4.5m to $47K.
- The estimated engine manufacturing cost was $0.5m instead of $7m.
- Normal cycle time was reduced from an average 3.5 years to 9 months.
- Predicted quality level was >6 Sigma, instead of the normal 2–3 Sigma.

(*Source*: Based on Knowledge Roundtable, 2001, 2004)

for which new products are being developed. However, many companies struggle with the many challenges they present. Often companies make the mistake of managing them as if they were teams operating in close physical proximity and having low cultural diversity (McDonough et al., 1999).

Global teams routinely cross boundaries. These may be national, organisational and/or cultural. Since these teams may need representation from a number of different functions and geographical areas, they tend to be larger than co-located teams. All of these elements represent significant challenges in two particular areas. The first set of challenges relates to managing the team, such as ensuring effective communication, building trust, and so forth. The second set relates to managing the project – its schedule, budget, tasks and so on. Firms need to recognise that by adopting global teams they need to prepare their managers and team members for working in different types of teams and in different ways of working.

Working in global teams presents a number of unique obstacles. First, distance between members can affect the co-ordination and control of teams (co-ordination refers to the integration of tasks and organisational units so that the team's efforts contribute to the over-all objectives, while control refers to the process of adhering to goals, policies and standards). Distance makes it more difficult to communicate and solve problems and build trust between team members. Most of the problems arise from the greater complexities caused by cultural, linguistic misunderstandings and the limitations of technology as a social interface. Secondly, and perhaps rather obviously, once the initial euphoria of foreign travel wears off, global team members can feel isolated. Constant travelling and distant attendance demanded by these teams can be demoralising and harmful to family life. Therefore, care must be taken to plan and support global teams, otherwise team members quickly suffer burn-out. Fortunately, the need to physically attend global team meetings can be alleviated by the use of modern technologies.

Recent research has suggested that not only is teamwork quality more difficult to achieve as team member dispersion increases, but that it is also more critical to team performance (Hoegl et al., 2007), and that these teams can outperform co-located teams if they can overcome this obstacle.

The use of information technologies to enable communication among team members can significantly reduce the cost of bringing global team members together. Different technologies have been found to be useful in facilitating communications across groups and between employees located at dispersed geographical locations. Various technologies have been successfully used (e.g. e-mail, video conferencing, electronic chat, teleconferencing, point-to-point video conference, etc.). Teams that use these technologies frequently exhibit higher performance than those who do not. Other than reduced cost, many of these tools support asynchronous communication, to allow team activities to progress without members being in contact at the same time. This is particularly important when teams have to combat time zone differences. However, as elsewhere, there is a need to guard against the tendency to overload team members. Additionally, the different technologies can accentuate cultural misunderstandings by their inability to capture or convey a social presence and information-rich non-verbal cues (e.g. facial expressions, voice inflections and gestures).

While many challenges exist, it is the problems around managing cultural diversity that prevent most global teams from being effective. Corporate culture defines the norms, attitudes, values and behaviour patterns that form the core identity of an organisation or operating unit and plays a key role in determining the working climate, style, strategy, behaviour and processes of the firm (Saffold, 1988). Within global teams, important social information, such as social status or level of expertise, may be lost in a virtual team environment characterised by high levels of anonymity. Lack of social context can alter or hinder the extent to which team members develop trust. This affects the ability to develop relational links amongst team members, and negatively affects creativity, morality and decision-making quality. Within multi-cultural global teams there can be considerable difficulty when resolving conflict, creating cohesion and building trust. Yet despite the apparent problems facing global teams, they have been found (due to their multi-cultural membership) to exhibit high levels of creativity and to be able to develop more and better solutions to problems than teams with lower cultural diversity (Watson et al., 1993).

Other structures for innovation

We have seen how different firm types are positioned to drive specific types of innovation, and therefore meet their unique business objectives. Within these firms, there are a number of different approaches that can be adopted to drive innovation. The most common approach is the use of cross-functional programme teams. However, there are other equally useful forms that a firm can use in parallel with, or completely outside, existing innovation frameworks. Some of these forms are geared towards solving a very specific problem, while others are far more general in their scope and applicability.

A common approach in many companies is the use of a *research laboratory*, or an equivalent advanced development group. Often staffed by highly skilled technical personnel, these forms explore new possibilities in the use of specific technologies, and work to reduce the company's exposure to damaging risk before allowing programmes to flow into the development funnel. These groups have a strategic focus and tend to be at their most successful when they are driven and supported by a strong market understanding. If, and when, this form is used it becomes a critical necessity to establish a linkage with the rest of the organisation. Specifically, an effective technology transfer competence is needed between the research laboratory and the company's engineering, marketing and production groups.

ILLUSTRATION

Bell Labs history

More than any other single institution, Bell Laboratories has helped weave the technological fabric of modern society. Since its founding in 1925, Bell Labs technology has shaped the ways people live, work and play. In fact, the technologies created by Bell Labs are so pervasive they are nearly invisible.

The countless millions of transistors quietly labouring behind the scenes in the workplace, in homes, cars, banks, gas pumps, stores, telephone and computer networks – just about everywhere – are all descended from the first transistors invented here between 1947 and 1952. And all digital communication of sound, images and data – whether on telephone wires, in optical fibres, through the atmosphere or between a PC's processor and its memory – rests on mathematical foundations of information theory laid here in the late 1940s.

Today's global economy rests on an infrastructure of networking, computing and software technology, much of which was invented and developed by Bell Labs. Some of the other important technological milestones of our age that were initiated by Bell Labs include: stereo recording, sound motion pictures, the first long-distance TV transmission, the first fax machine, the touch-tone phone, several generations of modems, communications satellites, lasers, solar cells, cellular telephony, lightwave communication systems, and software that operates, maintains and manages some of the most sophisticated public and private communications networks in the world.

(*Source*: Based on Bell Labs, 2005)

Companies with a strict focus on short-term profitability tend to have product divisions that are less likely to spend time and precious resources in developing new products, especially if they do not produce immediate profits. Some companies tackle this problem by establishing *incubator* departments. The incubator's role is to come up with ideas for and develop new technologies and products. These are then passed on to intermediate department(s) to conduct experiments on production methods, marketing and supporting processes. Only once senior management gives its approval can these new products and technologies get passed on to an existing, or new, product division.

Recognising that smaller organisations often produce more innovative solutions and do so more effectively, some companies put together *skunk works* or *tiger teams*. These are teams that are often located in a physically separate location and are responsible for getting the job done with little to no interference from the company's headquarters. These teams have been used very effectively in the past, and have been shown to be successful in situations where stretch project goals are set, especially with respect to lead time (Larson and Gobeli, 1988; McGrath et al., 1992).

ILLUSTRATION

Cuban Missile Crisis

On 16 October 1962, John F. Kennedy was notified that the Soviet Union was installing nuclear ballistic missiles in Cuba. Immediately after the CIA briefing he set up EXCOM, the executive committee of the National Security Council, to find solutions.

The EXCOM core group was carefully selected to include key players who also qualified as trusted advisors. EXCOM consisted of 14 members, some senior cabinet members, military, low-level staff and outside advisors. There were several floaters. Group selection was superb. For the next 13 days the EXCOM group wrestled continuously with how to resolve the crisis.

Robert Kennedy said the EXCOM had no leader, no co-ordinator. In fact, RFK was a nominal co-ordinator, reporting back to his brother and tasked to drive the group to reach a consensus. However, his team co-ordination role was weak and EXCOM suffered from a number of dysfunctions.

- While the conflict among members was always uninhibited, it was not always impersonal or constructive.
- EXCOM did not adopt a systematic search for solutions.
- The process was undisciplined; participants were distracted; people kept coming and going and bypassing the group to directly lobby the president.

On the positive side:

- The conflict was intense, uninhibited, open and honest. Commitment was extreme. People said what they thought, even if it was unkind.
- Questionable interpersonal trust was balanced by unquestionable loyalty; there were no leaks.
- The ability to debate without media pressure was invaluable.

From a problem-solving perspective, there was a deep ideological split between the hawks and the doves. They eventually reconciled this split using a Delphi approach. Each side wrote a position paper. These papers were exchanged back and forth, attacked and defended. It seemed that this technique was ad hoc, invented by the team. Eventually, the hawks realised that they did not need to bomb immediately. The group also synthesised a rather creative final solution.

→

EXCOM began its deliberations without JFK. His involvement in the debate increased with time. Towards the end he was a full-fledged participant and witnessed the nuances of the give and take between the hawks and the doves. While JFK demanded a consensus, when the consensus was weak he was the clear decision maker. He learned his lessons from the Bay of Pigs and did not repeat groupthink errors. In the final analysis JFK made no serious errors in judgement about Soviet intentions.

EXCOM is an excellent Tiger Team case study because there were no good solutions to the crisis. Every potential solution had serious risks and flaws. Throughout the crisis, no one maintained a consistent opinion. Group selection and the uninhibited constructive conflict were superb.

(*Source*: Pavlak, 2004)

The alternative structures are illustrated in Figure 8.6. Do note, however, that their use needs to be balanced with some potential adverse effects. First, the best staff are more often than not asked to serve on these high-profile teams. Thus, their existence may disrupt and demoralise everyone else in the company. Second, they tend to be created to address unknown challenges, and often in a very reactive way. This makes R&D budgeting less plannable and progress more difficult to assess. Finally, and perhaps most significantly, they cost more than other team structures and approaches. Despite these drawbacks, the use of these alternatives has been increasing over the years.

Another interesting, although rarely used, approach is the *internal venture team*. These teams are typically set up by the individual who conceived the original idea. This individual assumes leadership of the team and takes a share in any profits that are gained. This approach can provide strong motivation and encourages creativity but may tie up competent staff in risky projects. Interestingly, whilst this is a different structural approach to innovation, in practice it tends to be treated as any other project in the development funnel.

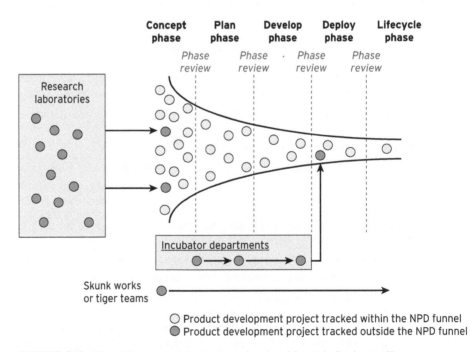

FIGURE 8.6 Alternative or complementary structural formats for innovation

Individuals in innovation

Specific roles and responsibilities of individuals differ across the various strata of the innovation framework, depending on each person's skills, knowledge, attributes, experience and seniority. We first briefly examine some key roles within innovation and then discuss two pivotal leadership roles – the executive (sponsor and/or review board member) and the champion.

The features that characterise a firm's approach and tendency toward innovation were discussed earlier in this chapter. The dimensions applied to the organisation are to an extent also of relevance to individuals. Innovative individuals tend to like, and are motivated by, the challenge of complex problems. Also, they prefer to build up a rich body of knowledge based on the specific problem domain. Since this can involve long-term, inquisitive explorations, innovative people are likely to be quite patient. In identifying solutions to problems, innovative individuals have a tendency to explore options from many different perspectives, which can lead to the generation of unusual ideas; and often they may spend considerable additional effort simply refining their ideas. At a personal level, innovative people generally consider themselves as different; they tend to be independent and non-conformist. Most of the time breakthrough innovations arise when people assert their individuality, break free of structural thinking and synthesise novel interpretations to move projects forward. Indeed, studies seem to indicate that innovation projects benefit greatly from unconventional individuals (e.g. Takeuchi and Nonaka, 1986). This is particularly the case for radical and high-risk innovation.

In one sense, an innovating firm can be usefully thought of as an independent communication network of individuals, where each member is a discrete pocket of knowledge. This knowledge includes facts, principles, experience-based insights, working procedures, research findings and ideas. Thus, an important challenge for a company is how these individuals (packets of knowledge) can be mobilised for the purposes of establishing a competitive advantage (at both the business and functional level) (Clark and Wheelwright, 1993). In trying to tap into these individuals' capabilities it is necessary to understand the roles and activities that individuals must enact for innovation. Regardless of the organisation structures used, the team formats employed or the additional support groups that enhance the innovative capabilities of the company, a number of common roles can be found to underpin most efforts for innovation. These are briefly described below.

The review board

The review board determines project selection, continuation, termination and funding of projects. Senior managers in the review board set the strategic direction and vision for the company, and through effective portfolio management align the company's investments towards meeting the long-term, sustainable, profitable goals of the company.

The technical advisory board

In addition to the review board, some companies also adopt a technical advisory board. This comprises of a number of senior technical personnel. They check, monitor and make decisions over the availability, readiness and source (external or internal development) of required technologies. They also ensure the 'engineering' part of the organisation appropriately assesses and scopes an innovation prior to significant resource deployment. Thus, they are responsible for driving a tight alignment of technologies to the company's ascribed strategies and architecture.

The executive sponsor

The executive sponsor is a senior member of the company's management team and is likely to be a member of the review board. The executive sponsor offers individual support for a specific product development project. He/she often supports the *champion* (see below) in removing barriers and ensuring that projects are tightly aligned to the company's business objectives.

The programme manager

The programme manager is generally responsible for the oversight of multiple projects, which are usually inter-related by similar business interests (e.g. market segments), technical solutions (e.g. product family) and customer base. Consequently, this role is relatively senior in the organisation and often carries ultimate responsibility for the success of a specific project. Due to the cross-functional responsibility of this role, the accountability for the financial return on the investment and the need to strongly influence the rest of the organisation, the programme manager is also sometimes referred to as the *project champion*.

The project manager

The project manager is responsible for the planning and execution through all phases of the product development lifecycle. The role involves managing project resource utilisation and performance, meeting milestones and budgetary constraints, identifying and managing risks and fulfilling project deliverables and objectives. In smaller scale projects, the project manager may assume the role of the programme manager/champion.

The project team members

Project team members are responsible for planning and executing tasks delegated by the project manager. These tasks may be in the context of the cross-functional team or specifically focussed on the functional area they represent. Generally, team members report directly to the project manager or through another project team member serving in an interim management or technical leadership position.

The skills, knowledge and experience of all these key players need to be brought together to drive innovation performance. This is illustrated by the study by Song et al. (1997). This study highlights that new product performance is positively influenced by marketing proficiency, technical proficiency and product quality. Marketing proficiency refers to the four stages of exploration (exploration, concept development, market development and market start-up), while technical proficiency refers to the four stages of development (prototype development, testing, manufacturing start-up and technical services). These proficiencies and the need for product quality are supported by the existence of specific skills brought together in an innovation team (see Figure 8.7).

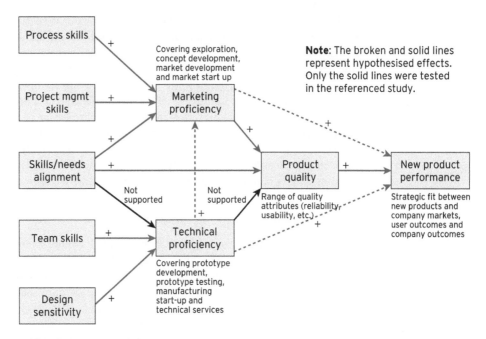

FIGURE 8.7 Basic skills and proficiencies for innovation
Source: Song et al., 1997

The important message for organisations is that they need to establish the right mix of technical, market and product quality skills in their innovation framework(s) through the competencies and capabilities of their people. People and the competencies that they bring to the task are vital in the game of innovation.

Leadership in innovation

Leaders tend to shape organisational culture by signalling what are the important priorities and values for the organisation. Leaders are expected to set and teach standards and live them in a way that inspires others to do likewise. Leaders generally set expectations for performance and by so doing provide a centre of focus for other's efforts. They reinforce the culture by using symbols (ideas, words, etc.) to define work and give it character.

Leadership involves thinking beyond the current problems of today and looking towards the possibilities of what the company can become in the future. At the same time, leaders must be capable of focussing on the few things that are important to the success of the company.

They influence followers to do what needs to be done to fulfil the organisational vision. To achieve this they must share their power with others. Good leaders are able to drive the organisation by tapping into something deep within stakeholders that moves them beyond motivation to a state of inspiration. They are able to place an authentic priority in caring about things (people, services, etc.). Nevertheless, it is important that leaders break their visions of excellence down into discrete tasks that can be communicated and executed. And since change takes time, leaders must be persistent and patient. During the process of change, leaders need to absorb and contain anxiety that is unleashed when things do not work out as intended, and provide answers or provide the temporary emotional reassurance and stability as the answers are being worked out.

Being a leader is a challenging and complex task. Leadership needs to be practised at many levels in the organisation. It cannot be confined solely to the top of the organisational hierarchy. So where might these leaders come from? Trait theory suggests that people have natural gifts that make them born leaders. A different view is that anyone can lead and different types of people lead differently. There is also an aspect of leadership that can be gained through knowledge, improving skills and experience. Therefore, it is important for companies to not only recognise what makes an effective leader but also to foster these attributes as part of the individual's career development as well as the organisation's succession planning process. Within innovation development projects there are two key types of leadership roles: the executive sponsor (CEO or senior member of the review board) and the champion (or programme manager). These leadership roles are further elaborated next.

Senior management role in innovation

New product programmes containing high levels of risk require senior managers to play a visible role for success. This role requires a vision to be provided to steer the new programme down the right road (Swink, 2000) and share responsibility in the success or failure of the programme. Some companies have gone as far as linking senior managers' remuneration to the success or failure of the programme. This is a signal of both involvement and commitment from the senior ranks.

As an organisation matures and grows, sub-groups can emerge with their very own sub-cultures. The different sub-groups and sub-cultures can affect the integration and co-ordination of activities. Senior management must therefore consider whether the emergence of these sub-groups is supportive or destructive to the company's broader goals and vision. Leaders must be sensitive to a range of issues and possess diagnostic skills to understand the nature of 'soft' and 'hard' organisational problems, have the capability to develop insights and possess the intervention skills to make the desired changes happen. Due to their position of power and influence senior managers play a key role in promoting interaction between different departments, particularly the marketing–technical interface.

Another key role of senior management is one of creating a network of management advocates who provide sponsorship for innovative projects. In some cases, these senior individuals may be able to enhance the company's reputation and products by personally interacting with strategic and lead-user clients (de Bretani, 2001). Most common of all, of course, senior management are involved in the formal screening and review of projects and key evaluation points and general innovation decision making and strategising.

Decision making in innovation

The key elements comprising common innovation frameworks were reviewed in Chapter 5. In order for the innovation framework to operate effectively, it is important that two critical elements (the senior management 'review board' and the 'decision process') are effectively brought together to support the company's innovation aspirations. The bureaucracy associated with the decision-making process, the information presented at pre-defined phase reviews, the assessment models and performance indicators used by the review board, and the pre-disposition towards risk all have a bearing on the success of the development project.

Decision making in many types of organisations, especially hierarchical ones, involves additional bureaucracy. Unfortunately, this is true for many decision-making processes in innovation. For example, it is common for innovation decision processes to be defined in terms of checklists (outlining specific deliverables needed for different phase reviews) and success criteria (outlining what hurdles need to be overcome before additional funding will be approved by the company). On the positive side, these procedures and screens can help protect against any personal impulses from senior managers to inappropriately approve or cancel a project. However, providing extensive documentary evidence and supporting plans can negatively affect the level of innovation in a company. Firstly, the need for significant documentation slows down decision making and ultimately delays the release of innovative products to the market. Secondly, employees will understandably recourse to standard historic protocols and problem-solving routines, knowledge of the current asset base and history-based personal paradigms of the business when constructing the review materials. This can limit the extent to which, and the way in which, innovative opportunities are explored, presented and operationalised.

The tendency to fall back on familiar paradigms is not limited to those who prepare materials for stage-gate, or phase, reviews. The review board can also exhibit higher comfort levels around existing technical and market knowledge and the company's current assets. This comfort and lack of understanding of new opportunities can either lead them to an overly optimistic assessment of the potential of a new project (because they base their assessments on the profits of current products) or over-cautiousness in supporting radical innovation(s) that may have the tendency to destroy existing competencies or involve significant switching costs. It is important to always place innovation decisions within the context in which they are taken. For instance, how the company measures performance and how it reinforces this by incentives and bonus programmes. In companies where success is measured on short-term financial yardstick the review board is likely to avoid investing in lengthy (and risky) radical innovation projects. One way of overcoming this problem would be to set aggressive goals in the business such that they raise aspirational reference points above simple survival and incremental innovation. However, this also has the potential to create considerable conflict and stress if short-term financial return strictures are imposed strongly and carry heavy penalties for employees at the coal-face for missing stretch targets.

Those involved in the decision process need to take great care when preparing and reviewing materials at phase reviews. Very often, the information is subject to a number of interesting phenomena, such as:

- *Imaginary precision* (see also Chapter 7) arises when decision makers place emphasis on information and scoring rather than the right decision to be made.

- *The halo effect* occurs when positive scoring on select variables leads to the neglect of others. Consequently, programmes may be approved because of the attractiveness of a minority of attributes yet a more balanced view of the totality may present a less wholesome picture.

- *Bold forecasting biases* are generally seen in asset-rich companies, which tend to be overly optimistic with regard to incremental innovations, or in de novo firms that are overly optimistic about the potential of radical innovations.

- *Programme persistence bias* is where the presence and support of programme advocates in the review board influences funding decisions beyond limits that are reasonably justified and validated.

Innovation champions

Trying to differentiate between a *team leader* and a *champion* can be confusing, particularly since the two roles can be assumed by one individual. Essentially, team leaders lead a group of people towards a specific objective within certain constraints (e.g. time, cost and quality) and take responsibility for the internal co-ordination of this group. *Team leadership* is inwardly focused on team operations and effectiveness. *Champions*, on the other hand, exhibit a strong external focus and look for opportunities to positively affect a team from outside (e.g. perhaps by influencing senior managers). To this extent, the champion must possess a wide range of leadership skills.

The team leader is someone who assumes leadership, whether it is formal or informal. Team leaders are responsible for securing and directing resources towards an agreed objective. They ensure the team remains focussed on what it is they are supposed to be doing. Team leaders must recognise and address problems as they arise. Sometimes this will require facilitation of the team to address internal issues. At other times it may be necessary to tackle issues that lie outside the team but nevertheless affect team performance. This may require the team leader to maintain effective channels of communication with external bodies or integrate the work of the team with that of other groups. An effective team leader ensures that the team members are clear about their individual actions and commitments. Good team leaders almost invariably contribute to the work of the team (as a team member) without over-influencing or pulling rank.

As team leaders move into a champion role, their perspective may change from one of leading to one of directing. The champion sets team direction by first setting a clear and engaging vision, with the details left unspecified. This allows the team the flexibility to decide how best to execute the details themselves. The champion assists in translating this vision into long-term strategies, short-term operational tactics and goals and tasks. As part of this framing, the champion needs to ensure that the relevant knowledge and skills are in place to meet the team's and project's needs over time. Organisationally, the team leader or champion roles must be supported by a reward system that encourages positive behaviour and provides positive consequences for good performance.

Champions have to be adept at managing external linkages. They must be good at networking, active in the process of sense making and represent the team in a broader environment. Networking involves the development and maintenance of information sources inside and outside the team. Sense making involves creating meaning of the information gathered so it is helpful to the team. Team representation involves representing the team to the outside world, safeguarding its interests and shaping the environment to maximise support for the team. This skill allows champions to forge informal co-operative ties across functional lines, and allows them to foster strong relationships across a diverse constituent base. Consequently, they are able to lobby strongly and extensively; for instance, when funding dries up and is much needed for the project to be put back on the map. Champions ensure that development teams are held together and protected, especially during difficult times. Champions provide the operational-level enthusiasm and persistence to keep projects alive in the trenches. This may involve protecting the project from financial and managerial restraints often imposed by corporate managers. The champion's role is a varied one. It involves directing and protecting teams in innovation, while also building strong ties with influential parties outside the team to drive a project that would otherwise come under threat.

Champions are much needed in companies where support systems, processes and infra-structure are lacking for managing innovation systematically. In these organisations it is the drive, flair and persuasion of the individual champions that is key to success. Champions appear to influence radical versus incremental innovation in different ways. Incremental projects speed up when there is a highly influential individual overseeing a portfolio of projects rather than one for each – the opposite is true for radical projects. Under highly uncertain conditions there tends to be a greater propensity for political activity and thus steering a high-risk innovation project requires the dedicated energy of a highly political champion who is able to promote its agenda by controlling information, co-opting management and building coalitions (Frost and Egri, 1991).

ILLUSTRATION

Champions at the core of innovation at Apple

Product champions have a vision for a product, and drive them to market, often working with others to do so. This vision is often bold, and may force companies to move in a new direction. A great example of this was seen at Apple, a computer company that moved into the personal entertainment industry with the Apple iPod.

In a world where MP3 players had existed for a number of years, it appeared that there was little room for any significant new entrants to the market. However, the designers of the iPod combined improvements in a number of key industries to make the iPod a massive success.

Firstly, Apple improved the state of their basic product by designing the click wheel interface, which was a significant improvement over the traditional interfaces. By bundling the product with iTunes, a software product that leveraged Apple's strong computer-based competencies, expectations were changed around how easy it was to purchase and download music to the player. They also changed the industry in the way that they allowed firmware updates to be easily performed on the player. The iPod was not a new-to-the-world product, but iTunes was.

During this time, the manufacturers of MP3 players were spending their time concentrating on their players, and the software to drive them. The product champions at Apple were integrating advancements in electronics, audio compression, internet technology, service and software. They saw the opportunity to cross-pollinate between different industries to create a market-dominating product, but also one where switching costs are prohibitive, further protecting their leading position in the market.

(*Source*: Adapted from Roland, 2008)

Conclusion

In this chapter we discussed characteristics associated with innovative organisation. Depending on the nature of the challenges and the availability of competencies to exploit innovation, firms can be organised differently. We describe a number of such firm types: individual inventors, multi-product hierarchical firms, Silicon Valley, virtual corporations and conglomerate formats. All of these differ in their approaches but ultimately all are geared to achieve the same objective: profitable growth through innovation.

After reviewing the different firm types, we looked at how organisations may be structured internally to deal with innovation. After briefly dealing with common structures (e.g. functional, matrix, etc.), we considered how to develop the functional integration necessary to support the cross-functional challenge of managing innovation. A key issue covered is how to create alignment between marketing, R&D and manufacturing. However, cross-functional integration is not a 'magic bullet' to meet all innovation challenges. Consequently, we reviewed both the advantages and drawbacks of integration and looked at how integration and involvement might change as we move through the innovation process.

Moving down a level in aggregation, the chapter examined the use of teams in executing innovation projects. Cross-functional teams are the cornerstone of most innovation frameworks, and their structure and use was elaborated in detail. As companies become global in their operations the capacity to co-locate cross-functional teams becomes constrained. Many companies have dealt with this by developing global/virtual teams. The challenges and benefits of global team forms were presented. Besides teams, companies use other structures to drive innovation. These include research laboratories, incubator departments and skunk works/tiger teams.

As we crossed the divide from teams to individuals, the issue of reward and compensation was highlighted. The major individual roles commonly found in innovation projects were briefly elaborated before discussing the leadership roles of the executive sponsor and the project champion. In this context, we noted that the leadership qualities exhibited in one role closely mirrored those in the other, and differed only in scope. The extended role of the executive sponsor as a review board member was also discussed, particularly in the context of decision making.

In summary, this chapter has shown how organisations are structured to address their innovation challenges, and how the progressive decomposition of the organisation into departments, groups and individuals demands careful consideration from everyone if the company is to successfully innovate.

QUESTIONS

1. Outline the characteristics that can be used to describe a company as innovative, citing examples in each case.

2. Discuss the advantages and disadvantages of applying different firm types to address innovation, and provide examples where possible.

3. In the context of organisational structures, show how you would address the challenges of cross-functional integration in innovation. What benefits would you expect to see as a result?

4. Describe the challenges an organisation might face when moving from traditional co-located innovation teams to ones that are global/virtual in nature.

5. Describe the role of the project champion in innovation. Discuss how this role is linked either to the traditional team leader role or that of the executive sponsor.

6. Indicate the factors that could lead to flawed innovation decision making. Suggest how you would correct these problems.

CASE STUDY

Remedy for a malady

The number of new medicines has steadily dropped, while the cost of bringing each one to market has risen sharply to more than $1bn (£605m, €700m). The debate has never been more urgent. Pharmaceutical companies face the disappearance of billions of dollars in revenues in the next few years as patents expire on their existing medicines, undermining the sales that have kept them in business. Meanwhile, state and private healthcare systems alike are seeking ways to cut costs and are balking at the rising price of new medicines.

A first tactic companies are adopting to deal with their troubled drug 'pipelines' is to overhaul internal processes. Stephan Danner of Roland Berger, a consultancy, says drug development has begun to receive the cost-cutting scrutiny previously given to operations such as sales forces. At the centre of this approach is speeding up the clinical trials that are required to test experimental drugs on patients. The more quickly that promising new medicines are launched, the greater the revenues generated before their patents expire. By the same token, the more swiftly drugs with problems are identified, and abandoned before expensive late-stage testing begins, the lower the wasted development times.

Greater computerisation of the results of drug tests in patients is a start, says Patrice Matchaba, head of drug safety at Novartis, another big producer. Much data is still collected on paper, which takes longer to process. He also sees a sharp rise in trials taking place in developing countries such as China, where costs are lower and it is quicker to find patients.

Companies are also seeking to create structures that foster innovation. Chris Viehbacher, who has been overhauling Sanofi-Aventis since he became chief executive late last year, says: 'We had 11 management levels in research and development and you had to dig down quite a few before you found anyone doing research. We need to reconfigure. We've just been tweaking things. We have to change how people think and interact.'

Many other industry leaders have tried to do the same, although no clear winning model has emerged. When he took charge of GlaxoSmithKline at the start of the decade, Jean-Pierre Garnier introduced a series of smaller 'centres for excellence in drug discovery' focussed on types of therapy. Andrew Witty, who replaced him last year, says these groups now need to be sub-divided further to deliver better results.

A second approach to boosting innovation involves intensified collaboration between companies. Eli Lilly has signed cost- and revenue-sharing deals with operators including Covance and Quintiles. AstraZeneca has agreed development projects with Bristol-Myers Squibb on a diabetes drug and with Merck for a cancer treatment.

GSK this year went much further, announcing a deal with Pfizer to pool all of their existing and experimental drugs for HIV. They must share future revenues – but also stand to gain more than either could separately, by combining expertise and funding and sharing the high risks of failure. By making their venture a separate entity, they also strip out other overheads, boosting accountability and focus.

Some of the more radical drug company partnerships are taking place with non-profit organisations. Cancer Research, a UK charity, has lately signed three deals, including two with AstraZeneca, to test experimental treatments that the company was unwilling to pursue on its own.

Their approach also raises a third, and still more radical, way of tackling the innovation drought: collaborative alliances that go beyond individual partnerships to span the entire pharmaceutical industry as well as academic researchers and regulators. One advantage is greater information sharing to cut costly duplication.

In the US through the Critical Path Initiative, and more recently in Europe via the Innovative Medicines Initiative – both in tight co-operation with their respective regulators – progress has been made in identifying common 'biomarkers' by which competing companies agree on the best ways to measure an experimental drug's efficacy or safety.

'Companies have recognised there is no comparative advantage in safety', says Ray Woosley, Critical Path president. But he concedes that they are most willing to co-operate in areas where they are failing to make much headway on their own, such as treatments for Alzheimer's disease. 'If they had a magic bullet, they would not share data.'

(*Source*: A. Jack, 'Remedy for a malady', *FT*, 14 August 2009)
© The Financial Times Limited 2009

QUESTIONS

1. This case describes a number of approaches to organisational structure in pharmaceutical companies. What could be the advantages and disadvantages of each approach?

2. To what extent might those approaches be relevant in other industries?

3. How might organisational or national culture impact on the effectiveness of the various approaches?

References

Allen, T.J. (1979), *Managing the flow of Technology: technology transfer and the dissemination of technological information within the R&D organization*, Cambridge, MA: MIT Press.

Anon (2005), 'Motorola – Pretty in pink', *Economist*, 5 November, 84.

Ayres, D., Dahlstrom, R. and Skinner, S.J. (1997), 'An exploratory investigation of organisatioal antecedents to new product success', *Journal of Marketing Research* 34: 107–116.

Bell Labs (2005), Bell Labs History, **www.bell-labs.com/about/ history/**.

Boutellier, R., Gassman, O., Macho, H. and Roux, M. (1998), 'Management of dispersed product development teams: The role of information technologies', *R&D Management* 28(1): 13–25.

Briggs, H. (2001), 'Profile: Marconi, the wireless pioneer', *BBC News Online*, 11 December.

Chappell, L. (1995), 'Being there (Honda of America Manufacturing Inc's co-location strategy)', *Automotive News*, February: 21–22.

Clarke, K.B. and Wheelwright, S.C. (1993), *Managing new product and process development*, New York: The Free Press.

Connelly, M. (1995), 'Like minded (Ford Motor Company's co-location strategies for vehicle development teams)', *Automotive News*, February: 2–5.

Coombs, G. and Gomez-Mejia, L.R. (1991), 'Cross-functional pay strategies in high-technology firms', *Compensation and Benefits Review* 23: 40–48.

Cooper, R.G. and Kleinschmidt, E.J. (1987), 'New products: What separates winners from losers', *Journal of Product Innovation Management* 4: 169–184.

Cooper, R.G. and Kleinschmidt, E.J. (1991), *Formal processes for managing new products: The industry experience*, Hamilton, Ontario: Faculty of Business, McMaster University.

De Brentani, U. (2001), 'Innovative versus incremental new business services: Different keys for achieving success', *Journal of Product Innovation Management* 18(3): 169–187.

Donnellon, A. (1993), 'Cross-functional teams in product development: Accommodating the structure to the process', *Journal of Product Innovation Management* 10(5): 377–392.

Easley, R.F., Deveraj, S. and Crant, M. (2003), 'Relating collaborative technology use to teamwork quality and performance: An empirical analysis', *Journal of Management Information Systems* 19(4): 247–68.

Ford, R.C. and Randolph, W.A. (1992), 'Cross-functional structures: A review and integration of matrix organisation and project management', *Journal of Management* 18: 267–294.

Frost, P.J. and Egri, C.P. (1991), 'The political process of innovation', in L.L. Cummings and B.M. Staw (eds), *Research in Organisational Behaviour*, Greenwich, CT: JAI Press.

Griffin, A. (1992), 'Evaluating QFD's use in U.S. firms as a process for developing products', *Journal of Product Innovation Management* 9(1): 171–187.

Griffin, A. (1997), 'PDMA research and new product development practices: Updating trends and benchmarking best practices', *Journal of Product Innovation Management* (14): 429–458.

Griffin, A. and Hauser, J.R. (1996), 'Integrating R&D and marketing: A review and analysis of the literature', *Journal of Product Innovation Management* 13: 191–215.

Gupta, A.K., Raj, S.P. and Wilemon, D. (1986), 'A model for studying R&D–marketing interface in the product innovation process'. *Journal of Marketing* 50: 7–17.

Henard, D.H. and Szymanski, D.M. (1999), 'Why are some new products more successful than others? A meta-analysis of empirical evidence', Unpublished Working Paper, Texas: Texas A&M University, College Station.

Hoegl, M. and Proserpio, L. (2004), 'Team member proximity and teamwork in innovative projects', *Research Policy* 33(8): 1153–1165.

Hoegl, M., Ernst, H. and Proserpio, L. (2007), 'How teamwork matters more as team dispersion increases', *Journal of Product Innovation Management* 24(2): 156–165.

IBM (2005), IBM Archives, **www-03.ibm.com/ibm/history/history/decade_1990.html**.

Jack, A. (2009), 'Remedy for a malady' *Financial Times*, 14 August.

Karagozoglu, N. and Brown, W.B. (1993), 'Time-based management of the new product development process', *Journal of Product Innovation Management* 19(3): 204–215.

Katz, R. and Allen, T.J. (1985), 'Project performance and the locus of influence in the R&D matrix', *Academy of Management Journal* 28: 67–87.

Knowledge Roundtable (2000), **www.knowledge-roundtable.com**.

Knowledge Roundtable (2001), **www.knowledge-roundtable.com**.

Knowledge Roundtable (2004), **www.knowledge-roundtable.com**.

Kono, T. and Clegg, S. (2001), *Trends in Japanese management: Continuing strengths, current problems and changing priorities*, New York: Palgrave MacMillan.

Larson, E.W. and Gobeli, D.H. (1988), 'Organising for product development projects', *Journal of Product Innovation Management* 5: 180–190.

Larson, E.W. and Gobeli, D.H. (1986), 'Organizing for product development projects', *Journal of Product Innovation Management* 3: 180–190.

Lorsch, J.W. and Lawrence, P.R. (1965), 'Organizing for product innovation', *Harvard Business Review*, January–February: 109–120.

McDonough, E.F., Kahn, K.B. and Griffin, A.J. (1999), 'Managing global product development teams: Achieving effective performance by linking communications speed, complexity and scope', *IEEE Transactions on Engineering Management* 46(4): 1–12.

McGrath, M.E., Anthony, M.T. and Shapiro, A.R. (1992), *Product development: Success through product and cycle-time excellence*, Boston, MA: Butterworth-Heinemann.

Moenaert, R.K. and Souder, W.E. (1990), 'An information transfer model for integrating marketing and R&D personnel in new product development projects', *Journal of Product Innovation Management* 7(2): 91–107.

Page, A.L. (1993), 'Assessing new product development practices and performance: Establishing crucial norms', *Journal of Product Innovation Management* 10: 273–290.

Pavlak, A. (2004), Modern Tiger Teams: Team problem solving for the 21st century, Thales Research Inc., 2 December. **http://mywebpages.comcast.net/apavlak/MTT_12-21-04.pdf**

Parry, M.E. and Song, X.M. (1991), 'Integrating R&D and marketing: A comparison of practices in the Japanese and American chemical industries', *IEEE Transactions on Engineering Management* 41(1): 5–20.

Roland, M. (2008), 'Product design speak 101: product champions', Carolina Newswire, RTP Product Development Guild, 25 July. Sourced from **http://carolinanewswire.com/news/News.cgi?database=pipeline.db&command=viewone&id=6**

Ross-Flanigan, N. (1998), 'The virtues and vices of virtual colleagues', *Technology Review*, March/April: 53–59.

Saffold, G.S. (1988), 'Culture traits, strength, and organizational performance: Moving beyond "strong" culture', *Academy of Management Review* 13(4): 546–558.

Song, X.M. and Parry, M. (1993), 'Determinants of R&D–marketing integration in high-tech Japanese firms', *Journal of Product Innovation Management* 10(1): 4–22.

Song, X.M. and Parry, M.E. (1996), 'What separates Japanese new product winners from losers', *Journal of Product Innovation Management* 13(5): 422–439.

Song, M.X., Souder, W.E. and Dyer, B. (1997), 'A causal model of the impact of skills, synergy and design sensitivity of new product performance', *Journal of Product Innovation Management* 14: 88–101.

Souder, W.E. (1987), *Managing new product innovations*, Lexington, MA: Lexington Books.

Swink, M. (2000), 'Technological innovativeness as a moderator of new product design integration and top management support', *Journal of Product Innovation Management* 17(3): 208–220.

Takeuchi, H. and Nonaka, I. (1986), 'The new product development game', *Harvard Business Review* 66(1): 137–146.

Taylor, W. (1911), *The principles of scientific management*, New York: Harper Brothers.

Teece, D.J. (2000), *Managing intellectual capital: Organisational, strategic and policy dimensions*, Oxford: Oxford University Press.

Tuckman, B.W. and Jensen, M.A. (1977), 'Stages of small group development revisited', *Group and Organizational Studies* 2(4): 419–427.

Trygg, L. (1993), 'Concurrent engineering practices in selected Swedish companies: A movement or an activity for the few?', *Journal of Product Innovation Management* 10(5): 403–415.

Udy, S.H. Jnr. (1959), *Bureaucracy and rationality in Weber's organisation theory: An empirical study*, Washington, DC: American Sociological Association.

Watson, W.E., Kumar, K. and Michealson, L.K. (1993), 'Cultural diversity's impact on interaction process and performance', *Academy of Management Journal* 36: 590–602.

Zettelmeyer, F. and Hauser, J.R. (1995), Metrics to evaluate R&D groups: Phase 1, Qualitative interviews working paper', Cambridge, MA, International Centre for Research on the Management of Technology, MIT.

9 Culture and climate for innovation

Learning outcomes

When you have completed this chapter, you should be able to:

- Appreciate the importance and impact of organisational culture and climate on innovation.

- Understand the difference between organisational culture and climate.

- Appreciate ways of managing culture to drive innovative behaviour.

- Understand the norms and values that encourage innovation, and those that stifle innovation.

- Recognise the role leadership needs to play in driving innovation through culture.

- Recognise structures, systems and processes that enable a culture for innovation.

Introduction

In boardrooms and corporate corridors across the world there is talk about innovation and the importance of 'doing' innovation. Many companies try to do it but only a few succeed. The reality is that innovation, for the most part, frightens organisations because it is inevitably linked to risk. Whilst there is a lot of talk about the power and benefits of innovation, most companies remain averse to the aggressive investment and commitment demanded to succeed. A typical scenario is one of debates and discussion by senior management over the vital importance of innovation, and often the matter ends there. Some go a step further and commit occasional resources and R & D funds, but do so in a piecemeal and ad hoc manner. However, to become an innovative company requires more than just debate and resources; it requires an organisational culture and climate that constantly guides organisational members to strive for innovation.

As highlighted previously, innovation is an activity that is cross-functional in nature and spans a wide range of activities across the business chain to provide value to customers and a satisfactory return to the business. Up until now, in dealing with structures and process activities for innovation we have focussed on tangible aspects of innovation. However, innovation is equally about the environment and culture of the company. Innovation is a spiritual force that exists in a company that impels it forward in value creation (Buckler, 1997). The spiritual force is the energy driving organisational innovativeness. It is probably best described as the pervasive organisational attitude that allows the business to see beyond the present to create the future. In short, innovation success is not just governed by the hard tangible enactment of process and structures, but just as much about the soft dimension of employee perceptions, actions and attitudes. Implementing structures and systems for innovation is challenging, but this is small compared to the arduous task of making these structures and systems work through elicitation of the desired behaviour and actions from employees. Simply deciding that the organisation has to be innovative is not sufficient. The decision has to be backed by actions that create an environment that drives desired behaviours. People in the company must be made to feel so comfortable and drawn to innovation that they create it.

ILLUSTRATION

Microsoft at the top of the table

Microsoft became the world's leading software producer through a lot of hard work, astute technological and business acumen, and careful management of its organisational culture. Microsoft's founder and CEO, Bill Gates, based the firm's culture on the principle of empowerment. Managers delegate power to the developers, who write and design software. The firm is managed in such a way that managers interact as little as possible with the developers, although the managers do provide mentors to help newly recruited developers to understand the firm's culture.

Microsoft's physical layout facilitates creativity and innovation. Corporate headquarters resembles a college campus, with playing fields, an outdoor eating area, and a basketball court. Almost every office has a window, and almost every door is open. Employees work hard (80-hour weeks) and play hard (parties, pranks, picnics, sports and good-natured fun).

(*Source*: Based on Higgins, 1995)

Whilst much of discussion in boardrooms centres around the concrete structures and systems little direct consideration is given to the way these affect innovation. Even when culture's role as a primary determinant of innovation is acknowledged, it still is underplayed. As we shall see in this chapter, possessing a positive cultural predisposition towards creative behaviour is an essential ingredient for success. Culture consists of multiple elements that interweave to enhance or inhibit the tendency to innovate. What type of culture is needed to breed business success is not an easy question, since the answer depends on each company's environment, history, current actions and future aspirations. To examine organisational culture in isolation from its context is a mistake, and to simply identify one type of culture and propose it as the panacea to the company's lack of innovation is to compound that mistake.

 ## Culture and climate

Visiting companies like 3M, Hewlett-Packard, Sony, Honda, and the Body Shop, one is left with a feeling that is not often encountered in ordinary companies. This 'feeling' often defies definition, yet despite its intangibility contains organisational concreteness as real as the machinery on the shop-floor. This feeling usually is found rooted in the prevailing psyche of each organisation. A company like 3M feels dynamic whilst some of its counterparts feel rather staid and unexciting. The feel of the organisation reflects both its climate and culture. The term climate originates from the work of organisational theorists such as Kurt Lewin (i.e. leadership styles create social climates), and Douglas McGregor (Theory X and Y), who used the term to refer to social climate and organisational climate, respectively. The climate of the organisation is inferred by its members through the organisation's practices, procedures and rewards systems and is indicative of the way the business runs itself on a daily and routine basis. In one sense it is the encapsulation of the organisation's true priorities.

Human beings are active participants of the environments in which they live. They shape, and are reciprocally shaped by, their environments. Through action and observation employees make sense of the organisational environments they live in and from their experience of it they infer organisational priorities. Their perceptions, and understanding, of the environment guide their decisions and behaviours. From their understanding they create postures to achieve their own particular ends. At times individuals may find that their personal ends are coincident with those of the organisation or they may find a conflict between the two. Either way, the interaction with the organisation and the procedures and practices that define the environment affect individuals' behavioural postures. The organisational practices and procedures that come to define these perceptions are labelled climate. Schneider et al. (1996a) defines four dimensions of climate (see Figure 9.1).

It is primarily from these sources that employees draw inferences about the organisational environment in which they reside and understand the priorities accorded to certain goals that the organisation espouses.

Closely allied to the concept of climate is culture. Organisational culture refers to deeply held beliefs and values. Culture is, in a sense, a reflection of climate but operates at a deeper level. Whereas climate is observable in the practices and policies of the organisation, the beliefs and values of culture are not visible at that level but exist as cognitive schema which govern behaviour and actions to given environmental stimuli. To illustrate the interlinkage, 3M has the practice of setting aside a certain amount of time for employees to do creative work on their own initiatives. To support this, specific seed funding is provided and the individuals are encouraged to share and become involved in each other's projects. These practices and support (climate) make individuals believe that senior management values

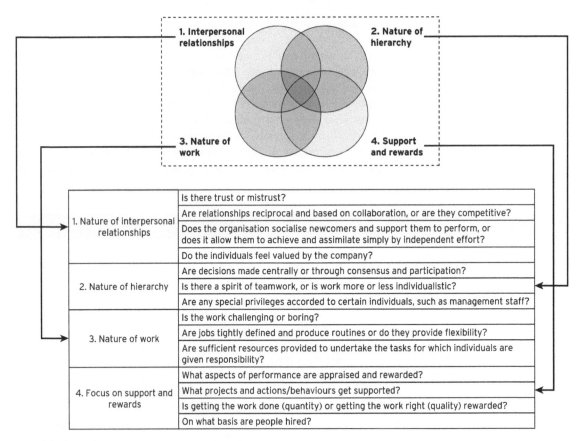

FIGURE 9.1 Four dimensions of climate
Source: Schneider, Gunnarson and Niles-Jolly, 1996

innovation (culture). Culture thus stems from the interpretations that employees give to their experience of organisational reality (why things are the way they are, and the how and why of organisational priorities).

If the notion of innovation culture is to be useful, it is important to be clear about what we mean by the term. Failure to specify it clearly leads to confusion and misunderstanding. The question of what is innovation culture is pertinent yet complex. The reason for this is partly to do with the way the concept of culture has evolved and partly to do with the inherent complexity within the concept itself. It is perhaps important to remember that the concept of corporate culture has developed from anthropological attempts to understand whole societies. The term over time came to be used for other forms of social groupings, ranging from whole nations, corporations, departments and even teams within businesses. There are a multitude of definitions of culture, and most suggest culture is the pattern of arrangement or behaviour adopted by a group (society, corporation or team) as the accepted way of solving problems. Culture includes all the institutionalised ways and the implicit beliefs, norms, values and premises that underlie and govern behaviour.

Culture can be thought of as having two components: explicit or implicit. The distinction between explicit and implicit components of culture is important in that it allows a better understanding of how to analyse and manage it. *Emplicit* culture represents the typical patterns of behaviour by people and the distinctive artefacts that they produce and live within.

Implicit culture refers to values, beliefs, norms and premises that underline and determine the observed patterns of behaviour (i.e. those expressed within explicit culture).

The distinction is necessary because it serves to highlight that it is easier to manipulate explicit aspects when trying to fashion organisational change. For example, in trying to make a company customer orientated, it may be possible to elicit certain actions and behaviours from employees through relatively simple training in customer-facing techniques but not necessarily effect any change in implicit culture. A change in implicit culture would necessitate altering the value set of the individual members to the extent that it becomes an unconscious norm of action, rather than guided by procedural or other organisational control routines. The degree and extent to which this happens is dependent on the strength of the culture. The strength of culture depends primarily on two things:

1. Pervasiveness of the norms, beliefs and behaviours in the explicit culture (i.e. the proportion of members holding strongly to specific beliefs and standards of behaviours).

2. Match between the implicit and explicit aspects of culture.

Another way of looking at culture is in terms of cultural norms. Creating culture through use of words is seldom enough. Essentially, norms vary along two dimensions (O'Reilly, 1989):

1. The intensity: amount of approval/disapproval attached to an expectation.

2. Crystallisation: prevalence with which the norm is shared.

For instance, when analysing an organisation's culture it may be that certain values are held widely but there is no intensity, i.e. everyone understands what top management wants, but there is no strong approval/disapproval. By way of contrast, it may be that a given norm, such as innovation, is positively valued in one group (marketing and R&D) and negatively valued by another (say manufacturing). In this case, there is intensity but no crystallisation. It is only when both intensity and consensus prevail that strong cultures exist. This is why it is difficult to develop or change culture. Strong cultures score highly on the intensity and crystallisation attributes. Moreover, really strong cultures work at the implicit level and exert a greater degree of control over people's behaviour and beliefs.

Strong cultures can be beneficial as well as harmful depending on the circumstances in which the organisation finds itself. The value of strong cultures is that by virtue of deeply held assumptions and beliefs the organisation is able to facilitate behaviours in accordance with organisational principles. Companies with strong cultures possess a large proportion of employees who hold common beliefs and opinions over a large number of organisational matters, such as attitudes towards its products, its customers and its processes. However, organisations need also to be wary of strong cultures. As well as being a strength, a strong culture can in some circumstances be a hindrance. To effectively use culture over the long term organisations need to also possess certain values and assumptions about *accepting change*. These values must be driven by the strategic direction in which the company is moving. Without these a strong culture can be a barrier to recognising the need for change, and being able to reconstitute itself even if the need is recognised. Supporting this apparently contradictory facet of culture, Denison (1984) in a longitudinal study found evidence that suggests incoherent and weak cultures at one point in time were associated with greater organisational effectiveness in the future, and that some strong cultures eventually led to decline in corporate performance. Clearly, balance and understanding of context is important. Cultures with strong drive for innovation and change can lead to problems when market circumstances and customer requirements demand predictability and conformance to specifications. John Scully's rescue of Apple Computers from the highly innovative but less predictable culture created by Steve Jobs is a good example of the weakness of a strong culture. Many years later, when market circumstances changed, it was the re-instatement of Steve Jobs that brought innovative flair and creativity back into Apple Corporation.

Generally, we can say that because culture can directly affect behaviour it can help a company to prosper. An innovative culture can make it easier for senior management to implement innovation strategies and plans. The key benefit is that often it can do things that simple use of formal systems, procedures or authority cannot. Moreover, given the nature of culture and climate it is clear that senior managers play a critical role in shaping culture. They are able to give priority to innovation by allocating resources and rewarding innovative behaviours and guarding against complacency. Employees take the priorities set by what management values, and use these to guide their actions. The challenge for management then is to make sure that the employees make the right type of attributions, since any mismatches or miscommunication quite easily lead to confusion and chaos.

ILLUSTRATION

A tale of two cultures

Culture has important bearing for organisations. The approaches adopted by General Motors Corp. (GM) and Southwest Airlines exemplify two highly contrasting cultures.

During the Alfred P. Sloan's presidency of GM, the company's corporate culture under-valued both its customers and employees. GM's culture was driven by a widespread belief that:

- GM is in the business of making money, not cars.
- Cars are primarily status symbols. Styling is therefore more important than quality to buyers who will, after all, trade up every year.
- Workers do not have an important impact on productivity or product quality.
- Consumer, environmental, and other social concerns are unimportant to the American public.
- Managers should always be developed from inside the company.

During the Sloan era General Motors paid too much attention to systems, policies and procedures, with little value placed on employees and their needs. This culture had a powerful debilitating effect on the firm's ability to compete. GM found itself in a rigid culture because it was a culture that had done so well for the company in the past. However, with the Japanese invasion of the US auto market GM was forced to re-evaluate the assumptions underlying its culture.

GM's culture sharply contrasts that of Southwest Airlines. Consider CEO Herb Kelleher's message to the Airlines Associates:

When you're sitting around with your grandchildren, I want you to be able to tell them that being connected to Southwest Airlines was one of the finest things that ever happened to you in your entire life. I want you to be able to say, Southwest Airlines ennobled and enriched my life; it made me better and bigger and stronger than I ever could have been alone. And if, indeed, that happens with your grandchildren, then that will be the greatest contribution that I could have made to Southwest Airlines and to its future.

Sloan was a technical genius, but Kelleher understood the importance of corporate culture.

(*Source*: Based on Locander, 2005)

Organisational culture and effectiveness

Having examined the issue of defining culture, it is necessary to check the attributes that make for its effectiveness. The topic of culture and effectiveness is of central importance, yet the area is beset by a formidable set of research problems. Any theory of cultural effectiveness must encompass a broad range of phenomena extending from core assumptions to visible artefacts, and from social structures to individual meaning. In addition, the theory must also address culture as symbolic representations of past attempts at adaptation and survival, as well as a set of limiting or enabling conditions for future adaptation. Even though attempts at integration have been made there is still very limited consensus regarding a universal theory, and a great deal of scepticism exists about whether culture can ever be 'measured' in a way that allows one organisation to be compared with another.

Innovation and culture effectiveness

Empirical work on organisational culture can be traced back to the early work of classical organisation theorists such as Lawrence and Lorsch (1967). In more recent times a vast base of popular literature on the subject was started by writers such as Peters and Waterman (1982) who espoused a theory of excellence that purports to identify cultural characteristics of successful companies.

Numerous studies have produced evidence highlighting the importance of culture to organisational performance and effectiveness. To cite a handful of exemplary studies, Gordon (1985) highlighted that high and low performing companies in the banking and utilities industries had different culture profiles. Kotter and Heskett (1992) present an analysis of the relationship between strong cultures, adaptive cultures and effectiveness. Deshpande et al. (1993) link culture types to innovativeness. They define four generic culture types: market culture, adhocracy culture, clan culture and hierarchical culture. They suggest that certain forms of culture are more able to enhance innovativeness than other types. Market and adhocracy cultures score highly for high performance companies, exhibiting a statistically significant relationship.

Deshpande et al.'s typology of culture into four archetypes is based on the seminal work of Quinn and Rohrbaugh (1983), who found that clusters of values reproduced Jung's (1923) psychological archetype dimensions. This typology is often referred to as the 'Competing values model' of organisational effectiveness. The competing values model typology frames shared beliefs in terms of organisational attributes, leadership styles, mechanisms of organisational bonding and overall strategic emphasis (see Figure 9.2). The model uses two dimensions to define culture types. The vertical axis describes the continuum from organic to mechanistic processes. This captures the extent to which the organisation is biased toward flexibility, spontaneity and individuality in contrast to control, stability and order. The horizontal axis describes the relative emphasis on internal maintenance (smoothing activities, integration, etc.), as opposed to external positioning (competition, environmental differentiation, etc.).

The market culture quadrant (lower right) emphasises competitiveness and goal achievement. It is assessed primarily in terms of productivity and market objectives. In stark contrast, the clan culture (upper left quadrant) emphasises teamwork, cohesion and participation (hence the reference to this as the competing values model). In this culture type, commitment of organisational members is through involvement and participation, and organisational cohesiveness and personal satisfaction are valued more highly than financial

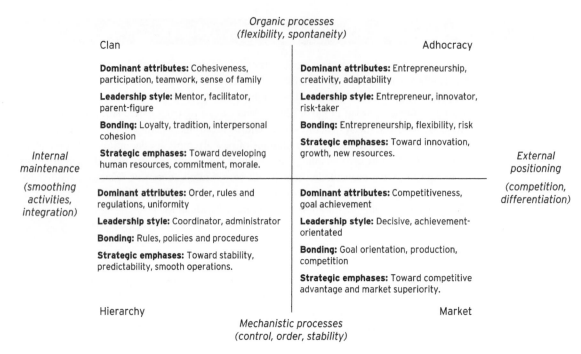

FIGURE 9.2 Competing values model of organisational culture
Source: Deshpande et al., 1993

or market share objectives. The other two polar culture types are adhocracy and hierarchy. The adhocracy culture emphasises values of entrepreneurship, creativity and adaptability. Flexibility and tolerance are important beliefs and organisational effectiveness is determined by movement and development of new growth opportunities. The hierarchy culture, in contrast, stresses order, rules and regulations. Effectiveness under the hierarchy culture is measured by consistency and achievement of clearly stated goals. It is important to keep in mind that these four types are not mutually exclusive. Firms can, and often do, possess elements of several cultural types (perhaps even across different business units of the same firm), but over time it is likely that one form will become dominant over the other traits.

More generally, Denison and Mishra (1995) identify four cultural traits and values that are associated with cultural effectiveness (see Figure 9.3). These are:

1. Involvement is a cultural trait which is positively related to effectiveness.
Involvement of a large number of participants appears to be linked with effectiveness by virtue of providing a collective definition of behaviours, systems, and meanings in a way that calls for individual conformity. Typically, this involvement is gained through integration around a small number of key values. This characteristic is popularly recognised as a strong culture. Involvement and participation create a sense of ownership and responsibility. Out of this ownership grows a greater commitment to the organisation and a growing capacity to operate under conditions of ambiguity.

2. Consistency is a cultural trait that is positively related to effectiveness.
Consistency has both positive and negative organisational consequences. The positive influence of consistency is that it provides integration and co-ordination. The negative aspect

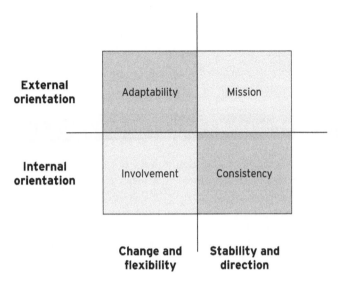

FIGURE 9.3 Model of culture traits
Source: Denison and Mishra, 1995

is that highly consistent cultures are often the most resistant to change and adaptation. Additionally, the concept of consistency allows us to explain the existence of sub-cultures within an organisation. Sources of integration range from a limited set of rules about when and how to agree and disagree, all the way to a unitary culture with high conformity and little or no dissent. Nonetheless, in each case the degree of consistency of the system is a salient trait of the organisation's culture.

3. Adaptability, or the capacity for internal change in response to external conditions, is a cultural trait that is positively related to effectiveness.
Effective organisations must develop norms and beliefs that support their capacity to receive and interpret signals from their environment and translate them into cognitive, behavioural and structural changes. When consistency becomes detached from the external environment firms develop into insular bureaucracies, and find it difficult to adapt.

4. Sense of mission or long-term vision is a cultural trait that is positively related to effectiveness.
This contrasts sharply with the adaptability notion, in that it emphasises the stability of an organisation's central purpose and de-emphasises its capacity for situational adaptability and change. A mission appears to provide two major influences on the organisation's functioning. First, a mission provides purpose and meaning, as well as a host of non-economic reasons why the organisation's work is important. Second, a sense of mission defines the appropriate course of action for the organisation and its members. Both of these factors reflect and amplify the key values of the organisation.

Denison and Mishra propose that, for effectiveness, organisations need to reconcile all four of these traits. The four traits together serve to acknowledge two contrasts: the contrast between *internal integration and external adaptation*, and the contrast between *change and stability*. Involvement and consistency have as their focus the dynamics of internal integration, while mission and adaptability address the dynamics of external adaptation. This focus is consistent with Schein's (1985) observation that culture is developed as an organisation learns to cope with the dual problems of external adaptation and internal integration. In addition, involvement and adaptability describe traits related to an organisation's capacity to change, while consistency and mission contribute to the organisation's capacity to remain stable and predictable over time.

Managing culture for innovation and creativity

It is through interaction with the organisation that an individual makes sense of the organisation. And the nature of the interaction between the individual and the organisation defines the nature of outcomes in the shape of his/her actions or behaviour. We can perhaps see this more clearly if we conceptualise organisations as a collection of many behaviour episodes, each making up a slice of 'organisational life', that come together over time to constitute the organisation. Within this, an individual's accumulated experience with the organisation leads him/her to develop an interpretative schema of the preferences, expectations and knowledge of the organisation.

Individuals try to understand their environments through a (process) cycle of continuous information seeking, meaning ascription and action (Gioia and Manz, 1985). This process of reciprocal interaction is known as sense-making. Sense-making processes are guided by schema, which impose meaning and structure on information in order to facilitate comprehension and action. Schemas are developed based on the common features of relevant instances (behaviour episodes), and become more abstract and complex as experiences are repeated (Fiske and Taylor, 1984). Behaviour episodes are the building blocks of schema. They guide interpretations and actions in new behaviour episodes, which further refine schemas and so on. Well organised schemas, based on the common features of behaviour episodes, facilitate the imposition of habitual interpretations and actions on familiar circumstances even in the face of considerable ambiguity. If this thesis can be accepted, and there seems to be compelling evidence for it, then the critical importance of organisational culture and leadership actions that provide the cues, which ultimately govern organisational function and activity, become of prime importance in nurturing creativity and innovation (Pfeffer, 1981). According to this form of theoretical logic, actions result from the joint influence of sense-making, motivation, knowledge and ability.

The importance of cueing particular schema in organisations places at centre stage the role of organisational culture as a key determinant of innovation. Organisationally, cueing (activation) of the schema is heavily shaped by triggers, such as signals from leadership and the practices in an environment that surrounds employees.

An appreciation of the importance of signalling is a clue as to how culture can be developed and managed in organisations. All organisations possess a culture but few systematically attempt to manage it. Three generic mechanisms play an important role in this: (i) actions and behaviours, (ii) communication, and (iii) rewards and punishment (see Figure 9.4). What varies across companies is not what is done but only in the nature and degree to which such mechanisms are utilised.

The process, typically, begins with the words of senior management. These words represent the decisions that have been taken by management. However, for these words to have meaning they must be communicated into the organisation. The communication may be explicit, as encapsulated by mission and philosophy statements, or implicit in which case it is inferred by those lower down the organisational ladder by discerning between actions that are approved and rewarded within the organisation against those that are not. Over time,

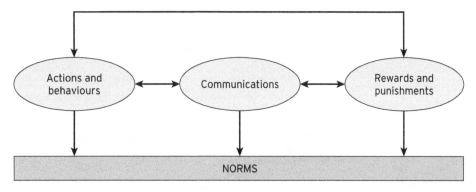

FIGURE 9.4 Basic mechanisms for managing organisational culture

from management's actions and words organisational members begin to develop consistent interpretations over what is deemed to be important by the organisation. When the resulting behaviour is consistently rewarded (or punished) over time norms begin to form. For norms to either develop or change, individuals go through a staged process of interpretation and commitment (see Figure 9.5):

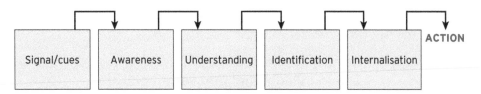

FIGURE 9.5 Simple stage process in the development of norms

At the first stage, individuals simply become aware of the signal being given from the actions and behaviours of management. Next, an appreciation and understanding of implications arising from these cues begins to be formed. Individuals position themselves relative to the implication(s) through a process of identification. The positioning may be an acceptance or a rejection depending on the individual's appreciation and standing with respect to the act that is being requested through communications. Strong identification leads to positive acceptance of the requested acts. Weak identification with the cue(s) is indicative of conflict or rejection. The identification (or lack of it) forms the basis from which internalisation takes place. Internalisation leads to the solidification of specific actions and beliefs. Solidification results if there is a match between the individuals' values and beliefs and organisation's values and requests for action. Employees under 'match' conditions feel a higher sense of belonging and pride, and consequently derive higher satisfaction. The person and the organisation start to act in synchrony when the individual finds the values of the organisation to be intrinsically rewarding and congruent with his/her own personal values. At the point when solidification of beliefs and values translates into actions, norms begin to emerge. If this final stage is reached for a majority of the organisation's employees then one may rightly say that the culture is being affected.

We now turn to consider in more detail a number of key factors (individual, leadership and organisational) and their role and impact in effecting organisational culture.

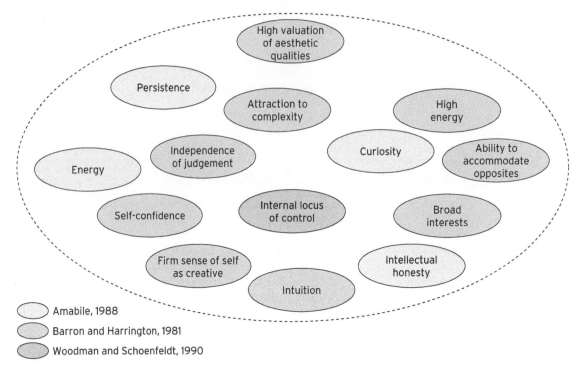

FIGURE 9.6 Personality traits for innovation

The individual and innovation culture

People are central in organisational culture. Organisations must consider the type of employees that can most effectively drive innovation. From a diverse range of research (psychology to management) it has been found that a core of reasonably stable personality traits characterise creative individuals. A select set of personality traits for innovation are illustrated in Figure 9.6.

Although there appears to be general agreement that personality is related to creativity, attempts to try and use this inventory type of approach in an organisational setting as predictor of creative accomplishments is fraught with dangers, and is hardly likely to be any more useful than attempts at picking good leaders through the use of trait theory approaches. Nevertheless, it does highlight the need to focus on individual actors and to try and nurture such characteristics or at least bring them out, if necessary, in an organisational setting.

Cognitive factors also appear to be associated with the ability to innovate. Research appears to indicate a number of cognitive factors are associated with creativity. For instance, medical psychology indicates differences in cognitive processing; ascribing the left cerebral cortex to rational thinking, and the right brain to intuition. A few cognitive parameters affecting idea production are illustrated in Figure 9.7.

Personal motivational factors affecting innovation

At the individual level numerous motivation-related factors have been identified as drivers of innovation and creative production. These are briefly discussed next.

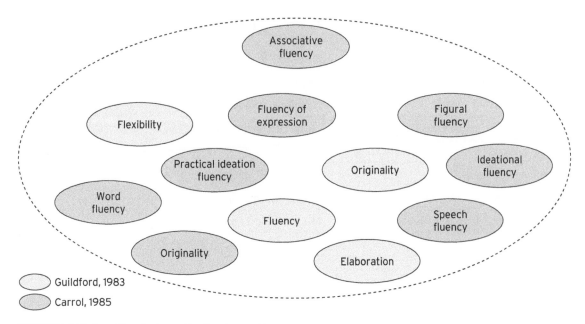

FIGURE 9.7 Cognitive factors affecting innovation

Intrinsic versus extrinsic motivation

Intrinsic motivation is a key driver of creativity (Amabile, 1988; Barron and Harrington, 1981). In fact, extrinsic interventions such as rewards and evaluations can adversely affect innovation motivation because they appear to redirect attention from 'experimenting' to following rules or technicalities of performing a specific task. Furthermore, apprehension about evaluation appears to divert attention away from the innovation because individuals become reluctant to take risks since these risks may be negatively evaluated. Contrarily, in order to be creative individuals need freedom to take risks, play with ideas and expand the range of considerations from which solutions may emerge.

Challenging individuals

Open-ended, non-structured tasks engender higher creativity than narrow jobs. People respond positively when they are challenged and provided sufficient scope to generate novel solutions. It appears that it is not the individual who lacks creative potential but it is organisational expectations that exert a primary debilitating effect upon the individual's inclination to innovate (Shalley and Oldham, 1985).

Skills and knowledge

Innovation is affected by relevant skills such as expertise, technical skills, talent, etc. However, domain-related skills can have both positive as well as negative consequences. Positively, knowledge enhances the possibility of creating new understanding. Negatively, high domain-relevant skills may narrow the search heuristics to learnt routines and thereby constrain fundamentally new perspectives. This can lead to functional 'fixedness'.

At a more macro-level, organisations tend to attract and select persons with matching styles (Schneider et al., 1996b). Organisational culture, as well as other aspects of the organisation, can be difficult to change because people who are attracted to the organisation

TABLE 9.1 Organic and mechanistic structures influencing innovation

Organic structures promoting innovation	Mechanistic structures hindering innovation
Freedom from rules	Bureaucratic
Participative and informal	Many rules and set procedures
Many views aired and considered	Long decision chains and slow decision making
Face-to-face communications (little red tape)	Communication via the written word
Cross-functional teams	Rigid departmental separation and functional specialisation
Emphasis on creative interaction and aims	Little individual freedom of action
Outward looking – take on external ideas	Formal reporting
Flexibility concerning changing needs	Information flow upwards, directives flow downwards
Non-hierarchical	Hierarchical
Information flow downwards and upwards	

may be resistant to accepting new cognitive styles. When a change is forced, those persons attracted by the old organisation may leave because they no longer match the newly accepted cognitive style. Among other things, the culture–cognitive style match suggests that organisational conditions (including training programmes) supportive of innovation and creativity will be effective only to the extent that the potential and current organisational members know of and prefer these conditions.

Structure and innovation culture

Although much research appears to agree that innovation is influenced by social processes, research in this area often has taken a back-seat to research on psychological differences between innovative and non-innovative individuals. Generally, it can be said that innovation is enhanced by organic structures rather than mechanistic structures (Burns and Stalker, 1961). The simple characteristics associated with each format of structure are depicted in Table 9.1.

Innovation is increased by the use of highly participative structures (e.g. high performance–high commitment work systems). For instance, an idea champion must be made to feel part of the total innovation. At the very least he/she must be allowed to follow the progress of the innovation. This builds involvement via ownership and enhances attachment and commitment at the organisational level. There is also a case to let the individual lead the project from the beginning to the end. This level of flexibility and involvement is generally available only within the fluidity of organic structures.

Creating structures and systems to empower people to innovate is one of the most effective ways for organisations to mobilise the creative energies of their people. Combined with leadership support and commitment, empowerment gives people freedom to take responsibility for innovation. Empowerment in the presence of a strong innovation culture produces both energy and enthusiasm to consistently work towards producing innovative outcomes. Employees themselves are able to devise ways that allow them to innovate and accomplish

ILLUSTRATION

Safeguarding innovation at Magma International

For automotive components and system supplier Magna International, innovation is built into a 'corporate constitution' that outlines the company's core principles: one of which is to foster inventive thinking on the part of employees. 'Incremental innovation requires the right environment – one built on fairness, security, safety and proper communications', said Belinda Stronach, president and CEO of the $11 billion company. According to Stonach, a comprehensive incentive programme helps motivate its 72,000 employees to be creative.

'We slice up the pie of profits before it's baked', she said. Six per cent of profits are distributed to Magna's management team, all of whom – Stronach included – receive low base salaries. 'Employees receive 10 per cent of profits, of which a portion is in shares and a portion is in cash', she notes. 'We're all motivated to generate profit because we receive a percentage, and we're also required to hold shares so that we look out for the long-term interests of the company.'

Aware that profit incentives alone won't deliver innovation, Magna also encourages creative thinking and idea sharing by promoting open communications and a sense of security among employees. To facilitate dialogue and collect ideas, for example, each division holds monthly meetings between employees and the general manager. 'We recently created an employee advocate position – an individual jointly selected by the employees and by management who cannot be fired by management, only by an employee ballot vote – to foster communications between employees and management', Stronach said. 'The mandate is to facilitate communications, keep employees happy and bring forward new ideas.'

'Without safeguards, employees will not have the confidence or the motivation to come forward with new ideas', she added. 'We found that by making employees stakeholders and providing the right entrepreneurial environment, incremental innovation is a by-product.'

(*Source*: Based on Anon, 2003)

their tasks. The only serious problem with empowerment occurs when it is provided within an organisation without a strong value system directing activities in a unified and aligned manner to the super-ordinate goals of the organisation. Under such conditions, empowerment becomes little less than abdication of responsibility, and when responsibility and power is pushed downwards chaos typically ensues.

Empowerment can, however, be easily incapacitated. Consider, for example, the impact of common utterances by bosses, as shown in Figure 9.8.

The impact of these so-called 'killer phrases' can be quite devastating in puncturing employee initiative. Additionally, people are bound by social and psychological barriers that inhibit initiative taking, and hence innovation. Some typical barriers of this form are:

- *Self-imposed barriers*: A lack of belief in self to have the potential to be creative and innovative.

- *Unwarranted assumptions*: an acceptance of tradition, or a blinkered approach, which does not question fundamental assumptions of things.

- *One correct answer thinking*: Assuming the first solution found is the best, or there is only one solution to the problem.

- *Failing to challenge the obvious*.

FIGURE 9.8 Killing empowerment

- *Pressure to conform*: Wishing not to stand out from the group.
- *Fear of looking foolish*.

A number of actions can be taken to structure empowerment and participation to contribute to innovation. These include the following and are discussed next:

- Establishing meaningful 'actions' boundary.
- Defining risk tolerance.
- Structure involvement.
- Accountability.
- Action orientation.

Establish meaningful 'actions' boundary

For employees to be creative and innovative they need to understand the primacy of the innovation agenda, and know how far they are being empowered to achieve these ends. Successful companies need to draw an 'actions' boundary through a process of explicitly defining the domain of action and the priority, and the level of responsibility and empowerment provided to reach these ends. Most often such transmission occurs through mission and vision statements. Devised correctly these statements can act as powerful enablers. Devised incorrectly they are powerful disablers, breeding cynicism and discontent.

Define risk tolerance

Employees need to know the level of risks that they can safely take. This helps them to define the space within which they are allowed to act in an empowered manner and the occasions on which they need to get organisational ratification. For example, employees need to know how much time they can spend on their pet projects, and how much effort they should expend to ensure that their 'routine' operations are not made sub-optimal. They need, also, to understand the penalties if inefficiencies creep into aspects of their task. In this way, understanding of risk provides a clearer definition of the priority and space for innovative actions. Without knowing the risk tolerance that exists within the organisation, employees tend not to be willing to try to innovate or engage in activities that are a departure from desired standard.

Structure involvement

Involvement is not something that just occurs on its own. Organisations must design into their structures and systems ways of buying involvement. Involvement requires emotional encouragement, as well as an infrastructure, to create possibilities of involvement. Organisational design and layout can be used to create a physical environment to enhance interaction. Awards and special recognition schemes are other mechanisms to encourage 'buy-in' to the philosophy of innovation as a way of organisational life. Establishing specific mechanisms for structured involvement, such as quality circles, is yet another device to encourage active participation into the programme. Without direct structures to induce innovation, the commitment to innovation remains an empty exhortation and produces empty results.

Accountability

A very common problem in empowered innovation is that everyone is encouraged to participate in cross-functional processes to the extent that many lose track of who is accountable for what. The result of unrestricted and uncontrolled empowerment is chaos. As new processes are put in place, new forms of behavioural guidance must be provided and must be accompanied by redefinitions of responsibility. Empowerment on the surface looks like an unstructured process yet, in reality, it is anything but that. In fact, it demands a clear definition of domains in which individuals are allowed to exert creative discretion and the level of responsibility that they must execute whilst engaging in their total task as employees of the organisation.

Action orientation rather than bureaucracy orientation

To help innovation take place, organisations must avoid creating bureaucratic bottlenecks that have the effect of suffocating innovation. One primary culprit is overly bureaucratic procedures for rubber-stamping approval or reporting requirements. Faced with such obstacles a lot of employee ideas fail to make it past the first few hurdles. In fact, a large proportion of suggestion schemes fail not because there is a lack of ideas but because of protocols and the failure of the protocols to process with sufficient speed either a favourable or unfavourable response. Lack of employee innovativeness is rarely the stumbling block. More usually it is the organisational processes and structures, which are so burdensome and unwieldy that they create high level of unresponsiveness. Companies must root out unfruitful elements of bureaucracy, processes and structure. Structures, systems and processes help to lay the basic infrastructural foundations for creative behaviour to take place.

Leadership and innovation culture

Leading-edge organisations consistently innovate, and do so with courage. It is the task of organisational leaders to nurture the culture and provide a climate that acknowledges innovation at every level. Notwithstanding the fact that leadership is critically important, leaders cannot on their own build a culture of continuous improvement and innovation. A culture of innovation requires the buy-in of a majority of employees. This requires spreading the innovation message into all corners of the organisation. One way is to recruit and train innovation champions, who are made responsible for constantly and continuously encouraging innovation throughout the organisation.

To build a successful and sustainable culture of innovation, leadership needs to accomplish two broad tasks. First, they need to be acutely sensitive to their environment and acutely aware of the impact that they themselves have on those around them. This sensitivity enables them to provide an important human perspective to the task at hand. Sensitivity is critical because it is only within this awareness that the leader can begin to bridge the gap between 'leaderspeak' and the real world of organisational culture. The second factor is the ability of leaders to accept and deal with ambiguity. Innovation cannot occur without ambiguity, and organisations and individuals who are not able to tolerate ambiguity in the workplace environment and its relationships end up reproducing routine actions. Organisational routines, almost by definition, cannot have all attendant problems and scenarios worked out in advance. Leaders must appreciate this fact, otherwise they risk creating a risk-averse culture. Tolerance of ambiguity allows space for risk-taking and exploration of alternative solution spaces that do not always produce business results. Tolerance of ambiguity and risk hedges against constant deployment of tried and tested routines for each and every occasion. Peters and Waterman (1982) came close to the mark in highlighting that the most successful managers have an unusual ability to resolve paradox, to translate conflicts and tensions into excitement, high commitment and superior performance. Developing this further, Mills and Delbecq (1996) identify characteristics that distinguish characteristics of highly innovative firms against less innovative companies:

- Top management commits both *financial and emotional support* to innovation, and promotes innovation through champions and advocates for innovation.

- Top management has to ensure that *realistic and accurate assessments* of the markets are made for the planned innovation. Highly innovative firms are close to their end users and are accurately able to assess potential demand.

- Top management ensures that innovation projects get the necessary *support* from all levels of the organisation.

- Top management ensures that *structured methodology/systems* are set in place so that each innovation goes through a careful screening process prior to actual implementation.

The above suggests that senior management play a pivotal role in enhancing or hindering organisational innovation. If senior management can install all of the above types of procedures and practices then they effectively seed a climate conducive to innovation. It is important to note that it is not sufficient to only emphasise one or few practices. Climates are created by numerous elements coming together to reinforce employee perceptions. Weaknesses or contradictions even along single dimensions can quite easily debilitate efforts. This is so because perceptions of the climate are made on aggregates of experience. For example, if rewards are not structured for innovation but are given for efficient performance of routine operations then no matter how seductive are other cues, employees are likely to respond with caution and hesitation when attempting to innovate.

Additionally, management create a climate not just by what they say but also by their actions. It is through visible actions over time rather than through simple statements that employees begin to cement perceptions. It is only when employees see things happening around them and to things that push them towards innovation that they begin to internalise the values of innovation. At innovative companies, the whole systems of organisational function are geared up to emphasise innovation (who gets hired, how employees are rewarded, how the organisation is designed and laid out, what processes are given priority and resource back-up, and so on).

ILLUSTRATION

The value of mistakes

It is important to have a 'no-blame' culture; one in which employees have the freedom to fail. As we noted before, as far back as 1941, William McKnight, former president of 3M, said: 'Management that is destructively critical when mistakes are made kills initiative, and it is essential that we have people with initiative if we are to continue to grow.'

Accidents and mistakes often lie behind new products, although companies can be reluctant to admit that a slip-up, rather than hours of methodical testing, is behind its latest launch.

Scotchgard

The Scotchgard range was discovered by a lab assistant who was working on a new liquid coolant and accidentally spilled a few drops on her shoes. When no amount of scrubbing would remove the stain she realised that the solution would make a good rain repellent, and the Scotchgard Protectors range was born.

Wispa

Cadbury reportedly stumbled upon the ingredients for Wispa when it was trying to match the consistency of Aero, but failed to put enough raising agent into the mixture and so ended up with a slightly denser version.

Corporate missions, philosophy statements and innovation culture

Having a clear corporate philosophy enables individuals to co-ordinate their activities to achieve common purposes, even in the absence of direction from their managers. One impact of corporate statements is their influence in creating a strong culture capable of appropriately guiding behaviours and actions. However, there is also a degree of doubt as to whether statements of credo have any value in driving organisations forward. Most statements are of little value because they fail to grab people's attention or motivate them to work toward a common end (Collins and Porras, 1991).

Despite these concerns, Ledford et al. (1994) suggest that, if correctly formulated and expressed, philosophy statements can provide three advantages. First, the statements can be used to guide behaviours and decision making. Second, philosophy statements express organisational values and norms, which can help employees interpret ambiguous stimuli. Third, they may contribute to organisational performance by motivating employees or inspiring feelings of commitment. Importantly, it is worth bearing in mind that the mission statement does not have to move mountains to make a cumulative difference in firm performance. If individual employees become just a little bit more dedicated to innovation, exert just a little bit more effort towards creativity goals, care just a little bit more about their work, then the statement may produce a positive return on the investment needed to create it. So what makes a statement effective? According to Ledford et al., an effective statement consists of four basic guiding principles to bring a statement to life:

1. Make it a compelling statement. Avoid boring details and routine descriptions.
2. Install an effective communication and implementation process.
3. Create strong linkage between the philosophy and the systems governing behaviour.
4. Have an on-going process of affirmation and renewal.

ILLUSTRATION

Gillette's leadership tablet

When James Kilts joined Gillette in 2001, the 100-year-old company already had a respectable legacy of inventive thinking, with headline products like the Atra, Sensor, Venus and the Mach series under its innovation belt. Yet Kilts wasted no time introducing into the firm his four building blocks for innovation: communicate a vision, get the right people, stay clear of building consensus, and look externally.

'It starts with communication', Kilts said. 'You need to ensure that your organisation understands that innovation is not confined to the R&D function or to other technical areas. We created a simple vision two years ago: build total brand value by innovating to deliver consumer value and customer leadership faster, better and more completely than the competition.'

But having a clearly articulated message only works if you have the right people – and give them the freedom to take chances. 'You've got to hire and retain people with energy and people who love to change and learn', Kilts said. 'And you need to encourage risk taking. One of the themes in our company is to remember that the opposite of success is not necessarily failure but inertia.'

While risky ventures often spark debate, contention comes with the territory. 'Real creativity can be very contentious, and you need to encourage people to challenge [current thinking] and maintain an attitude that they're unafraid to disagree with authority figures', Kilts said. 'Consensus building is not always the best way to promote innovation.'

In fact, sometimes the popular consensus can be dead wrong. Kilts, who prior to joining Gillette held top positions at Nabisco and Kraft Foods, recalled that when Oscar Mayer looked at possible modifications to its Lunchables line of children's lunch packages, the product group considered – and rejected as terrible – the idea of adding a drink to the product. Shortly thereafter, the president of that division met with a customer who voiced the same idea. 'The president went back and told the product group, who said they thought it was the worst possible idea, "Well, I'm going to do it anyway"', Kilts said. 'That little idea, called the Fun Pak or Lunchables, doubled the size of the business.'

Kilts notes 'companies need to look outside their own doors and use benchmarking as a source of new ideas'. 'Talk with people in other industries about what they're doing and what they're accomplishing', he urges. 'I've gotten a lot of good ideas from other industries.'

(*Source*: Based on Anon, 2003)

Cultural norms for innovation

Keeping in mind that the external environment strongly influences an organisation, and reciprocally the intrinsic creativity inherent in the organisation defines its ability to adapt to, and even shape, the environment, we need to ask how can culture promote innovation? Indeed, does culture hinder or enhance the process of creativity and innovation? The answer lies in the norms that are widely held by the organisation. If the right types of norms are held and are widely shared then culture can activate and promote creativity and innovation. Just as easily if the wrong form of culture exists, no matter the level of effort and good intention, little in the way of innovation will be forthcoming.

Perhaps what is most important to remember is that in reality, despite all the mystique, there is little that is magical or indeed elusive about culture. The problem is primarily about deciding clearly what are the appropriate norms, the specific attitudes and behaviours that are desired and then identifying and building norms to reach out to these expectations. A variety of research studies (e.g. Schneider et al., 1996a; Judge et al., 1997; O'Reilly, 1989) appear to identify a relatively similar set of critical norms involved in promoting and implementing innovation and creativity. This is summarised in Table 9.2.

TABLE 9.2 Norms promoting innovation and facilitating implementation

Norms that promote creativity	Norms that promote implementation
Freedom and risk-taking: the degree to which the individuals are given latitude in defining and executing their own work. Key attributes: • freedom to experiment • challenge the status quo • expectation that innovation is part of one's job • freedom to try things and fail • acceptance of mistakes • allow discussion of dumb ideas • no punishment for mistakes **Dynamism and future orientation**: the degree to which the organisation is active and forward looking. Key attributes: • forget the past • willingness not to focus on the short term • drive to improve • positive attitudes towards change • positive attitudes towards the environment • empower people • emphasis on quality not quantity **External orientation**: the degree to which the organisation is sensitive to customers and external environment. Key attributes: • adopt customers' perspective • build relationships with all external interfaces (suppliers, distributors, etc.)	**Challenge and belief in action**: the degree to which employees are involved in executing daily operations and the degree of 'stretch' required. Key attributes: • not being obsessed with precision • emphasis on results • meeting one's commitments • anxiety about timeliness • value getting things done • hard work is expected and appreciated • eagerness to get things done • cut through bureaucracy **Leadership commitment and involvement**: the extent to which leadership exhibits real commitment and leads by example and actions rather than just empty exhortation. Key attributes: • senior management commitment • walk the talk • declaration in mission/vision **Awards and rewards**: the manner in which successes (and failures) are celebrated and rewarded. Key attributes: • ideas are valued • top management attention and support • respect for embryonic ideas • celebration of accomplishments, e.g. awards • suggestions are implemented • encouragement

TABLE 9.2 *Continued*

Norms that promote creativity	Norms that promote implementation
Trusts and openness: the degree of emotional safety that employees experience in their working relationships. When there is high trust, new ideas surface easily. Key attributes: ● open communication ● listen better ● open access ● encourage lateral thinking ● intellectual honesty ***Debate***: the degree to which employees feel free to debate issues actively, and the degree to which minority views are expressed readily and listened to with an open mind. Key attributes: ● expect and accept conflict ● accept criticism ● don't be too sensitive ***Cross-functional interaction and freedom***: the degree to which interaction across functions is facilitated and encouraged. Key attributes: ● move people around (job rotation) ● teamwork ● manage interdependencies ● flexibility in jobs, budgets, functional areas ***Myths and stories***: the degree to which success stories are collected and celebrated. Key attributes: ● symbolism and action ● build and disseminate stories and myths	***Resources (innovation time and training)***: the amount of time and training employees are given to develop new ideas and new possibilities and the way in which new ideas are received and treated. Key attributes: ● built in resource slack ● funds/budgets ● time ● opportunities ● promotions ● tools ● infrastructure, e.g. rooms, equipment, etc. ● continuous training (encourage lateral thinking, creativity training, etc.) ● encourage skills development ***Corporate identification and unity***: the extent to which employees identify with the company, its philosophy, its products and customers. Key attributes: ● sense of pride ● willingness to share the credit ● sense of ownership ● eliminate mixed messages ● shared vision and common direction ● build consensus ● mutual respect and trust ● concern for the whole organisation ***Organisational structure: autonomy and flexibility***: the degree to which the structure facilitates innovation activities. Key attributes: ● decision-making responsibility at lower levels ● decentralised procedures ● freedom to act ● expectation of action ● belief the individual can have an impact ● delegation ● quick, flexible decision making ● minimal bureaucracy

Despite the interest in the field of innovation much of the research evidence concerning practices that encourage innovation cultures and creative climate remains unsystematic and anecdotal. As mentioned earlier, the importance of culture has been emphasised by organisational theorists, such as Burns and Stalker (1961), who present a case for organic structures as opposed to mechanistic structures. In popular literature, Peters and Waterman (1982) similarly suggest that in order to facilitate innovation, work environments must be simultaneously tight and loose. Burgleman and Sayles (1986) highlight the dependency of innovation with the development and maintenance of an appropriate context within which innovation can occur. Judge et al. (1997), in presenting findings from a study of R&D units, compare cultures and climates between innovative and less innovative firms. They argue that the key distinguishing factor between innovative and less innovative firms is the ability of management to create a sense of community in the workplace. Highly innovative companies behave as focussed communities whereas less innovative companies behave more like traditional bureaucratic departments. They suggest four managerial practices that influence the making of such goal-directed communities. These include:

- Balanced autonomy.
- Personalised recognition.
- Integrated socio-technical system.
- Continuity of slack.

Balanced autonomy

Autonomy is defined as having control over the means as well as the ends of one's work. This concept appears to be one of central importance. There are two types of autonomy:

- *Strategic autonomy*: the freedom to set one's own agenda
- *Operational autonomy*: the freedom to attack a problem, once it has been set by the organisation, in ways that are determined by the individual self.

Operational autonomy encourages a sense of the individual and promotes entrepreneurial spirit, whereas strategic autonomy is more to do with the level of alignment with organisational goals. It appears that firms that are most innovative emphasise operational autonomy but retain strategic autonomy within the senior management strata. Top management appear to specify ultimate goals to be attained but thereafter provide freedom to allow individuals to be creative in the ways they achieve goals. Pushing strategic autonomy lower down, in the sense of allowing individuals a large degree of freedom to determine their destiny ultimately leads to less innovation because of an absence of guidelines and lack in direction and focus of effort. On the other hand, giving too little operational autonomy also has the effect of creating imbalance. Here the roadmap becomes too rigidly specified, and the heavy control drives out innovative flair, leading eventually to bureaucratic strait-jackets. What works best is a balance between operational and strategic autonomy.

Personalised recognition

Rewarding individuals for their contribution to the organisation is widely used by corporations. Recognition can take many forms but generally falls into one of two categories: rewards can be either extrinsic or intrinsic. Extrinsic rewards are things such as pay increases, bonuses, and shares and stock options. Intrinsic rewards are those that are based on internal feelings of accomplishment by the recipient. For example, being personally thanked by the CEO, or being recognised by the peer group.

Innovative companies appear to rely heavily on personalised intrinsic awards, for individuals as well as groups. Less innovative companies tend to place almost exclusive emphasis on extrinsic awards. It appears that motivating individuals more through their intrinsic desires rather than extrinsic desires leads to greater creative thought and action. Nevertheless, extrinsic rewards have to be present at a base level, in order to ensure that individuals are at least comfortable with their salary. Beyond the base-salary thresholds innovation is primarily driven by levels of self-esteem rather than external monetary rewards. It appears that extrinsic rewards often yield only temporary compliance. Extrinsic rewards promote competitive behaviours that disrupt workplace relationships, inhibit openness and learning, discourage risk taking, and can effectively undermine interest in work itself. When extrinsic rewards are used individuals tend to channel their energies in trying to get the extrinsic reward rather than unleash their creative potential.

Integrated socio-technical system

Highly innovative companies appear to place equal emphasis on the technical side as well as the social side of the organisation. They look to nurture not only technical abilities and expertise but also promote a sense of togetherness. Fostering group cohesiveness requires paying attention to the recruitment process to ensure social 'fit' beyond technical expertise, and also about carefully integrating new individuals through a well designed socialisation programme. Less innovative firms, on the other hand, appear to be more concerned with explicit, aggressive individual goals. Less innovative firms tend to create environments of independence, whereas innovative ones create environments of co-operation.

Continuity of slack

Highly innovative companies set goal expectations that are perceived to be reasonable in that they try not to overload individuals with projects. Too many projects spread effort too thinly, leading individuals to step from the surface of one to the next. These conditions create time pressures that militate strongly against innovativeness.

Slack is the cushion of resources that allows an organisation to adapt to internal and external pressures. Slack has been correlated positively to innovation. Judge et al. (1997) note that it is not just the existence of slack but the existence of slack over time that appears to have a positive impact upon innovation. They find less innovative firms have slack, but these firms experienced significant disruptions or discontinuities of slack in their past or were expecting disruptions in the future. Therefore, innovativeness seems to be linked with both experience and expectations of slack resources. It can be hypothesised that slack, and future expectations of uninterrupted slack, provide scope for the organisation and its members to take risks that they would take under conditions of no slack, or interruptions in slack. Organisationally this would appear to indicate the need for generating a base-line stock of slack in a variety of critical resources (such as time and seed funding for new projects).

ILLUSTRATION

Innovation culture par excellence: the 3M way

3M's success is primarily based on creating a culture of innovation, structures and human resources pool necessary to support and nourish a climate of consistent creativity and innovation.

3M is probably the most cited example of innovation culture. Despite the masses written on the company, its culture embodies a number of what appear to be simple principles.

Importance of flexibility

New ideas and new tactics are embraced, celebrated, developed and tested. If they don't work the plug is quickly pulled, and the company moves on. This flexibility starts at the top and suffuses all organisational levels.

Importance of goals and missions

More than 30 per cent of revenues must be generated by products introduced in the last four years. Such lofty goals are set by many companies but few achieve them like 3M. How? The answer is both simple and complicated. From top management down, 3M hires the best people, and then *respects*, *supports* and *insists* on their efforts to *think*, *learn* and *create* – in short to innovate.

Importance of free time

3M technicians spend 15–50 per cent of their time researching pet projects. Promising concepts are awarded *genesis grants* (These can be £25,000+) to help move an idea to next stage.

Importance of the BIG team: sharing and interaction

Individual creativity is enhanced through collaboration among different disciplines. Salespeople are in continuous dialogue with customers to find out what they need or want (preferably, even before the customer knows it). Then they talk with technicians to initiate the creation of new products. This emphasis on *team* mentality and the *sharing* of ideas is a fundamental tenet of 3M's culture.

Importance of celebration

3M actively celebrate successes, and regales stories of success throughout the organisation. Post-it Note pads Art Fry, and Silver Spence, Steve Okie and the waterproof sandpaper, etc., have become legends to motivate, direct and guide actions.

Importance of challenge and stretch

3M's leadership sets challenges and signal emphasis on innovation. During the 1990s recessionary period, CEO Livio D. DeSimone, instead of cutting staff like other companies, increased the R&D budget, and raised his expectations even higher. The old 25 per cent new products goal became 30 per cent, and the period was shortened by one year. The results: 50 new products were identified and more than half were brought to the market (some in record times!). Example: The Scotch-Brite scrubbing pads, which in two years captured approximately 25 per cent market from competitors!

 ## Conclusion

In attempting to build an enduring company, it is vitally important to understand the key role of the soft side of the organisation in innovation. Companies like IBM have seen their original positions of dominance overturned because of their inability to focus upon innovation, and more importantly to understand the importance of culture and climate in innovation. One of the reasons for this was that their leaders narrowly focussed their total efforts in trying to come up with the next great innovation. Instead their time would have been better spent designing and creating an environment that would be able to create innovations of the future. Companies aspiring towards innovative goals need to learn from the examples of highly successful companies like 3M, and the Body Shop, whose leaders spend their energy and effort in building organisational cultures and climates that perpetually create innovation.

In accepting this viewpoint, the key question in innovation begins to change from the traditional issue of focussing effort on the next great innovation to one that asks whether you are creating an environment that stimulates innovation. Are you simply focussing on your product portfolio or are you focussed on building a culture that cannot be copied? Are you busy inventing a narrow base of products, or are you experimenting with creating *innovativeness*. Without doubt, the most innovative companies of the future will be dominated by those that do not simply focus energies upon product and technical innovation, but those who have managed to build enduring environments of human communities striving towards innovation through the creation of appropriate cultures and climate. This will be the energy of renewal and the drive to a successful future.

In this chapter the importance of innovation culture and climate has been highlighted. As competitive pressures increase, the need to continuously adapt, develop and innovate has become a basic building block for organisational excellence. Failure to innovate eventually leads businesses to stagnate and wither away in the face of a dynamic environment. The chapter emphasised the need to understand the softer factors that lead to innovation excellence.

The chapter highlighted numerous practices that characterise highly innovative organisations. Broadly speaking, innovation requires a company to simultaneously excel along two key dimensions, namely:

1. *Hard innovation practices*: This dimension is concerned with the company putting in place structures for innovation, such as innovation stage-gate methodologies, suggestion schemes, reward schemes, quantitative goals, organisational systems and procedures for interaction, physical infrastructures and resources to enhance co-operation and collaboration.

2. *Soft innovation practices*: This dimension stresses proper and effective management of the hard aspects of innovation. The soft aspects include managing the culture and climate of the organisation to create an innovation orientation and positive behaviours. The soft side of innovation requires careful management through sensitive leadership, who is responsible for setting the agenda for innovation and reinforcing the agenda in the behaviours of its people by signalling these behaviours by symbolic, as well as 'hard', resource allocations.

It is quite difficult to strike the correct balance between soft and hard actions upon which innovation success is built. Too often, firms stress hard aspects of innovation but neglect addressing the vague yet vital soft aspects of innovation. The emphasis and attention toward the hard aspects is given because of the ease of identifying these actions and the physical manifestation of these actions once they have taken place. Unfortunately, implementing the hard elements of practice alone yields only partial benefits, and these tend to plateau after a short period. Long-term and full benefits can only be accrued if the hard aspects are complemented by soft aspects, which provide the underlying behavioural impulse towards innovation. Indeed, it is the soft aspects that ensure that the organisation is innovative in the long term. In the end, success is not a question of either–or but is based on a complement of actions. The identification of climate and culture affecting practices highlights some of the key issues that need to be addressed to create the soft–hard complement of actions to move towards innovation excellence.

QUESTIONS

1. Discuss why culture is so important in developing an innovative organisation.

2. What is the difference between organisational culture and climate?

3. How can you tell a strong culture from a weak culture?

4. Identify the basic characteristics associated with clan, hierarchy, market and adhocracy culture types.

5. Explain the cultural traits model. What insights does this provide about an innovative business culture?

6. How can leaders drive and shape an innovative culture? What must they do, and what must they not do?

7. Why is the individual so important for an innovative organisation? What individual factors and considerations should be taken into account when managing an organisation for innovation?

8. Discuss the design of systems and practices necessary to drive innovation.

9. From your experience, identify five organisational norms. Assess how each affects innovation.

10. Why are communications, actions, and rewards so important in an organisation?

CASE STUDY

Chinese manufacturers bullish on exports

The Huajian Group, a Sino-Taiwan shoe maker, is precisely the type of Chinese exporter that should be on its knees. Huajian exports 95 per cent of its output to the US, focus of the global financial crisis.

'Christmas orders are coming in and probably won't be as high as last year', says Zhang Huarong, Huajian's founding chairman. 'But things are getting better these days. Our profit margin has decreased but orders are up 10 per cent from our worst period [earlier this year].' The company, he adds, has recently increased its workforce by more than 20 per cent – to 22,000 workers from 18,000 – and raised salaries 3 per cent.

It is a similar story across town at Dongguan's Songshan Lake high-tech park, a model business development zone. There, Celestica, a former IBM division, makes teleconferencing equipment and Xbox computer game consoles for Microsoft.

According to company officials, Xbox shipments are down about 15 per cent compared with last year. 'That's why we're putting a lot of emphasis on efficiency', says one manager. Celestica has not made any employees redundant, relying instead on natural attrition.

While Huajian and Celestica may be surviving rather than thriving, their performances are encouraging, considering the wider pain across china's export sector. In Guangdong, which is China's largest export centre, accounting for about a third of national shipments, exports fell 18.3 per cent in the first six months of this year from 2008, to $153.4bn.

This macro performance would seem to validate Beijing's hopes that the financial crisis is helping to speed a flight to quality, benefiting large exporters such as Huajian and Celestica at the expense of smaller, less efficient factories.

'The global financial crisis has made enterprises realise that they need to restructure', said Wang Yang, the Chinese Communist party's most senior representative in Guangdong, 'Factories that have patented products are doing better, for example.'

'Our main focus is not on [gross domestic product] growth but on how to transform the city, especially our industrial structure', added Zhu Xiaodan, party secretary of Guangzhou, the provincial capital. 'Even if we have to sacrifice part of our GDP, we want to pay this price.'

Mr Wang and Mr Zhu's quality-over-quantity mantra is not necessarily the rule. The mayor of Dongguan, for example, is sticking by his city's 10 per cent growth target in spite of having achieved just 0.6 per cent growth over the first half of this year. Growth appears to be even more of an obsession at Guangzhou's premier development zone, where officials calculate and boast of such statistical nonsense as economic output per square metre of land area.

In companies such as Vtron Technologies, zonal planning can point to something more meaningful: high-tech enterprises established by local entrepreneurs. Vtron makes interactive, wall-sized display terminals that would not look amiss on the bridge of the Enterprise in a *Star Trek* film.

Vtron's customers include Azerbaijan's air traffic control centre and Chinese police departments, which combine Vtron's technology with their closed-circuit surveillance systems to zoom in and out of street corners. Annual sales are growing at 10 per cent compared with 20–30 per cent before the crisis.

'Vtron is a hidden champion in a niche market', says Tiger Tang, the company's public affairs director. The government is hoping many more like it will emerge. As Mr Wang, Guangdong's party secretary, puts it: 'The cruel reality of the market is that innovation is essential to survival.'

(*Source*: Based on T. Mitchell, 'Chinese manufacturers bullish on exports', *FT*, 11 August 2009)
© The Financial Times Limited 2009

QUESTIONS

1. From your reading of the case, what different approaches to quality and innovation occur in China?

2. Discuss which of these approaches are most likely to lead to success in (a) China and (b) your own country.

References

Amabile, T.M. (1988), 'A model of creativity and innovation in organisations', in B.M. Straw and L.L. Cummings (eds), *Research in organisational behaviour*, Greenwich: JAIPress, Vol.10.

Anon (2003), 'Winning through incremental innovation', *Chief Executive*, January/February: 10–13.

Barron, F.B. and Harrington, D.M. (1981), 'Creativity, intelligence, and personality', *Annual Review of Psychology* 32: 439–476.

Blau, J. (1996), 'Siemens refocusing R&D on products', *Research Technology Management* 39(1): 4–5.

Buckler, S.A. (1997), 'The spiritual nature of innovation', *Research-Technology Management*, March–April: 43–47.

Burgleman, R.A. and Sayles, L.R. (1986), *Inside corporate innovation: Strategy, structure and managerial skills*, New York: Free Press.

Burns, T. and Stalker, G.M. (1961), *The management of innovation*, London: Tavistock Publications.

Carroll, J.B. (1985), 'Domains of cognitive ability', paper presented at the meeting of American Association for the Advancement of Science, Los Angeles.

Collins, J.C. and Porras, J.I. (1991), 'Organisational vision and visionary organisations', *California Management Review* 34: 30–52.

Denison, D.R. (1984), 'Bringing corporate culture to the bottom-line', *Organisational Dynamics*, Autumn: 4–23.

Denison, D.R. and Mishra, A.K. (1995), 'Toward a theory of organisational culture and effectiveness', *Organisation Science* 6(2): 204–223.

Deshpande, R., Farley, J.U. and Webster, F.E. (1993), 'Corporate culture, customer orientation and innovativeness in Japanese firms: A quadrad analysis', *Journal of Marketing* 57: 23–27.

Fiske, S.T. and Taylor, S.E. (1984), *Social cognition*, Reading, MA: Addison Wesley.

Gioia, D.A. and Manz, G. (1985), 'Linking cognition and behavior: A script processing interpretation of vicarious learning', *Academy of Management Review* 10: 527–539.

Gordon, R. (1985), 'The relationship between corporate culture to industry sector and corporate performance', in R.H. Kilman, M.J. Saxton, R. Serpa and assoc. (eds), *Gaining control of corporate culture*, San Francisco, CA: Jossey-Bass.

Guildford, J.P. (1983), 'Transformation abilities or functions', *Journal of Creative Behaviour* 17: 75–83.

Higgins, J.M. (1995), 'Innovate or evaporate', *The Futurist* 29(5): 42–49.

Judge, W.Q., Fryxell, G.E. and Dooley, R.S. (1997), 'The new task of R&D management: Creating goal directed communities for innovation', *California Management Review* 39(3): 72–84.

Jung, C.G. (1923), *Psychological types*, London: Routledge.

Kotter, J.P. and Heskett, J.L. (1992), *Corporate culture and performance*, New York: Free Press.

Lawerence, P.R. and Lorsch, J. (1967), *Organisation and environment: Managing differentiation and integration*, Boston, MA: Harvard University Press.

Ledford, G.E., Wendnhof, J.R. and Strahley, J.T. (1994), 'Realising a corporate philosophy', *Organisational Dynamics*, Autumn: 5–19.

Locander, W.B. (2005), 'Staying with the flock', *Marketing Management* 14(2): 23–32.

O' Rielly, C.O. (1989), 'Corporations, culture and commitment: Motivation and social control in large organisations', *California Management Review*, Summer: 9–25.

Mills, P. and Delbecq, A. (1996), 'Managerial practices that enhance innovation', *Organisational Dynamics*, Summer: 24–34.

Mitchell, T. (2009), 'Chinese manufacturers bullish on exports', *Financial Times*, 11 August.

Peters, T. and Waterman, R. (1982), *In search of excellence: Lessons from America's best run companies*, New York: Warner Books.

Pfeffer, J. (1981), 'Management as symbolic action: The creation and maintenance of organisational paradigms', in L.L. Cummings and B.M. Straw (eds), *Research in organisational behaviour*, Vol.3. Greenwich: JAI Press.

Quinn, R.E. and Rohrbaugh, R. (1983), 'A spatial model of effectiveness criteria: Toward a competing values approach to organisational analysis', *Management Science* 29(3): 363–377.

Schein, E.H. (1985), *Organisational culture and leadership*, San Francisco, CA: Jossey Bass.

Shalley, C.E. and Oldham, G.R. (1985), 'Effects of goal difficulty and expected evaluation on intrinsic motivation: A laboratory study', *Academy of Management Journal* 28: 628–640.

Schneider, B., Gunnarson, S.K. and Niles-Jolly, K. (1996a), 'Creating the climate and culture of success', *Organisational Dynamics* 23(1): 17–29.

Schneider, B., Brief, A.P. and Guzzo, R.A. (1996b), 'Creating a climate and culture for sustainable change', *Organisational Dynamics*, Spring: 7–19.

Woodman, R.W. and Schoenfeldt, L.F. (1990), 'An interactionist model of creative behaviour', *Journal of Creative Behaviour* 24: 279–290.

10 Innovation in a global world

Learning outcomes

When you have completed this chapter, you should be able to:

- Appreciate the drivers of industry globalisation and innovation.

- Communicate the underlying reasons for the evolutionary trend towards transnational configuration for innovation.

- Understand the advantages and limitations of different structural configurations for global innovation.

- Appreciate the factors that are required to implement and work the transnational form for innovation.

- Describe the role of subsidiaries in the global roll-out of an innovation.

- Appreciate the issues involved in the R&D location decision.

- Recognise the added challenges in managing people and teams in an international environment.

- Describe the roles and responsibilities of managers in global innovation projects.

Drivers of globalisation

By almost every indicator available (international trade, FDI, technology flow) globalisation is becoming pervasive. Proponents of the global world view (often labelled globalists) note a number of technological, social, political and economic trends that are driving towards a commonality of features across the world (Ohmae, 2000; Yip, 1992). Globalisation involves:

- A convergence of tastes and product preferences that allows development and offers a standard product or service worldwide.
- The process of integrating purchasing, manufacturing and marketing on a global scale to achieve economies of scale.
- Organisations with global operations, global cultures and global mindsets.
- Markets and industries dominated by a few large players.

The process of industry globalisation is influenced by a number of drivers, which can be grouped into market, cost, economic and governmental, and competitive (Yip, 1989). The trends taking place within the industry drivers determine the globalisation potential of an industry and the appropriate strategic action for firms to take. In other words, the industry drivers influence the shape of organisational strategy and structure.

Market drivers

Globalisation depends on consumer behaviour, and the nature and structure of channels to reach consumers. Market factors driving industry globalisation are:

- *Homogeneous customer needs*: Customers in different countries who desire the same type of product or service provide an opportunity for firms to standardise their product(s). It may be that only parts of the product can be standardised, and therefore building an understanding of which part needs to be standardised and which needs to be customised is important for success.
- *Global customers*: Customers who source and buy globally facilitate the push to a uniform global offering. This is often the case in the domain of industrial markets, where centralised and co-ordinated buying helps to force down purchase prices. However, with the advent of new technologies global purchasing is fast becoming a widespread phenomenon, even in the consumer community.
- *Global channels*: The existence of channels of distribution that facilitate getting goods to customers scattered worldwide plays a role in driving forward globalisation. For instance, a trip to the local food store clearly demonstrates the relevance of this capability in the food and retail industry.
- *Transferable marketing*: Certain products and product categories are highly amenable to uniform marketing. For example, a strong brand with unique brand values often requires little local adaptation.

Cost drivers

The economics of business depend heavily on cost drivers. Important cost drivers for globalisation are:

- *Economies of scale and scope*: It may be that a single country is not large enough to provide significant economies of scale or a new level of scale-effect can be derived by access to a larger market (i.e. global economies of scale).

- *Learning and experience*: Beyond economies of scale it may be possible that learning and experience effects continue to take place, thus necessitating access to a larger market.

- *Sourcing efficiency*: Global purchasing can provide the purchaser bargaining and negotiating power, making it possible to dictate conditions of purchase.

- *Favourable logistics*: If products can be transported with ease and cost effectiveness, they fuel the global trend. For instance, before freeze technology was available it was not possible to transport fresh flowers across the globe. With innovations in wrapping technologies, freshness can be maintained in otherwise perishable commodities. This makes global transfer easier. The viability of this proposition depends on whether the value of the good relative to transportation costs is positive.

- *Technology development costs*: In some industries the costs of innovation are so high that recouping investment requires a global market. The airline and auto sector are good illustrations of this, where the development costs can be monumental.

Governmental and economic drivers

Government policies can directly and indirectly influence organisational strategy levers pushing for a globalised approach. Key amongst these are:

- *Trade policies*: Policies that promote world trade encourage use of a global strategy. Protectionist policies constrain company actions and ability to internationalise their operations fully.

- *Integration of world capital markets*: Transactions on a global market require efficient and integrated financial market(s).

- *Globally binding rules of law*: Safe business transactions occur if rules can be globally applied and upheld.

- *Compatible technical standards*: Differing product standards imposed by governments make it difficult to use a standard product.

Competitive drivers

What happens in the competitive marketplace is not totally under the control of a firm. Nevertheless, as far as possible firms do try to influence and drive competitive change in their favour. Firms can precipitate globalisation directly by the actions that they take. Competitive drivers are:

- *Globalised competitors*: When competitors adopt globalised approaches, often it is necessary for others to match or pre-empt their move by following a similar route.

- *Interdependence of countries*: Companies taking actions in one country usually find they are being closely monitored by customers and competitors alike in other countries. Introduction of a new model in one country may fuel market demand in others, which needs to be filled quickly before local competitors jump in.

While globalisation may fast be becoming a fact of life, in the sense we are able to discern its trends and external drivers, the nature of its impact is hotly debated. Some critics reject the globalist convergence thesis (e.g. Hirst and Thompson, 1999), arguing that there is little empirical evidence to support the assertion that there is more globalisation now than predecessor epochs and economic systems. Other commentators adopt a more benign position. They accept that the forces of change are transforming the world map, but the nature of this transformation is much more complex than the convergence thesis of the globalists (e.g. Giddens, 1999). According to this group of tranformationalists, the direction and outcome of the forces of global change is uncertain, and is likely to result in oppositional and contradictory development. There will be winners and losers in the new globalised world order, and this world order will be much more fragmented and integrated or connected at the same time. The old dualities of the North and the South, the First World and the Third World are being replaced by complex interconnected stratifications ruled by an emerging elite, with the periphery occupied by the marginalised and voiceless fringes. Others, whilst not questioning the force of globalisation, question the need for standardised global strategies and products that feature centrally in the arguments of globalisation proponents. For instance, Douglas and Wind (1987) argue that there are many barriers to standardisation of products and strategies, and greater returns may be achieved by adapting products, production and marketing strategies to the needs of specific markets. Moreover, only some markets are clearly becoming global, many others are not.

The global dynamic contains tremendous implications not just on the world economy but also for business practice and organisation. Multi-national companies (a general term used here as an umbrella term to cover a variety of organisational forms which operate in more than once country) account for a growing proportion of the world's GNP. The top

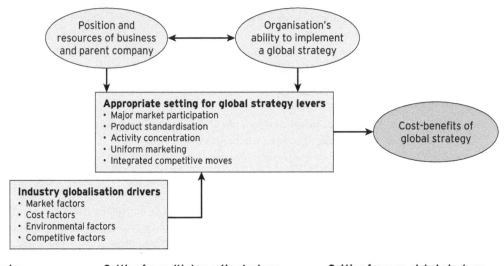

Dimension	Setting for multi-domestic strategy		Setting for pure global strategy
Market participation	No particular pattern	←→	Significant share in major markets
Product offering	Fully customised in each country	←→	Fully standardised worldwide
Location and value-added activities	All activities in each country	←→	Concentrated – one activity in each (different) country
Marketing approach	Local	←→	Uniform worldwide
Competitive moves	Stand-alone by country	←→	Integrated across countries

FIGURE 10.1 Forces of global strategy
Source: Adapted from Yip, 1989

450 companies accounted for more than 80 per cent of their total investment from activities outside their home countries, and more than a quarter of the world's GNP, as far back as 1996 (Bartlett and Ghoshal, 2000).

In general, there is a growing body of evidence indicating that many markets are becoming increasingly international or global in their nature. Interestingly, simultaneous to the development of global markets is the emergence of more sophisticated, more demanding consumers desiring highly differentiated and customised products and services rather than standardised ones. This means that organisational responses must be flexible and responsive rather than rigidly standardised. Flexibility of strategy and management is central to meeting the polar demands of local responsiveness and economies from standardisation. This led to the development of notions such as *total global strategy* and *transnational strategy*. Deciding on the strategy for global operation requires making choices along a number of strategic dimensions (see Figure 10.1). Yip (1989) refers to these dimensions as strategy levers, and they necessitate structural and strategic adaptation. Companies use these strategy levers to create firm-specific marketplace and competitive benefits. These can be achieved through cost reduction, enhanced customer preference, improved quality, or simply positions to attack competitors.

ILLUSTRATION

China stretches its internationalisation muscle

The automobile industry has been a major sector supporting China's industrialisation and modernisation efforts for a number of years. In the 1980s, the central government decided to open China's auto market to international companies. Aware that its domestic manufacturers would not be able to compete against the more sophisticated and experienced foreign rivals, the government only allowed foreign automakers to enter the Chinese market through joint ventures, usually forming 50-50 partnerships between themselves and domestic, state-run firms. The Chinese hoped that these arrangements would allow their domestic car manufacturers to tap the technological and management expertise of their foreign partners. In exchange, the foreign automakers would gain access to the vast Chinese market.

In 1983, American Motors Corporation (AMC) signed a joint venture agreement with China's Beijing Automotive Works, the first such major manufacturing deal reached by a western industrial company in China. Since this time, a number of partnerships have grown between the Chinese and foreign automakers to foster technological cooperation. Some of the players here include Volkswagen, General Motors (GM), Toyota, Honda, Nissan, Mazda, Hyundai and Kia.

GM is the US automotive manufacturer which has made the biggest investment and achieved the most success in the Chinese auto market. In 2009, GM had nine joint ventures in China, along with a wholly owned parts distribution centre. GM now employs more than 32,000 employees in China, and in July 2009 it announced that it was relocating its international operations from Detroit to Shanghai. GM commands 11 per cent of the market, and has sold 1.46 million vehicles into this market during the first 10 months of 2009, an increase of over 60 per cent compared to the first 10 months of 2008.

From a Chinese perspective, the results have been equally impressive. In recent years, China has become the world's fastest growing automotive producer. Annual vehicle output has increased from less than 2 million vehicles in the late 1990s to 9.5 million in 2008. In terms of production volume, China has now surpassed Korea, France, Germany and the United States, trailing only Japan. China is

→

also well ahead of the other developing countries that are considered potential automotive producers. In the so-called BRIC countries (Brazil, Russia, India and China), the net combined growth of auto producers of three of the four BRIC countries was only slightly over a quarter of the total volume growth in China (over the period 2000-2008). China's automobile industry has continued to expand despite the recent global economic downturn - from January to October (2009), 10.89 million vehicles were sold in China.

In the two-and-a-half decades since these joint ventures were introduced, the perception of the domestic Chinese automakers is that their foreign partners have benefited more from the relationships than they have. The domestic firms have had difficulty in creating their own designs and meeting world standards in terms of product quality, safety and environmental requirements. As a result, the domestic cars have generally been built on platforms from global automakers, or developed as a result of reverse engineering of international models.

To overcome these hurdles, the Chinese are now reversing the trend of inward Foreign Directed Investment (FDI) by allowing domestic Chinese automakers to acquire foreign brands. The first attempt of this kind was the purchase of the MG Rover Group by SAIC (Shanghai Automotive Industry Corporation) in 2005. As a result, SAIC now have access to the technologies and designs which will allow them to enter international markets, and leverage known international brands. In September 2008, the former MG Rover Group plant in Longbridge (England), employing around 380 workers, began assembling MG Roadster kits imported from China.

 ## Evolution of business in the global environment

Traditional explanations for international operations are based on Raymond Vernon's classical product life cycle theory, in which the starting point of internationalisation is typically an innovation in the home country (Vernon, 1966). In the second stage the home market becomes saturated, and the innovating firm looks to develop exports in similar markets as a supplement. The third stage is characterised by product standardisation and the arrival of a large number of competitors leading to a focus on price and cost competitiveness. This triggers companies to seek low-wage developing countries as potential places to locate production. These countries are also potential markets since pockets of demand begin to emerge in these regions. In the final stage, the developing nations may become net exporters to the developed regions. Whilst numerous shortcomings of this theory can be easily discerned, it constitutes an instructive frame of reference for the motivation to internationalise corporate operations. Taken together these motivations and drivers have led to a pattern of evolutionary organisational development: from being domestic to international, then to multi-national or global, and ultimately to transnational. The evolutionary path is depicted in Figure 10.2.

The link between strategy and structure has been long established. Alfred Chandler (1962) noted that change in a firm's product-market strategy should be accompanied by shift in organisational structure to support the implementation of its strategy. As a company grows it becomes necessary to introduce structures capable of achieving co-ordination and integration of geographically disperse operations (Stopford and Wells, 1972). The pattern of structural change is dependent on the diversity of the company's foreign product range and the relative amount of foreign sales (see Figure 10.3). When only a limited range of the company (innovations) products are sold abroad and constitute only a small proportion of total

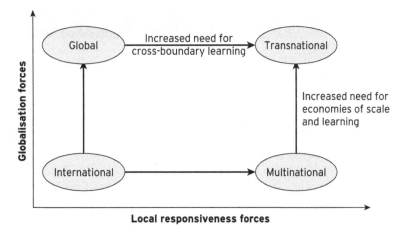

FIGURE 10.2 Evolutionary organisational response to global drivers of change

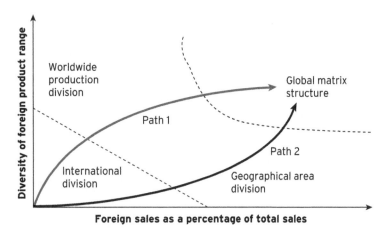

FIGURE 10.3 Stopford and Wells model of stages of international structural development
Source: Stopford and Wells, 1972

sales, companies can quite easily cope by setting up an international division. Going beyond a certain point on either dimension leads to other structural formats becoming more appropriate. If product diversity is low and geographic markets become larger and account for significant sales, setting up geographic area divisions is a highly feasible solution. On the other hand, product range increases beyond a certain point require the setting up of a worldwide product division to cope with the increasing product complexity. Development along either path eventually culminates in a global matrix structure, which is able to provide benefits of local responsiveness and product-based economies through appointment of a manager responsible for each product and a manager for each area. While in theory this proposition works well, in practice it leads to numerous intractable problems. Problems in the practice of global matrix structure emanate primarily from an unclear reporting hierarchy resulting from an overlap of responsibilities, conflicting objectives and power struggles for decision-making dominance, and compromise decisions that serve neither party well.

Configurations and structure for global innovation

Multi-national firms manage their innovation by organising and controlling their operations through different organisational formats. Formal organisational structures, as captured in an organogram (diagram of the organisational hierarchy), are powerful instruments of control but are poor at capturing the multi-dimensional flows involved in multi-national management of innovation. Clearer depiction of the multiple exchanges and control can be observed from organisational configurations. Boutellier et al. (1999) propose five organisational configurations for the management of R&D. The configurations are classified along two dimensions of difference: dispersion of internal competencies, and the degree of co-operation between R&D sites. The five configurations for innovation are: ethnocentric, geocentric, polycentric, R&D hub, and integrated R&D network.

Ethnocentric centralised R&D

The ethnocentric centralised R&D organisation is one in which R&D activity is concentrated in the home nation. The company adopts the stance that the home country centre is superior in technology and knowledge compared to its subsidiaries in other countries. The centre is the think tank where new ideas are thought up, progressed and developed. These innovations are eventually rolled out as new products or services to be manufactured in different locations and subsequently distributed worldwide. The core knowledge base is protected within the home environment, see Figure 10.4.

Japanese companies, internationalising in the 1970s typically grew as centralised hubs because their strategies depended on tight centralised control of activities to secure cost advantages. Additionally, this configuration protects against unplanned technology transfer. The knowledge assets of the company, key personnel and activities are co-located. Innovation is managed through a strong shared identity, vision, and systems of management and operation.

Due to its inward focus, the ethnocentric form suffers from a lack of sensitivity to emerging pockets of international demand and trends, and is often plagued by the not-invented-here

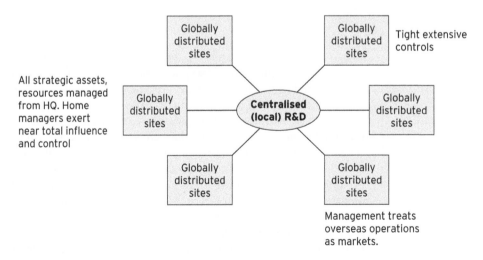

FIGURE 10.4 Ethnocentric centralised R&D

(NIH) syndrome. Despite the obvious shortcoming, this configuration can be highly effective for innovation. For example, Microsoft used it to build its breathtaking success. Microsoft was, however, able to do so because it enjoyed an abundance of local talent and had a product that was globally accepted. This allowed Microsoft to leverage its centralised software development. Another company that has used this configuration to good effect is Toyota. The ethnocentric configuration is commonly deployed by companies entering newly emerging markets. For example, VW's entry into China.

ILLUSTRATION

R&D at Samsung

By 2004 Samsung Electronics was spending more on research and development than any other Asian company outside Japan. Its R&D investment rose to $4.6bn (£2.5bn, 8.3 per cent of sales) in 2004 from $1.6bn (5.8 per cent of sales) in 2000. The South Korean giant recruited 3000 scientists and engineers a year to its 25,000-strong R&D workforce.

Although Samsung started carrying out R&D abroad from around 2000, Kim Chuljin, head of corporate technology strategy, said 93 per cent of the work was carried out in six R&D centres in Korea. The heart of Samsung's corporate research effort remains in Suwon, 50km south of Seoul, where the company was founded in 1969 to make black-and-white televisions.

A distinctive feature of Samsung's approach was its Value Improvement Programme, based in Suwon. Individual business units submitted provisional details of their significant product and process innovations to the VIP Centre, where each one would undergo intensive scrutiny by a team of scientists, engineers and other specialists seconded to the project from across the company (or in some cases hired as sub-contractors).

A team normally had between 15 and 80 members, who worked together on a project for a few months. The centre handled about 40 projects a year.

'Team members were freed from their normal duties and worked full-time on the project', said Jung Kyunghan, VIP senior manager. The work could be all-consuming, so the top floor of the centre was a dormitory.

The team looked at every aspect of a proposed innovation, trying to cut production costs and improve performance. Cost savings are usually the easiest way to measure success, said Mr Jung. Some cost reductions achieved included 31 per cent for Samsung's plasma-display televisions and 35 per cent for the SPH-A680 mobile phone. 'Altogether the centre saved $2.5bn in 2004 and with further planned savings of $3.5bn for the following year', he said.

(*Source*: Based on C. Cookson, 'The invention house in the East – R&D in Asia', *Financial Times*, 17 June 2005, p. 14)

Geocentric centralised R&D (centralised hub)

As the company becomes more dependent on foreign sales, sensitivity to local markets rises in importance. Under these circumstances the geocentric format becomes more appropriate. The geocentric model attempts to overcome some of the problems of home-country focus. It attempts this by recruiting a more multi-cultural, multi-national workforce, and engages in listening activities in external markets whilst trying to maintain efficiency advantages of a

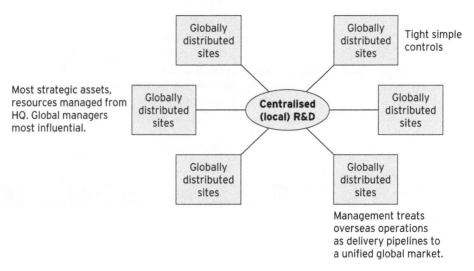

FIGURE 10.5 Geocentric model for R&D

centralised innovation and knowledge base. Often, such companies send personnel abroad to collaborate with local manufacturers, suppliers and lead customers.

By the mid-1990s, Nissan had adopted this approach in the development of the Primera for the European market. Nissan's R&D centre formed a core team who were sent out to Europe. The core team was supported by hundreds of engineers in Japan, all of whom had experience of European culture through exchange visits to European outposts. Extensive scanning of the European market was conducted coupled with market research and workshops with lead users to feed back local requirements.

The geocentric format (see Figure 10.5) is the first tentative step towards internationalising R&D, whilst trying to maintain advantages of high degree of central control.

Polycentric decentralised R&D (decentralised federation)

For those companies for whom local responsiveness is of primary importance the polycentric decentralised R&D approach is most appropriate. European companies, especially those internationalising during the 1920s and 1930s, faced with limited transport, communications and an era of protectionism, typically adopted a decentralised federation approach. This approach (shown in Figure 10.6) is still widely prevalent in European multi-national companies.

Within this configuration the centre provides capital investment to set up subsidiaries, which then operate as independent fully integrated business units with considerable management and strategic autonomy. R&D innovation activity takes place in foreign subsidiaries, responding directly to local product tastes. The subsidiary firm fully 'delivers' on all components of the innovation: from research, development, manufacture to marketing. There is an absence of a central co-ordinator of R&D, and all units are allowed to develop and engage in their own research and development strategies. There is little exchange of knowledge between the various units. If exchange does occur it tends to be at late stages of projects. Often there is duplication of effort and the corporate parent is typically late in receiving information about projects. Examples of companies utilising this format are Shell, Philips in the 1980s, and Sulzer.

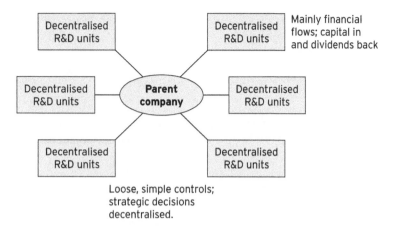

FIGURE 10.6 Polycentric decentralised R&D

R&D hub model (co-ordinated federation)

This form is characterised by a strong central R&D home base supported by R&D outposts (see Figure 10.7). Tight central control and co-ordination of R&D is provided from the centre. The centre acts as the *lead* in most innovations and technical developments. Foreign R&D units are directed to specific technological domains defined by the centre, or simply used as listening outposts and/or technical support units to foreign operations. In this configuration, foreign subsidiaries are able to adapt products and strategies to account for local market tastes but they depend on the parent for new products, processes and ideas. This format requires considerably more co-ordination and control than the ethnocentric, geo-centric or polycentric forms. The subsidiary units have to possess critical mass in R&D to engage fruitfully in the specified field of research, yet not grow so large as to create redun-dancy and replication. The centre has to create excellent communication links and establish itself as the technology leader to sustain the balance of power and ideas flow. Examples of

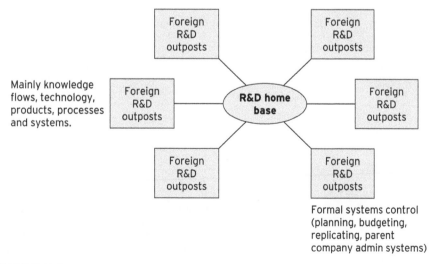

FIGURE 10.7 R&D hub model

companies that have deployed this format are Kao, Matshushita, NEC, Sharp, Bosch, Zeneca and Daimler Benz.

The integrated R&D network

This form is characterised by dispersed competencies that are highly interconnected (see Figure 10.8). Domestic R&D is no longer the centre of control of innovation, but is one of many units that are interconnected. Each unit within the network specialises and leads in a particular product, technology or function. This makes it the *lead centre* in developing and sustaining competence in that specified role. Many variations of this format can be found. For instance, a unit may be accorded a world product mandate, in which case it leads on the entire value generation of that product, not just for its product-related R&D. Thus, it becomes responsible for co-ordinating all key activities: manufacturing, introduction and marketing of the product, and its subsequent generations. A unit may, on the other hand, be responsible for only leading research in a specific product category, and then have its research translated into manufactured products in other units that possess a higher capability to deliver global efficiency in production. Companies successfully using this approach are ABB, IBM, Roche and Canon.

Whilst there are advantages to the integrated network, a number of co-ordinative and structural problems can surface. In integrated networks, the practice of creating a product in one unit and exploiting it in another can raise problems of 'taxation'. R&D is investment intensive, but the fruits of a unit's R&D labour can be exploited by others in the network. By applying the principle of treating each unit as a legally independent unit accruing its own profit but not having to incur R&D expenditure leaves the 'originator' to incur a loss. To overcome this, transfer prices have to be introduced. If these transactions do not follow open market conditions or do not correctly reflect costs then a tax correction is needed. In other words, the decision on R&D location may be influenced by tax considerations by the controller, over and above technology or market advantages. The network can overcome this by setting up a central technology to which all R&D units sell their technology, and the central company makes its revenues from selling technical assistance to manufacturing arms. For

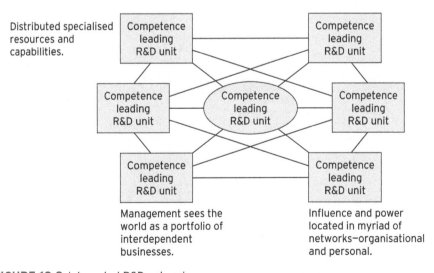

FIGURE 10.8 Integrated R&D network

example, Nestlé manages its research centres and research units (which together constitute 50-plus operations across 10 countries, with annual R&D budget exceeding half a billion Swiss Francs) through Nestec. Nestec, which co-ordinates all worldwide activities and exploits synergies, is managed by fewer than 20 people. Nestec is the legal owner of all Nestlé technologies and is responsible for co-ordinating the effort of receiving knowledge from the research centres, which specialise in specific technologies, and disseminating it globally to the 300 or so dispersed production units through licensed contract.

Different global pressures are driving the shift towards different configurations, but Boutellier et al. (1999) note that the move ultimately is toward the integrated R&D network. Pressures from the forces of globalisation necessitate that companies simultaneously optimise efficiency and local responsiveness, and learn. The need to balance what appears to be pushing in different directions, forces evolution to a transnational form. The transnational form attempts to balance product, function and area (geography). In the global environment the issue is not to be globally integrated or locally responsive, but how to be both at the same time. According to Boutellier et al. (1999), the trend towards integrated R&D occurs because it delivers, at lowest total cost, a balance of local responsiveness and global efficiency (see Figure 10.9).

Managers operating in global environments must therefore be able to reconcile interdependence of functions with different geographies and co-ordinate the overall activities to build and sustain competitive advantage. This requires a multi-dimensional approach, one that allows:

- Tasks to be systematically differentiated by allowing different businesses, functions and areas to be treated differently, and organised differently.

- Relationships between the different parts of the business to be based on interdependence rather than independence.

- Co-ordination of differentiated and interdependent oganisational sub-units through a strong shared vision and development of integrative mechanisms.

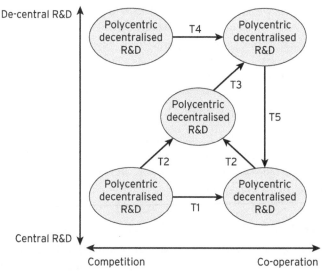

Trend 1. External orientation – when companies become aware of the need to be more sensitive to exports and foreign markets.

Trend 2. Establishing listening posts – when companies want to be aware of technological developments across the world.

Trend 3. Empowerment of foreign R&D – when companies want to foster and utilise local creativity and innovation.

Trend 4. Integration of decentralised R&D sites. When companies want to ensure that they leverage and make full use of their R&D potential.

Trend 5. Re-centralisation. When the cost pressures force companies to focus and exploit scale effect more fully, by concentrating on a few leading research centres and re-centralising decisions to a few key competence centres.

FIGURE 10.9 Evolutionary trend to integrated R&D form
Source: Adapted from Boutellier et al., 1999

The multi-dimensional approach leads to the development of an integrated network, which represents the transnational form. The integrated network possesses three key elements:

- *Multi-dimensional perspectives*: The diverse and complex nature of the environment requires a heightened sensitivity and response capacity. This requires (1) developing capabilities in subsidiaries to respond to local needs; (2) developing competitive capability to co-ordinate at a global level and respond to the global strategies of competitors; (3) possessing competitive capability to create and leverage new competencies through innovation and facilitate their transfer amongst other units.

- *Distributed and interdependent capabilities*: The transnational configuration tries to avoid the problems of other international forms. The transnational approach is to allow different parts to develop expertise that can be leveraged across all units. For instance, global scale can be achieved by making a local plant into the global 'production' centre for all of the company's units. For example, a particular R&D centre can be made the centre of excellence for the whole of the business, and a particular marketing group be the lead for a specified product category across all the operations of the business. In other words, the company becomes an integrated network of distributed, yet interdependent, capabilities working to the benefit of the whole of the organisation.

- *Flexible integrative processes*: To weave the interdependent network of capabilities with multiple perspectives requires processes that facilitate integration. This is done through three interconnected management processes:

  - *Centralisation*, which is sensitive to the groups within the organisation but allows senior management to intervene in certain decisions to ensure overall co-ordination.

  - *Formalisation*, which allows different parts of the organisation to play a role in key decisions.

  - *Socialisation*, norms and procedures that provide an overall direction and frame of reference for delegated decision making to take place.

Developing the capability to innovate, learn and leverage is not an easy task for most multi-national companies. Companies historically have fallen into either the *centre for global innovation* process model (the ethnocentric, geocentric and R&D hub configurations) in which innovation is located in the home country, or at the other end the *local for local innovation* model (the polycentric decentralised configuration) in which the subsidiary innovates for the local market. Matshushita's worldwide strategy for VCR and NEC's global strategy exemplifies the centre for global innovation approach, whereas Unilever's approach until recent years exemplifies the local-for-local innovation approach, in which products are developed and tailored to the specific needs of the market. For example, Unilever's soap for the Indian market was customised to make it suitable for washing in streams. In between these two extremes is the integrated network, which captures new ways of developing and diffusing knowledge and innovation. The integrated approach constitutes transnational innovation processes (Bartlett and Ghoshal, 2000); and, these processes fall into two broad categories: locally leveraged and globally linked innovation processes.

Locally leveraged innovation processes

This ensures that the special resources and competencies are available not only for the local subsidiary but are spread and used throughout the multi-national companies' worldwide operations. This process ensures that the outcomes of local subsidiary's innovation are made widely available and leveraged to maximum effect.

Globally linked innovation processes

This process pools together the resources and talents of the many different multi-national companies' units to jointly engage and manage the innovation activity. This process attempts to combine complementary skills in the innovation effort. This type of approach was used by P&G in the development of the detergent Vizir; market intelligence from one unit was coupled with the development capability of another and marketing prowess of another for a highly successful and seamless product launch.

These two transnational processes are becoming widespread but do not entirely replace the traditional *local for local* and *centre for global* processes but rather supplement them to a greater or lesser extent. As the organisation becomes more transnational and networked, the transnational innovation processes become the dominant modes of operation. To make these innovation processes work requires surmounting a number of challenges. Actions in making these processes effective are discussed next.

Making central innovations effective

To make central innovations effective, three factors need attention:

- *Gain the input of subsidiaries into centralised activities*: The linkages (processes and people) with the centre must be multiple and multi-faceted. Individuals, occupying different hierarchical positions, from the centre can be re-located into the subsidiary. There they occupy dual roles and responsibilities. They work for the subsidiary but still sit on the parent company's committees. Japanese companies are masters of establishing and maintaining such interlinkages.

- *Respond to local–national needs*: While pushing for centralised control it is necessary to ensure that local market needs are not ignored. Japanese companies that successfully operate the centre-to-global approach are able to do so because they take pains not to blunt local sensitivity. They do so by creating a split research budget between technology-led and market-led research projects. Technology-led projects are those which are directed toward long-term strategic goals of the company, and are useful across a number of the multi-national companies' units. Market-led projects are geared to the local market needs of specific divisions. Half of the total budget is allocated to central research. The remaining half is for short-term market-led projects. The market-led budget is allocated by competition and negotiation. Groups from the central research laboratories indicate the research they wish to undertake, and the product divisions express their interest by negotiating which projects they would sponsor. Through a process of negotiation, research expertise is matched to product division needs. Competition for market projects is intense, and ensures that market orientation is maintained.

- *Manage responsibility-personnel flow*: Personnel rotation should be used to ensure cross-functional integration. Rotation is systematically deployed by Japanese companies: development scientists are moved into production, or marketing, and vice versa. Often enough, the rotated individual takes his/her project with them but has to adopt a new functional role. This enhances the specific effects of the transfer, since learning is transferred from the individual to other team members, while he/she is also learning new skills from them.

Making local innovation efficient

To capitalise on local innovation, a number of key mechanisms and processes are necessary.

- *Empowering local management*: Managers and individuals in the subsidiary need to be provided with adequate space to experiment and seek solutions to their local problems. The centre, thus, must release resources as well as authority.

- *Link local managers to corporate decision-making processes*: Local-to-local innovation requires resources and autonomy but this should not be done in a wasteful manner from the parent company's point of view. To ensure a central perspective is embedded into local management, it is necessary to involve local managers in central decision making. In this way, not only can local managers inform the centre of their priorities but they reciprocally take to their subsidiaries the priorities and values of the parent.

- *Force tight inter-functional integration*: Just as cross-functional integrative mechanisms are required to make centre to global innovation efficient, they are needed for efficient local-to-local innovations. Rotation and cross-functional teams at different levels of the organisation are required.

Innovation subsidiary location and management

Decisions over home and subsidiary configurations and strategies are based on two principal questions (Kogut, 1985):

- In which functional activities should the firm focus its efforts? What should be the firm's focus for R&D and innovation?

- Where should each part of the value chain be conducted? Where should the R&D take place?

The answer to the first question depends on the individual firm's specific competitive advantage, and the answer to the second on the firm's comparative advantage. Competitive advantage defines firm-specific advantages, or areas in which the firm possesses distinctive skills and competences that it can employ against competitors (Hamel and Prahalad, 1990; Porter, 1980). Firm-specific advantages are defined by specific product-market decisions that the firm takes. The decisions include the competitive premise (differentiation or cost), the focus of attention (value chain activity) and market (customer segment and market strategies). Comparative advantage defines location-specific advantages, and influences where to source and base operations (this theory is based on Ricardo, 1817). The two forms of advantages, and hence the answers to the questions, interact with each other. Firms locating in certain geographic areas may acquire competitive advantage by exploiting their comparative advantage to better effect than their competitors.

The international environment differs from domestic environments primarily along two dimensions: firstly, institutional and cultural differences; and secondly, factor costs. In international settings, cultural and institutional barriers can easily change the balance of firm-specific advantages. Marketing programmes may need to be redesigned, and work practices re-engineered to accommodate local proclivities of practice and institution. Second, factor costs (labour, source material, and capital costs) differ significantly from one country to the next, and can have important effects on the firm's parity with competitors. Countries differ in their factor endowments, and because of this they may possess comparative advantage in a specific factor for a specific type of value chain activity that the firm needs. For example, R&D requires highly trained human capital, and only those countries that possess this factor in abundance are able to serve the firm's needs competitively. In the case of manufacturing, on the other hand, countries with comparative advantage may either possess process

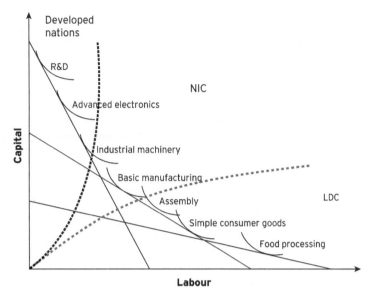

FIGURE 10.10 Value added chain of comparative advantage
Source: Kogut, 1985

technologies that are key to the manufacturing process (i.e. have capital and process advantage), or are able to offer cheaper labour (i.e. possess labour-intensity advantage).

Utilising classical economics principles, Kogut (1985) derives a chain of comparative advantage (see Figure 10.10). On the basis of isoquant boundaries of comparative advantage, Kogut shows that developed countries, newly industrialising countries and less developed countries occupy different positions of comparative advantage across different industry sectors and value chain activities. Developed nations maintain advantage for R&D activity, advanced electronics and industrial machinery, while newly industrialising countries (NICs) are best placed in basic manufacturing, assembly and simple consumer goods, and less developed countries (LDCs) are better placed for highly labour-intensive activities.

Two key factors can affect the neat ordering of the chain of comparative advantage: (1) costs of transportation and tariffs, which can create strong barriers between nations and allow domestic firms to survive despite being at a disadvantage; and (2) firm-specific competitive advantages (especially economies of scale, scope and learning). For instance, economies of scale may outweigh disadvantage in factor costs despite a poor location. Even from this basic discussion, it is clear that which subsidiary of the company should be involved in R&D and where this should be located is quite a tricky decision requiring consideration of the intermeshed issues of comparative and competitive advantage.

Roles of subsidiaries in innovation management and roll-out

Once the decision about R&D location has been taken, the task of managing innovation in a multi-national company's operation remains. This, however, is neither simple nor straightforward. With national units operating as complex, self-sufficient and interdependent units, trying to balance multiple axes of pressure requires re-assessment of the simple HQ–subsidiary relationship. Subsidiaries, in the more complex configuration demanded by the global marketplace, take on a range of responsibilities and roles. Bartlett and Ghoshal (2000)

Moving up the economic curve!

When people talk about the dramatic rise of science and technology in Asia, they normally have electronics and information technology in mind. They think, for example, of Bangalore's emergence as a great software engineering centre, Samsung's growth into a corporate powerhouse in consumer electronics, Lenovo's takeover of IBM's personal computer business and Taiwan's domination of global semiconductor manufacturing.

Most of the world's electronic products are already made in Asia, and the region is moving rapidly into their design and development. Fundamental research and innovation still tend to be the province of US and European companies and universities, but Asia plays a hidden role even here: many of the best IT researchers in the West - especially in the US - are Asian expatriates.

Paul Horn, who runs IBM Research, the world's most prolific IT research organisation, says about 30 per cent of IBM scientists and engineers working in the US come from Asia, mainly from India and China. A similar proportion of Silicon Valley entrepreneurs are Asian. Most expect to stay in the West, but enough return home to provide vital scientific and managerial leadership for IT companies and research labs in Asia. This is a useful conduit for technical interchanges between their original and adopted countries.

South Korea has gone further than any other Asian country in generating big, integrated electronics and IT companies - Samsung and LG - in the mould of the Japanese giants such as Sony, Toshiba and Matsushita. The inspiration for the Korean electronics industry is no mystery, says Robert Laughlin, president of the Korea Advanced Institute for Science and Technology: 'Its ascendancy was inherited from Japan. The Koreans are reaping the benefits of Japanese investments.'

While the Korean electronics industry has moved rapidly upmarket and is now emphasising original research and innovation, it is caught in the 'nutcracker' of its bigger neighbours, Japan (which still has a reputation for superior quality) and China (with undeniably lower costs), says Lee Gam-Yoel, chief executive of the Korea Electronics Association.

China has a much more diverse IT and electronics industry, with a few big companies making a global impact, such as Lenovo in personal computers and Huawei in telecommunications equipment, and many more that can sell into the fast-growing domestic market but are not innovative enough to be internationally competitive. Most of the country's IT exports are from foreign-owned plants.

George He, head of Lenovo's Beijing-based R&D operation, believes the global IT market is changing in ways that will help Chinese companies, with less emphasis on technical performance and more on meeting customers' needs. 'For the past two decades the IT industry has been driven by technology through improvements in speed, memory and so on', he says. 'But now it is becoming more applications-driven - which is a big opportunity for companies like Lenovo that have a strong design team and user research lab.'

Mr He mentions a home computer designed to alter its speed and power consumption according to the application running. When the user plays a computing-intensive game it runs extremely fast but at the cost of noise from the cooling fan; when gently browsing the Web, the computer runs slowly and silently.

Meanwhile, the state-funded Chinese Academy of Sciences is making progress at the top end of computer technology. The academy's National Research Centre for Intelligent Computing Systems in Beijing has developed the 'Dawning' series of supercomputers. The latest model, Dawning 4000A, carries out scientific number-crunching jobs - for example, in climate and geological modelling - at the Shanghai Supercomputer Centre. It currently ranks 17 in the Top 500 list of the world's most powerful computers.

(*Source*: Based on C. Cookson, 'The invention house in the East - R&D in Asia', *Financial Times*, 17 June 2005, p. 14)

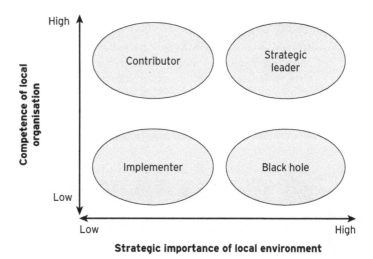

FIGURE 10.11 Subsidiary roles and responsibilities
Source: Adapted from Bartlett and Ghoshal, 2000

identify these roles into four primary types: Strategic leader, Contributor, Implementer and Black hole, on the basis of their local strategic importance and local competence (see Figure 10.11).

Strategic leader

This is a role for those companies which are highly competent and situated in strategically important markets. In this role, the subsidiary can become a partner to the centre in developing an innovation and implementing strategy, or it may even be allowed to assume a total lead role (if the centre is simply a co-ordinative unit). The subsidiary acts as the key sensor of the environment, and formulates and executes strategies that others may emulate.

Contributor

A subsidiary possessing distinctive competences, but operating in unimportant markets, can play a support role in the development of innovations and strategies for innovation. Its local environment may endow it with some specific insight or competence that can be used to good effect for the benefit of the company. For instance, the Swedish company Ericsson's development of the digital telecommunication AXE system received major help from its Australian subsidiary. The Australian subsidiary was spurred on by the government's push to make Australia the leader in digital technology capability.

Implementer

Subsidiaries with low competences in research and development and operating in strategically unimportant markets take on the role of implementer. Since the potential of the market is limited, the investment from the centre to the subsidiary is likewise. Quite a sizeable proportion of subsidiaries are given this role. Often they tend to be operating in developing markets or small countries. Implementers are efficient at executing the strategy of the leaders. The implementers are important in realising economies of scale and tend to be manufacturing or assembly operations, rather than the innovator or think-tank operations.

Black hole

Subsidiaries that operate in important markets for the company but lacking in a capability base eat up resources without making significant returns. One reason to maintain them, despite large expenditures and little return, is to have a presence in markets that are highly sophisticated and lead the advance of new innovations. This is why many European and American firms have small units operating in Japan. They monitor technological developments and assess local innovations for global roll-out potential through a fast follower strategy.

CASE STUDY

Electrolux's outpost in the East

Electrolux, the world's largest appliance maker, set up an 'Asian Team' as part of the Swedish company's attempt to unify its marketing strategies in the region.

The new business structure installs an Asian team, with 15 people from various countries, including Thailand, Malaysia, India and Sweden. The regional team's role is to look after the development of a plans and strategy for regional product development, marketing, customer service to suit Asian culture, says Fredrik Ramen, president for Asian region.

Moving away from the 'country-based' approach, Electrolux's restructuring is also aimed at benefiting the opening of trade in the region in line with the Asian Free Trade Area (AFTA) agreement.

'We want to offer the best business structure to the region, which will encourage us to provide better benefits to local customers in term of cheaper prices and faster service', said Ramen.

Ironically, Electrolux has taken the initiative while many other companies remain cautious over whether the 'Asian culture' actually exists. Car companies, for example, have witnessed a variety of tastes in each Asian country. (The pick-up truck, for example, is the No. 1 market in Thailand, while the saloon car leads in Malaysia, and the sport utility vehicle in the Philippines). Some analysts, though, point to different taxes in each country to account for the differences.

Ramen said that setting up manufacturing facilities in Asia is not a primary target for the company. He said he believed in a good combination between sourcing products locally via sub-contract manufacturing and importing products from original factories.

Electrolux has its own factories for appliances in Australia, China and India. The company has so-called collaborated factories in Thailand, Malaysia and Indonesia. Electrolux is dealing with four to five collaborated factories in Thailand for the production of refrigerators, microwave ovens, table-top gas cookers, and water heaters.

Ramen said Electrolux is also collaborating with Toshiba both regionally and globally in supplying different products to one another.

'We have many subcontract manufacturing facilities here so we need to be close with them. Our regional office in Singapore will look after for logistics works', said Ramen.

Electrolux achieved total sales of about US$1.2 billion (Bt540 billion) in the Asia Pacific last year, including about $100 million in Asian countries.

QUESTION

1. Is Electrolux's Asian Team unit set up as a strategic leader, contributor, implementer or black hole? Explain your reasoning.

(*Source*: Based on Anon, 2001)

People and teams for global innovation

Many of the challenges of managing people and teams are similar in the global context to what they are in the domestic context. For instance, misalignment of individual skills to project requirements, lack of clarity in team objectives, failures of leaders to align and motivate the visions of employees. Nevertheless, in the global context they face additional challenges resulting from differences in geography, scale, language and culture. Management of people in multi-national companies is prone to problems of misunderstanding and trust. However, diversity of culture and perspective should not be just seen as a problem. It can open up opportunities for better innovation. The traits of national cultures, such as the Japanese pragmatism, Italian flair for design, German systematic rigour, and British inventiveness can be used to innovate faster and more effectively. Many companies deliberately try to blend culturally derived skills to improve their innovation. For example, the logic in establishing Hitachi Europe was on the belief that a mixture of European and Japanese mentalities would improve speed and effectiveness of innovation. Cultural diversity is in itself, however, not sufficient for more productive innovation. Innovation in culturally diverse environments demands culturally sensitive management, i.e. it is the approach to cultural diversity that is important, not diversity itself (Lane and Di Stephano, 1992).

Research indicates that people trust one another more when they share similarities, communicate frequently and operate in a common cultural context (Kramer and Tyler, 1996). Key in this is communication. Unfortunately, multi-national companies suffer from communication obstacles arising from geographical or spatial separation, language and cultural differences. Cultural predispositions in the form of person-nation traits such as risk tolerance, individualism, power distance, and time disposition (Hofstede, 1991), that combine to define high- and low-context cultures, can affect innovation. Process, technology and person factors must be matched with each other for effective team functioning (Boutelleir et al., 1999).

Team diversity brings to bear different skills and distinct knowledge from different subsidiaries in different countries. This creates a high level of cognitive diversity (Govindarajan et al., 2001). This can be a strong source of strength but it must be coupled with cognitive integration. Without cognitive integration, cognitive diversity can bring incompatibility and difficulty (See Figure 10.12).

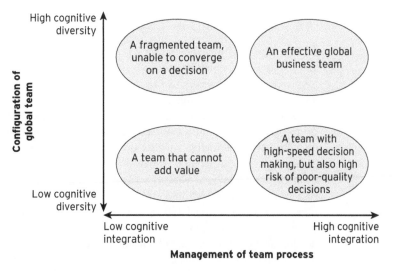

FIGURE 10.12 Global team effectiveness
Source: Adapted from Govindarajan and Gupta, 2001

TABLE 10.1 Improving communication and cultivating trust

Overcoming communications barriers	
1. Language and cross-cultural training	This fosters more direct and spontaneous communication
2. Agreement on norms of behaviour	Establishing explicit ground rules for communication induces better interaction
3. Adopting data-driven decisions	Rather than relying on opinion, discussions should be based on fact
4. Developing alternatives to enrich debate	Surfacing alternatives is a useful way to follow expression of diverse views
5. Rotating meeting location	This helps to enrich the cognitive system of individuals, as well as legitimate the expression of divergent positions
Cultivating a culture of trust	
1. Scheduling face-to-face meetings	This is the richest form of communication, and helps to build a solid foundation of trust. It is critical that the first few meetings of global teams occur face-to-face
2. Rotating and diffusing team ledership	By rotating and diffusing team leadership across countries, managers from subsidiaries can gain an appreciation for cross-border coordination and cooperation. This also fosters a sense of mutual interdependence and dampens 'us and them' attitudes
3. Linking rewards to team performance	Linking rewards to team performance encourages members to focus on the problem and resolve conflicts
4. Build social capital	At any one time, a multi-national company will have many projects ongoing. By taking multi-national, rather than country-wide, initiatives, the company can create interpersonal familiarity, which ultimately feeds trust and creates social capital for the future

To achieve cognitive integration it is necessary to recognise and anticipate the problems, and put in place mechanisms to reconcile diverse perspectives. One way is to improve communication, and the second is to cultivate trust. Several ways of tackling these issues exist, and are summarised in Table 10.1.

An added challenge in the management of global projects is the spatial spread of different competences in different subsidiaries. In dealing with this, many companies have increasingly resorted to bringing together the required competences for a specific project from different parts of the parent organisation, and even from external parties, if the competences do not exist internally, in what are termed *virtual teams*. Virtual project teams enable organisations to pool the talents and expertise of employees, and non-employees, by eliminating time, space, organisational and geographic boundaries. Virtual teams source the skills and resources to execute rapid product development projects, and therefore can be used in the development of projects that fall outside the capability of a single firm. These teams tend to be entrepreneurial and create a possibility for the firm to break away from its traditional stream of innovations by bringing together in a single team a wider competence portfolio than before. Notwithstanding the potential of these teams, they can be difficult to manage because typically people in virtual teams are not co-located, often come from varying backgrounds, and have little face-to-face contact. Because of such issues there is growing evidence that virtual teams fail more often than they succeed (Furst et al., 2004). This makes communication and trust building even more pertinent. In order to overcome the lack of face-to-face contact and facilitate communication, managers use technology (such as virtual whiteboards, collaborative document editors and instant messaging) to build 'virtual work-spaces' (Malhotra and Majchrzak, 2005).

CASE STUDY

Kraft's food matrix

A row of coffee makers stood on a sideboard in Roger Deromedi's office at Kraft Foods' headquarters in Northfield, Illinois. This was not because the company's chief executive had a serious caffeine habit. Rather, he said, brewing a cappuccino, it was so that he could test the performance of Kraft's own product, the Tassimo – a system of producing café-quality coffee at home from pre-packed 'pods' – against rivals from other manufacturers.

Kraft badly needed Tassimo to be a success. The biggest food maker in North America and the second biggest in the world after Nestlé had experienced a challenging couple of years. Hit products had been thin on the ground: a series of product launches in the previous year had disappointed, under-lining what critics said was Kraft's paucity of real innovation and sluggishness in bringing ideas to market. Growth in important categories, such as biscuits, has been clobbered by the low-carbohydrate diet trend. Prices for important raw materials, such as cheese, had shot up. Earnings had fallen year-on-year for the previous four quarters. And the Kraft chief was out of the office for six weeks after being admitted to hospital with a viral infection and acute dehydration.

In response, Kraft tried to reinvent itself. Previously, it was split into two halves with two chief executives: an international arm, based in Rye Brook, New York, headed by Mr Deromedi; and a bigger North American arm, based in Northfield and run by Betsy Holden. Since Mr Deromedi was appointed sole chief executive in December 2003, the dual structure had been swept away in an attempt to create a unified, global business.

At the same time, Kraft was closing 20 factories worldwide, laying off 6000 of its 100,000 workers, and aiming to plough the expected $400m (£224m) annual savings by 2006 into innovation and marketing to improve its performance.

Mr Deromedi's restructuring was designed to make Kraft truly global, cut costs and crank up innovation. Step one, announced in January 2004, just 23 days after Mr Deromedi became sole CEO, was the re-organisation. That created five global product sectors – beverages, snacks, cheese and dairy, convenient meals and grocery – backed by two regional commercial units covering North America and elsewhere, and focussed on marketing and sales. The model bore strong similarities to the revamp of Procter & Gamble that began in the late 1990s.

Kraft also created global units handling functions such as supply chain and technology and a new global marketing and product development unit – headed by Betsy Holden, formerly Mr Deromedi's co-CEO.

When Kraft decided to re-organise itself, it chose a model that was familiar from restructuring exercises at other consumer goods companies: the matrix. Most of all, its approach resembled the shake-up of Procter & Gamble – though Roger Deromedi, Kraft chief executive, says he did not specifically study the P&G model. Under Durk Jager and then A.G. Lafley, P&G shifted away from a country-by-country

→

organisation as a way of breaking down national fiefdoms. It moved to three global business units, responsible for product categories, working with a network of regional 'market development organisations' charged with local marketing.

Kraft was split into North American and international arms – though its largest product categories had 'global councils' to cover best practices and sourcing. It re-organised itself into five global product sectors and two regional commercial units, with global units handling supply chain management, technology and other central functions.

This matrix approach worked well, Mr Deromedi said, for consumer goods groups that had to deal with three 'dimensions': product categories, geographies and functions. But the appropriate structure depended on a company's specific needs and its spread of products and markets.

Kraft created a global marketing and product development unit to kick-start innovation. Unlike P&G, which gave profit-and-loss responsibility to its global product units, Kraft left it with the regional marketing arms. Food, said Mr Deromedi, remained a more 'local' business with many more local brands than the household and personal care goods business in which P&G mainly operated. 'Our general manager in Germany competed against a different competitor from our general manager in France', he added.

Barely three weeks later, Mr Deromedi unveiled step two: factory closures and job cuts designed to save $400m a year by 2006. He also lowered Kraft's annual earnings growth target from 8–10 per cent to what analysts see as a more realistic 6–9 per cent again following the example of companies such as Gillette and P&G.

The big focus was on innovation. That, Mr Deromedi said, was vital not only to persuade consumers to buy its products, but to maintain the relationship with powerful global retailers such as Wal-Mart, Tesco and Carrefour. These had their own private-label products and looked to branded manufacturers to provide something different.

'The success of Wal-Mart requires us to do more in terms of bringing true innovation to the consumer', he said. 'If you are not bringing that to the retailer today and tomorrow, what do they need your brand for?'

Ms Holden's global marketing and product development unit, Mr Deromedi said, was giving a new impetus to innovation, with Ms Holden visiting consumers' homes around the world in search of new ideas. So, too, was a new 'innovation leadership team' consisting of Mr Deromedi, Ms Holden and four other executives to approve the allocation of resources.

QUESTIONS

1. Why and how was Kraft trying to re-invent itself?
2. In your opinion should the change help Kraft's efforts to boost innovation? How?

(*Source*: N. Buckley, 'Search for the right ingredients', *Financial Times*, p. 15, October 2004)

Leadership for global innovation

The challenges of managing and co-ordinating innovation within multi-national companies are enormous. Global strategies can easily crumble if managers are not able to fully cope with the new challenges of global co-ordination and control, and their associated roles and responsibilities. These roles and responsibilities span the entire spectrum of organisations: front-line, middle and senior management. Despite the importance of these roles and responsibilities surprisingly little study has been conducted. Bartlett and Ghoshal (2000) highlight the challenges and responsibilities of leaders in managing global innovation. These are elaborated next.

Role and responsibilities of the global business manager

Global business managers have to develop global efficiency by finding ways of securing global economies of scale and leveraging worldwide market position. This places demands on them to fulfil the following roles.

- *Worldwide business strategist*: Attempts to create global efficiency require the manager to be able to see opportunities and risks across countries and functional specialisms, and have the skills to co-ordinate and integrate these activities across divisions. This requires that the manager is able to reconcile and integrate different points of view and interests into an integrated strategy of how the business will compete in the specific product-market category. Companies have encountered problems in this when they have simply given old product division managers a new titular status. In these instances, subsidiary managers from other countries found the 'new' managers to be insensitive to non-domestic perspectives.

- *Architect of asset and resource configuration*: The global manager cannot just strategise, but needs to be able to co-ordinate resources and assets to support the attainment of global efficiency objectives. This does not mean possessing unilateral power, but taking a lead role in incorporating and winning the support of key geographic and functional area managers. After getting support at this level, the global manager needs the mandate from top-level management to appropriate the necessary resources and assets to implement the proposed strategy.

- *Cross-border co-ordinator*: The global manager must ensure that the flow of information, people and goods between the interlinked units occurs smoothly. This co-ordination can involve direct control or an oversight role in the setting of transfer prices.

Roles and responsibilities of worldwide functional manager

The need to develop and diffuse innovations throughout the multi-national company's worldwide units takes functional managers from their hitherto background role into an active role in the transnational organisation. The specific task facing each functional manager depends on their specific area of expertise (transfer of marketing prowess, transfer of technology insight, etc.). The key roles and responsibilities of these managers are:

- *Worldwide intelligence scanner*: The majority of innovations are conceived in response to stimuli from environmental threats or perceived opportunity. Functional managers need to be aware of any developments that may provide an opportunity or pose a threat, no matter how slight or futuristic the trend. The gains of the green movement in Germany's political arena was a signal for the highly market-sensitive German companies to prepare to define new corporate policies, adjust processes, and develop environmentally friendly products. They also quickly filtered this signal to their worldwide subsidiaries.

- *Cross-pollinator of best practices*: Functional managers not only have the expertise to be able to detect and assess the value of best practices from within and external to the organisation, but their knowledge makes them best placed to be able to facilitate the transfer into the organisational network.

- *Champion of transnational innovation*: Functional managers can, because of their deep expertise and capability, champion the use and leverage of their capability by innovatively combining it with other functional capabilities to produce novel and innovative solutions.

Roles and responsibilities for geographic subsidiary managers

Geographic managers are at the centre of conflicting demands facing the multi-national company. They have to ensure that they do not lose out to locally responsive competition, while at the same time defending themselves against global competitors and complying with the host-nation policies and circumstances. The key roles for the geographic manager involve being a:

- *Bi-cultural interpreter*: The country manager needs to be cognisant of the postures adopted by competitors in their 'home territory' and also build a deep appreciation of local customs in relation to the firm's organisational culture. The country manager must ensure that the values, priorities and strategies of the company are clearly understood by local employees, and that these employees are motivated appropriately toward implementation of these policies.

- *National defender and advocate*: In multi-national companies where the pressure for a standardised approach is very strong, the country manager needs to argue the case for local responsiveness. Otherwise national demands and pressures can be ignored in the parent company's map of strategic consideration, i.e. the manager must act as an advocate for the subsidiary's role in the multi-national company's integrated network.

- *Front-line implementer of corporate strategy*: Implementing the chosen strategy in any scenario is difficult, but is made more difficult in the subsidiary because complex demands arise from highly diverse constituents. Moreover, these demands need to be translated into specific actions within national settings that may differ widely in their demands upon the organisation. The country manager is pressurised from outside and constrained from within. The task is made even more difficult, since implementation decisions are not dictated by the country managers alone. The country manager may have a say in the formulation and discussion, but once the decision has been taken, the country manager must justify and implement this decision in his/her national organisation.

Roles and responsibilities of top-level corporate managers

At the senior level, the questions posed by the global environment are most severe. Top-level managers have to cope not only with providing direction and ensuring integrated action from diverse units, but also institute new ways of doing things, new norms and new values, and even grapple with the legitimacy of their own roles within the altered configurations. The key challenges are to balance seemingly contradictory pushes.

- *Providing direction and purpose*: Senior management must provide guidance and direction for innovation yet leave sufficient space to allow experimentation. The ability to create and communicate a vision that is able to energise staff is key.

- *Leveraging corporate performance*: It is not enough for senior staff to align the organisation to long-term goals through crafting visions. They must also balance this with defining potential courses of action for short-term results. To do so top managers need control mechanisms. Traditional control systems rely on responding to below-budget financial results. New forms of control involve pro-active personal mechanisms. Rather than being top-down controllers, senior managers must now take on the role of corporate-level support. This requires clarity of responsibilities, delegation and alignment of reward systems to responsibilities.

- *Flow of resources (capital, personnel and knowledge)*: One of the biggest challenges facing senior managers is one of co-ordinating the diverse flow of activities. The flow of goods (resourcing, scheduling, distribution) involves processes that can be pushed down into the organisation. However, the flow of resources (capital allocation, key personnel assignments) are decisions that top managers need to be directly involved in, to ensure they maintain control. The key flow is that of knowledge and information, and senior managers have to be active agents in this flow. These three flows are essential to the co-ordinative well-being of the organisation. Senior staff must enact a balance in these flows by adopting the correct level of formalisation, centralisation and socialisation.

● *Ensuring continual renewal*: The first two roles need to be carefully supplemented by the third, namely that of continuous organisational renewal. Without this the organisation can easily become highly profitable in the short run but rigid and incapable for the long term. Managers can address this by reducing bureaucracy, constantly fixing the organisation lens outwards and stirring the organisation by asking challenging questions that impel organisational innovation and learning and focus it firmly onto the future.

The emergent networked transnational configuration requires three core processes that characterise its management and approach: entrepreneurial, integration and renewal processes (see Figure 10.13). All three processes demand a new approach from senior, middle and front-line managers. The *entrepreneurial process* drives opportunity-seeking behaviour of the organisation. It is an externally focussed sensitivity to markets and general environment shifts. It involves searching for potential new opportunities to create new products, markets or entire businesses. The *integration process* is responsible for creating and leveraging links between dispersed capabilities and resources. This process is responsible for maximising advantage of selected opportunities. The third process is the *renewal process*. This process is key to ensuring that the organisation refreshes and revitalises itself. It requires fundamental questionsing of how things are done, what things are done, and why they are done.

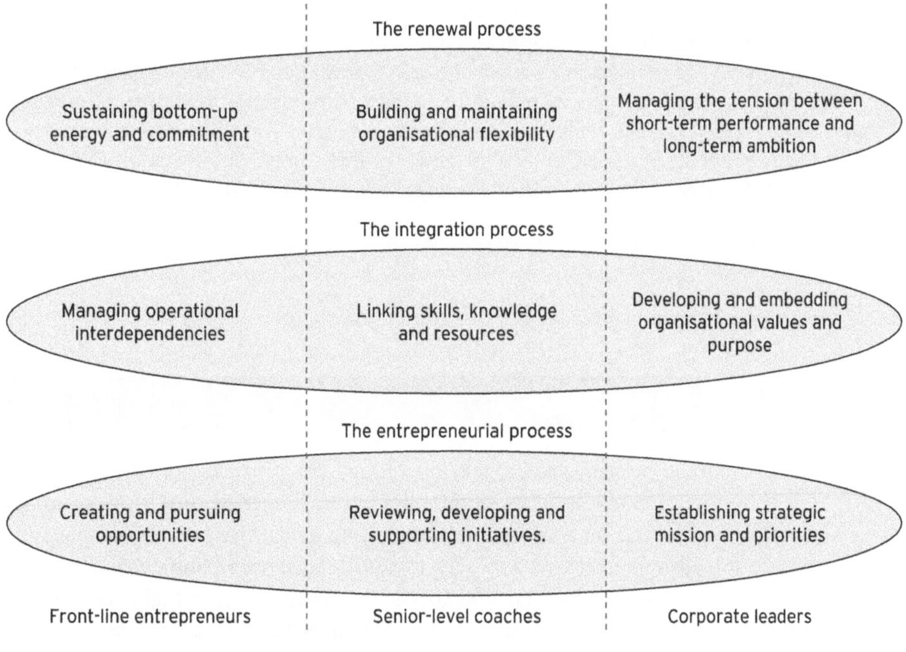

FIGURE 10.13 Roles and responsibilities for managers
Source: Adapted from Bartlett and Ghoshal, 2000

ILLUSTRATION

Japan's economic engine: process and strategic innovation

After Japan's economic downturn many people had written off Japanese companies. But these views should take heed of the fact that Japanese companies had been busily working away in the background developing organisational innovations, very much in the fashion of Kaisen and lean manufacturing that left their Western counterparts reeling in previous eras. Many Japanese companies 'very successfully' pioneered a twin-track approach in shifting more production towards high-value niche products while doing more to build plants elsewhere in Asia where costs were lower.

An important part of this strategy was greater investment in developing new product and manufacturing processes, following in the footsteps of leading exemplars such as Ricoh (an office-equipment company), Keyence (suppliers of automation equipment), and the electronic groups of Seiko, Sharp and Sanyo.

While manufacturing accounted for 19.5 per cent of Japanese output, only slightly above the average for all the 30 nations in the Organisation of Economic Co-operation and Development, more than half Japan's total was accounted for by high- and mid-technology goods – almost twice as high as the OECD norm. Such products included instruments, cars, electronic equipment and drugs.

Also, the research intensity of Japanese industry, measured by the number of researchers compared with other workers, was growing faster than in almost any other OECD country. Japan had 10.2 researchers per 1000 industrial employees, against the OECD average of 6.5.

Among those whose performance stood out were Toyota, Nissan and Honda, Japan's biggest car producers. All earned operating profits of above 10 per cent of sales, much higher than for most manufacturers, and were increasing market shares in the US.

Canon – manufacturer of cameras and semiconductor production machines – in 2002 recorded net income of ¥190bn (£1bn), six times more than in 1994. It spent highly on research and development and was estimated to own the seven most valuable patents of all time, all to do with ink-jet printing.

These companies, like other Japanese manufacturers, were spreading their influence to the rest of Asia, which in 2002 received a quarter of Japan's foreign direct investment, from 7 per cent in 2000.

Minebea, the world's biggest maker of miniature industrial bearings, also moved increasingly to high-technology products while building strength in Asia. The development centre was a small plant in Karuizawa, northern Japan, where ideas were worked out, and transferred to other Minebea plants in Thailand, Singapore and China that were responsible for most of the company's production.

(*Source*: Based on P. Marsh, 'Japanese groups engineer high-technology comeback', *FT*, 22 October 2003, p. 28)

Conclusion

The pressures for global operations are constant, and increasingly demand appropriate corporate responses. Companies can no longer succeed by innovating just in their domestic markets, since competitors exploiting global markets can gain significant market and cost advantages. Faced with such pressures, many companies have evolved structures and systems to co-ordinate their operations. In this chapter, we highlighted five organisational approaches that have been used by companies to manage their innovation efforts: ethnocentric, geocentric, polycentric, R&D hub, and integrated network. Depending on the firm's objectives and context each of these configurations can lead to success. However, the nature of the global pressures is such that it is forcing a gradual shift to the integrated network structural configuration. The move toward the integrated network, also known as the transnational structural form, occurs because it provides a balance between global efficiency and local responsiveness. Because this form is likely to become more pervasive into the future, it was considered in detail within this chapter.

The chapter examined the key challenges of managing a multi-national company for innovation. The issue of what types of R&D and where within the parent company's subsidiary units R&D ought be located was raised and discussed. This was followed by an examination of the roles that subsidiaries play in innovation roll-out. Inevitably, this led to discussion of the challenge of managing a diversity of people and project teams. The chapter concluded by defining the role and responsibilities that different strata of management need to discharge for the management of global innovation.

QUESTIONS

1. Identify the key drivers of globalisation. Discuss what are the implications of these for innovation.

2. List the different organisational configurations for global innovation. Examine the relative advantages and disadvantages of each. Is there a trend towards any one form? If so, state why.

3. Discuss what actions are necessary to make the integrated R&D network (or the transnational form) effective.

4. Why is the decision to conduct R&D in a particular location/subsidiary complex? What type of factors must be taken into account for this decision?

5. Discuss the different roles a subsidiary can play in the roll-out of an innovation.

6. What additional difficulties exist in managing global innovation team projects? What actions are needed to overcome these problems?

7. Define and discuss the different leadership responsibilities and roles in the management of global innovation projects.

CASE STUDY

The Dell model

Of all the business innovations explorer Marco Polo discovered in thirteenth century China, he was perhaps most surprised by the use of paper money. It was worth dozens of times the weight of the heavy coins that European traders lugged around. Today's multinational technology companies could learn a similar lesson: Bring only what's needed when entering China.

That's what Dell did under Phil Kelly, Dell Asia Pacific's first senior executive. In 1998, he introduced just a portion of Dell's famous business model to the Chinese marketplace, adding capabilities and staff as growth dictated. As a result, Dell's share of the PC market grew more than 60 per cent a year in 2000 to 2005. By 2009 Dell's China sales were growing 28 per cent per year, accounting for about 5 per cent of the company's global business.

The world's second largest personal computer maker also purchased about $23 billion of products in 2008 from China, Dell's largest overseas market.

Kelly's strategy allowed the company to mitigate the risks of trying to force-fit its model to China or abandoning its valuable experience, two common pitfalls for multinationals. Moreover, it allowed the company to localise operations, cement relationships with customers and government officials, and control costs in ways that account for the country's often unpredictable quirks and opportunities.

Dell's approach is worth studying. Companies that want to import their business model as-is are following a natural instinct: they believe they will succeed by continuing to do what they do well. In theory, the company's value chain, core capabilities and values would all come along in a type of pallet-ised, business-in-a-box. Managers would simply adjust downward to satisfy local requirements.

Alternatively, companies that invest in a new business model for China are responding to what they see as unique conditions. They often arrive at an initial arrangement that's very different from their traditional one. Once again, managers intend to incorporate their best capabilities whenever such standardisation would not diminish the custom model for China.

Unfortunately, importing a company's business model lock, stock and barrel generally means importing costs as well. Doing things the old way often costs too much in China. But customisation can result in a nearly similar outcome, because so much efficiency is lost through the abandonment of a well-proven model.

While Dell avoided these pitfalls, it still hit some bumps in the road, sometimes literally. Mr Kelly, a no-nonsense leader and former executive with Motorola in Asia, felt Dell needed to set up shop in China rather than simply export into the country from its Malaysian plants.

Headquarters thought differently, and initially rebuffed Mr Kelly's proposal to put a factory in China. Not only was Dell's model all but untested in China, they surmised, but also they had concerns around costs, skills and suppliers.

Mr Kelly remained convinced that Chinese customers would ultimately find Dell's business model compelling, and finally won approval.

He settled on Xiamen, a city along China's east coast, in 1997. But first, Mr Kelly and his team worked closely with the local leaders to create mutually attractive conditions for investment, tax relief, and production increases. Mr Kelly credits these initial discussions with setting the right tone, saying 'the economic model started well before we collected on our first invoice.'

Next, Mr Kelly and his team roughed out the basics of the business model. There was never any doubt it would be based on the US model. But they used a simpler form of it 'about 35–40 per cent, worth', Mr Kelly recalls. At first, this meant that Dell sold only a limited line of products – desktops emphasis-ing corporate buyers. Dell then built call centres and sales teams, but in a way that was focussed on the initial target market.

Mr Kelly had to adjust the model to accommodate local idiosyncrasies, a challenge that continued well beyond his tenure. For instance, even though eligible customers could order PCs online or via phone, low credit card penetration meant that most were unable to pay with credit cards. Dell created a flexible model that allowed customers to pay on delivery.

Dell also addressed unexpected order-fulfilment glitches. In one case, Dell hired a trucking company to deliver PCs in the northern part of the country. After two weeks, Mr Kelly's team discovered that PCs were arriving at customer locations in pieces. After some digging, managers learned they needed to specify that deliveries be made only on trucks with new springs.

The larger lesson is that business models must be adapted thoughtfully to the Chinese context. The key watch-out involves cost. If the business model can only be executed at high cost, the company is probably importing too much of the model and needs to consider possible adjustments to processes, standards and techniques. Paring the model to its core elements, then adding back local pieces over time, allows companies to carefully build on experience.

Consider how Mr Kelly used this insight to minimise the cost of talent. Early on he brought his management team up from Southeast Asia to set up the factory, support services and suppliers. Then he switched to local talent at the managerial level. He reached full localisation of all direct reports to the production head within the first year and full localisation across all posts within a few years of operation.

The challenges facing companies in China are substantial, but not insurmountable. The country is growing less opaque by the day, and multinationals more experienced by the hour about how to break into this underdeveloped IT market – one that will continue to grow at least four times faster than the US tech sector over the next two years. Defining the exact way to adapt to China depends on each company's situation. As with most issues, the devil is in the details. The heartening message is that multinationals are now beginning to succeed in China.

QUESTIONS

1. Evaluate Dell's entry into the China markets. What lessons can be learnt from Dell's global market entry strategy?
2. In your opinion is Dell's approach to entering the China market an innovation?

(*Source*: Paul Di Paola and T. Manning, 'Doing business in China', *Financial Times*, 11 February 2005, p. 1 and Reuters, 2009)

References

Anon (2001), 'Electrolux eyes "Asian culture"', *The Nation* (Thailand), 8 June, 36.

Barlett, C.A. and Ghoshal, S. (2000), *Transnational management: Text cases, and readings in cross-border management*, Boston: McGraw-Hill.

Boutellier, R., Gassmann, O. and Von Zedtwitz, M. (1999), *Managing global innovation: Uncovering the secrets of future competitiveness*, Berlin: Springer.

Buckley, N. (2004), 'Search for the right ingredients'. *Financial Times*, October, 15.

Chandler, A. (1962), *Strategy and structure*, Cambridge, MA: MIT Press.

Cookson, C. (2005), 'The invention house in the East – R&D in Asia', *Financial Times*, 17 July 14.

Di Paola, P. and Manning, T. (2005), 'Doing business in China', *Financial Times*, 11 February, 1.

Douglas, S.P. and Wind, Y. (1987), 'The myth of globalisation', *Columbia Journal of World Business*, Winter: 19–29.

Furst, S.A., Reeves, M., Rosen, B. and Blackburn, R.S. (2004), 'Managing the life cycle of virtual teams', *Academy of Management Executive* 18(2): 6–20.

Giddens, A. (1999), *Runaway world: How globalisation is reshaping our lives*, London: Profile Books.

Govindarajan, V. and Gupta, A.K.D.E. (2001), 'Building an effective global business team', *Sloan Management Review* 42(2): 63–71.

Hamel, G. and Prahalad, C.K. (1990), 'The core competence of the corporation', *Harvard Business Review*, May–June: 79–91.

Hirst, P. and Thompson, G. (1999), *Globalisation in question*, Cambridge: Polity Press.

Hofstede, G. (1991), *Cultures and organisations: Software of the mind*, London: McGraw-Hill.

Kogut, B. (1985), 'Designing global strategies: Comparative and competitive value-added chains', *Sloan Management Review* 26(4): 15–28.

Kramer, R.M. and Tyler, T.R. (1996), *Trust in organisations: Frontiers of theory and research*, Thousand Oaks, CA: Sage.

Kripalani, M., Ewing, J. and Einhorn, B. (2004), 'Huawei: More than a local hero', *Business Week*, 11 October: 180–181.

Lane, H.W. and Di Stephano, J.J. (1992), *International management behaviour: From policy to practice*, Oxford: Blackwell.

Marsh, P. (2003), 'Japanese groups engineer high-technology comeback', *Financial Times*, 22 October, 28.

Malhotra, A. and Majchrzak, A. (2005), 'Virtual workspace technologies', *Sloan Management Review* 46(2): 11–14.

Ohmae, K. (2000), *The invisible continent: Four strategic imperatives of the new economy*, London: Nicholas Brearley.

Porter, M.E. (1980), *Competitive strategy*, New York: Free Press.

Reuters (2009), 'Dell's China sales take a leap', 26 March.

Ricardo, D. (1817), 'Principles of political economy and taxation'. Reprinted in P.

Sraffa (ed.) (1951), *The works of David Ricardo*, London: Cambridge University Press.

Stopford, J.M. and Wells, L.T. Jr. (1972), *Managing the multinational enterprise: Organisation of the firm and ownership of subsidiaries*, New York: Basic Books.

Vernon, R. (1966), 'International investment and international trade in the product cycle', *Quarterly Journal of Economics* 80: 190–207.

Yip, G.S. (1989), 'Global strategy . . . in a world of nations?'. *Sloan Management Review* 31(1): 29–41.

Yip, G.S. (1992), *Total global strategy: Managing for a worldwide competitive advantage*, Englewood Cliffs, NJ: Prentice Hall.

PART 5

Execution within a structured development process

11 Market learning

Learning outcomes

When you have completed this chapter you should be able to:

- Recognise the importance of market learning for innovation.

- Appreciate the difference between incremental and discontinuous change and its implications for innovation.

- Appreciate an organisational process for market learning that is robust enough to deal with complex and highly dynamic environments.

- Appreciate the strengths and limitations of conventional tools and techniques for market understanding.

- Understand the key advances taking place in the tools and techniques for market learning and understanding.

- Recognise the variety of customer needs.

- Appreciate Kano's ideas of customer satisfaction and their role in defining and developing innovation.

- Understand a methodology of translating customer needs into organisational actions, and aligning the business to the market.

Introduction

Innovation is a source of vitality and advantage, but its impact on the bottom line is only produced if it delivers to the market an outcome that customers desire. The outcome is most commonly in the form of a product, but the innovation could be a process or strategy that enhances the value delivered to the end customers. With the growth of a global economy and emergence of the digital economy, important changes have been taking place in the nature of consumer demand and the means to serve these demands. On the demand side of the equation, new market dynamics are emerging: ever more sophisticated consumers, highly specific need segments, and rapid shifts in tastes. On the supply side companies are trying to out-compete one another through speed-to-market product development strategies and flexible operations and processes. As markets become more complex, dynamic and discontinuous, it becomes increasingly difficult to predict important aspects of the future, including customer desires and needs. The changes are re-defining the competitive landscape. Managers are put under greater pressure to observe, interpret and act upon market intelligence than ever before.

Global markets, unpredictable competitor moves, rapid technological change and ubiquitous information has increased the importance of marketplace learning, and simultaneously raised questions about the conventional approaches to marketplace understanding. As noted in Chapter 5, many failures in product innovation occur through poor assessment and understanding of the market (Cooper, 1988). However, companies, especially in fast changing discontinuous environments, need to move beyond just collecting lots of market data and information. Data must provide insights beyond mere reinforcement of already known and superficial facts. It is no longer sufficient to simply know what consumers say they want or need. Needs must be deeply understood and contextualised within future environments. This involves taking information about customers, competitors, communities and the organisation itself as raw material and processing it through the lens of experience to create a meaningful picture of marketplace reality. The stress is on the word meaningful: 'The picture of market reality is more than a collection of random information; it is a picture that conveys understanding' (Barabba, 1996, p. 155). Market learning requires market intelligence to move beyond consideration of 'discrete' components of the market in isolation. It requires the parts to be fitted into a systemic whole so as to allow construction of a closer and clearer view of reality (Pourdehnad and Robinson, 2001), and the reality itself is not fixed but is a changing landscape.

ILLUSTRATION

The risk and unpredictability of markets

Boeing began its launch of the 7E7 with the announcement of a contract with Japan's All Nippon Airways (ANA). ANA had placed the first order for 50 of the mid-sized 7E7 aircraft, worth $6bn (£3.5bn) at list prices, with the first deliveries scheduled for 2008. The 7E7, branded the Dreamliner, was urgently needed to revive Boeing's fortunes in the commercial aerospace sector, where it had been losing market share to its European rival Airbus.

Airbus had been outspending Boeing on product development and was in the midst of a $12bn development for its A380 superjumbo, which would be the world's largest commercial jet when it was scheduled to enter service with Singapore Airlines in 2006.

Airbus had outsold Boeing in four of the previous five years. In the previous year, Airbus had delivered more aircraft than the US group for the first time in its history. Airbus' jetliner market share had gone from 15 per cent in the 1980s to over 50 per cent, with more than 3300 Airbus jets in service worldwide. Airbus provided 50,000 jobs, representing Europe's ability to compete in high-technology manufacturing. But that success had a price – it was estimated Europe had spent $25bn (£13bn) in public resources on Airbus since 1970.

Mike Bair, Boeing 7E7 Senior VP, said the group expected further orders for the 7E7 before the end of the year by airlines in Asia, Europe and the US. It had made firm sales proposals to more than a dozen airlines. American Airlines and Northwest Airlines were seen as two of the most likely initial US customers while Singapore Airlines and Emirates were leading candidates in Asia and the Middle East.

Mr Bair also raised the prospect of low-cost airlines buying the aircraft who were interested in the opportunity to take their business model beyond a domestic or regional service. Boeing also forecast sales of 3500 aircraft in the mid-market over the next 20 years, in which the 7E7 was expected to compete. Mr Bair said it was confident of winning a share of more than 50 per cent.

The big question lay around which way the market would go. Would it swing towards the mid-range market predicted by Boeing or head in the direction of the super-jumbo? Both companies had placed their bets. The game was now to wait and see, and during this period they would jockey for competitive position through every means possible. In this game, Boeing had tactically tried to unbalance Airbus' footing by taking it to the World Trade Organisation (WTO) on the grounds of European subsidies, even though it too received favourable treatment from its domestic institutions. When the gains and losses were so huge, shifting the market in one's favour could mean the difference between life and death.

(*Source*: Based on C. Daniel et al., 'Boeing $6bn deal secures future for 7E7 aircraft: US group aims to win back market share from Airbus', *FT*, 27 April 2004, p. 21; R. Aboulafia, 'The transatlantic politics of aircraft subsidies, *FT*, 11 November 2004, p. 19)

Innovation and change

Markets and technology very rarely stand still. They are under constant change, and this dynamic holds important consequences for innovation. The critical factor in change is the nature and level of change. First, change can be either incremental and continuous or disruptive and discontinuous. Second, it can be across technologies or markets. Discontinuities in technology have always been perceived as an important dynamic of competition. However, market discontinuity is an equally important method of overturning rules of competition. Thus, we can define two dimensions of change: market change and technology change (see Figure 11.1). By mapping these two dimensions against level of change a matrix of different innovation patterns can be discerned.

For most of the time, markets and technologies change incrementally and continuously. Consequently, companies are engaged in innovative efforts within this domain of relatively stable markets and technologies. This is essentially a steady-state position of innovation. It involves continuous innovation in which incremental changes are made to the current offering. It is the domain that we most frequently encounter, and represents the comfort zone of operation for most companies. Simple shifts in customer needs and minor improvements in technology are used to develop new offerings. Innovation occurring in this domain is also sometimes referred to as sustaining innovation.

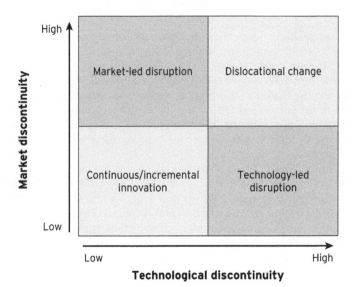

FIGURE 11.1 Dimensions of change

Now and then, however, disruptions to the steady state occur with the development of new technology that overthrows or displaces the dominance of the existing technological paradigm or through a sharp shift in market demand. In order to drive or keep pace with these changes companies must be sensitive and capable of adapting to discontinuous technology or discontinuous market change. The problem of discontinuous innovation is that it is difficult to predict and detect. Often it emerges from the periphery of the marketplace or from the fringes of basic research, hence it is commonly labelled as 'blue skies' research. Not surprisingly, most companies by their very nature prefer to focus on areas that lead to hard profit returns in the here and now rather than grapple with the long-term potentiality of uncertain gains into the future. Discontinuous shift, whether technological or market, means major upheaval for companies in the sector. Discontinuity makes many of the old ways of doing things redundant.

In dealing with uni-dimensional discontinuities we have used the terms disruptive or discontinuous innovation. We can call these first-order discontinuities. In the case of the multi-dimensional discontinuity we have a higher order change, which we call dislocational change. Dislocational innovation is a second-order change. It involves truly revolutionary and radical shifts. Firms facing discontinuities in both technology and markets have to deal with large-scale upheaval. The rules of the game are not just changed but an entirely new market induces much greater uncertainties. Often this type of change is a precursor to the creation of a new industry. New markets with very different and new needs are created through the development and application of radically new technologies. It is dislocational in the sense that it creates new industries and makes old industries and markets obsolete. The change is sharp and few of the older companies have the capabilities or the time to make the transition into the emerging landscape. A large number of companies, and sometimes all the old sector firms, perish. They just do not have the wherewithal to withstand multi-dimensional disruptive change.

Figure 11.2 maps the paths of firm approaches to accommodate the environmental shifts. Path P1 is the approach by a company that is acutely sensitive to its market. Its market intelligence antennae are able to pick up even weak signals of future change. The firm is able to

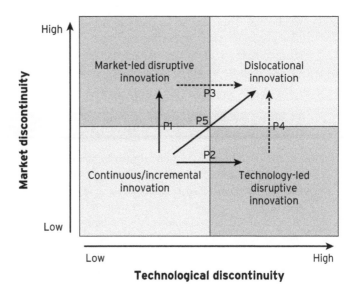

FIGURE 11.2 Change and paths of innovation

sift out from the background noise the patterns from which disruptive market change is likely to emerge. These firms possess a high-level sensing and learning capability.

Path P2 is the approach that firms take to either drive a technological shift or keep abreast with it. These firms focus on creating or acquiring technological competence through speculative investment in long-term research and development. There are advantages and problems with each of these paths. Following path P2 is a high-risk approach if uncertain and radical market shifts are likely to occur (i.e. those indicated by path P4). The real risk is if the markets do not emerge or move away from the technology being developed or invested. These shifts, therefore, may make speculative investments in technology highly risky. Thus, failure to be attuned to the market can lead to high investment loss. However, if the firm correctly predicts the shifts it places itself in a commanding position to dictate and control the industry.

On the other hand, reading the market carefully and being close to it allows the firm to know where the markets are heading, but without the technology capability the company is at risk of being left behind or locked out. If the company has the financial muscle, it may of course be able to overcome this hurdle by purchasing the technology know-how through licensing or firm merger and acquisition. This would allow it to successfully manoeuvre path P3.

The real challenge is to be attuned and capable of dealing with both of these sources of disruptive change simultaneously. Companies able to do this must balance not just multidimensional shifts but also maintain a balance with incremental or evolutionary innovation. This type of company is ambidextrous (Tushman and O'Reilly III, 1996). The ambidextrous innovator is best poised to take advantage of dislocational sources of change. The fact is that most companies find it difficult to build an ambidextrous capability. Most even fail in being able to spot and deal with uni-dimensional discontinuous shifts in their markets or technologies. They are ill-prepared to meet the challenge of path P5. To be able to follow path P5 companies must be excellent readers of markets and also have correctly placed investment bets on the right technologies. Many of the companies that do well in steady state incremental innovation do so by focussing on purely short-term needs and incremental technology. They find it extremely difficult to adjust to dislocational change; unless they have deep pockets and capabilities to make rapid transitions they are doomed to fail. In this chapter we focus on the importance of being closely attuned to and understanding markets. In later chapters we examine the implications of technological discontinuities and change.

Market learning and understanding

Success in innovation is underpinned by the need to stay close to one's markets and fully understand the needs of the customers within these markets. Yet many products fail because the company has failed to understand fully the markets in which it operates. Companies need a deep appreciation of their customers, their competitors, the changes occurring within their channels, the technologies on the horizon, and the institutional and regulatory environment within which they exist. Successful firms are highly attuned to the market; they continuously sense and act on events and trends in their markets. These are market-driven companies. They anticipate and react to changes in their markets and in so doing they are able to better define new product ideas, retain and attract customers, take appropriate advantage of emerging technologies and pre-empt competitor actions. Day (2002) highlights that successful companies continuously learn about their markets through a process of (i) market sensing, (ii) sense making, and (iii) reflection (see Figure 11.3). The way a company senses its markets is key in defining its ability to spot environmental discontinuities. Those companies that rely just on conventional methods of market learning are quite likely to miss out on small cues of emergent change occurring in the periphery of the marketplace.

Market sensing

Mastery of the complete market learning process is rare. Most firms suffer from some form of disability along the full market-learning spectrum. Some probe the market with a narrow

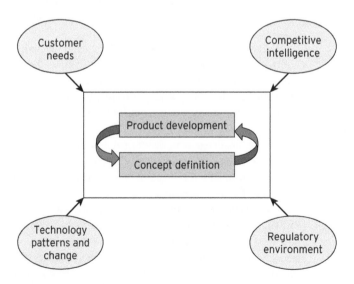

FIGURE 11.3 The different angles of the market environment
Source: Day, 2002

lens, others unintentionally use systems that constrict information flow, and some continually repeat their mistakes. A few are, however, able to master the full process, and reap the benefits of being able to anticipate market opportunities, and respond strategically and in a timely manner to changes in the environment.

Market sensing involves two key activities. It begins with an open-minded approach to the market rather than inquiry simply to confirm pre-existing beliefs about the environment. The second activity of market sensing is to disseminate information and insights throughout the organisation, such that it becomes a collective understanding of the marketplace. Ensuring that market information is understood requires ensuring that the market-sensing activity is followed by a sense-making activity. This involves an act of interpretation and is dependent on mental models of the organisational collective. When there exists shared understanding and shared assumptions the actions that follow are coherent and aligned. Without a common frame, different reactions and priorities are pressed, and the focus of organisational strategy peters out in fragmented actions.

Market sensing can be achieved through numerous devices to 'open' the collective mind.

1. Create a spirit of open-minded enquiry

Market learning companies have an openness to change. They perceive change with the lens of opportunity. They even take hold of threats and work at them to see if there are any potential windows of opportunity from even the threat itself. In contrast arrogant companies, occupied by the myopia of current success, are blind to market discontinuities and usually so until it is too late.

2. Carefully analyse competitor actions

Most companies keep a watchful eye on their competitors. They constantly tear down and reverse-engineer competitor products and monitor their marketing actions in the marketplace. Unfortunately, more often than not such exercises create superficial understanding: a collation of news clippings, price and market share trends. With their energies focussed thus, these companies can miss out on what is happening behind the scenes in terms of new capabilities that their competitors are building, the innovations in their processes and the shifts in their strategies. Some of these shortcomings can be addressed by the correct use of benchmarking. Yet even when benchmarking is applied, it is rare to see it being used to address the entire value chain. Without systematic benchmarking of the entire business value chain many important insights are overlooked. The result is a narrow focus on competitor product(s) rather than building an understanding of competitor processes and capabilities.

3. Listening to the market pulse

Companies that are able to use every means possible to create a picture of the market enjoy an enriched and deeper understanding of the marketplace and its dynamics. The changes in the markets are both subtle and complex and it is not enough to rely on simple examinations of the market. A number of market pulse measures must be taken to construct the picture. Over-reliance on a single market pulse (source of market intelligence) can easily lead to one-sided appreciation of a multi-sided picture. One important method of checking the market pulse is to listen to market front-line. For instance, customer complaints can be a source for product improvement. Front-line staff, such as sales teams, are excellent conduits of such knowledge. Additionally, the information in-flow must be made useful. This can be done by linking the information in-flow to the information up-flow. Technology can enhance information flow. However, technology alone is unable to make the system work. Technology can only succeed if there are appropriate supporting systems that encourage and reward individuals for their role in knowledge collection and utilisation.

4. Seeking out latent needs

It is necessary to go beyond the surface of consumer needs. Market research must be able to produce a deeper and richer understanding of customer needs. Many structured methods of market research, particularly quantitative forms, suffer from the straitjacket of numbers. Even qualitative methods, such as focus groups, are easily distorted by the view of one or a few effusive members. Research must be focussed to uncover the deeper needs and fuller pictures of a product concept and its use. The focus of conventional market research tools and techniques must be altered to this aim, as well as supplemented by the development of newer tools for this purpose.

5. Actively scan the market periphery

All companies scan their environment to some extent. What makes successful companies stand out from the not so successful ones is the focus of their scanning activity. Market learning companies do not focus attention on the obvious and the familiar. Doing so simply re-inforces understanding of the current market boundary, not *what it can be* or *may become*. Market-sensitive companies look at the edges of the market and check on the periphery for any cues of impending change. Often weak signals go un-noticed by the multitude of companies engaged in syndicated studies of current market patterns. This problem is compounded by a heavy reliance on traditional sources and methods of market information. Market research agencies as suppliers of market information are not attuned to the periphery of a company's market. Even worse they are hardly ever asked to investigate the periphery, and so they continue to supply the information they have been asked to provide.

6. Encouraging experimentation and improvement

Innovative organisations are constantly experimenting. They work hard at creating environments that encourage trial and error. When individuals in the organisation feel safe to try out things they begin to build richer understanding of what works and what does not, what the market needs, and what it does not. This involves a process of probe and learn (see Lynn et al., 1996 for an exposition of the probe and learn method).

ILLUSTRATION

The future will bring more of the past?

A fundamental problem with many companies is, once successful, they begin to believe what was successful in the past will continue to be successful in the future. These blinkers can be rational as well as emotional.

Success often clouds the ability to see and take advantage of new opportunities. For instance, Barnes & Noble and Borders, national booksellers, failed to perceive the internet as a significant threat to their book sales. Had they done so they could have pre-empted much of Amazon.com's success. Both were riding high on their success in driving many independent bookstores out of business. The internet was unproven and didn't fit neatly into their business model. As a result, they entered cautiously and very slowly. This gave Amazon sufficient time to become a formidable competitor.

To try and catch up with Amazon, Borders created a separate online division. Unfortunately, this separate organisation was so divorced from its bricks-and-mortar sister part that Borders missed the opportunity to adopt a bricks-and-clicks strategy that combined the strengths of its online and offline capabilities. Eventually, Borders sold its online unit to Amazon.

(*Source*: Based on Berggren and Nacher, 2001)

Organisational sense making

Collecting good market information is only a starting point. Companies must make use of this information. To do this they must give meaning to the information, as well as disseminate it. The key is to add value to the market data. Meaning and value depend on the way the information is processed by the cognitive lens of the organisation. These organisational cognitive filters are called mental models. Mental models organise, structure and pattern given information in particular ways. Thus, different mental models can embody the same information with very different meanings. Because of this, mental models can have important ramifications for organisational action. If many different types of mental models exist within the organisation then the outcome can be a cacophony of interpretations. This is typically the case in companies where functional mindsets and functional chimneys exist. The secret of aligned action is to ensure that a mutually shared mindset exists in the company. However, mental model sharing must be tempered because it can also quite easily lead to the dominance of a singular viewpoint in which alternative interpretations are foreclosed (an antithesis of open-minded enquiry). In the extreme this can result in decision-making myopia. This is usually compounded by a tendency to look for self-fulfilling prophecies, in which more market facts are gathered to reinforce, justify and ratify currently held beliefs.

To avoid such pitfalls and improve their mental models, companies should look to understand what mental models they are using and the nature of impact of their use. The most important way to understand and even change mental models is to surface them. This means bringing out into the open the assumptions that underlie actions. In others words, the nature and logic of the justification for specific accepted courses of action, beliefs and behaviours needs to be questioned and probed. Such a process opens up the possibility for process and strategic innovation to occur.

Reflection

Once decisions have been reached and implemented, the outcomes of these must also be monitored as a basis of further learning. This should involve a systematic deconstruction of actions to distil out learning. By taking action the firm is positioned to learn. However, actions do not of themselves become learning unless they are accompanied by a systematic process of de-briefing. Furthermore, new insights are easily lost, especially over time, if they are not captured and stored as readily retrieval knowledge within the organisational memory.

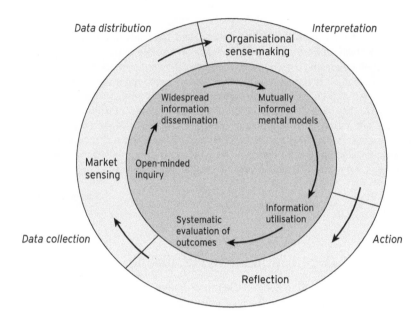

FIGURE 11.4 Organisational process for market learning

Conventional probes for market understanding

In view of the importance and costs of innovation it is not surprising that so much effort is directed at trying to build detailed understanding of the market. The business environment must be assessed from a number of different perspectives (see Figure 11.4). Customer needs and their reactions to new offerings must be assessed. Changes in technologies, current and on the horizon need to be evaluated. Competitor moves needs to be monitored. The regulatory environment needs to be noted and its implication for the business incorporated. Understanding of each of these has a very significant bearing upon the success of the corporate effort to successfully innovate.

The innovation (new product development) process can be broken into two basic parts: (i) an early market-product definition part, sometimes called the fuzzy front end (FFE), and (ii) the product development phases. Success requires due diligence to be paid to both phases. Whilst research suggests the importance of ensuring a robust early part (Gupta and Wilemon, 1990) often in practice much of the time and effort is directed to the second part of the process: the development stage (Bacon et al., 1994). The early phase, however, is important not least because it holds significant strategic consequences for downstream activities that follow. Poor reading of the market and the environment trends can set the organisation off on the wrong path. Once started down a path, companies find it incredibly difficult to stop or even change course.

Good information and deep understanding of the market play a key role in lowering innovation failure. Yet all too often if market research in the new product process is done at all, it is done as an afterthought. To be effective it must be used as an input into real-time decisions and not as an after-the-event check. If used well market information fuels organisational innovation and learning.

The amount and type of information needed depends on the newness of the product and the nature of the dynamic in the market or technology. These features guide the type of

From little niches can come big markets

The challenge for suppliers to the large and small 'cosmetic and personal care' market is to keep pace with changes in needs and emerging markets by developing innovative solutions.

Ingredient suppliers know it is imperative that they anticipate trends in the market, particularly emerging segments that are likely to be the major impetus behind growth in cosmetic sales. They must do this in order to 'buy' time to develop and leverage their technological innovations. One emergent market has been the men's cosmetics sector, in which technology-orientated manufacturers of a new breed are establishing themselves as major operators. Leading European players such as L'Oréal, Beiersdorf and Clarins are bidding for a firm foothold in the market, while SMEs are already creating niches.

New opportunities are being created by changes in a wide variety of markets. For instance, in teenagers' cosmetics, expanding segments include colorants and skin care, in which young people have a relatively wide range of needs. Ciba, which is already active in hair colorants for older age groups, has recently introduced an ingredient that helps to enhance the colours in young consumers' hair. L'Oréal uses the ingredient in its Feria Booster product to achieve more vibrant and intense red and copper tones. 'Hair dyes are now extending right across the age spectrum and are no longer mainly concerned with covering up grey hairs', says Mr Tim Schlange, head of Ciba Speciality Chemicals' Home and Personal Care division.

(Source: Based on Milmo, 2004)

questions that need to be asked. The basic type of key questions and accompanying research tools (Nijssen and Frambach 1998; Sultan and Barczak, 1999) are summarised in Table 11.1.

The main categories of intelligence-gathering tools commonly used across the development process are shown in Figure 11.5 and are briefly elaborated next.

TABLE 11.1 Key questions and research tools

NPD stage	Key questions	Suitable tools
Idea generation	● What product to develop? ● How to improve existing products?	Brainstorming, morphological analysis, synectics, focus groups, user-observation, Delphi method, benchmarking, observation, multi-dimensional scaling (MDS), benefit–needs analysis.
Concept development and testing	● How must the product be designed? ● How can the product deliver improved value?	Conjoint analysis, quality policy deployment, concept test, prototype test, in-home use test, observation, use-cases and scenarios.
Market testing	● How to introduce the product? ● What marketing strategies to use?	Mini tests, simulated market test, limited roll-out, scanner market research, test marketing, observation, antennae shops.
Market launch	● What is the new product's anticipated success? ● How to manage the product over its lifecycle?	Market prediction models, diffusion models, economic models (ROI analysis, payback time, etc.), observation.

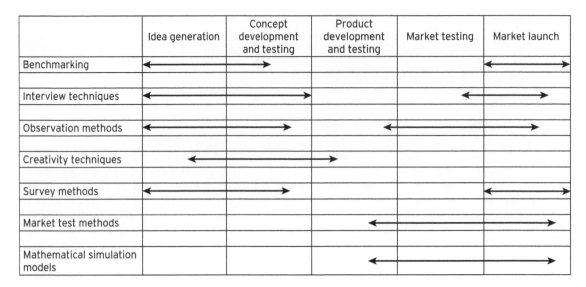

FIGURE 11.5 Market intelligence tools across the product development process

Benchmarking intelligence

Benchmarking is a systematic process of learning and comparing performance. Here we illustrate two simple ways of building market understanding.

Secondary sources

Information can be gained from monitoring the external environment. Secondary information can be easily gained by carefully checking patent disclosures, university and government research publications, trade journals as well as competitor product launches.

Product teardown (reverse engineering)

Product teardowns provide a basic insight into the strengths and weaknesses of a product or technology. Product teardown is a process of taking apart a product in order to understand its form and function. It can be done with a number of objectives: to understand how a product functions, how it fulfils its functions, costs of components and assembly, how it can be improved or developed, etc. Teardowns are often done as part of a larger competitive benchmarking process.

Interview techniques

There is a whole host of interview techniques that can be used to develop better understanding of the market. The most common ones for product development use either a direct questioning format or an indirect format. We elaborate an example of each.

Focus groups

Focus groups are a means of generating new product ideas. Focus groups involve getting together a group of customers in a relaxed environment and then directing them to react and discuss a number of topics. The main aim is usually to uncover needs, wants, etc.

Projective techniques

Projective techniques are interview techniques, which through an indirect approach of questioning attempt to define needs, fears and product use. This method is used in product areas that are likely to evoke emotional involvement. Common techniques include word-association tests, sentence completion, cartoon tests, thematic apperception tests and third-person techniques.

Creativity methods

Creativity techniques can be used to develop insights of the marketplace that could easily be missed by structured techniques. Creativity techniques are not just relevant for building external insights but are important in the problem-solving process inside the organisation.

Brainstorming

Brainstorming is typically carried out in a group and is designed to elicit suggested solutions to a presented problem. For instance, asking individuals to come up with new products, new use for existing products. Brainstorming can be conducted through a variety of techniques (such as synectics, word association, etc.).

Morphological analysis

This is an approach to find a large number of alternative solutions to a problem by dividing it into smaller sub-parts. For every sub-part problem a solution is defined, and eventually the solutions to the sub-parts are interlinked to solve the problem as a whole. It is especially appropriate for complex or multi-dimensional problems. The technique involves first listing all product/problem attributes, then defining as large a number of possible alternatives that can be used to fulfil the function of each attribute, and finally considering and evaluating the different combinations in order to arrive at the final decision.

Survey-based statistical methods

Surveys using direct questions are one of the most common methods of building market understanding. Surveys can vary greatly in the form and way they are conducted and the level of understanding they lead to. Most, however, are concerned with defining customer needs, product gaps and the value that the market places on features. From amongst the variety, three common yet sophisticated methods are benefit–needs analysis, multi-dimensional scaling (MDS) and conjoint analysis.

Benefit–needs analysis

Survey methods involve asking questions, usually on a rating scale that contains a list of needs or desired benefits deduced from secondary or prior research. Respondent profile information is also usually collected. Respondents rank or rate the needs and benefits. The data is then subject to advanced statistical techniques such as factor analysis and clustering to define segments and their associated needs.

Multi-dimensional scaling (MDS)

Another advanced technique based on survey-led input is multi-dimensional scaling (MDS). MDS allows definition of segments and indicates gaps in existing product lines.

Conjoint analysis

Conjoint analysis is an advanced method (like MDS) that allows decomposition of a customer's attitude towards a product to be broken down into his/her attitude to the component attribute (or product feature) through a process of comparing different combinations of attributes. The evaluative comparisons (e.g. ranking of the individual's disposition to buy or not) lead to an indication of the value that is associated with each attribute. From this the features to bundle in a product can be defined and assessed. An introductory discussion of this method can be found in Green and Wind (1975).

Mathematical methods

A number of methods develop understanding of markets through generalisation of insights from past evidence and theory.

Simulation models

Market patterns can be predicted from mathematical prediction using computer modelling. This involves using mathematical simulation to estimate the market share of a new product, usually over time by taking into consideration factors such as customer preference, market mix parameters and competitive intensity and competitor reactions. By altering the parameters, for example changing price elasticity of the product, the likely pattern of impact on the product's entry into the market and over its life cycle can be defined.

Diffusion models

This method focusses on the pattern of adoption of a new product. It is based on the theory of innovation diffusion which suggests that customers adopt with different speeds due to their personal dispositional perceptions of the relative advantages of the new product. Several mathematical approaches are used in diffusion models. One major group of models utilises what is known as penetration models. These predict the level of penetration by a new product in a given time period by using early sales results. Another group of models use an epidemiological approach in which the new product diffusion pattern is determined by a process of social interaction through which early adopters 'infect' the rest of the market population. This approach models diffusion as an analogous process to the spread of disease through a population (an excellent review of these can be found in Mahajan and Peterson, 1985 and Mahajan et al., 1990). A number of adoption models have been developed which incorporate market structure variables to predict market introductions (Urban et al., 1993). They use test market data and early market sales to forecast future sales and profitability of the new product. Many of these models have evolved from academic research and have been widely adopted by large blue-chip companies.

Market testing methods

Market testing methods are used to get market feedback on developed concepts, prototypes and actual products. The two main categories of test are those that simulate the environment and those that conduct real-life tests.

Simulated market test

Market tests can be performed in research laboratories, in which the traditional shopping process is compressed into a short time span. Consumers visit the research lab and are exposed to the various selected marketing mix elements (e.g. shown an advert) and then asked to shop in a room that looks like a supermarket aisle. From this researchers are able to estimate trial purchase rates and re-purchase based on their findings from the experimental store.

Mini tests

Companies can check on the likely impact of a new product introduction by conducting a mini-test before going for a full-scale launch. The mini-test involves distributing the product in a controlled manner in a small locality or in a few outlets. The objective is the same as that for the simulated market test: assess awareness, trial and repeat purchase behaviour and positioning via-à-vis the competition.

Observation methods

Observation is a rich medium for market information. It is relatively time-consuming but because it can yield different insights to quantitative approaches its use is preferred by many market researchers, especially in Europe. American research tends to be more orientated toward quantitative research whereas European companies show a preference for qualitative research (Nijssen and Frambach, 1998).

Observation studies can be of a variety of types: direct or indirect, verbal or non-verbal, participative and non-participative. For instance, indirect observation can be made through scrutiny of the physical trace of some past occurrence or event. It may be a content analysis of the artefacts of a product's use, its advertising, or media/newspaper evaluation. In other instances, it may be direct observation through actual participation of an event or through a mechanical medium such as a videotape, people-traffic counters, or scanner data from the retail checkout desks.

Additionally, observation may be at the physiological level of the individual. For instance, the oculometer monitors eye movements; the pupilometer measures changes in pupil dilation of subjects; the psychogalvonometer measures galvanic skin response (GSR), which is the involuntary change in electrical resistance of the skin; and voice pitch analysis detects changes in voice response to assess emotional states.

Observation allows for a wide variety of information about people, objects, spatial relations, temporal patterns and so on to be collected. However, whilst it is deemed to be a rich medium, it has its shortfalls beyond the yardstick of time and cost. One major disadvantage of observation studies is that cognitive phenomena such as attitudes, expectations, intentions and preferences are not observable. Observation study often captures overt expressions, especially when conducted over short durations as is typical in most market studies.

Consumption or use-analysis observation

This involves observation of how a product is used. Often observation is supplemented by interviews with the users. By observing consumers in use situations it is often possible to derive ideas for the improvement of current offerings.

In-house use tests

This method provides potential customers with a new product that is used/consumed in their home environment. Afterwards the experiences of use/problems are discussed. In some cases, with the participant's permission, the in-house test is combined with direct observation through use of appropriate mechanical devices.

TABLE 11.2 Limitations of some market research models

Market research model/key limitation	Market complexity not captured	Too much time to implement	Forecast inaccuracy	Expensive, complexity not captured
Focus groups/panel	✓			
Limited roll-out		✓		
Concept tests			✓	
Show test/clinic		✓		
Attitude/usage studies			✓	
Conjoint analysis				✓
QFD		✓	✓	
Home usage test		✓		✓
Life cycle models			✓	
Synectics			✓	✓

Source: Sanchez and Sudharshan, 1993

Limitations of conventional approaches

Attempts to improve the rate of new products through increased market research spend is widespread but unfortunately deep insight is not easily forthcoming. Problems with conventional approaches became evident during the 1990s. Despite vast spending on market research there were considerable shortcomings in the reliability and validity of traditional market research, such that they can compromise significantly the decisions of product development managers (Mahajan and Wind, 1991). Many companies, frustrated with lack of success in NPD and customer focus, had raised questions over the value of the consumer-driven NPD process and the associated marketing research and modelling used to assess customer needs (Wind and Mahajan, 1997). Much of this failure stemmed from shortcomings in the traditional approach to market research. Sanchez and Sudharshan (1993) highlighted the key limitations of traditional market research models as shown in Table 11.2.

Some critics suggest that the deficiencies of these techniques made them redundant (Hamel and Prahalad, 1994). However, the solution is not to reject these tools and techniques. The challenge instead is to develop new research and modelling approaches capable of dealing with the new problems arising from increased complexity and uncertainty.

Market research: following customers or leading customers

Thus far, we have assumed that extra information aids decision making within the NPD process and, therefore, leads ultimately to success. However, the nature of the relationship between conducting market research and performance is not all that straightforward. A number of studies have indicated either a tenuous or non-existence of such a relationship (e.g. Nijssen and Frambach, 1998). However, the failure of market research to show a positive effect on performance may be due to poor commissioning and use of market research as well as problems of implementation. Nijssen and Frambach (1998) indicated that when care-fully designed and aimed, market research could help the process of NPD. As noted earlier, other researchers have found that market research was most effective in the early phases of the NPD process (e.g. Cooper and Kleinschmidt, 1986).

Further question-marks over the value and relevance of market research have been raised. Market research can help in the process of fine-tuning existing products but its relevance for radical innovations has been questionable (Hamel and Prahalad, 1994). The value of the research has been considered to be contingent on a particular type of innovation, as well as the stage within the NPD process at which it was used. The relevance of market research was particularly questioned with regard to radical innovations involving big shifts in technology. In situations involving discontinuous technological development, customers were unlikely to understand the technology or its potential applicability. Scientists close to the technolog-ical development were the first to articulate the development and therefore, by inference of their expertise, best placed to define the initial set of potentialities. Consumers may have found the initial technological breakthrough too far removed from the reality of everyday consumption for them to make sense of its potential. This position changes with time as consumers begin to be educated about the 'technology'. Once consumers see and trial initial versions of a product concept they are able to anchor these in the world of consumption and use. Thereafter, they play an ever-increasing role in defining and shaping the market potential.

Companies simply focussing on understanding the needs that customers are able to arti-culate are prone to a tendency to innovate incrementally. They develop slight variants upon existing offerings. By focussing their energies narrowly on expressed and expressible con-sumer needs they run a huge risk of neglecting products arising from tomorrow's techno-logies and tomorrow's needs. Building on the work of a number of researchers (Hamel and Prahalad, 1994; Wind and Mahajan, 1997; Trott, 2001), we define a matrix along two axes to help assess the role and usefulness of market research (see Figure 11.6). The y-axis maps the

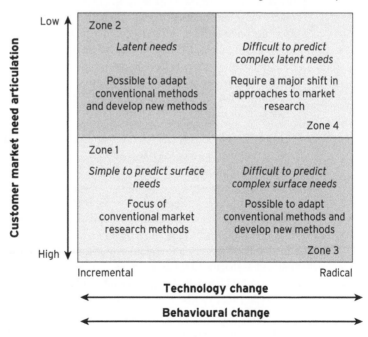

FIGURE 11.6 Customer needs and market research

extent to which the market or consumers are able to articulate their needs and the x-axis maps the level of discontinuity of change (technology or behavioural).

- *Zone 1*: Needs can be articulated and the 'change' shift is incremental (technologically or behaviourally). This is where the main focus of conventional NPD methods and techniques is directed. Here current tools are most effective and have the greatest impact in delivering incisive and insightful information.

- *Zone 2*: Here there is continuous change in technology or consumer behaviour but the problem is one of investigating needs and desires that consumers find it difficult to articulate. These are deep needs that exist at the sub-conscious or even pre-conscious level or are needs that have not been thought about because they do not as yet exist. This area represents unexploited opportunities. Current tools and methods can be used here but may lack in reliability and validity. This quadrant is one in which companies need to re-focus their market research attention to enable innovation over and above, e.g., changing the taste of the toothpaste or the shape of the dispenser nozzle. This requires developing new techniques as well as adapting conventional ones.

- *Zone 3*: Here the shift in technology or behaviour is discontinuous. However, given that consumers are able to express their needs in terms of what the technology can do for them, or able to countenance the behaviour change, many of the conventional techniques remain relevant.

- *Zone 4*: This poses the greatest challenge for the market research community. Here customers are unable to express or even know their needs and the change/shift is discontinuous. In these circumstances, there are only a few expert individuals and a handful of lead-users who are familiar with the discontinuous technology. Scientists and developers (or the advanced lead-users) are the ones who define the range of use possibilities for the technology. The challenge for market research companies is thus doubled. First, searching for a radical shift in technology (or behaviour), and second linking this to unknown or unexpressed needs. Companies able to do both are the ones able to transform the boundaries of the market and displace current competitive rules and positions. This is the region capturing disruptive or discontinuous innovation. To build understanding of this market zone requires major shifts in the way market research is currently conducted. This domain primarily (and to a lesser extent Zone 2 secondarily) and Zone 3 require what Wind and Mahajan (1997) refer to as 'knowledge-based marketing research and modelling'.

Under discontinuous change traditional market research is not able to provide accurate market understanding. However, we believe, in line with Wind and Mahajan (1997), that the solution is not to reject the value of consumer-driven NPD market research but the challenge is to adapt these tools and to develop new research methods and modelling approaches.

A number of shortcomings of traditional research make it necessary to re-define marketing research and market modelling beyond the traditional scope of qualitative methods (such as focus groups), consumer surveys and experiments, and move to use more encompassing tools of market knowledge acquisition about customers as well as stakeholders (Wind and Mahajan, 1997). Some new approaches and adaptations of conventional methods are already at hand. Building on Wind and Mahajan (1997), Figure 11.7 shows the range of approaches that can be used to aid the market intelligence and product development decision-making process. These emerging techniques help reduce the traditional reliance on focus groups and survey techniques. In the section that follows we examine a select number of these advances of approach and newly piloted techniques.

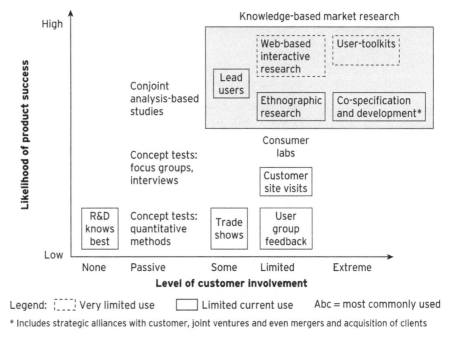

FIGURE 11.7 Developing the role of market research in innovation

New techniques for market understanding

There have been a number of developments attempting to address some of the shortcomings of conventional techniques in more dynamic and complex environments. We examine some of the key developments arising from opportunities created by new technology such as the Web, new co-development user-based methodologies, deeper insights arising from ethnographic approaches to the market and cognitive methods to surface customer needs.

Technology-led interactive research

Growth of internet use has created significant opportunity for online market research. Informed marketing and product development decision making requires estimating multi-variate relationships, such as the behaviour of a response variable to change in another product or marketing variable. Typically, data is collected through conventional methods such as direct mailings, telephone and shopping centre interviews, and focus groups. The conventional methods are slow and essentially represent a one-off interaction. Web-based customer input overcomes problems of conventional methods by enhanced capability across three dimensions (Dahan and Hauser, 2001).

1. It allows more rapid interaction, moving communication from a slow sequential mode to enable fast simultaneous interaction.

2. It enhances product conceptualisation by moving it from a primarily verbal test to one enabled by graphic and audio capabilities of multi-media computers to depict virtual products and product features. With rich virtual prototypes, product development teams can test their ideas and designs well before they go to the prototype stage.

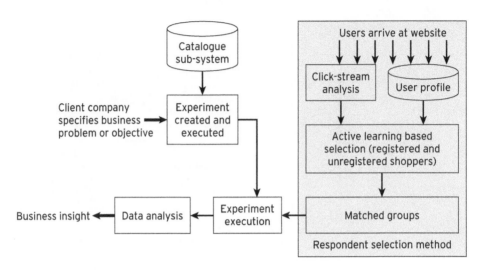

FIGURE 11.8 Online market research schema
Source: Agrawal et al., 2004. Reprint courtesy of International Business Machines Corporation © 2004 International Business Machines Corporation

3. Real-time computation is enabled, allowing a shift from fixed survey designs to dynamically adapting web pages. Real-time computation also allows stimuli presented to customers to become dynamic and interactive, thus facilitating instantaneous feedback from user to designer. Feedback allows the end user to understand better the trade-offs, say between price and function, and so improve the accuracy of decisions on 'ideal design'.

In web-based market research, changes in the product and marketing variables are executed online and the responses are collected online as part of content on a web page. The web page guides the customer through the process to engage in transactions or evaluations. A schematic of this type of system, from Agrawal et al. (2004), is provided in Figure 11.8. The process begins with specification of an objective from the firm (or the market research team on behalf of the firm). The objective could be, for example, to assess demand as a function of price for a new product. Let us say, sales of new brand A as the price of brand B is reduced, or the impact of introducing a new product on existing market brands. This data gathering is called an 'experiment'. The online web pages are then changed along the specified dimension(s) to set the experiment up for selected visitors to the website. The customer/visitors are broken into two groups. This is done to create a matched control and experimental group. The matched groups are set up to allow observation of the response resulting from changes in product or marketing variables (price, bundle of functions, etc.). To observe the effect of a change along the variable under scrutiny requires removing the effects of any other compounding factors by use of a matched control group. The groups are formed on the basis of visitor (user) profiles to remove differences in population characteristics. The user profile can be constituted from the click-stream pattern (navigator) along with the user's historical transactions (if available from their log-on records) and any other relevant information. The visitor simply proceeds through the website, and the user's response is measured either explicitly or indirectly. The experiment is then executed for a set amount of time, or until no further useful information is forthcoming.

The range of possibilities for using web-based research is large: it can be used for assessing price sensitivity, determining brand loyalty, product cannibalisation, defining market penetration patterns for product categories, as well as deriving attribute utilities for product functions.

Major work in this field is being conducted at the Massachusetts Institute of Technology (MIT) by a group of researchers within the Virtual Customer Initiative (VCI) centre. Their work has made several significant breakthroughs. The group, working with other eminent researchers, has developed a number of novel methods of gathering customer input for product development (for detailed discussion see Dahan and Hauser, 2001; Urban and Hauser, 2004). By taking advantage of new computational algorithms, multi-media visualisation tools and web interactivity, the tools and methods help product development teams to generate and evaluate new concepts and prototypes quickly, accurately and inexpensively. We briefly highlight the key developments from amongst these.

Web-based or adaptive choice-based conjoint analysis

This method takes the well-established conjoint analysis tool for probing customer trade-offs and adapts it for the Web. Customers are presented with a set of products with specific bundle of features and are asked online to indicate their comparative preferences. From analysis of the online survey information it becomes possible to assess how much value customers place on specific features of a product. This method can be used for a wide range of product types, and has been piloted to assess automobile features and laptop computer bag features.

FastPace or (fast-polyhedral-adaptive conjoint) question selection

Web visitors tend to be impatient. Conventional conjoint analysis requires a significant number of questions for estimation of attribute utilities. FastPace uses an algorithm that allows accurate estimates of attribute (feature) utilities with a set of fewer questions.

Virtual concept testing

The facilities of web-based media-rich presentation allows testing of concepts without having to actually build the product prototype.

Virtual brainstorming

This is a web-based asynchronous ideation system that overcomes the constraints of co-location. Consumers or team members are invited to participate in an idea-generation exercise. To work well, the system needs to ensure that for each exercise incentives are fine-tuned to get individuals to think of ideas that are relevant.

Information pump

This is a web-based interactive game designed to get participants to think hard and describe their needs in detail and truthfully by use of a finely tuned variable incentive system. For example, reward is increased when they tell the truth and articulate new customer needs that are not redundant with previously stated needs. In pilot studies this process has shown promise to outstrip extant qualitative methods in creative output.

User design

This exploits the flexibility of the Web to enable users to design their own virtual products. Customers can design a product by use of a drag and drop function. As desired features are added (or removed) costs and constraints automatically define the price. This allows the product development team to understand more fully the complex interactions of features, and also allows customers to clarify and understand their own preferences. The technique is useful for defining opportunities for product design improvement especially in the early phases of product development.

Securities trading concepts

This method combines virtual concepts with customers' interaction with each other in a stock market type of game. Customers buy and sell stocks of virtual product concepts. Initial research suggests that the security price is a good predictor of how the market will accept the product. This is a novel way to identify winning concepts.

Genetic algorithms

This technique is based on genetic algorithms. The US firm Affinnova has developed an interactive design by evolutionary algorithms (IDEA) that combines market research and design into one. In genetic algorithms product features are treated as genes, and the algorithm searches for an optimal progeny design concept through a process of 'mating' current concepts. The idea is based on an evolutionary process to arrive at optimal design. Using the IDEA technology, a product concept (e.g. packaging, print copy of an advert, or product) is defined by a number of attributes, each of which can have a number of different values, to assemble a total product design. For instance, a bottle can be broken down into a top, neck base, general contours, colour, label, etc.). Respondents in real time select the pressures that drive the evolutionary process towards the fittest design candidates. The pressures are defined by respondent selections on a simple preference rating scale of likes and dislikes. As consumers express their preferences and indifferences the system iterates and explores the design universe (which for complex products with many attributes can involve many hundreds of thousands of design possibilities) to generate an image of a product that scores optimally, i.e. a picture of their true preferences.

Customer listening in

The internet allows passive observation of customers. By manipulating the website structure and design (e.g. via 'data miners') it is possible for an engineer to 'listen in' to the way customers navigate and search for attributes that are not being satisfied by current offerings.

Distributed systems of product development

Previously, considerable time and effort was spent in communications, especially when different teams of expertise were situated in geographically disperse locations. New technologies enable integration of different expertise and information in real time. Distributed Object Modelling Environment (DOME) is a system that enhances and accelerates the information and expertise flow. It works by setting up a common platform between the distributed teams, each of which feeds its expertise, knowledge and decisions into a central platform as knowledge inputs. As these knowledge inputs are posted they enhance the knowledge base of other team members (who may be situated in distant locations) in terms of product parameters, constraints and possibilities. This allows formation of virtual cross-functional teams. Systems such as DOME are potentially useful for large organisations with dispersed operations.

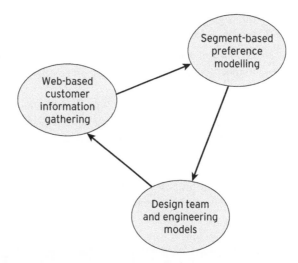

FIGURE 11.9 Distributed object modelling environment (DOME)
Source: Dahan and Hauser, 2001

For example, DOME has been implemented by Ford Motor company (Dahan and Hauser, 2001) (see Figure 11.9).

Non-web-based customer-led methods

A number of customer-led research methodologies can also be used to better understand customer needs and wants. Two examples are discussed here: 'lead users' and 'user toolkits'.

Lead users

Traditional methods of market research are limited in their ability to deal with really novel or discontinuous innovations. This is particularly the case for high-tech products, in which the average consumer is likely to have low awareness. Urban and von Hippel (1988) propose the deployment of 'lead users' as a solution to this problem. Lead users belong to a select group of individuals whose current needs within a product category are highly likely to become general in the marketplace months or years into the future. These individuals, also, are ones who benefit significantly by obtaining a solution to their needs. Because of the combination of these two characteristics this sub-set is likely to have the deepest understanding of the need and will strive to select the optimal solution. This makes them a valuable target sample for discontinuous market research enquiry.

Urban and von Hippel (1988) suggest a four-step process to incorporate lead users into the market research process:

1. *Identify an important trend or technical trend*: In order to define advanced users in the market it is important first to define the trend that one is interested in. This means looking at an important dimension of the product category and assessing trends with respect to it. Trend identification may be achieved through a variety of means. A poll of experts or Delphi panel are two methods for this.

2. *Identify lead users who lead the trend in terms of (i) experience and (ii) intensity of need*: This can be achieved by conducting a survey of the population, and then clustering them

into a group of users who show advanced understanding of the trend and possess high-level needs along this dimension.

3. *Obtain and analyse lead-user data*: From the cluster analysis of lead users select a small number to participate in a group discussion to develop one or more concepts along the trend-line trajectory.

4. *Test and validate the value of lead-user needs data*: From the point of commercialisation new product ideas from lead-users are only interesting if they are also preferred by the general marketplace. To test this it is necessary to check the general population's preference toward the lead-users concept and other concepts and existing offers. If the general market shows a preference for the lead users' concepts in their rating then there is potential in their proposed concepts, i.e. if non-lead users show a similar preference to lead users then the idea should be considered for further development.

ILLUSTRATION

Customers are doing it for themselves

Traditionally, firms send out market researchers to discover 'unmet needs' of their customers. The researchers report back and the firm peruses the data, decides which ideas to develop, and assigns them to development teams. Professor Eric Von Hippel (1989) argues that harnessing the customer more effectively can reduce the number of project failures. Instead of engaging a representative sample of customers, firms must identify the few special customers who innovate. Researchers call such customers 'lead users'.

The healthcare division of General Electric (GE) refers to these 'lead users' as 'luminaries', and they tend to be well-published doctors and research scientists from leading medical institutions. GE brings up to 25 of these 'luminaries' together at regular medical advisory board sessions to discuss the evolution of GE's technology. GE then shares some of its advanced technology with a sub-set of luminaries who form an 'inner sanctum of good friends', resulting in the release of new products as a consequence of this collaboration.

Staples, an American office-supplies retailer, held a competition amongst its customers to come up with new product ideas, and received 8300 submissions. Lead users were identified from this group, and subsequently played a major role in the development of a number of products, including the 'word-lock' – a padlock that uses words instead of numbers.

An interesting facet of this method is that it challenges a widely held notion that people expect to be paid for their creative work, hence the need to protect and reward the creation of intellectual property, and it appears that customers are willing to donate their creativity freely. This may be because some people value the enhanced reputation and network effects of freely revealing their work more than any money they can make out of patenting.

(Source: Based on Economist, 2005)

User toolkits

Another technique for increasing the involvement of users into the development process is the concept of a user toolkit developed by Eric von Hippel and Ralph Katz (2002). Many companies have found it difficult to come to terms with fast-changing consumer needs and the superficiality of conventional techniques to understand user needs, and the expense and time needed for ethnographic approaches. Faced with this scenario, von Hippel and Katz developed a method that allows companies to 'abandon' research into user needs. Instead, they 'outsource' the research to the users themselves. To facilitate outsourcing, users must be provided with the capability and tools to develop the initial designs and product proto- types (virtual or tangible) by themselves. The process involves equipping users with a 'user- friendly' toolkit which enables them to define and develop features according to their needs. To work, the toolkits have to be specifically geared to the product category or field. Allowing users to come up with and specify solutions themselves enables companies to pick up early on user needs. If these changes become apparent late on in the process this leads to high-cost re-work and correction. Use of toolkits has enabled faster and more efficient development, cutting time to market, in some cases by two-thirds in certain product categories (von Hippel, 1998).

ILLUSTRATION

DIY innovation

BMW has begun prototyping 'telematics' (combining computing and telecommunications) and online services for a new generation of luxury cars, in which its customers played a major role as designers. This effort to harness the creativity of its customers began in 2003, when BMW posted a toolkit on its website allowing ideas to be developed to take advantages in 'telematics' and in-car online services.

From the 1000 customers who used the toolkit, BMW chose 15 and invited them to meet its engineers in Munich. Some of their ideas (which remain under wraps for now) have since reached the prototype stage, says BMW. Customers were delighted to be invited into this scheme, and did not expect payment. This success has led BMW to broaden its customer-innovation efforts further, and more and more com- panies are looking toward active customer engagements of this kind.

Westwood Studios, a developer now owned by the computer games company Electronic Arts (EA), first noticed its customers innovating its products after the launch of the game 'Red Alert' in 1996. Gamers were making new content and posting it freely on fan websites. Westwood made a conscious decision to embrace this phenomenon, and was soon shipping basic development tools with its games. Three years later, it had a dedicated department to feed designers and producers working on new pro- jects with customer innovations.

(*Source*: Based on Economist, 2005)

Ethnographic methods

Qualitative research plays a key role in building market understanding. Many companies such as P&G, and L'Oréal have found that no matter how much data is collected some insights can only be gained by 'deeper' observation of customers in their natural habitats (Sykes, 1990). Qualitative research contains a wide variety of techniques and methods derived from two broad schools. One group of methods borrows from psychology and its major concern has been to explore the subconscious. The second group is derived from soci- ology, social anthropology, linguistics and semiology. It emphasises building an under- standing of the 'world view' of people by probing their experiences and feelings.

In engaging in qualitative research one is involved in what is commonly called the interpretive paradigm. This contrasts sharply with deciphering quantitative information (which is part of the positivist paradigm, in which objectivity and scientific logic and experimentation play a key role in developing insight and understanding). Interpretive research adopts an inductive frame in which multiplicities of reality are accepted and the subjective nature of knowledge is accepted as a starting assumption. Interpretive research is based on induction, and inference is made from specific instance(s) and then considered for potential generalisation. In contrast, positivist approaches are driven by deductive criteria that demand postulating a frame or theory and then validating it through a systematic process of data gathering (sampling and control) such that the inference (proven or unproven) can be generalised.

Ethnography is an approach that falls under a broad and general research umbrella that covers observation and interviews. Ethnographic inquiry is defined as 'a descriptive, qualitative market research methodology for studying the customer in relation to his or her environment to acquire a deep understanding of customers' lifestyles or cultures as a basis for better understanding their needs and problems (Belliveau et al., 2002). Ethnography is distinguished from general observation and interview methods by its requirement of spending a large amount of time observing a certain group or 'population' of people, and even perhaps sharing a way of life with them. The origins of ethnography originate from cultural anthropology. The organising principle relies on building an understanding of behaviour from detailed longitudinal observation. It is essentially a technique that involves entering the target's (for our purposes this could be customer, employee, competitor, etc.) natural environment (work, home, shopping, etc.). For example, in an attempt to understand the lifestyle of customers of its Lynx deodorant, Unilever's Home and Personal Care division sends out its market research representatives to clubs and raves. Market insights such as language and behaviour that are easily missed out by conventional techniques are picked up through such assignments.

In Europe particularly, there has been a growing trend to use ethnographic methods to study customer habits in retail and home environments. Ethnographic approaches allow the researcher to break away from the artificiality of the laboratory and study the consumer in their natural habitat/environment. The approach allows building richer, more rounded and more nuanced understanding of customers. Ethnography grew from attempts to understand different cultures, but its techniques of immersion, direct on-site observation and assumption-free interviewing are turning out to be highly applicable for exploring markets.

Ethnography can, when used correctly, build a deeper understanding than numbers. To grasp people's motivations and underlying meanings often requires going beyond that which can be articulated. A group of techniques are evolving from anthropology that present opportunities for product development. This group of techniques is often referred to as empathic design or contextual inquiry.

They allow the world to be viewed with a new set of eyes; a view of the world through your customer's lens. From such approaches two important types of learning for product development innovation can be derived (Perry, 1998).

1. *The out-there view*: Comprehending the world through another's eyes, hearing and sharing their stories and experiences, begins the process of building deeper understanding of motivation and behaviour. Through a glimpse of customers' real lives can come insights for innovation, often of their latent subconscious needs.

2. *In-here learning*: Understanding the world through a different lens allows us to challenge our own mental models. It forces surfacing of baseline assumptions and taken-for-

TABLE 11.3 Summary of ethnographic approaches and techniques

Approach/technique	Strength	Limitation
Field observation (passive)	Unobtrusive.	Need skilled observers/Cannot probe.
Written field notes	Record meaning of events as they occur. Relatively unobstrusive.	Limited recording of events. Cannot probe for insights without creating a break in the subject's action.
Full video recording	Comprehensive visual and sound data.	Limited angle of view. High evaluation costs. Respondents may be apprehensive. Laws or ethics may prohibit use.
Disguised field observation	Less obstrusive. View true behaviour.	Possible ethical concerns. No opportunity to probe or confirm interpretation with the subject.
Enthographic interview (active) observation and interview of individuals	Preselected subjects and script. Thorough inquiry.	High screening costs depending on difficulty to recruit. Possible Hawthorne effect.
Spontaneous intercept interviews	Action triggered with natural transition to interview. No recruitment cost.	Complex logistics results in increased on-site labour hours. Lack of pre-screening can yield gaps in sample of subjects.
On-site observation and interviews of affinity groups	Observe joint action and peer relationships.	Complex coordination effort is common. Effort required to gain acceptance. Possible bias due to dominant group member.
Participant observation direct involvement in events	Potential for surprise findings is high. Stresses empathic understanding.	Need skilled observers, access to right events. Limited exploration of researcher observations.

Source: Rosenthal and Capper, 2006

granted truths. Left unquestioned these assumptions and dominant mental models easily lead to organisational myopia. A summary of ethnographic approaches and techniques is offered in Table 11.3.

Empathic design

This approach creates understanding of users' needs through a process of building empathy with the customer's world, rather than relying on them to verbalise their needs. The process recognises that customers are often unaware of their own psychological and cultural predispositions and therefore fail to describe what developers want. Empathic design goes beyond traditional focus groups and surveys to a state requiring an immersion in the customer's world. Product developers first develop a deep understanding of the user's environment, and then they use this knowledge to extrapolate the environment that may evolve in the future. From this they can define technologies and product features that will be required to satisfy these needs.

Contextual inquiry

This is a technique in which the investigative team conducts an on-site interview (e.g. at home or at work) with a customer, while the customer performs real tasks. The investigators can interrupt the customer as the task is performed under scrutiny and ask them to explain their actions. The results of the methods are then mapped on to affinity diagrams and work-flow charts, and the findings can then be disseminated into the organisation (Holtzbaltt and Beyer, 1993).

Other variants of contextual inquiry are the beeper approach and the shadowing approach (Stevens, 1999). Shadowing involves following participants with a rolling camera, like a investigative crew for a TV documentary. In beeper studies participants are given a beeper, a logbook and a disposable camera and asked to go about their daily activities. When the beeper buzzes they are asked to take a picture of what they are doing, and answer questions such as what they are doing, how and why.

By complementarily adding to the conventional market research it becomes possible to break the sole focus on incremental market-led innovation and start getting a glimpse into sources of radical discontinuous innovation.

ILLUSTRATION

The new research

Anthropologists who observe people shopping – 'streetologists' – are among some innovative methods, including cameras and video diaries, being used by market researchers to delve into consumers' minds.

Frustrated by a lack of new insights into product or service categories such as food, drink and banking, research company Link Consumer Strategies, whose clients include Diageo, Kraft and Tesco, asked consumers to take a more active part in product development.

'It used to be enough to show a consumer a new brand of milkshake, say, and to record that he or she liked the packaging simply because pink had always been their favourite colour', said Louise Southcott, chairman of Link. 'Today though, with so many of our basic needs already met by marketers, it is necessary to go beyond the standard superficialities and tap into people's subconscious. If pink is their favourite colour because it reminds them of a happy childhood, that is something marketers can work with.'

Link asked its research subjects to complete complex 'self-investigative' or homework assignments before they attended research sessions, in order to gain greater insight into consumer behaviour than traditional market research provides. Ms Southcott said: 'Increasingly pernicious marketing problems require more in-depth, powerful tools to unlock them and while consumer dialogue is important, it needs to be made to work much harder. By asking consumers to really think about their lives, we can get genuine insights into subconscious motivations.'

Link cited Hovis Crusty White, launched by British Bakeries three years earlier. 'We established early on that most people thought white sliced bread was tasteless, nasty stuff and then asked them for the sorts of things that would make them feel better about white sliced bread.

'Many of them came up with words like 'love', 'comfort' and 'homeliness' and some showed a beautiful crusty loaf. The feeling of homeliness associated with the crust was an important hook and the resulting product has done very well in a crowded marketplace.'

(*Source*: Based on V. Matthews, 'How to dig deeper into the consumer mind', *FT*, 9 October 2003, p. 17)

Cognitive methods

Metaphor elicitation technique was developed by Zaltman (1997) in response to the recognition that important cognitive processes tend to be missed in traditional research because it fails to capture emotion, non-verbal communication, visual imagery and metaphor. Zaltman suggests that the hidden meanings and motivations driving behaviour can easily be missed. To overcome this he developed a method that relies less on verbal means to compile understanding of managers and customers but stresses much more a visual form of self-expression.

The basic procedure of the process involves getting participants to collect images and pictures to describe what they seek from a product category. The technique makes participants active in determining and compiling their own portfolio. In other words, the research stimulus is handed over to them to express meaning and attitudes through their own lens. The portfolio forms the basis upon which the researcher conducts interviews.

Initially participants are briefed to collect a portfolio of pictures for a product category. The brief defines a problem in the product category but ensures it is vaguely defined. They are given 7–10 days to collect the images. The procedure involves eight steps.

1. *Story telling*: Pictures are used as an entry point to explore customer concepts. The participants are asked to relate each picture to the product category being studied. In describing ideas a story about the associations and relationships to the construct (being studied) begin to emerge.

2. *Missed images*: Participants are asked if they wanted to bring other pictures, but because of time constraints were not able to do so. Any missed pictures that are deemed fundamental to the person's desired imagery are incorporated into the portfolio at this point.

3. *Sorting*: Participants are asked to arrange the portfolio of pictures in meaningful groups. They are then asked to check if any picture in the set duplicates the same story or message. If so it is removed.

4. *Construct elicitation*: The interviewer randomly selects three pictures and asks why two are similar and the third different in relation to the ill-defined problem. This typically produces one or two constructs. Further questions are used to ladder meaning to the constructs. Essentially, this step employs Kelly Repertory Grid methods to ladder constructs.

5. *Metaphor elaboration*: The participants are asked select a picture and widen its frame. They may add or subtract. The meaning and reasons for doing so in context to the problem are explored. This step breaks the equilibrium set by the pictures and allows stimulus from the sub-conscious to enter into the problem domain.

6. *Sensory images*: Participants are asked to introduce a sensory event (smell, taste, touch, sound, etc.) and elaborate it onto the imagery of picture. Linguistic analysis of the imagery can bring out important additional insights.

7. *The vignette*: This step brings into play elements involving psychodrama. Participants are asked to develop a short film about the topic. By adding movement into the imagery different sensory and cognitive elements are brought into play.

8. *The digital image*: Here participants are requested to produce a summary image or montage that captures the problem/subject under study. The summary actively manipulates (distorts, extends, cuts) existing totalities into a synthesis of a newer totality. This process can elicit new ideas, intentions or thoughts or reinforce and deepen existing ones. Participants are then asked to recount the story of the image, and describe it as if they were explaining it to someone who had not been present at any of the interviews.

The market and customer needs: peering into the looking glass

Thus far, we have talked about the importance of the market and of methods to explore what the customer needs and wants. We have assumed customer needs as a unitary concept. However, customer needs are not singular or simple. They can be both complex and varied. Needs can be classed in a variety of ways, though the most common grouping is one of explicit or latent needs. Three basic classification of needs (Otto and Wood, 2001) can be discerned:

Group 1: Observability

Needs differ on the ability of the individual to define them.

1. *Surface (or articulate) needs*: These are needs that consumers can easily articulate. They constitute needs that can be identified with conventional methods of consumer research, such as direct and indirect questions.

2. *Latent needs*: These needs consumers find difficult to express because they exist at a sub-conscious or pre-conscious level. These needs are typically not linked directly to the product but are associated with the sub-conscious need states of the individual. The link to the product occurs through the 'system' within which the product operates.

Group 2: Use needs

This group of needs differ on changebility.

1. *Generic (or task) needs*: These needs are integral to the task executed by a product category. For example, the intrinsic task of soap is to remove dirt. This need is a generic constant of the task. These needs are also sometimes labelled as constant needs. Often they represent the fundamental needs of human beings. Needs such as those associated with desire to satiate hunger, the need for clothing, the need to be able to travel, etc. These basic needs exist in constancy, but can be fulfilled by a variety of means. For example, the need to satiate hunger can be fulfilled by a variety of foods. However, basic needs are not just those to be associated with people but can be associated with products. For instance, for a car there is a generic need that it must possess a mechanism to stop (i.e. brakes of some type), and an ability to steer and so on.

2. *Extension (or augmentation) needs*: These needs go beyond the basic task of a product category. For example, whilst the task need of a washing powder (soap) is to remove dirt, the need of users to get the right quantity for a wash-load led to the development of washing powder tablets by Unilever's Home and Personal Care products division. These needs can be variable and can change over time or with shifts in technology. For example, the need for horses as means of transport began to disappear with the invention of other forms of transport such as the bicycle and especially the automobile. Digital photography has begun to eliminate the need for film-processing firms. Given their changing nature, these needs are difficult to define precisely in advance, though once they transpire people often take them for granted and as being constant.

Group 3: Segment needs

This grouping system distinguishes needs on the basis of differences across sub-parts of the population.

1. *Population needs*: These needs exist in the entire market population of interest. For example, all cars manufactured across the world possess a night-light, an air supply to the passenger cabin, and so on.

2. *Niche needs*: These are needs that apply only to a segment(s) of the population. For example, cars in warmer climates, for instance the Far East, require air conditioning as standard.

As can be observed from the above categories, each of the groups is not entirely distinct in domain terms but the categorisation does enable different types of insight to be drawn.

From customer satisfaction to customer delight

The primary role of innovation and new product development is to satisfy customer needs. Up until now we have assumed, just as we did with needs, that customer satisfaction is a singular. However, the Japanese quality proponent Noriaki Kano highlighted that there exist three generic levels of customer satisfaction depending on how well (the extent to which) a product (and its bundle of functions) fulfils customer expectation of performance (Kano, 1995). Kano's work shows that the performance expectations of a product and, secondly, the nature of customer needs, can and often do change over time.

Kano links customer satisfaction to product function in a two-dimensional map (see Figure 11.10). The customer satisfaction dimension is mapped on a spectrum from customer disgust to customer delight. The product function dimension moves from an absence of the feature/function to its full implementation. If one considers the level of presence of a product function as a one-to-one proxy of a customer's needs, we can trace a 45-degree line that defines what is called one-to-one quality or linear quality. The linear quality line defines the expected performance that the customer assumes or wishes to derive from a new product (or new function). On the other hand, Kano argues that one can define a line that traces the condition in which the minimum or basic level of satisfaction from the product (or product function) is being derived. This is the basic performance of the product (or its functionality) that the customer must have. Otherwise, customer satisfaction will fall into the disgusted or dissatisfied zone (also known as 'must-have' quality). If, on the other hand, the product is able to exceed the desired expectation from the customer, there is a move into the zone of

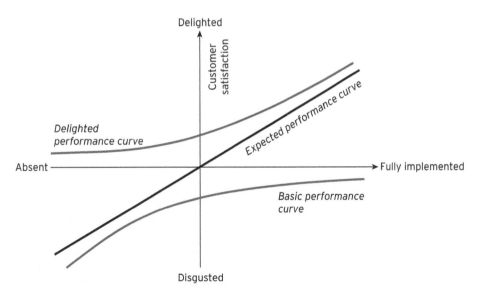

FIGURE 11.10 Kano's customer delight diagram
Source: Kano, 1995

customer delight. This is traced as the upper curve on the Kano diagram. Thus, Kano defines three states of customer satisfaction: customer delight, customer satisfaction and customer disgust. As desired functionalities are implemented, and depending on how well these functionalities meet customer expectations, it is possible to reach different levels of customer satisfaction.

In developing new products or new products with new functions the aim of the developer should be to delight the customer. First, to create products that possess the required type of functionalities (*basic* or *must-have* quality), secondly to ensure that these functionalities perform to a minimum expectation, and third to build enhancements into the product that allow it to go beyond the expectation of customers.

Additionally, the Kano diagram shows that the more a product function is implemented (moving from left to right for the curves), the more the customer expects. For instance, when a product function that exceeds expectation is initially introduced it gives a large delight differential. However, as more and more of it is provided (by the company, and also perhaps by competitors) the delight differential gets eroded. In other words, it becomes harder to delight the customer because the customer has come to expect more. Over time, as provision of the delight feature becomes commonplace, it drops downward into a basic satisfier category. Therefore, over time it becomes harder to supply the basic expected performance.

Let us use two simple examples to illustrate. First, a car with mechanical brakes that take an inordinate amount of time and distance to bring it to halt. The brakes fail to meet basic performance criteria. The customer is rightly unhappy with the car and the brakes. If the brakes bring the car to a stop, but perhaps with some locking when the brakes are applied hard, the condition could generally be considered to be acceptable performance. Now, when ABS (anti-lock braking system) brakes were first developed and fitted into cars it brought them to a quick and controlled halt. The new ABS product function exceeded customer expectation and represented a delight factor. As more and more automakers began to fit ABS into their cars the level of delight differential decreased. Over time it will become an expected function, and further over time it may even fall to become part of the basic performance criteria. A hair shampoo is the second illustrative example. The basic function of a shampoo is to clean hair. When Head & Shoulders came out with a formulation to remove dandruff it initially represented a delight factor for customers. With time, however, a shampoo possessing anti-dandruff capability was considered nothing too special. Most shampoos were able to deliver this capability. What was required in this category of products was another delight feature. Subsequently, Pantene developed its Pro-V with a nutrient formulation to make hair healthy, giving added bounce and shine. This then became the gold standard for customer delight.

Although Kano's diagram is very simple, it points to an important insight for product developers: customer expectations increase over time. By extension of this logic we can also note that customer needs thus develop and extend over time.

QFD: putting the voice of the customer into the process

Gathering market knowledge and information is a redundant activity if that information is not then used. Moving from the stage of defining and appreciating customer needs to taking action involves circulating the knowledge inside the organisation in a meaningful way. Put simply, there is no point just collecting market information if it is not put to good effect. One important method, devised by the Japanese to do just this, is quality function deployment (QFD) or house of quality.

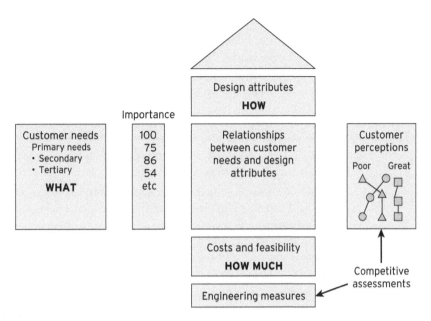

FIGURE 11.11 The house of quality

When customer needs are captured by market research they are usually defined in the 'voice' of the customer, i.e. customers talk about needs in their own terms and language. Product designers and development engineers cannot always accurately translate these needs into product specifications and functions. For example, a consumer may talk about bounce or shine when discussing hair but to the development scientist these terms hold little precise meaning. Usually a gap emerges between the voice of the customer and the voice of the process. The voice of the process determines the actions and activities, i.e. what actually get done. Thus, it is imperative to translate the voice of the customer into the voice of the process.

Yoji Akao, a Japanese professor, developed QFD in the late 1960s as a highly structured method to translate customer requirements into specific product and service characteristics, which are then fed systematically into the processes and systems that produce them (Akao, 1990). By the mid-1980s QFD was being used by a large number of Japanese companies. Many western companies such as Procter & Gamble, Hewlett-Packard, AT&T and Ford, from their benchmarking activity, observed this methodology and soon implemented it themselves. Besides its role in customer need translation, QFD has been found to improve communications between departments. This aspect makes QFD even more pertinent to product development since effectiveness in product development demands close co-operation between engineering, production and marketing.

The primary aim of QFD is twofold. First, to translate needs specified in the customer language into detailed technical requirements, and second to define priorities in customer need fulfilment. QFD helps direct organisational processes to engage in specific activities to deliver to customer wants. QFD achieves this by what is called a 'What–How' matrix (see the relevant sections of Figure 11.11). This matrix lists customer wants (the 'What'), technical requirements (the 'How'), and competitive assessments using customers' subjective perceptions and the firm's own objective engineering measurements. The process is one in which customer needs are translated via the matrix into a language that engineers and the development team can understand. The construction of the matrix requires a considerable amount of prior market and technical research to provide input data. The input data must pay particular attention to potential design trade-offs that influence the balance between quality, cost and functional performance. The basic construction of the QFD matrix is essentially a two-stage process, each with a number of key steps (Hauser, 1993):

Stage 1. Voice of the customer

1. *Identify customer needs*, requirements and dislikes (For instance, information collected from personal interviews or focus groups).

2. *Class the needs* as primary (of strategic importance to the product) and secondary (of tactical importance in the functions of the product). For example, ease of use of a product is a primary need. A secondary need is usually an elaboration of the primary need. Each primary need is usually broken down into around 3–10 secondary needs. For instance, ease of use can be broken up into 'quick to set up', 'easy to operate', 'fast to use'. If necessary, secondary needs can be further broken down into tertiary needs.

3. *Rank the requirements* (and dislikes) according to importance.

4. *Compare customer perceptions of the product with competitor offerings*. This helps to highlight how well needs are fulfilled and which features of the product are doing favourably relative to competition.

Stage 2. Voice of the engineer

1. *Translate needs into specific design characteristics*. This involves identifying design attributes associated with each customer need, and specifying them as measurable characteristics. For example for a car door, ease of use may be broken down into 'handle – size of human hand', 'door – comfortable weight', 'door – right size for average person', etc.).

2. *Assess and compare* engineering measures of product against competitors.

3. *Develop the relationship matrix*. It is now necessary to specify which design attributes influence (or deliver) which customer need. This involves specifying the relationship between customer requirement and technical attributes. The key is to look for the strongest relationships, thus leaving most of the matrix (about 60 per cent blank).

4. *Develop the roof of the matrix*. This involves estimating the strength of the relationship. For instance, if a particular design attribute is highly capable of delivering upon a particular customer functionality it is assigned a high rating (strong relationship), and a medium rating or low rating (weak relationship). Usually, symbols are used to show the strength of the relationship.

5. *Make other estimates*. In addition to the above, it is necessary to estimate and compare the company's ability to produce the product on other criteria such as cost, feasibility and technical difficulty.

There is more to QFD than just compiling the house of quality matrix. Filling the matrix is the first step. The QFD matrix must then be cascaded down into the organisation by developing a series of matrices, each one translating customer needs into the next level of actions required from the organisation (see Figure 11.12). The measures of customer needs are first translated into design attributes. The design attributes act as the basis of defining product/service features. In turn, the features are then used to define activities in the manufacturing

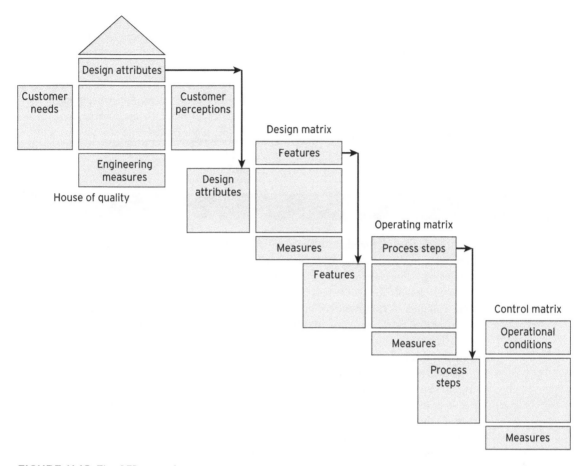

FIGURE 11.12 The QFD cascade process

process and operations to deliver value to the customer. Each cascade step is linked in order to ensure that the initial customer needs of the first matrix are interlinked to all the actions that occur subsequently in the delivery processes.

By making different departments work together, in collecting data and then matching customer needs to specific engineering dimensions, QFD integrates different departmental activities at a system level. In this way, QFD helps to implement a customer-orientated philosophy. Whenever deviations to specifications occur, personnel from different departments must come together to eliminate them. Getting different functional areas to compare their activities against competitors along the entire spectrum of specifications also helps to set in motion a product improvement momentum. This is further amplified by the cascade process, in which engineering specifications are fed into the manufacturing process and so on. Through its translation, alignment and improvement actions QFD can substantially improve product development. Toyota managed to reduce its time to market by more than 40 per cent, reduce almost by half its production costs as well as almost entirely eliminate rust warranty claims (Sullivan, 1986). Use of QFD by US and European firms has resulted in gains, but not for all companies (Griffin, 1992). One reason for this, especially for western companies, is the significant effort required to effectively implement QFD into the system and culture. Notwithstanding this, those who managed to overcome the implementation hurdle realised benefits in terms of improved decision making, more highly motivated teams, and faster, more timely movement of information to those who needed it.

To place QFD in its correct organisational context it is important to note that it fits in as part of a strategic context defined by vision or policy deployment. Policy deployment itself is a cascade process (very much like the QFD cascade) in which the strategic aims of the organisations are translated systematically into the major process and sub-processes of the organisation.

 ## Conclusion

In this chapter we highlight the necessity for companies to stay close to their market when engaging in the act of innovation. When market environments and technologies are slow changing, being close to the market whilst challenging is not difficult since there are at hand numerous tools and techniques to facilitate this. The type of innovation occurring in these environments is continuous or incremental. This is also sometimes referred to as sustaining innovation. However, when the change in markets and technologies is discontinuous the challenge is much more severe. Most companies find it very difficult to deal with this type of environment. One explanation for this is that many companies living in relatively stable markets concentrate simply on incremental innovation. They do this because, first, it brings them success and returns on investment in the short term, and second, they are good at it. Due to this they tend to follow traditional routines and reinforce behaviours and actions. Over time these can become rectified. Unfortunately, when disruptive change arrives these firms are caught off-balance and are not able to react or adjust sufficiently to ensure continued prosperity. They undergo a period of struggle and usually only a few of them survive it. In this chapter we elaborated upon an organisational process of market learning and understanding that helps to overcome such market blindness.

The conventional tools and techniques of building market understanding were elaborated upon, and highlight that these tools are deficient in fast-changing and complex environments. In appreciation of discontinuous and complex market environments a number of new techniques have been developed. One group of techniques utilise new technologies to enhance the market learning and understanding capability. A second group of techniques have begun to involve the customer much more directly in the innovation process, whilst others have taken to examining the market in much greater detail than hitherto through the use of ethnographic methods, or have tended toward widening the research frame to incorporate a wider breadth of sensory elicitation.

The chapter highlighted that market needs are not unitary, as they are often treated, but complex. They are also not static, and change over time. These notions were developed by examination of the multiplicity that underlies the concept of customer satisfaction. Noriaki Kano's ideas of customer delight, customer satisfaction and customer disgust are elaborated to highlight this. We concluded by indicating that it is not enough just to develop market understanding. The innovating company must be capable of circulating its market insights and changing them into new product development actions. We discussed one structured method of doing this, namely quality function deployment. We also highlighted that the QFD method is itself part of a larger process of alignment of the business to the market, called quality policy deployment.

QUESTIONS

1. What are the implications of continuous and discontinuous change for innovation?

2. What is an ambidextrous innovator, and why are these firms most capable of dealing with dislocational change?

3. What are the common causes of market blindness? Describe an organisational process for market learning, which is appropriate for fast-changing, complex and disruptive environments.

4. Highlight four conventional methods of market research, and define their strengths and weaknesses.

5. Why are new methods for market learning and understanding necessary? Identify the main types of development to improve market understanding and consequently innovation success.

6. What are the different ways of classifying customer needs? Find an illustrative example of each.

7. Describe the basic diagram developed by Noriaki Kano. What are its implications for innovation?

8. What role does QFD play in the organisational market learning and innovation process?

CASE STUDY

HP hits the right note with celebrities and piano-black case

When Todd Bradley was appointed to lead Hewlett-Packard's $28bn personal computer division in 2005, the conventional wisdom was that PCs were a rapidly commoditising business that held little potential for innovation.

Bruising competition from Dell, HP's biggest PC rival, and three difficult years spent trying to manage the integration of Compaq, the PC maker HP bought for $19bn in 2002, had dented morale and left the group with slumping margins and slowing sales growth.

Bradley, a gruff, no-nonsense manager said: 'I didn't fundamentally believe the rhetoric that was in the marketplace about PC commoditisation', he says. 'I was pretty confident that, with awesome people, awesome technology focused on turning that technology into innovation that matters to customers, that we could reset the marketplace.'

In the spring of 2006, HP launched an advertising campaign called 'The Computer is Personal Again' featuring celebrities demonstrating how they used their HP computers to manage their digital lives. The campaign, which featured artists including Jerry Seinfeld, the comedian, and Jay-Z, the rap star, drew rave reviews and helped kick-start a sales revival.

'We were laser-focused on taking a leadership position from a product and a thought perspective, and that campaign was really the rallying point', Mr Bradley says.

→

HP built on the success of its ad campaign by unveiling new designs for its PCs. The designs, which feature a distinctive 'piano-black' finish, were meant to bring a sense of 'timeless elegance' to the often dull world of the personal computer, according to Mr Chahil.

Taken together, the results have been impressive: last year, HP overtook Dell as the world's biggest PC maker by sales. The group's operating margin – a vital measure of profitability – has jumped from an anaemic 3.9 per cent to 5.8 per cent.

But not all of HP's PC revival can be attributed to its successful ad campaign or improved design, according to Richard Gardner, an analyst at Citigroup.

Even before Mr Bradley arrived on the scene, HP had embarked on a revamp of its PC supply chain. Jim Burns, the former head of HP's supply chain operations and now chief of investor relations, developed a system that allowed HP to outsource its notebook manufacturing to Taiwan while retaining internal control over procurement. By keeping procurement in-house, HP was able to get better prices on components.

HP may be well positioned in the PC market but rivals are racing to catch up. These include Dell, which is trying to bounce back from two years of slower sales growth with an aggressive new retail strategy.

'Dell has gone into 12,000 retail outlets in the past six months. HP has 80,000 touch points globally. Lenovo is competing with consumer products and Acer is coming into retail aggressively', Mr Gardner says. 'If you get slower market growth rate at the same time you get all these other guys into retail, it could get tougher over the next year or two.'

Mr Bradley says that technology is likely to remain a key differentiator as companies compete for customers. HP's plans for the new year in the PC arena include a focus on mobility and the 'digital home'.

(*Source*: K. Allison, 'HP hits the right note with celebrities and piano-black case', *Financial Times*, 11 January 2008)

QUESTIONS

1. Critically evaluate what is happening in the PC market.
2. Based on the HP scenario, how would you compare the impact of marketing or technology on the PC market?
3. Carry out your own further research to consider that question in relation to other technology-based products.

References

Aboulafia, R. (2004), 'The transatlantic politics of aircraft subsidies', *Financial Times*, 11 November, 19.

Agrawal, A., Basak, J., Jain, V., Kothari, R., Kumar, M., Mittal, P.A., Modani, P.A., Ravikumar, K., Sabharwal, Y. and Sureka, R. (2004), 'Online marketing research', *IBM Journal of Research and Development* 48(5/6): 671–677.

Akao, Y. (1990), *Quality function deployment: Integration of customer requirements into product design*, Cambridge, MA: Productivity Press.

Allison, K. (2008), 'HP hits the right note with celebrities and piano-black case', *Financial Times*, 11 January.

Bacon, G., Beckman, S., Mowery, D. and Wilson, E. (1994), 'Managing product definition in hi-tech industries; A pilot study', *California Management Review*, Spring, 36/3, 32–56.

Barraba, V.P. (1995), *Meeting of the minds*, Cambridge, MA: Harvard Business School Press.

Belliveau, P., Griffin, A., and Somermeyer, S. (2002), 'The PDMA Toolbook for New Product Development', New York: Wiley.

Berggren, E. and Nacher, T. (2001), 'Introducing new products can be hazardous to your company: use the new solutions delivery tools', *Academy of Management Executive*, 15/3, 1–12.

Cooper, R.G. (1988), 'Predevelopment activities determine new product success', *Industrial Marketing Management* 17: 237–247.

Cooper, R.G. and Kleinschmidt, E.J. (1986), 'An investigation into the new product process: Steps, deficiencies and impact', *Journal of Product Innovation Management* 3: 71–85.

Dahan, E. and Hauser, J.R. (2001), 'Product development – managing a dispersed process', in B. Weitz and R. Wensley (eds), *Handbook of marketing*, **http://mitsloan.mit.edu/vc.**

Daniel, C., Done, K. and Sanchanta, M. (2004), 'Boeing $6bn deal secures future for 7E7 aircraft: US group aims to win back market share from Airbus', *Financial Times*, 27 April, 21.

Day, G.S. (2002), 'Managing the market learning process', *Journal of Business and Industrial Marketing* 17(4): 240–252.

Economist (2005), 'The rise of the creative consumer: The future of innovation', *Economist*, 12 March, 374(8417): 75.

Green, P.E. and Wind, Y. (1975), 'New ways to measure consumer judgements', *Harvard Business Review*, July/August: 107–117.

Griffin, A. (1992), 'Evaluating QFD's use in US firms as a process for developing products', *Journal of Product Innovation management* 9: 171–187.

Gupta, A.K. and Wilemon, D.L. (1990), 'Accelerating the development of technology-based new products', *California Management Review* 32(2): 24–44.

Hamel, G. and Prahalad, C.K. (1994), 'Competing for the future', *Harvard Business Review* 72(4): 122–128.

Hauser, J.R. (1993), 'How Puritan-Bennett used the house of quality', *Sloan Management Review* 34(3): 61–70.

Holtzblatt, K. and Beyer, H.R. (1993), 'Making customer-centred design work for teams', *Communications of the ACM* 36(6): 93–103.

Kano, N. (1995), 'Upsizing the organisation by attractive quality', *Proceedings of the First World Congress for Total Quality Management*, Sheffield, UK, April.

Lynn, G., Marone, J. and Paulson, A. (1996), 'Marketing and discontinuous innovation: The probe and learn process', *California Management Review* 38(3): 8–37.

Mahajan, V. and Peterson, R.A. (1985), Innovation diffusion: Models and applications, Beverly Hills, CA: Sage Publications.

Mahajan, V. and Wind, G. (1991), 'New product models: Practice, shortcomings and desired improvements', Report Number 91–125, Marketing Science Institute, Cambridge, MA, October.

Mahajan, V., Muller, E. and Bass, F.M. (1990), 'New product diffusion models in marketing: A review and directions for research', *Journal of Marketing*, 54: 1–26.

Matthews, V. (2003), 'How to dig deeper into the consumer mind', *Financial Times*, 9 October, 17.

Milmo, S. (2004), 'In Europe, margin pressures are balanced by dramatic growth in niches', *Chemical Market Reporter*, 12 May, 263(19): 10.

Nijssen, E.J. and Frambach, R.T. (1998), 'Market research companies and new product development tools', *Journal of Product and Brand Management* 7(4): 305–318.

Otto, K.N. and Wood, K.L. (2001), *Product design: Techniques in reverse engineering and new product development*, Upper Saddle River, NJ: Prentice Hall.

Perry, B. (1998), 'Seeing your customers in a whole new light', *Journal of Quality and Participation* 21(6): 38–43.

Pourdehnad, J. and Robinson, P.J. (2001), 'Systems approach to knowledge development for creating new products and services', *Systems research and Behavioural Science* 18: 2–40.

Rosenthal, S. and Capper, M. (2006), 'Ethnographies in the front end: Designing for enhanced customer experiences', *Journal of Product Innovation Management*, 23(3): 215–237.

Sanchez, R. and Sudharshan, D. (1993), 'Real-time market research', *Marketing Intelligence and Planning* 11(7): 29–38.

Stevens, T. (1999), 'Lights, camera, innovation', *Industry Week* 248(14): 32–36.

Sullivan, L.P. (1986), 'Quality function deployment', *Quality Progress* 19(6): 36–50.

Sultan, F. and Barczak, G. (1999), 'Turning marketing research high-tech', *Marketing Management*, Winter: 25–30.

Sykes, W. (1990), 'Validity and reliability in qualitative market research: A review of the literature', *Journal of the Market Research Society* 32(3): 289–239.

Trott, P. (2001), 'The role of market research in the development of discontinuous new products', *European Journal of Innovation Management* 4(3): 117–125.

Tushman, M.L. and O'Reilly III, C.A. (1996), 'Ambidextrous organisations: Managing evolutionary and revolutionary change', *California Management Review* 38/4: 8–30.

Urban, G.L. and Hauser, J.R. (2004), '"Listening in" to find and explore new combinations of customer needs', *Journal of Marketing Research* 64: 72–87.

Urban, G.L., Hulland, J.S. and Weinberg, B.D. (1993), 'Pre-market forecasting for new consumer durable goods: Modelling categorisations, elimination and consideration phenomena', *Journal of Marketing* 57: 47–63.

Urban, G.L. and Von Hippel, E. (1988), 'Lead user analysis for the development of new industrial products', *Management Science* 34(5): 569–582.

Von Hippel, E. (1998), 'Economics of product development by users: The impact of "sticky" local information', *Management Science* 44(5): 629–644.

Von Hippel, E. and Katz, R. (2002), 'Shifting innovation to users via toolkits', *MIT Sloan Management Working Paper 4232-02*, April.

Von Hippel, E. (1989), 'New product ideas from "lead users"', *Research Technology Management* 32(3): 24–27.

Wind, J. and Mahajan, V. (1997), 'Issues and opportunities in new product development: An introduction to the special issue', *Journal of Marketing Research*, February: 1–12.

Zaltman, G. (1997), 'Rethinking market research: Putting people back in', *Journal of Marketing Research*, November: 424–437.

12 Design and manufacture for innovation

Learning outcomes

When you have completed this chapter, you should be able to:

- Appreciate the importance of design, and the steps involved in design practice.

- Articulate the reasons for failure in design and innovation.

- Understand the concept of design latitude and its importance for downstream manufacturing.

- Understand concurrent engineering and the advantages it provides over traditional engineering approaches.

- Appreciate how manufacturing and design affect innovation.

- Recognise the importance of estimating production costs, and understand the methodology for setting meaningful target costs.

- Appreciate product architecture, modular design and platforms in product development, and the benefits they offer.

- Show how process-led manufacturing customisations can enhance market strategies.

- Appreciate a series of tools and techniques employed within total quality management systems that play a role in product and process innovation.

- Understand the latest approaches that help drive greater flexibility in product development.

Importance of design

For many companies design and manufacture is a nightmare. It is a fragmented process in which power struggles between different departments and delays are the norm. Yet design and manufacturing are highly strategic activities. They have wide-ranging and pervasive effects, affecting the efficiency of production all the way through to sales strategies, and speed of repair. Design and manufacturing decisions taken in the early stages of the development process become increasingly interwoven and interdependent as the development process evolves over time. This creates a historical chain in which later decisions are conditioned by those made previously.

In many sectors, such as automobiles and white goods, design decisions determine 60–80 per cent of final production costs. Despite this, many senior managers put most of their energy and effort into analysing current production rather than product design. In doing this they are focussing on the 'window dressing', not the 'window'.

What is design?

Delivering better products and faster to the market requires effective execution of design. But what is design? The *Oxford English Dictionary* describes design as 'a preliminary sketch or picture'. Academics and practitioners close to the discipline often describe it as a multi-disciplinary iterative process; a process that translates an idea or market need into a successful product.

In design, the customer is central; in the sense that design is the set of processes that translate customer requirements into manufacturable outcomes such that they fully meet customer requirements. From the many definitions a number of common issues about design can be teased out, namely:

- It is a creative process.
- It is a multi-disciplinary process.
- It is an iterative evolutionary process.
- It serves human needs.

The competitive environment has forced the realisation upon many companies that the practice of a design team handing over a 'design sketch' to manufacturing is not the way to do it. Long gone are the days when the product designer's work was over with the delivery of a set of drawings for the manufacturing department to make. The 'hand-over' practice recalls scenarios in which manufacturing personnel would be asked to produce to a design that had no consideration of the manufacturing process, product quantities, tooling etc. Concurrent engineering (or simultaneous engineering) now represents the norm of practice. This embodies communications and interactions with a wide variety of functions (marketing, manufacturing, supply chain, business planning, commercial/legal, finance and servicing). All of these functions play a role in the activities of product delivery, and work together and communicate in parallel to bring quality to the process.

The word 'design' is popularly used in a very broad sense. It is used to denote anything from an example of new fashion to a complex new machine. There is, also, an increasing use of the word 'designer' to give a product market appeal and credibility. The presumption that is implied is that a designer has spent time creating the product especially for the customer. In contrast, an assembly device, such as a robot, will have been designed almost entirely with the function in mind, with little concern for the appearance of the device. This highlights a

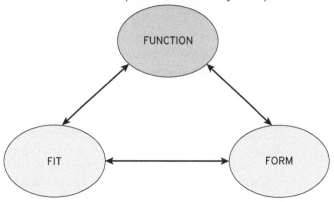

This aspect of design is responsible for executing the product task. It is the aspect that most commonly dissatisfies customers because failure of poor performance in execution of the basic task indicates that the product is not meeting the requirements.

FUNCTION

FIT

FORM

This is part of the design that deals with how things go together, how they integrate to form the whole system. It tackles engineering parameters and deals with analysis of product limits and tolerances.

This is the aesthetic or artistic end of the design spectrum. It is what the public today usually means by design. The shape and appearance of the product is quite often regarded as 'the design'.

FIGURE 12.1 Basic elements of design

spectrum of design. Every product that is designed contains three elements of design: form, fit and function:

The idea that design is a combination of form, fit and function leads to an appreciation that the design process de facto has an element of activities ranging from the aesthetic to the practical or operational. Form, function and fit may be arranged in a pyramid (as in Figure 12.1). Fit is an aspect that customers do not always come into contact with. It is an attempt to make sure that the parts come together to make a 'functionable' product. Poor fit typically leads to poor function. Function defines the basic requirement from a product, and customers most commonly use function as a primary yardstick for assessing a product. It is simply no good if a product looks good but fails to execute the task expected of it. Form is at the top of the pyramid. Only after a product is able to satisfy the basic requirement(s) do aesthetic considerations enter into the equation. Because of this, firms typically consider function and fit aspects first before turning their attention to form. However, for customers the reverse is the case. Their initial impressions of the product arise primarily from form attributes. If the form aspect is 'strong' it can facilitate purchase and trial from among a variety of competing offerings. Once purchased the customers proceed to assess the function aspect of design. During function assessment reinforcement or disconfirmation of the customers' initial predisposition toward the form aspect occurs. Only if form, function and fit assessments are positive does the product stand a chance as a candidate for future repurchase.

Requirements engineering to balance form, fit and function

Before proceeding, it is important that we clarify how the needs of the customer are captured, distilled and validated before entering any design activity. The details of this are covered in Chapter 11 of this book, but it is important to understand what is often termed the marketing–R&D interface, one of the most common points of failure in NPD frameworks.

Marketing and design have been recognised as being key contributors to new product development and commercial success (see Kotler, 2003). There is a widespread belief that marketing plays a significant role in the early development of products and that it is combined with other areas of expertise, such as industrial design, to address critical user-product interaction issues (Ulrich & Eppinger, 2000). However, while new product development would ideally involve an interdisciplinary, collaborative, effort, Oliver (2002) points out that 'differences in orientation between disciplines with respect to timescales, style of working and objectives may all lead to tensions'. However, Veryzer (2005) takes a more specific view (when discussing discontinuous, or radical, innovation) by finding that it is the marketing–industrial design linkage that is the one which offers one of the greatest challenges in innovation.

An overview of some of the potential impacts in the marketing–R&D interface is outlined earlier in this book. However, a more detailed summary of potential issues and impacts, as they relate to requirements engineering, are provided in Table 12.1.

To address these problems, it is important for any organisation to have an effective requirements engineering process, ably manned by skilled marketing and technical professionals who can operate in an environment of ambiguity and uncertainty, and turn this into a distinct competitive advantage. How this might be achieved will be discussed next.

Managing different types of requirements

Requirements for a new product, process or service tend to flow through an innovation framework quite freely. However, if you ask different stakeholders what these requirements are, you are likely to get different, and in some cases conflicting, answers. The reason for this is quite simple; an innovation framework cannot operate effectively unless it can adequately collect the needs of the customer (or market) and translate them into a language that the design team understand, and blended with underlying requirements which may already be known to the team (e.g. legal and regulatory requirements). The various requirements are illustrated in Figure 12.2.

This represents the critical marketing–R&D boundaries which so often undermine a company's ability to compete effectively. In most cases, the customer will express their internal and external needs in normal, everyday language, which collectively will define a conceptual solution to their specific business problem. They tend to express the 'Whats' of what the customer needs (see the description of the 'house of quality' in Chapter 11). There are, of course, many different approaches which can be used to gather these requirements, including customer workshops, customer surveys, pilots, antennae shops, customer advisory boards, market research, etc. Additionally, the priorities of the customer's needs can be assessed using such tools as QFD, Kano modelling, or conjoint analysis.

Regardless of the technique used, we need to ensure we capture some basic information such a description of the need, the benefits of the need to be derived, and additional supporting information which will help us manage the definition of these requirements over time (e.g. owner, originator, due date, a unique identifier or reference, etc.).

On the other hand, the requirements to design a product, process or service need to be expressed in precise technical terms. These requirements define the 'hows' outlined in QFD analyses, indicating how customer needs will be met. A translation process is therefore required to convert the needs of the customer into the language of the design team. During this technical definition of requirements, other activities may take place to drive further business value, such as:

- *Quality attribute analysis*: Where technical requirements are assessed in measurable terms of how they need to perform (e.g. availability, usability, reliability, inter-operability,

TABLE 12.1 Problems encountered in inefficiency requirements engineering processes

Area	Problem	Causes	Result
Elicitation	Uncoordinated elicitation of requirements across different groups in the company (marketing, product management, engineering, business leads, etc.)	Duplicated effort in gathering requirements Gaps in gathering requirements	Customers dissatisfied in being asked the same questions many times Innefficient use of company resources repeating tasks Customers dissatisfied with the solutions they are offered. Wasted development effort in delivering solutions which do not meet customer needs
Specification	Requirements are defined in terms of the solutions (the 'hows' rather than the 'whats') Critical information is not collected during capture and specification	May lock the company into a commitment to deliver an inappropriate/sub-optimal solution May drive unnecessary content in the solution Understanding of the customer need is limited Additional effort required to recapture customer needs	Customers dissatisfied with the solutions they are offered Adds unnecessary cost into the solution Deliver the wrong solution Wasted effort and time to collect information
Analysis	Limited use of analytical techniques used Techniques used are manually intensive	May drive unnecessary content in the solution May miss critical customer needs (unstated needs) Takes significant effort to analyse and approve requirements	Adds unnecessary cost into the solution Customers are dissatisfied with the solutions they are offered Product development and release are delayed
Validation	Limited use of validation techniques employed Limited formal validation of the solution with the customer (or validation conducted too late)	May miss critical requirements May drive unnecessary content in the solution Unable to assess how effective the solution has been in meeting the customer's needs	Customers dissatisfied with the solutions they are offered Adds unnecessary cost into the solution Customers dissatisfied with the solutions they are offered.
Management	High levels of administration in managing requirements No clear route in who/where requirements are to be transmitted to in the organisation Ownership of requirements within the organisation is unclear	Tools not integrated or accessible Information held in different places and in different formats Performance measurement is manually intensive Requirements can be lost when they enter the business Delays in acting on a critical customer need	Multiple translations of information across different groups Product development is delayed Miss improvement opportunities, and reinforces current inefficiencies Customers dissatisfied with the solutions they are offered Solutions released into the market too late

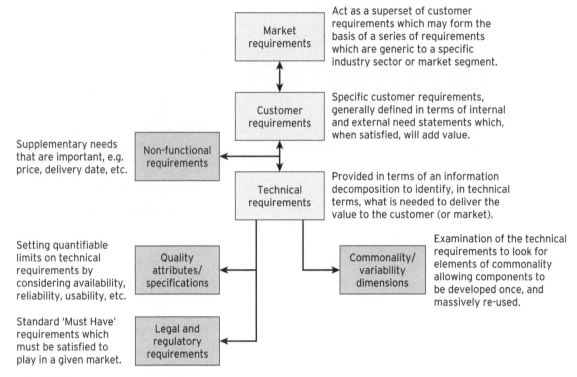

FIGURE 12.2 Hierarchy of requirements to manage

serviceability). Many elements of DFX (design for excellence, covering design for manu-facturability (DFM), design for serviceability (DFS), design for testability (DFT) and design for assembly (DFA) can be addressed here.

- *Commonality/variability analysis*: Looks for commonality in requirements across different customer needs and technical requirements. This can uncover opportunities for developing a component (or solution) once, and massively re-using the assets across the customer base. This is strongly enabled by companies adopting 'platforming' or 'architectural' developments as a cost reduction strategy.

Many different approaches can be employed to achieve this translation, and a deeper under-standing on how the customer's needs can be satisfied, such as:

- Functional decomposition of requirements into lower level, more detailed descriptions.
- The use of rapid prototyping to give shape and form to ideas, and remove ambiguity. This can be achieved using easy-to-build physical models, or re-use of objects to develop software prototypes.
- Visualisation of designs using computer aided design (CAD) tools, and historical schematics of components, assemblies and sub-assemblies.
- Use of specific design methodologies to define and visualise requirements, such as the Unified Modelling Language (UML) employed in object-orientated software development, and using techniques such as use-cases and scenarios to drive detailed understanding.

It is important to realise that the process for capturing and distilling these requirements is a time-consuming, and cyclical event (see Figure 12.3).

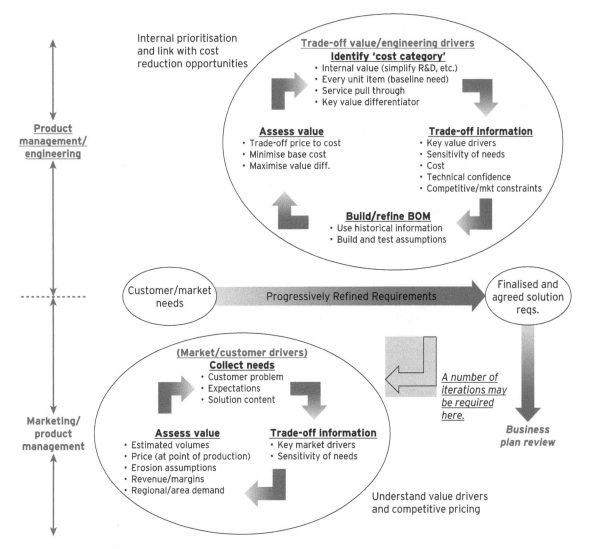

FIGURE 12.3 The iterative nature of requirements engineering

The first cyclical event involves understanding the needs of the customer (or market) (the 'whats'), before moving into a concurrent translation and cyclical analysis of the technical requirements (the 'hows'). At any point, the process can cycle back to the beginning for further refinement. Eventually, the objective will be to have a stable and clearly defined set of requirements which articulates the customer's detailed needs, and provides the design team with sufficient information to then construct a suitable solution. From an innovation efficiency perspective, it is important that requirements can be defined and stabilised as early in the innovation process as possible, and any subsequent changes managed quickly and effectively.

Generic requirements engineering framework

There are a number of very specific steps which must exist in any requirements engineering framework, these include elicitation, analysis, specification, validation and requirements management. These are illustrated in Figure 12.4.

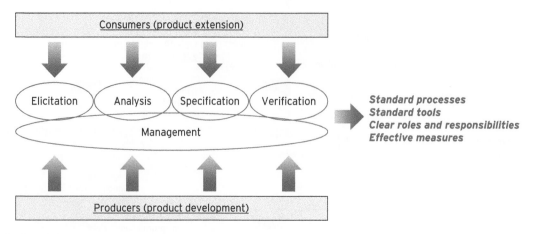

FIGURE 12.4 Generic requirements engineering framework

In this framework, the elicitation of requirements represents the pro-active capture of customer needs and wants, and ensuring sufficient information is gathered in terms of stated and unstated needs. The analysis activity can include the translation of customer requirements into technical requirements, or more detailed analysis of the technical requirements to ensure a deep understanding. Specification represents those tasks required to adequately capture the definition of the requirements and their traceability through the translation process. Verification involves those tasks which allow a company to ensure it continues to meet its customers needs. These four activities operate concurrently and independently. As a result, a management framework is needed to ensure the requirements are ultimately captured, reviewed, approved and frozen, and any changes are managed according to sound principles (change control boards, formal approval levels, contract re-negotiations at specific trigger points, and so on).

Benefits of an effective requirements engineering capability

Effectively eliciting requirements, translating them into technical requirements and validating them at key check-points is critical to the success of any innovation framework. Yet, with so many potential points of failure, this is an area which often results in disappointing innovation performance. However, by addressing many of the problems found here with sound structure and practices, the requirements engineering practices in a company can become a powerful competitive weapon.

So what do customers have to gain from this capability? Quite simply, they are likely to get the solutions they need to their complex business problems faster. Consequently, the business with strong requirements engineering capabilities can expect to see increased market share, margins and revenue by being able to release optimal solutions to market ahead of the competition. This then leads to increased customer retention and satisfaction, thus raising entry barriers for the competition.

Additionally, by operating a more efficient requirements engineering framework, and stabilising requirements sooner, companies will see productivity increases as the 'cost of quality' (scrap, re-work, etc.) is massively reduced. Using more advanced techniques will also allow companies to more effectively realise their business strategies (e.g. cost reduction driven by platforming/re-use and enabled by commonality/variability analysis).

Finally, by improving business performance in this manner, employees will have an increased sense of security, and morale will increase as they feel part of a winning and successful team. It is by ensuring this strong requirements engineering capability that we can now confidently move into the realm of design in more detail.

The design spectrum

Pugh (1991) highlights the existence of a spectrum of design activity. He notes two polar boundaries for design: boundary A is concerned with radical and innovative conceptual design and boundary B represents conventional design, characterised by incremental refinement of the existing system and sub-system design, materials and production methods. Figure 12.5 shows this spectrum in terms of the differing core design models for this spectrum. The innovative pole is about overturning existing notions of design. The mid-point model shows that whilst there may be conceptual innovation, this may meet resistance from conventional manufacturing practice. This situation is fine as long as the product is static. The failure of the Swiss watch industry to respond to the electronic-quartz revolution spearheaded from the Far East shows the weakness of boundary B type rigidity.

The two types of boundary rigidities can apply to any of the three design dimensions: form, function and fit. For example, Swatch took a highly innovatory approach to the form aspect of watches, in styling them in colourful and fashionable designs using cheap materials. By doing so they challenged the conventional design practice of watches. Challenging or innovating across the fit may appear a little unfamiliar at first, but if one remembers that fit is about the way components combine or come together, it becomes easier to see how this can be considered along the conventional practice or radical design spectrum.

A useful way of looking at the design spectrum is through the lens of the Henderson and Clark model of innovation. Although Henderson and Clark did not develop their ideas to specifically highlight the spectrum, their ideas are an insightful way of defining and scrutinising approaches along the design spectrum. Henderson and Clark (1990) classify innovation along two dimensions (see Figure 12.6). The horizontal dimension captures an innovation's impact on components, while the vertical captures its impact on the linkages between components. Framed in this way, radical and incremental innovation are extreme points along the two dimensions. Radical innovation establishes a new design format, in which a new set of core design concepts are embodied within a new architecture. Incremental innovation refines and extends an established design. Improvement occurs in individual components but the underlying core design concepts and the links between them remain the same. On the basis of these two dimensions, Henderson and Clark elaborate two further types of innovation:

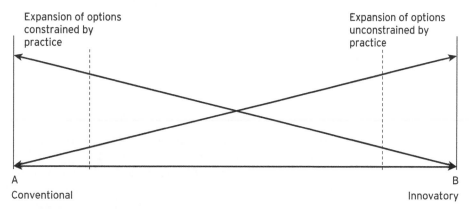

FIGURE 12.5 The design spectrum

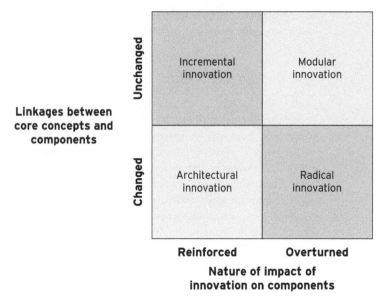

FIGURE 12.6 The Henderson and Clark framework for defining innovation
Source: Henderson and Clark, 1990, *Administrative Science Quarterly*, The Johnson School at Cornell University

- innovation that *changes only the core* design concepts of a technology (*modular innovation*).

- innovation that *changes only the relationships* between the components (*architectural innovation*).

Replacement of mechanical components with electronic circuits is an example of a modular innovation. To the degree that one can simply replace the mechanical parts with electronic part(s), it is an innovation that changes the core design concept without changing the product's architecture. In contrast, the essence of architectural innovation involves the re-configuration of an established system such that it links together existing components in a new way.

Take for instance, a ceiling air-fan. Improvements in its blade design or insulation to reduce noise represent incremental innovation. A move to central air conditioning constitutes radical innovation. A move to a portable fan is an architectural innovation. A replacement of the mechanical components with electronic components (as in auto-fan) is modular innovation.

Failure in design and innovation

There is abundant research evidence that a large proportion of new product introductions either fail in the marketplace or fail to make it to the marketplace. The reasons for these are fourfold, covering the market, manufacturing, design and technology.

Market failure is due to the product not fulfilling the needs of the customers adequately. This implies that designers were not able to translate customer requirements or that the customer requirements identified (via marketing research) were faulty in the first place. A second possible cause of failure, of course, is that the competitor offerings fulfil the needs of customers much more effectively, thereby once again indicating a failure in marketing research and marketing, or a flaw in the design and execution of the product development process. Clive Sinclair's C5 is a famous example of market failure. The C5 was a low-speed single-person vehicle. It was truly fuel efficient but not even the most ardent of the green environmentalists wanted it.

Manufacturing failure arises from manufacturing defects. These arise from failure(s) in the manufacturing process to meet the specification for parts manufacture or the assembly process. This could be attributable to an error in the manufacturing process itself, such as a setting, an adjustment or human error in the assembly of parts.

Design failure arises from design faults. Typically, they occur from a failure to follow design principles. The design principles stipulate the constraints of applying a particular design embodiment. They represent a failure of the designer to apply known constraints in the design, such as the correct selection of materials, adequate allowance for stress, etc. The case of Ford Pinto is a well-known example of a design flaw – in which the Pinto's petrol tank exhibited a tendency to catch fire on rear impact collisions.

Technology failure occurs as a result of the design system or sub-system trying to operate outside the latitude for which it was originally designed. For example, on 28 January 1986 the space shuttle Challenger exploded 73 seconds after lift-off due to high-temperature failure of the seals on the booster engines.

ILLUSTRATION

BMW: not as easy as it looks

When the fourth-generation 7 series was launched in 2001, BMW purists said BMW designer Chris Bangle was out to destroy their sacred brand. In 2005 BMW AG launched a mid-life facelift of the 7-series saloon. The new car was expected to please critics who found the initial version of the 7 series too radically styled and too complicated. This newer version of BMW's flagship was tweaked in response to criticisms of the current model's styling and features.

Addressing sore points:

Design aesthetics

For those who found the controversial styling of the fourth-generation BMW 7 series hard to swallow, the company responded by softening the styling touches, particularly at the rear, where a new boot lid received a horizontal chrome that made it look lower, even though it was a fraction of an inch higher. At the front, the kidney shaped grille was wider and more deeply integrated into the bumper. Head-lights and tail-lights were also changed.

Design function

Secondly, for those who found navigating the equally controversial iDrive electronic control system frustrating and confusing, BMW made changes. The iDrive system drew harsh criticism for being so complex that it forced drivers to take their eyes off the road to click through multiple steps just to perform simple functions such as changing the radio station. The new iDrive received new buttons that made it easier for occupants to change functions quickly.

(*Source*: Based on Bradford, 2005)

Despite, these potential failure points, the value of design as a 'potent' marketing variable is heralded in leading managerial marketing textbooks (e.g. Kotler, 2003), and is viewed widely as helping to provide a sustainable competitive advantage. Indeed, analysis reveals that firms rated as having 'good' design were stronger on a number of financial performance metrics (returns on sales, returns on assets, net income, cash flow and stock performance) than those of a 'low' design capability (Hertenstein et al., 2005).

The interconnection between design and manufacturing

In product development, an important consideration is the concept of design latitude. Design latitude specifies the engineering parameter range within which a product is able to perform its desired function. Outside this range product failure occurs.

Why does a design need latitude? It is obvious that parameters that control an object's function must be capable of being tolerated by overall design. This is the basis of robust design. At first sight, design latitude (or design tolerance) seems like a luxury that is not essential for good design. In a way latitude can be thought of as unimportant when one is thinking of a single product item operating according to the functions prescribed by design. However, as soon as design is thought of in terms of manufacture of a number of units, the concept of latitude takes on a more significant role. First, it is important to understand that no parameter has one absolute value. Every parameter has a nominal value and a range over which this nominal value can vary. Correctly worked out this range is what can be tolerated in order to satisfy the function in which it plays a part, and is thus termed the tolerance of the dimension (or parameter). For example, let us say that a product component should be 5cm long to assemble a product. When this component is being produced, not every component is going to be exactly 5cm. Some components will be say, 4.8cm, 4.9cm, 5.00cm, 5.1cm, and 5.2cm. This represents the manufacturing variability (or range of production) in producing the component. However, for the product to be assembled and function properly the component cannot be shorter than say 4.9cm or longer than 5.1cm. This defines the design tolerance (or latitude).

A good designer works out what is the tolerable range for each of the parameters in order to ensure that the total product functions correctly once it is assembled. The designer wants to make sure that these tolerances are as wide as possible to make the part easier to manufacture, but also to be sure that even when the parameter departs from its nominal value the part will function as required. In contrast, the manufacturing engineer aims to strive towards an arrangement of equipment that attempts to keep all of the parameters as close as possible to the nominal value. In other words, the manufacturing engineer is trying to arrange the production process such that there is minimum variation since each part is made one after the other. This is done so that parts delivered are more likely to be within ranges that the designer set and will therefore contribute to a more reliable performance once all the parts have been assembled together to form the final product.

At the start of a product's development, designers specify a tolerance range for the product parameters that is usually quite narrow. This precision and tightness of specification occurs because the designers are trying to create a product that they are sure can deliver performance. Sometimes these initial design specifications may even be narrower than the variance that the manufacturing process can achieve. This of course is not a viable state since it would result in a product that is highly susceptible to failure. The design engineering challenge, therefore, is to attempt over time to broaden latitude. In contrast the manufacturing

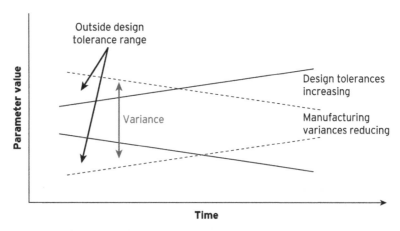

FIGURE 12.7 The role of latitude in design and manufacturing

challenge is to try and narrow the variances in the manufacturing process (see Figure 12.7). This is usually achieved as production experience grows.

Besides the understanding of design latitude there is another important issue at stake here. Quite often, companies think product robustness is the responsibility solely of manufacturing, i.e. manufacturing must provide parts well within design tolerances. The concept of latitude, however, shows that this responsibility must be shared. The designer needs to seriously consider the tolerance ranges that are defined and not just state tolerances that are thought to be those achievable by manufacturing. This indicates the need for designers and engineers to work closely at as early a point in time as possible. Furthermore, for the product to be successful in the marketplace, it must embody design characteristics that appeal to the end customer. This requires up-front collaboration with marketing people.

Engineering and design in the generic development processes

The development processes described thus far have been generic. However, companies must approach the task of development differently depending on the requirements of the product being developed and the firm's unique context. The actual development methodologies used by companies must be in accordance to the specific challenges they face. For instance, design starts to play an active role at different stages depending on the nature of the product being designed. To explain the nature of the task, it is convenient to classify products according to the nature of dominant challenge that faces the development team. This ranges on a spectrum from technology-driven to user-driven. User-driven products require more aesthetic design input while technology-driven products are dominated by function-driven design input. Of course, these classifications can be dynamic. Take for instance, the Sony Walkman. The core benefit of the first Walkman model was its technology (miniature tape player). As competition entered, Sony moved on to create aesthetic appeal and enhanced utility as additions in its subsequent models.

The design and engineering activities that need to take place to develop a new product vary from company to company, and industry to industry – i.e. they are context contingent. However, four generic steps exist in any development process: design, implementation, integration and testing. In the first step, the designers prepare the plans and specifications that translate customer and market needs into functional requirements, which can then be addressed by the engineering community. The implementation activity sees the designs and

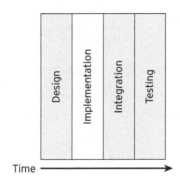

FIGURE 12.8 Waterfall development model

specifications being translated into tangible deliverables (or product components). These components are then integrated into a final product, and then tested against various criteria (e.g. against customer requirements, legal and regulatory needs, etc.).

The stability of market needs, the understanding of these needs, and the ability to create effective product solutions determines the way a company will deploy these steps in its innovation framework. When working in conditions of relative market stability on traditional projects, in which product features can be defined completely and specifications can be frozen early, a 'waterfall' methodology is most appropriate (see Figure 12.8).

The waterfall development process begins with a long design phase to define the entire project and all the product features. During this phase, in-depth planning and requirements analysis take place. Once the design is 'frozen' the implementation phase is initiated. During the implementation phase development of the product components and desired features occurs. Once created, the features described in the design are integrated into a working product, which is then tested. After it passes the test the product is ready to be manufactured for the customer. In this type of development model, project scope is defined up-front and attempts are made not to deviate from this baseline. Since the content of the development work is well defined, and the necessary information is at hand to set a realistic schedule and budget, project teams in this form of development typically are free from the surprises that often throw projects off-track. The waterfall approach is the most efficient and economically sound choice when building a well-defined and stable solution.

In many cases, however, it is difficult to fully define up-front a project's scope. This is especially true when working on truly ground-breaking opportunities. In this environment development teams do not have a clear view of what the finished article will look like, so they need to explore possibilities and pass through many revisions before an effective design and product solution evolves. Under vague and unpredictable conditions an iterative (*spiral* or *incremental*) development approach should be adopted.

The iterative approach involves a series of frequent iterations of the design–implementation–integration–test cycle. In other words, it is a series of waterfall models (see Figure 12.9).

Even though the spiral and incremental approach share common features (and are often referred to interchangeably), strictly there is difference between the two. The *spiral* approach uses the sequence of iterations to refine the same features, while the *incremental* process attempts to implement different features that the customer requests. Both processes are well suited to innovative projects because the short iterations allow development teams to quickly show customers the results of their latest requests, or new possibilities. The 'spiral' model provides a useful framework when working in 'white space' with a customer (i.e. an area of opportunity where no one clearly understands the need, or the design to meet that need). In

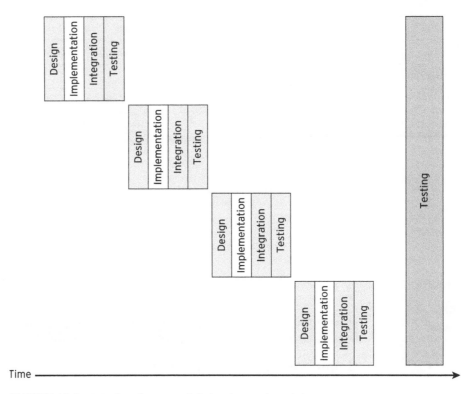

Time ——→

FIGURE 12.9 'Spiral' or 'incremental' development model

these instances, the opportunity to develop a strong relationship with the customer through a journey of exploration can yield far greater benefits than the immediate financial return of the current development project.

Each of these development approaches may be used at different times in the innovation process. During advanced development, where new concepts are being born and explored, the incremental model applies best, while a combination of either waterfall or iterative models may be used for the mainstream product development activity. Once a basic product has been built, a series of customisations or re-configurations may be applied to incrementally add functionality to meet specific customer needs. In this instance, the use of a spiral or incremental approach would work best. The use of the different approaches is illustrated in Figure 12.10.

It is necessary to appreciate that the generic development model should not be applied naively. The development process must be adjusted to the specific challenges of the project as well as be aligned to the strategic aspirations and goals of the firm (for instance, to be the first to market). It is therefore imperative that cognisance is taken of the firm's strategy, its environment and the challenges of the specific project before initiating the execution of the innovation process. By taking into account the full range of factors that define any particular innovation project, the company becomes better placed to select the most appropriate development methodology to translate customer needs into effective and profitable solutions. By carefully attuning the innovation project to the variety of demands it becomes possible to ensure that the development project is managed appropriately inside the organisation, and the product is released into the market at a timely moment so as to improve its chances of success.

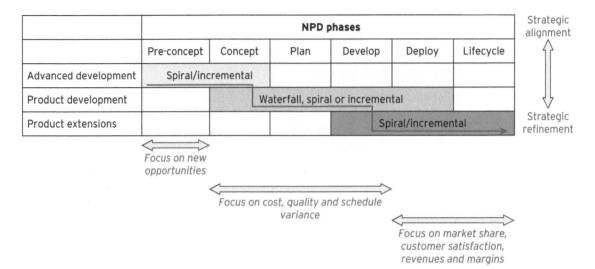

FIGURE 12.10 Applying different development approaches in innovation

ILLUSTRATION

Spiral design versus spiralling costs?

The cost of developing a larger, more powerful unmanned aerial vehicle (UAV), the Global Hawk RQ-4B, increased by as much as $150 million over initial estimates of production. This prompted the Pentagon official who oversaw the project to withhold nearly $400 million until the US Air Force formulated a plan to keep down the escalating costs.

The RQ-4B was expected to feature a fuselage roughly 3 ft longer and a wingspan nearly 15 ft wider than the RQ-4As already produced by Northrop Grumman. The estimate to expand the vehicle's size was about $275 million, according to programme officials. The RQ-4B was designed for missions like those of the legendary U-2 reconnaissance aircraft, and was intended to carry 3000 lb of payload – 30 per cent more than its predecessor the RQ-4A. The B model was to contain more on-board power to operate sophisticated sensors and a 'plug-and-play' information architecture designed to let operators easily switch to-be-built modular payloads on-board the aircraft as needed. Eventually, the UAV was expected to employ a new advanced radar built by a Northrop Grumman-Raytheon team, which would find and target moving objects on the ground.

The majority of the cost increase lay in producing the designs for the 'B' model and in changes made to the production of the new vehicle's wings.

The growing cost raised questions about how the Pentagon could better manage a spiral development programme while controlling price. Spiral development encourages a flexible schedule to field new technologies as they become available. Although a 100 per cent solution may not be fielded when needed, spiral development would have allowed the Pentagon to field a near-total solution to get new equipment into the hands of commanders as soon as possible.

This flexibility, however, could have led to a spiralling of cost. The Global Hawk was almost becoming a victim of its own success. It has been dogged by shifting requirements as air commanders' input new requirements from tests in the field.

One estimate was that the completely finished Global Hawk, with its spare parts and logistics, could cost as much as $5.8 billon by 2012. Auditors noted the total price was difficult to estimate because the advanced sensors now in development for Global Hawk had not yet been firmly priced.

(*Source*: Based on Butler, 2005)

Concurrent engineering: integrating design and manufacturing into the NPD process

As discussed above, design and manufacturing must work closely with each other. Unfortunately, the classical linear innovation model (recall generations 1–3 covered in Chapter 5) that prevails widely in corporate practice is poor at integrating design of the product with the manufacturing process, even when manufacturability is considered to be a primary consideration. In this system whilst the various techniques of manufacturing, such as value engineering, are highly useful for cost reduction and improving manufacturability, they come into play late in the development process. Therefore, they fail to offset the fundamental problems with this approach: sub-optimal manufacturing system with a large wastage of time and resources in re-work, which could have been avoided with proper design. To overcome these problems, a new process of manufacturing engineering emerged in which the key functional activities for product development are conducted concurrently. This approach, spearheaded by Japanese companies, is called concurrent engineering (see Figure 12.11). Unfortunately, the term is used rather loosely and is often used interchangeably with numerous expressions to encompass it. This can cause confusion, and in this text we shall use the term concurrent engineering (CE) as far as possible to connote parallel or synchronous process activity.

The average practice in the West relies heavily on a conventional linear sequential design process. Decision making is highly centralised and occurs within functional silos. Due to weak incorporation and poor dove-tailing of decisions (customer preferences, marketing, design and manufacturing) the number of engineering changes that occur in the best US and European companies is more than 40–60 per cent higher than the best Japanese companies (see Figure 12.12). This is due to the absence of an efficient decision-making process (Prasad, 1995).

a. Classical linear model

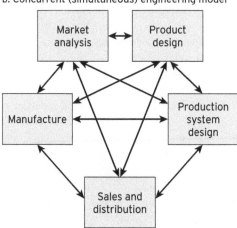

b. Concurrent (simultaneous) engineering model

FIGURE 12.11 Classical linear engineering vs concurrent engineering

FIGURE 12.12 Engineering change profiles

Winner et al. (1988) coined the term concurrent engineering to explain the systematic method of concurrently designing both the product and the downstream production and support processes. This definition is now widely accepted, even though the related aspects of concurrent engineering implementation are still not fully understood, and are evolving.

The practice of CE is widespread in Japan, where it is referred to as doki-ka. The meaning of doki-ka is narrower in the West, as it tends to focus on technical matters and does not include the marketing domain. As practised in Japan, the idea for a product comes from the marketing department into the design and development process. At this stage the idea is not in a technical format that can be used by manufacturing or other operations but is stated in the language of consumption attributes (e.g. price, performance, quality and functional capability). These ideas are passed into the development process through engineers who are joint members of the marketing, design and development departments. This begins the process of development through the initiation of multi-directional information flows (Figure 12.13). This process has been adopted by many Japanese companies, such as Matsushita, Sony and Fujitsu. Toyota, however, is the company that is most often cited, because of its impressive achievements in using this, as well as other complementary process innovations in building a platform for sustained marketplace success.

Success in product development is underpinned by how well companies integrate the various functional areas along the entire product development and business operation chain. For example, the integration of R&D with production is a critical step in the capture of global markets. In highly competitive environments a product's functionalities are essential for the marketplace, but they are meaningless unless a product can be manufactured to the standard demanded by customers and at a price that allows the companies to recoup costs with surplus profit. In the past, the lack of integration between product design and other functions led to products that were difficult to manufacture, install, service and maintain. The price of this was high re-design, production and market entry delay costs (Poli, 2001).

CE is an integrated approach for designing products and processes for cost-effective, high-quality downstream operations. Under a CE regime, product and process design are

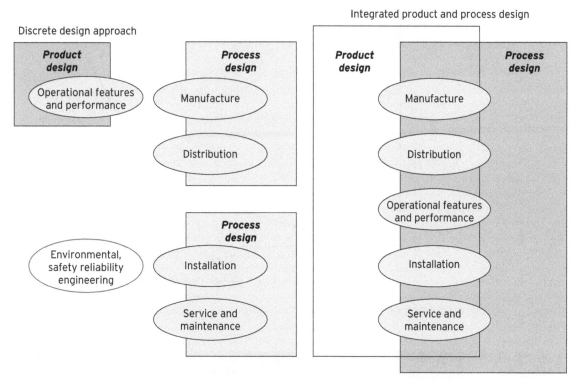

FIGURE 12.13 Marrying product design to the process

integrated from end to end. Integration of the product development process and the entire business operations value chain facilitates ease of manufacture, distribution, installation and service, whilst at the same time improving quality, reducing cost and even reducing time to market. CE reduces the product development by cutting down the frequency of redesign iterations, and instituting parallel processing and removing activities that do not add value. In essence, the CE environment marries product design (the design of product features, components, etc.) to process design (the design of activities to produce the products). Although simultaneous product and process design has inherent risks, correctly implemented the gains in speed to market can be fairly substantial. With respect to costs, 80–90 per cent of total life-cycle cost of a product (manufacturing, distribution, servicing, etc.) are determined in the design phase (Gatenby and Foo, 1990) yet the design phase efforts represent only 5 per cent of the life-cycle costs. Downstream functions account for a large proportion of the total cost outlay (Figure 12.14). Thus, products that are not designed for downstream function needs fail to optimise the business system.

For many companies, concurrent engineering has become a dominant feature of their manufacturing design and development process. CE implementation requires new and innovative forms of human resource practices and organisational designs. Institutional inertia and rigidity, failure to devolve and decentralise managerial authority, strict job designs, coupled with lack of knowledge of CE concepts and the initial costs of change, are major obstacles in its successful implementation (Shena and Derakshan, 1994). Hard technology alone is not sufficient. The way it is used is of paramount importance. This in turn is determined by the quality of the workforce and by other managerially determined factors, such as organisational design, division of labour and administrative processes.

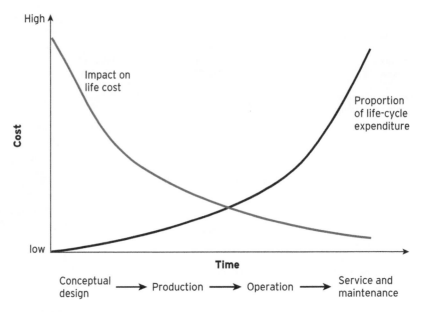

FIGURE 12.14 Costs over time

Manufacturing strategy and innovation

The traditional role of manufacturing was simply to be as cost efficient as possible and not obstruct the deployment of strategy. In more recent times, it has been realised that manufacturing must be more than a mere onlooker in the strategic process. Unfortunately, even when this was appreciated there remained a pervasive belief that for any given strategic posture a company ought to nurture only very specific types of competences, since no factory can be expected to perform well at everything. This logic flows from the field of strategy, in which it was emphasised that competitive advantage could only be built from pure strategy types, such as cost leadership or differentiation. Any mixture of these would lead to a condition of being 'stuck in the middle', and consequently poor performance. Using similar logic there was, and still remains in many industries in the West, a belief that there is a trade-off between efficiency and flexibility of the manufacturing process. This belief was transposed into manufacturing context in the product–process matrix devised by Hayes and Wheelwright (1979). This two-dimensional matrix traces the life cycle of products (from one of a kind to higher volume eventually to a standardised commodity) on one axis, and process (from jumbled to batch processing to assembly line to continuous flow) on the second axis (see Figure 12.15). Under this thinking, only those positions along the diagonal represent viable contingency arrangements, and all others are misfit positions. For example, high-volume products should be made in assembly mode and not job or batch mode. Any other configuration would be considered inefficient.

Flexible systems of manufacturing make production of non-standardised products in a quasi-continuous process possible via a flattening of the diagonal. The implications are important here as they undermine the proposition that there is fundamental tension between innovation and efficiency, making a choice between them no longer relevant. The de-maturation of a supposedly mature industry reinforces the challenge to traditional assumptions and the associated mechanical application of life-cycle theory (product and process).

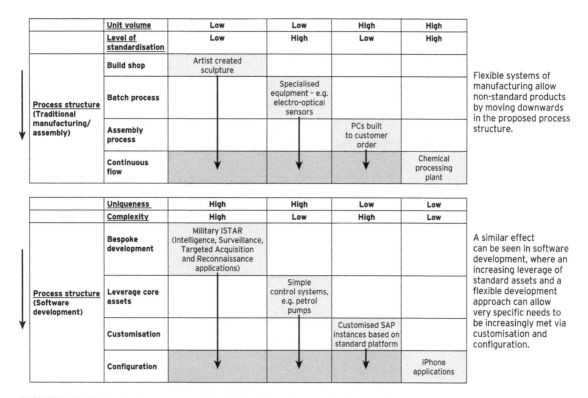

		Low	Low	High	High
	Unit volume	**Low**	**Low**	**High**	**High**
	Level of standardisation	**Low**	**High**	**Low**	**High**
Process structure (Traditional manufacturing/ assembly)	**Build shop**	Artist created sculpture			
	Batch process		Specialised equipment – e.g. electro-optical sensors		
	Assembly process			PCs built to customer order	
	Continuous flow				Chemical processing plant

Flexible systems of manufacturing allow non-standard products by moving downwards in the proposed process structure.

		High	High	Low	Low
	Uniqueness	**High**	**High**	**Low**	**Low**
	Complexity	**High**	**Low**	**High**	**Low**
Process structure (Software development)	**Bespoke development**	Military ISTAR (Intelligence, Surveillance, Targeted Acquisition and Reconnaissance applications)			
	Leverage core assets		Simple control systems, e.g. petrol pumps		
	Customisation			Customised SAP instances based on standard platform	
	Configuration				iPhone applications

A similar effect can be seen in software development, where an increasing leverage of standard assets and a flexible development approach can allow very specific needs to be increasingly met via customisation and configuration.

FIGURE 12.15 Product-process matrix adapted to software development
Source: Adapted from Hayes and Wheelwright, 1979

These developments show that it is possible to pursue a path of product and process innovation and 're-innovation' at speed (i.e. radical innovation) whilst simultaneously driving down cost efficiency.

In the new world of competition, manufacturing must deliver on a number of fronts. It must simultaneously reduce costs, increase quality, be capable of responding to rapidly changing customer needs as well as execute a seamless end-to-end process of production consistently and reliably. The old view captured in trade-offs and exclusive focus on specific dimensions (e.g. cost versus quality) is both false and is rapidly disappearing. Successful companies compete by re-thinking their products, processes and procedures in order to compete across multiple dimensions of competition. In making this link the key questions for manufacturing broadens from not just 'how can we reduce costs' but 'how can we compete'. This requires manufacturing to tackle three simultaneous challenges balancing quality, time and cost.

- *Quality*: The company must be able to provide high-quality products that fulfil needs of customers specifically and distinctively.
- *Time*: The company must be responsive to the marketplace. It must get to the marketplace with an appropriate product design before the competition.
- *Cost*: The company must be able to produce the desired product, with all the attributes and quality, at a price the market is willing to pay and at a cost which is lower than or in parity with the competition. It may use this to drive out competition or improve margin returns.

These challenges can generally be tackled by applying sound manufacturing technologies. These manufacturing technologies are classified as hard or soft. Hard technologies are hardware and software intensive, and include computer aided design (CAD), computer aided manufacture (CAM), computer numerically controlled (CNC) machines, flexible manufacturing systems (FMS), automated inspection tools, robots, WAN, LAN and so on. Soft technologies are manufacturing and production know-how, process design and improvement such as concurrent engineering, JIT manufacturing, manufacturing cells, TQM and so on (for more on these see Swamidass, 2002).

Delivering the product at the right price: market-based target costing

In this section we turn to look at the challenge of producing the desired product at a cost that is competitive and yields desired returns for the innovating company.

In the final analysis, the success of any innovation is assessed on the revenue–cost stream. One of the most difficult and important tasks in the development process is to be able to estimate the production cost of a new product. It is vitally important to get an appreciation of the cost as early as possible in order to make long-term revenue predictions. Cooper and Chew (1996) highlight that poor estimates of final target cost can have catastrophic consequences by elaborating on an example in which a 5 per cent error would have eliminated any return on the company's $200 million investment. Clearly, the establishment and underwriting of the target production cost at the onset of the design phase is an essential objective. Unfortunately, it is usually in error. Most of the time the desired target cost estimation is lower than the final cost. In the early phases of development only a rough estimation can be made, and this is refined as development matures to the final phases of the development process. Typically, the costs of production are made to decrease through the development cycle. At the start, the initial total cost (component and material cost, manufacture and assembly cost) tend to exceed the target cost envelope. One major task of engineering and design iterations (manufacturing improvement, design improvement, alternative material selection, etc.) is to reduce the final cost toward the target cost (see Figure 12.16).

Ulrich and Pearson (1988) show that the quality of design has a significant impact on manufacturing cost (see Figure 12.17). The consequences of design can change the cost of

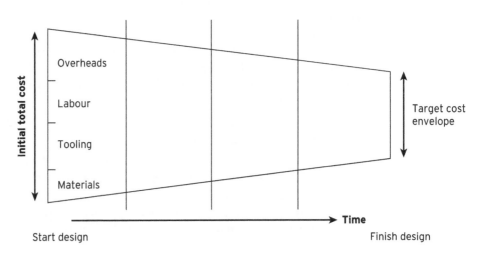

FIGURE 12.16 Target envelope

FIGURE 12.17 Effect of design on quality and manufacturing
Source: Ulrich and Pearson, 1988

manufacturing by as much as 50 per cent or more. It is also important to note that manufacturing unit costs fall with production volume, because of economies of scale, and experience curve effects. Good design and efficient and effective manufacture play an important role in determining the final production cost of a unit of product. From a product development point of view, it is critically important for designers and manufactures to work closely to ensure that the final target cost is achieved. If a product cannot be produced at the target cost, it becomes a liability rather than an asset. The firm begins to bleed rather than make a profit.

Numerous methods of costing can be used to deduce a target cost. The target cost can be defined by conventional activity based costing (ABC) or quality costing methods. Some companies even use simple heuristics and rules of thumbs, such as the Pareto principle, but these carry large error risks. Cooper and Chew (1996) propose a target–costing process which encompasses market factors such as timing of launch, prices that the market will withstand, cost of production, material supplies, and volume as variables.

The methodology for a market-based target-costing process is elaborated in the steps below.

- *Step 1. Define the product, and target the marketplace*
  The logic of target costing is not to minimise cost but to assess and maximise the product's total long-term profitability. This requires a deep understanding of the customer and market segments, and their evolution over time. To achieve this, it is important to appreciate the prices that customers will accept, the functionalities they will insist on, and what the competition will offer them.

- *Step 2. Compute overall target costs*
  The aim of this step is to compute the costs that must not be exceeded if acceptable margins from specific products at specific price points are to be guaranteed. Done late on in the product development process such financial analysis does little to inform the design and production team of what is required to make the product a success from the firm's perspective. Communicated early on in the process, it guides the design and production team's considerations of the various critical trade-off decisions that they have to make.

- *Step 3. Allocate target costs and define the gap between expected and target*
  After a target cost has been deduced, the next step is to apportion the cost among the various product functions. This is done by first calculating the gap between the target

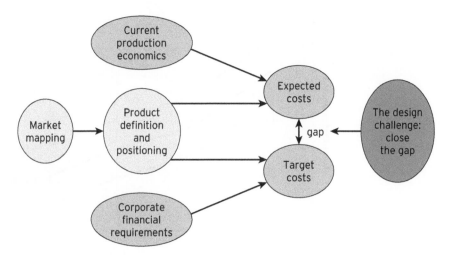

FIGURE 12.18 Market-based target costing
Source: Adapted from Cooper and Chew, 1996

cost, and what is estimated to be the cost for manufacturing the product with its present processes, material, productivity, etc. The gap highlights the difference that must be closed through re-iteration(s) of the design and development process.

● *Step 4. Understand and apply the cardinal rule*
The final cost target is unalterable. All design and development participants, irrespective of rank must obey this. Whilst the design and target costing process are iterative, the target cost should not be allowed to change downwards. Such drift makes it a game. The aim is to set 'stretch' targets so that design and development teams are forced to become highly creative in their solutions and value engineering and quality are pursued vigorously. The cardinal rule is: if the target costs cannot be met the product cannot be launched.

The target cost becomes the basis towards which all the functions involved in the product development process must strive through the deployment of a variety of methodologies and improvement techniques, such as process designs, quality improvement and creative problem solving. For the target costing process to work, the decisions and criteria through which targets are set must be made highly transparent. Organisational politics must be strictly minimised to build the necessary trust and commitment for success. All the different parties must work on the development project as a team to meet the goal of reducing the cost to the target, and if possible even beyond since it is one of the key factors in determining whether the product will yield a return for the company. Of course, the product's market desirability must not be compromised in the process either. If costs are kept down by omitting features desired by the customers or making a lower quality product, it is highly unlikely that the company will make any returns on investing in innovation. Customers will simply reject the product in the marketplace and turn to competitive offerings.

Strategic leverage of manufacturing and design formats

Understanding about different types of design manufacturing formats and innovations is important because each different format holds very different implications for designers,

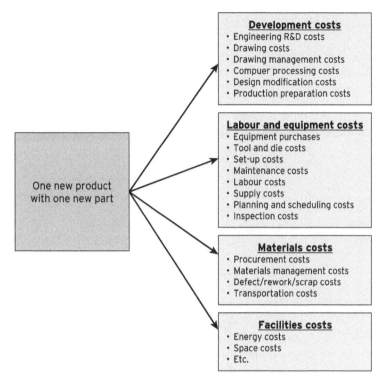

FIGURE 12.19 Product proliferation costs

management and the organisation. Even a simple design change, such as introducing a single new part to a product, can quite easily unleash a proliferation of change and costs (Galsworth, 1994). Figure 12.19 shows the potential ripple effect resulting from one new change or component. This highlights the need to approach design of products with extreme care. As the discussion below will highlight, there are numerous strategic implications depending on the type of innovation and design format an organisation follows. These formats are critical features in enabling competitive capability in environments that demand a higher intensity of new product introduction. If the appropriate design and manufacturing regimes are not adopted it is easy for the organisation to become crippled by product and parts complexity, high costs and organisational complexity as they attempt to cope with the increasing fragmentation of markets.

We elaborate two approaches to design and manufacturing that keep in check the complexity and cost, whilst allowing higher volume and faster release of distinctive new products: (i) product architecture and modular design, and (ii) platform manufacturing.

Product architecture and modular design

As customers around the globe become more and more sophisticated in their preferences, companies have had to respond by segmenting more aggressively. They have been able to do this by developing a greater number of differentiated and improved products. In diverse product markets (from financial services and consumer electronics to clothing) companies have had to adopt strategies of creating greater product variety and more frequent upgrading of products. Such has been the pressure that it has caused a dynamic that is bringing traditional models of innovation under great stress. A fundamental factor allowing the deployment of the new product strategies in dynamic markets is the concept of modularity in the design of products and organisations.

Most products are built from several functions, which in combination provide a set of product functionalities that differentiate one product from another in the eyes of the consumers. Once the decision surrounding the overall functionalities desired from a new product has been made, designers begin the task of creating a new product by decomposing the overall product functionality into a set of inter-related functional components. Decomposing a product design into functional components and specifying the interfaces that define the functional relationships between those components creates a *product architecture*. Product architecture is the assignment of functional elements of a product to the physical building blocks of the product (Ulrich and Eppinger, 2000). In product architecture, component interface specifications define, for example, how one component is physically connected to another (the attachment interface). Interfaces can be of many types, such as communication interface, spatial interface, environmental interface, etc.

There are two fundamental approaches to specifying the interfaces in product design: the conventional approach and the modular approach. The two approaches lead to fundamentally different kinds of product architectures.

The *conventional* approach involves development of a product architecture in which assemblies of components are first integrated and then improvements in performance or cost sought. Under this regime changing a component's design is time-consuming and costly because changing one component's design may require making compensatory changes in the designs of many inter-related components, i.e. there is a high degree of interdependence among components in a conventionally optimised product architecture.

A *modular* product architecture minimises the amount of interdependencies among component designs in a product design. It does this by specifying interfaces between components to allow for a range of *component designs* to be locked to the base. Another feature of a modular product architecture is that it is intentionally defined *at the beginning* of a development process. This allows for the substitution of different versions of components into a product. The substitutability allows creation of product variants endowed with different bundles of features. In this way, modular product architectures enable leverage of a basic product design to create multiple product variants. This 'designed-in' flexibility permits companies to:

- Produce greater product variety.
- Reduce time to market.
- Reduce development costs.

Appreciating the role of modularity in product architecture is important because it can be deployed strategically to combat competition. This appreciation is behind the radical transformation of product designs and product strategies, which are being utilised by a growing number of companies that are deploying design as a strategic tool.

Platform approach: manufacturing distinctive quality and reducing costs

Another way of meeting the challenges highlighted earlier is through the development of product platforms. A product platform generates responsiveness to a market by allowing the development of many product variants, whilst simultaneously holding costs down. Because of this the platform approach to new product development has become a central element in the success of many companies. Through a process of sharing components, production process, technology and know-how across a number of products makes it possible to minimise costs of development. The ability to release new products at marginal extra cost means that companies can respond to customer needs in fragmented niche markets.

The platform approach paves the path toward achieving mass customisation. It facilitates the manufacture of highly differentiated products without consuming excessive resources. Robertson and Ulrich (1998) define platforms as the collection of assets that are shared by a set of products. These assets can be any of four types:

● *Components:* Parts of product design.

● *Processes:* Equipment to design, produce, assemble components associated with the manufacturing and supply chain.

● *Knowledge:* Design, technical, and production know-how.

● *People and relationships:* Teams, structures, relationships with external partners (e.g. supplier networks).

Central to the platform approach is the notion of a product family, from which a stream of new products evolve (Meyer and Utterback, 1995). A product family is defined as a set of products that shares a common technology and addresses a related set of market applications. A commonly observed pattern of platform is one in which a product family undergoes successive product extensions (see Figure 12.20). Over time the product extensions may result in the development of new knowledge, skill or technology. These new skills, technologies and knowledge may be used to develop a new platform, which then goes on to evolve its own family of products. The commercial success of a product family not only sustains itself but also makes possible the development of new platforms. In this way, both incremental

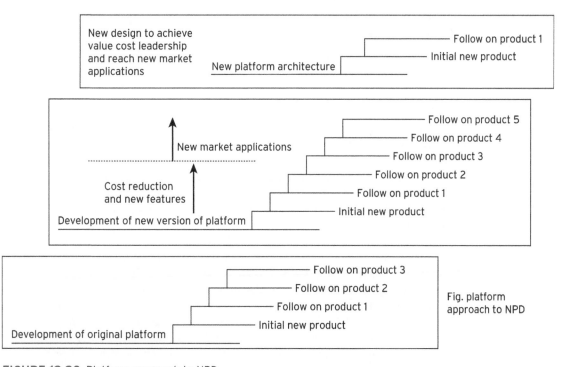

FIGURE 12.20 Platform approach to NPD

and radical innovations can be generated through the platform process. The simplest example of product family and platforms is perhaps cars. For example, the Ford Sierra constituted a product family comprising of variants such as Sierra 1.6, 1.8, 1.8l, 1.8GL etc. All of these cars were made on the same platform and shared common parts. The addition of different features allowed them to target different market segments and niches. By sharing common platform and modular components Ford was able to release a large number of variants without incurring high costs. After some time, the Sierra was replaced by the Ford Mondeo, which had a radically different design and incorporated state-of-the-art components. Effectively, the Mondeo started a new platform, from which numerous Mondeo variants were released. At times, the same car model with slight adjustment may be released in new geographic markets under a different brand name (e.g. GM's Vauxhall in the UK and Opel in Germany), even though it is essentially the same. In fact, cars that are very common may be released in the same markets under different brand names to target different segments. For example, currently the Skoda shares the same platform as VW, and the cars are virtually identical with only a few differences. Perhaps, one of the best examples of deploying a platform approach to innovation is Sony. More than 50 variants of the Sony Walkman were released, each with slightly different features, on the same basic platform.

Many companies and sectors use platforms to develop and manufacture their new products. Platforms are quite common in the auto sector, consumer electronics (e.g. Hewlett Packard for inkjet printers, Sony for portable cassette players), and the commercial aircraft sector.

Platforms allow companies to develop differentiated products efficiently, improve their flexibility and responsiveness of manufacturing, and win positions of market dominance against companies that develop one product at a time.

Production platforms, like design formats, can be of two types: conventional platforms or modular platforms. In a modular platform there is a high degree of sharing of resources, whereas in a traditional non-standardised architecture the sharing is modest.

Product development platforms are based on two key features:

- Distinctiveness of the product.
- Commonality contained within the product and its associated process.

These two elements result in what look to be two opposing pushes: product-led variety distinctiveness versus product commonality. Product distinctiveness is valuable in the market, but it is usually costly to deliver. Commonality drives down costs but often fails to impress the market. Use of modular platform architectures allows companies to manage the trade-off between distinctiveness and commonality. In a modular platform it is possible to easily substitute one component module with another to create a distinctive and customised product to fulfil the needs of the chosen segment(s) specifically. What is special about this process of substitution to create customisation is that the costs of creating this distinctiveness are kept low.

In conventional product architectures component commonality is low, thus making it difficult for them to be manufactured on a shared platform. Moreover, because they are integrated into a single entity it is very difficult to add or subtract features as desired by different market segments. Thus, these modes are highly constrained in their ability to offer a customised product. The only way to do so is to build afresh a new unique product. Of course, this has a high level of uniqueness because it is designed and uniquely optimised to meet the needs of the target segment. However, it also entails very high costs because the total product and its components must be re-designed from scratch. Different product

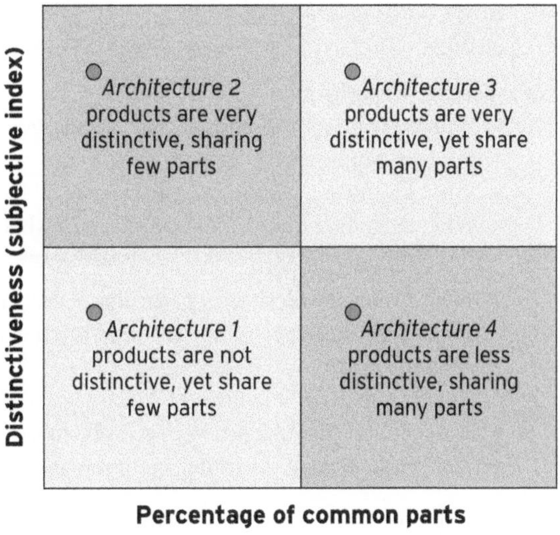

FIGURE 12.21 Product architecture and platforms for distinctiveness and sharing

architectures and their potential advantages and pitfalls are illustrated in Figure 12.21. The chosen product architecture has direct ramifications for the production architecture, and indirectly impinges upon marketing flexibility and architecture. The production architecture defines the range of product that can be produced. For instance, how many different models or variations of a particular model can be produced on the same production line. This in turn, imposes constraints on the marketing activity by defining activities (such as change in pack size, cover, etc.) that can be carried out within the manufacturing environment without incurring significant costs and disruption.

Extending Robertson and Ulrich (1998), product platform planning may be done by focussing upon four information plans. These plans tackle a number of simple yet key questions.

1. *The marketing plan*
   - What products do customers want?
   - What product features are required by which segments?
   - What value is placed on these features?
   - How will we differentiate the models from each other?
   - How will we make sure the models attract our customer target?

2. *The product plan*
   - What model and varieties do we wish to produce, and for which target customer niche?
   - What major options do we need to offer for each model?

3. *The design plan*
   - How can we improve the design?
   - How can we simplify and retain design performance?

In addition to these considerations the design plan has two sub-component elements:

3a. *The differentiation plan*
   - Which elements are to be distinct and different? Why? What value do they deliver?
   - What elements/components bestow differentiation?

- What components will be different? Why?
- What technologies will be different? Why?

3b. *The commonality plan*
- Which elements (components or sub-components) are to be common across the product family?
- What knowledge can be shared across products?
- What technology can be leveraged across what products?

4. *The manufacturing plan*
- What products will share a particular platform?
- What is the basis of creating the platform, i.e. what is being shared (knowledge? components? etc.)
- How can sharing be improved in the platform?
- How can the manufacturing process be improved?
- What is the long-term strategy to leverage the platform?

Each of these plans feeds into the other. There is little chance for success if they are tackled in isolation with little communication between the responsible functions. Platform planning and product architecture design requires full appreciation of all constraints and opportunities. Any gap in co-ordinated planning and action can have major repercussions since a key factor of successfully tapping the benefits of a modular design system is tight coupling of the parts into the total product architecture. Poor coupling and lack of co-ordinated action do not make for a seamless product development system. Indeed, the costs of failing to co-ordinate and couple the platform correctly can be much greater than the costs of not executing the conventional development model because of the consequent ripple effect. In other words, the jigsaw must fit; ill-fitting parts of the picture make for poor product quality.

Process-led customisation for market-based strategies

As we have discussed, increasingly sophisticated customers demand to have their needs fulfilled very specifically. This has led companies to innovate process systems capable of delivering customised products whilst maintaining cost advantages of standardisation. According to Pine (1993) four strategies can be developed to cope with this increase in product variety. Four possible customisation strategies that a firm might adopt are:

1. Point of delivery customisation.
2. Customisable product or service design.
3. Quick response (reducing lead times through supply chain management).
4. Modular product design.

Swaminathan (2001) proposes, on the basis of product modularity and process modularity, four standardisation approaches that can be used to implement mass customisation whilst minimising the cost effects of product variety and variability. These process-led strategies enable market customisation whilst minimising internal product and process changes.

1. *Part standardisation*
Through the use of common parts costs can be kept down (due to economies of scale, inventory reduction and risk reduction of inventory stock-out through pooling, and dampening of parts proliferation, etc.).

2. *Process standardisation*

This approach delays customisation as late as possible, so that the front part of the process can be standardised. This allows the early part of the process to be standardised to produce semi-finished inventory, before the final product is customised to specific customer requirements.

ILLUSTRATION

Examples of process standardisation

Hewlett Packard differentiates its Deskjet printer by adding a customised manual and power supplier late in the process (i.e. in a language and capability to carry the voltage appropriate to the country in which the product is being sold).

Benetton's strategy of dividing the sweater-making process into two stages of manufacture: knitting and dyeing, exemplifies this strategy. The company's knitting process is standardised, and the dyeing process is used to quickly respond to the fashion taste of specific segments of customers.

3. *Product standardisation*

This involves firms offering a large variety of products to customers yet stocking only a small inventory of them. In other words, the advertisement of product availability exceeds the stock. When a customer wants a product version that is not in stock, the firm must either manufacture to that order (from scratch or from sub-component assembly), or engage in a process called downward substitution. Downward substitution is a process in which the customer is offered a product from the available set but one which exceeds the features demanded by the customer.

On the positive side of this practice is the obvious benefit of low stock holding. There is also the side-benefit that a customer in receipt of an up-grade product at the price of the lower may be delighted by the offer. On the negative side, customers may become dissatisfied if the product is built from scratch and if this process involves a long wait.

ILLUSTRATION

Examples of downward substitution

1. A car-rental company offers a higher end car when the one requested is not available.
2. A computer manufacturer packages higher memory/speed specification when the lower end chips are not in stock.

4. *Procurement standardisation*

This strategy uses commonality in parts and components to pool purchasing demand. By pooling purchasing, companies are able to better spread risk of procurement across products with common components. The risk of carrying products whose demand is uncertain is in this way lowered. The strategy can also be used to purchase equipment that is capable of manufacturing a variety of final products, thus reducing the risk of investment in the wrong type of equipment.

Continuous improvement in innovation: total quality management of products and processes

The product that is delivered to the customer must be reliable and meet their needs completely. Developing new products is of no use at all if they are defective or fail to perform to expectations when the customers come to use them. Doing so simply amounts to squandering product development money and energy. From a customer point of view it is imperative that new products fulfil closely their needs. From an organisational point, it is imperative that the highest quality products are produced most efficiently. This requires highly effective processes. Both of these challenges can be tackled through quality management.

Quality and reliability engineering is needed in the product development process to ensure that delivery is made to the true needs of the customer. The modern view of quality is about accurately defining and then satisfying or exceeding customer expectations. This view of quality transcends the earlier narrower perspectives that focussed attention upon conformance to requirements and quality assurance through process control. The modern quality paradigm is holistic and draws upon a set of general principles to formulate practical techniques for continuous improvement. In its modern conceptualisation, quality management is a total organisational philosophy, and its techniques are relevant not just for design and manufacturing but also across the entire business processes system (Juran, 1992; Ishikawa, 1985).

So what is quality? In its essence quality:

- focuses upon continuous improvement of processes and products
- drives predictability by use of scientific methods (decision based on fact)
- changes culture through the involvement of everyone and every level in the organisation (total)
- strives for customer satisfaction (internal and external).

Quality techniques feature throughout the basic innovation process. The basic set of quality techniques and their use in relation to the various development stages are summarised in Figure 12.22. These can be categorised as online (active process improvement tools, such as the cause–effect fishbone, FMEA etc.) or offline activities (e.g. quality function deployment (QFD), quality policy deployment (QPD)).

The philosophy of quality has over time become more encompassing in its scope. Modern versions of quality are referred to as Total Quality Management to capture the belief that the quality philosophy applies to all aspects of an organisation and its activities. This is why it is 'total'. It is not relevant just for the shop-floor and manufacturing operations but for all of the organisation, including top-level processes and leadership. Indeed, the remit of total has been expanded even further to include society. Many companies have taken on board a more holistic and broader philosophy of quality. This is mirrored in their adoption of broad frameworks that direct quality improvement attention toward all organisational processes. The most common and widely recognised frameworks are the European Quality Foundation Excellence Model (EFQM), the Malcolm Baldridge model of the US, and the Japanese Deming Model. The models have many national variants, such as the British Excellence Model, the Swedish Model, etc. These models essentially consist of two categories: enablers and results. The models are predicated on the belief that results (shareholder return, customer satisfaction, employee satisfaction and societal well-being) are produced if the

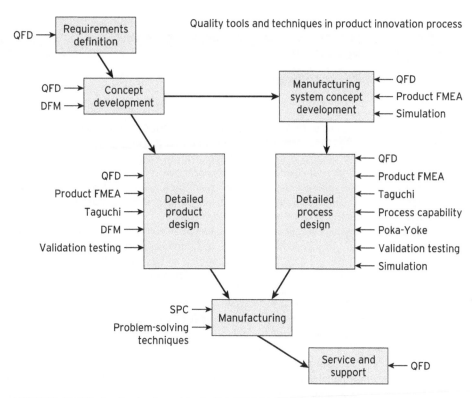

FIGURE 12.22 Quality tools and techniques in product development

enabling factors within the organisations are well managed and continually improved. For instance, the EFQM model indicates that bottom line performance is a consequence of keeping customers satisfied, employees happy and looking after the welfare of society though organisational actions. Leaders deploy strategy through the development and continuous improvement of processes aligned to customers' needs, within which employees are motivated to improve products and processes and external partnerships are constructed on a win–win basis.

The EFQM model stresses innovation and learning as an element of its improvement initiative. World-class firms are those that are really able to excel at the innovation and learning aspect. The stress on innovation is not narrowly focussed on product innovation, but echoes more the emphasis of the quality philosophy, namely process innovation. Moreover, the 'total' dimension of quality also indicates strategic innovation. Indeed, there is a close and reciprocal relationship between the different forms of innovation. This is particularly the case between process and strategic innovation. More often than not significant process innovations lead to strategic change, and strategic innovation holds de facto implications for processes.

Innovating the innovation process: building flexibility in the product development process

Flexibility and speed in business process execution is a key business challenge, and is widely observed as a way to gaining competitive advantage. However, the benefits of flexibility

ILLUSTRATION

Process improvement = profits!

Rick Wagoner took over as CEO of General Motors in 2000. Under Rick Wagoner's guidance, GM has been implementing lean manufacturing techniques that it learnt from Toyota in California throughout its operations. To set the process rolling Wagoner put out a stark warning to GM executives to improve quality: they could either deal with the problem or leave.

General Motors has applied Japanese lean manufacturing techniques, such as kanban (just-in-time manufacturing) and kaizen (continuous improvement) that it learnt from Toyota. These helped improve productivity and quality at GM's North American plants.

The second element in Wagoner's strategy has been to try and leverage GM's size. For decades GM had given its regions the freedom to design and engineer cars locally. Its cars could appeal to local tastes but it meant there were few global economies of scale. Competitors such as Toyota, Europe's Volkswagen and luxury manufacturers BMW and Mercedes-Benz use the same production system in every factory, share components and models between regions and have centralised engineering facilities. GM's size and breadth means the company has much to gain from sharing design expertise and components. Bob Lutz, GM vice-chairman, likens it to a Lego set, with one region able to draw on the gearboxes, engines or suspension of another to save designing everything from scratch. Some branding is also going global, led by Chevrolet and Cadillac.

The result: GM has improved its productivity and quality faster than rivals and has cut the size of its workforce. Having applied Japanese manufacturing techniques, GM pushed ahead of its domestic rivals on productivity. According to the annual Harbour Report, GM has cut hours worked per vehicle by 25 per cent over the past six years, the fastest improvement of any manufacturer, and has four of the top five factories in North America.

It has been in manufacturing and not products that Mr Wagoner's strategy has achieved most. GM's focus on manufacturing strategy seems to have worked. It survived the 2004 economic slowdown, remaining profitable whilst its counterparts Ford and Chrysler recorded huge losses in their automotive operations.

Yet there is a long way to go. GM's returns remain unacceptably low: just $125 profit per vehicle in 2003. Compare this with Toyota's return of ¥226,000 ($2000).

In fact the success story never really happened. In 2005, Toyota pulled ahead of GM as the world's leader in vehicle sales, widening the profitability gap even further. In the years 2005–8 GM lost around $70 billion, largely because they ignored industry wide trends towards more environment-friendly cars. GM only survived the 2008 economic crisis through major reductions in capacity and the input of US government funds.

(*Source*: Adapted from J Mackintosh, 'Paying the bill after the price war', *Financial Times*, 30 September 2004, p. 14)

depend on the environment in which the firm operates. For companies in stable environments the pay-off from investment in flexibility is much less than that gained by those companies in dynamic environments. In fast-changing environments the ability to accommodate evolving customer needs and technologies yields tremendous benefit. We observed this in our earlier discussion of the waterfall and iterative approach to design and engineering development.

When firm flexibility is low the economic cost of modifying a product, especially in the late stages, is high. Under this scenario, development teams have to engage in activities to minimise the risk of design changes. In other words, they have to expend effort up-front on expensive and time-consuming information-gathering activities (such as forecasting and market research) to reduce development uncertainty. If however, a firm is highly agile, the development team has the option of modifying the products as more information becomes available late into the development process. This not only improves conformance to customer requirements since accurate information from prototyping is available, but also speeds development time whilst reducing cost. For instance, in a dynamic environment large investment in early specification may only be of marginal use if customer needs are evolving during the development period itself. There are a number of studies that appear to indicate the ability to make changes close to product or process introduction is positively associated with higher customer quality and firm performance (e.g. Iansiti and MacCormack, 1997).

Thomke and Reinertsen (1988) make a compelling case for development process flexibility. They argue development flexibility has become important because product complexity has increased dramatically with increased customer sophistication. Modern products require many more functions, and this has made forecasting ever more difficult. Secondly, the life cycle of products is decreasing. Both these challenge the effectiveness of conventional forecasting methods. Consequently, managers need to re-define the problem of innovation from one of improving forecasting to one of eliminating the need for accurate long-term forecasts. As acquiring accurate information about the future becomes more difficult and prone to higher forecasting errors then the traditional approaches to forecasting begin to reach their limits of effectiveness. In such environments the role of flexibility as an agency of risk control increases. Development flexibility becomes a powerful alternative to forecasting the future. By selecting specific types of management strategies and design technologies companies are able to increase response agility. This makes them less reliant on long-term forecasting accuracy.

As we discussed earlier, one way of building flexibility is through leverage of modular design architecture. A second important way is to design and implement processes that are intrinsically capable of delivering flexible response.

An example of innovation process flexibility is Toyota. Whilst many companies have implemented a variety of continuous improvement and lean production techniques none have been able to parallel Toyota's development cycle time reduction or agility. We now turn to examine Toyota's approach (Sobek et al., 1999) in order to discern key principles that provide development process flexibility.

Development and design process flexibility at toyota: set-based concurrent engineering

Traditional development practice, whether concurrent or not, tends to quickly converge to a single solution, and then attempts are made to modify that solution until it meets the design objectives. This is an effective enough approach unless the selected starting point is incorrect. Under this scenario subsequent iterations to refine the selected solution are not only time-consuming but more often than not lead to a sub-optimal design. In contrast, what is referred to as 'set-based concurrent engineering' (SBCE) or 'set-based development' (SBD) begins by initially considering a wide set of possible solutions and gradually narrowing the possibilities to a single solution. The premise upon which the process is based is simple: by casting a wide net at the start, and by eliminating weaker solutions over time, you are more likely to identify better solutions. Ward and Seering (1989) coined the phrase set-based design in 1987, to refer to a process that was observed at Toyota, in which a large number of development specifications are gradually narrowed down until the final solution emerges. Ward and Seering call conventional concurrent engineering a point-based approach to design, and the new approach a set-based approach.

What is set-based development?

Traditional, linear innovation involves functions in a serial manner. Each function designs to a single solution or point. Thus, research and development generates its best single solution based on its criteria and 'throws it over the wall' to marketing, which then develops its marketing plan based on what development has passed on to them, and so on down the serial chain. This clearly is a simplified version of events because there are feedback loops. The feedback from downstream functions, however, comes into action only after upstream functions have already committed to a particular solution. This explains the costly and time-consuming re-work. Moreover, since the feedback is made on the basis of a single selected solution it often arrives back as a critique. Given the need to minimise expensive re-work the end result of this process is minor changes to the base design.

The concurrent engineering approach improves upon the serial approach because it is effective in reducing the time and length of the feedback loops, particularly for the most critical interdependencies. Despite improvements, the concurrent engineering approach represents only an incremental gain because it shares the base assumptions of the serial approach. The major difference, in the concurrent approach, is that it utilises a higher degree of parallel processing. Put simply, conventional CE remains within the paradigm of point-based engineering, i.e. CE is an improvement over serial engineering, but the basic picture remains the same: the design team iterates on one solution. This is why it is referred to as 'point-based concurrent engineering'.

Problems with the concurrent engineering approach often occur as the design passes from one group to the next for critique from a different functional expertise (and this is true even if the input occurs as a cross-functional team), because every request for a change ripples into further changes and analysis. It is also quite possible that once set in motion the 're-work' loop iterates indefinitely without convergence to a single solution. Experience from the world of practice indicates that most often the iterations only come to a halt when development time runs out. The major problem arises from the fact that the development organisation never gets a clear picture of the total set of possibilities, and the end result is that the final product and its design may be far from optimal. However, it is important to remember that despite its inherent weaknesses many companies have successfully deployed iterative, point-based models.

The set-based process, however, is quite different from conventional point-based approaches. In the set-based approach the development team participants consider, develop and communicate sets of solutions in parallel and do so relatively independently. Over time, as more information becomes available from development tests, customer research, and from the efforts of other team participants, the solution space is gradually narrowed down. As the solution space narrows toward a select number of designs, the participants of the development team are committed to stay within the set(s). This serves to ensure that others can rely on their communication.

Figure 12.23 illustrates the basic process of SBD. In the initial stage, three functions (marketing, design engineering and manufacturing engineering) define broad sets of feasible solutions from their domains of expertise (*principle 1: map the design space*). In the next stage, design engineering gradually refines the set by discarding ideas that are clearly not feasible from the manufacturing perspective, and marketing gets further feedback from customer response to the initial ideas (*principle 2: integrate by intersection*). Each function then continues the continuous improvement of the set. Following improvements the three groups continue to communicate about the sets under consideration to ensure producible product designs and also to ensure that these are desired by the market. This enables manufacturing to start planning for feasibility of the mass production process and marketing to start

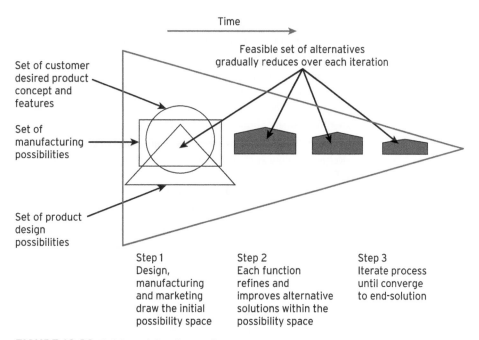

FIGURE 12.23 Set-based development process

planning product positioning and launch strategies (*principle 3: establish feasibility before commitment*). As sets are refined there is gradual convergence to a final design, based on highly informed decision making. The process of gradual convergence has the advantage of allowing both functions to work in tandem and thus significantly lowers the risk of re-work. The illustration is highly simplified, because it takes into account only two actors. The process works just as well with many actors.

The underlying premise of the set-based approach is that it assumes that reasoning and communicating about sets of ideas leads to more robust, optimised design as well as greater overall efficiency than working with a single idea at a time. In practice this appears to be the case, even though the individual steps look cumbersome and inefficient. Also, theoretically it is possible for SBCI to be conducted without any back-tracking or re-work. However, in practice, the cost of removing all back-tracking probably cannot be justified. The Pareto principle is particularly relevant. Toyota's approach of converging to a final solution from a set, rather than trying to optimise from a single chosen idea, appears to allow for dramatic reduction in time and cost of back-tracking.

Thomke and Reinertsen (1998) capture some of the key underlying principles for process flexibility. Examining these in relation to the Toyota practice it seems that the process architecture can be designed to accommodate flexibility in a number of ways:

- *Progressively lock down requirements*: Conventionally, companies utilise development models in which requirements must be defined before any design work can begin. The basis of this is that one should not begin to design until one knows precisely what one is designing. The effect of this is to force specification of items for which accurate information is unavailable at the time. This exposes them to making changes when accurate information does become available. In the alternative model of development, specifications are gradually locked down. Deferring decisions lowers the vulnerability of these companies to the appearance of more accurate specifications late in the process. These firms make decisions within a shorter time span, and their decisions are more efficient because the decisions are more likely to remain stable. This was the logic of operation in the iterative development methodology discussed earlier in the chapter.

- *Keep multiple back-up approaches viable even after concept selection*: Conventionally, only one single design concept is selected and everyone supports it or risks becoming an outcast from the team. Flexibility, however, requires at least one back-up is kept alive in case the primary concept encounters problems.

- *Provide a sound framework for making trade-off decisions*: Many of the problems in decision making are a consequence of people not having appropriate tools to make trade-off decisions. The longer it takes to make a decision, the higher the cost of change and the lower the flexibility. Development flexibility can be increased by providing IT-based decision-support systems that facilitate rapid decision making.

Process flexibility can also be created through the use of flexible technologies such as CAD, CAM, CAE tools and prototyping technologies. These enable significant reduction in development time, as well as reducing the costs of making changes. These new technologies lower iteration costs of design. In much the same way that word-processors dramatically altered the cost of iterations on documents, changes in design technology and processes have altered the economic cost of design iterations. However it is important to note that technology adoption does not automatically guarantee success. Many companies in the West implemented on a large scale flexible technologies such as CIM yet were unable to gain significant benefits. The Japanese, in contrast, have adopted these technologies as parts of small islands rather than large-scale plant renovations. The Japanese managed to make these technologies create process flexibility and have reaped benefits. The lesson emerging from this experience is that success is not just from the adoption of these technologies but in the nature of the way these are incorporated into the fabric of the organisation's systems and culture.

ILLUSTRATION

The car ahead . . .

Toyota Motor Corpation's culture of kaizen, or continuous improvement, includes a degree of paranoia, executives and observers of the automaker agree. This gives Toyota a big edge in product development and operating efficiencies around the world, they say.

'Because we're paranoid, because we chase very lofty goals and we gain energy from the pursuit', Toyota's employees 'never gain the arrogance because we never accomplish our goals', said Toyota US Division General Manager Jim Lentz.

Jim Press, COO of Toyota Motor Sales USA Inc., noted that Toyota is 'afraid of complacency'. What put Toyota above everybody was its relentless drive to move forward. This mind-set brought huge success. Toyota reported a record global net profit of about $11 billion in its fiscal year that ended 31 March, 2004. The company also set records for worldwide vehicle sales, revenue and operating profits.

But Toyota knew it could not let success go to its head. There were challenging times still ahead.

One major challenge Toyota faced was adapting its disciplined, rational business approach to more emotional activities such as vehicle styling and advertising. Another challenge was its sliding customer service ratings and an ageing owner base.

Jim Press argued Toyota had made progress in responding to criticisms that its styling was too bland. He cited Toyota's re-designed Avalon saloon car and its FT-SX sport wagon concept. 'We really turned the corner on styling with a lot more emotion', Press said. 'Lexus also is developing a new styling direction', he added.

Lentz conceded that Toyota traditionally devoted more time and resources to engineering than to styling, and, 'as a result, there was a problem'. But, he said, that imbalance had 'changed fairly rapidly' in the past few years.

(*Source*: Based on Halliday, 2004)

Conclusion

In this chapter it was highlighted that design and manufacturing are fundamental activities in the innovation process. Design must not only embody a product idea but also ensure that the designed product performs the functions expected of it. Design also plays an important aesthetic role and is very important in attracting customers. Good aesthetics are key influencers in the purchase decision of consumers. However, they must also be backed up by product quality and performance. Failing along any dimension of design can lead to a variety of design failures. A fundamental challenge in approach to design is to ensure that not only does it create market desirability but it also helps the company achieve its strategic objectives. This can be strongly influenced by an effective requirements engineering capability.

In the modern day of concurrent development practice, design and manufacturing are inextricably linked. Good design facilitates ease of manufacture, and for this to occur designers and engineers must work closely together. We showed this interlinkage by elaborating the concept of design latitude. Additionally, innovation processes should not be naively implemented. They must be adjusted to the circumstances of the firm and the needs of the specific project. This was illustrated by developing two models of contingent development: the waterfall model and the iterative model. The waterfall model is appropriate for stable market environments and projects for which requirements are clear and relatively fixed. The iterative model is more appropriate for situations in which there is greater uncertainty in the project and the market shows flux.

In the highly competitive modern environment it was shown that traditional notions of trade-offs between cost efficiency and innovation do not hold. Companies must be cost efficient and highly innovative simultaneously. Companies must respond faster than the competition in developing high-quality products and do this with utmost cost efficiency. The chapter highlighted that these challenges could be addressed by taking a variety of actions. The first step in this process was to have a clear view of the target costs that must be achieved by the development team to ensure return on project investment. Once this target is set it is necessary to start executing methodologies to ensure successful delivery to strategic goals. In recent times a number of methods have come into prominence to aid this process. One way of meeting these challenges is to leverage design and the manufacturing configuration. Product architecture can be strategically configured into a modular design format and the manufacturing process configured as a common platform that shares resources and know-how across product. Used together these two methodologies allow costs to be controlled whilst delivering product variety and distinctiveness. In addition to these, a company can adopt a number of market customisation strategies built on internal process standardisation. Another way of addressing the challenge is through quality management. Quality management focusses on continuously improving the efficiency and effectiveness of the internal process through the deployment of a number of relatively simple and practical techniques such that a high quality product is assured. The final way of meeting the challenges is to examine the innovation process itself and innovate it to provide a high level of flexibility, responsiveness and capability to deliver successful innovations. This was illustrated by scrutinising the approach developed by the exemplary process innovator, Toyota.

QUESTIONS

1. Provide examples from your experience of good and bad design. State why they were good or bad.

2. Under what circumstances would you wish to adopt the spiral design methodology? What are the advantages and limitations of this relative to the waterfall methodology?

3. What are the common causes of design failure?

4. Explain the concept of 'design latitude' and how it can affect manufacturing efficiencies.

5. Describe the advantages and disadvantages a company may experience by adopting a concurrent engineering approach over traditional serial development methods.

6. Describe the concept of platforming and the benefits to be gained from its successful implementation.

7. Using an illustrative example, describe the four possible customisation strategies that a firm might adopt.

8. Using a company from the industry sector of your choice, explain what the most appropriate manufacturing strategies might be, and how these reinforce broader strategic goals.

9. Explain the activities involved in setting production target costs.

10. Describe the concepts, and inter-relationships, of product architecture, platforms and modular design. Explain what benefits can be gained from adopting these approaches.

11. Explain how process-led manufacturing customisations can enhance market strategies.

12. What is the role of TQM in innovation?

13. Describe some of the latest approaches that help drive greater flexibility in product development.

CASE STUDY

Car manufacturing: vehicle makers appreciate the virtues of virtual design

Electronics may be responsible for about 90 per cent of innovation in automobiles, but they also provide vehicle makers with their biggest challenge – keeping up with innovation in consumer electronics. The success of Apple's iPod was one such challenge. Customers were asking how they could connect these tiny digital music players to their cars' audio systems.

Computer-aided design (CAD) and computer-aided manufacturing (CAM) systems have been standard for years, but the latest developments in digital technology are revolutionising motor vehicle design, manufacture, retailing and capabilities in ways that could only be hinted at by earlier, simpler systems.

The most popular CAD and CAM systems are now well established and have become critical elements of product life-cycle management software. PLM software includes CAD and CAM, tool design and manufacture, digital manufacturing, supply chain management and workflow management.

Primary manufacturers and component suppliers are modelling products in three dimensions using software before building physical prototypes. The ideal is to have a single digital mock-up of the vehicle to be used as the 'blueprint' by all suppliers. 'If you have many subcontractors and they are all producing prototype parts for your vehicle and you change an important part, how many will be affected and have to go back and re-engineer their part', he asks. 'If you can minimise that by using the digital model at the prototyping stage you can reduce costs. As soon as you go to hard prototyping, things slow down and costs rise.'

John Deere, the US maker of agricultural and other heavy equipment, is experimenting, in conjunction with the Iowa State University, with haptics, a technology that enables a user to 'feel' the experience of assembling and disassembling heavy components. Users hold a kind of motor-driven stylus, made by SensAble Technologies of Woburn, Massachusetts, in each hand while looking at 3D images of the components on a computer screen. When the two parts are put together, the user 'feels' the collision through the stylii.

The modern manufacturing line itself is significantly more flexible than in the past, turning out a cabriolet one moment, a van the next. This leads to complex logistics issues, as supplies of doors, wheels and other components have to be ready to be fitted to the correct vehicle. Barcoded adhesive labels are currently used to identify components but these can become dirty or scratched. Instead, Powerlase, a UK company, uses solid state lasers to engrave barcodes directly on to aluminium, and galvanised and stainless steel.

Technology is also having to reflect changes in the way dealers operate, as they now tend to sell a variety of vehicles. Dealer management systems allow buyers, when choosing a new car, to select options and accessories, automatically register the vehicle and create a link to a finance company. It will tell the buyer when the new car is to be delivered, help sell their old vehicle back to the dealer and set the after-sales market process running.

Manufacturers have developed sensors for detecting dangerous pressure levels in tyres and a dangerous lack of attention in the driver. A combination of global positioning equipment and mobile radio enables cars to be tracked and charged for their use of the roads.

KPIT Cummins designs software that automatically reduces speeds on wet roads and controls the oil inflow and level of emissions. NXP is developing the ignition key of tomorrow, whose chief advantage will be to tell drivers, via a tiny screen, if their cars are locked once they are in the supermarket.

QUESTIONS

1. How would you categorise the key benefits of using electronic-related innovations in car manufacturing?

2. Considering each of the categories in turn, investigate further some of the developments described in this case study. To what extent does each development benefit (a) the manufacturer and (b) the manufacturer's suppliers, and (c) the end customer.

References

Bradford, W. (2005), 'BMW 4 series gets a new look', *Automotive News*, 28 March, 79(6140): 8.

Butler, A. (2005), 'Spiralling cost', *Aviation Week and Space Technology*, 4 April, 162(14): 27.

Case, A. (2008), 'Car manufacturing: Vehicle makers appreciate the virtues of virtual design', *Financial Times*, 28 May.

Cooper, R. and Chew, W.B. (1996), 'Control tomorrow's costs through today's designs', *Harvard Business Review*, January/February: 88–97.

Deming W.E. (1986), *Out of crisis*, Cambridge: Cambridge University Press.

Gatenby, D.A. and Foo, G. (1990), 'Design for X (DFX): Key to competitive, profitable products', *AT&T Technical Journal*, May/June: 2–13.

Galsworth, G.D. (1994), *Smart, simple design: Using variety effectiveness to reduce total cost and maximise customer section*, Vermont: Oliver Wright Publication Inc.

Halliday, J. (2004), 'Toyota's drive keeps it in front', *Automotive News*, 4 April, 28F.

Hayes, R.H. and Wheelwright, S.C. (1979), 'Link manufacturing process and product life cycles' *Harvard Business Review*, January/February: 21–34.

Henderson, R.M. and Clark, K.B. (1990), 'Architectural innovation: The reconfiguration of existing product technologies and the failure of established firms', *Administrative Science Quarterly* 35: 9–30.

Hertenstein, J.H., Platt, M.B., and Veryzer, R.W. (2005), 'The impact of industrial design effectiveness on corporate financial performance', *Journal of Product Innovation Management* 22(1): 3–21.

Iansiti, M. and MacCormack, A. (1997), 'Developing products on internet time', *Harvard Business Review* 75(5): 108–117.

Ishikawa, K. (1985), *What is total quality control? The Japanese way*, Englewood Cliffs, NJ: Prentice Hall.

Juran, J.M. (1992), *Juran on quality design: The new steps for planning quality into goods and services*, New York: The Free Press.

Kotler, P. (2003), *Marketing management*, 11th edn, Upper Saddle River, NJ: Prentice-Hall.

Mackintosh, J. (2004), 'Paying the bill after the price war', *Financial Times*, 30 September, 14.

Meyer, M.H. and Utterback, J.M. (1995), 'Product development and cycle time and commercial success', *IEEE Transactions on Engineering Management* 40(4): 297.

Oliver, N. (2002), 'An organisational perspective', in M. Bruce and J. Bessant (eds), *Design in business: Strategic innovation through design*', Harlow, UK: Pearson Education Limited.

Pine, J.B. (1993), *Mass customisation: The new frontier in business competition*, Cambridge, MA: Harvard Business School Press.

Poli, C. (2001), *Design for manufacturing*, Boston, MA: Butterworth Heinemann.

Prasad, B. (1995), 'A structured approach to product and process optimisation for the manufacturing and service industries', *International Journal of Quality and Reliability Management* 12(9): 123–138.

Pugh, S. (1991), *Total design: Integrated methods for successful product engineering*, Workingham, UK: Addison-Wesley Publishing.

Robertson, D. and Ulrich, K. (1998), 'Planning for product platforms', *Sloan Management Review*, Summer: 19–31.

Shena, D.G. and Derakshan, S. (1994), 'Organisational approaches to the implementation of simultaneous engineering', *International Journal of Production Management* 14(10): 30–43.

Sobek, D.K. II, Ward, A.C. and Liker, J.K. (1999), 'Toyota's principles of set-based concurrent engineering', *Sloan Management Review*, Winter: 67–83.

Swamidass, P.M. (2002), *Innovations in competitive manufacturing*, New York: AMACOM.

Swaminathan, J.M. (2001), 'Enabling customisation using standardisation', *California Management Review* 43(3): 125–135.

Thomke, S. and Reinertsen, D. (1998), 'Agile product development', *California Management Review* 41(1): 8–30.

Ulrich, K. and Pearson, S.A. (1988), 'Assessing the importance of design through product archaeology', *Management Science* 44(3): 352–369.

Ulrich, K.T. and Eppinger, S.D. (2000), *Product design and development*, New York: McGraw-Hill.

Veryzer, R.W. (2005), 'The roles of marketing and industrial design in discontinuous new product development', *Journal of Product Innovation Management* 22(1): 22–41.

Ward, A. and Seering, W. (1989), 'Quantitative inference in a mechanical design compiler', *Proceedings of the first international conference on design theory and methodology*, Montreal, Quebec, Canada.

Winner, R.I., Pennel, J.P., Bertrand, H.E. and Slusarczuk, M.M.G. (1988), *The role of concurrent engineering in weapons systems acquisition* (IDA Report R-388), Alexandria, VI: Institute for Defence Analysis.

13 Supply chain management and innovation

Learning outcomes

When you have completed this chapter, you should be able to:

- Describe a generic supply chain model, along with its major components.

- Explain the major supply chain paradigms and how they support innovation.

- Describe how supply chains support innovation and a company's business growth objectives.

- Describe how value nets offer a competitive advantage over traditional innovation approaches.

- Show how supply chains can be enabled, or constrained, by technology.

Introduction

Innovation (at the firm level) is a value-adding process that concerns itself with a series of activities starting from the generation of an idea to the fruitful commercialisation of that idea. NPD frameworks have been employed to drive innovation in the past, but the nature of some of the external challenges facing companies now demands approaches beyond traditional product development models.

Firstly, customers are demanding more sophisticated solutions to their increasingly complex needs, often broadening the scope beyond traditional product development. For example, you only need to experience buying a car to see how the sale now incorporates flexible financing, extended warranty services and road accident cover in one attractive offer. Companies have to either expand their development competencies or source the required competencies from alternative sources to meet customer expectations.

Additionally, customers are turning to new ways of purchasing products, especially through the internet. Customers are increasingly using the internet to specify which configuration of products they need, and set their own delivery requirements. A good example of this is Dell's online PC ordering approach. Dell's model builds PCs to user specifications and delivers directly to the customer's house. This model offers a new value proposition that traditional development and manufacturing approaches find hard to compete with.

Finally, customers are demanding lower prices as technology becomes commoditised, especially when there is an increased access to global competitors. One only needs to access websites like 'Kelkoo' (where you search for products of your choice, compare prices across many suppliers in an instant, and select the cheapest option) to see this.

All of these factors can have a crippling effect on companies: development costs are rising as product complexity increases, product life cycles (and therefore ROIs) are shrinking, and competitive solutions are being made available sooner. The only way of addressing these problems simultaneously is to effectively align the product, and demand for that product, through an effectively configured and aligned supply chain. More specifically, companies need to consider innovative changes at a product, process and strategic level within the supply chain that complement, rather than conflict, with their innovation frameworks. This can take a number of forms:

- Supplier involvement earlier in the innovation process to co-design, or to provide, important solution components where the company is reluctant to build a strong competence internally.

- Collaborative, symbiotic ventures with other companies to provide important solution components, or to extend the scope of a solution to deliver even greater value to the customer.

- Introduction of practices and integrated technologies that can accelerate processes and information flow throughout the customer–supplier value chain in a way that can reduce cycle time, reduce costs, and increase flexibility. In this way, additional value propositions are offered to customers beyond those of the basic solutions on offer.

- Sourcing of solution components after initial release which will reduce costs and/or extend functionality (and therefore life-cycle revenue).

In this chapter, we explore these issues, highlighting what needs to be considered, and what can be achieved through the management of supply chains within an innovation framework.

ILLUSTRATION

There is no innovation if it never reaches the customer

Product innovation counts for little unless the products reach the customer. This means the innovation must be distributed quickly and in a way that fulfils customer needs. The most respected companies are not the cheapest or the most innovative but those that actually deliver the products – literally.

Take, for example, Dell the PC manufacturer. Its PCs are little different from those of IBM and Hewlett-Packard. Yet Dell's business model has revolutionised the industry and made Dell the PC leader.

In the fashion sector, Zara, the Spanish clothes retailer, has grown to be an international phenomenon. Zara sources much of its production locally. While that may cost more on a unit basis, it gives Zara a more responsive supply chain, enabling it to bring out new lines as fashions change.

Good supply chain management can translate into lower prices. For example, Payless Shoes, the US footwear retailer which has 5000 stores and maintains an average of 800 different styles and colours. Payless can get a pair of shoes all the way from China to the US and sell it for just $15.

(*Source*: Based on Anon, 'Product distribution', *FT*, 1 October 2003, p. 5)

Supply chains

Before examining how supply chains interface with innovation, it is important to build an understanding of a generic supply chain model. The supply chain is the set of inter- and intra-company processes that produce and deliver goods and services to customers. It includes activities such as materials sourcing, production, scheduling, and the physical distribution system, backed up by the necessary information flows. Procurement, manufacturing, inventory management, warehousing and transportation costs are typically considered part of the supply chain organisation. Marketing, sales, finance and strategic planning are not. Product development, demand forecasting, order entry, channel management, customer service and accounts payable and receivable lie in a grey area; in theory, they are part of the supply chain process, but they are seldom included within the supply chain organisation (Bovet and Martha, 2000).

Definitions of supply chains highlight complementary inter-relationships to innovation. Supply chains are life-cycle processes supporting physical, information, financial, and knowledge flows for moving products and services from suppliers to end users. This definition indicates the importance of the end customer and the importance in delivering solutions to customers. Without the capability to deliver new innovations to the customers, in the places where they purchase and also with the additional services that make up the solution to their problem, the innovation becomes meaningless. Clearly, any innovation must take into account the delivery process and make sure that the delivery process is configured to the desired solution requested by the customer.

Internally, the relationship between product development with supply chain is equally important to the success of innovation as the links between product development and marketing, or of design to manufacturing. If one considers that supply chain and purchasing costs can represent as much as 70–80 per cent of their operating costs (Reese et al., 2002),

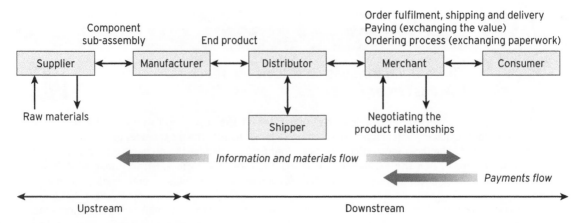

FIGURE 13.1 The generic supply chain model

it is easy to appreciate the importance of this field. To elucidate this, we begin by describing a generic supply chain model.

In any generic supply chain model (see Figure 13.1), there are a number of specific roles played by different organisations. The 'Supplier' is responsible for providing raw material components to be used by the 'Manufacturer', who subsequently makes the consumer ready end-product. The 'Distributor' delivers the end-product to the 'Merchant' or 'Consumer'. Distributors may also use other 'Shippers' to get the end-product to the correct destination. The 'Merchant' then sells the product to the end customer and provides guidance and helps set consumer expectations. Finally, the 'Consumer' gets to consume the product, which fulfils the reason the product was manufactured in the first place.

Within this framework, information (and knowledge) and materials flow both up and down the supply chain, while payments tend to flow in a single direction. This reflects the view of Handfield and Nichols (1999), who propose two types of supply chains: (i) upstream (or incoming materials), and (ii) downstream (or outgoing distribution). It is important in this framework that materials can move quickly and freely to prevent unnecessary build-up of inventory at any point. Efficiencies can be achieved by allowing inventory to flow only when necessary, exchanging knowledge, removing bottlenecks, balancing capacity and generally co-ordinating the smooth flow of materials. This is the role of the 'materials management' group. Within the category of upstream supply chains, the technology supply chain and component supply chains have been identified (Ettlie and Resa, 1992). At each point in the chain, it is expected that organisations deliver and add value to the end product. To achieve this, individual organisations must inter-relate and interact within this network.

In support of this model, there are some key exchanges that need to take place. For the sake of simplicity, the roles of distributor, supplier and manufacturer can be combined. These key exchanges include:

1. *Negotiating the product and relationships*: This is the process necessary for establishing the business relationship (e.g. trading partner agreement).

2. *Ordering process (exchanging paperwork)*: The transmittal and receipt of purchase orders, invoices and shipping notices, credit information and the like.

3. *Component sub-assembly*: Where raw materials and sub-components are sourced and transformed into a more valuable component to be used by the manufacturer.

4. *Paying (exchanging the value)*: At the heart of the merchant–consumer relationship are problems around security of payment.

5. *Order fulfilment, shipping and delivery*: This is the process of getting the order and getting it to the customer through an appropriate distribution path.

The model presented here is very simplistic, as supply chains can be decomposed into many levels. There could be a single supply chain that includes only the immediate set of suppliers and customers, or we may go down any number of levels to include the raw material suppliers at one end and the disposal of used finished products at the other. Generally, the term 'product' describes a basic product or service. An 'extended product' includes the basic product or service, but additionally includes the value-adding activities of the supply chain and incorporation of any other features necessary to augment the basic product before it gets to the final consumer. Companies, therefore, need to consider carefully what products and extended products will comprise their innovation portfolio, and the source of the various value-adding activities. It is important to remember that:

- In the absence of internal development capability, the supply chain offers an alternate approach for sourcing important components to build the product solution.

- Collaboration through early design, or component integration constitute part of the supply chain and feed into the development effort. This can lead to accelerated development cycle times and/or reduced costs.

- The nature of the market, the solution being offered and a company's competencies feature as key determinants of the nature of the NPD model (particularly in design, development and manufacturing), and these in turn dictate the best configuration of the supply chain.

There are a number of different ways of configuring supply chains. These range from the simplistic functional paradigm to the sophisticated strategic approach. Each paradigm affects different companies in different industry sectors in different ways. We discuss these issues and then go on to examine the alignment between supply chains and NPD.

Supply chain paradigms

An understanding of the basic approaches to the management of supply chains is necessary before its importance and link to innovation can be illustrated. We do this by discussing the different approaches to configuring supply chains.

The different ways companies may implement and support their supply chains is driven by strategic business objectives, the complexity of products, and the internal competencies they can leverage in releasing these products to targeted markets. As a result, they vary in complexity and the nature of the benefits they drive. A diagrammatic view of the different approaches and levels is provided in Figure 13.2.

If we adopt a sequential view to the process, the various supply chain approaches progress from the most basic functional level through to the most complex (strategic) level. As new challenges arise, companies build on the previous level to improve their performance. Interestingly, this progression follows the broad steps defined by many NPD maturity models, such as Carnegie-Mellon's Software Engineering Institute's (SEI) CMMI (Capability Maturity Model – Integrated) model – which cites supply line management practices as a key area supporting NPD (Carnegie Mellon University, 1999). More specifically, the Supply-Chain Reference model (SCOR) has been developed and endorsed by the Supply Chain Council as the cross-industry standard diagnostic tool for supply chain management, spanning

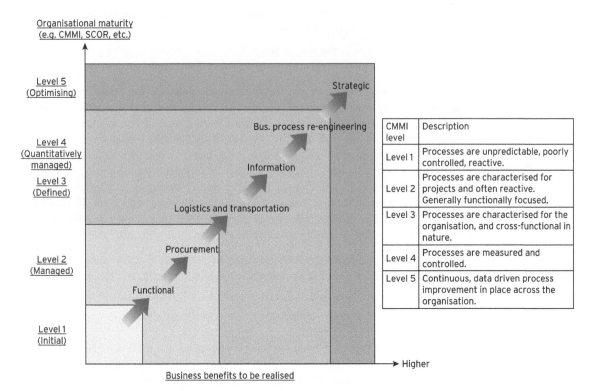

FIGURE 13.2 Supply chain paradigms alignment to business maturity

from the supplier's supplier to the customer's customer (see **http://www.supply-chain.org/ cs/root/home** for more information).

Increasing levels of capability are driven by moving from a chaotic and fragmented environment (Level 1), through to functional definition and optimisation (Level 2), then leading to an integrated environment where optimisation occurs at a company/firm level (Levels 3 and 4). Finally, the company reaches world-class performance through alignment of all the processes to strategic goals (Level 5). Over time companies are increasingly evolving their supply operations as they leverage the power of the supply chain as a competitive weapon. In doing so, they move from one paradigm to another at a higher level.

As we move through these maturity levels, the links between the supply chain and NPD models become stronger. In the initial level there is little coupling to the innovation process, but for the higher levels there is a tighter coupling of the delivery process to the innovation process. In order to prevent any organisational imbalance, it seems obvious that any improvement or development in NPD model should be accompanied by a corresponding improvement in the supply chain (and vice versa).

Each of these supply chain paradigms will be discussed next. Following this, we show how supply chains are connected to the innovation process.

Functional paradigm

The functional paradigm represents the most basic state in supply chain management. It is characterised by companies which procure materials, convert them and sell them on. In this approach individual departments of companies attempt to maximise their own objectives (generally cost reduction), without any strong linkages to other upstream or downstream departments. This generally results in the department that is most dominant/powerful to control the process and drive the greatest cost reductions for itself. Unfortunately, this often does not translate into improvements across the total supply chain.

This represents a starting point for most companies, and the approach tends to predominate in functional organisations whose primary objective is to release a 'basic' product to the customer at a lower price than competitive offerings. While it may make sense for some organisations to possess traditional organisation structures there is a move away from this approach driven by increased customer segmentation, which demands processes to be tailored to meet customer needs.

From an innovation perspective, this supply chain configuration is primarily about simply sourcing components and materials at the lowest possible cost that are needed for initial development and subsequent manufacturing operations.

Procurement paradigm

Since materials are a major cost in any product organisation, some companies find it necessary to move from a functional to a procurement supply chain paradigm. Under the procurement paradigm, the supply chain is considered in terms of suppliers and procurement of materials from them. The difference between this and the functional paradigm is in the approach to purchasing. Under the functional paradigm sourcing occurs in a fragmented manner with individual supplier deals whereas the procurement approach undertakes systematic and planned sourcing. Vendors are screened and managed for efficient purchasing. The focus is to create efficiencies through sourcing improvements, reduced vendor bases and the adoption of vendor-managed inventory levels.

Under this paradigm, depending on the importance of the products and/or services being sourced, the company needs to determine if a single or multiple sourcing strategy will be adopted. Each carries its own specific advantages and disadvantages, and these need to be weighed in the context of the company's broader business objectives.

From the illustration in Figure 13.3, it can be seen that advantages of one approach map onto disadvantages of the other. Each element needs to be carefully weighed before an

	Single sourcing	Multiple sourcing
Advantages	• Stronger relationships • More commitment and effort • Better communications • Economies of scale • Higher confidentiality	• Ability to drive prices down • Switch sources if problems arise • Wide source of knowledge of access
Disadvantages	• Supplier can exert upward pressure • Supplier affected by demand fluctuations	• Difficult to drive commitment • More effort required in communications • Difficult to obtain economies of scale

FIGURE 13.3 Advantages and disadvantages of sourcing strategies

approach is adopted. Companies attempting to shrink the supplier base generally dominate the supplier and any partnership negotiations are focussed on price reductions, often in a way that shifts profits from one company to another, rather than driving any fundamental improvement in the supply chain.

This paradigm provides an extended cost reduction capability for the NPD team in a way that transcends internal functional boundaries. Additionally, the use of single or multiple sourcing of components may help address areas of risk to the product development team (e.g. availability of components, cost competitiveness, etc.) by ensuring a consistent supply of components and raw materials. In some cases, the supplier base may be extended to support broader geographical and market needs.

Logistics and transportation paradigm

Logistics management activities typically include inbound and outbound transportation management, fleet management, warehousing, materials handling, order fulfilment, logistics network design, inventory management, supply/demand planning, and management of third party logistics services providers. To varying degrees, the logistics function also includes sourcing and procurement, production planning and scheduling, packaging and assembly, and customer service. It is involved in all levels of planning and execution – strategic, operational and tactical. Logistics management is an integrating function, which coordinates and optimises all logistics activities, and also integrates logistics activities with other functions including marketing, sales manufacturing, finance and information technology.

Under this paradigm, the supply chain is a physical path of a product enacted through a set of facilities linked by a transportation network. These facilities include factories, warehouses, sales offices, trucks and ships and distribution centres. The major objective here is to lower logistics costs (e.g. transportation costs), but other objectives may also exist to support this effort, e.g. simplifying contacts for customer enquiries.

It is within this paradigm that channel management becomes increasingly influential. Channel management means the adjustment of scheduling, materials movement, stock levels, pricing and other sales strategies so as to bring all the operations into line with each other. The growing reliance on suppliers to assure the appropriate quality levels of their materials means that upstream suppliers are increasingly managing the inventories of downstream customers. This is known as vendor managed inventory (VMI) or a continuous replenishment programme.

This paradigm continues the theme of driving costs out of the supply chain. However, it can disrupt engineering and manufacturing practices if it is not properly optimised. An important consideration for NPD is to ensure how products are manufactured and delivered to end customers for the lowest possible cost. In some instances this requires employing global manufacturing facilities to address local customers. In this instance, NPD teams would need to plan for a handover between engineering and manufacturing which may span many miles, different time zones, different facilities and cultures. The supply chain process must be configured to handle this and support any customisation of the base products to different regional needs by sourcing local components and services.

Information paradigm

This paradigm attempts to improve the links within a company and within the broader supply chain through the use of integrated IT applications and improved IT communications. Implemented effectively, this environment 'without paper' can help reduce errors in communication, speed information flow, reduce mailing costs, increase opportunity costs, and makes business processes more effective.

In this paradigm the supply chain is integrated by the movement of information among the many participants. An integrated supply chain has a common information base as well as the mechanisms to share this information among participants. The major objective here is to minimise information processing costs and collapse cycle times.

Accuracy is particularly crucial and is often addressed by inbuilt validation procedures. While some companies may lack the advanced technology to operate an effective supply chain network, they can still begin to think of approaches that move them down this path (e.g. company intranets, e-mail, business-to-business communications, radio frequency booking systems, etc.).

There are two key elements in understanding an IT-enabled supply chain management, namely (i) the 'communication of information', and (ii) the 'applications architecture'. A number of different techniques are available to communicate information from one computer to another, allowing different companies with different IT infrastructures to establish an effective supply chain alignment. Additionally, a large number of integrated applications have been created to support the needs of different companies in many different industries. Depending on the specific needs, these applications can be implemented in a specific sequence and can be configured to better support internal supply chain processes.

ILLUSTRATION

Integrating the supply chain sub-process through IT

The warehouse is at the heart of any supply chain, and a good warehouse management system can play an essential role in ensuring the speed and accuracy of inventory movements. This is a fact that is often overlooked by companies that see the planning, sourcing and manufacturing portions of the supply chain as the only areas to focus their drive for efficiencies.

In addition, warehouse management tends to be treated as an isolated process, and not integrated with other links in the supply chain, such as transportation management systems. Manhattan Associates, a company that specialises in warehouse management, recently announced a suite of software that it claims integrates transportation management with warehouse management. 'Gone are the days of warehouse management activities happening in isolation from transportation management activities', says Pervinder Johar, vice-president of transportation product development at the company. 'Now the two systems act as one, exchanging information and providing customers with more flexibility to determine how their supply chain processes are executed.'

(*Source*: Based on J. Shillingford, 'Warehouse management', *FT*, 26 November 2003, p. 12)

The information paradigm facilitates the rapid flow of digital information across functional groups, and supply chain members, and by so doing can help create an aligned and integrated NPD environment. Ideally, linked via engineering plans for a new concept, all product-related information can be made instantly accessible by all participants in NPD effort (e.g. availability of procurement specifications for suppliers). This allows the key players to take informed decisions over the variety of trade-offs in the development process and also build, in advance, plans and schedules for the development and launch of the new product. A number of enterprise-level applications are appearing on the market that support end-to-end organisational workflow and offer a single company knowledge repository.

Strategic paradigm

This paradigm highlights that the supply chain needs to be integral to the achievement of a company's strategic objectives. In other words, the supply chain should not just be optimised to achieve efficient supply chain goals such as cost efficiency but its metric of success is how well it supports the company's strategic goals, only one of which may be cost efficiency. The strategic paradigm takes into account the chain of resources across the entire business value chain needed to support a product's market positioning in terms of the target customer, pricing and promotion mix. By establishing goal congruence through the supply chain resource chain, the desired positional advantage can be achieved, cost reductions can be realised and risks systematically minimised.

In developing the supply chain from a strategic vantage point, it is necessary for the company to take into account two factors: the product-market characteristics and the company's supply chain capability. The product excellence dimension rates the product against competitive products in its chosen market. The best in class will rank the highest in terms of functionality, reliability, and value for price, and the supply chain excellence dimension depends on the efficiency and responsiveness of the company's supply chain vis-à-vis competitor supply chains. Thus, the supply chain design depends on the strategic nature of the product and its positioning on the grid (see Figure 13.4).

When positioned in quadrants D or B, products are sold at low margins, and the supply chain needs to focus on efficiency rather than delivery and availability. Alternatively, those products positioned in grids A or C tend to be innovative products that sell at higher margins, and the supply chain needs to be responsive.

Companies with a wide portfolio of products may have some that fall in each category. As a matter of fact, most companies prune underachieving products and businesses – characterised by 'D's.

Most products we buy today lie in the 'B' category. Competition is intense because there is little difference among products, so success requires some innovation in the supply chain (e.g. process innovation to change workflows, or product innovation to change solution components). 'B' products may be former 'A' products whose early success attracted

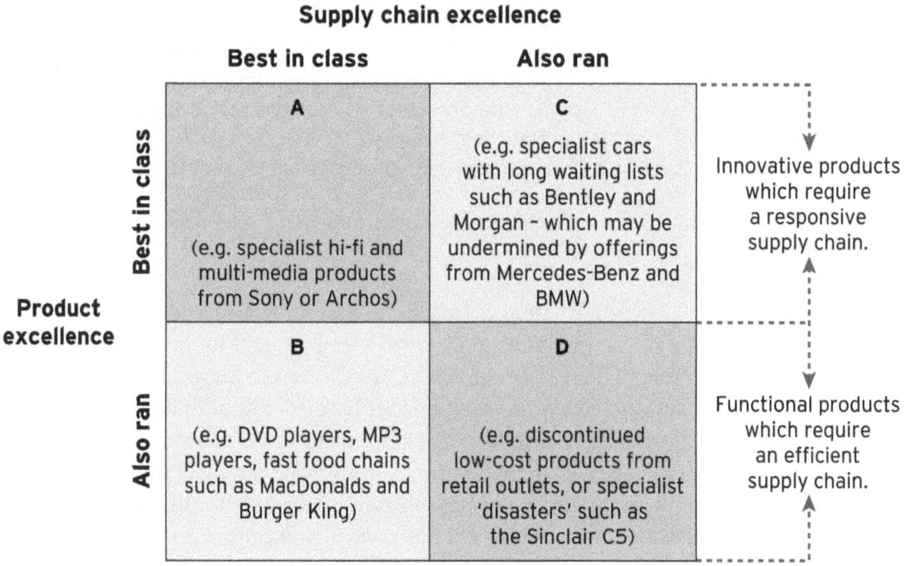

FIGURE 13.4 Supply chain design options

competitive offerings. B products have efficient supply chains but strong competitive reaction means they no longer represent the standard for product excellence necessary to allow the company to charge premium prices.

Wonderful products supported by sloppy operations populate the 'C' category. Such companies are vulnerable to copycat competitors. Unless they move to another category, they will not survive.

Fischer (1997) prescribes a way to implement these strategies. Fischer points out that supply chain design depends on the nature of the product. He divides products into functional and innovative categories. Functional products sell at low margins – equivalent to categories 'B' and 'D' on the grid. Supply chains for functional products should be highly efficient since customers buy on the basis of price. When high costs are a dominant feature, investments should concentrate more on gaining advantages through process innovations of the supply chain in order to improve productivity (Jones and Davis, 2000).

Innovative products – equivalent to categories 'A' and 'C' – command higher margins. Delivery and availability, not efficiency, drive the supply chain design. With a strategic goal of differentiation, in which the unique qualities of the product are expected to provide value to the customer, the supply chain has to be capable of delivering high levels of responsiveness and service to match the strategic positioning of the offering.

Performance is seriously affected if the supply chain is not aligned to the characteristics of the market. In high-volume markets, companies tend to operate an 'efficient' supply chain. However, when relative contribution margins, or the level of product variety, are high, it is necessary to implement a 'responsive' supply chain. Companies will also deploy a 'responsive' supply chain when demand or technological uncertainty exists.

From the above, we can observe that companies need to be aware of their market requirements and characteristics in order to select the most appropriate supply chain model to source, integrate and deliver solutions profitably to customers. Any misalignment significantly undermines previous work performed in developing the innovation and negatively affects the company's business performance. The relationship between supply chain types and market requirements is shown in Figure 13.5.

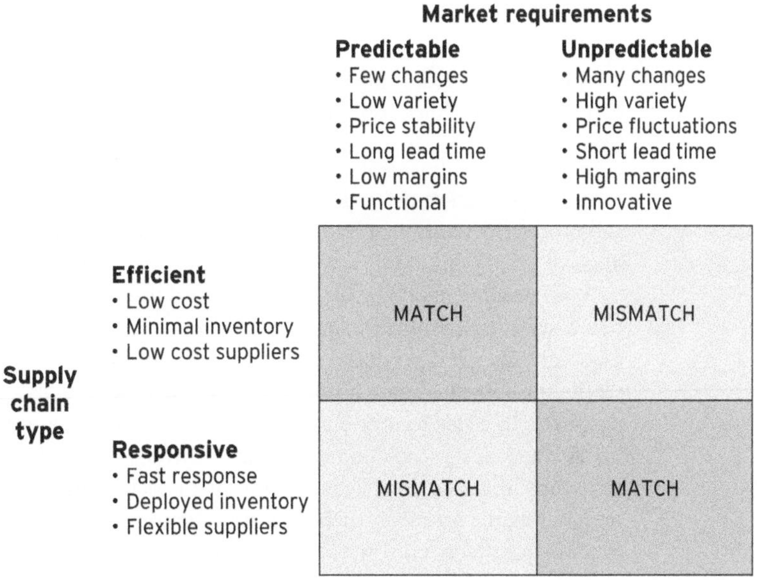

Market requirements

	Predictable • Few changes • Low variety • Price stability • Long lead time • Low margins • Functional	**Unpredictable** • Many changes • High variety • Price fluctuations • Short lead time • High margins • Innovative
Efficient • Low cost • Minimal inventory • Low cost suppliers	MATCH	MISMATCH
Responsive • Fast response • Deployed inventory • Flexible suppliers	MISMATCH	MATCH

Supply chain type

FIGURE 13.5 Supply chain alignment to the market

Using this simple alignment, companies can take into account market characteristics – market growth rates, levels of product variety, relative contribution margins and uncertainty – when making an initial supply chain investment. However, as solutions are developed and released into markets that subsequently mature, so the company moves from one supply chain approach to another to maximise profitability and extend product life-cycle revenue.

Supply chain interface with innovation

As mentioned earlier, the term 'supply chain' can mean many things to different people. Generally, it is agreed that it encompasses the integration of organisations and activities to drive greater customer responsiveness and push down overall costs to achieve a sustainable competitive advantage. It encompasses the management of logistical activities, customer–supplier relationships, new product development and introduction, inventory management and facilities. Doing so involves the design, maintenance and operation of supply chain processes aligned to meet end customer needs.

Appreciating the various features of the paradigms of supply chains is the basis from which to understand how the supply chain affects innovation. Product development concerns itself with the identification, design, development, release and on-going life cycle of products. Traditionally, most focus has been placed on the use of R&D to develop products and product extensions internally within companies. However, effectively aligned supply chains offer an alternative approach to delivering innovations to customers.

Srivatava and Fahey (1999) identify three key ways supply chains support creation of customer value. These are:

● The development of new solutions, or the re-invigoration of existing solutions, accomplished through the product development process.

● The purchase of components and competencies through a supply chain process, which are then transformed into desired customer outputs, and delivered according to customer needs.

● A customer relationship management process that links the company to end customers in order to build relationships and shape perceptions.

Figure 13.6 outlines some of the key changes that are driving companies to move towards the sixth-generation network innovation system. In order to take advantage of these shifts, the product development and supply chain management frameworks must be effectively aligned.

With product development, there is a need to capture customer needs and wants. These needs are then channelled through a development process. To develop new innovation, especially complex products, often requires integration of skills and components from within the company (base product or knowledge) with skills and components from outside suppliers. In order to create the optimal solutions, the company has the option to either 'make' the necessary solution components through internal development and manufacture, or to 'buy' them via an effective supply chain. Depending on the nature of the components in question, the decision may be to source the components or skills needed early in the NPD process (e.g. to support first-mover advantages), or after the initial release (e.g. to reduce costs or extend life-cycle revenue). This is illustrated in Figure 13.7.

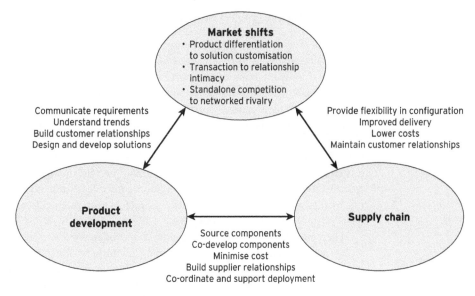

FIGURE 13.6 Key drivers of supply chains

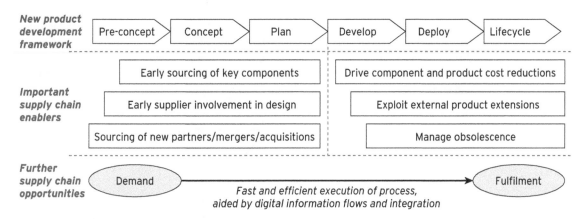

FIGURE 13.7 New product development and supply chain enablers

The 'make–buy' conundrum is one that can potentially be addressed by the functional or procurement supply chain paradigms, as discussed earlier. However, customers are increasingly looking for additional satisfiers other than a good product. Faster and more flexible delivery, lower costs and cheaper solutions are also entering the customer's value equation, but these are often contradictory to traditional NPD frameworks where standardisation of products and long lead times are used to drive costs down. To achieve this the supply chain needs to adopt a higher level configuration, such as that captured by the information paradigm or the strategic paradigm involving a network of suppliers engaged in a collaborative venture (such as value nets).

The area of 'make–buy' decisions is discussed next, followed by a review of how new customer value drivers can be better supported through a more effective supply chain model.

Supply chains and the make–buy decision

A number of ways exist in which companies can deliver value to their customers. Internal design, development and manufacture is one approach, but sourcing competencies from outside the company is another important and viable approach.

Companies increasingly face a market-orientated imperative to incorporate the best technology into their 'extended' products. However, they can rarely do this alone through internal R&D. This is particularly so for complex products incorporating a wide range of new product technologies. Moreover, differentiated products require further augmentation in the form of high levels of customisation and services. Even large companies find it difficult to maintain research efforts simultaneously along all technological fronts. The increasing cost and complexity of new product development makes it difficult for companies to build the 'totality' of assets needed for successful development, forcing them to look outside their own companies for potential solutions.

When making the 'make–buy' decision, the company needs to look carefully at the consequences (see Figure 13.8). Adopting a 'make' philosophy allows companies to take control of their destiny and may allow them to dominate a market, but this strategy can carry significant costs. Alternatively, a 'buy' philosophy will help reduce costs, but also reduces the influence and differentiation a company can bring to the market. Table 13.1 provides a brief summary of alternatives and potential consequences.

It is important that a company has flexibility in deciding upon 'make' and 'buy' in order to support its strategic growth objectives.

In a rapidly changing technological environment, critical technologies necessary for innovation and new product development that are not held currently within the boundaries of a firm can be obtained through purchasing components, or entering into a collaborative agreement which can split in three different ways: (1) mergers or acquisitions, (2) strategic alliances, and (3) internal co-development with early supplier involvement. Mergers and

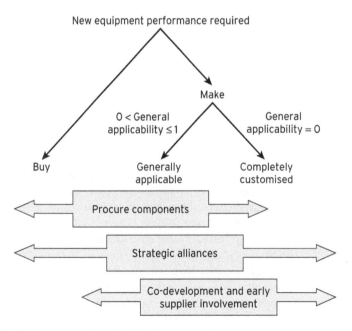

FIGURE 13.8 The make or buy decision in supply chains

TABLE 13.1 Make-buy consequences for the buyer

Consequence for buyer	Buy		Make-customise		Make-generally	
	Effect on buyer's profits		Effect on buyer's profits		Effect on buyer's profits	
	+	−	+	−	+	−
Tailored to production process		X	X			X
Generates upgrades and field support	X			X	X	
Economies of scale from large runs of production equipment	X			X	X	
Price premium from early access to equipment		X	X		X	
Improved yields from previewing equipment		X	X		X	
Potential licensing revenue		X		X	X	
Sponsorship costs	X			X		X

acquisitions can be too expensive when factoring in the uncertainty about the future value of any acquired technology (Lambe and Spekman, 1997). Purchasing components, strategic alliances and early supplier involvement in design are discussed next as viable approaches to support innovation.

ILLUSTRATION

Supply chain practice in the auto sector

The auto sector has led development in supply chain management, and is often used as a benchmark of practice. The sector is one of the most complex, with products and supply chains as complicated as aerospace or defence, but with ever shorter product development times.

According to Gary Turner, a Director in the automotive consultancy practice at PWC. 'It is proportionally more prone to risk management issues than other sectors.'

Companies like GM, Ford and the other large auto manufacturers have to understand the fine balance of risk and opportunities in the make–buy decisions constructed within their supply networks.

The biggest change has been the move from 'make to drawing', where the car maker provides a design to the supplier, to 'engineer to requirement'. Under this model, the supplier designs and manufactures a component or, increasingly, an entire module – for example, the dashboard, front end or the suspension. Now, the financial risk is pushed down to tier one (first-level supplier) right from the early stages.

As a matter of course, suppliers who make a mistake with design bear the cost of problems that such an error causes. Even suppliers building parts to a car maker's design are often asked to meet part or all of the costs of warranty claims from manufacturing problems. Suppliers also bear much of the risk of a new vehicle succeeding or failing. Because the supplier usually pays for the tooling and is reimbursed through a payment of a few cents extra for each part supplied, if demand is lower than forecast they may never recoup their investment. On top of that, it is becoming the norm for suppliers to have to pay for manufacturers' costs if parts cannot be delivered for any reason.

'It is quite common for a clause to be included that if the production line is stopped, carmakers can say to the supplier we will charge you £50,000 an hour', says Mr Turner.

But with auto suppliers in a financially troubled state, car makers need to be careful not to push them beyond their ability to meet obligations. The danger of a supplier going bust is not a new one, and has frequently led to vital parts makers being bought out by their customers to ensure continuity of supply.

As more risk is transferred to suppliers, the car makers are putting even more effort into analysing the financial position of their suppliers to spot potential problems. 'The big carmakers have a ranking of risk of suppliers and a system to flag up when a supplier hits a certain number of points on the distress scale', says Mr Turner. Alerts typically bring in the financial risk management team.

(*Source*: Based on J. Mackintosh, 'Drive to offload risks on to the suppliers', *Financial Times*, 1 October 2003, p. 4)

Component sourcing – support from the purchasing function

In many industries, a substantial proportion of a product's value is purchased from external sources, in some cases as much as 80 per cent (Smith and Reinertsen, 1991). In many companies, a purchasing and supply chain management department is given the responsibility to source these components and services, drive sourcing improvements, reduce vendor bases, and ultimately cut costs. In this capacity, they act as the company's interface with its suppliers. They receive requests from engineering, manufacturing and operations, and are then responsible for preparing requests to suppliers, which in turn return quotations and supporting documentation (e.g. statements of work, quotations, statements of understanding, etc.). After an examination of the quotes, and negotiation over terms and conditions, suppliers are selected and receive payment according to agreed terms. The purchasing department is responsible for performing vendor assessments, raising the necessary purchase orders, ensuring all legal and regulatory terms are concluded, and managing delivery of the products and services into operations.

Purchasing or supply chain managers have always needed to possess an intimate knowledge of their products and components. Traditionally, they have been measured on their ability to win discounts and their efficiency in handling transactions. They tended to be involved so late in the NPD process that they were constrained in the way they could work with suppliers. They often had to act as gatekeepers and thus had to attempt to keep the production process running smoothly. Almost inevitably because of the reactive manner in which they were being involved they ended up introducing delays into the process.

Over time their role has expanded. This reflects the increasing importance placed by supply chain management in supporting NPD. Buyers are now involved in the whole business chain, and are focussed on total cost containment rather than unit price. This requires them to focus on a wider area including material costs, buying price, labour costs, transportation costs, quality costs, etc. As a result, they are now being assessed on their selection of suppliers to meet internal needs, the reduction of supplier base, a reduction in transactions and the value they add to the total business.

In this expanded role, they support NPD by sourcing new components and/or suppliers for early integration into a company's solutions, or their ability to drive supply chain cost reductions and address obsolescence issues after new products have been released. To carry out this role they must work closely with engineering and other innovation team members to select the correct specification and materials for cost-effective manufacturing.

Strategic alliances

One response to challenges in the market is for companies to enter into alliances to access complementary assets and knowledge. Strategic alliances are inter-organisational relationships that firms enter voluntarily with one another. They help companies to pool risks and reduce uncertainty, to build new competencies, to access complementary assets, to enhance organisational learning, and to adapt to new technologies. Furthermore, strategic alliances allow partner companies to build relational capital over time and this allows them to succeed in areas where they would fail if they attempted to go it alone.

ILLUSTRATION

Where would the PC business be without IBM, Microsoft and Intel?

In the early days of the personal computer, a number of manufacturers appeared with proprietary hardware, software and operating systems. Companies like Apricot, Apple, Sinclair and Commodore all introduced models which allowed computers into the home, but they were not interchangeable.

IBM was one of the first companies to realise that they could not become world leaders in all the components that make up a viable PC business. As a result, the company entered into a strategic partnership with Intel, which provided the 8088 microprocessor. Similarly, Microsoft developed the 'Disk Operating System' (DOS) to drive the various modules and associated applications for IBM.

As a result of these partnerships, Intel continues to lead the market in providing Pentium and Celeron processors to the PC market, while Microsoft offers its Windows platform as a basis for running applications and controlling increasingly sophisticated devices. Who would have guessed that it would be IBM that would suffer most from this relationship as more competitors realised they could enter the PC manufacturing business – but would never be able to master the microprocessor or operating system components of the PC.

Strategic alliances are positively associated with innovativeness and new product development, financial performance and wealth creation.

Two forces are known to improve alliance performance over time:

1. Strategic partners have the tendency to invest in the development of skills and routines adapted to the specific relationship as the partners interact with one another over time. Increased interaction and exchanges between partners leads to increased investments in co-specialised assets and in the level of bilateral dependence between the parties (Teece, 1986). Such specialised assets improve the information flow between partners, which may lead to an increase in the performance of the alliance over time.

2. The second force to improve alliance performance is the relationship between alliance performance and alliance mortality. Prior research has found a high level of mortality during the first 4–5 years of inter-organisational relationships, which can be interpreted as a liability of newness. Alliances that are performing poorly are likely to have a higher probability of dissolution because the parties in the alliance will be unwilling to continue to commit resources to a poorly performing alliance.

The relationship between age and alliance performance seems to be U-shaped curvilinear rather than linear, with the minimum point of alliance performance occurring after approximately four and one-half years (see Figure 13.9). Thus, strategic alliances appear to

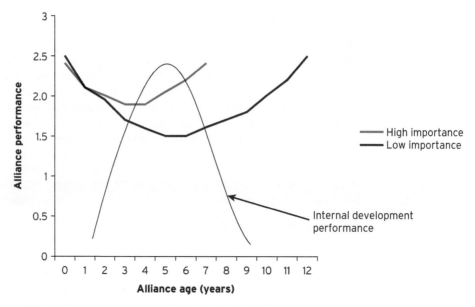

FIGURE 13.9 The relationship between alliance age and alliance performance

face a liability of adolescence rather than a liability of newness. Contrary to expectations, important alliances exhibit shorter honeymoon periods (Deeds and Rothaermel, 2003). This may be because they receive more attention from top management and there is lower inertia in the reassessment of alliances that are of high importance to both parties since the consequences of failure are much higher.

The challenge for innovation alliances is to build and nurture a strong sense of symbiosis which is strongly supported by senior executives from the company and suppliers alike. An early and active identification of the optimal points of interface between both parties needs to be established, and reinforced with clear objectives and a common 'code of conduct'. Regardless of how effectively strategic alliances are initially constructed, they will run into difficulty at some point. It is important under these circumstances to ensure that any short-term problems are quickly resolved, and the impacts are not allowed to distort the common purpose and benefit to be gained by all participants.

This is well illustrated in the work conducted by Bstieler (2006), who examined the effect of trust in new product development and the effect on performance. The findings suggested that communication behaviour and perceived fairness were positive contributors to trust, while conflicts during the development and perceived egoism of partners appeared to have a detrimental effect. Importantly, high levels of trust were found to create conditions for successful collaborative outcomes.

Interestingly, the time it takes to reach the minimum performance point for R&D alliances is about the time Katz and Allen (1985) found R&D teams took to reach their maximum performance points (inverted U-shaped). In other words, when the teams start becoming most effective is when, ironically, most of the alliances begin a path toward dissolution. This trend should be kept in mind when making the initial alliance/build decisions, but also recognised when the relationships are strained and the gulf between internal development teams and strategic partners seems at its widest.

One element which can affect the timing and impact of the maximum performance point is the extent that partner organisations engage in intensive, mutual learning (Grunwald and

Kieser, 2007). However, care must be taken when establishing the range and extent of this learning, and by focussing on the following elements, it is possible to reduce the levels of this learning without jeopardising success. These elements are:

- Modularisation, which allows specialists of different domains to develop modules to a large extent independently of each other and to concentrate communication between themselves on the design of interfaces between the modules.
- Storing of knowledge in artefacts instead of in organisational members' memories.
- Localisation of knowledge not present in the project team, but for which a need has arisen through transactive memory.
- Knowledge integration by prototyping.

Although these four mechanisms reduce the need for cross-learning between specialists of different domains, some common knowledge and some cross-learning between the partner specialists are still required.

Internal development and early supplier involvement

The phenomenon of downstream buyers co-operating with upstream suppliers to either introduce new products or improve the quality of existing product lines is common across a spectrum of industries. Through co-development projects, the supplier in effect serves as a conduit of knowledge between buyers. This conduit has been described as a form of leakage of knowledge via equipment suppliers, and has been characterised as a 'kind of tax' but also a benefit because innovation costs are spread over multiple buyers.

Supplier involvement refers to the resources (capabilities, investment, information, knowledge, ideas) that suppliers provide, the tasks they carry out and the responsibilities they assume regarding the development of a part, process or service for the benefit of a buyer's current or future product development projects (van Echtelt et al., 2008).

Involving suppliers in product development has been argued to contribute to short-term project performance through improved product quality, reduction in development time and a reduction in development and product costs (e.g. Primo and Admundson, 2002; Ragatz et al., 1997).

Besides the typical short-term benefits, some authors have pointed at some longer term, or strategic, benefits. Firstly, a long-term relationship in which experience is accumulated between two partners can result in a more efficient and effective collaboration in future projects (Sobrero and Roberts, 2002). A second long-term benefit occurs with the creation of permanent access to suppliers' new technology, which may be of strategic importance for future product development activities (Wynstra et al., 2001). A further long-term benefit is the alignment of technology strategies with key suppliers through roadmaps, thus allowing new market opportunities to be exploited more effectively (Monczka et al., 2000).

There are a number of conditions that need to be considered when electing to enter into an 'early supplier' relationship rather than a joint venture. Early supplier involvement provides an environment where the company retains more control of the innovation process and the end product, and thereby allows the company greater control in driving its growth objectives. Early supplier involvement can also be established sooner, and at lower cost, than a joint venture. Supplier involvement is also useful when deploying 'revolutionary' technology, as it has stronger and more immediate benefits (market impact and internal learning), but also allows critical intellectual property to be protected (Neale and Corkindale, 1998).

Supplier integration involves 'suppliers providing information and directly participating in the decision making for purchases used in new products, processes and services. This has been identified as a critical factor in achieving a high level product development performance' (Clark and Fujimoto, 1991). The earlier this participation can take place, the more effective the supplier involvement will be, resulting in higher levels of productivity and a greater probability that the end product will be successful. The objectives of the innovation project need to be considered from many perspectives before opting for early supplier integration (Tao and Wu, 1997).

While companies and their suppliers can bring a wealth of knowledge and experience to an innovation framework, the ability of companies to inwardly transfer technology and associated knowledge in these engagements is an essential competence. Product technology transfer entails movement of the product technology (and knowledge about it) from source to recipient. Therefore, the technology transfer process begins at the point of commitment to a specific technology by the recipient firm and concludes when that technology has been incorporated satisfactorily into the recipient's new product. This 'product technology trans-fer' process is difficult to master and conduct, and can be fraught with unanticipated prob-lems and excessive risk, leading to milestone slippages, cost over-runs and functionality problems. While this is recognised as a critical competence, the product technology transfer process is often conducted in an ad hoc manner (Sheridan, 1999).

Successful management of the technology supply chain in product development allows faster and more efficient component sourcing as well as trouble-free incorporation of the technology into the innovation. In this sense, effective management of the technology sup-ply chain enables a more effective implementation of component technologies into the

ILLUSTRATION

Suppliers as innovators

Automotive suppliers were expected to be responsible for nearly 60 per cent of the industry's research and development by 2010, up from about 40 per cent in 2004, a report by the consultancy firm Roland Berger suggested.

The findings, from a study of 40 companies worldwide, underscore the increasing complexity of vehicle technology and the pressure felt by suppliers to remain competitive as car makers demand price cuts. The study highlighted the knock-on effect among the supplier community of car makers' increasing attempts to develop a broad range of niche vehicles, each with different types of content designed to appeal to smaller groups of customers.

Wim van Acker, Managing Director of Roland Berger's Detroit-based automotive practice, said 'New model proliferation and product complexity' would increase, along with pressure to reduce costs and cut product development lead times. The electronics content of an average car in the 1970s, for example, was less than 10 per cent and it was expected to top 40 per cent by 2010.

Much of the innovation would be driven by suppliers because car makers' R&D expenditures as a percentage of sales had remained flat at about 4 per cent over the past 4–5 years. At the same time, car makers had cut the amount of time needed to develop new vehicles from about 36 months in the mid-1990s to 24 months or less currently.

(*Source*: Based on J. Grant, 'Vehicle suppliers to extend R&D role', *FT*, 22 July 2004, p. 27)

product and allows faster transition to downstream phases in a given new product development project. This in turn helps achieve faster and lower cost product development with greater marketplace potential.

Once companies have the know-how in the supply chain network they then have the choice of how best they will exploit the knowledge. Subsequently, the knowledge may be 'embodied' within a product or product upgrades (with premium pricing), or 'unembodied' via enhanced field support.

Supply chain network: value nets – an emerging competence in NPD

Traditional supply chains and innovation models have attempted to meet customer demand through a fixed product line (with options for downstream customisation where needed) resulting in the development of a relatively undifferentiated product providing an average service to average customers. These products have generally been manufactured and pushed through distribution channels to the awaiting customers. During this process, materials are seen to flow sequentially through the supply chain, with subsequent time delays and multiple hand-offs. Inventories tend to build up along the chain, providing useful but costly buffers against supply chain failures and inaccurate demand forecasts. Consequently, the traditional objective within the supply chain (in the 'functional' and 'procurement' paradigms) is to drive cost efficiency, often through conventional (perhaps adversarial) customer–supplier relationships.

With the advent of the internet and e-commerce, customers are looking for flexibility to order what they want, at the lowest possible cost, and delivered according to their own needs. Anyone who has purchased a PC from Dell will testify to the ease of being able to purchase what they want, for the right price, and have it delivered when they want. Consequently, companies not only need to provide superior solutions, but must also meet the extended customer choices that drive customer satisfaction.

It seems a statement of the obvious to note that no single company can match the combined skills and capabilities of a network of firms dedicated to co-operatively serve a chosen market. In the supply chain field, the concept of firm networks has led to the development of a configuration that is being referred to as value nets (see Figure 13.10). Value nets involve a symbiotic and value-enhancing relationship between companies that perform some (or all)

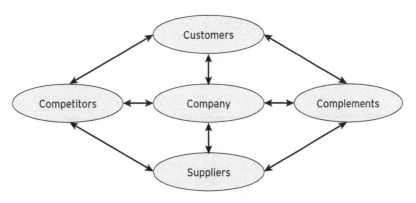

FIGURE 13.10 The value net

sourcing, assembly and delivery activities. Led by a single company, which manages the customer relationship, this model stimulates new levels of trust and co-operation that transcend the traditional 'win-or-lose' mentality in which costs are transferred from one participant in the supply chain to another. Since value nets view every end customer as unique and allow them to choose the product/service they value most, they can help all the network partners to earn greater profits and competitive position.

Value nets allow the selection of the best companies to fulfil specific areas in the supply chain. Value nets can utilise business process re-engineering techniques, digital information, and integration of IT solutions to integrate working practices to a point where costs are minimised and cycle times significantly reduced. This allows customers to place orders for configured solutions to meet their specific needs, which can be built to order and delivered very efficiently. As market needs change, the value net can either adjust elements within it, or engage new partners to ensure customer responsiveness.

Suppliers and customers are clearly part of the production process. Competitors obviously influence the environment within which the company or organisation does business. However, the often overlooked players in the game are the 'complements' – other organisations with which reciprocal and mutually advantageous relationships exist. Hardware and software manufacturers are a simple example; both depend upon each other (to the point where they could not exist separately; they are mutually dependent).

Though the idea of complements may be apparent in the context of hardware and software, the principle is universal. A complement to one product or service is any other product or service that makes the first one more attractive. Hot dogs and mustard, cars and auto loans, televisions and DVD players, fax machines and phone lines. Central to the concept of complements, therefore, is the notion of added value, which is essentially the incremental benefit that a company brings to the game.

Value nets are characterised by five elements which give them the edge over traditional models (Bovet and Martha, 2000). These are:

1. A strong alignment to customers, who dictate what they want and how it will be delivered. They then receive customised solutions with customised service 'wraps' that drives customer satisfaction.

2. Systematic assignment of tasks to partners, who execute and collaborate in order to drive increased value to the customer.

3. An ability to rapidly re-design and re-scale the net in the event of market changes, supported by rapid information flows.

4. Collapsed processes supported by rapid information flows, which allow order-to-delivery cycles to be reduced, and inventories to be minimised.

5. Use of digital information and rule-based event-driven tools to automate operational decisions, and provide data analysis to guide executive decision making.

Mastery of value nets allows faster operations and optimisation of activities which contribute to improved capital efficiency, and shorter cycle times. In turn, the ability to be more flexible in meeting customer requirements helps win market share and grow revenue. By enabling higher responsiveness to customers, value nets (supplier networks) have altered the terms of competition in a way that severely tests the traditional single-firm approach to innovation. Firms following the traditional approach must either change or suffer decline in the face of supplier networks that draw on a vastly greater source of capabilities, and do so in a dynamic and flexible manner.

Supply chains and information technology

Information technology (IT) has some fairly generic and well understood roles to play in any business. It can help increase scale efficiencies of the company, process basic business transactions, and collect and provide information for managerial decision making by monitoring and reporting organisational performance. The movement of information is a fundamental element of any supply chain. If this is burdened with inefficient practices, administrative delays and data incompatibilities, then the supply chain – and the business, can grind to a halt.

In the past, this information was characterised by costly and time-consuming movement of paper from one department to another, and from one company to another. Initial attempts to move data using IT initially proved to be successful. EDI (electronic data interchange) offered an automated method for transmitting information from one computer to another in a pre-internet environment which reduced costs and accelerated data flow. However, the implementation of EDI was complicated by different applications being used throughout the supply chain, different networking environments, variable data formats and the use of different integration standards. This caused particular difficulties. For instance, when one company in the supply chain changes an aspect of its IT solution, it force changes downstream to ensure the data can continue to flow effectively.

Recent standardisation in IT architectures has helped address many of these problems. Standard application development languages (e.g. Visual Basic, Java and HTML), integration standards (e.g. JMS) and common messaging protocols (e.g. .NET and .COM) have allowed greater inter-operability between IT environments. Application vendors have also begun to provide enterprise-wide, configurable, workflow tools that can be extended beyond the functional boundaries offered by earlier applications. In this way, functional activities are aligned via a common IT tool to support cross-functional activities, e.g. aligning supply chain activities to product development to manufacturing, etc.

With a more effective IT infrastructure put in place, a company can expect to see improvements in three areas. Firstly, an improvement in linkage and communication results in faster and cheaper data flows. Secondly, as communities in the supply chain grow, new suppliers can be found, quickly assessed and integrated into the supply chain faster than ever before. Thirdly, further efficiency gains are realised through the tighter coupling of processes and systems by reducing administration, eliminating redundancy and minimising buffers, e.g. inventory within the supply chain.

While the benefits offered appear obvious, they also provide a basis upon which new competencies can be developed which further support innovation. Design is best achieved by the co-location of product development teams, an assertion supported by Clark and Fujimoto (1991) who found that engineers and suppliers working together during early design create superior products. Improved supply chain integration can have the effect of bringing companies and their suppliers closer together, resulting in a richer sharing of knowledge and experience (rather than simple data transfer) during early innovation phases. IT can help overcome the barrier to co-location by facilitating the formation of virtual teams across a globally dispersed supply chain. Many IT tools already offer features to help overcome time, space and relationship limitations (e.g. e-mail, discussion boards, etc.).

Additionally, new development methodologies advocating 'modular or component'-based designs and platforming lend themselves to using a greater number of small suppliers to more effectively provide individual components to a complex and integrated solution. With integrated systems in place, it becomes possible for engineers to prepare designs and specifications, and then quickly validate them with potential suppliers in order to secure the right components for the right price.

ILLUSTRATION

Technology as a driver of supply chain innovation

When Tesco announced, in 2001, that it expected to save £55m a year – equivalent to around 3.5 per cent of non-food turnover – by switching to direct global sourcing, there were plenty of raised eyebrows. Direct importation, and accompanying customs hassles, are things retailers like to avoid and in 2001 most still regarded supplier portals as too experimental to risk on critical business.

As Tesco's subsequent performance confirmed, its direct sourcing model – developed with the help of Retek, a software supplier to the retail sector, and consultants Kurt Salmon Associates – has continued to add to the on-going profit growth. The portal now handles approximately 40 per cent of globally sourced non-food products using real-time links to track merchandise from supplier, via shippers and customs clearance, to distribution centres.

Supplier portals and global sourcing models are now becoming the norm. In the UK, companies such as Argos, Selfridges and Debenhams have already taken this route. In France Carrefour is establishing a supplier portal for global data synchronisation, and in the US chains such as Federated Department Stores, Lowes and Dillard's have developed similar initiatives.

Exchanging data with suppliers is nothing new; retailers have been using electronic data interchange (EDI) for decades. The big retailers and manufacturers tend to have extensive overseas buying offices – although here, too, things are changing: 'The needs are very different in, say, Hong Kong or Bangladesh', says Wolfgang Wanning, principal with Kurt Salmon Associates, in Dusseldorf, and involved in a number of global sourcing projects with European retailers.

'In Hong Kong it is more about joint product development, whereas in less well-developed markets the issue is quality control and order processing which has different IT needs and can be more fully automated.'

Technology is also enabling common product catalogues, which are improving global sourcing opportunities, and web-based portals allowing even the smallest suppliers to link directly with their retail customers.

Software companies such as QRS and GXS have developed product catalogues giving a standard definition of lines, linked to global product codes, which retailers can access to aid sourcing and to improve data exchange with suppliers. Using QRS's Tradeweave Showroom application, for example, suppliers can post details of the products available. 'Buyers can see what's on offer before they go to market', says William Holden, CIO responsible for implementing the QRS system at Dillard's.

Fashion house Liz Claiborne has adopted similar systems from GXS, linking its suppliers in Latin America and the Caribbean and then providing an electronic catalogue of merchandise for its retail customers. 'We use different solutions to ensure that we include as many of our business partners as possible but in the way that works for them', says David Persson, director of B2B commerce at Liz Claiborne.

In the UK, the Debenhams department store chain went live in April 2003 with a supplier portal built on the Collaborator platform from UK-based software house Eqos. The 'B2B.net' portal gives offshore suppliers immediate web-based access to relevant orders, despatch instructions or product design information and is cutting weeks from production cycles of own-label lines.

Debenhams is using electronic advanced shipping notices (ASN) to track shipments from supplier to carrier. 'Because the system is visible, our buyers are alerted to any problems so that urgent items can be switched to air freight if need be', says business systems controller, Dominic Nash.

(*Source*: Based on P. Coy, 'World is an oyster for sourcing goods', *FT*, 12 May 2004, p. 6)

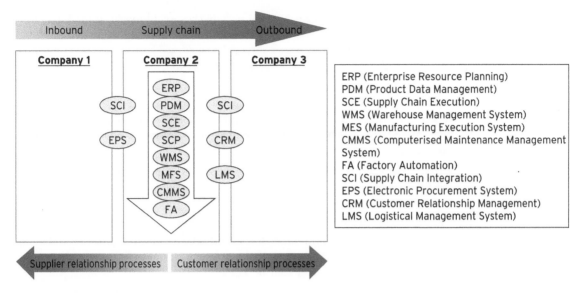

FIGURE 13.11 Potential technology applications in the supply chain

IT offers a way of optimising the supply chain, and its linkages to other functions – including innovation. It can also be used to increase the visibility of the company outside its own operations. This offers a huge business opportunity as the company's innovations can become more accessible to a larger customer base. It is always important to keep uppermost in one's mind that the choice of IT and its application should be made wisely and as part of a company-wide IT strategy, not limited to one specific area.

Overview of some applications that support the supply chain

The potential benefits of integrated applications supporting the supply chain have been discussed already. A generic view of some key applications is offered here to illustrate the complexity and variability of this area. An illustration of how these different applications may be positioned in the context of the supply chain is shown in Figure 13.11, along with an explanation of some of the applications available.

- *ERP* (enterprise resource planning) has evolved as a result of the increasing need to integrate internal operations while also decentralising the company's internal IT infrastructure (e.g. mainframes being replaced by distributed servers). Consequently, individual system modules providing different functionality can be implemented to meet a company's needs, and be installed on a distributed IT infrastructure where multiple servers could be co-located at different sites, but remain 'connected'.

- *PDM* (product data management) technologies have evolved from the need to create, store, distribute, update, re-use and obtain information from data associated with the design and manufacture of products. These tools accomplish this by managing data and the associated workflows.

- *SCE* (supply chain execution) technology generally help execute transactions related to warehouse management, transportation management, logistics management and distribution management.

- *WMS* (warehouse management systems) technologies were brought to market to help manage the efficient and rapid control and movement of materials that are purchased and created by the manufacturing process. Activities supported here include order tracking, fulfilment notifications, receiving, storage, order selection, loading, shipping and inventory management.

- *MES* (manufacturing execution system) has been evolving since the 1990s and includes a variety of functionality associated with the control, monitoring and reporting of factory floor processes (e.g. labour tracking, production reporting, product and workflow management, etc.).

- *CMMS* (computerised maintenance management system) help manage and control the utilisation, repair and tracking of the equipment used in a manufacturing facility. Maintenance management software can extend equipment life, reduce downtime, reduce repair costs and capital investment, increase productivity and product consistency.

- *FA* (factory automation) forms the actual link between the material, processes and information in a production line and includes robotics, computerised numerical control (CNC) and programmable logic control (PLC).

- *SCI* (supply chain integration), also known as 'enterprise application integration' (EAI), supports application-to-application and customer-to-business integration. It includes generic software services for security management, protocol management, data mapping and software connector modules that allow internal process software to communicate with external process software.

- *EPS* (electronic procurement system) attempts to reduce purchasing costs in a company by improving the efficiency of purchasing decisions and transactions, and by sourcing low-cost alternatives (e.g. online auctions or using online catalogues).

- *CRM* (customer relationship management) addresses the selling and marketing functions in a business enterprise, and typically includes sales force automation, call centre management, customer profile management, data mining, product configuration, proposal generation, proposal management and order entry features.

- *LMS* (logistics management system) helps in the management of warehousing, storage, transportation and materials tracking.

With the increasing number, and emphasis placed on them, it is increasingly likely that most applications will support several features, and this presents a problem when trying to select the right software to use. A decision to adopt these applications must take into account not only the most important features needed for the business but also what the potential needs downstream might be. This is necessary to ensure that any significant capital investment will yield a return in the longer term.

Conclusion

Innovation frameworks have been established to help companies capture ideas, and drive them through design, development and release in order to meet specific commercial objectives of the company. They involve cross-functional alignment of key areas to execute the processes that will result in customers receiving effective solutions to their business problems.

Supply chains are a set of integrated processes that transcend company boundaries, and are intended to produce and deliver goods and services to customers. They have evolved from basic functional paradigms (offering cost reduction opportunities) to strategic choices on how best to service targeted customers and markets by offering optimal choices in a flexible and efficient way. As supply chains evolve, they increasingly interact and support innovation frameworks.

Supply chains play a key role to source the components and materials to 'build' the innovation into an effective solution to a customer problem, and to do so at the lowest possible cost through efficient purchasing, sourcing and distribution. This allows either the cost savings to be passed to the customers (and increase market share), or to be withheld within the company (increasing profits). Supply chains also play a role in reducing life-cycle costs, address component obsolescence and ensure life-cycle revenues and margins are protected.

From simple sourcing and supply of components the supply chain can be extended to include earlier involvement of suppliers in design efforts. In this way, specific expertise can be introduced to the early stages of innovation in a way that yields an optimised innovation solution and provides an effective sharing of knowledge amongst the participants. Relationships with suppliers may move beyond this significant involvement to a more strategic level, where synergy and symbiosis drives joint objectives of companies and suppliers alike.

Supply chains are key in driving more effective operations by streamlining processes across many functions and integrating them through effective IT systems. By effectively managing the supply chain, operating costs and cycle times can be reduced. Increasingly, enterprise-wide IT applications such as SAP and MatrixOne support a company's information and workflow from end to end, and at comparatively lower cost than past IT solutions.

The emergence of value nets, a symbiotic network community of suppliers that is capable of being integrated into a cohesive group to collectively meet the needs of end customers, offers a new value proposition that exceeds the capabilities of the single-firm approach to innovation. Their ability to deliver customised innovation solutions at the lowest cost enhances the ability to satisfy customers. The challenge for companies in the next 5–10 years will be to try to get more effective integration of innovation and supply chain processes.

QUESTIONS

1. Describe the major components of a generic supply chain, and explain how they are connected using a real-life example.

2. Explain how a company may progressively move from one supply chain paradigm to another, stating how this will increasingly support innovation.

3. Choose an example, and use it to explain how supply chains can be used to support and extend innovation frameworks.

4. Describe how value nets may undermine traditional approaches to innovation.

5. Explain the critical role information technology plays in enabling supply chains, giving examples to illustrate your answer.

CASE STUDY

Control of the supply chain turns critical

An efficient supply chain is a prize worth striving for. According to Accenture, the consultancy firm, 'supply chain leadership' can increase a company's market capitalisation by between 7 and 26 per cent above the industry average.

But for a business, even competing for that prize demands a significant investment in resources. An efficient supply chain is a must for a widening range of businesses. Fashion, hi-tech and grocery retailers grasped early on the importance of ensuring the right stock reached the right store at the right time. No one wants a warehouse full of summer dresses in October, or indeed shelves of last season's mobile phones in the run-up to Christmas. But the supply chain is now moving up the agenda in slower-moving sectors such as heavy manufacturing.

Effective supply chain management is the only way to make efficient use of global sourcing strategies and especially, the huge manufacturing capacity of China and the Pacific Rim. 'Our internal systems handle more than 700 suppliers', says Christian Verstraete, worldwide supply chain expert at Hewlett-Packard. 'We have to be able to exchange messages not just with them, but with their suppliers.'

Supply chain managers in many sectors are looking for greater visibility of what is happening in their supply chains and faster access to more accurate data. This means that if there is an unexpected event, be it storms affecting shipping or a production shortfall, companies can divert stocks or bring in alternative suppliers.

'Companies are not just asking suppliers why there is a problem with an order', says Sanjiv Sidu, president of supply chain management software vendor i2. 'They are asking: "When did you first know, and why did you surprise me?"'

In heavy or complex manufacturing, supply chain problems can lead to cancelled orders running into billions of dollars, or severe penalties for late delivery. As manufacturers move away from vertically integrated production, the supply chain suddenly becomes critical.

'In aerospace and defence, we are 10 years behind the hi-tech or even automotive sectors and how we improve the performance of our supply chain is quite a challenge', explains Bill Black, chief quality officer at aerospace manufacturer EADS.

'The cost of running our supply chain logistics is minor, set against the $100m cost of an aircraft. But the cost of failure is enormous. About 80 per cent of the cost of an aircraft is accounted for by suppliers and partners', says Black, making EADS 'architects of complex products'.

'I need to know if an event can affect our master schedule and that means that I need to know what is happening, not just with my tier one, but with tier four, five or six suppliers.'

Visidot is one of a number of new technologies that are helping businesses improve supply chain visibility and the speed at which they collect supply chain data. Others include radio frequency identity (RFID) tags as well as three-dimensional and even colour bar codes.

'In the past, for manufacturers [supply chain] visibility stopped at the batch or lot level', says Krish Mantripragada, head of RFID and Auto-ID solutions at enterprise software vendor, SAP. 'But recalls and quality issues are putting a lot of pressure on companies to make their data more granular, and to be able to track single items.'

The response to RFID, however, differs from industry to industry. Mr Mantripragada says that interest is greatest in sectors such as pharmaceuticals, aerospace and defence 'where complete traceability and product integrity are the priorities'.

In other industries, some companies are looking to use RFID to make their supply chains more efficient, but they are finding the costs to be higher than expected. The costs of RFID tags may be heading downwards, but there is far more to a supply chain project than the tags alone.

RFID, for example, produces a unique serial number for each product, while conventional tracking systems may be designed just to record a product's stock code, and assume that each product with the same code is identical.

'It is partly an infrastructure problem, with the need to deploy sensors. But the second problem is serialised data management', says Mr Mantripragada. 'Many production processes batch supplies, so business processes need to adapt to handle serialisation.'

For businesses considering their supply chains, the most important step is to look at the business process and how it could be improved, and then pick the technology that fits best.

Nick Costides, portfolio manager for UPS Supply Chain Solutions, based in Atlanta, says: 'As an express delivery company, barcodes meet our needs. But in the long term, there are opportunities. For example, if every item in a warehouse had an RFID tag, it would make taking physical inventories much easier.'

Companies also need to consider how access to item-level data, or indeed more up-to-date status information from the supply chain will support decision making.

'Distribution centre operators clearly have different needs from C-level executives', says Mr Costides. 'We give them the information they want to see, so they are not overwhelmed.'

Fortunately, modern enterprise IT systems have the capacity to handle the increased data coming in from systems such as RFID. But technologists caution against relying on a single change to improve supply chain performance.

'There is not one killer application but rather a series of incremental steps before we see the ground shift', says SAP's Mr Mantripragada. 'Some customers have seen significant returns on investment from better data accuracy and visibility, but no two customer scenarios are the same.'

(*Source*: S. Pritchard, 'Control of the supply chain turns critical', *FT*, 19 September 2007)
© The Financial Times Limited

QUESTIONS

1. Why is supply chain management important for innovation?
2. Explain in what way the supply chain process is connected to the innovation process.
3. Identify the advantages and disadvantages of an integrated supply chain system?
4. What role does technology play in the supply chain?

References

Anon (2003), 'Product distribution', *Financial Times*, 1 October, 5.

Bovet, D. and Martha, J. (2000), *The power of value nets*, Chichester: John Wiley & Sons.

Bstieler, L. (2006), 'Trust formation in collaborative new product development', *Journal of Product Innovation Management* 23(1): 56–72.

Carnegie Mellon University (1999), Software Engineering Institute, The capability maturity model (Guidelines for improving the software process), Massachusetts: Addison-Wesley.

Clark, K. and Fujimoto, T. (1991), *Product development performance*, Boston, MA: HBS Press.

Council of Supply Chain Management Professionals (2010), **http://cscmp.org/aboutcscmp/definitions.asp**.

Coy, P. (2004), 'World is an oyster for sourcing goods', *Financial Times*, 12 May, 6.

Deeds, D.L. and Rothaermel, F.T. (2003), 'Honeymoons and liabilities: The relationship between age and performance in research and development alliances', *Journal of Product Innovation Management* 20: 468–484.

Ettlie, J.E. and Resa, E.M. (1992), 'Organisational interaction and process innovation', *Academy of Management Journal* 35(4): 795–827.

Fischer, M.L. (1997), 'What is the right supply chain for your product?', *Harvard Business Review*, March–April: 105–116.

Grant, J. (2004), 'Vehicle suppliers to extend R&D role', *Financial Times*, 22 July, 27.

Grunwald, R. and Kieser, A. (2007), 'Learning to reduce interorganisational learning: An analysis of architectural product innovation in strategic alliances', *Journal of Product Innovation Management* 24(4): 369–391.

Handfield, R.B. and Nichols, E.L. (1999), *Introduction to supply chain management*, Upper Saddle River, NJ: Prentice Hall.

Jones, G.K. and Davis, H.J. (2000), 'National culture and innovation: Implications for locating global R&D operations', *Management International Review* 40(1): 11–39.

Katz, R. and Allen, T.J. (1985), 'Project performance and the locus of influence in the R&D matrix', *Academy of Management Journal* 28: 67–87.

Lambe, C.J. and Spekman, R.E. (1997), 'Alliances, external technology acquisition and discontinuous technological change', *Journal of Product Innovation Management* 1(2): 102–116.

Mackintosh, J. (2003), 'Drive to offload risks on to the suppliers', *Financial Times*, 1 October, 4.

Monczka, R.M., Handfield, R.B., Scannell, T.V., Ragatz, G.L. and Frayer, D.L. (2000), *New product development strategies for supplier integration*, Milwawkee: ASQ Quality Press.

Neale, M.R. and Corkindale, D.R. (1998), 'Codeveloping products: Involving customers earlier and more deeply', *Long Range Planning* 31(3): 418–425.

Primo, M.A. and Admundson, S.D. (2002), 'An exploratory study of the effects of supplier relationships on new product development outcomes', *Journal of Operations Management* 20(1): 33–52.

Pritchard, S. (2007), 'Control of the supply chain turns critical', *Financial Times*, 19 September.

Ragatz, G.L., Handfield, R.B. and Petersen, K.J. (2002), 'Benefits associated with supplier integration into product development under conditions of technology uncertainty', *Journal of Business Research* 55(5): 389–400.

Ragatz, G.L., Handfield, R.B. and Scannell, T.V. (1997), 'Success factors for integrating suppliers into new product development', *Journal of Product Innovation Management* 14(3): 190–202.

Reese, S.J., Speare, N. and Wilson, K. (2002), *Global procurement and supply chain management*, London: Kogan Page.

Sheridan, J.H. (1999), 'Managing the chain', *Industry Week* 248(16): 50–54.

Shillingford, J. (2003), 'Warehouse management', *Financial Times*, 26 November, 12.

Smith, P.G. and Reinertsen, D.G. (1991), *Developing products in half the time*, New York: Van Nostrand Reinhold.

Sobrero, M. and Roberts, E.B. (2002), 'Strategic management of supplier–manufacturer relations in product development', *Research Policy* 31(1): 159–182.

Srivatava, S. and Fahey, L. (1999), 'Marketing, business processes, and shareholder value: An embedded view of marketing activities and the discipline of marketing', *Journal of Marketing* 63: 168–179.

Tao, S. and Wu, C. (1997), 'On the organisation of cooperative research and development: Theory and evidence', *International Journal of Industrial Organisation* 15(5): 573–596.

Teece, D.J. (1986), 'Profiting from technological innovation, implications for integration, collaboration, licensing and public policy', *Research Policy* 15(6): 285–305.

Van Echtelt, F.E.A., Wynstra, F., Van Weele, A.J. and Duysters, G. (2008), 'Managing supplier involvement in new product development: A multiple case study', *Journal of Product Innovation Management* 25(2): 180–201.

Wynstra, J.Y., Finn, V.W., Arjan, J. and Weggeman, M. (2001), 'Managing supplier involvement in product development: The critical issues', *European Management Journal* 19(2): 157–167.

14 Knowledge management and learning for innovation

Learning outcomes

When you have completed this chapter you should:

- Understand the emergence of the knowledge economy and the development of knowledge management.

- Understand what knowledge management and learning is in the innovation context.

- Identify different schools of knowledge management thought, knowledge processes and knowledge management strategies.

- Appreciate internal and external knowledge management processes.

- Understand how to organise internally for managing knowledge for innovation.

- Understand the role of benchmarking in innovation.

The knowledge-based economy

In the modern day the primacy of the traditional factors of production, land and labour has been challenged by knowledge. The logic is simple: as long as one possesses knowledge other production factors are easy to obtain. Accordingly, knowledge becomes a primary resource of the new economy. Clearly, if knowledge is the driving force of the modern economy then it is critical for organisations to find ways of accessing existing knowledge and creating new knowledge. Thus, the most important challenge of the knowledge-based economy is finding a methodology, a discipline or a process through which information can be made productive. Three fundamental changes in knowledge can be observed during the twentieth century (Drucker, 1993):

- *Shift 1. The industrial revolution*, in which knowledge was applied to tools, processes and products.
- *Shift 2. The productivity revolution*, within which scientific principles of management were applied to human labour, by individuals such as F.W. Taylor and Henry Ford.
- *Shift 3. The knowledge revolution*, the third shift is one we are witnessing currently. It is a management revolution in which knowledge is being applied to the creation and management of knowledge itself.

Global competition has eroded organisational competencies that historically provided business success. The historical preoccupation with business optimisation through efficiency is no longer sufficient. Companies are having to face up to this new reality. As they do so they have begun to recognise the importance of possessing high levels of knowledge. They find knowledge provides them with critical competences for modern-day competition: pre-cognition and adaptation (Castells, 1996). Pre-cognition prepares the company for the future. It is the capability of being ready for tomorrow's needs by building a competency to innovate new products and services. This endows the firm a capacity to adapt to future environments and circumstances.

Emergence of knowledge management and learning

Beginning around the 1980s many corporate practices to manage individual and team skills and corporate learning started to converge into what is now commonly called knowledge management. The term 'knowledge management' was first used at the 1986 Swiss conference (sponsored by the United Nations International Labour Organisation (ILO)) by Karl Wiig, a prominent advocate and the likely founder of this field.

Management of knowledge is not really new. Throughout history, owners of family businesses have passed on their commercial wisdom to their children, master craftsmen have painstakingly taught their trades to apprentices, and workers have exchanged ideas and know-how on the job. However, it was not until the 1990s that company executives started discussing the concept of knowledge management. By the mid-to-late 1990s many companies became acutely sensitive to the fact that inside their own organisations lay vast pools of untapped knowledge, know-how, and best practices, which they had thus far failed to employ or even recognise (Ernst & Young, 1997 survey reported in Ruggles, 1998). This realisation led organisations to search for ways to leverage knowledge to enhance business success. It was not long thereafter that many began to describe themselves as knowledge-intensive businesses and prioritise management of knowledge and learning as a core competency. This movement received a major push when Nonaka (1994), in his now seminal work, declared that organisations wishing to become strategically innovative must move beyond the traditional model of processing information to one that incorporates the creation and management of knowledge.

With the emergence of the global economy the push toward knowledge management and learning gained particular momentum. Facing intense global competition a large number of companies re-organised and restructured. In the 1980s, over 50 per cent of the Fortune 500 underwent some form of restructuring exercise (Field and Yang, 1990). However, companies engaging in the practice of optimising (efficiency) through de-layering did not appreciate the full ramifications of their actions. In shedding employees many companies lost individuals with tacit knowledge gained over many years through their unique experiences. The hiring and teaching of new recruits is hugely expensive and undermines the cost-cutting objectives that the shedding of employees had originally intended to drive. These companies had adopted short-term solutions to long-term problems. This led some companies to begin searching for a new business paradigm. They were not convinced that these new 'de-layered and lean' structures were likely to meet the challenges ahead. De-layering could not create the capability to match the speed of foreign competitors' product development, deliver higher levels of customer service or achieve leaps in productivity. Moreover, it was highly unlikely to provide the skills and sensitivity to manage a diverse workforce and motivate the company's best employees.

Knowledge management is a process that enables a company to adapt and survive discontinuous environmental change. In essence, it is a process to capture the collective expertise and intelligence in an organisation in order to foster innovation through continued organisational learning (Nonaka, 1991; Davenport et al., 1998). This it does by capturing an organisation's *know-how* and *know-what* through creation, collection, storage, distribution, and application of knowledge. In practice, knowledge management seeks to synergistically combine the data and information processing capacity of information technologies with the creative and innovative capacity of human beings.

If conducted well knowledge management prevents, or at least reduces the impact of, the loss of critical knowledge due to retirement, downsizing, de-layering and employee mobility to other firms. The focus is not just to ameliorate negative change. Its major role is positive. It improves decision making and also motivates employees to better themselves. Properly developed and executed knowledge management programmes can have numerous potential benefits, such as:

- Improved decision making.
- Quicker problem solving and fewer mistakes.
- Reduced product development time.
- Improved products and services.
- Improved customer service and satisfaction.
- Reduced research and development costs.
- Improved rate of innovation.

ILLUSTRATION

Shell: knowledge management for speed of technology leverage

'The challenges facing E&P [exploration and production] professionals of the 21st century will be increasingly attuned to those of knowledge management, as we strive to improve our ability to identify, access and recover increasing volumes of hydrocarbons in response to global demands ... Continued improvements in current E&P technical capability will be complemented by effective data management, in its broadest sense, as the industry seeks to enhance the management of hydrocarbon reservoirs' (John Darley, Director of Shell Technology EP, 2002).

Shell's Exploration and Production employed about 30,000 people in 2002. Shell's E&P business was a worldwide activity (across 45 countries), with operations in areas such as North America, Europe, the North Sea, The Netherlands, Africa, the Middle East, the Far East and Australia. 'Deploying technology on such a global spread contributes to successful implementation by speeding applications up the learning curve', Darley said. 'For example, experience gained in horizontal gravel packing in the Gulf of Mexico has been quickly and effectively applied in Shell operations in both the Far East and Middle East. Building on those experiences allows us to improve the original concepts and move up a continuous circle of global improvements.'

Shell exploration and production activities were directed toward increasing value in Shell's E&P business through the rapid application of key technologies, providing technology and technical solutions to Shell operating units and partners worldwide. 'We have focused expertise and funding to make sure that these technologies are quickly applied across Shell's businesses', Darley said. 'It has proven extremely effective. We have a very rapid takeoff on all of those technologies around the world, and see corresponding value generation in terms of reduced well costs, higher oil and gas productivity and increased reserves.'

(*Source*: Based on Anon, 2002)

Defining knowledge and learning

To be able to manage knowledge and learning it is necessary to have at least a basic understanding of their nature and characteristics. We discuss these issues next.

What is knowledge?

Knowledge is a multi-faceted construct and one that some find difficult to come to grips with. There is general agreement that three levels define what is commonly referred to as the knowledge hierary: data, information and knowledge (see Figure 14.1).

We will confine our attention to these levels. However, it is important to note that some researchers have added 'wisdom: applied knowledge' as a fourth level, and others have even expanded the hierarchy to five levels by including 'Expertise: Fast and accurate advice' and 'Capability: Organised expertise' as fourth and fifth levels respectively. Unfortunately, these additions compound the extant confusion rather than provide any further significant insight.

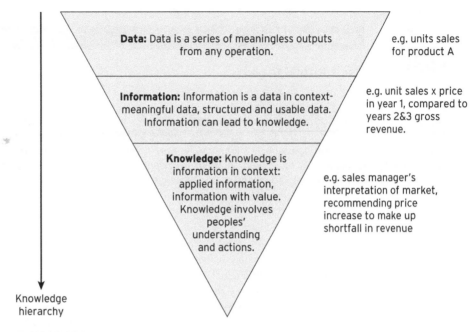

Data: Data is a series of meaningless outputs from any operation.

e.g. units sales for product A

Information: Information is a data in context-meaningful data, structured and usable data. Information can lead to knowledge.

e.g. unit sales x price in year 1, compared to years 2&3 gross revenue.

Knowledge: Knowledge is information in context: applied information, information with value. Knowledge involves peoples' understanding and actions.

e.g. sales manager's interpretation of market, recommending price increase to make up shortfall in revenue

Knowledge hierarchy

FIGURE 14.1 The knowledge hierarchy

Types of knowledge: tacit versus explicit knowledge

There are two types of knowledge, explicit and tacit:

- *Explicit knowledge* is clearly formulated, easily expressed without ambiguity or vagueness, and can be codified and stored in a database.

- *Tacit knowledge* is the unarticulated knowledge that is often difficult to describe and transfer. Tacit knowledge includes lessons learned, know-how, judgement, rules of thumb, and intuition (O'Dell and Grayson, 1998).

In contrast to explicit knowledge, tacit knowledge cannot be explicated fully, even by an expert. It is transferred from one person to another only through a long process of apprenticeship. Tacit knowledge is work-related practical know-how, i.e. that learned informally on the job. It is the knowledge which is usually transferred by demonstration rather than description, and encompasses such things as skills. For example, it is difficult to explain to another person how to walk a tightrope or ride a bike. To become an adept practitioner of an art, let us say a martial art such as Aikido or Tai Chi Chuan, requires more than instruction. It requires years of practice until the 'knowledge' becomes deeply internalised. Only then is it possible to produce the flawless outward expression as self-defence. Although initially conceived at the individual level, tacit knowledge exists in organisations as well. Much organisational knowledge remains tacit because it is impossible to describe all aspects necessary to successfully perform a task (Nelson and Winter, 1982).

Organisations have traditionally focussed on the explicit part of knowledge whilst ignoring tacit knowledge although it is estimated that only 10 per cent of an organisation's knowledge is explicit (Grant, 1996). One major reason why tacit knowledge is rarely managed is because it is much more difficult. It involves extraction of personal knowledge that is

ILLUSTRATION

Tacit knowledge

This is a story of an experienced engineer who spent a lifetime working on the North Sea oil rigs. This story has become part of folklore at BP. Even while landing on the platform from a helicopter he could detect if the rig was operating properly simply by the burn colour of the flame and the noise of the rig. This knowledge he had accumulated from years of experience. Try as he would, it was difficult for him to pass this auditory and visual knowledge on to the new engineers.

difficult to express and communicate. It is deeply embedded within individual experience, judgement and intuition involving impenetratable intangibles such as personal beliefs, perspectives and the individual's value system. Yet, the success of any knowledge and learning programme to produce the much vaunted competitive advantages depends heavily on how well the organisation manages its tacit knowledge. According to Nonaka and Takeuchi (1995), tacit knowledge lies at the very heart of organisational knowledge.

Knowledge and learning

Knowledge and learning are interconnected concepts. As we shall see from the discussion, new knowledge is the outcome of learning, and new knowledge when it is applied feeds into the process of building a higher level of insight and learning.

Learning is a process of using existing insight or knowledge to produce new insight or knowledge. Learning is embodied in a state of action, i.e. it is an act. Knowledge, on the other hand, is an awareness and understanding based on interpretation of data and information. It is a state of understanding (explicit and tacit) that helps guide the form and shape of action(s). Knowledge is shaped by the interpretive focus of the individual or organisation, and is thus dependent on experience and mental models used to process the data and information. Thus, knowledge is a state of possession or being.

Learning and knowledge, therefore, mutually reinforce each other in a cycle. The act of learning provides knowledge and understanding, which in turn feeds further learning. Moreover, companies are routine-based, history-dependent systems that respond to experience. In other words, they are experiential learning systems. A company's past affects its future capability of change. It is a fact that all organisations learn, but only learning organisations *consciously* learn. Working in concert, the two create a virtuous spiral of knowledge learning. To put it simply: at an overall level, data and information are accepted into an organisation from different sources. The organisation conceptualises the information based on its norms, cognitive framework, context and culture. This conceptualisation, which is part of the learning process, leads to knowledge that supports the decision taking process. This leads to actions or group of actions that constitute the organisation's behaviour. The feedback in the process creates opportunity for creating new information, new knowledge and new learning process (see Figure 14.2).

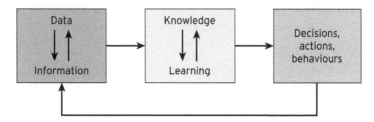

FIGURE 14.2 The knowledge–learning connection

Types of learning: adaptive v. generative

There exist two types of learning: *Adaptive* or *Generative*.

Adaptive learning, or single-loop learning, focusses on solving problems without examining the appropriateness of current learning behaviours. Adaptive learning does not question the fundamental assumptions underlying the existing ways of doing work. Because of this focus the main outcome is narrow improvements. Adaptive learning is only the first stage of organisational learning. The next level is double-loop learning (or generative learning), which ought to be the main pre-occupation for companies (Argyris, 1990).

Double-loop learning emphasises continuous experimentation and feedback over the very way organisations go about defining and solving problems. The essential difference between the two views is between being adaptive and having adaptability. To maintain adaptability, organisations need to operate themselves as experimenting or self-designing organisations, i.e. maintain themselves in a state of frequent, near-continuous change (in structures, processes, domains, goals, etc.), even in the face of apparently optimal adaptation (Hedberg et al., 1976).

ILLUSTRATION

Single-loop learner

As a student I used to own a well-known brand motor car that kept 'missing' whilst driving, making for a very jolty experience. I took it to a garage which specialised in that brand. The mechanic, on hearing the problem and the make of the car, instantly knew what the problem was. It was carbon in the carburetter, he exclaimed. Within a few minutes the problem was fixed. All that was required was a quick blow with an air jet to unblock the fine holes of a pin. The car drove well for a while but some weeks later the same problem reappeared. I took the car back to the garage and the same treatment was quickly applied. Unfortunately, the problem kept repeating, and it was not that long before even I became adept at executing the simple operation at home. The mechanics at the branded garage were engaging in single-loop learning. They could instantly recognise and fix the problem but even with all the recurrences they did not ask why it occurred and how to prevent it from happening. This was so even after I had passed my concern to the manufacturing company. Had it taken action to examine the carburetter design so as to prevent the problem occurring it would have been engaging in double-loop learning.

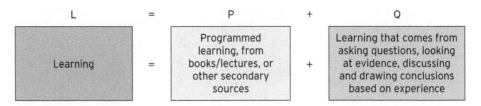

FIGURE 14.3 Revans' formula for learning

An additional insight to this issue can be developed from Reg Revans' attempts to explore the dimensions of learning. Reg Revans, a father figure in the field of action learning, proposed a simple formula for learning (shown in Figure 14.3).

According to Revans, learning builds primarily through an emphasis on 'Q'. Revans' basic idea was to ensure that work teams undertook two fundamental activities: (1) solve a problem or complete a project, and, (2) learn from the job. After the completion of each project learning was to be written down and shared with the planning group or CEO (Revans, 1983). The key to successful execution of projects was to get the team to ask questions whenever a problem was encountered. These questions were the source from which learning would arise. It is perhaps no coincidence that Japanese quality circles, which are renowned for process improvements work on the same basic principles.

Knowledge as competence

The theory of competitive advantage is based on the simple axiom: a firm's resources must perform better than the competition. Internal resources belonging to a particular organisation, such as human resources or machinery, are assets. To provide a competitive benefit these assets must perform their task more effectively than the competition. Prahalad and Hamel (1990) use this view to promulgate the notion of core competencies, which are responsible for competitive advantage.

The resource-based view (RBV) specifies that there are two types of assets: strategic and non-strategic. Non-strategic assets are widely available and common, whereas strategic assets are unique and possessed by only a few. A strategic asset is one that contributes to the organisation's long-term success.

Knowledge meets the four characteristics of a strategic asset in the following ways (Audrey and Robert, 2001):

- *Valuable*: New organisational knowledge contributes to the improvement of products, services, processes, technologies, and staff competencies. Organisations can attain valuable strategic advantage and remain competitive by being the first to acquire new knowledge, by exploiting an opportunity or thwarting a threat.

- *Rare*: Organisational knowledge depends on not only the sum of employee know-how, know-what, and know-why, but also on organisation-specific culture, organisation's history and even the experiences of past employees. That is why it is rare.

- *(Imperfectly) inimitable*: The knowledge contribution of individuals in the organisation depends not only on personal interpretation of information but also the organisational culture, history and the organisation's accumulated experiences. Group interpretations and assimilation of knowledge are dependent on the synergy of the total membership of the group. Therefore, different groups or organisations do not think or function in identical ways.

- *Non-substitutable*: Since the group/organisations distinctive competence is a critical successful factor for the organisation achievements, the knowledge behind this success is non-substitutable.

Thus to build and sustain competitive advantage, core competencies must be difficult to imitate, non-substitutable, durable, and non-transparent. Collis (1996) identifies organisational capability as the firm's dynamic routines that enable it to generate continuous improvement in efficiency or effectiveness, and that it embodies a firm's tacit knowledge of how to initiate or respond to change. It is in the science of developing core competencies that organisational learning and knowledge management are most intimately associated. In order for a resource to yield competitive advantage the firm must utilise it in a unique way, or have some unique knowledge about its function. From this perspective, the organisational capability of managing knowledge and learning is a core competence.

Managing knowledge and learning for innovation

In the sections that follow we examine how knowledge and learning can be managed to foster innovation. Knowledge and learning for innovation can be driven by two primary ways: internally or externally. First, we deal with the internal challenges of managing knowledge and learning to improve efficiency and effectiveness of the product development process, and then go on to examine the sources and the way of managing external knowledge and learning.

In many discussions of knowledge management and learning the focus of attention is simply on the internal aspects. However, as noted above, there is an external dimension to the management of knowledge. Knowledge resides within the macro-environment as well as in the supra-structures of environment (see Figure 14.4). Operating at the macro-level are competitor firms, potential competitors, customers and other agencies that possess specific types of knowledge that can impact the firm. The firm must recognise these and take steps to ensure that it inwardly transfers this knowledge to succeed into the future. The inward transfer of knowledge is called *absorptive capacity* (Cohen and Levinthal, 1990). Without this inward transfer the company will fail to keep up with competition. Inward transfer can be

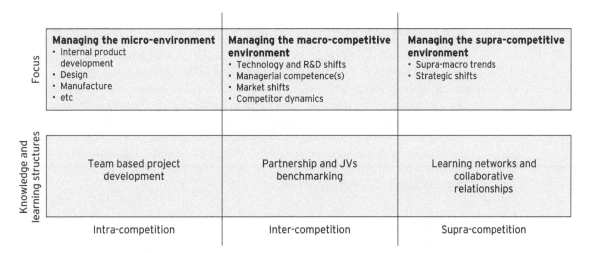

FIGURE 14.4 Array of the knowledge transfer challenge: from internal creation to external absorption

made via a number of routes such as building and sustaining collaborative partnerships and benchmarking. At the supra-environment level strategic shifts and changes occur that can re-define the very nature of competition and firm boundaries. National-level institutional infrastructures, networks and relationships are key sources of knowledge in the supra-environment. In other words, competitive advantage is not solely built from the firm operating in isolation, but through the competitive resilience of the institutional network acting in concert.

ILLUSTRATION

The importance of knowledge management for service industries

Business service improvements and new service introductions are significantly associated with collectively held knowledge, such as codified service solutions or team-based competencies and procedures. The emphasis of the knowledge management approach should depend on whether the company's innovation strategy is geared towards incremental improvements to existing services or development of new services. First, the probability of improvements to existing services is enhanced by the ability to codify knowledge into service solutions and explicit technologies. To achieve codification of services, firms may apply project management techniques that standardise service delivery processes and stages, and may develop metrics for client satisfaction measurement.

For services businesses operating in a very rapidly changing market, or in many different markets, this approach may not be worthwhile because services cannot be standardised to any significant degree, where there will be a greater reliance on the tacit knowledge of an experienced service delivery practitioner.

Consider this in the context of any successful consultancy company, who will offer different 'customer engagement' contacts at the early stages of a business relationship, then change the personnel as the more routine and standard analysis/planning/ execution phases are enacted.

(*Source*: Adapted from Leiponen, 2006)

The generic knowledge management process

As noted earlier, knowledge management is a process and knowledge needs to be managed via a process (Davenport et al., 1996). The generic goal of the knowledge and learning process is in the development of core competencies to support strategic intent. Managing knowledge and learning helps the company to own, control and properly maintain competencies as state of the art, and also helps it to tailor them to specific projects and business initiatives.

The management of knowledge and learning involves five key generic processes: finding existing knowledge, creating new knowledge, acquiring new knowledge, storing and retrieving knowledge, applying and re-using (or leveraging) knowledge. This is illustrated in Figure 14.5, and will be discussed next.

Find existing knowledge

A basic task of knowledge management is to identify what and where knowledge resides. If the company does not know what knowledge exists within itself it is not possible for it to

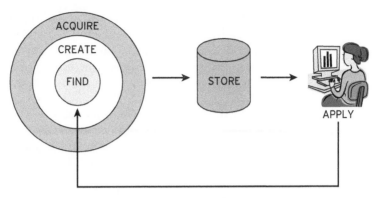

FIGURE 14.5 Framework for a knowledge management process

capitalise upon it. Consequently, the company has a tendency to re-invent the wheel or keep on making the same mistakes. It is important for the company to take stock of the competences and capabilities that it needs. Equally important, it must pinpoint capability gaps that need to be filled. Finding existing knowledge, however, is not just an internally focussed task. Some knowledge exists out in the external environment. It is just as important to know what and where external knowledge exists and how this will shape future competitive dynamics.

Create knowledge

It is not sufficient just to identify the sources of knowledge. Companies must continuously refresh their knowledge base if they are to survive the dynamic of the competition. Thus, creation of new competencies and capabilities is a core part of knowledge management. The creation process is primarily manifest as innovation. Most visibly it is product innovation, but just as importantly, if not more, are process and strategic innovation. Without constant updating of knowledge, corporate competences become outdated and obsolete.

Acquire knowledge

It is not always possible, or even the right thing, to create internally all knowledge. If a company does not have the knowledge that it requires, it must acquire this knowledge from external sources.

Store knowledge

In order not to lose knowledge it is necessary to capture knowledge and store it in a form that is retrievable into the future. This act is about creating an organisational memory. The key characteristic of a good organisational memory system is storage capacity plus ease of retrieval capability. Due to developments in IT, organisational memory is usually constituted as an electronic repository. Modern organisational memory systems are based on intranet platforms, and so enable wide access and dissemination.

Apply (and re-use) knowledge

There is no point collecting and storing knowledge if it is not used. One of the essences of knowledge management and learning is to improve organisational functioning by leveraging existing knowledge. This means existing knowledge must be used in business activities, and in our case the activity is creating innovation. The act of applying knowledge in business leads to further experience, which is a source from which new learning can be gleaned, i.e. application of knowledge in business operations leads to creation of new knowledge. This is a slightly different source of creation than pure knowledge creation, which is often the domain of R&D departments or other efforts aimed to specifically create new knowledge or competencies. Here, creation of knowledge is a side benefit of producing business outcomes, such as new products. To obtain maximum benefit knowledge should be used and re-used. In other words, once a pertinent insight or 'know-how' is gained it should be shared throughout the organisation. Only if this knowledge is made widely available can it be made use of by those who may benefit from it. Access to knowledge should be open and not restricted since it is not possible beforehand to define who would or would not find a particular piece of knowledge useful. To confine access to specialists or select departments goes against the grain of learning and knowledge management.

As we shall see later, the effective execution of these processes requires other sub-processes such as assembling and packing knowledge to facilitate efficient storage and re-use.

The internal challenge: the knowledge creation process

In 1995, Nonaka and Takeuchi published what is now one of the key texts on the creation of organisational knowledge. They assert that making new knowledge available to others ought to be a central activity for organisations, and is the defining characteristic of the phenomenon of knowledge management. According to Nonaka and Takeuchi, knowledge is created in the interaction of explicit and tacit knowledge. This process of knowledge creation occurs through a spiral, moving from tacit knowledge to explicit knowledge and back to tacit (see Figure 14.6).

The spiral starts with socialisation through which people share their internal knowledge with others. Through deep immersion and interaction, tacit knowledge in one person is converted into tacit knowledge of another. This process of knowledge sharing creates new knowledge inside the receiver. Socialisation is the key part for capturing tacit knowledge. The next stage in the spiral is externalisation. This is when tacit knowledge is converted or made explicit through metaphors, images, and analogies. Stage three is called combination. In this

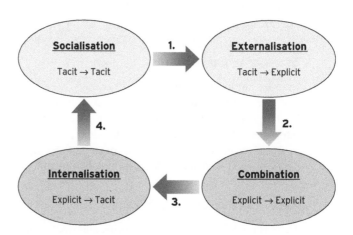

FIGURE 14.6 Modes of knowledge generation

stage explicit knowledge is combined with other explicit knowledge to create databases, documents, numbers, spreadsheets, and files. The last stage is known as internalisation, in which explicit knowledge is converted back to tacit knowledge. Internalisation involves knowledge transfer from documents, manuals and stories into deep-seated understanding through practice or learning by experimenting and doing.

Nonaka (1991) suggests that any combination of part of the four processes may leave an incomplete picture of the learning process and fail to cover all the relevant opportunities for knowledge creation that are available. Rather a systematic use of all four processes in strict rotation serves to cover all opportunities at each stage. Additionally, the sequence is iterative rather than distinct, i.e. after each full cycle of the four processes an improvement is made. The process, if continuously repeated, builds knowledge. This precipitates the 'Spiral of Organisational Knowledge Creation'.

In sum, insights and knowledge exist in the mind and body of the individual. To make use of this knowledge, beyond the exercise of it by the individual, necessitates making this internalised understanding explicit. By harvesting tacit knowledge from the individual and transforming it as explicit knowledge renders that knowledge available to a much wider audience of individuals. Social interaction and connection with knowledge sources creates a forum for nurturing the transformation process. Thus, organisations should amplify these processes by enabling social interaction and connection to knowledge to take place. They can do so by building systems and support for the fundamental processes that facilitate these interactions.

While this process seems fairly simplistic, the circumstances which may trigger its use can be highly varied. Nonaka (1991) suggested the following conditions which could propagate the knowledge creation process:

- *Creative chaos*: Creative chaos (or tension) can act as a strong motivator to bring about improvement and change. This tension can be either genuinely brought about by such things as the rapid loss of market share or artificially created by the setting of tight deadlines. The result is, however, the same: promoting team cohesiveness in the face of adversity.

- *Reflective action*: In developing new solutions to problems it is necessary to clearly define the problem. Often, however, problem definition is constrained by the view of the person defining it. Reflection over one's beliefs and boundaries leads to better problem definition and by extension to a better solution.

- *Information redundancy*: Information redundancy, in this instance, is the over-publication of information. Rather than selective distribution on a 'need-to-know' basis, information (even non-essential information) is disseminated to all participants in a project. In this way the problem is brought to the attention of a much wider audience than would normally examine it. Consequently, a greater variety of perspectives can be brought to bear upon the problem. This type of information dissemination can help overcome hierarchical and departmental barriers.

- *Internal rivalry*: To guard against the acceptance of the first solution that comes along, the problem should be given to multiple teams. Each team's proposed solutions are the basis for debate in deciding which is the best solution. This also generates the social interaction required for knowledge creation.

- *Strategic rotation*: Staff rotation exposes individuals to differing perspectives and appreciation of the language of the others in the organisation. In this way organisational knowledge becomes more dynamic and fluid.

These concepts are tied to several theories of organisational structure to create context-sensitive selection, i.e. in certain circumstances it is better to see the organisation or the problem in one way whilst at other times it may be more relevant to view it differently, i.e. structures should be created and selected to suit the problem. This is described as hypertext organisation because of its similarities to a page of hypertext. Hypertext organisation allows looking at a problem from different angles and provides knowledge and information in different ways and from different perspectives, i.e. the problem and organisational knowledge can be viewed in several differing ways, each imparting a slightly differing meaning.

Organising knowledge and learning for innovation

Knowledge and learning in the innovation process can be conceptualised to occur at three different levels: Individual, team and corporate (or strategic). In modern corporate settings some individuals (such as scientists involved in basic research) may learn and create in isolation but for the most part individual competence enhancement occurs within team environments. Innovation teams are organised on a project basis, and teams learn through the experience of completing a project. After completion of a product development project, experience can be captured and consolidated into the company as part of its corporate intellectual assets (see Figure 14.7). This intellectual asset base can subsequently be re-used by individuals and teams to create yet more insight and learning.

In the past very little knowledge and learning took place in the innovation process. For the most part each development project was executed in isolation. At the end of a project, the team responsible for the development was disbanded and individuals returned back to their functional departments without any assessment of the learning (from success or failure) that had taken place or account of how individual skills and organisational competencies had developed.

To stop the same mistakes being made, and improve products, effective use and re-use of knowledge through sharing of experience and collective learning must be mandated. To achieve this the three levels of knowledge and learning can be structurally organised into two key organisational components: (1) Innovation Management Planning System (IMPS), and (2) Innovation Knowledge Repository (IKR).

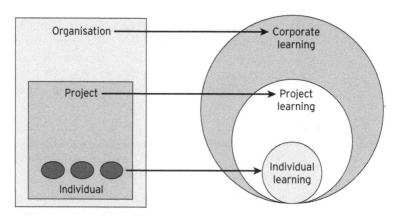

FIGURE 14.7 The three knowledge-learning improvement levels

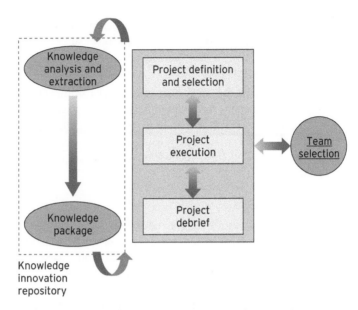

FIGURE 14.8 Innovation management planning system framework

Innovation management planning system

As noted earlier, the new product development process is essentially an intricate project management system, in which each product development is a project. To become highly efficient at new product development, an organisation must possess a structure/system for the control and execution of innovation projects. This structure must be able to efficiently execute a number of key tasks if it is to deliver a strong product development capability. These key activities are illustrated in Figure 14.8 and discussed next.

Project definition and selection

The IMPS system must be able to identify the portfolio of projects that align with business strategy, and resource those that it wishes to progress to development.

Team selection

The IMPS must, from the available pool of expertise, form teams that are made responsible for the development task. The challenge is to select members with the appropriate set of skills and capabilities demanded by the project. This requires an understanding of individual skills and talents. Despite what one may think at first sight, this is no easy task. In most companies, an individual is rarely allocated to only one project. Often they are given a few projects; an average of 8–10 projects is quite commonplace. Practice shows, however, that individuals cannot cope with more than four projects and give them the due care and diligence required to succeed. Overburdening individuals can result in severe deleterious consequences. Additionally, the company may find the right individual is not available because he/she is already on other projects. One remedy sometimes used is to re-assign the person half way through. This is not a good solution because it breaks project continuity. Thus, even if the IMPS has a very good understanding of individual skills and competencies, assigning the right person to the right project is not easy. Often this means that the group, and hence the competency mix set to deliver the task, is sub-optimal from the beginning. It is important for the IMPS to ensure the best mix of skills is blended for the development task at hand. Doing so improves the likelihood of success.

Project execution

To be effective the IMPS must exert overall control of the innovation process. The control is exerted generally, in its classic form, via the stage-gate structured system. Project control requires keeping track of decisions and communicating these to all concerned. The information collected at each stage-gate meeting can be placed onto the innovation knowledge repository. This enhances dissemination and keeps a record that can be used in later project debriefs.

Project de-brief

For each innovation project (successful or unsuccessful) there is a need to conduct a project de-brief, in which lessons learnt can be drawn out. The main de-brief occurs at project-end. However, mid-stage de-briefs can also be undertaken. The de-brief should take place with the project team plus executive members responsible for overseeing the project. The aim of the de-brief is to try and uncover what worked well, what didn't, what problems were encountered, why and how they were resolved. Thus, the learning that has taken place in the execution of the project must first be drawn out if it is to be shared later.

Knowledge analysis and extraction

This stage is closely linked with and follows up on the work started in the de-brief stage. Essentially, this stage further distils and refines the information gained from the project de-brief. The focus here is on high-level analysis to build deeper and more holistic understanding. By attempting to build a deeper understanding of what worked, and also to probe why it worked, and under what conditions and situations this new knowledge could be used in the future a higher level of learning is being attempted, i.e. generative learning, as opposed to single-loop learning. At this point in time, the IMPS must also gather information on personal competencies developed from the experience of the project. This information will be vital when it comes to selecting team members for future projects. This information is placed in a people part of the knowledge repository, which acts like a yellow pages directory of 'who knows what' within the company.

Knowledge package

Once knowledge has been collected from the de-brief it needs to be made re-useable, and not just stored. This involves taking the knowledge and packing it in a format that allows it to be stored but also retrieved and understood by the multiple of potential audiences who may require it into the future (this is a way of creating hypertext features). The basic task at this stage is to create packets of knowledge that can be used by new project teams and innovation managers. The packets of knowledge must be put together in a way that makes them highly useful and accessible to the potential clients (the project teams, management planners, etc.). For example, highly technical reports must be made accessible, and tags to experts in the organisation for further advice and guidance toggled on to the knowledge packet.

Innovation knowledge repository

The innovation knowledge repository can be divided into two inter-related parts: a section responsible for storing technical and project experience information, and a section for persons' competence and expertise. As projects get executed, the team gains experiences with products, plans, processes and models that have been used in their attempt to achieve project aims. The data, insight and knowledge gathered during the development and execution of a project can subsequently be deposited in the innovation knowledge repository. Both successes and failures are useful learning experiences. They show what worked and what did not. The projects are thus a supply source of knowledge to the innovation repository. The repository transforms the insights and learning into re-usable units (through the process of *analysing* experiences) and supplying them back to the project organisation (through a process of *packaging* useful insights and knowledge).

Analysis involves screening carefully the experience collected, in order to uncover any genuinely new knowledge and learning. Once new knowledge is uncovered, it must be converted into a useable form. This is called packaging.

Packaging involves taking the new knowledge and converting it into a usable form. This is achieved through three activities: *generalise, tailor* and *formalise.*

- *Generalise* means taking the knowledge from its specific context and making it more generic. If this can be done, it makes that specific knowledge available for more general use.
- *Tailoring* is to customise the knowledge packet to the specific needs of a team, unit or individual.
- *Formalising* a knowledge solution involves taking steps to make the discovered new knowledge a standard throughout the organisation, because it is considered to represent best practice.

The individuals responsible for the innovation repository can play a number of roles. For example, besides specific monitoring they can provide consulting support to the IMPS team. The individuals may also take a lead in exploring/mining external knowledge and information nuggets. As noted earlier, the innovation knowledge repository also has a role in keeping information on the developing competencies of project team members. This information can subsequently be used in the selection of personnel for future engagements. See Figure 14.9 for a summary of the process.

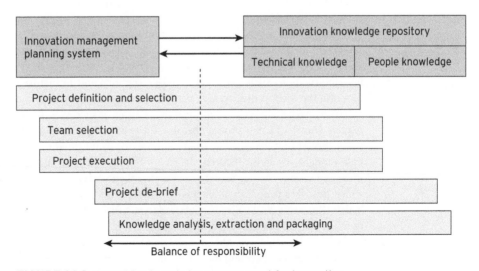

FIGURE 14.9 Organising knowledge management for innovation

The innovation knowledge repository (IKR) is thus an important part of the knowledge-led organisation. It supports re-use of experience and collective learning by developing, updating and providing 'packets' of competencies. These packages of competencies are built from previous 'learning and knowledge experience' derived from individuals and teams executing projects. The 'packets' can be later utilised by teams to carry out new projects. In this way the company makes effective re-use of its existing knowledge and also updates its corporate learning as new insights are developed from experience.

The process is first one of discovering where knowledge exists (i.e. which people possess what skills) and then creating new knowledge (via project experience). The second key part of the process is, as far as possible, to make knowledge explicit (via the activities of the IKR) so as to enable sharing to take place. If knowledge cannot be made explicit, sharing must take place by creating a connection to the individual so that sharing occurs through socialisation and apprenticeship. In this interplay (between the individual, the project and the organisation) a tacit-to-explicit cycle is constantly turned. This interplay facilitates what Nonaka (1991) termed the spiral of knowledge creation.

Structuring the organisation as a innovation management planning system and innovation knowledge repository, in which people's specific competencies can be leveraged and developed, offers the company an opportunity to learn from every project. In this way, as the company matures it constantly rejuvenates and re-invigorates itself with a constant flow of fresh insight and learning. Over the long term this supports the evolution of the organisation from task-based, where all activities are aimed at the successful execution of current project tasks, to knowledge and learning capability-based. Knowledge and learning-based capability endows the company with continuous energy for improvement and change. It makes the organisation adaptive and resilient to its environment.

Unlearning and innovation

Unlearning appeared almost 30 years ago as a sub-process of the organisational learning process, but has received only limited attention in academic research (see Akgun et al., 2006). Organisational unlearning and memory are closely related concepts, and are viewed as the changing of beliefs, norms, values, procedures and operationalised as changes in beliefs and routines in organisations.

Rigid product development processes and group beliefs, as well as the preservation of pre-determined routines and mindsets throughout a project inhibit the reception and evaluation of new markets and technology information, and reduce the value of the perceived new information. Such narrow-minded perceptions and immature decision making can diminish the chances of success of new products, particularly in turbulent environments.

Firstly, fixed routines can diminish the chances of success in the development and subsequent launch of a new product because the team cannot integrate new information effectively. Project routines facilitate fixed responses to any information in a manner that requires little thought. Secondly, incorrect beliefs or mindsets tend to incorporate errors in judgement and actions because team members alter their perception of reality to fit their schema, which describes people's willingness to focus on information that supports their current beliefs (Rousseau, 2001). Fixed beliefs lead to perception rigidity or inaccurate causal attributions, which make teams slower to recognise changes.

In researching this area, Akgun et al. (2006) found that unlearning is directly and positively affected by team anxiety and the turbulence of the environment in which the team operates. Consequently, managers can enhance unlearning by creating a sense of urgency by introducing an artificial crisis. Additionally, training in lateral thinking, or bringing in an outsider, can help avoid the groupthink phenomenon and challenge existing policies and procedures. However, this type of interaction needs to be conducted with careful considered evaluation – otherwise, the subsequent changes in beliefs and routines can cause information/knowledge loss.

Knowledge management strategies

Knowledge management means many different things to many different organisations, each facing unique challenges. We will discuss the different schools of thought on knowledge management before focussing on the various strategies that exist.

Knowledge management school of thought

Researchers and academics have taken different perspectives on knowledge management, ranging from technological solutions to communities of practice and the use of the best practices. There are currently three major perspectives defining what constitutes an organisational knowledge management system. One is the technical perspective. The technical perspective emphasises the use of advanced software, hardware and infrastructure for supporting knowledge and organisational learning. This perspective relies on technological tools to increase the accessibility to information and knowledge. The technology-centred knowledge management system utilises different technologies such as electronic messaging, intranet/internet web browsing, electronic task management, document management, shared databases, video conferencing and visualisation tools, group discussion tools, data mining, and many other emerging tools to facilitate finding, storing, creating and using knowledge. However, while the use of these tools is important, many of these technological tools are not rare and therefore they are not strategic assets in themselves. The second school suggests that knowledge management is more of a human resource issue with emphasis on organisational culture and teamwork. A strong, positive organisational culture is critical to promoting learning, development and the sharing of skills, resources and knowledge. The third school argues what makes assets strategic is to be found in the interplay between technology and humans within specific organisational culture. Under this perspective knowledge management is a socio-technical system of tacit and explicit business policies and practices which are enabled by strategic integration and complex combination of technology infrastructure, business processes, human intellectual capacities and the organisation culture.

Specific knowledge management strategies

Managing knowledge creation requires getting individuals and teams to share information, experience and insight. New technologies facilitate this process. In the knowledge creation process companies must tackle two key activities: collection and connection. The connecting dimension involves linking people who need to know with those who know, and so develop new capabilities for nurturing knowledge and acting knowledgeably. Connecting is necessary because knowledge is embodied in people, and in the relationships within and between organisations. In carrying out collection and connection the company must focus on getting a balance between the two.

For many companies the rapidly falling costs of communications and computing together with the growth and accessibility of the World Wide Web has been instrumental in catalysing opportunities for knowledge sharing. The best information environments make it easier for people to work together irrespective of geographic location and time. They do this by providing immediate access to the organisational knowledge base and thus create value to the user. For example, electronic networks can give access to experts on a worldwide basis; teams can work together without being together. Help-desks and advisory services can be very effective, in the short term, in connecting people and getting quick answers to questions, thus accelerating cycle time, and adding value for clients. Organisational yellow pages can enable staff to connect to the right people and their know-how more efficiently. However, an organisation that focusses entirely on connecting, with little or no attempt at collecting, can be very inefficient. Such organisations fail to get full leverage of sharing, and waste time in 'reinventing wheels'.

The collecting dimension relates to the capture and dissemination of know-how. Information and communication technologies facilitate codification, storage and retrieval of content. Through such collections of content, what is learned is made readily accessible to future users. However, even where comprehensive collections of materials exist, effective use still requires *knowledgeable* and *skilled* interpretation and alignment with the local context to get effective results. This occurs through people. Therefore, organisations which concentrate completely on collecting and which make little or no effort to foster people connections end up with a repository of static documents. Knowledge management programmes must have the aim of an integrated approach to managing knowledge. This can be achieved through a balance between connecting individuals who need to know with those who do know, and collecting what is learned as a result of these connections and making that easily accessible to others. For example, if collected documents are linked to their authors and contain other interactive possibilities they become dynamic and hence much more useful.

Examining knowledge-performance outcomes of knowledge programmes, Ahmed (2001) identifies four main generic knowledge management strategies: *reactive, mechanistic, organic, adaptive* (see Figure 14.10). The reactive knowledge management strategy, as the name implies, characterises companies that simply react to shifts in the environment and the strategies adopted by others. Mechanistic knowledge management strategies are those that are heavily driven by the implementation and use of IT infrastructures to implement the

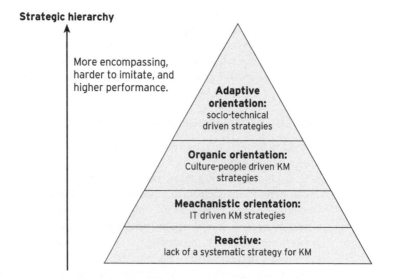

FIGURE 14.10 The strategic orientation hierarchy

knowledge management programme, i.e. technology-driven strategies. Organic knowledge management strategies emphasise the people and cultural side of the organisation to build and implement their knowledge management programmes, i.e. culture–people-driven strategies. Adaptive knowledge management strategies are an emerging format, which balance the human side with the technical side of the organisation to optimise learning and organisational flexibility, i.e. they are socio-technical-driven strategies. Ahmed (2001) notes that not only is there an evolution over time towards adaptive strategic forms as companies mature in their practice of knowledge management, but also there are performance ramifications. Adaptive strategic forms outperform organic, which outperform mechanistic, which in turn outperform reactive strategies. These strategies can be mapped along two axes (connection and collection) – see Figure 14.11. The mapping process highlights that companies in their attempts to implant knowledge management into their organisations can follow many possible routes. Over time there is a move towards adaptive knowledge management strategies that meld the IT drivers with people and culture. This is the balanced socio-technical approach to strategy for sustained knowledge-led performance.

ILLUSTRATION

Different pathways to knowledge management

Mechanistic knowledge management

Ernst & Young, a leading consultancy company, relies heavily on IT to drive its knowledge management. All its consultants are briefed to tap into their intranet-based knowledge repository before going out on any assignment. This ensures that the consultants are well briefed on the industry sector and all previous work and projects done with the client. Typically projects are done in teams, with a senior consultant or partner leading the project. At the end of each project every team must produce a de-brief document of the project, especially if new procedures or findings were discovered. Projects new to the firm are given considerable attention in constituting team membership since this is an opportunity to create new knowledge. Consultants are clearly informed of their duty to both check the knowledge intranet and update it. Each individual is monitored on how often they check the knowledge repository and upload new content onto it.

Organic knowledge management

CMG is a fast growing IT consultancy. Whilst it advises on IT its own approach to knowledge management is very different. It relies on informal person-to-person connection. CMG believes that the foundation of good knowledge management is predicated on sharing, and sharing does not occur without trust. Whilst it does have an intranet portal for knowledge management, most of CMG's efforts are at creating an open atmosphere based on personal connection from the very bottom to the very top of the organisation. CMG uses many devices from open meeting to regular lunches in the pub to generate a close tightly knit community. These 'get-togethers' act as a springboard to share experiences and foster high-trust relationships.

Adaptive knowledge management

Companies like IBM and Xerox exemplify adaptive knowledge management. They stress the technology but they stress people equally or more. These companies abound with 'communities of practice', some of which are formally created by the company and some that spring up informally around common interests of employees.

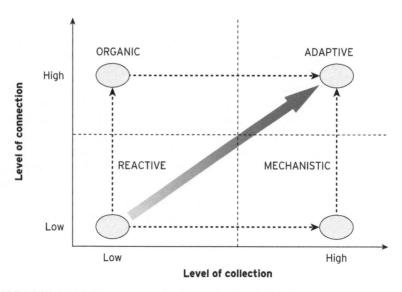

FIGURE 14.11 Knowledge management strategy paths over time

Thus, we observe that no matter how great their information processing capabilities, computers are merely tools. Peter Drucker contends that the confusion between knowledge and information has caused managers to sink billions of dollars in information technology ventures that have yielded marginal results (Drucker, 1993). Knowledge is actually created not through technology, rather it is through the social processes of collaborating, sharing knowledge, and building on each other's ideas. It seems therefore, notwithstanding its importance, that technology is not the biggest challenge in implementing effective knowledge management. Indeed, there is some evidence that there is no direct correlation between IT investments and knowledge management, or business performance (Malhotra, 1998).

Unfortunately, most conceptions of IT do not adequately address the human aspects of knowledge, particularly the tacit dimension (Nonaka and Takeuchi, 1995). Interpretations of knowledge management based primarily on rules and procedures embedded in technology seem mis-aligned with a dynamically changing business environment. In this sense, IT systems have hampered the management of knowledge because IT management has led to an inward focus to the exclusion of changes in the external reality of business (Drucker, 1993). The bigger challenge is of organisational cultural issues such as functionalism that often divide allegiances and block the transfer of knowledge from individual minds into the organisation at large. Another barrier is senior management, which often fail to support knowledge and learning behaviours.

 ## Managing external knowledge

Faced with an increasingly complex and knowledge-intensive environment companies have to engage in more than just internal knowledge management. They need to manage the external interface of knowledge management. This means transferring knowledge from outside sources and implanting and leveraging it inside the organisation. There are essentially two ways to achieve this. One is to source knowledge through purchase or collaboration. The second is to transfer knowledge by developing mechanisms and processes to absorb and assimilate knowledge. One major modern method of achieving this aim is benchmarking.

Sourcing external knowledge and learning

Beyond tapping into internal knowledge, it is also necessary for a company to access and use external knowledge. This can be done through a number of routes. There are two major ways of acquiring knowledge: either through purchase of knowledge or by sourcing it by building a partnership with those that possess it.

Purchase-based arrangements to acquire knowledge

A number of arrangements to acquire new knowledge involve making investments.

- *Equity investment*: Involves share investment by a firm (usually a large firm) in another firm (usually a smaller firm). Equity investments, especially if they are significant, give the company control and therefore access to knowledge.

- *Client-sponsored research contract*: One company pays another (typically a smaller firm) to conduct research on a specific field of interest to them (product, process and project). Here, knowledge creation is contracted out to a specialist firm. Typically, the contract is with a research laboratory.

- *University agreement*: This involves agreement with a university (or research institute) to conduct research on behalf of the firm. It is quite common to find university research being funded or part-funded by companies. Most notably it occurs as sponsorship or scholarships. In this way companies can build close links and therefore enjoy privy access to basic science and research, which may be part-funded by government and other bodies.

- *Licensing*: Another way of acquiring knowledge is to simply buy another's proprietary know-how. The common method of purchasing knowledge on the open market is through licensing. Licensing involves a contractual agreement through which a firm gains access to another company's patents, technology or knowledge for a fee. Licensing is *inwards* when the firm pays a fee for access to another knowledge and *outward* when the firm receives a fee for giving access to its proprietary knowledge to another.

Co-operative arrangements to acquire knowledge

Besides purchasing knowledge, new knowledge can be sourced from a variety of collaborative arrangements.

- *Joint venture*: An independent third party enterprise formed by one company with another. Assets are contributed by both parties and risks are shared. The goal is to share knowledge and expertise. Often joint ventures are between companies with complementary knowledge and skills.

- *Co-operative development or R&D consortia*: Partnerships which involve the coming together of a number of firms or institutes to undertake a joint programme (usually a large-scale project) which requires pooling of resources, expertise, or coming together to pioneer and set dominant industry standards. This includes a variety of activities in which firms (governments or other agencies) co-operate to make better use of their collective R&D resources. They feature technical information exchange, harmonising of requirements, complementary R&D, and agreement on standards. A variety of co-operative development arrangements can be formed, and a select few are described below:

- *Co-development*: Development of a system by two or more firms (or nations) in which the costs of development as well as design are shared. For example, the development of Concorde involved multi-national co-development.
- *Manufacturing agreement or co-production*: An agreement whereby one company agrees to manufacture products for another firm. In this a firm acquires the technical information and know-how to manufacture or assemble technology or components developed by another. Two basic variations can arise: *fully integrated co-production* in which each partner purchases the same system and produces parts for each other's units, or *production under licence* in which a partner (typically foreign) produces the technology under licence from the originating partner.
- *Complementary partnership*: This concept was developed as a cost effective way of developing related but complementary technologies. Participating partners develop different but complementary items that contribute to a specific project or mission. The resulting products are then available for purchase or co-production.

- **Innovation relationship network**: This is a structural form that is based on relationships between a firm and other firms. The firm, under this perspective, is part of an embedded set of structural relationships that can be either loose or tight. Tight coupling implies the use of formal control and co-ordination. Tight coupling depicts the situation found in conventional vertical or horizontal integration based on contract.

- **Corporate venturing**: This involves a process that differs slightly from the alliance co-operative arrangement. In a corporate venture rather than acquiring competences through collaboration with another firm, the company sets up a separate organisation within itself. This internal structural unit is charged with developing new competence(s). This structure, often called an incubator, typically possesses systems and policies that encourage entrepreneurial behaviour.

As we can see from the above, many different terms are used to describe the collaborative relationships that exist between companies. Terms such as strategic alliance, strategic partnership, collaborative or co-operative agreement are common and are often used interchangeably. We use the term strategic alliance here to refer to various types of co-operative arrangements. These alliances can be broadly categorised into the following groups (Forrest and Martin, 1992):

- *Technological alliances*: designed to access and expand R&D knowledge of the firm, and thus ensure that it remains leading edge.

- *Operation-based alliances*: designed to provide the firm with and/or expand its operational/ manufacturing capabilities. These can include co-development, licensed production, etc.

- *Market-based alliances*: are those that are used to build or complement market strengths through gaining access to markets or developing marketing expertise.

- *Managerial alliances*: based on sharing management expertise and learning between partner companies and institutions.

- *Financial alliances*: are built to provide a source of monetary support in order to execute technology acquisition or commercialisation strategies.

Why should firms collaborate? Amongst the many reasons for collaboration, innovation is a primary rationale. The most frequently cited reason for co-operation is to develop or transfer new technologies. A key driver of collaborative arrangements in many sectors is development of new products or exchange of new technology. Collaborative alliances facilitate innovation (Bidualt and Cumming, 1994) by:

- Allowing companies to develop new products and processes cheaper and facilitate speed of market entry.

- Allowing partners to reach a critical mass of human and financial resources needed to undertake large projects. This spreads the risks of development, and increases efficiency of production through economies of scale.

- Merging technological skills and knowledge from different companies, thereby improving the innovation process.

ILLUSTRATION

Procter & Gamble's external focus to learning

Procter & Gamble (P&G) have an initiative labelled *Connect and Develop*. Part of this initiative is to drive an outward learning focus to capture and capitalise on all opportunities. There are a number of critical elements of this initiative.

Joint technology developments

P&G uses 'Joint Technology Developments' with other companies and institutions. This is particularly the case in its pharmaceuticals operations, where joint development is a way of life. The pharmaceutical sector has the highest development cost of any product field, and so partnerships are used to identify and develop scientific leads. One example within P&G is the joint clinical development with Alexion scientists designed to reduce heart tissue damage that occurs as a result of heart attacks. P&G matched the cardiovascular science and clinical expertise of its scientists with the biotech know-how from Alexion to create a highly complementary partnership.

Licensing

In the past P&G was inward looking and insular with regard to its policy toward licensing. P&G didn't really reach for outsiders' ideas, and had little intention of selling its own. Three years previously, P&G's Technology Acquisition Group was created to give the company an external door through which it could actively seek out new technologies and products. P&G hoped that stepping up the licensing of technologies would allow it access to complementary technologies that would fill gaps in its intellectual property portfolio. TAG, as it is called, has become a primary portal for soliciting external technologies. It provides a vehicle for inventors and technologists to submit their ideas for prompt evaluation.

University research

P&G funding of joint university research goes back a long way. One of the earliest and most productive was P&G's 1950s collaborative work at Indiana University, which led to the development of Crest, the first fluoridated toothpaste.

(*Source*: Based on Sakkab, 2002)

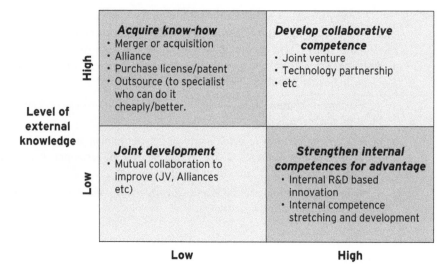

FIGURE 14.12 Knowledge acquisition options

The decision with regard to the most appropriate format for knowledge transfer and knowledge management can be usefully mapped along two dimensions. These are the level of internal knowledge and understanding (in the specific field of interest – technology, product, market, process, etc.), and the level of external knowledge or understanding. The matrix of the two dimensions indicates strategic approaches that may be utilised under different circumstances. These strategic options are summarised in Figure 14.12. If the firm and its external counterparts both possess low levels of knowledge, the best option is either to simply continue independently or engage in joint development of new knowledge. If, however, the firm possesses greater knowledge than others in the sector then the optimal strategy is for it to further strengthen and expand its current competencies. When others possess greater knowledge it becomes necessary for the firm to take steps to ensure that it is not behind. This requires it to actively transfer external knowledge into itself. This can be done through a variety of knowledge acquisition strategies, such as partnership alliance, licensing or even taking a decision to outsource that activity if purchase or internal development are not feasible options for the firm at that time. In a situation where both the firm and external agencies have a high degree of knowledge, it serves the interests of the firm to engage in partnerships that lead to win–win competitive advantage outcomes, such as a complementary technology partnership or joint ventures.

Absorbing knowledge and learning through benchmarking

Gathering knowledge/intelligence from competitors is not a new phenomenon, but its systematic and formal use is relatively recent. Companies like Xerox, Motorola and Ford attribute significant improvements as a result of the practice of benchmarking, and greater definition of what constitutes key areas of knowledge management practices can be found in evolving standards (such as PAS2001 within the British Standards Guide).

Benchmarking is an improvement methodology which functions by getting organisations to compare themselves to how other companies are carrying out business and use this as a source of knowledge and stimulus to improve themselves. Benchmarking in this sense is a learning and developmental process. It works on the principle of identifying best practices, improving them, adapting them to the needs of the company and then implementing them. Benchmarking is not exclusively about quantitative measurements, although unfortunately in the majority of practice it has tended to be so. In its true sense benchmarking is much more about general improvements than it is about hard metric-based comparisons. In fact some of the most useful information for organisations tends to be 'soft' knowledge about organisational practices and procedures. While benchmarking can be used to set targets it is more than just a target-setting device by management. Because it is based on what is being achieved by other organisations it allows an objective assessment of *what* can be achieved, *how* it can be achieved and *where* the organisation is in relation to these criteria. The understanding of the others' practices often serves to provide inspiration and impetus to move the company forward. In essence, benchmarking is about continuously striving for improvement by learning from others better than oneself. Definitionally, 'benchmarking is the ongoing structured and objective process of measuring and improving products/services, practices and processes against the best that can be identified worldwide in order to achieve and sustain competitive advantage' (Grinyer and Goldsmith, 1995, p. 5).

Benchmarking has a variety of meanings attached to it. There remains a certain degree of confusion and even mysticism about what benchmarking really is about. For companies such as Xerox, which was responsible for the early development of the concept and is a leader in the application of this methodology, benchmarking has provided significant improvements. However, for others the experience has been rather ephemeral and somewhat elusive. Many of the problems of failure can be related to the lack of clarity in its method of use and application.

In general there exist four basic types of benchmarking approaches (Camp, 1995), each with its own specific limitations and advantages.

Internal benchmarking

This is based on conducting comparisons with other parts of the same organisation. This is possible if the organisation is large enough and its sub-parts are different enough to allow possibilities of learning from one another. This approach is relatively simple in that access and depth of information is easily obtainable. Moreover, it is possible to continue monitoring progress on a continuous basis. The major limitation is in being able to find examples of practice that yield significant improvement opportunities.

Competitor benchmarking

This form of benchmarking requires examining competitive companies and using their indexes of performance and practice to fashion improvement programmes. The advantage of this form of benchmarking is that the comparisons are much more direct because they pertain to a specific industry sector. Due to this the learning is likely to be more relevant as well as much more easily adaptable to the context of the client organisation. Of course, the major problem with this form of benchmarking is (because of the nature of competition) that much of the information will be sensitive in nature, and the likelihood of disclosure limited. Moreover, there are possibilities that competitors may purposely mislead each other. Despite these drawbacks, large organisations do exchange information in select areas of joint interest.

Functional benchmarking

This is a form of benchmarking which involves making comparison of like functions but with non-competitor organisations. This type of benchmarking has several advantages:

- Information is accessible because the competitive angle is absent, and often leads to the development of partnerships.
- Learning on a function by function basis facilitates adaptation and ease of implementation.
- Functional leaders are easy to identify.

The drawback or limitation of this approach is that the learning that takes place is narrow, and holistic aspects cutting across functional areas get missed.

Generic benchmarking

Generic benchmarking is the most complex form of benchmarking in that often it cuts across narrow functional boundaries, leading to comparisons of business processes across a wide variety of industries. This form offers the potential for making radical improvements and truly searches for best practices. The problem of this type of benchmarking is the level of complexity involved. Companies undertaking this form would need to have a deep experience of benchmarking coupled with an understanding of their own vision and competence, and a sensitivity to be able to recognise broad processes from different sectors that may be of relevance and potential. Additionally, the integration of radical and novel concepts into the company is likely to present a great adaptation and implementation challenge.

Benchmarking is often seen by organisations as a solo effort (internal benchmarking). Unfortunately, this offers very limited opportunities for learning and process improvement. Compounding this is the thinking that companies must find 'like' organisations to benchmark, and it involves primarily quantitative data collection. This leads to narrow benchmarking

ILLUSTRATION

Benchmarking airlines

Airline profitability is determined by two key factors: the loading (average percentage of number of passengers carried to total number of seats) and how long the aircraft is in the air. Passenger bookings are strongly dictated by issues such as the on-board quality of service. Flying time is determined by how long the aircraft sits on the ground, i.e. the time taken to make all the safety checks, clean the aircraft, load meals and conduct all other activities that prepare the aircraft for take-off. A flagship carrier like British Airways could use benchmarking in a number of ways.

- *Competitive benchmarking*: BA could benchmark with best-in-class carriers such as Emirates or Singapore Airlines to improve its in-flight service quality.
- *Functional benchmarking*: BA could examine how other non-competitors manage similar operations. For example it could benchmark against Stagecoach, which faces a similar loading and transport challenge but in the coach sector. Or it could scrutinise the processes leading to the operational efficiency of German and Japanese trains.
- *Generic benchmarking*: An excellent example of generic benchmarking in the airline sector is the benchmarking against the Ferrari Grand Prix racing team. Pit-stops can make the difference between winning or losing a race. The process used by the Ferrari team to fuel up, change tyres, and conduct all necessary checks and changes was studied carefully and proved to be inspirational for the airline in reducing dramatically its time on the tarmac.

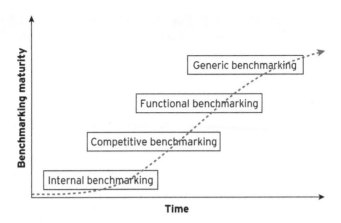

FIGURE 14.13 Benchmarking approach maturity curve

practice, which often overlooks qualitative aspects of processes. This situation can be improved by engaging in the higher level functional and generic benchmarking activities. In benchmarking there appears to be a maturity curve (see Figure 14.13). Most firms start benchmarking by engaging in simple discrete measurements, typical of internal benchmarking, and competitive benchmarking, and with time and experience move to higher level functional and generic benchmarking. The move to functional benchmarking requires a qualitative transition, and to generic benchmarking an even bigger jump in order to exploit good practice from what appears to be radically different contexts.

The most common pitfalls of benchmarking are (DeToro, 1995):

- Lack of adequate planning.
- Establishing inappropriate performance measures.
- Appointing inappropriate personnel to the benchmarking team.
- Lack of depth in the benchmarking studies.
- Inappropriate or inaccurate data gathering methods.
- Failure to plan for implementation.
- Failure to adapt the benchmarking partner's process to one's organisational culture.
- Failing to involve employees in decision making about benchmarking and its implementation.

Benchmarking has become an integral part of business for many successful companies. Notwithstanding its growing popularity, particularly in conjunction with quality initiatives to drive business improvements, benchmarking remains a relatively under-utilised tool in the field of innovation. Despite the existence of a vast literature base identifying success or failure factors in product development (e.g. de Bretani, 1996; Cooper and Kliendschimdt, 1995) few have tried to explicitly incorporate a benchmarking best practice methodology. An exception to this is Pierz (1995), who uses a benchmarking methodology to examine best practices for new product development funding in the telecommunications industry.

To date, the primary focus of most benchmarking efforts has been external screening and collecting knowledge. However, to fully benefit from benchmarking, companies must pay due diligence to the inward transfer of knowledge. Without this capability it is not possible to reap benefits. Sadly, many benchmarking attempts remain focussed just on external identification of best practice and neglect the internal transfer dimension.

Knowledge dissemination, co-location and IT

Innovation can be explained as the transformation of knowledge embedded in different places in an organisation into knowledge embedded in a new product. It is not surprising, therefore, that a positive association between the exchange of knowledge and information and innovation performance has been found to exist (Keller, 1994).

The primary strategy for ensuring a high level of knowledge dissemination has been the co-location of R&D staff, where co-location is defined as the positioning of departments and offices of R&D personnel in close proximity to each other. However, with the increased dispersion of innovation activities on a global scale, more companies are using information and computer mediated communication (CMC) to replace, or augment, co-location and face-to-face contact (Malhotra at al., 2001). CMC are information technologies that enable, intensify or expand the interactions of those involved in the execution of a planning, design, decision, or implementation task. Many CMC technologies are being used in innovation, and include e-mail, content management systems, groupware (e.g. collaborative notebooks, forums, electronic whiteboards), web pages, file transfer systems, and videoconferencing.

The value in investing heavily in CMC is a matter of debate, with some studies documenting the successful use of IT in innovation projects (Malhotra et al., 2001) while others cite various limitations (e.g. Cooper, 2003). The argument for co-location is equally open. McDonough et al. (2001) supported the assertion that the probability of communication between individuals decreases as distance increases. However, Moenaert and Caeldries (1996) found no such significant relationship between proximity and technological communication on the department level, and Rafii (1995) believed that the value of co-location may be greatly exaggerated. To add to the confusion here, research has suggested that groups using electronic communications systems communicate less effectively in many circumstances than groups who meet face-to-face.

Recent studies have suggested that there is a high impact of CMC technologies on knowledge dissemination compared to co-location, and while it was thought that companies must choose between co-location (face-to-face communications) and the use of IT, there is now evidence that they interact and strengthen each other (Song et al., 2007). There has also been a suggestion that co-location and electronic communication are better suited for particular types of communication: electronic communication for uncertainty reduction and face-to-face communication for ambiguity resolution; co-location for building trusted relationships and spontaneous encounters, and CMC technologies for bridging time and space. This has important implications for innovation, as the first phases of technology development projects are more characterised by ambiguity about project goals and technological feasibility than later phases and it is important to build trust at this point, so co-location would be more appropriate in this instance, while technical knowledge dissemination in later phases would be better supported by CMC technologies.

Conclusion

In this chapter, the role of knowledge management in innovation has been highlighted. Knowledge has an explicit part and a tacit part, each with specific requirements in terms of management. World class companies are able to harness both in the innovation process. This requires building effective internal processes to capture, create, share and leverage knowledge. The innovation systems needs to be organised to ensure that knowledge is captured and learning takes place systematically. This may be achieved by structuring the innovation system into two components: a planning and execution component and a knowledge repository component. Working in concert these two structures ensure that each innovation project is optimally organised for success and is controlled and tracked for knowledge and learning.

The management of knowledge is not just an internal challenge, as is so often assumed. It is also an external challenge of transferring the knowledge from outside and embedding it within the organisation. Success in innovation is heavily dependent upon how effective an organisation is in building a knowledge capability and then being able to leverage it. Managing knowledge is a critical process in enhancing the capacity to innovate.

QUESTIONS

1. Are knowledge and knowledge assets really a primary resource as suggested by Peter Drucker? Under what circumstance might this assertion not hold?

2. What is the difference between knowledge and learning?

3. Identify the key elements of a knowledge system to manage innovation. How should they be organised?

4. What types of information would you keep in an innovation knowledge repository? List the types of items under each category. How would you organise and manage it to make it more effective?

5. Define the basic generic knowledge strategies? What dimensions underlie their definition/classification? Comment on how/why the evolutionary trajectory of the knowledge strategies may break down.

6. How can benchmarking be used for innovation? What are the advantages and disadvantages associated with each type? Give examples of the types of benchmarking in relation to specific innovation projects.

7. Under what situations should you look to source knowledge externally and under what circumstances should it be created internally?

8. Identify the key challenges of collaborating for innovation. How can these be overcome and managed?

CASE STUDY

Keeping the know-how of a retiring generation

If the average age of the scientists in your company's R&D department is 48, surely there is no need to worry yet about losing expertise if one of them retires? Wrong, says David DeLong: 'I want to know which of the key people are 56, 58 or 60 – who is getting ready to walk out the door.' Mr DeLong, a research fellow at MIT's AgeLab, is one of several experts urging organisations to work harder at ensuring that the knowledge held only in employees' heads is not lost when they leave the company or retire.

Judging by Accenture's (2005) global study nearly four in 10 respondents said their organisations did not have a formal process and/or tools for capturing their workplace knowledge. 27 per cent said they expected to retire without any transfer of knowledge and only 17 per cent expected an intensive, months-long process of knowledge transfer.

Northrop Grumman is very similar to many other aerospace companies, as a large proportion of its workforce are baby-boomers. Mr Cheese of Northrop Grumman says the technology has not been flexible enough to support the very real challenges of KM [knowledge management], and companies have often focused on technologies that act like libraries – giving a structure and taxonomy to corporate information – when KM is really about tacit knowledge retained by individual employees.

This 'social context of knowledge' is often overlooked, says Eric Lesser, an expert in human capital issues at IBM Business Consulting Services. 'Performance in highly competitive marketplaces requires workers armed with knowledge that goes beyond the explicit information contained in manuals and databases. There is an increasing need to tap into the experience, intuition and social networks of employees', says Mr Lesser. 'Technology can enable and help, but if a company does not have a culture of knowledge sharing and collaboration, all the technology in the world isn't going to help', he says.

'Managers as a whole have not been educated to see intellectual property as an asset in the way that money is', agrees John Kay, a member of the management group at PA Consulting Group. 'If the average company managed its money in the way it managed its IP, it wouldn't be in business.'

There is, finally, the question of who takes responsibility for implementing KM within organisations. Some companies have appointed, at boardroom level, knowledge managers who can influence the direction of the company, says Mr Kay, but others in the role have been glorified IT managers, who can organise the information but cannot influence the cultural aspects of KM.

Experts such as Mr Kay and Mr DeLong point to several instances of companies that have recognised the need for effective KM. BP wins praise on the technology side for its expert locator system that helps employees find the right specialist within the company on a given issue, such as a particular type of oil drilling problem. The UK oil major is also commended on the touchy-feely front for making it part of a specialist's job to help a successor, rather than simply getting on with his or her new job. Mr Kay contrasts that approach with the attitude in some parts of the UK civil service, where 'people are deemed to be the expert in a field at the instant they step into it'.

Mr DeLong cites the in-depth interviews carried out by Rolls-Royce, the UK aero-engine group, on soon-to-retire Concorde engine designers, to ensure their expertise was preserved for future customers – irrespective of Concorde's own retirement. But getting experts to articulate their knowledge is no simple process, he warns, noting how one US organisation spent $1m on videotaping retiring experts but did not think about how future users would access the information they needed. The tapes now sit on a shelf, unused.

IBM has been active in the KM field, too, both on its own account and on behalf of its customers. Internally, its ThinkPlace intranet tool, devised by Nick Donofrio, executive vice-president for innovation and technology, helps the company to marshal and share innovation, and is combined with several cultural and management approaches, including incentive and recognition schemes.

Nothing illustrates better the struggles many companies have had with KM than the prevalence of what is euphemistically termed 'knowledge recovery'. In plain English, this means bringing back people whose knowledge has been lost, as contractors and consultants.

One US study found that 60 per cent of organisations have been doing this, says Mr DeLong, not that companies are too keen to talk about it – 'nobody wants to advertise that they've made a mistake', he says. Mr Kay at PA says he is often called in by companies that have lost knowledge or are about to do so, and says this shows they have failed to build KM into their cultures.

Another idea, recommended by Mr Kay, is a 'friendly-leaver' policy for early retirees, ensuring that successors are fully briefed, and he advocates creating a culture in which older people feel it is an important part of their job to bring on a new generation. This could be encouraged through financial incentives or simply, in a professional context, by the feeling of enrichment at having helped a younger colleague.

Perhaps the biggest challenge, especially for big companies with a long history of downsizing, job cuts and corporate upheaval, is to develop or rebuild the trust that encourages employees to share knowledge rather than hoard it.

'People will share with their colleagues if it is presented as helping colleagues with their career and keeping their own legacy alive in the company', says Mr Shaffar. 'As people get closer to retirement, and are presented with an opportunity to be a mentor to a new hire, I think we find they are pretty available.'

(*Source*: A. Baxter, 'Keeping the know-how of a retiring generation', *FT*, 24 January 2006)
© The Financial Times Limited

QUESTIONS

1. What types of knowledge are discussed in this case?
2. What difficulties exist if those different types of knowledge are to be captured and used by future employees?
3. What further challenges exist for organisations that want to share knowledge between existing employees?

References

Accenture (2005), The aging workforce, www.accenture.com/Global/Services/By_Subject/Workforce_Performance/R_and_I/AchievingWorld.htm.

Ahmed, P.K. (2001), 'Competing in the knowledge economy', *Proceedings of the 6th conference on ISO and TQM*, Scotland, April.

Akgun, A.E., Lynn, G.S. and Byrne, J.C. (2006), 'Antecedents and consequences of unlearning in new product development teams', *Journal of Product Innovation Management* 23(1): 73–88.

Anon (2002), 'Overview with John Darley, Director of Shell Technology EP (STEP)', *Oil and Gas Investor*, May: 6–10.

Argyis, C. (1990), *Overcoming organisational learning differences: Facilitating organisational learning*, Boston, MA: Allyn & Bacon.

Audery, S. and Robert, D. (2001), 'Managing organisation knowledge as strategic assets', *MCB Journal of Knowledge Management* 5(1): 8–18.

Baxter, A. (2006), 'Keeping the know-how of a retiring generation', *Financial Times*, 24 January.

Bidault, F. and Cumming, T. (1994), 'Innovating through alliances: Expectations and limitations', *R&D Management* 24(1): 33–45.

Camp, R.C. (1995), *Business process benchmarking: Finding and implementing best practices*, Milwaukee, WI: ASQC Quality Press.

Castells, M. (1996), *The rise of the network society*, Cambridge, MA and Oxford: Blackwell Books.

Cohen, W. and Levinthal, D. (1990), Absorptive capacity: A new learning perspective on learning and innovation', *Administrative Science Quarterly* 35: 128–152.

Collis, D. (1996), *Organisational learning and competitive advantage*, London: Sage.

Cooper, L.P. (2003), 'A research agenda to reduce risk in new product development through knowledge management: A practitioner perspective', *Journal of Engineering and Technology Management* 20(1–2): 117–140.

Cooper, R.G. and Kleinschmidt, E.J. (1995), 'Benchmarking the firms' critical success factors in new product development', *Journal of Product Innovation Management* 12: 374–391.

Davenport, T.H., Jarvenpaa, S.L. and Beers, M.C. (1996), 'Improving knowledge work processes', *Sloan Management Review* 37(4): 53–65.

Davenport, T.H., Delong, D.W. and Beers M.C. (1998), 'Successful knowledge management projects', *Sloan Management Review* 39(2): 43–57.

De Bretani, U. (1996), 'Success factors in developing new business services', *European Journal of Marketing* 15(2): 33–59.

De Toro, I. (1995), 'The 10 pitfalls of benchmarking', *Quality Progress*, January: 61–63.

Drucker, P.F. (1993), *Post-capitalist society*, New York: Harper & Row.

Elmuti, D. (1998), 'The perceived impact of the benchmarking process on organisational effectiveness', *Production and Inventory Management Journal* 39(3): 6–11.

Field, N.E. and Yang, H. (1990), 'The organisation that learns', *Fortune*, 12 March, 133.

Forrest, J.E. and Martin, M.J. (1992), 'Strategic alliances between large and small research intensive organisations', *R&D Management* 22(1): 41–53.

Grant, R. (1996), 'Toward a knowledge-based theory of the firm', *Strategic Management Journal* 17, Winter Special Issue: 109–122.

Gringer, P. and Goldsmith, R. (1995), 'Generating major change in companies', *Strategic Management Journal*, special issue: 131–146.

Hedberg, B., Nystrom, P.C. and Starbuck, W.H. (1976), 'Camping on seesaws: Prescriptions for a self-designing organisation', *Administrative Science Quarterly* 21: 41–65.

Keller, R.T. (1994), 'Technology-information processing fit and the performance of R&D project groups', *Academy of Management Journal* 37(1): 167–179.

Leiponen, A. (2006), 'Managing knowledge innovation: The case of business-to-business services', Journal of Product Innovation Management, 23(3): 238–258.

Malhotra, Y. (1998), 'Knowledge management for the new world of business', **www.brint.com/km/whatis.htm.**

Malhotra, A., Majchrzak, A., Carman R. and Lott V. (2001), 'Radical innovation without colocation: A case study ar Boeing-RocketDyne, *MIS Quarterly* 25(2): 229–249.

McDonough III, E.F., Kahn, K.B., and Barczak, G. (2001), 'An investigation on the use of global, virtual and co-located new product development teams', *Journal of Product Innovation Management* 18(2): 110–120.

Moenaert, R.K. and Caeldries, F. (1996), 'Architectural design, interpersonal communication and learning in R&D', *Journal of Product Innovation Management* 13(4): 296–310.

Nelson, R. and Winter, S.G. (1982), *An evolutionary theory of economic change*, Cambridge, MA: Belnap.

Nonaka, I. (1991), 'The knowledge creating company', *Harvard Business Review*, November–December: 96–104.

Nonaka, I. (1994), 'A dynamic theory of organisational knowledge creation', *Organisation Science* 5(1): 14–37.

Nonaka, I. and Takeuchi, H. (1995), *The knowledge-creating company: How Japanese companies create the dynamics of innovation*, New York: Oxford University Press.

O'Dell, C. and Grayson, C.J. (1998), 'If only we knew what we know: Identification and transfer of internal best practices', *California Management Review* 40(3): 154–174.

Pierz, K.A. (1995), 'Benchmarking new product development funding', *Journal of Product Innovation Management* 12: 43–53.

Prahalad, C.K. and Hamel, G. (1990), 'The core competence of the corporation', *Harvard Business Review* 68(3): 79–91.

Rafii, F. (1995), 'How important is physical location to product development success?', *Business Horizons*, January/February: 78–84.

Revans, R. (1983), *The A.B.C. of action learning*, Bromley: Chartwell-Bratt.

Rousseau, D.M. (2001), 'Schema, promise and mutuality: The building blocks of the psychological contract', *Journal of Occupational and Organisational Psychology* 74(4): 511–541.

Ruggles, R. (1998), 'The state of the notion: Knowledge management in practice', *California Management Review* 40(3): 80–89.

Sakkab, N.Y. (2002), 'Connect and develop complements research and develop at P&G', *Research Technology Management* 45(2): 38–46.

Song, M., Berends, H., Van Der Bij, H. and Weggeman, M., (2007), 'The effect of IT and co-location on knowledge dissemination', *Journal of Product Innovation Management* 24(1): 52–68.

INDEX